AUDIT & ACCOUNTING GUIDE

Property and Liability Insurance Entities

NEW EDITION AS OF
JANUARY 1, 2013

Copyright © 2013 by

American Institute of Certified Public Accountants, Inc.
New York, NY 10036-8775

All rights reserved. For information about the procedure for requesting permission to make copies of any part of this work, please e-mail copyright@aicpa.org with your request. Otherwise, requests should be written and mailed to the Permissions Department, AICPA, 220 Leigh Farm Road, Durham, NC 27707-8110.

1 2 3 4 5 6 7 8 9 0 AAP 1 9 8 7 6 5 4 3

ISBN 978-1-93735-208-0

Preface

About AICPA Audit and Accounting Guides

This AICPA Audit and Accounting Guide has been developed by the Property and Liability Insurance Guide Task Force to assist management of property and liability insurance entities in preparing financial statements in conformity with generally accepted accounting principles (GAAP) and statutory accounting principles and to assist practitioners in performing and reporting on their audit engagements.

The Financial Reporting Executive Committee (FinREC) is the designated senior committee of the AICPA authorized to speak for the AICPA in the areas of financial accounting and reporting. Conforming changes made to the financial accounting and reporting guidance contained in this guide are approved by the FinREC Chair (or his or her designee). Updates made to the financial accounting and reporting guidance in this guide exceeding that of conforming changes are approved by the affirmative vote of at least two-thirds of the members of FinREC.

This guide

- identifies certain requirements set forth in Financial Accounting Standards Board (FASB) *Accounting Standards Codification*™ (ASC).
- describes FinREC's understanding of prevalent or sole industry practice concerning certain issues. In addition, this guide may indicate that FinREC expresses a preference for the prevalent or sole industry practice, or it may indicate that FinREC expresses a preference for another practice that is not the prevalent or sole industry practice. Alternatively, FinREC may express no view on the issue.
- identifies certain other, but not necessarily all, industry practices concerning certain accounting issues without expressing FinREC's views on them.
- provides guidance that has been supported by FinREC on the accounting, reporting, or disclosure treatment of transactions or events that are not set forth in FASB ASC.

Accounting guidance for nongovernmental entities included in an AICPA Audit and Accounting Guide is a source of nonauthoritative accounting guidance. FASB ASC is the authoritative source of U.S. accounting and reporting standards for nongovernmental entities, in addition to guidance issued by the Securities and Exchange Commission (SEC). Accounting guidance for governmental entities included in an AICPA Audit and Accounting Guide is a source of authoritative accounting guidance described in category *b* of the hierarchy of GAAP for state and local governmental entities, and has been cleared by the Governmental Accounting Standards Board. AICPA members should be prepared to justify departures from GAAP, as discussed in Rule 203, *Accounting Principles* (AICPA, *Professional Standards*, ET sec. 203 par. .01).

Auditing guidance included in an AICPA Audit and Accounting Guide is recognized as an interpretive publication as defined in AU-C section 200, *Overall Objectives of the Independent Auditor and the Conduct of an Audit in Accordance with Generally Accepted Auditing Standards* (AICPA, *Professional Standards*). Interpretive publications are recommendations on the application of generally accepted auditing standards (GAAS) in specific circumstances, including engagements for entities in specialized industries.

An interpretive publication is issued under the authority of the AICPA Auditing Standards Board (ASB) after all ASB members have been provided an opportunity to consider and comment on whether the proposed interpretive publication is consistent with GAAS. The members of the ASB have found the auditing guidance in this guide to be consistent with existing GAAS.

Although interpretive publications are not auditing standards, AU-C section 200 requires the auditor to consider applicable interpretive publications in planning and performing the audit because interpretive publications are relevant to the proper application of GAAS in specific circumstances. If the auditor does not apply the auditing guidance in an applicable interpretive publication, the auditor should document how he or she complied with the requirements of GAAS in the circumstances addressed by such auditing guidance.

The ASB is the designated senior committee of the AICPA authorized to speak for the AICPA on all matters related to auditing. Conforming changes made to the auditing guidance contained in this guide are approved by the ASB Chair (or his or her designee) and the Director of the AICPA Audit and Attest Standards Staff. Updates made to the auditing guidance in this guide exceeding that of conforming changes are issued after all ASB members have been provided an opportunity to consider and comment on whether the guide is consistent with the Statements on Auditing Standards.

Recognition

Property and Liability Insurance Entities Audit and Accounting Guide Overhaul Task Force (2005–2012)

(members when this edition was completed)	(former members who contributed to the development of this edition)
Mark Parkin, *Chair*	Ken Croarkin
Michelle Avery	Martin John
Keith Bell	Scott Lewis
Alissa Choi	William Lowry
Maureen Downie	Marc Smith
William Ferguson	Ramin Taraz
Daniel Grady	
Richard Lynch	
Coleman Ross	
E. Daniel Thomas	
Magali Welch	

AAG-PLI

AICPA Senior Committees
Financial Reporting Executive Committee

(members when this edition was completed)

Richard C. Paul, *Chair*
Aaron Anderson
Linda Bergen
Adam Brown
Terry Cooper
Lawrence Gray
Randolph Green
Mary E. Kane
Jack Markey
Joseph D. McGrath
Rebecca Mihalko
Steve Moehrle
Angela Newell
Mark Scoles
Brad Sparks
Dusty Stallings

(former members who contributed to the development of this edition)

Jay Hanson, *Former Chair*
Benjamin S. Neuhausen, *Former Chair*
David Alexander
Robert Axel
Rick Arpin
Kimber Bascom
Glenn Bradley
Neri Bukspan
Brett Cohen
Pascal Desroches
James A. Dolinar
L. Charles Evans
Faye Feger
Bruce Johnson
Richard Jones
Carl Kampel
Lisa Kelley
David Morris
Jonathon Nus
Richard Petersen
Roy Rendino
Terry Spidell
Randall Sogoloff
Richard K. Stuart
Enrique Tejerina
Robert Uhl
Dan Weaver
Dan Zwarn

(continued)

Auditing Standards Board

(members when this edition was completed)

Darrel R. Schubert, *Chair*	David Morris
Brian Bluhm	Kenneth R. Odom
Robert E. Chevalier	Don M. Pallais
Sam K. Cotterell	Brian R. Richson
Jim Dalkin	Mike Santay
David Duree	Kay W. Tatum
Jennifer Haskell	Kim L. Tredinnick
Ed G. Jolicoeur	H. Steven Vogel
Barbara Lewis	Kurtis A. Wolff
Carolyn H. McNerney	

The AICPA and the Property and Liability Insurance Entities Audit and Accounting Guide Overhaul Task Force gratefully acknowledges the contributions of Evan Cabat, Jean Connolly, Jennifer Englert, Robert Evans, Danielle Fandrey, Thomas Fekete, Julie Gould, Andy Gray, Linda Healy, Jay Muska, Mary Saslow, Lisa Slotznick, and Deborah Whitmore.

The AICPA and the Property and Liability Insurance Entities Audit and Accounting Guide Overhaul Task Force gratefully acknowledge those members of the AICPA Insurance Expert Panel who reviewed or otherwise contributed to the development of this guide: Jill Butler, Darryl Briley, Kathleen Enright, Matthew Farney, James Greisch, Kenneth N. Hugendubler, Margie M. Keeley, Joshua Keene, Rick Sojkowski, Robert Tarnok, Anthony Valoroso, and Jennifer Yaross. Additionally, the AICPA and the Property and Liability Insurance Entities Audit and Accounting Guide Overhaul Task Force thank those past members of the AICPA Insurance Expert Panel who reviewed or otherwise contributed to the development of this guide but rotated off the Insurance Expert Panel prior to the guide being completed: Amy Corbin, Elaine Lehnert, Sandra Peters, and Donald Schwegman.

AICPA Staff

Kim Kushmerick, *Senior Technical Manager*, Accounting Standards, and *Staff Liaison* to the AICPA Insurance Expert Panel	Dan Noll, *Director*, Accounting Standards

Guidance Considered in This Edition

Authoritative guidance issued through January 1, 2013, has been considered in the development of this edition of the guide. Authoritative guidance that is issued and effective for entities with fiscal years ending on or before January 1, 2013, is incorporated directly in the text of this guide. Authoritative guidance issued but not yet effective for fiscal years ending on or before January 1, 2013, is presented as a guidance update. A guidance update is a shaded area that contains information on the guidance issued but not yet effective and serves as a reference to appendix D, "Guidance Updates," where appropriate. The distinct presentation of this content is intended to aid the reader in differentiating content that may not be effective for the reader's purposes.

This includes relevant guidance issued up to and including the following:

- FASB Accounting Standards Update (ASU) No. 2012-06, *Business Combinations (Topic 805): Subsequent Accounting for an Indemnification Asset Recognized at the Acquisition Date as a Result of a Government-Assisted Acquisition of a Financial Institution (a consensus of the FASB Emerging Issues Task Force)*
- Statement on Auditing Standards (SAS) No. 126, *The Auditor's Consideration of an Entity's Ability to Continue as a Going Concern* (Redrafted) (AICPA, *Professional Standards*, AU-C sec. 570)
- NAIC Statement of Statutory Accounting Principles No. 103, *Accounting for Transfers and Servicing of Financial Assets and Extinguishments of Liabilities*
- Public Company Accounting Oversight Board (PCAOB) Auditing Standards No. 8–16 (AICPA, *PCAOB Standards and Related Rules*, Auditing Standards)

Users of this guide should consider guidance issued subsequent to those items listed previously to determine their effect on entities covered by this guide. In determining the applicability of recently issued guidance, its effective date should also be considered.

Defining Professional Responsibilities in AICPA Professional Standards

Audit Engagements

AICPA professional standards applicable to audit engagements use the following two categories of professional requirements, identified by specific terms, to describe the degree of responsibility the requirements impose on auditors:

- *Unconditional requirements.* The auditor must comply with an unconditional requirement in all cases in which such requirement is relevant. GAAS uses the word *must* to indicate an unconditional requirement.
- *Presumptively mandatory requirements.* The auditor must comply with a presumptively mandatory requirement in all cases in which such a requirement is relevant except in rare circumstances. GAAS uses the word *should* to indicate a presumptively mandatory requirement.

In rare circumstances, the auditor may judge it necessary to depart from a relevant presumptively mandatory requirement. In such circumstances, the auditor should perform alternative audit procedures to achieve the intent of that requirement. The need for the auditor to depart from a relevant presumptively mandatory requirement is expected to arise only when the requirement is for a specific procedure to be performed and, in the specific circumstances of the audit, that procedure would be ineffective in achieving the intent of the requirement.

Prior to SAS No. 122, the terms *is required to* or *requires* were used to express an unconditional requirement in GAAS (equivalent to *must*). With the issuance of SAS No. 122, the terms *is required to* and *requires* do not convey a requirement or the degree of responsibility it imposes on auditors. Instead those terms are used to express that a requirement exists. The terms are typically used in the clarified auditing standards to indicate that a requirement exists elsewhere in GAAS.

Attest Engagements

AICPA professional standards applicable to attest engagements use the following two categories of professional requirements, identified by specific terms, to describe the degree of responsibility they impose on a practitioner:

- *Unconditional requirements.* The practitioner is required to comply with an unconditional requirement in all cases in which the circumstances exist to which the requirement applies. The terms *must* and *is required* are used to indicate an unconditional requirement.

- *Presumptively mandatory requirements.* The practitioner must comply with a presumptively mandatory requirement in all cases in which the circumstances exist to which the requirement applies; however, in rare circumstances the practitioner may depart from the requirement provided that the practitioner documents his or her justification for the departure and how the alternative procedures performed in the circumstances were sufficient to achieve the objectives of the requirement. The word *should* is used to indicate a presumptively mandatory requirement.

It is important to note that upon the effective date of the clarified auditing standards the terms describing professional requirements for audit engagements are revised and are different than those used for attest engagements. See the preceding section for information on defining professional requirements related to auditing standards.

Applicability of GAAS and PCAOB Standards

Audits of the financial statements of *nonissuers* (those entities not subject to the Sarbanes-Oxley Act of 2002 or the rules of the SEC—that is, private entities) are conducted in accordance with GAAS as issued by the ASB, the designated senior committee of the AICPA with the authority to promulgate auditing standards for nonissuers. The ASB develops and issues standards in the form of SASs through a due process that includes deliberation in meetings open to the public, public exposure of proposed SASs, and a formal vote. The SASs and their related interpretations are codified in AICPA *Professional Standards*. Rule 202, *Compliance With Standards* (AICPA, *Professional Standards*, ET sec. 202, par. .01) of the AICPA Code of Professional Conduct requires an AICPA member who performs an audit to comply with the standards promulgated by the ASB. Failure to follow GAAS, and any other applicable auditing standards, is a violation of that rule.

Audits of the financial statements of *issuers*, as defined by the SEC (those entities subject to the Sarbanes-Oxley Act of 2002 or the rules of the SEC—that is, public entities), are conducted in accordance with standards established by the PCAOB, a private sector, nonprofit corporation created by the Sarbanes-Oxley Act of 2002 to oversee the audits of issuers. The SEC has oversight authority over the PCAOB, including the approval of its rules, standards, and budget.

References to Professional Standards

In citing GAAS and their related interpretations, references use section numbers within *Professional Standards* and not the original statement number, as appropriate. In those sections of the guide that refers to specific auditing standards of the PCAOB, references are made to the AICPA's *PCAOB Standards and Related Rules* publication.

AICPA.org Website

The AICPA encourages you to visit the website at www.aicpa.org and the Financial Reporting Center at www.aicpa.org/FRC. The Financial Reporting Center supports members in the execution of high quality financial reporting. Whether you are a financial statement preparer or a member in public practice, this center provides exclusive member-only resources for the entire financial reporting process. The Financial Reporting Center also provides timely and relevant news, guidance, and examples supporting the financial reporting process, including accounting, preparing financial statements, and performing compilation, review, audit, attest or assurance, and advisory engagements. Certain content on the AICPA's website referenced in this guide may be restricted to AICPA members only.

Select Recent Developments Significant to This Guide

ASB's Clarity Project

To address concerns over the clarity, length, and complexity of its standards, the ASB has made a significant effort to clarify the SASs. The ASB established clarity drafting conventions and redrafted all of its SASs in accordance with those conventions, which include the following:

- Establishing objectives for each clarified SAS
- Including a definitions section, where relevant, in each clarified SAS
- Separating requirements from application and other explanatory material
- Numbering application and other explanatory material paragraphs using an A- prefix and presenting them in a separate section that follows the requirements section
- Using formatting techniques, such as bulleted lists, to enhance readability
- Including, when appropriate, special considerations relevant to audits of smaller, less complex entities within the text of the clarified SAS
- Including, when appropriate, special considerations relevant to audits of governmental entities within the text of the clarified SAS

In addition, as the ASB redrafted standards for clarity, it also converged the standards with the International Standards on Auditing (ISAs), issued by the International Auditing and Assurance Standards Board. As part of redrafting the standards, they now specify more clearly the objectives of the auditor and the requirements with which the auditor has to comply when conducting an audit in accordance with GAAS.

With the release of SAS Nos. 117–120 and Nos. 122–126, the project is near completion. As of the date of this guide, the only SAS remaining to be clarified is SAS No. 65, *The Auditor's Consideration of the Internal Audit Function in an Audit of Financial Statements*.

Note that SAS No. 122 withdraws SAS No. 26, *Association With Financial Statements*, as amended.

SAS Nos. 122–126 are effective for audits of financial statements for periods ending on or after December 15, 2012. Refer to individual AU-C sections for specific effective date language.

As part of the clarity project, current AU section numbers have been renumbered based on equivalent ISAs. Guidance is located in "AU-C" section numbers instead of "AU" section numbers. "AU-C" is a temporary identifier to avoid confusion with references to existing "AU" sections, which remain effective through 2013 in AICPA *Professional Standards*. The "AU-C" identifier will revert to "AU" in 2014, by which time the clarified auditing standards become fully effective for all engagements. Note that AU-C section numbers for clarified SASs with no equivalent ISAs have been assigned new numbers. The ASB believes that this recodification structure will aid firms and practitioners that use both the ISAs and GAAS.

All auditing interpretations corresponding to a SAS have been considered in the development of a clarified SAS and incorporated accordingly, and have been withdrawn by the ASB except for certain interpretations that the ASB has retained and revised to reflect the issuance of SAS No. 122. The effective date of the revised interpretations aligns with the effective date of the corresponding clarified SAS.

Important Notice to Reader

This AICPA Audit and Accounting Guide has been fully conformed to reflect the new standards resulting from the Clarity Project. This year's edition of the guide fully incorporates the clarified auditing standards into all guide content so that auditors can further their understanding of the clarified auditing standards, as well as begin updating their audit methodologies, resources, and tools prior to the clarified auditing standards' effective date. Additionally, this approach gives auditors the opportunity to review and understand the changes made by their third-party audit methodology and resource providers, if applicable. The clarified auditing standards are effective for audits of financial statements for periods ending on or after December 15, 2012 (calendar year 2012 audits).

See the previous section titled "Guidance Considered in this Edition" for more information related to the guidance issued as of the date of this guide. Also see appendix E, "Mapping and Summarization of Changes—Clarified Auditing Standards." This appendix cross references extant AU sections with AU-C sections and indicates the nature of changes made in the clarified standards.

International Financial Reporting Standards

AICPA governing council voted in May 2008 to recognize the International Accounting Standards Board (IASB) as an accounting body for purposes of establishing international financial accounting and reporting principles. This amendment to appendix A, *Council Resolution Designating Bodies to Promulgate Technical Standards*, of the AICPA's Code of Professional Conduct (AICPA, *Professional Standards*), gives AICPA members the option to use International Financial Reporting Standards (IFRS) as an alternative to GAAP. As a result, private entities in the United States can prepare their financial statements in accordance with GAAP as promulgated by FASB; an other comprehensive basis of accounting (OCBOA), such as cash- or tax-basis; or IFRS, among others. However, domestic issuers are currently required to follow GAAP and the rules and regulations of the SEC. In contrast, foreign private issuers may present their financial statements in accordance with IFRS as issued by the IASB without a reconciliation to GAAP, or in accordance with non-IFRS home-country GAAP reconciled to GAAP as permitted by Form 20-F.

The growing acceptance of IFRS as a basis for U.S. financial reporting could represent a fundamental change for the U.S. accounting profession. Acceptance of a single set of high quality accounting standards for worldwide use by public companies has been gaining momentum around the globe for the past few years. See appendix F, "International Financial Reporting Standards," of this guide for a discerning look at the status of convergence with IFRS in the United States and the important issues that accounting professionals need to consider now.

Insurance Contracts Project

The IASB split its insurance contract project into two phases so that some components of the project were completed by 2005 without delaying the rest of the project. Phase I addresses the application of the existing IFRS to entities that issue insurance contracts. Phase II, initiated in September 2004, is a comprehensive project on accounting for insurance contracts. The issuance of IFRS No. 4, *Insurance Contracts*, along with *Basis for Conclusions on IFRS 4* and *Implementation Guidance to IFRS 4* brought phase I of the international insurance project to a close.

Effective for the aforementioned international insurers for annual periods beginning on or after January 1, 2005, IFRS No. 4 provides the framework for accounting for insurance contracts until the IASB completes phase II. IFRS No. 4 generally allows insurance contracts to be accounted for under the insurer's existing local accounting with some enhancements to those local standards. Although IFRS No. 4 permits the continuation of the existing local accounting for insurance contracts, the standard has imposed a requirement that the contract must contain significant insurance risk to qualify as an insurance contract under IFRS No. 4. The standard applies to reinsurance contracts as well as insurance contracts. IFRS No. 4 does not apply to other assets and liabilities of an insurer. Readers with international reporting situations should continue to be alert to potential developments in international accounting standards for insurance contracts.

On August 2, 2007, FASB issued an invitation to comment on *An FASB Agenda Proposal: Accounting for Insurance Contracts by Insurers and Policyholders, Including the IASB Discussion Paper, Preliminary Views on Insurance Contracts*. That invitation to comment included a discussion paper issued by the IASB, *Preliminary Views on Insurance Contracts*, which set forth its preliminary views on the main components of an accounting model for an issuer's rights and obligations (assets and liabilities) under an insurance contract. FASB issued the invitation to comment to gather information from its constituents to help decide whether there was a need for a comprehensive project on accounting for insurance contracts and whether FASB should undertake such a project jointly with the IASB.

In October 2008, FASB decided to join the IASB's insurance contract project.

In July 2010, the IASB issued the exposure draft *Insurance Contracts*. In developing the IASB's exposure draft, most of the discussions about the proposed insurance accounting approaches were held jointly with FASB. Although the boards reached common decisions in many areas, they reached different conclusions in others. Some FASB members prefer the IASB's proposed measurement approach; however, the majority prefers an alternative approach. Regardless of FASB members' individual views and uniform commitment to convergence, FASB determined that additional information was needed about whether the possible new accounting guidance would represent a sufficient improvement to GAAP to justify issuing new guidance. On September 17, 2010, FASB issued, for public comment, the discussion paper *Preliminary Views on Insurance Contracts.*

The boards are redeliberating significant issues based on feedback received on the IASB exposure draft and FASB discussion paper. FASB is expected to release an exposure draft, and the IASB is expected to issue a targeted revised exposure draft, during the first half of 2013. Readers should be aware that the tentative conclusions discussed in this project could significantly change accounting for insurance contracts, and remain alert to any final pronouncements.

For more specific information, visit the FASB website at www.fasb.org and the IASB website at www.iasb.org.

TABLE OF CONTENTS

Chapter		Paragraph
1	Nature, Conduct, and Regulation of the Business	.01-.96
	General Nature of the Business	.01-.03
	Kinds of Insurance	.04-.08
	Legal Forms of Organization	.09
	Methods of Producing Business	.10-.17
	Major Transaction Cycles	.18-.36
	Underwriting of Risks	.18-.27
	Pooling, Captives, and Syndicates	.28-.30
	Processing and Payment of Claims	.31-.32
	Investments	.33-.36
	Accounting Practices	.37-.96
	State Insurance Regulation	.37-.45
	National Association of Insurance Commissioners	.46-.47
	Federal Regulation—Securities and Exchange Commission	.48-.53
	Federal Regulation—The Dodd-Frank Wall Street Reform and Consumer Protection Act	.54-.63
	Federal Regulation—Terrorism	.64-.68
	Industry Associations	.69
	Statutory Accounting Practices	.70-.88
	Generally Accepted Accounting Principles	.89-.95
	Comparison of SAP and GAAP	.96
2	Audit Considerations	.01-.180
	Introduction	.01
	Scope of the Audit Engagement	.02-.11
	General Considerations	.02-.04
	PCAOB Integrated Audit of Financial Statements and Internal Control Over Financial Reporting	.05-.08
	Additional PCAOB Audit Standards	.09-.11
	Planning and Other Auditing Considerations	.12-.69
	Audit Planning	.13-.14
	Audit Risk	.15-.19
	Risk Assessment Procedures	.20-.25
	Understanding the Entity, Its Environment, and Its Internal Control	.26-.43
	Common Industry Ratios and Performance Metrics	.44-.56
	Identifying and Assessing the Risks of Material Misstatement	.57-.60
	Performing Audit Procedures In Response to Assessed Risks	.61-.67
	Use of Assertions in Obtaining Audit Evidence	.68-.69

Chapter		Paragraph
2	Audit Considerations—continued	
	Other Risk Assessment Activities and Considerations	.70-.74
	Planning Materiality	.70-.72
	Performance Materiality and Tolerable Misstatement	.73-.74
	Consideration of Fraud in a Financial Statement Audit ...	.75-.76
	Insurance Industry—Fraud Risk Factors	.77-.99
	The Importance of Exercising Professional Skepticism	.79
	Discussion Among Engagement Personnel Regarding the Risks of Material Misstatement Due to Fraud	.80-.83
	Obtaining the Information Needed to Identify the Risks of Material Misstatement Due to Fraud	.84-.85
	Identifying Risks That May Result in a Material Misstatement Due to Fraud	.86-.90
	Assessing the Identified Risks After Taking an Evaluation of the Entity's Programs and Controls That Address the Risks Into Account	.91-.92
	Responding to the Results of the Assessment	.93
	Evaluating Audit Evidence	.94
	Responding to Misstatements That May Be the Result of Fraud	.95-.96
	Communicating About Possible Fraud to Management, Those Charged With Governance, and Others	.97-.98
	Documentation and Guidance	.99
	Use of Information Technology	.100-.103
	Going Concern Considerations	.104-.112
	Evaluating Misstatements	.113-.116
	Audit Documentation	.117-.125
	Consideration of the Work of Internal Auditors	.124-.125
	Communication of Matters Related to Internal Control ...	.126-.133
	Identification of Deficiencies in Internal Control	.127-.128
	Communication of Deficiencies in Internal Control	.129-.133
	Communication of Other Matters With Those Charged With Governance	.134-.138
	Matters To Be Communicated	.136-.138
	Communications by Successor Auditors	.139
	Auditor Independence	.140
	Auditing Fair Value Measurements and Disclosures	.141-.143
	Considerations for Auditors to Comply With the NAIC Model Audit Rule	.144-.165
	Awareness	.145-.146

Chapter		Paragraph
2	Audit Considerations—continued	
	Change in Auditor	.147
	Auditor's Letter of Qualifications	.148
	Qualifications of the Auditor	.149
	Indemnification	.150
	Partner Rotation	.151
	Prohibited Services	.152-.154
	Consideration of Internal Controls in a Financial Statement Audit	.155
	Notification of Adverse Financial Condition	.156-.157
	Report on Internal Controls	.158-.160
	Working Papers	.161
	Communications to Audit Committees	.162
	Management's Report on Internal Controls Over Financial Reporting	.163-.165
	Auditor's Consideration of State Regulatory Examinations	.166-.170
	Auditor's Consideration of Permitted Statutory Accounting Practices	.171-.175
	SEC Requirements for Management's Report on Internal Control Over Financial Reporting	.176-.180
3	Premiums	.01-.132
	Background	.01-.29
	Types of Premiums Adjustments	.04
	Summary of Premium Transaction Flow	.05-.26
	Involuntary Markets	.27-.29
	Accounting for Premiums and Acquisition Cost	.30-.110
	Premium Revenue and Premium Adjustments	.30-.49
	Premium Receivable	.50-.55
	Acquisition Costs	.56-.83
	Premium Deficiencies	.84-.97
	Medicare Part D	.98-.102
	Accounting for Contracts That Do Not Transfer Insurance Risk	.103-.104
	Disclosure Considerations	.105-.110
	Auditing Premiums and Acquisition Costs	.111-.132
	Audit Planning	.111
	Consideration of Fraud in a Financial Statement Audit	.112
	Audit Risk Factors—Premiums and DAC	.113-.116
	Management Estimates	.117-.119
	Risk of Material Misstatement—Inherent Risk Factors	.120-.121

Contents

Chapter		Paragraph
3	Premiums—continued	
	Internal Control	.122-.124
	Control Environment	.125-.126
	Risk Assessment Process	.127-.128
	Control Activities	.129
	Audit Procedures Responsive to the Assessed Risks of Material Misstatement	.130-.131
	Audit Consideration Chart	.132
4	The Loss Reserving and Claims Cycle	.01-.191
	Introduction	.01-.02
	Types of Businesses and Their Effect on the Estimation Process	.03-.14
	Policy Duration	.04
	Type of Coverage	.05
	Kind of Insurance Underwritten: Line of Business or Type of Risk	.06-.14
	The Transaction Cycle	.15-.32
	Claim Acceptance and Processing	.16-.18
	Claim Adjustment and Estimation	.19-.24
	Claim Settlement	.25-.28
	Reinsurance Receivable	.29-.30
	Salvage and Subrogation	.31-.32
	Components of Loss Reserves	.33
	Estimating Methods	.34-.53
	Illustrative Projection Data	.44-.53
	LAE Reserves	.54-.62
	DCC Reserve Calculation Approaches	.56-.59
	AO Reserve Calculation Approaches	.60-.62
	Changes in the Environment	.63-.66
	Critical Accounting Policies and Estimates Disclosure	.67-.68
	Use of Specialists by Management in Determining Loss Reserves	.69-.71
	Guaranty Fund and Other Assessments	.72
	Accounting Principles	.73-.93
	Discounting Loss Reserves	.75-.82
	Structured Settlements	.83-.85
	Reinsurance Receivables	.86
	SAP	.87-.93
	Disclosures of Certain Matters in the Financial Statements of Insurance Enterprises	.94-.99
	Applicability to Statutory Financial Statements	.94
	Relationship to Other Pronouncements	.95

Chapter		Paragraph
4	The Loss Reserving and Claims Cycle—continued	
	Liability for Unpaid Claims and Claim Adjustment Expenses	.96-.99
	Auditing Loss Reserves	.100-.191
	Planning Considerations—Overview	.100-.105
	Consideration of Fraud in a Financial Statement Audit	.106-.108
	Risk of Material Misstatement—Inherent Risk Factors	.109
	Internal Control	.110-.112
	Control Environment	.113
	The Entity's Risk Assessment Process	.114-.115
	Information Systems	.116
	Control Activities	.117-.118
	Identifying and Assessing the Risks of Material Misstatement	.119
	Audit Procedures Responsive to the Assessed Risks of Material Misstatement	.120-.128
	Use of Loss Reserve Specialists	.129
	Loss Reserve Specialists Engaged by the Auditor	.130-.132
	Use of Management Specialists by Auditors in Evaluating Loss Reserves	.133-.135
	Auditor's Response to Management's Use or Non-Use of a Loss Reserve Specialist	.136
	Evaluating the Reasonableness of the Estimates	.137
	Analytical Procedures	.138-.143
	Testing the Data, Assumptions, and Selection of the Estimate	.144-.148
	Auditing the Underlying Data Used in the Loss Reserving Process	.149-.154
	Develop a Point Estimate or Range to Evaluate Management's Estimate	.155-.156
	Loss Reserve Ranges	.157-.163
	Factors That Could Affect a Range of Reasonably Possible Outcomes	.164-.170
	Evaluating the Financial Effect of a Reserve Range	.171-.179
	Auditor Uncertainty About the Reasonableness of Management's Estimate and Reporting Implications	.180-.181
	Evaluating the Reasonableness of Loss Adjustment Expense Reserves	.182-.183
	Ceded Reinsurance Recoverable and Receivable	.184-.189
	Understanding the Impacts of Foreign Exchange	.190
	Audit Consideration Chart	.191

Chapter		Paragraph
5	**Investments and Fair Value Considerations**	.01-.228
	Introduction	.01-.08
	Overview	.01
	Investment Evaluation	.02-.03
	Recordkeeping and Key Performance Indicators	.04-.05
	The Transaction Cycle	.06-.07
	Safekeeping	.08
	Regulation	.09-.14
	Statutory Limitations	.10-.14
	Financial Accounting Standards Board *Accounting Standards Codification* 820 and 825	.15-.40
	Definition of *Fair Value*	.16-.22
	Application to Liabilities and Instruments Classified in a Reporting Entity's Shareholders' Equity	.23-.25
	The Fair Value Hierarchy	.26-.30
	Fair Value Determination When the Volume or Level of Activity Has Significantly Decreased	.31-.33
	Disclosures	.34-.35
	Fair Value Option	.36-.38
	Statutory Accounting	.39-.40
	Accounting Practices	.41-.202
	Significant Differences Between GAAP and Statutory Accounting	.42
	Cash and Cash Equivalents	.43-.49
	Debt and Equity Securities	.50-.93
	Mortgage Loans	.94-.107
	Real Estate	.108-.118
	Derivatives, Including Futures, Options, and Similar Financial Instruments	.119-.131
	Joint Ventures and Partnerships	.132-.144
	Investments in SCA Entities	.145-.156
	Investment Income Due and Accrued	.157-.161
	Asset Transfers and Extinguishments of Liabilities	.162-.179
	Repurchase Agreements	.180-.192
	Securities Lending	.193-.201
	Other Information	.202
	Auditing Investments	.203-.228
	Audit Planning	.203
	Consideration of Fraud in a Financial Statement Audit	.204
	Audit Risk Factors—Investments	.205-.208
	Risk of Material Misstatement—Inherent Risk	.209-.211
	Internal Control	.212-.214

Chapter		Paragraph
5	Investments and Fair Value Considerations—continued	
	Control Environment	.215
	Risk Assessment Process	.216-.217
	Information System	.218-.219
	Control Activities	.220
	Service Organizations	.221-.224
	Audit Procedures Responsive to the Assessed Risks of Material Misstatement	.225-.226
	Audit Consideration Chart and Procedures	.227-.228
6	Reinsurance	.01-.119
	Types of Reinsurance	.07-.08
	Reinsurance Contracts	.09-.19
	Bases of Reinsurance Transactions	.15-.18
	Frequently Used Terms in Reinsurance Contracts	.19
	Accounting Practices	.20-.81
	Generally Accepted Accounting Principles Accounting Practices	.20-.75
	Statutory Accounting Principles	.76-.81
	Special Risk Considerations	.82-.86
	Auditing Reinsurance	.87-.119
	Audit Planning	.87
	Consideration of Fraud in a Financial Statement Audit	.88
	Audit Risk Factors—Reinsurance	.89-.91
	Risk of Material Misstatement—Inherent Risk	.92
	Internal Control	.93-.94
	Control Environment	.95
	Risk Assessment Process	.96-.97
	Information and Communication	.98-.99
	Control Activities	.100
	Audit Procedures Responsive to the Assessed Risks of Material Misstatement	.101-.102
	Internal Control of the Ceding Entity	.103-.104
	Internal Control of the Reinsurer	.105-.106
	Auditing Procedures for the Ceding Entity	.107-.109
	Auditing Procedures for the Assuming Entity	.110-.113
	Pools, Associations, and Syndicates	.114
	Reinsurance Intermediaries	.115-.118
	Audit Consideration Chart	.119
7	Income Taxes	.01-.77
	Introduction	.01-.02
	Federal Income Taxation	.03-.20

Chapter		Paragraph
7	**Income Taxes—continued**	
	Statutory Accounting Practices and Taxable Income	.05-.07
	Special Income Tax Provisions	.08-.20
	State Taxation	.21-.22
	GAAP Accounting for Income Taxes	.23-.55
	Basic Principles of GAAP Accounting for Income Taxes	.25-.45
	Disclosure Requirements Contained in GAAP Literature	.46-.55
	Statutory Accounting for Income Taxes	.56-.61
	Disclosure Requirements Contained in Statutory Literature	.61
	Changes in Tax Law	.62
	Auditing Income Taxes	.63-.77
	Audit Planning	.63
	Consideration of Fraud in a Financial Statement Audit	.64
	Audit Risk Factors—Income Taxes	.65-.67
	Risk of Material Misstatement—Inherent Risk	.68
	Internal Control	.69-.70
	Control Environment	.71
	Risk Assessment Process	.72-.73
	Control Activities	.74
	Audit Procedures Responsive to the Assessed Risks of Material Misstatement	.75-.76
	Audit Consideration Chart	.77
8	**Insurance-Related Expenses, Taxes, and Assessments**	.01-.52
	Introduction	.01-.05
	Premium and State Taxes	.06-.12
	Guaranty Fund and Other Assessments	.13-.30
	Generally Accepted Accounting Principles	.19-.22
	Statutory Accounting Principles	.23-.30
	Capitalized Costs and Certain Nonadmitted Assets	.31-.35
	Pensions	.36-.37
	Audit Considerations	.38-.52
	Audit Planning	.38
	Consideration of Fraud in a Financial Statement Audit	.39
	Audit Risk Factors	.40-.42
	Internal Control	.43-.45
	Audit Procedures Responsive to the Assessed Risks of Material Misstatement	.46-.52

Table of Contents

Chapter		Paragraph
9	Captive Insurance Entities	.01-.43
	Introduction	.01-.06
	Types of Captive Organizations	.07-.26
	Captive Operations	.27-.29
	Specific Transaction Considerations and Accounting Principles	.30-.35
	Taxes	.33-.35
	Audit Considerations	.36-.43
	Audit Planning	.36
	Consideration of Fraud in a Financial Statement Audit	.37
	Audit Risk Factors	.38-.40
	Internal Control	.41-.42
	Audit Procedures Responsive to the Assessed Risks of Material Misstatement	.43
10	Reports on Audited Financial Statements	.01-.85
	Reports on Financial Statements	.01-.02
	Unmodified Opinions on GAAP Financial Statements	.03-.05
	Modified Opinions	.06-.28
	Qualified Opinion	.10-.11
	Disclaimer of Opinion	.12-.14
	Adverse Opinion	.15-.17
	Emphasis-of-Matter Paragraphs	.18-.27
	Evaluating Consistency of Financial Statements	.28
	Additional Guidance When Performing Integrated Audits of Financial Statements and Internal Control Over Financial Reporting	.29-.32
	Reporting on Whether a Previously Reported Material Weakness Continues to Exist	.32
	Auditors' Reports on Statutory Financial Statements of Insurance Entities	.33-.54
	NAIC—Codified Statutory Accounting	.34-.36
	Regulatory Basis Financial Statements Intended for General Use	.37-.42
	Regulatory Basis Financial Statements Intended for Limited Use	.43-.48
	Regulatory Basis Financial Statements—Other Issues	.49-.54
	Correction of Error	.55-.60
	Correction of an Error—Regulatory Basis Financial Statements Intended for General Use	.59
	Correction of an Error—Regulatory Basis Financial Statements Intended for Limited Use	.60

Chapter		Paragraph
10	Reports on Audited Financial Statements—continued	
	Opinion on Supplemental Schedules	.61-.67
	Other Reports	.68-.85
	Accountant's Awareness Letter	.69-.71
	Change in Auditor Letter	.72-.75
	Notification of Financial Condition Letter	.76-.79
	Auditor Reports for Communicating Unremediated Material Weaknesses in Internal Control to Insurance Regulators	.80-.83
	Accountant's Letter of Qualifications	.84-.85

Appendix

A	Property and Liability Insurance Entity Specific Disclosures
B	Examples of Development Data
C	List of Industry Trade and Professional Associations, Publications, and Information Resources
D	Guidance Updates
E	Mapping and Summarization of Changes—Clarified Auditing Standards
F	International Financial Reporting Standards

Glossary

Index of Pronouncements and Other Technical Guidance

Subject Index

Chapter 1

Nature, Conduct, and Regulation of the Business

General Nature of the Business

1.01 The primary purpose of the property and liability insurance business is the spreading of risks. The term *risk*[1] generally has two meanings in insurance—it can mean either a *peril insured against* (for example, fire is a risk to which most property is exposed) or a *person or property protected* (for example, a home or an automobile). For a payment known as a premium, insurance entities agree to relieve the policyholder of all or part of a risk and to spread the total cost of similar risks among large groups of policyholders.

1.02 The functions of the property and liability insurance business include marketing, underwriting (that is, determining the acceptability of risks and the amount of the premiums), billing and collecting premiums, investing and managing assets, investigating and settling claims made under policies, and paying expenses associated with these functions.

1.03 In conducting its business, an insurance entity accumulates a significant amount of investable assets. In addition to funds raised as equity and funds retained as undistributed earnings, funds accumulate from the following:

- Premiums collected
- Sums held for the payment of claims in the process of investigation, adjustment, or litigation
- Sums held for payment of future claims settlement expenses

The accumulation of these funds, their investment, and the generation of investment income are major activities of insurance entities.

Kinds of Insurance

1.04 Kinds of insurance, generally referred to as *lines of insurance*, represent the perils that are insured by property and liability insurance entities. Some of the more major lines of insurance offered by property and liability insurance entities include the following:

- *Accident and health* covers loss by sickness or accidental bodily injury. It also includes forms of insurance that provide lump-sum or periodic payments in the event of loss by sickness or accident, such as disability income insurance and accidental death and dismemberment insurance.

---

[1] This definition differs from the definition of *insurance risk* stated in the Financial Accounting Standards Board (FASB) *Accounting Standards Codification* (ASC) glossary, which describes insurance risk as the risk arising from uncertainties about both underwriting risk and timing risk. Actual or imputed investment returns are not an element of insurance risk. Insurance risk is fortuitous; the possibility of adverse events occurring is outside the control of the insured. It is the definition in the FASB ASC glossary that determines the proper accounting when considering risk transfer. See chapter 6, "Reinsurance."

- *Automobile* covers personal injury or automobile damage sustained by the insured and liability to third parties for losses caused by the insured.
- *Fidelity bonds* cover employers against dishonest acts by employees. Blanket fidelity bonds cover groups of employees.
- *Fire and allied lines* includes coverage for fire, windstorm, hail, and water damage (but not floods).
- *Home insurance* provides coverage for damage or destruction of the policyholder's home. In some geographical areas, the policy may exclude certain types of risks, such as flood or earthquake, and require additional coverage.
- *Inland marine* covers property being transported other than trans-ocean. (It also includes floaters, which are policies that cover movable property, such as a tourist's personal property.)
- *Miscellaneous liability* covers most other physical and property damages not included under workers' compensation, automobile liability, and multiple peril policies. Damages include death, cost of care, and loss of services resulting from bodily injury, as well as loss of use of property.
- *Multiple peril*, a package coverage, includes most property and liability coverage except workers' compensation, automobile insurance, and surety bonds.
- *Ocean marine* includes coverage for ships and their equipment, cargos, freight, and liability to third parties for damages.
- *Professional liability* covers physicians, surgeons, dentists, hospitals, engineers, architects, accountants, attorneys, and other professionals from liability arising from error or misconduct in providing or failing to provide professional service.
- *Surety bonds* provide for monetary compensation to third parties for failure by the insured to perform specifically covered acts within a stated period. (Most surety bonds are issued for persons doing contract construction, persons connected with court actions, and persons seeking licenses and permits.)
- *Workers' compensation* compensates employees for injuries or illness sustained in the course of their employment.

1.05 In addition to these lines, insurance is provided by excess and surplus lines:

- *Excess liability* covers the insured against loss in excess of a stated amount, but only for losses as covered and defined in an underlying policy. The underlying amount is usually insured by another policy but can be retained by the insured.
- *Surplus lines* include coverage for risks that do not fit normal underwriting patterns, risks that are not commensurate with standard rates, or risks that will not be written by standard carriers because of general market conditions. These kinds of policies are generally written by carriers not licensed in the jurisdiction where the risk is located and generally are not subject to regulations governing premium rates or policy language.

Nature, Conduct, and Regulation of the Business

1.06 The lines and premium volume that may be written by an entity are generally restricted by state insurance regulations. States also use risk-based capital standards for regulating solvency and capacity and also monitor the amount of premium written as a ratio of the entity's surplus.

1.07 Insurance written by property and liability insurance entities may be broadly classified as *personal lines*, which consist of insurance policies issued to individuals, and *commercial lines*, which consist of policies issued to business enterprises. Personal lines generally consist of large numbers of relatively standard policies with relatively small premiums per policy. Examples are homeowner and individual automobile policies. Commercial lines involve policies with relatively large premiums that are often retroactively adjusted based on claims experience. The initial premium is often only an estimate because it may be related to payroll or other variables. Examples are workers' compensation and general liability. Many large insurance entities have separate accounting, underwriting, and claim-processing procedures for these two categories.

1.08 Insurance is generally available to the individual as a means of protection against loss. There are instances, however, in which a person cannot obtain insurance in the voluntary insurance market. States have established programs to provide insurance to those with high risks who otherwise would be excluded from obtaining coverage. The following are some of the more common programs that provide the necessary coverage:

- *Involuntary automobile insurance.* States have a variety of methods for apportioning involuntary automobile insurance. The most widely used approach is the Automobile Insurance Plan (formerly called the Assigned Risk Plan). Under this plan, all entities writing automobile insurance in a state are allocated a share of the involuntary business on an equitable basis. Each automobile insurer operating in the state accepts a share of the undesirable drivers, based on the percent of the state's total auto insurance that it writes. For example, an entity that writes 5 percent of the voluntary business in a state may be assigned 5 percent of the involuntary applicants. It is then responsible for collecting the premiums and paying the claims on the policies issued to these applicants. Other states use a reinsurance plan under which each insurer accepts all applicants but may place high-risk drivers in a reinsurance pool, with premiums paid to and losses absorbed by the pool. Still another approach is a joint underwriting association, in which one or more servicing entities are designated to handle high-risk drivers. States may require insurers to participate in the underwriting results.

- *Fair Access to Insurance Requirements (FAIR) plans.* FAIR plans are state-supervised programs established to provide coverage for property in high-risk areas. Entities that operate in the state are required to participate in the premiums, losses, expenses, and other operations of the FAIR plan.

- *Medical malpractice pools.* These pools were established when healthcare professionals and institutions were experiencing difficulty in obtaining liability insurance in the voluntary insurance market. The pools were established by law and currently exist in the majority of states. All insurers writing related liability insurance in such states are considered mandatory participants in the pools as a condition for their continuing authority to transact business in such states.

- *Workers' compensation pools.* These pools are similar to FAIR plans. As with FAIR plans, companies operating in a given state are assessed a proportionate share, based on direct writings, of the underwriting results of the pool.

Legal Forms of Organization

1.09 The principal kinds of property and liability insurance organizations are

  a. *stock companies*, which are corporations organized for profit with ownership and control of operations vested in the stockholders. Generally, the stockholders are not liable in case of bankruptcy or impairment of capital.

  b. *mutual companies*, which are organizations in which the ownership and control of operations are vested in the policyholders. On the expiration of their policies, policyholders lose their rights and interests in the entity. Many states require the net assets of a mutual insurance entity in liquidation to be distributed among the current policyholders of the entity, and the prior policyholders have no claim against the assets. Most major mutual entities issue nonassessable policies as provided under state laws. If a mutual entity is not qualified to issue such policies, however, each policyholder is liable for an assessment equal to at least one annual premium in the event of bankruptcy or impairment of minimum equity requirements. Many mutual insurance entities are seeking enhanced financial flexibility and access to capital to support long-term growth and other strategic initiatives. Because of many economic and regulatory factors, as well as increased competition, some mutual insurance entities have chosen to demutualize or to form mutual insurance holding entities.

  c. *reciprocal or interinsurance exchanges*, which are composed of a group of persons, firms, or corporations, commonly termed *subscribers*, who exchange contracts of insurance through the medium of an attorney-in-fact. Each subscriber executes an identical agreement empowering the attorney-in-fact to assume, on the subscriber's behalf, an underwriting liability on policies covering the risks of the other subscribers. The subscriber assumes no liability as an underwriter on policies covering his or her own risk; the subscriber's liability is limited by the terms of the subscriber's agreement. Customarily, the attorney-in-fact is paid a percentage of premium income, from which he or she pays most operating expenses, but some exchanges pay his or her own operating expenses and compensate the attorney-in-fact at a lower percentage of premiums or by some other method.

  d. *public entity risk pools*, which are cooperative groups of governmental entities joining together to finance exposures, liabilities, or risks. Risk may include property and liability, workers' compensation, employee health care, and so forth. A pool may be a stand-alone entity or be included as part of a larger governmental entity that acts as the pool's sponsor. Stand-alone pools are sometimes organized or sponsored by municipal leagues, school associations, or other kinds of associations of governmental entities. A stand-alone pool is frequently operated by a board that has as its membership one member from each participating government. It typically has no publicly

Nature, Conduct, and Regulation of the Business

elected officials or power to tax. Public entity risk pools normally should be distinguished from private pools, which are organized under the Risk Retention Act of 1986. These private pools, or risk retention groups, can provide only liability coverage, whereas public entity risk pools organized under individual state statutes can provide several kinds of coverage. The four basic kinds of public entity risk pools are

   i. *risk-sharing pools*, which are arrangements by which governments pool risks and funds and share in the cost of losses.

   ii. *insurance-purchasing pools*, which are arrangements by which governments pool funds or resources to purchase commercial insurance products. These arrangements are also called *risk-purchasing groups*.

   iii. *banking pools*, which are arrangements by which money is made available for pool members in the event of loss on a loan basis.

   iv. *claims-servicing* or *account pools*, which are arrangements by which pools manage separate accounts for each pool member from which the losses of that member are paid.

A pool can serve one or several of those functions. Pools that act only as banking or claims-servicing pools do not represent transfer of risk. Those pools are not considered insurers and do not need to report as such.

    e. private pools. Because of the unavailability and unaffordability of commercial liability insurance, Congress enacted the Risk Retention Act of 1986. This act allows the organization of private pools for the purpose of obtaining general liability insurance coverage. Two basic types of private pools are allowed:

   i. *Risk retention groups.* An insurance entity formed by the members of the private pool primarily to provide commercial liability insurance to the members.

   ii. *Purchasing groups.* Members of a private pool purchase commercial liability insurance on a group basis.

Methods of Producing Business

1.10 The marketing department of an insurance entity is responsible for sales promotion, supervision of the agency or sales force, and sales training. Property and liability insurance entities may produce business through a network of agents (agency companies) or through an employee sales force (direct writing companies), or they may acquire business through insurance brokers or through direct solicitation. A combination of methods may also be used. The distinctions among an agent, a broker, and a salesperson are based on their relationships with the insurance entity.

1.11 *Agents.* Insurance agents act as independent contractors who represent one insurance entity (exclusive agents) or more than one entity (independent agents) with express authority to act for the entity in dealing with insureds.

1.12 General agents have exclusive territories in which to produce business. They agree to promote the entity's interest, pay their own expenses, maintain a satisfactory agency force, and secure subagents. They may perform a significant portion of the underwriting. They may also perform other services in connection with the issuance of policies and the adjustment of claims, including negotiating reinsurance on behalf of the insurer, which neither local agents nor brokers are authorized or expected to do.

1.13 Local and regional agents are authorized to underwrite and issue policies but are not usually given exclusive territories. They usually report either to entity branch offices or directly to the entity's home offices. Agents are generally compensated by commissions based on percentages of the premiums they produce. Because of their greater authority and duties, general agents usually receive higher percentages than local or regional agents.

1.14 Agents have the power to bind the entity, which means that the insurance is effective immediately, regardless of whether money is received or a policy is issued. Generally, agents are considered to have vested rights in the renewal of policies sold for insurance entities. The entity cannot, however, compel independent agents to renew policies, and the agents may place renewals with other entities.

1.15 *Brokers.* Insurance brokers represent the insured. As a result, brokers do not have the power to bind the entity. Brokers solicit business and submit it for acceptance or rejection with one or more insurance entities. Brokers may submit business directly to an entity, through general or local agents, or through other brokers. Brokers are compensated by commissions paid by insurance entities, normally percentages of the premiums on policies placed with the entities, or through fees paid by the insured. A growing trend among large brokers is toward fee agreements, wherein commissions are either not accepted from the respective insurer or commissions received from the insurer by the broker are offset against the fees to be paid by the insured.

1.16 *Direct writing.* Direct writing entities sell policies directly to the public, usually through salespeople or Internet sales, thus bypassing agents and brokers. Direct writing may be done from the entity's home office or through branch sales offices. Underwriting and policy issuance may also be done from the home office or branches. The salespeople may be paid commissions, straight salaries, or a commission incentive with a base salary. Salespeople generally have the power to bind the entity; however, the entity retains the right to cancel the policy, generally for up to 60 days.

1.17 Direct response advertising or mass marketing is also used for producing business. This results in sales to many people simultaneously, with single programs to insure a number of people or businesses. Such methods use direct billing techniques that may also permit individuals to pay premiums by salary deductions, credit cards, or as a direct draft against a checking account.

Major Transaction Cycles

Underwriting of Risks

1.18 Underwriting includes evaluating the acceptability of the risk, determining the premium, and evaluating the entity's capacity to assume the entire risk.

Nature, Conduct, and Regulation of the Business

1.19 *Evaluating risks.* Evaluating risks and their acceptance or rejection involves (*a*) a review of exposure and potential loss based on both the review of policies, past claims experience, and the endorsements to existing policies and (*b*) an investigation of risks in accordance with procedures established by entity policy and state statutes. For example, applicants for automobile insurance may be checked by reference to reports on driving records issued by a state department of motor vehicles. A commercial enterprise wanting to purchase property insurance coverage may need to provide certain types of information when applying for coverage, for example, claims history, an engineering survey, a fire hazard survey, or similar investigations. In addition, an entity's underwriting policy may establish certain predetermined criteria for accepting risks. Such criteria often specify the lines of insurance that will be written as well as prohibited exposures, the amount of coverage to be permitted on various kinds of exposure, the areas of the country in which each line will be written, and similar restrictions.

1.20 *Setting premium rates.* Establishing prices for insurance coverage is known as the rate-making process, and the resultant rates that are applied to some measure of exposure (for example, payroll or number of cars) are referred to as *premiums*. Determining premiums is one of the most difficult tasks in the insurance business. The total amount of claims is not known at the time the insurance policies are issued and, for many liability policies, is not known until years later. Determining proper premium rates is further complicated by the fact that no two insurable risks are exactly alike. The intensity of competition among hundreds of property and liability insurance entities in the United States is also significant in setting premiums.

1.21 Premium rates may be established by one of three methods:

> a. *Manual rating*, which results in standard rates for large groups of similar risks and is used, for example, in many personal lines such as automobile insurance
>
> b. *Judgment rating*, which depends on the skill and experience of the rate-maker and, generally, is used for large or unusual risks such as ocean marine insurance
>
> c. *Merit rating*, which begins with an assumed standard or "manual" rate that is adjusted based on an evaluation of the risk or the insured's experience in past or current periods and is used in many commercial lines such as workers' compensation

1.22 The transaction cycle for premiums is described in detail in chapter 3, "Premiums."

1.23 *Reinsurance.* Insurance entities collect amounts from many risks subject to insurable hazards; it is expected that these amounts will be sufficient in the aggregate to pay all losses sustained by the risks in the group. To do so, the number of risks insured needs to be large enough for the law of averages to operate.[2] However, insurance entities are often offered, or may be compelled to accept, insurance of a class for which they do not have enough volume in the aggregate to permit the law of averages to operate. Further, entities often write policies on risks for amounts beyond their financial capacities to absorb. An entity also may write a heavy concentration of policies in one geographic area

---

[2] That is, the statistical tendency of expected losses over a large population of risks.

that exposes the entity to catastrophes beyond its financial capabilities. Ordinarily, all or part of such risks are passed on to other insurance or reinsurance entities.

1.24 Spreading of risks among insurance entities is called *reinsurance*. The entity transferring the risk is called the *ceding entity* and the entity to which the risk is transferred is called the *assuming entity*, or the *reinsurer*. Although a ceding entity may transfer its risk to another entity through reinsurance, it does not discharge its primary liability to its policyholders. The ceding entity remains liable for claims under the policy; however, through reinsurance, the ceding entity reduces its maximum exposure in the event of loss by obtaining the right to reimbursement from the assuming entity for the reinsured portion of the loss. The ceding entity is also exposed to the possibility that the reinsurer will not be able to reimburse the ceding entity.

1.25 The term *portfolio reinsurance* is applied to the sale of all or a block of an entity's insurance in force to another entity. This kind of reinsurance is frequently used when an entity wishes to withdraw from a particular line, territory, or agency. In portfolio reinsurance, the assuming entity generally undertakes responsibility for servicing the policies—collecting the premiums, settling the claims, and so on—and the policyholder subsequently deals directly with the assuming entity.

1.26 *Fronting*. Fronting is a form of an indemnity reinsurance arrangement between two or more insurers whereby the fronting entity will issue contracts and then cede all or substantially all of the risk through a reinsurance agreement to the other insurer(s) (the fronted entity) for a ceding commission. Such arrangements must comply with any regulatory requirements applicable to fronting to ensure avoidance of any illegal acts. As with other reinsurance contracts, the fronting entity remains primarily liable on the insurance contract with the insured. Fronting arrangements usually are initiated by fronted companies that are not authorized to write insurance in particular states.

1.27 The principal kinds of reinsurance agreements and the mechanics of reinsurance are discussed in detail in chapter 6, "Reinsurance."

Pooling, Captives, and Syndicates

1.28 *Pooling*. The term *pooling* is often used to describe the practice of sharing all, or portions of, business of an affiliated group of insurance entities among the members of the group. Each premium written by the affiliated companies is customarily ceded to one entity; after allowing for any business reinsured outside the group, the premiums are in turn ceded back in agreed-upon ratios. Claims, claim adjustment expenses, commissions, and other underwriting and operating expenses are similarly apportioned. Each member of the group shares pro rata in the total business of the group, and all achieve similar underwriting results. Another kind of pooling involving sharing of risks among governmental entities is discussed in paragraph 1.09*d*.

1.29 *Underwriting pools, associations, and syndicates*. Underwriting pools, associations, or syndicates are formed by several independent entities or groups of entities in joint ventures to underwrite specialized kinds of insurance or to write in specialized areas. These groups are often operated as separate organizations having distinctive names and their own staff of employees. The pools, associations, or syndicates may issue individual or syndicate policies on behalf of the member entities, which share in all such policies in accordance with an agreement, or policies may be issued directly by the member entities and then

Nature, Conduct, and Regulation of the Business

reinsured among the members in accordance with the agreement. The agreement stipulates the group's manner of operation and the sharing of premiums, claims, and expenses. Such groups customarily handle all functions in connection with the specialized business that would otherwise have to be handled by specific departments in each of the member companies. This kind of arrangement usually is more economical in handling the business for the members.

1.30 *Captives.* Noninsurance businesses[3] try to use various methods to minimize their cost of insurance. Other than retaining the risk (that is, self-insurance), perhaps the most conventional method is the use of captive insurers. Captive insurers are wholly owned subsidiaries created to provide insurance to the parent entities. Captives were originally formed because no tax deductions are allowed if risks are not transferred, whereas premiums paid to insurers are tax deductible. Captive domiciles in the United States continue to expand as states pass legislation to facilitate the formation of domestic captives. The growth in the capital that captives control is also on the rise. The domiciles in the United States that contain the largest number of captives are Vermont, South Carolina, Hawaii, Arizona, the District of Columbia, and Nevada. Captives are discussed in detail in chapter 9, "Captive Insurance Entities."

Processing and Payment of Claims

1.31 An insurance entity's claim department accepts, investigates, adjusts, and settles claims. Although specific procedures vary from entity to entity, a common pattern exists to the flow of transactions through the claims cycle, which consists of the following major functions: claim acceptance and processing, claim adjustment and estimation, and claim settlement.

1.32 The transaction cycle for claims, including a claims process flowchart, is discussed in more detail in chapter 4, "The Loss Reserving and Claims Cycle."

Investments

1.33 A property and liability insurance entity collects funds from those who desire protection from insured loss and disburses funds to those who incur such losses. During the time between receiving premiums and the payment of losses, the entity invests the funds. These investments consist primarily of debt and equity securities. They may include mortgage loans, real estate, repurchase agreements, and derivative instruments. They may also include investments in mutual funds, hedge funds, joint ventures, and partnerships. In addition to holding long-term investments, insurance companies generally maintain short-term portfolios consisting of assets with maturities of less than one year to meet liquidity needs. Short-term investments of property and liability insurance entities typically consist of commercial paper, repurchase agreements, certificates of deposit, Treasury bills, and money market funds.

1.34 Because insurance entities must be able to meet the claims of their policyholders, their investments generally should be both financially sound and sufficiently liquid. To ensure that entities will be able to meet their obligations, statutory restrictions have been placed on their investment activities. Although statutes and regulations vary from state to state, most states specify maximum

---

[3] Technical Questions and Answers sections 1200.06–.16 (AICPA, *Technical Practice Aids*) provide information on finite insurance products utilized by noninsurance enterprises. The guidance provides information to assist insurance customers and practitioners in identifying the relevant literature to consider in addressing their specific facts and circumstances.

percentages of an entity's assets, surplus, or both that may be placed in various kinds of investments. In addition, regulatory authorities may require that some investments be deposited with the state insurance departments as a condition for writing business in those states. Investment standards and restrictions for public entity risk pools differ significantly from standards for insurance entities. In some jurisdictions, public entity risk pools must follow regulations governing the investment of public funds. Invested assets consist primarily of bonds and marketable equity securities, but investments are also commonly made in mortgage loans and income-producing real estate. In addition, the insurance industry has been increasingly utilizing options, financial futures, and other instruments in its investment activities.

1.35 Many insurance entities have separate investment departments responsible for managing the entities' investable funds. However, they may also use outside advisers or portfolio managers. The evaluation for purchase and subsequent purchase or sale of investments is based on the judgment of the entity's investment and finance committees.

1.36 The transaction cycle for investments is discussed in more detail in chapter 5, "Investments and Fair Value Considerations."

Accounting Practices

State Insurance Regulation

1.37 The insurance industry is deemed to be a business vested with the public interest and is regulated by the states. Statutes in each state provide for the organization and maintenance of an insurance department responsible for supervising insurance entities and enforcing compliance with the law. Property and liability insurance entities are subject to formal regulation by the insurance department of the state in which they are domiciled and are also subject to the insurance regulations of the states in which they are licensed to do business.

1.38 Although statutes vary from state to state, they have as their common principal objective the development and enforcement of measures designed to promote solvency, propriety of premium rates, fair dealings with policyholders, and uniform financial reporting. State statutes (*a*) restrict investments of insurance entities to certain kinds of assets, (*b*) prescribe methods of valuation of securities and other assets, (*c*) require maintenance of reserves, risk-based capital, and surplus, and (*d*) define those assets not permitted to be reported as admitted assets.

1.39 The states regulate insurance premium rates to ensure that they are adequate, reasonable, and not discriminatory. In a 1944 decision, the U.S. Supreme Court held that insurance is interstate commerce and as such is subject to regulation by the federal government. However, in 1945 Congress passed the McCarran-Ferguson Act, which exempts the insurance business from antitrust laws. Although Congress insisted that the federal government has the right to regulate the insurance industry, it stated in the McCarran-Ferguson Act that the federal government would not regulate insurance as long as state legislation provided for the supervision of insurance entities, including rate making. The following practices are protected by the McCarran-Ferguson Act:

Nature, Conduct, and Regulation of the Business

- Pooling of statistical data for rate making
- Standard policy forms and standardized coverage
- Joint underwriting and joint reinsurance (such as insurance pools for exceptional hazards)
- Tying of various lines of insurance, that is, making the purchase of lines of insurance that are unprofitable to the insurance entity conditional on the purchase of profitable lines (***Note:*** Tying is not permitted in certain states)

1.40 All states have passed legislation requiring insurance commissioners to review, with or without prior approval, most rates charged by insurance entities. An entity must file most rates with the insurance department of each state in which it is authorized to do business. A number of states also require formal or tacit approval of rates by respective state insurance departments.

1.41 To promote fair dealing with policyholders, state statutes provide for certain standard provisions to be incorporated in policies and for the insurance departments to review and approve the forms of policies. State insurance departments review and approve contract forms and perform market conduct examinations involving pricing policies and notifications to contract holders as required by law. Insurance agents, brokers, and salespeople must qualify for and obtain licenses granted by the insurance department of a state before they may conduct business in the state.

1.42 To promote uniform financial reporting, as previously discussed, the statutes provide for annual or more frequent filings with the insurance departments in a prescribed form.

1.43 In a majority of states, insurance entities may not be organized without the authorization of the insurance department and, in states in which such authorization is not necessary, approval by the insurance department is necessary for the completion of organization.

1.44 An insurance department generally consists of an insurance commissioner or superintendent in charge, one or more deputies, and a staff of examiners, attorneys, and clerical assistants. Many larger insurance departments also employ actuaries to review rate filings and to assist in the monitoring of financial solvency, principally relating to loss reserves. The head of the state insurance department, generally referred to as the commissioner, is either appointed by the governor or elected. The state legislature is responsible for enacting laws and statutes; however, the commissioner usually holds many discretionary powers, including the authority to issue the rules and regulations necessary to ensure compliance with the state's statutes. A commissioner is not bound by precedent; that is, the commissioner may disregard his or her own previous decisions as well as the decisions made by predecessors. Formal acts of an insurance regulatory authority are set forth either as adjudications or rulings. *Adjudications* are a commissioner's decision in a particular situation, such as a denial of a provision in a certain contract form requested by an insurer. *Rulings*, or regulations, are regulatory decisions concerning situations that have widespread implications; they apply to all activities over which the state insurance department has jurisdiction. The insurance commissioner also has the power to take remedial action against any entity in noncompliance with the regulations of the affected state, including actions that would preclude the insurance entity from writing further business in a particular state.

AAG-PLI 1.44

1.45 States generally conduct periodic financial examinations of property and liability insurance entities. These examinations are conducted under the supervision of the state insurance department of the entity's state of domicile with the participation of other zones on request from other states in which the entity is licensed to write business. Examinations generally are conducted every three to five years, at the discretion of the state department of insurance. At the conclusion of the examination, a detailed report, including any adjustments to statutory surplus required by the state examiners, is issued. Generally, such adjustments are not retroactively recognized in an entity's financial statement. Regulators may deem a property and liability insurance entity unable to continue doing business as a result of inadequate statutory surplus levels, and force the entity into receivership, rehabilitation, or liquidation.

National Association of Insurance Commissioners

1.46 To create greater uniformity both in the laws and their administration and to recommend desirable legislation in state legislatures, the state commissioners of insurance organized an association that is known today as the National Association of Insurance Commissioners (NAIC). The activities of the NAIC include monitoring financial conditions and providing guidance on financial reporting and state regulatory examinations. The work of the NAIC over the years has helped to eliminate many conflicts of state law and to promote more uniform and efficient regulation of insurance entities. In June 1989, the Financial Regulation Standards were developed, which established baseline requirements for an effective regulatory system in each state. The NAIC Financial Regulation Standards and Accreditation Program was subsequently developed by the NAIC to provide states with guidance regarding these standards. The standards are divided into three categories: (*a*) laws and regulations, (*b*) regulatory practices and procedures, and (*c*) organizational and personnel practices. Accounting, financial reporting, and auditing requirements are included in the standards. Mandating certain requirements and certifying that the states are in compliance provides a degree of assurance that regulators have adequate authority to regulate insurers, have the resources to carry out that authority, and have in place administrative practices designed for effective regulation.

1.47 *Insurance Regulatory Information System.*[4] The NAIC Insurance Regulatory Information System (IRIS) was developed to assist the state insurance departments in monitoring financial conditions of property and liability insurance entities. The system uses financial ratios to identify entities that may be having financial difficulties. Such priority entities can then be targeted for closer surveillance or perhaps for onsite examination. IRIS ratio results are kept confidential through the period when the ratios are calculated. They are made available only to the entity and to the state of domicile insurance department. After a period of review by the entity and the domiciliary state regulator, the ratio results are published by the NAIC.

Financial Ratios

Financial ratios can be categorized as overall ratios, profitability ratios, liquidity ratios, or reserve ratios. A brief description of each of the individual ratios and the acceptable results (based on the NAIC guidance in effect in 2012) follows.

---

[4] From the National Association of Insurance Commissioners Insurance Regulatory Information System, Kansas City, Kansas.

Nature, Conduct, and Regulation of the Business

Overall Ratios

Gross premiums written to policyholders' surplus. An entity's policyholders' surplus provides a cushion for absorbing above-average losses. This ratio measures the adequacy of this cushion, net of the effects of premiums ceded to reinsurers. The higher the ratio, the more risk the entity bears in relation to the policyholders' surplus available to absorb loss variations. This ratio is calculated by dividing gross premiums written by policyholders' surplus. The results of this test should include results up to 900 percent.

Net premiums written to policyholders' surplus. An entity's surplus provides a cushion for absorbing above-average losses. This ratio measures the adequacy of this cushion. The higher the ratio, the more risk the entity bears in relation to the surplus available to absorb loss variations. This ratio is calculated by dividing net premiums written by policyholders' surplus. The results of this test should be less than 300 percent.

Change in net writings. Major increases or decreases in net premiums written indicate a lack of stability in the entity's operations. A large increase in premium may signal abrupt entry into new lines of business or sales territories. In addition, such an increase in writings may indicate that the entity is increasing cash inflow in order to meet loss payments. A large decrease in premiums may indicate the discontinuance of certain lines of business, scaled back writings due to large losses in certain lines, or loss of market share due to competition. The usual range for this ratio is from –33 percent to 33 percent.

Surplus aid to policyholders' surplus. The use of surplus aid reinsurance treaties may be taken as an indication that entity management believes policyholders' surplus to be inadequate. In addition, the continued solvency of entities with a large portion of policyholders' surplus deriving from surplus aid may depend upon the continuing cooperation of the reinsurer. The usual range for the test is less than 15 percent.

Profitability Ratios

Two-year overall operating ratio. The overall operating ratio is a measure of the operating profitability of an insurance entity. Over the long run, the profitability of the business is a principal determinant of the entity's financial solidity and solvency. The usual range for this test is less than 100 percent.

Investment yield. In addition to measuring one important element in profitability, the investment yield also provides an indication of the general quality of the entity's investment portfolio. The usual range for this test is greater than 3 percent and less than 6.5 percent.

Change in policyholders' surplus. The change in policyholders' surplus is, in a sense, the ultimate measure of the improvement or deterioration of the entity's financial condition during the year. The usual range for this test is from a decrease of 10 percent to an increase of 50 percent.

Liquidity Ratios

Liabilities to liquid assets. The ratio of total liabilities to liquid assets is a measure of the entity's ability to meet the financial demands that

AAG-PLI 1.47

may be placed upon it. It also provides a rough indication of the possible implications for policyholders if liquidation becomes necessary. The usual range for this test is less than 100 percent.

Gross agents' balances to policyholders' surplus. The ratio of agents' balances to policyholders' surplus measures the degree to which solvency depends on an asset that frequently cannot be realized in the event of liquidation. In addition, the ratio is reasonably effective in distinguishing between troubled and solid entities. The usual range for this test is less than 40 percent.

Reserve Ratios

One-year reserve development to policyholders' surplus. This ratio measures the accuracy with which reserves were established one year ago. The usual range for this test is less than 20 percent.

Two-year reserve development to policyholders' surplus. The two-year reserve development to surplus ratio is calculated in a manner similar to the calculation in the one-year reserve development test. The two-year reserve development is the sum of the current reserve for losses incurred more than two years prior, plus payments on those losses during the past two years minus the reserves that had been established for those losses two years earlier. The usual range for this test is less than 20 percent.

Estimated current reserve deficiency to policyholders' surplus. This ratio provides an estimate of the adequacy of current reserves. The usual range for this test is less than 25 percent.

Unusual circumstances precluded, an entity would be considered a priority entity if it failed four or more ratios. As previously discussed, the results of the NAIC IRIS financial ratios should be reviewed and results outside the usual ranges investigated and explained.

Federal Regulation—Securities and Exchange Commission

1.48 Because property and liability insurance entities are subject to state insurance department supervision and regulations, the Securities Exchange Act of 1934 contains certain provisions exempting stock property and liability insurance entities from registration with the Securities and Exchange Commission (SEC). However, a large number of entities have registered under the act, either in connection with the listing of their shares on a national securities exchange or because they have formed holding companies that do not qualify for exemption under the act. Property and liability insurance entities registered under the act must comply with the SEC's periodic reporting requirement and are subject to the proxy solicitation and insider-trading rules. Insurance entities making public offerings are required to file under the Securities Act of 1933 and must thereafter comply with the annual and periodic reporting requirements of the Securities Exchange Act of 1934. However, these entities are not under the proxy solicitation or insider-trading rules of the Securities Exchange Act of 1934 as long as they meet the attendant provisions for exemption. Insurance entities that are SEC registrants should follow Article 7 of SEC Regulation S-X, SEC Industry Guide 6, and applicable Staff Accounting Bulletins, which prescribe the form and content of financial statements.

1.49 Additionally, the aforementioned entities subject to SEC rules and regulations are required to follow the provisions of the Sarbanes-Oxley Act of

Nature, Conduct, and Regulation of the Business

2002 and related SEC regulations that implement the act. Their outside auditors are also subject to the provisions of the act and to the rules and standards issued by the Public Company Accounting Oversight Board (PCAOB), subject to SEC oversight. For further information on these rules and regulations, see chapter 2, "Audit Considerations."

1.50 *Disclosure information—general recommendations.*[5,6] SEC staff recommendations for improved disclosures include, but are not limited to the following:

> a. *Loss reserves.* The SEC staff desires improved explanations for changes in reserve estimates. More specifically, disclosure should show changes in estimates by line of business, discussion of the range of estimates by line of business, improved explanations of the facts involved in the reserve estimates, or new information since the last report date underlying the improved insight on estimates and a more robust discussion of the entity's remaining exposure to uncertainty. Additional disclosure for incurred, but not reported, reserves and case reserves and by line of business should also be considered. The staff has expressed concern that investors expect a higher degree of precision on loss reserve estimates than exists. Therefore, investors should be provided with more detailed information relating to uncertainties inherent in the estimates.
>
> Note that disclosures for the liability for unpaid claims and claim adjustment expenses and reinsurance recoverables on paid and unpaid claims should enable the reader to understand (i) management's method for establishing the estimate for each material line of business and how the methodology is appropriate for the reporting, development, and payment patterns inherent in the business line; (ii) any changes to significant assumptions used to determine the current period estimate from the assumptions used in the immediately preceding period, the reason for the change, and the impact of the change; and (iii) the reasonably likely variability inherent in the current estimate and the impact that variability may have on future

---

[5] The Division of Corporation Finance of the Securities and Exchange Commission (SEC) has distributed several illustrative letters to public entities identifying a number of disclosure issues they may wish to consider in preparing Management's Discussion and Analysis for their reports on Forms 10-Q, Form 10-K, or Form 20-F. Readers should familiarize themselves with these letters that can be found on the SEC website:

- January 2012 letter reminding public entities of the Division of Corporation Finance's views regarding disclosures relating to registrants' exposures to certain European countries: www.sec.gov/divisions/corpfin/guidance/cfguidance-topic4.htm
- October 2010 letter reminding public entities of the disclosure obligations to consider in their upcoming Form 10-Qs and subsequent filings, in light of continued concerns about potential risks and costs associated with mortgage and foreclosure-related activities or exposures: www.sec.gov/divisions/corpfin/guidance/cfoforeclosure1010.htm
- March 2010 letter requesting information about repurchase agreements, securities lending transactions, or other transactions involving the transfer of financial assets with an obligation to repurchase the transferred assets: www.sec.gov/divisions/corpfin/guidance/cforepurchase0310.htm
- March and September 2008 letters surrounding the fair value of financial instruments: www.sec.gov/divisions/corpfin/guidance/fairvalueltr0308.htm and www.sec.gov/divisions/corpfin/guidance/fairvalueltr0908.htm

[6] During several speeches in 2010, the SEC staff stated that it will increase its scrutiny of registrants' loss contingency disclosures, looking for compliance with existing loss contingency disclosure requirements. The staff raised concerns that some registrants may not be disclosing an estimate of the possible loss or range of loss in circumstances where such an estimate could be made, and that other registrants, in circumstances where an estimate cannot be made, may not be stating that fact.

AAG-PLI 1.50

reported results, financial condition, and liquidity. Disclosure about the liability for unpaid claims and claim adjustment expenses should identify underlying causes, not just intermediate effects, and should include a quantitative as well as qualitative discussion. Disclosure should be concise and to the point and should avoid unnecessary repetition. Readers should refer to Section II R of the SEC's *Current Accounting and Disclosure Issues in the Division of Corporation Finance*, which can be accessed at www.sec.gov/divisions/corpfin/cfacctdisclosureissues.pdf.

b. *Other than temporary impairments of securities (general).*[7] Discussion should include the entity policy for evaluating other than temporary impairments, the amount of impairment, and whether those factors would affect other investments. The SEC staff expressed an expectation for this level of disclosure for each quarter for all material impairments.

c. *Realized losses on investments.* Discussion should include the amount of loss and the fair value at the date of sale as well as the reasons for sales if the entity previously asserted the ability and intent to hold the investment to maturity, in order to justify the lack of an impairment loss. The SEC expressed an expectation for this level of disclosure each quarter for all material losses.

d. *Unrealized losses on investments.* Discussion should include concentrations of securities with a loss. Additionally, disclosure should include the length of time that securities have been recorded with an unrealized loss, in tabular format, by class of security, and broken out between investment and noninvestment grade investments. The SEC staff expressed an expectation for this level of disclosure each quarter for all material unrealized losses.

e. *Accounting policy disclosures.* Registrants should provide more specific information regarding critical accounting policies, especially if the policies are in areas where there is known diversity in practice.

f. *Contractual obligations.* The SEC staff recommended increased disclosures regarding insurance contracts in the contractual obligations table in Form 10-K. Disclosures include variables such as future lapse rates and interest crediting rates.

g. *Loss contingencies.* The guidance in Financial Accounting Standards Board (FASB) *Accounting Standards Codification* (ASC) 450-10-50 should be followed when determining what information related to legal proceedings and loss contingencies should be disclosed.

h. *Mortgage and foreclosure-related activities or exposures.* Discussion should include the impact of various representations and warranties regarding mortgages made to purchasers of the mortgages (or to

---

[7] For the application of generally accepted accounting principles (GAAP), refer to FASB ASC 320, *Investments—Debt and Equity Securities*.

For statutory accounting practices, refer to the impairment sections of Statement of Statutory Accounting Principles (SSAP) No. 26, *Bonds, Excluding Loan-Backed and Structured Securities*; SSAP No. 32, *Investments in Preferred Stock (including investments in preferred stock of subsidiary, controlled or affiliated entities)*; and SSAP No. 34, *Investment Income due and Accrued*. For additional specifics, see chapter 5, "The Investment Cycle."

Nature, Conduct, and Regulation of the Business

purchasers of mortgage-backed securities) including to the government-sponsored entities (GSEs), private-label mortgage-backed security (MBS) investors, financial guarantors, and other whole loan purchasers.

  i. *Repurchase agreements, securities lending transactions, or other transactions involving the transfer of financial assets.* Discussion should include information about whether repurchase agreements were accounted for as sales for accounting purposes or collateralized financing, and additional details as per the March 2010 sample letter sent by the Division of Corporation Finance of the SEC.

1.51 *SEC disclosures—Sarbanes-Oxley Act of 2002 implementation.* In response to passage of the Sarbanes-Oxley Act of 2002, the SEC and PCAOB have issued (or are issuing) additional rules and regulations specifying compliance. Additionally, in June 2006, state regulators adopted changes to the Annual Financial Reporting Model Regulation effective in 2010 by considering certain provisions of the act. For additional information, see chapter 2. Sections of the act that contain disclosure requirements include Sections 302, 401(a), 401(b), 404, 406, and 407:

  a. Section 302—Certification of disclosure in companies quarterly and annual reports CEOs and CFOs (or their equivalents) are now required to certify the financial and other information contained in quarterly and annual reports and make certain disclosures. Additionally, Department of Justice certifications (governed by Section 906 of the act) became effective upon enactment of the act.

  b. Section 401(a)—Disclosure in management's discussion and analysis about off-balance sheet arrangements and aggregate contractual obligations. This section of the act requires that each annual and quarterly financial report disclose specific material transactions and relationships.

  c. Section 401(b)—Conditions for use of non-GAAP financial measures. This section discusses the disclosure of pro forma financial information in any report filed with the SEC, or in any public disclosures or press releases. The use of the phrase *non-GAAP financial measures* rather than *pro forma financial information* is used to eliminate confusion with pro forma disclosures that are required under existing SEC rules and regulations. As required by the act, whenever an entity presents a non-GAAP financial measure, Regulation G will require presentation of a numerical reconciliation to the most directly comparable measurement calculated using GAAP. Regulation G also explicitly prohibits the presentation of inaccurate or misleading non-GAAP financial measures. Rule 401(b) defines a *non-GAAP financial measure* as a numerical measure of an entity's historical or future financial performance, financial position, or cash flows that excludes (includes) amounts, or is subject to adjustments that have the effect of excluding (including) amounts, that are included (excluded) in the most directly comparable measure calculated in accordance with GAAP.

  d. Section 404—Management's reports on internal control over financial reporting and certification of disclosure in exchange act periodic reports. See chapter 2 of this guide for additional information about this section.

Property and Liability Insurance Entities

e. Sections 406 and 407—Disclosure required by Sections 406 and 407 of the Sarbanes-Oxley Act of 2002. These sections discuss code of ethics and audit committee financial expert disclosures, respectively.

1.52 *Additional insurance industry information for non-GAAP financial measures.* The definition of non-GAAP financial measures specifically excludes measures that are required to be disclosed by GAAP, SEC rules, or an applicable system of regulation imposed by a government, governmental authority, or self-regulatory organization. Therefore, ratios (for example, statutory) used by insurance registrants in SEC filings to describe the results of operations are considered outside the scope of the non-GAAP rules so long as those ratios are identical (in terms of both formula and result) to those presented in required filings with insurance regulators.

1.53 In addition to Regulation G, the SEC also amended Regulation S-K Item 10(e) to impose additional requirements and restrictions on the disclosure of non-GAAP financial measures included in a filing with the SEC. Among other things, the amendments to Regulations S-K prohibit the presentation of performance measures that exclude charges or gains identified as *nonrecurring*, *infrequent*, or *unusual*, unless the excluded items meet certain conditions. In the past, many insurance entities had used the term *operating earnings* (or similar non-GAAP terms) in discussing financial results included in a filing with the SEC. Operating earnings can be defined in a variety of different ways; however, the most common definition is net income excluding after-tax realized investment gains and losses. Under non-GAAP rules, the term "operating earnings" is now prohibited from being used in SEC filings because it is considered a performance measure that is adjusted to eliminate or smooth items (realized investment gains and losses), which have either occurred in the prior two years or are likely to recur within two years from the balance sheet date.[8]

Federal Regulation—The Dodd-Frank Wall Street Reform and Consumer Protection Act

1.54 The Dodd-Frank Act created new regulations for companies that extend credit to customers, exempt small public companies from Section 404(b) of the Sarbanes-Oxley Act of 2002, make auditors of broker-dealers subject to PCAOB oversight, and change the registration requirements for investment advisers. Some of the highlights of the Dodd-Frank Act are summarized in the following paragraphs.

1.55 The Dodd-Frank Act created a new systemic risk regulator called the Financial Stability Oversight Council (FSOC). The FSOC identifies any company, product, or activity that could threaten the financial system. It is chaired by the Treasury secretary and members are heads of regulatory agencies, including the chairmen of the Federal Reserve, the Federal Deposit Insurance Corporation (FDIC), and the SEC, among others. For those large entities deemed a threat to the U.S. financial system, the FSOC can, under the authority of a new orderly liquidation authority, authorize the FDIC to close such entities under the supervision of the Federal Reserve. The FSOC, through the Federal Reserve, has the power to break up large firms, require increased reserves, or

---

[8] Readers should be aware of the revised SEC Compliance and Disclosure Interpretation *Non-GAAP Financial Measures* (specifically question 102.03 that addresses adjusting a non-GAAP financial performance measures), issued in January 2010, that can be found on the SEC website at www.sec.gov/divisions/corpfin/guidance/nongaapinterp.htm.

Nature, Conduct, and Regulation of the Business

veto rules created by another new regulator, the Bureau of Consumer Financial Protection, with a two-thirds vote.

1.56 The new Bureau of Consumer Financial Protection (BCFP) consolidates most federal regulation of financial services offered to consumers. The director of the BCFP replaces the director of the Office of Thrift Supervision (OTS) on the FDIC board. Almost all credit providers, including mortgage lenders, providers of payday loans, refund anticipation loan providers, other nonbank financial companies, and banks and credit unions with assets over $10 billion, will be subject to the new regulations.

1.57 The Dodd-Frank Act recognizes that CPAs providing customary and usual accounting activities (which include accounting, tax, advisory, or other services that are subject to the regulatory authority of a state board of accountancy) and other services incidental to such customary and usual accounting activities are already adequately regulated and, therefore, are not subject to the BCFP's authority.

1.58 The Dodd-Frank Act amends the Sarbanes-Oxley Act to make permanent the exemption from its Section 404(b) requirement for nonaccelerated filers (those with less than $75 million in market capitalization) that had temporarily been in effect by order of the SEC. Section 404(b) of the Sarbanes-Oxley Act requires companies to obtain an auditor's report on management's assessment of the effectiveness of the company's internal control over financial reporting. In September 2010, the SEC issued Final Rule Release Nos. 33-9142; 34-62914, *Internal Control Over Financial Reporting in Exchange Act Periodic Reports of Non-Accelerated Filers*, to conform its rules to this resulting change from the Dodd-Frank Act.

1.59 The Dodd-Frank Act gives the FSOC the duty to monitor domestic and international financial regulatory proposals and developments, including insurance and accounting issues, and to advise Congress to make recommendations in such areas that will enhance the integrity, efficiency, competitiveness, and stability of the U.S. financial markets. The FSOC may submit comments to the SEC and any standard setting body with respect to an existing or proposed accounting principle, standard, or procedure.

1.60 Previously, the Investment Advisers Act of 1940 required investment advisers with more than $30 million in assets under management to register with the SEC. Under the Dodd-Frank Act, this threshold for federal regulation has been raised to $100 million, with certain exceptions. This change will increase the number of advisers under state supervision.

1.61 Because it lowers the legal standard from "knowing" to "knowing or reckless," the Dodd-Frank Act may make it easier for the SEC to prosecute aiders and abettors of those who commit securities fraud under the Securities Act of 1933, the Securities Exchange Act of 1934, the Investment Company Act of 1940, and the Investment Advisers Act of 1940. Additionally, the Dodd-Frank Act authorizes two studies on these matters. One of the studies directs the Government Accountability Office to investigate the impact of authorizing private rights of action for aiding and abetting claims and to release its findings within 1 year. The second study directs the SEC to examine whether private rights of action should be authorized for transnational or extraterritorial claims, and that study is to be completed within 18 months.

1.62 The Dodd-Frank Act requires a nonbinding shareholder vote on executive pay. Management must give shareholders the opportunity to vote on how frequently shareholders will have a "say on pay" (that is, annually, every

AAG-PLI 1.62

two years, or every three years). Compensation based on financial statements that are restated must be returned for the three years preceding the restatement in an amount equal to the excess of what would have been paid under the restated results. Listing exchanges will enforce the compensation policies. The Dodd-Frank Act also requires directors of compensation committees to be independent of the company and its management and requires new disclosures regarding compensation.

1.63 In addition to the previously mentioned regulations, the Dodd-Frank Act also

- provides for the PCAOB to create a program for registering and inspecting the auditors of broker-dealers, including standard setting and enforcement.
- requires standardized swaps to be traded on an exchange, or in other centralized trading facilities, to better promote transparency in this complex market.
- eliminates the private adviser exemption under the Investment Advisers Act of 1940, which will consequently result in more advisers having to register with the SEC. Advisers to venture capital funds remain exempt from registration, as well as advisers to private funds if such an adviser acts solely as an adviser to private funds and has less than $150 million in U.S. assets under management. The Dodd-Frank Act also amends the Investment Advisers Act of 1940 to specifically exclude family offices from registration as an investment adviser.

Federal Regulation—Terrorism

1.64 Property and liability entities must follow the Terrorism Risk Insurance Act of 2002 (TRIA) and its amendments, the Terrorism Insurance Extension Act of 2005 and the Terrorism Risk Insurance Program Reauthorization Act of 2007. TRIA created a federal backstop for property and casualty insurance entities covering acts of terrorism in excess of $5 million. Insurance entities would pay a deductible equal to 7 percent, 10 percent, and 15 percent of prior year premiums in 2003, 2004, and 2005, respectively. The government would then cover 90 percent of losses exceeding the deductible with insurance entities liable for the other 10 percent. Federal payments would be capped at $90 billion, $87.5 billion, and $85 billion in 2003, 2004, and 2005, respectively. Among other matters, the updated TRIA also mandates that insurers should make terrorism insurance available under all of its property and casualty insurance policies on the same terms and conditions as the underlying policy.

1.65 Effective January 1, 2006, the Terrorism Insurance Extension Act of 2005 added new program years 4 and 5 (2006 and 2007, respectively) to the definition of insurer deductible. The insurer deductible is set as the value of an insurer's direct earned premiums for (newly defined) commercial property and casualty insurance over the immediately preceding calendar year multiplied by 17.5 percent and 20 percent for 2006 and 2007, respectively. A program trigger prohibits payment of federal compensation unless the aggregate industry insured losses from an act of terrorism exceeds $50 million and $100 million for 2006 and 2007, respectively. Additionally, subject to the program trigger, the federal share is 90 percent and 85 percent of an amount that exceeds the applicable insurer's deductible in 2006 and 2007, respectively.

Nature, Conduct, and Regulation of the Business

1.66 In January 2006, the NAIC adopted two model disclosure forms to assist insurers in complying with the Terrorism Risk Insurance Extension Act of 2005. The model disclosure forms may be used by insurers to meet their obligation under the rules and provide policy holders of the status of current coverage. Insurers must comply with state law and this act and are encouraged to review the disclosure forms in light of their current policy language, state legal requirements, and the provisions of this act.

1.67 On December 26, 2007, the Terrorism Risk Insurance Program Reauthorization Act of 2007 was signed into law. This act extends the provisions of the revised TRIA through December 31, 2014. As discussed in paragraph 1.66, subject to the program trigger, the federal share remains at 85 percent of an amount that exceeds the applicable insurer's deductible (the value of an insurer's direct earned premiums for commercial property and casualty insurance over the immediately preceding calendar year multiplied by 20 percent).

1.68 Additionally, the NAIC's Terrorism Insurance Implementation Working Group adopted a model bulletin intended to help state insurance regulators advise insurers about regulatory requirements related to the extension of the TRIA. The model bulletin provides guidance to insurers related to rate filings and policy language that state regulators would find acceptable to protect U.S. businesses from acts of terrorism. The model bulletin describes important changes that are contained in the Terrorism Insurance Extension Act of 2005 and informs insurers regarding whether rate and policy form filings might be needed.

Industry Associations

1.69 The property and liability insurance industry has many industry associations to help with the multitude of technical problems that arise in the course of business. These organizations also monitor regulatory developments and provide public relations for the industry. See appendix C, "List of Industry Trade and Professional Associations, Publications, and Information Resources," for a list.

Statutory Accounting Practices

1.70 *NAIC codified statutory accounting.* Statutory financial statements are prepared using accounting principles and practices prescribed or permitted by the insurance department of the state of domicile, referred to in this guide as statutory accounting practices. The insurance laws and regulations of the states generally require insurance entities domiciled in those states to comply with the guidance provided in the NAIC *Accounting Practices and Procedures Manual* (the manual) except as otherwise prescribed or permitted by state law. The NAIC codified statutory accounting practices for certain insurance entities, resulting in a revised *Accounting Practices and Procedures Manual*. States generally require insurers to comply with most, if not all, provisions of the manual. Preparers of financial statements and auditors of an insurance entity should continually monitor the status of the new guidance adopted as part of the manual and the effects on the prescribed practices of the domiciliary state.

1.71 The manual is published annually as of March containing all updates adopted through December 31 of the preceding year. Changes adopted during the year are available on the NAIC website under the Accounting Practices and Procedures Task Force, notably the Statutory Accounting Principles Working Group and the Emerging Accounting Issues Working Group. The primary

AAG-PLI 1.71

Statutory Accounting Principles (SAP) material in the manual is presented in Statements of Statutory Accounting Principles (SSAPs) and with interpretations of the Emerging Accounting Principles Working Group. Other related material is also included in the manual. State insurance laws and regulations require insurers to comply with the guidance provided in the manual except as prescribed or permitted by state law. States adopted the manual in whole, or in part, as an element of prescribed SAP in the states. If, however, the requirements of state laws, regulations, and administrative rules differ from the guidance provided in the manual or subsequent revisions, those state laws, regulations, and administrative rules will take precedence. The NAIC also published *States' Prescribed Difference from NAIC Statutory Accounting Principles*, organized by state including reference to each state's applicable statute or regulation, as a means of providing further information to regulators, public accountants, and entity personnel regarding these differences.

1.72 The NAIC took into consideration FASB Statement No. 168, *The FASB Accounting Standards Codification™ and the Hierarchy of Generally Accepted Accounting Principles—a replacement of FASB Statement No. 162*, which essentially reduces the GAAP hierarchy to two levels (one that is authoritative and one that is not). The preamble of the manual notes the following as the statutory hierarchy, which is not intended to preempt state legislative or regulatory authority:

Level 1

- The SSAPs, including GAAP reference material, to the extent adopted by the NAIC from FASB ASC[9] (FASB ASC or GAAP guidance)

Level 2

- Consensus positions of the Emerging Accounting Issues Working Group as adopted by the NAIC

Level 3

- NAIC annual statement instructions
- *Purposes and Procedures Manual of the NAIC Securities Valuation Office*

Level 4

- Statutory Accounting Principles Statement of Concepts[10]

Level 5

- Sources of nonauthoritative GAAP accounting guidance and literature, including (*a*) practices that are widely recognized and prevalent either generally or in the industry, (*b*) FASB concept statements, (*c*) AICPA Issue Papers, (*d*) International Financial Reporting Standards, (*e*) pronouncements of professional associations or regulatory agencies, (*f*) Technical Questions and Answers included in AICPA *Technical Practice Aids*, and (*g*) accounting textbooks, handbooks, and articles.

---

[9] Effective September 15, 2009, FASB ASC is the source of authoritative GAAP. As of that date, FASB ASC superseded all then-existing non-SEC accounting and reporting standards. All other nongrandfathered, non-SEC accounting literature not included in FASB ASC is nonauthoritative.

[10] The Statutory Accounting Principles (SAP) Statement of Concepts incorporates by reference FASB Concept Nos. 1, 2, 5, and 6 to the extent they do not conflict with the concepts outlined in the statement. However, for purposes of applying this hierarchy, the FASB concepts statements shall be included in level 5 and only those concepts unique to statutory accounting as stated in the statement are included in level 4.

Nature, Conduct, and Regulation of the Business

If the accounting treatment of a transaction or event is not specified by the SSAPs, preparers, regulators, and auditors of statutory financial statements should consider whether the accounting treatment is specified by another source of established SAP. If an established SAP from one or more sources in level 2 or 3 is relevant to the circumstances, the preparer, regulator or auditor should apply such principle. If there is a conflict between SAP from one or more sources in level 2 or 3, the preparer, regulator or auditor should follow the treatment specified by the source in the higher level—that is, follow level 2 treatment over level 3. Revisions to guidance in accordance with additions or revisions to the NAIC statutory hierarchy should be accounted for as a change in accounting principle in accordance with SSAP No. 3, *Accounting Changes and Corrections of Errors*.

1.73 The manual, the NAIC's annual statement instructions, *Examiners Handbook*, *Valuation of Securities Manual*, committee minutes, model rules, regulations, and guidelines provide sources of SAP. Some states may issue circular letters or bulletins describing their positions on various areas of accounting. In areas in which specific accounting practices are not prescribed, widely recognized practices may be permitted in a given state or specific accounting applications may be approved by the state insurance department, either orally or in writing. Auditors are able to review state examiners' reports to obtain evidence of accounting practices that have either been explicitly or implicitly accepted on examination.

1.74 Each state insurance department requires all insurance entities licensed to write business in that state to file an annual statement, also referred to as the convention blank, statutory blank, or, simply, the blank, with the state insurance commissioner for each individual insurance entity. Most states require the blank to be filed by March 1 of the following year. All states require that the annual statement for the calendar year be comparative, presenting the amounts as of December 31 of the current year and the amounts as of the immediately preceding December 31. The annual statement includes numerous supplementary financial data, such as analysis of operations by lines of business and detailed schedules of investments, losses, and reinsurance. The NAIC's instructions to the annual statement require that insurance entities file in conjunction with their annual statement (*a*) an opinion by a qualified actuary concerning the adequacy of reserves and other actuarial items and that such reserves conform with statutory requirements and (*b*) a narrative document captioned "management discussion and analysis" discussing material changes in significant annual statement line items and material future operating events, similar to the disclosures currently required by the SEC for public entities. The management discussion and analysis is due April 1 of the following year.

1.75 The NAIC requires most insurance entities in all states to file, by June 1, an audited financial report with the insurance commissioners of their state of domicile and all other states in which they are licensed. Exemptions to requirements to file include insurance entities that write less than one million dollars in direct premiums. The financial statements included in the audited financial report should be prepared in a form and using language and groupings substantially the same as the relevant sections of the annual statement of the insurer. The annual audited financial report is to include a reconciliation of differences, if any, between the audited statutory financial statements contained in that report and the annual statement filed with the state commissioner and a written description of the nature of the differences.

AAG-PLI 1.75

1.76 The NAIC Revised Model Audit Rule requires insurance entities to have their auditors prepare and file a report on material weaknesses, if any, in the entity's internal controls, an accountant's awareness letter, an accountant's letter of qualification, and a separate report by the entity's management on internal controls over financial reporting.

1.77 It may not be necessary for some public entity risk pools and captive insurers to prepare reports on a SAP basis. Enabling legislation generally sets forth such entities' reporting requirements and may require reporting to the state insurance commissioner or state agency. Separate rules may apply to reporting, capitalization requirements, and so forth.

1.78 Insurance entities are examined regularly by state or zone (a group of states) insurance examiners, usually once every three to five years. The annual statements filed with the regulatory authorities are used to monitor the financial condition of insurance entities in the period between examinations and to provide the financial data to help regulate the industry.

1.79 In addition to the audits of financial statements, insurance examiners review compliance with laws or regulations concerning policy forms, premium rates, kinds of investments, composition of the board of directors, members' attendance at board meetings, reinsurance contracts, intercompany transactions, and fair treatment of policyholders. Insurance examiners use the *Examiners Handbook*, a publication of the NAIC that outlines the procedures for conducting an examination as a guide in performing examinations and in preparing reports. Significant revisions were made to the examination approach outlined in the handbook that are effective for examinations conducted in 2010. The revisions incorporate a risk-focused framework and approach to the conduct of examinations. Some of the steps followed in the examination are similar to those followed by independent auditors as the handbook specifies that auditors should consider and include appropriate procedures described in the handbook as the auditor deems necessary.

1.80 Insurance entities prepare their statutory financial statements in accordance with accounting principles and practices prescribed or permitted by the insurance department of their state of domicile, that is, SAP. Paragraph .07 of AU-C section 800, *Special Considerations—Audits of Financial Statements Prepared in Accordance With Special Purpose Frameworks* (AICPA, *Professional Standards*), states that financial statements prepared on a statutory basis are considered special purpose financial statements (prepared in accordance with a special purpose framework).

1.81 Prescribed SAP are practices incorporated directly or by reference in state laws, regulations, and general administrative rules applicable to all insurance enterprises domiciled in a particular state.

Permitted Statutory Accounting Practices[11]

1.82 Permitted SAP include practices not prescribed in paragraph 1.71 but allowed by the domiciliary state regulatory authority. An insurance entity may request permission from the domiciliary state regulatory authority to use a specific accounting practice in the preparation of its statutory financial statements if either of the following occur:

---

[11] For additional information, see the NAIC *Accounting Practices and Procedures Manual* preamble and its section "Permitted Practices Advance Notification Requirement Question and Answers."

Nature, Conduct, and Regulation of the Business

  a. The entity wishes to depart from the prescribed SAP

  b. The prescribed SAP does not address the accounting for the transaction specifically

Accordingly, permitted accounting practices differ from state to state, may differ from entity to entity within a state, and may change in the future.

1.83 In instances where the domiciliary state regulator is considering approval of a request for an accounting practice that departs from the NAIC *Accounting Practices and Procedures Manual* and state prescribed accounting practices, the domiciliary regulator must provide notice (to other states) under the requirements as defined in paragraphs 55–57 of the manual's preamble.

1.84 Paragraph 56 of the manual's preamble states that the notice must disclose the following information regarding the requested accounting practice to all other states in which the insurer is licensed prior to the financial statement filing date:

  a. The nature and a clear description of the permitted accounting practice request.

  b. The quantitative effect of the permitted accounting practice request with all other approved permitted accounting practices currently in effect as disclosed in appendix A-205, "Illustrative Disclosure of Differences Between NAIC Statutory Accounting Practices and Procedures and Accounting Practices Prescribed or Permitted by the State of Domicile," for that insurer in the domiciliary state.

  c. The effect of the requested permitted accounting practice on a legal entity basis and on all parent and affiliated U.S. insurance entities, if applicable.

  d. Identify any potential effects on and quantify the potential impact to each financial statement line item affected by the request. The potential impact may be determined by comparing the financial statements prepared in accordance with NAIC SAP and the financial statements incorporating the requested permitted accounting practice.

1.85 Paragraph 57 of the manual's preamble states that the granting of approval for an accounting practice request by the domiciliary state regulator does not preempt or in any way limit any individual state's legislative and regulatory authority.

1.86 The disclosures in this paragraph should be made if (*a*) state prescribed SAP differ from NAIC SAP or (*b*) permitted state SAP differ from either state prescribed SAP or NAIC SAP. The disclosures should be made if the use of prescribed or permitted SAP (individually or in the aggregate) results in reported statutory surplus or risk-based capital that is significantly different from the statutory surplus or risk-based capital that would have been reported had NAIC SAP been followed. If an insurance enterprise's risk-based capital would have triggered a regulatory event had it not used a permitted practice, that fact should be disclosed in the financial statements. Insurance enterprises should disclose, at the date each financial statement is presented, a description of the prescribed or permitted SAP and the related monetary effect on statutory

AAG-PLI 1.86

surplus of using an accounting practice that differs from either state prescribed SAP or NAIC SAP.[12]

1.87 Financial statements prepared on a regulatory basis of accounting should include all informative disclosures that are appropriate for the basis of accounting used. That includes a summary of significant accounting policies that discuss the basis of presentation and describe how that basis differs from GAAP. As noted in the preamble of the manual, paragraph 59 states the following:

> To the extent that disclosures required by an SSAP are made within specific notes, schedules, or exhibits to the annual statement, those disclosures are not required to be duplicated in a separate note. Annual statutory financial statements which are not accompanied by annual statement exhibits and schedules (for example, annual audit report) shall include all disclosures required by the SSAPs based on the applicability, materiality and significance of the item to the insurer. Certain disclosures, as noted in individual SSAPs, are required in the annual audited statutory financial statements only.

Additionally, the provisions of the manual as well as the NAIC Emerging Accounting Issues Working Group Interpretation 04-1, *Applicability of New GAAP Disclosures Prior to NAIC Consideration*, state that GAAP pronouncements do not become part of SAP until and unless adopted by the NAIC. However, provisions of the manual or any other explicit rejection of a GAAP disclosure do not negate the requirements of paragraph .17 of AU-C section 800. For further information, see exhibit 1-1, "Evaluation of the Appropriateness of Informative Disclosures in Insurance Entities' Financial Statements Prepared on a Statutory Basis." The interpretation provides guidance in evaluating whether informative disclosures are reasonably adequate for financial statements prepared on a statutory basis.

Nonadmitted Assets

1.88 SSAP No. 4, *Assets and Nonadmitted Assets*, paragraph 2 defines an *asset* under SAP, "For the purposes of statutory accounting, an asset shall be defined as: probable future economic benefits obtained or controlled by a particular entity as a result of past transactions or events.... These assets shall then be evaluated to determine whether they are admitted." Paragraph 3 of SSAP No. 4 discusses nonadmitted assets as follows:

> As stated in the Statement of Concepts, "The ability to meet policyholder obligations is predicated on the existence of readily marketable assets available when both current and future obligations are due. Assets having economic value other than those which can be used to fulfill policyholder obligations, or those assets which are unavailable due to encumbrances or other third-party interests should not be recognized on the balance sheet," and are, therefore, considered nonadmitted. For purposes of statutory accounting principles, a nonadmitted asset shall be defined as an asset meeting the criteria

---

[12] Disclosures in this paragraph should be applied by a U.S. insurance enterprise, a U.S. enterprise with a U.S. insurance subsidiary, or a foreign enterprise with a U.S. insurance subsidiary, if the enterprise prepares GAAP financial statements. If a foreign insurance enterprise that does not have a U.S. insurance subsidiary prepares GAAP financial statements or is included in its parent's consolidated GAAP financial statements, the notes to the financial statements should disclose permitted regulatory accounting practices that significantly differ from the prescribed regulatory accounting practices of its respective regulatory authority, and their monetary effects.

in paragraph 2 above, which is accorded limited or no value in statutory reporting, and is one which is:

  a. Specifically identified within the *Accounting Practices and Procedures Manual* as a nonadmitted asset; or

  b. Not specifically identified as an admitted asset within the *Accounting Practices and Procedures Manual.*

A nonadmitted asset should be charged against surplus unless specifically addressed in the NAIC *Accounting Practices and Procedures Manual*. The asset shall be depreciated or amortized against net income as the estimated economic benefit expires. In accordance with the reporting entity's written capitalization policy, amounts less than a predefined threshold of furniture, fixtures, equipment, or supplies, shall be expensed when purchased.

Generally Accepted Accounting Principles[13]

1.89 FASB ASC 944, *Financial Services—Insurance*, classifies insurance contracts as short-duration or long-duration contracts. The classification depends on whether a contract is expected to provide coverage for an extended period. As noted in FASB ASC 944-20-15-2, insurance contracts shall be classified as short- or long-duration contracts depending on whether the contracts are expected to remain for an extended period. As discussed in FASB ASC 944-20-15-7, the factors that shall be considered in determining whether a particular contract can be expected to remain in force for an extended period are as follows for a short-duration contract:

  a. The contract provides insurance protection for a fixed period of short duration

  b. The contract enables the insurer to cancel the contract or adjust the provisions of the contract at the end of any contract period, such as adjusting the amount of premiums charged or coverage provided

1.90 Also discussed in FASB ASC 944-10-15-10, the factors that shall be considered in determining whether a particular contract can be expected to remain in force for an extended period are as follows for a long-duration contract:

  a. The contract generally is not subject to unilateral changes in its provisions, such as a noncancelable or guaranteed renewable contract

  b. The contract requires the performance of various functions and services, including insurance protection, for an extended period

---

[13] Readers should refer to the section "Insurance Contracts Project" in the preface of this guide. In July 2010, the International Accounting Standards Board (IASB) issued the exposure draft *Insurance Contracts*. In developing the IASB's exposure draft, most of the discussions about the proposed insurance accounting approaches were held jointly with FASB. Although the boards reached common decisions in many areas, they reached different conclusions in others. Some FASB members prefer the IASB's proposed measurement model; however, the majority prefers an alternative model. Regardless of FASB members' individual views and uniform commitment to convergence, FASB determined that additional information was needed about whether the possible new accounting guidance would represent a sufficient improvement to GAAP to justify issuing new guidance. On September 17, 2010, FASB issued, for public comment, the discussion paper *Preliminary Views on Insurance Contracts.*

The boards are redeliberating significant issues based on feedback received on the IASB exposure draft and FASB discussion paper. FASB is expected to release an exposure draft and the IASB is expected to release a revised targeted exposure draft during the first half of 2013. Readers should remain alert to any final pronouncements.

1.91 Determining whether a contract is short-duration or long-duration requires both judgment and an analysis of the contract terms. Most property and liability insurance contracts currently issued are classified as short-duration contracts.

1.92 Under FASB ASC 944-605-25-1, premiums from short-duration contracts should be recognized as revenue over the contract period in proportion to the amount of insurance provided. For those few types of contracts for which the period of risk differs significantly from the contract period, premiums should be recognized as revenue over the period of risk in proportion to the amount of insurance protection provided. That generally results in premiums being recognized as revenue evenly over the contract period (or the period of risk, if different), except for those few cases in which the amount of insurance protection declines according to a predetermined schedule.

1.93 As noted in FASB ASC 944-30-25-1A, an insurance entity shall capitalize only certain acquisition costs related directly to the successful acquisition of new or renewal insurance contracts. As discussed in FASB ASC 944-30-25-1 and 944-30-35-1, acquisition costs should be capitalized and charged to expense in proportion to premium revenue recognized. (Particular sections of this guide discuss the requirements of FASB ASC 944, but the reader should refer to FASB ASC 944 itself for specific guidance.)

1.94 FASB ASC 944 provides guidance on accounting by insurance enterprises for deferred acquisition costs on internal replacements of insurance and investment contracts.

1.95 Governmental Accounting Standards Board (GASB) Statement No. 10, *Accounting and Financial Reporting for Risk Financing and Related Insurance Issues*, as amended and interpreted by various GASB pronouncements, sets forth the accounting and financial reporting requirements for public entity risk pools. GASB Statement No. 10, as amended and interpreted, is based primarily on FASB ASC 944, but includes certain accounting and financial reporting requirements that differ from FASB ASC 944. In addition to the requirements of GASB Statement No. 10, there are other GASB pronouncements that affect accounting and financial reporting by public entity risk pools. For example, GASB Statement No. 3, *Deposits with Financial Institutions, Investments (including Repurchase Agreements), and Reverse Repurchase Agreements*, requires pools to make certain disclosures about the credit and market risks of their investments. Further, GASB Statement No. 9, *Reporting Cash Flows of Proprietary and Nonexpendable Trust Funds and Governmental Entities That Use Proprietary Fund Accounting*, requires pools to present a statement of cash flows using cash flows categories that differ from those required by FASB Statement No. 95, *Statement of Cash Flows*. This guide does not attempt to highlight the areas in which different accounting or reporting is required for public entity risk pools.

Comparison of SAP and GAAP

1.96 The differences between SAP and GAAP result from their differing emphasis, as noted in the preamble of the manual paragraph 10:

> GAAP is designed to meet the varying needs of the different users of financial statements. SAP is designed to address the concerns of regulators, who are the primary users of statutory financial statements. As a result, GAAP stresses measurement of emerging earnings of a business from period to period... while SAP stresses measurement of the ability to pay claims in the future.

Adequate statutory surplus provides protection to policyholders and permits an entity to expand its premium writing. Accordingly, SAP places a great deal of emphasis on the adequacy of statutory surplus. Table 1-1, "Summary of Statutory Accounting Practices and Generally Accepted Accounting Principles," presents a summarized comparison of the major differences in accounting treatment between SAP and GAAP for selected financial statement components. The reader ordinarily should, however, refer to the actual pronouncements for explicit guidance in accounting for transactions in each of the areas.

Table 1-1

Summary of Statutory Accounting Practices and Generally Accepted Accounting Principles

The following are highlights of significant differences in accounting treatment between SAP and GAAP for certain financial statement components. As described in paragraph 1.82, statutory accounting may vary by state. The SAP and GAAP references in the chart pertaining to each area are not necessarily inclusive of all guidance applicable to the subject matter.

	Codified Statutory Accounting Practices	*Generally Accepted Accounting Principles*[14]
Bonds	Debt securities with a National Association of Insurance Commissioners (NAIC) designation of 1 or 2 should be reported at amortized cost; all other debt securities (NAIC designations 3–6) should be reported at the lower of amortized cost or fair value. See Statement of Statutory Accounting Principles (SSAP) No. 26, *Bonds, Excluding Loan-backed and Structured Securities*, and SSAP No. 43, *Loan-backed and Structured Securities*, as amended.	Classified as trading securities or securities available for sale at fair value; classified as held-to-maturity at amortized cost, if positive intent and ability to hold to maturity exist. See Financial Accounting Standards Board (FASB) *Accounting Standards Codification* (ASC) 320, *Investments—Debt and Equity Securities*.[15]

---

[14] GAAP in this chart contain numerous references to both financial and nonfinancial assets and liabilities that are subject to fair value measurement. FASB ASC 820, *Fair Value Measurement*, establishes a framework for measuring fair value that applies broadly to financial and nonfinancial assets and liabilities and improves the consistency, comparability, and reliability of the measurements. The guidance in FASB ASC 820 applies under other accounting pronouncements that require or permit fair value measurements. Accordingly, FASB ASC 820 does not require any new fair value measurements but the application of it will change current practice. For further information, see www.fasb.org and chapter 5, "Investments and Fair Value Considerations."

[15] FASB and the IASB have a joint project on the accounting for financial instruments. The objective of this project is to significantly improve the decision usefulness of financial instrument reporting for users of financial statements. The project will replace FASB and the IASB's respective financial instruments standards with a common standard. The boards believe that simplification of the accounting requirements for financial instruments should be an outcome of this improvement.

The project has effectively been split into three components: classification and measurement, impairment, and hedge accounting projects.

    a. Classification and Measurement. On May 26, 2010, FASB issued proposed Accounting Standards Update (ASU) *Accounting for Financial Instruments and Revisions to the Accounting for Derivative Instruments and Hedging Activities—Financial Instruments (Topic 825) and Derivatives and Hedging (Topic 815).*

    b. Credit Impairment. On January 31, 2011, FASB and the IASB proposed a common solution for impairment accounting in the supplementary document *Accounting for Financial Instruments and Revisions to the Accounting for Derivative Instruments and Hedging Activities—Impairment.*

    c. Hedge Accounting. On February 9, 2011, FASB issued the discussion paper *Invitation to Comment—Selected Issues about Hedge Accounting* to solicit input on the IASB's exposure draft *Hedge Accounting* in order to improve, simplify, and converge the financial reporting requirements for hedging activities.

Summary of Statutory Accounting Practices and Generally Accepted Accounting Principles—continued

	Codified Statutory Accounting Practices	Generally Accepted Accounting Principles
Common stock	Investments in unaffiliated common stock are generally reported at fair value as stated by the NAIC's Securities Valuation Office. See SSAP No. 30, *Investments in Common Stock (excluding investments in common stock of subsidiary, controlled or affiliated entities)*.	Fair value. See FASB ASC 320.
Nonredeemable preferred stock	Perpetual preferred should be valued based on the underlying characteristics of the security, the quality rating as designated by the NAIC, and whether an asset valuation reserve is maintained by the reporting entity. See SSAP No. 32, *Investments in Preferred Stock (including investments in preferred stock of subsidiary, controlled, or affiliated entities)*.	Fair value. See FASB ASC 320.
Mortgages	First mortgages that are not in default with regard to principal or interest are carried at outstanding principal balance, or amortized cost if acquired at a discount or premium less impairment. See SSAP No. 37, *Mortgage Loans*.	Unpaid balance plus unamortized loan origination fees as prescribed by FASB ASC 310, *Receivables*.
Real estate—investment	Properties occupied or held for the production of income are reported at depreciated cost less encumbrances less impairment. See SSAP No. 90, *Accounting for the Impairment or Disposal of Real Estate Investments*. Additional information can be found in SSAP No. 40, *Real Estate Investments*.	Depreciated cost, after impairment write-down as per FASB ASC 360, *Property, Plant, and Equipment*.
Real estate—held for sale	Report at the lower of depreciated cost or fair value less encumbrances and estimated costs to sell the property.	Lower of carrying value or fair value less cost to sell.

(continued)

Summary of Statutory Accounting Practices and Generally Accepted Accounting Principles—continued

	Codified Statutory Accounting Practices	*Generally Accepted Accounting Principles*
	See SSAP No. 90, as amended by SSAP No. 95, *Exchanges of Nonmonetary Assets, A Replacement of SSAP No. 28—Nonmonetary Transactions*. Additional information can be found in SSAP No. 40.	
Investment in affiliates	Investments in subsidiary, controlled, or affiliated entities should be reported using either a market valuation approach or one of the equity methods. See SSAP No. 97, *Investments in Subsidiary, Controlled, or Affiliated Entities, A Replacement of SSAP No. 88*	Consolidated, equity basis, or cost as appropriate. See FASB ASC 970-323; FASB ASC 835-20; FASB ASC 810, *Consolidations*; and FASB ASC 272, *Limited Liability Entities*.
Unrealized gains (losses) for securities	Unrealized gains (losses) on investments held at other than amortized cost are recorded directly to surplus. Guidance comes from a variety of sources, including but not limited to, SSAP Nos. 26, 30, 32, 43R, and 86.	Recorded in net income for trading, or other comprehensive income for available for sale, as appropriate (except for held-to-maturity). See FASB ASC 320 and FASB ASC 220, *Comprehensive Income*.
Other-than-temporary impairment issues (for marketable debt and equity securities)	Under SSAP No. 26, if it is determined that a decline in fair value of a bond is other-than-temporary, an impairment loss should be recognized as a realized loss equal to the entire difference between the bonds carrying value and its fair value at the balance sheet date of the reporting period for which the assessment is made. The new cost basis shall not be changed for subsequent recoveries in fair value. Future declines in fair value which are determined to be other than temporary, shall be recorded as realized losses. An impairment shall be considered to have occurred if it is probable that the reporting entity will be unable to collect all amounts due according to the contractual terms of a debt security in effect at the date of acquisition.	For debt securities, if an other-than-temporary impairment has occurred, the amount of the other-than-temporary impairment recognized in earnings depends on whether an entity intends to sell the security or more likely than not will be required to sell the security before recovery of its amortized cost basis less any current-period credit loss. If an entity intends to sell the security or more likely than not will be required to sell the security before recovery of its amortized cost basis less any current-period credit loss, the other-than-temporary impairment shall be recognized in earnings equal to the entire difference between the investment's amortized cost basis and its fair value at the balance sheet date. If an entity does not intend to sell the security and it is not more likely than not that the entity

Nature, Conduct, and Regulation of the Business 33

**Summary of Statutory Accounting Practices and
Generally Accepted Accounting Principles—continued**

	Codified Statutory Accounting Practices	Generally Accepted Accounting Principles
	For loan backed and structured securities, the impairment guidance within SSAP No. 43R, *Loan-backed and Structured Securities—Revised*, requires bifurcation of "interest" and "noninterest" components for impairment recognition in situations when the entity does not have an intent to sell and has the intent and ability to hold the investment for a period of time sufficient to recover the amortized cost basis: • When an other-than-temporary impairment has occurred because the entity intends to sell or has assessed that they do not have the intent and ability to retain the investments in the security for a period of time sufficient to recover the amortized cost basis, the amount of the other-than-temporary impairment recognized in earnings as a realized loss shall equal the entire difference between the investment's amortized cost basis and its fair value at the balance sheet date. • When an other-than-temporary impairment has occurred because the entity does not expect to recover the entire amortized cost basis of the security even if the entity has no intent to sell and the entity has the intent and ability to hold, the amount of the other-than-temporary impairment recognized as a realized loss shall equal the different between the investment's amortized cost basis and the present value of cash flows expected to be collected, discounted at the loan-backed or structured	will be required to sell the security before recovery of its amortized cost basis less any current-period credit loss, the other-than-temporary impairment shall be separated into both of the following: *a.* The amount representing the credit loss *b.* The amount related to all other factors The amount of the total other-than-temporary impairment related to the credit loss shall be recognized in earnings. The amount of the total other-than-temporary impairment related to other factors shall be recognized in other comprehensive income, net of applicable taxes. The previous amortized cost basis less the other-than-temporary impairment recognized in earnings shall become the new amortized cost basis of the investment. That new amortized cost basis shall not be adjusted for subsequent recoveries in fair value. However, the amortized cost basis shall be adjusted for accretion and amortization as prescribed in FASB ASC 320-10-35-35. See FASB ASC 320. For equity securities, if it is determined that the impairment is other than temporary, then an impairment loss shall be recognized in earnings equal to the entire difference between the investment's cost and its fair value at the balance sheet date of the reporting period for which the assessment is made. The measurement of the impairment shall not include partial recoveries after the balance sheet date. The fair

(continued)

AAG-PLI 1.96

**Summary of Statutory Accounting Practices and
Generally Accepted Accounting Principles—continued**

	Codified Statutory Accounting Practices	*Generally Accepted Accounting Principles*
	security's effective interest rate. • SSAP No. 43R has been amended to revise the definition of a loan-backed security. In June 2010, nonsubstantive revisions were also adopted to paragraphs 27 and 36 of SSAP No. 43R to clarify the accounting for gains and losses between AVR and IMR for SSAP No. 43R securities. Both revisions were effective for January 1, 2011. See SSAP No. 26; No. 30 (excluding investments in common stock of subsidiary, controlled, or affiliated entities); and No. 32 (including investments in preferred stock of subsidiary, controlled, or affiliated entities), See also NAIC Interpretation 06-7, *Definition of Phrase "Other Than Temporary."*	value of the investment would then become the new amortized cost basis of the investment and shall not be adjusted for subsequent recoveries in fair value See FASB ASC 320.
Nonadmitted assets	Excluded from the statutory balance sheet and charged to surplus. Major nonadmitted assets include agents' balances/uncollected premiums over three months due, certain amounts of deferred tax assets, certain intangible assets and furniture, fixtures, and equipment. See SSAP No. 4, *Assets and Nonadmitted Assets*; No. 6, *Uncollected Premium Balances, Bills Receivable for Premiums, and Amounts Due from Agents and Brokers*; No. 10, *Income Taxes*; No. 19, *Furniture, Fixtures and Equipment; Leasehold Improvements Paid by the Reporting Entity as Lessee; Depreciation of Property and Amortization of Leasehold Improvements*; No. 20, *Nonadmitted Assets*; No. 29, *Prepaid Expenses*; No. 68, *Business Combinations and Goodwill*; No. 87,	Not applicable.

AAG-PLI 1.96

Summary of Statutory Accounting Practices and Generally Accepted Accounting Principles—continued

	Codified Statutory Accounting Practices	Generally Accepted Accounting Principles
	Capitalization Policy, An Amendment to SSAP Nos. 4, 19, 29, and 73; and No. 96, *Settlement Requirements for Intercompany Transactions, An Amendment to SSAP No. 25—Accounting for and Disclosures about Transactions with Affiliates and Other Related Parties.*	
Loss reserves	Claims, losses, and loss/claim adjustment expenses should be recognized as expense when an event occurs. Liabilities should be established for any unpaid expenses, with a corresponding charge to income. See SSAP No. 55, *Unpaid Claims, Losses and Loss Adjustment Expenses*; No. 62R, *Property and Casualty Reinsurance*; and No. 65, *Property and Casualty Contracts.*	Accrued when insured events occur and based on the estimated ultimate cost of settling the claims. Estimated recoveries are deducted from the liability for unpaid claims. See FASB ASC 944 and Securities and Exchange Commission Staff Accounting Bulletin No. 62, *Discounting by Property and Casualty Insurance Companies.*
Premium balances receivable	Uncollected premium balances, and bills receivable for premiums meet the definition of an asset as defined in SSAP No. 4, and are admitted assets to the extent they conform to the requirements of SSAP No. 6.	Due and uncollected premiums are recorded as assets. An appropriate allowance should be established. See FASB ASC 944.
Contract holder dividend liability	Dividends to policyholders immediately become liabilities when they are declared and should be recorded as a liability. See SSAP No. 65.	If limitations exist on the amount of net income from participating insurance contracts of insurers that may be distributed to stockholders, provision is made for accumulated earnings expected to be paid to contract holders, including pro rata portion of dividends incurred to valuation date; If there are no net income restrictions, the future dividends are accrued over the premium-paying period of the contract. Accounting varies depending on the applicability of FASB ASC 944.

(continued)

Summary of Statutory Accounting Practices and Generally Accepted Accounting Principles—continued

	Codified Statutory Accounting Practices	Generally Accepted Accounting Principles
Reinsurance	Full credit generally given for authorized reinsurers; net reporting required; reinsurance recognized based on adequate risk transfer; liability for unauthorized reinsurers. See SSAP No. 62R.	Reinsurance recognized based on adequate transfer of risk; provision for uncollectible reinsurance and gross reporting of balance sheet amounts required under FASB ASC 944, net reporting is not allowed unless a right of offset exists as defined in FASB ASC 210-20.
Deferred taxes	SSAP No. 101 (effective January 1, 2012) establishes SAP for current and deferred federal and foreign income taxes and current state income taxes. In general, SSAP No. 101 adopts the concepts of FASB ASC 740, with modifications. A reporting entity's balance sheet should include deferred income tax assets (DTAs) and liabilities (DTLs), the expected future tax consequences of temporary differences generated by statutory accounting. SAP reporting requires an admissibility test, in addition to the statutory valuation allowance, to determine how much of the gross DTAs should be admitted.	Under FASB ASC 740, *Income Taxes*, provision made for temporary differences, net operating losses, and credit carryforwards. It is necessary to determine if a DTA valuation allowance is needed. DTAs are reduced by a valuation allowance if, based on all available evidence (both positive and negative), it is more likely than not (a likelihood of more than 50 percent) that some portion or all of the tax benefit will not be realized. The weight given to the potential effect of negative and positive evidence should be commensurate with the extent to which it can be objectively verified. The valuation allowance should be sufficient to reduce the DTA to the amount that is more likely than not to be realized.
Leases	All leases, except leveraged leases should be considered operating leases. See SSAP No. 22, *Leases*.	Classified as capital or operating according to the provisions of FASB ASC 840, *Leases*.[16]

---

[16] FASB and the IASB initiated a joint project to develop a new approach to lease accounting that would ensure that assets and liabilities arising under leases are recognized in the statement of financial position. The comment period for the discussion paper ended on July 17, 2009. The proposals in the discussion paper have been refined based on comment letters received and input from preparers, auditors, users, regulators, and other interested parties during other outreach activities. On August 17, 2010, the Boards published, for public comment, an exposure draft, *Leases*. In July 2011, the Boards announced that they agreed unanimously to reexpose their revised proposals for a leases standard. The Boards are currently redeliberating based on comments received and currently plan to release an exposure draft during the first half of 2013.

Summary of Statutory Accounting Practices and Generally Accepted Accounting Principles—continued

	Codified Statutory Accounting Practices	Generally Accepted Accounting Principles
Liability for postretirement benefits other than pensions	An employer should account for its postretirement benefits for vested employees only, on an accrual basis. See SSAP No. 14, *Postretirement Benefits Other Than Pensions*, which adopted FASB Statement No. 106, *Employers' Accounting for Postretirement Benefits Other Than Pensions*, and No. 132 (revised 2003), *Employers' Disclosures about Pensions and Other Postretirement Benefits—an amendment of FASB Statements No. 87, 88, and 106*, with some modifications.[17]	Expected postretirement benefit obligations are recognized over the working life of employees; liability based on vested and nonvested benefits under FASB ASC 715, *Compensation—Retirement Benefits*.
Pension benefits	For defined benefit plans, reporting entities should adopt FASB ASC 715 with a modification to exclude nonvested employees and account for additional minimum pension liability. The excess of plan assets over obligations should be treated as a nonadmitted asset. Net plan obligations must be accrued irrespective of funding. For defined contribution plans, the reporting entity should expense contributions required by the plan over the period in which the employee vests in those contributions. Contributions to plan participants' accounts made prior to vesting should be treated as prepaid expenses and should be nonadmitted. Contributions required after participants terminate or retire should be accrued and an expense should be recorded over the working lives of the participants.	Pension costs calculated based on the projected unit credit method under FASB ASC 715.

(continued)

---

[17] At the NAIC spring 2012 meeting, the SAP Working Group adopted SSAP No. 92, *Accounting for Postretirement Benefits Other than Pensions*, and SSAP No. 102, *Accounting for Pensions*, with an effective date of January 1, 2013, with early adoption permitted and the ability to elect a 10 year phase-in period.

Summary of Statutory Accounting Practices and Generally Accepted Accounting Principles—continued

	Codified Statutory Accounting Practices	Generally Accepted Accounting Principles
	See SSAP No. 89, *Accounting for Pensions, A Replacement of SSAP No. 8*, which adopts FASB ASC 715, with some modifications.[18]	
Contract acquisition costs	Charged to expense when incurred. See SSAP No. 71, *Policy Acquisition Costs and Commissions*.	Under FASB ASC 944-30-25-1A, an insurance entity should capitalize only certain acquisition costs related directly to the successful acquisition of new or renewal insurance contracts. Such costs are amortized in relation to the revenue generated (premiums or estimated gross profit, as appropriate) if recoverable from such revenue. See FASB ASC 944.
Consolidation	Generally not applied given financial statement focus on presentation from a liquidity of assets standpoint for regulatory purposes. Majority-owned subsidiaries are not consolidated for individual entity statutory reporting. See SSAP No. 97, *Investments in Subsidiary, Controlled and Affiliated Entities, A Replacement of SSAP No. 88*.	Generally required in accordance with FASB ASC 810.[19]

---

[18] See footnote 17.

[19] On November 3, 2011, FASB issued the proposed ASU *Consolidation (Topic 810): Principal versus Agent Analysis*. The comment period ended February 15, 2012. The objective of this project was to consider comprehensive guidance for consolidation of all entities, including entities controlled by voting or similar interests. This included an evaluation of guidance for determining the capacity of a decision maker.

Exhibit 1-1

Evaluation of the Appropriateness of Informative Disclosures in Insurance Entities' Financial Statements Prepared on a Statutory Basis

Question—Insurance entities issue financial statements prepared in accordance with accounting practices prescribed or permitted by insurance regulators (a *statutory basis*) in addition to, or instead of, financial statements prepared in accordance with generally accepted accounting principles (GAAP). All states have adopted the National Association of Insurance Commissioners' (NAIC's) *Accounting Practices and Procedures Manual* as the primary basis of prescribed statutory accounting principles (SAP). The *Accounting Practices and Procedures Manual*, as revised by NAIC's codification project along with any subsequent revisions, is referred to as the manual. The manual contains extensive disclosure requirements.

After a state adopts the manual, its statutory basis of accounting includes informative disclosures appropriate for that basis of accounting. The NAIC annual statement instructions prescribe the financial statements to be included in the annual audited financial report.

How should auditors evaluate whether informative disclosures in financial statements prepared on a statutory basis are appropriate?

Interpretation—Paragraph .07 of AU-C section 800, *Special Considerations—Audits of Financial Statements Prepared in Accordance With Special Purpose Frameworks* (AICPA, *Professional Standards*), states that financial statements prepared on a statutory basis (regulatory basis) are considered special purpose financial statements (prepared in accordance with a special purpose framework).

Paragraph .17 of AU-C section 800 states the following:

> Section 700 requires the auditor to evaluate whether the financial statements achieve fair presentation. In an audit of special purpose financial statements when the special purpose financial statements contain items that are the same as, or similar to, those in financial statements prepared in accordance with GAAP, the auditor should evaluate whether the financial statements include informative disclosures similar to those required by GAAP. The auditor should also evaluate whether additional disclosures, beyond those specifically required by the framework, related to matters that are not specifically identified on the face of the financial statements or other disclosures are necessary for the financial statements to achieve fair presentation.

The provisions of the manual preamble that state, "GAAP pronouncements do not become part of Statutory Accounting Principles until and unless adopted by the NAIC," or any other explicit rejection of a generally accepted accounting principles disclosure does not negate the requirements of paragraph .17 of AU-C section 800.

Question—What types of items or matters might be considered by auditors when evaluating whether informative disclosures similar to those required by GAAP are reasonably adequate?

Interpretation—Paragraph .11 of AU-C section 800, states the following:

> Section 210 requires the auditor to establish whether the preconditions for an audit are present. In an audit of special purpose financial statements, the auditor should obtain the agreement of management

that it acknowledges and understands its responsibility to include all informative disclosures that are appropriate for the special purpose framework used to prepare the entity's financial statements, including

 a. a description of the special purpose framework, including a summary of significant accounting policies, and how the framework differs from GAAP, the effects of which need not be quantified.

 b. informative disclosures similar to those required by GAAP, in the case of special purpose financial statements that contain items that are the same as, or similar to, those in financial statements prepared in accordance with GAAP.

 c. a description of any significant interpretations of the contract on which the special purpose financial statements are based, in the case of special purpose financial statements prepared in accordance with a contractual basis of accounting.

 d. additional disclosures beyond those specifically required by the framework that may be necessary for the special purpose financial statements to achieve fair presentation.

Question—How does the auditor evaluate whether "informative disclosures similar to those required by GAAP" are appropriate for

 a. items and transactions that are accounted for essentially the same or in a similar manner under a statutory basis as under GAAP?

 b. items and transactions that are accounted for differently under a statutory basis than under GAAP?

 c. items and transactions that are accounted for differently under requirements of the state of domicile than under the manual?

Interpretation—Disclosures in statutory basis financial statements for items and transactions that are accounted for essentially the same or in a similar manner under the statutory basis as under GAAP should be the same as, or similar to, the disclosures required by GAAP unless the manual specifically states the NAIC codification rejected the GAAP disclosures. The provisions of the manual preamble that state, "GAAP pronouncements do not become part of Statutory Accounting Principles until and unless adopted by the NAIC," or any other explicit rejection of a GAAP disclosure does not negate the requirements of paragraph .17 of AU-C section 800.

Disclosures should also include those required by the manual.

Disclosures in statutory basis financial statements for items or transactions that are accounted for differently under the statutory basis than under GAAP, but in accordance with the manual, should be the disclosures required by the manual.

If the accounting required by the state of domicile for an item or transaction differs from the accounting set forth in the manual for that item or transaction, but it is in accordance with GAAP or superseded GAAP, the disclosures in statutory basis financial statements for that item or transaction should be the applicable GAAP disclosures for the GAAP or superseded GAAP. If the accounting required by the state of domicile for an item or transaction differs from the accounting set forth in the manual, GAAP or superseded GAAP, sufficient relevant disclosures should be made.

Informative disclosures similar to those required by GAAP include disclosures related to matters that are not specifically identified on the face of the financial statements, such as (*a*) related party transactions, (*b*) restrictions on assets and owners' equity, (*c*) subsequent events, and (*d*) uncertainties. Other matters could be disclosed if such disclosures are necessary to keep the financial statements from being misleading.

Chapter 2
Audit Considerations

Introduction

2.01 In accordance with AU-C section 200, *Overall Objectives of the Independent Auditor and the Conduct of an Audit in Accordance With Generally Accepted Auditing Standards* (AICPA, *Professional Standards*), an independent auditor plans, conducts, and reports the results of an audit in accordance with generally accepted auditing standards (GAAS). This chapter of the guide provides guidance and general auditing considerations for audits of financial statements of property and liability insurance entities. In particular, the audit guidance focuses on the risk assessment process, which includes obtaining an understanding of the entity and its environment and its internal control, Audit guidance is also included in the chapters that discuss the cycles of the property and liability insurance process, including selected control and auditing procedures the auditor may wish to consider.

Scope of the Audit Engagement

General Considerations

2.02 AU-C section 210, *Terms of Engagement* (AICPA, *Professional Standards*), states the auditor should agree upon the terms of the audit engagement with management or those charged with governance, as appropriate. The agreed upon terms of the audit engagement should be documented through a written communication with the property and liability insurance entity in the form of an audit engagement letter. As discussed in paragraph .10 of AU-C section 210, the understanding should include the following:

- The objectives of the engagement
- Management's responsibilities
- The auditor's responsibilities
- A statement illustrating that because of the inherent limitations of an audit, along with the inherent limitations of internal control, an unavoidable risk exists that some material misstatements may not be detected even though the audit is properly planned and performed in accordance with GAAS
- Identification of the applicable financial reporting framework for the preparation of the financial statements
- Reference to the expected form and content of any reports to be issued by the auditor and a statement that circumstances may arise in which a report may differ from its expected form and content

2.03 The auditor should be aware that certain state regulations require specific language within the engagement letter. For example, one state requires the auditor to confirm that an opinion on the financials will be provided prior to the regulatory filing deadline; some states require the auditor to confirm they will inform the state insurance department if they become aware of a material misstatement or if the insurance company no longer meets minimum capital and surplus requirements.

Considerations for Audits Performed in Accordance With Public Company Accounting Oversight Board (PCAOB) Standards

Paragraphs 5–7 of PCAOB Auditing Standard No. 16, *Communications with Audit Committees*, (AICPA, *PCAOB Standards and Related Rules*), provides requirements for establishing an understanding of the terms of the audit engagement with the audit committee.

2.04 In defining the scope of audit services, the auditor may consider matters relating to specific reporting responsibilities of the engagement, including

    a. the legal structure or organization of the insurance entity and the number and kind of entities that need separate reports on statutory accounting principles (SAP) or generally accepted accounting principles (GAAP) financial statements, or both, or that need consolidated GAAP financial statements;

    b. regulatory reporting and filing requirements for local, state, and other regulatory authorities; and

    c. reporting requirements—of a foreign parent or subsidiaries—such as those for which requirements and guidance are provided in AU-C section 910, *Financial Statements Prepared in Accordance With a Financial Reporting Framework Generally Accepted in Another Country* (AICPA, *Professional Standards*), for the auditor practicing in the United States, who is engaged to report on the financial statements of a U.S. entity that have been prepared in conformity with accounting principles that are generally accepted in another country for use outside the United States.

PCAOB Integrated Audit of Financial Statements and Internal Control Over Financial Reporting[1]

2.05 Many property and liability insurance entities or their holding companies are public issuers; the scope requirements for audits of issuers have been expanded. As described in paragraph 2.133, pursuant to Section 404 of the Sarbanes-Oxley Act of 2002 (SOX), the Securities and Exchange Commission (SEC) requires a PCAOB registered public accounting firm to provide an attestation report on the effectiveness of an entity's internal control over financial reporting. PCAOB Auditing Standard No. 5, *An Audit of Internal Control Over Financial Reporting That Is Integrated with An Audit of Financial Statements* (AICPA, *PCAOB Standards and Related Rules*, Auditing Standards), establishes requirements and provides directions that apply when an auditor is engaged to audit both an entity's financial statements and the effectiveness of internal control over financial reporting. However, Section 989G of the Dodd-Frank Act added SOX Section 404(c) to exempt smaller issuers that are neither accelerated filers nor large accelerated filers from the attestation requirement under Rule 12b-2. Section 404(c) essentially provides that a

---

[1] This service is referred to as an integrated audit throughout the guide. Certain areas of Public Company Accounting Oversight Board (PCAOB) Auditing Standard No. 5, *An Audit of Internal Control Over Financial Reporting That Is Integrated with An Audit of Financial Statements* (AICPA, *PCAOB Standards and Related Rules*, Auditing Standards), provide guidance that corresponds to guide topics. These topics are discussed as indicated but the discussion is not all inclusive.

Audit Considerations

nonaccelerated filer will not be required to include an attestation report from its registered public accounting firm on internal control over financial reporting in the annual reports it files with the SEC.

2.06 More specifically, for integrated audits, paragraph 3 of PCAOB Auditing Standard No. 5 states that

> The auditor's objective in an audit of internal control over financial reporting is to express an opinion on the effectiveness of the entity's internal control over financial reporting. To form a basis for expressing such an opinion, the auditor must plan and perform the audit to obtain appropriate evidence that is sufficient to obtain reasonable assurance about whether material weaknesses exist as of the date specified in management's assessment. The auditor should integrate the audit of internal control over financial reporting with the audit of the financial statements. Maintaining effective internal control over financial reporting means that no material weaknesses exist; therefore, the objective of the audit of internal control over financial reporting is to obtain reasonable assurance that no material weaknesses exist as of the date specified in management's assessment.

2.07 PCAOB Auditing Standard No. 4, *Reporting on Whether a Previously Reported Material Weakness Continues to Exist* (AICPA, *PCAOB Standards and Related Rules*, Auditing Standards), establishes requirements and provides directions that apply when an auditor is engaged to report on whether a previously reported material weakness in internal control over financial reporting continues to exist as of a date specified by management. The engagement described by the standard is voluntary and the standards of the PCAOB do not require an auditor to undertake an engagement to report on whether a previously reported material weakness continues to exist.

2.08 PCAOB Auditing Standard No. 4 amended paragraph .04 of AT section 101, *Attest Engagements* (AICPA, *PCAOB Standards and Related Rules*, Interim Standards), to clarify that PCAOB Auditing Standard No. 4 must be used for reporting on whether a material weakness continues to exist for any purpose other than an entity's internal use.

Additional PCAOB Audit Standards

2.09 The PCAOB has issued additional standards that are applicable to both audits of financial statements only and integrated audits. PCAOB audits of financial statements only may also occur for specific SEC registrants (for example, certain investment entities and brokers and dealers as noted in PCAOB Release No. 2011-001, *Temporary Rule for an Interim Program of Inspection Related to Audits of Brokers and Dealers*). These standards are intended to cover the entire audit process from initial planning activities to forming the opinion(s) to be expressed in the auditor's report.

2.10 The PCAOB issued a suite of eight auditing standards, Auditing Standards Nos. 8–15 (AICPA, *PCAOB Standards and Related Rules*, Auditing Standards), with the goal to enhance the effectiveness of the auditor's assessment of, and response to, the risks of material misstatement in financial statements. Appendix 11, "Comparison of the Objectives and Requirements of the Accompanying PCAOB Auditing Standards with the Analogous Standards of the International Auditing and Assurance Standards Board and the Auditing Standards Board of the American Institute of Certified Public Accountants," of PCAOB Release No. 2010-004, *Auditing Standards Related to the Auditor's*

Assessment of and Response to Risk and Related Amendments to PCAOB Standards (AICPA, *PCAOB Standards and Related Rules*, Select PCAOB Releases), discusses certain differences between the objectives and requirements of the PCAOB risk assessment standards and the analogous standards of the International Auditing and Assurance Standards Board and the Auditing Standards Board (ASB). The following are summaries of each standard:

- Auditing Standard No. 8, *Audit Risk*, discusses the auditor's consideration of audit risk in an audit of financial statements as part of an integrated audit or an audit of financial statements only. It describes the components of audit risk and the auditor's responsibilities for reducing audit risk to an appropriately low level in order to obtain reasonable assurance that the financial statements are free of material misstatement.

- Auditing Standard No. 9, *Audit Planning*, establishes requirements including assessing matters that are important to the audit, and establishing an appropriate audit strategy and audit plan.

- Auditing Standard No. 10, *Supervision of the Audit Engagement*, sets forth requirements including supervising the work of engagement team members. It applies to the engagement partner and to other engagement team members who assist the engagement partner with supervision.

- Auditing Standard No. 11, *Consideration of Materiality in Planning and Performing an Audit*, describes the auditor's responsibilities for consideration of materiality in planning and performing an audit.

- Auditing Standard No. 12, *Identifying and Assessing Risks of Material Misstatement*, establishes a process that includes information-gathering procedures to identify risks and an analysis of the identified risks.

- Auditing Standard No. 13, *The Auditor's Responses to the Risks of Material Misstatement*, establishes requirements for responding to the risks of material misstatement in financial statements through the general conduct of the audit and performing audit procedures regarding significant accounts and disclosures.

- Auditing Standard No. 14, *Evaluating Audit Results*, establishes requirements regarding the auditor's evaluation of audit results and determination of whether the auditor has obtained sufficient appropriate audit evidence. The evaluation process includes, among other things, evaluation of misstatements identified during the audit; the overall presentation of the financial statements, including disclosures; and the potential for management bias in the financial statements.

- Auditing Standard No. 15, *Audit Evidence*, explains what constitutes audit evidence and establishes requirements for designing and performing audit procedures to obtain sufficient appropriate audit evidence to support the opinion expressed in the auditor's report.

2.11 In August 2012, the PCAOB adopted Auditing Standard No. 16, *Communications With Audit Committees* (AICPA, *PCAOB Standards and Related Rules*, Auditing Standards). The standard establishes requirements that enhance the relevance and timeliness of the communications between the auditor and the audit committee and is intended to foster constructive dialogue between the two on significant audit and financial statement matters. The new standard and related amendments are effective for public company audits of fiscal periods beginning after December 15, 2012.

Planning and Other Auditing Considerations

2.12 An audit of a property and liability insurance entity's financial statements provides financial statement users with an opinion by the auditor on whether the financial statements are presented fairly, in all material respects, in accordance with an applicable financial reporting framework, which also enhances the degree of confidence that intended users can place in the financial statements. To accomplish that objective, GAAS require the auditor to obtain reasonable assurance about whether the financial statements as a whole are free from material misstatement, whether due to fraud or error. Reasonable assurance is a high, but not absolute, level of assurance. It is obtained when the auditor has obtained sufficient appropriate audit evidence to reduce audit risk (that is, the risk that the auditor expresses an inappropriate opinion when the financial statements are materially misstated) to an acceptably low level. Reasonable assurance is not an absolute level of assurance because there are inherent limitations of an audit that result in most of the audit evidence, on which the auditor draws conclusions and bases the auditor's opinion, being persuasive rather than conclusive. This section addresses general planning considerations and other auditing considerations relevant to property and liability insurance entities.

Audit Planning

2.13 AU-C section 300, *Planning an Audit* (AICPA, *Professional Standards*), establishes standards and guidance on the considerations and activities applicable to planning an audit conducted in accordance with GAAS, including preliminary engagement activities (for example, appointment of the independent auditor); preparing a detailed, written audit plan; and determining the extent of involvement of professionals with specialized skills. The auditor should establish an overall audit strategy that sets the scope, timing, and direction of the audit and that guides the development of the audit plan. The nature, timing, and extent of planning vary with the size and complexity of the entity and with the auditor's experience with the entity and understanding of the entity and its environment, including its internal control.

2.14 The auditor should plan the audit so that it is responsive to the assessment of the risks of material misstatement based on the auditor's understanding of the entity and its environment, including its internal control. Paragraph .A2 of AU-C section 300 states that planning is not a discrete phase of the audit, but rather a continual and iterative process that often begins shortly after (or in connection with) the completion of the previous audit and continues throughout the completion of the current audit engagement. Planning, however, includes consideration of the timing of certain activities and audit procedures that need to be completed prior to the performance of further audit procedures.

> *Considerations for Audits Performed in Accordance With PCAOB Standards*
>
> PCAOB Auditing Standard No. 9 provides guidance on the responsibility of the engagement partner for planning, considerations for companies with operations in multiple locations or business units, and the involvement of persons with specialized skill or knowledge. In addition, the auditor should refer to paragraph 9 of PCAOB

Auditing Standard No. 5 regarding planning considerations for integrated audits.

Audit Risk

2.15 Paragraph .A1 of AU-C section 320, *Materiality in Planning and Performing an Audit* (AICPA, *Professional Standards*), states that audit risk is the risk in which the auditor expresses an inappropriate audit opinion when the financial statements are materially misstated. Audit risk is a function of the risks of material misstatement and detection risk.[2] Materiality and audit risk are considered throughout the audit, in particular, when

    a. determining the nature and extent of risk assessment procedures to be performed;

    b. identifying and assessing the risks of material misstatement;[3]

    c. determining the nature, timing, and extent of further audit procedures;[4] and

    d. evaluating the effect of uncorrected misstatements, if any, on the financial statements[5] and in forming the opinion in the auditor's report.

Audit Risk Factors

2.16 AU-C section 320 addresses that the overall objectives of the auditor are to obtain reasonable assurance about whether the financial statements as a whole are free from material misstatement, whether due to fraud or error. The auditor is thereby enabled to express an opinion on whether the financial statements are prepared, in all material respects, in accordance with an applicable financial reporting framework and to report on the financial statements and communicate, as required by GAAS, in accordance with the auditor's findings. As discussed in paragraph .A1 of AU-C section 320, the auditor obtains reasonable assurance by obtaining sufficient appropriate audit evidence to reduce audit risk to an acceptably low level. *Audit risk* is the risk that the auditor expresses an inappropriate audit opinion when the financial statements are materially misstated. Audit risk is a function of the risks of material misstatement and detection risk. Materiality and audit risk are considered throughout the audit when

    a. determining the nature and extent of risk assessment procedures to be performed;

    b. identifying and assessing the risks of material misstatement;

    c. determining the nature, timing, and extent of further audit procedures; and

---

[2] See paragraph .14 of AU-C section 200, *Overall Objectives of the Independent Auditor and the Conduct of an Audit in Accordance With Generally Accepted Auditing Standards* (AICPA, *Professional Standards*).

[3] See AU-C section 315, *Understanding the Entity and Its Environment and Assessing the Risks of Material Misstatement* (AICPA, *Professional Standards*).

[4] See AU-C section 330, *Performing Audit Procedures in Response to Assessed Risks and Evaluating the Audit Evidence Obtained* (AICPA, *Professional Standards*).

[5] Paragraph .11 of AU-C section 450, *Evaluation of Misstatements Identified During the Audit* (AICPA, *Professional Standards*).

Audit Considerations

    d. evaluating the effect of uncorrected misstatements, if any, on the financial statements and in forming the opinion in the auditor's report.

2.17 Experience has demonstrated that audit risk may be greater in certain areas than in others. Significant transaction cycles of property and liability insurance entities include the premium cycle, the claims cycle, the reinsurance cycle, and the investment cycle. Risk factors specific to these cycles include the appropriateness of revenue recognition methods for premium earned including estimated premiums and those related to adjustable features, valuation and recoverability of deferred acquisitions costs, valuation of loss and loss and expense reserves, the appropriateness of the determination of risk transfer, the completeness and accuracy of the computation of reinsurance recoverable, the valuation of reinsurance recoverable, the valuation of investments, and the recording of declines in investment valuations below cost basis. There are also significant risk factors associated with determining that the provision for income taxes and the reported income tax liability or receivable are properly measured, valued, classified. Additional significant risk factors are associated with deferred tax liabilities and assets accurately reflecting the future tax consequences of events that have been recognized in the property and liability insurance entity's financial statements or tax return. The preceding risk factors, as well as other audit risk factors, are described in separate chapters contained within this guide.

2.18 Although the summary of the risk potential in these operating areas is not all-inclusive, the summary does present major areas of recommended concentration in determining the nature and extent of audit procedures described in other chapters of this guide. The auditor's preliminary conclusions regarding the degree of audit risk may be modified by the results of audit work performed. The procedures described throughout this guide for each major operating cycle focus on the preceding overall risks as well as on other kinds of audit risks, and the auditor may refer to those chapters for additional guidance. Further discussion regarding the understanding of the entity and describing the consideration of fraud within an audit of a property and liability company are subsequently described to further assist the auditor in the planning process.

2.19 In order to obtain a general understanding of the industry, the auditor may refer to chapter 1, "Nature, Conduct, and Regulation of the Business," of this guide, which discusses the nature of the property and liability insurance business and many characteristics of operations in the industry. Although conditions will vary from entity to entity, the independent auditor may consider the conditions discussed in the Audit Risk Alert *Insurance Industry Developments* for the current year.

Risk Assessment Procedures

2.20 As described in AU-C section 315, *Understanding the Entity and Its Environment and Assessing the Risks of Material Misstatement* (AICPA, *Professional Standards*), audit procedures performed to obtain an understanding of the entity and its environment, including the entity's internal control, to identify and assess the risks of material misstatement, whether due to fraud or error, at the financial statement and relevant assertion levels are referred to as *risk assessment procedures*. Paragraph .05 of AU-C section 315 states that the auditor should perform risk assessment procedures in order to provide a basis for the identification and assessment of risks of material misstatement at the financial statement and relevant assertion levels. Risk assessment procedures by themselves, however, do not provide sufficient appropriate audit evidence on which to base the audit opinion.

2.21 In accordance with paragraph .06 of AU-C section 315, the auditor should perform the following risk assessment procedures to obtain an understanding of the entity and its environment, including its internal control:

    a. Inquiries of management and others within the entity who, in the auditor's professional judgment, may have information that is likely to assist in identifying risks of material misstatement due to fraud or error

    b. Analytical procedures

    c. Observation and inspection

Identification of Significant Risks

2.22 As part of the assessment of the risks of material misstatement, the auditor should determine which of the risks identified are, in the auditor's judgment, risks that require special audit consideration (such risks are defined as *significant risks*). One or more significant risks normally arise on most audits. In exercising this judgment, the auditor should consider inherent risk to determine whether the nature of the risk, the likely magnitude of the potential misstatement including the possibility that the risk may give rise to multiple misstatements, and the likelihood of the risk occurring are such that they require special audit consideration.

2.23 As noted in paragraph .22 of AU-C section 330, *Performing Audit Procedures in Response to Assessed Risk and Evaluating the Audit Evidence Obtained* (AICPA, *Professional Standards*), if the auditor has determined that an assessed risk of material misstatement at the relevant assertion level is a significant risk, the auditor should perform substantive procedures that are specifically responsive to that risk. When the approach to a significant risk only consists of substantive procedures, those procedures should include tests of details.

Information From Previous Audits

2.24 As discussed in paragraph .10 of AU-C section 315, when the auditor intends to use information obtained from the auditor's previous experience with the entity and from audit procedures performed in previous audits, the auditor should determine whether changes have occurred since the previous audit that may affect its relevance to the current audit.

Communication With Engagement Team

2.25 In accordance with paragraph .11 of AU-C section 315, the engagement partner and other key engagement team members should discuss the susceptibility of the entity's financial statements to material misstatement and the application of the applicable financial reporting framework to the entity's facts and circumstances. The engagement partner should determine which matters are to be communicated to engagement team members not involved in the discussion. This discussion could be held concurrently with the discussion among the audit team that is specified by AU-C section 240, *Consideration of*

Fraud in a Financial Statement Audit (AICPA, *Professional Standards*), to discuss the susceptibility of the entity's financial statements to fraud.

Understanding the Entity, Its Environment, and Its Internal Control

The Entity and Its Environment

2.26 AU-C section 315 requires that the auditor obtain an understanding of the entity and its environment, including its internal control. As discussed in paragraph .12 of AU-C section 315, the auditor should obtain an understanding of the following:

    a. Relevant industry, regulatory, and other external factors, including the applicable financial reporting framework.

    b. The nature of the entity, including

        i. its operations;

        ii. its ownership and governance structures;

        iii. the types of investments that the entity is making and plans to make, including investments in entities formed to accomplish specific objectives; and

        iv. the way that the entity is structured and how it is financed,

to enable the auditor to understand the classes of transactions, account balances, and disclosures to be expected in the financial statements.

    c. The entity's selection and application of accounting policies, including the reasons for changes thereto. The auditor should evaluate whether the entity's accounting policies are appropriate for its business and consistent with the applicable financial reporting framework and accounting policies used in the relevant industry.

    d. The entity's objectives and strategies and those related business risks that may result in risks of material misstatement.

    e. The measurement and review of the entity's financial performance.

The Entity's Internal Control

2.27 As discussed in paragraph .13 of AU-C section 315, the auditor should obtain an understanding of internal control relevant to the audit. Although most controls relevant to the audit are likely to relate to financial reporting, not all controls that relate to financial reporting are relevant to the audit. It is a matter of the auditor's professional judgment whether a control, individually or in combination with others, is relevant to the audit.

2.28 An understanding of internal control assists the auditor in identifying types of potential misstatements and factors that affect the risks of material misstatement and in designing the nature, timing, and extent of further audit procedures. When obtaining an understanding of controls that are relevant to the audit, the auditor should evaluate the design of those controls and determine whether they have been implemented by performing procedures in addition to inquiry of the entity's personnel.

2.29 Obtaining an understanding of the entity and its environment, including its internal control, is a continuous, dynamic process of gathering, updating, and analyzing information throughout the audit. Throughout this process, the auditor should also follow the guidance in AU-C section 240, as discussed in paragraphs 2.75–.99.

Considerations for Audits Performed in Accordance With PCAOB Standards

PCAOB Auditing Standard No. 12 paragraph 8, states the auditor should evaluate whether significant changes in the company from prior periods, including changes in internal control over financial reporting, affect the risk of material misstatement.

2.30 Paragraph .04 of AU-C section 315 defines internal control as

> a process effected by those charged with governance, management, and other personnel that is designed to provide reasonable assurance about the achievement of the entity's objectives with regard to the reliability of financial reporting, effectiveness and efficiency of operations, and compliance with applicable laws and regulations. Internal control over safeguarding of assets against unauthorized acquisition, use, or disposition may include controls relating to financial reporting and operations objectives.

2.31 Internal control consists of the following five interrelated components:

   a. Control environment

   b. The entity's risk assessment process

   c. The information system, including the related business processes relevant to financial reporting and communication

   d. Control activities relevant to the audit

   e. Monitoring of controls

Components of Internal Control

2.32 As discussed in paragraph .15 of AU-C section 315, the auditor should obtain an understanding of the control environment. As part of obtaining this understanding, the auditor should evaluate whether

   a. management, with the oversight of those charged with governance, has created and maintained a culture of honesty and ethical behavior, and

   b. the strengths in the control environment elements collectively provide an appropriate foundation for the other components of internal control and whether those other components are not undermined by deficiencies in the control environment.

2.33 As noted in paragraph .16 of AU-C section 315, related to the entity's risk assessment process, the auditor should obtain an understanding of whether the entity has a process for

   a. identifying business risks relevant to financial reporting objectives;

   b. estimating the significance of the risks;

Audit Considerations

    c. assessing the likelihood of their occurrence; and

    d. deciding about actions to address those risks.

2.34 As noted in paragraph .17 of AU-C section 315, if the entity has established a risk assessment process (referred to hereafter as the entity's risk assessment process), the auditor should obtain an understanding of it and the results thereof. If the auditor identifies risks of material misstatement that management failed to identify, the auditor should evaluate whether an underlying risk existed that the auditor expects would have been identified by the entity's risk assessment process. If such a risk exists, the auditor should obtain an understanding of why that process failed to identify it and evaluate whether the process is appropriate to its circumstances or determine if a significant deficiency or material weakness exists in internal control regarding the entity's risk assessment process. If the entity has not established such a process or has an ad hoc process, the auditor should discuss with management whether business risks relevant to financial reporting objectives have been identified and how they have been addressed. The auditor should evaluate whether the absence of a documented risk assessment process is appropriate in the circumstances or determine whether it represents a significant deficiency or material weakness in the entity's internal control.

2.35 The auditor should obtain an understanding of the information system, including the related business processes relevant to financial reporting, including the following areas:

    a. The classes of transactions in the entity's operations that are significant to the financial statements.

    b. The procedures within both information technology and manual systems by which those transactions are initiated, authorized, recorded, processed, corrected as necessary, transferred to the general ledger, and reported in the financial statements.

    c. The related accounting records supporting information and specific accounts in the financial statements that are used to initiate, authorize, record, process, and report transactions. This includes the correction of incorrect information and how information is transferred to the general ledger. The records may be in either manual or electronic form.

    d. How the information system captures events and conditions, other than transactions, that are significant to the financial statements.

    e. The financial reporting process used to prepare the entity's financial statements, including significant accounting estimates and disclosures.

    f. Controls surrounding journal entries, including nonstandard journal entries used to record nonrecurring, unusual transactions, or adjustments.

2.36 In understanding the entity's control activities, the auditor should obtain an understanding of how the entity has responded to risks arising from information technology. See additional discussion on the use of information technology by property and liability insurance entities in paragraphs 2.100–.103.

2.37 The auditor should also obtain an understanding of how the entity communicates financial reporting roles and responsibilities and significant matters relating to financial reporting, including *a.* communications between management and those charged with governance, and

b. external communications, such as those with regulatory authorities.

2.38 As discussed in paragraph .21 of AU-C section 315, the auditor should obtain an understanding of control activities relevant to the audit, which are control activities the auditor judges necessary to understand in order to assess the risks of material misstatement at the assertion level and design further audit procedures responsive to assessed risks. An audit does not require an understanding of all the control activities related to each significant class of transactions, account balance, and disclosure in the financial statements or to every assertion relevant to them. However, the auditor should obtain an understanding of the process of reconciling detailed records to the general ledger for material account balances.

2.39 The auditor should obtain an understanding of the major activities that the entity uses to monitor internal control over financial reporting, including those related to those control activities relevant to the audit, and how the entity initiates remedial actions to deficiencies in its controls.

2.40 If the entity has an internal audit function, the auditor should obtain an understanding of the following in order to determine whether the internal audit function is likely to be relevant to the audit:

a. The nature of the internal audit function's responsibilities and how the internal audit function fits in the entity's organizational structure

b. The activities performed or to be performed by the internal audit function

2.41 The auditor should obtain an understanding of the sources of the information used in the entity's monitoring activities and the basis upon which management considers the information to be sufficiently reliable for the purpose.

Tests of Controls

2.42 Paragraphs .08–.09 of AU-C section 330 discuss tests of controls and state that the auditor should design and perform tests of controls to obtain sufficient appropriate audit evidence about the operating effectiveness of relevant controls if

a. the auditor's assessment of risks of material misstatement at the relevant assertion level includes an expectation that the controls are operating effectively (that is, the auditor intends to rely on the operating effectiveness of controls in determining the nature, timing, and extent of substantive procedures), or

b. substantive procedures alone cannot provide sufficient appropriate audit evidence at the relevant assertion level.

2.43 In designing and performing tests of controls, the auditor should obtain more persuasive audit evidence the greater the reliance the auditor places on the effectiveness of a control.

Audit Considerations 55

Common Industry Ratios and Performance Metrics

2.44 Discussed in the following paragraphs are some unique characteristics of property and liability insurance entities that the auditor may consider when obtaining an understanding of the entity and its environment in order to assess the risks of material misstatement.

Combined and Operating Ratios

2.45 The combined and operating ratios of an insurance entity can be used as measures to assess the performance of an insurance entity. The accounting treatment for acquisition costs is not consistent between GAAP and SAP; therefore, a company will have a different combined ratio under the two financial accounting standards. A listing of commonly used ratios and information on how they are computed includes the following:

- *Loss ratio.* Total incurred losses divided by premium earned on both a GAAP and statutory basis.
- *Expense ratio.* Total underwriting and general expenses divided by premium earned on a GAAP basis. Total general expenses incurred and acquisition costs divided by premium written on a statutory basis.
- *Dividend ratio.* Policyholder dividends divided by earned premium on both a GAAP and statutory basis.
- *Combined ratio.* The sum of the loss ratio, expense ratio, and dividend ratio.
- *Investment income ratio.* Investment income divided by premium earned.
- *Operating ratio.* Combined ratio, less investment income ratio.

2.46 The auditor may consider using the combined and operating ratios—both for the industry and for the insurance entity whose financial statements are being audited—in evaluating the risk of material misstatement at the financial statement level. For example, these ratios may provide information about the entity's performance relative to the industry and about the economic conditions prevalent in the industry as a whole.

Risk-Based Capital

2.47 Property and liability insurance entities operate in a highly regulated environment. The regulation of property and liability insurance entities is directed primarily toward safeguarding policyholders' interests and maintaining public confidence in the safety and soundness of the property and liability insurance system. One of the primary tools used by state insurance departments for ensuring that those objectives are being achieved is risk-based capital (RBC).

2.48 Solvency regulation of property and liability insurance entities has historically focused on their capital. The National Association of Insurance Commissioners (NAIC) requires property and liability insurance enterprises to disclose RBC in their statutory filings. The RBC calculation serves as a benchmark for the regulation of property and liability insurance enterprises' solvency by state insurance regulators. RBC requirements set forth dynamic surplus formulas similar to target surplus formulas used by commercial rating agencies. The formulas specify various weighting factors that are applied to

AAG-PLI 2.48

financial balances or various levels of activity based on the perceived degree of risk. Such formulas focus on four general types of risk:

    a. Asset risk. The risk related to the insurer's assets.[6]

    b. Credit risk. The risk related to the collectability of insurance recoverables and miscellaneous receivables.

    c. Underwriting risk. The risk of adverse insurance experience with respect to the insurer's liabilities and obligations including excessive premium growth.

    d. Other risk. All other business risks (management, regulatory action, and contingencies).

2.49 The amount determined under such formulas is called the authorized control level (ACL) RBC.

2.50 RBC requirements establish a framework for linking various levels of regulatory corrective action to the relationship of a property and liability insurance enterprise's total adjusted capital (TAC) (equal to the sum of statutory capital and surplus and such other items, if any, as the NAIC's RBC instructions[7] may provide) to the calculated ACL.

2.51 The levels of regulatory action, the trigger point, and the corrective actions are summarized as follows:

RBC Levels and Corrective Actions

Level	Trigger	Corrective Action
Company Action Level RBC (CAL)	Total adjusted capital (TAC) is less than or equal to 2 × ACL, or TAC is less than or equal to 2.5 × ACL with negative trend	The property and liability insurance enterprise must submit a comprehensive plan to the insurance commissioner.
Regulatory Action Level RBC (RAL)	TAC is less than or equal to 1.5 × ACL, or unsatisfactory RBC plan	In addition to the action mentioned, the insurance commissioner is required to perform an examination or analysis deemed necessary and issue a corrective order specifying corrective actions required.
Authorized Control Level RBC (ACL)	TAC is less than or equal to 1 × ACL	In addition to the actions described, the insurance commissioner is permitted but not required to place the property and liability insurance enterprise under regulatory control.

---

    [6] This risk also includes risk of default.

    [7] The National Association of Insurance Commissioners' (NAIC's) risk-based capital (RBC) instructions may be amended by the NAIC from time to time in accordance with procedures adopted by the NAIC.

Audit Considerations

Level	Trigger	Corrective Action
Mandatory Control Level RBC (MCL)	TAC is less than or equal to 0.7 × ACL	The insurance commissioner is required to place the property and liability insurance enterprise under regulatory control.

2.52 Under the RBC requirements, the comprehensive financial plan should

  a. identify the conditions in the insurer that contribute to the failure to meet the capital requirements.

  b. contain proposals of corrective actions that the insurer intends to take and that would be expected to result in compliance with capital requirements.

  c. provide projections of the insurer's financial results in the current year and at least the four succeeding years, both in the absence of proposed corrective actions and giving effect to the proposed corrective actions.

  d. identify the key assumptions impacting the insurer's projections and the sensitivity of the projections to the assumptions.

  e. identify the quality of, and problems associated with, the insurer's business, including its assets, anticipated business growth and associated surplus strain, extraordinary exposure to risk, mix of business, and use of reinsurance in each case, if any.

2.53 Because of the importance of RBC to property and liability insurance entities, RBC may be considered in assessing the risks of material misstatement and planning the audit. The auditor may obtain and review the client's RBC reports to further his or her understanding of the RBC requirements for preparing such reports and the actual regulations associated with RBC.

NAIC Insurance Regulatory Information System

2.54 Many insurance laws and regulations address insurance entities' financial solvency, and insurance departments consequently monitor reports, operating procedures, investment practices, and other activities of insurance entities. One of the main purposes of the monitoring system is to detect, at an early stage, entities that are insolvent or may become insolvent.

2.55 To assist state insurance departments in monitoring the financial condition of property and liability insurance entities, the NAIC Insurance Regulatory Information System (IRIS) was developed by a committee of state insurance department regulators. It is intended to assist state insurance departments in identifying insurance entities whose financial condition warrants close surveillance. The system is based on 12 tests for property and liability insurance entities. The tests are based on studies of financially troubled entities compared to financially sound entities. Usual ranges have been established under each of the tests for a property and liability entity, but the ranges may be adjusted to reflect changing economic conditions. The results of the tests of all entities are compared, and those entities with 3 or more results outside of the usual range are given a priority classification indicating that a close review of the entity be undertaken. In addition, a regulatory team annually reviews the results and recommends regulatory attention if needed. One or more results outside the usual range do not necessarily indicate that an entity is in unstable financial condition, but the entity may need to explain the circumstances causing the unusual results. Annually, the NAIC publishes the booklet "NAIC Financial Solvency Tools—Insurance Regulatory Information System (IRIS)," which explains the IRIS ratios in detail. (Each of the individual ratios and the acceptable results is briefly described in chapter 1.) The auditor may consider IRIS test results when performing analytical procedures in the planning stage of an audit. IRIS ratios are no longer required to be filed separately with the NAIC due to current electronic filing requirements of NAIC annual statements.

2.56 Other industry sources useful in the preliminary assessment of risk evaluation include annual and quarterly statements filed with regulatory authorities, regulatory examination reports, IRS examination reports, and communications with regulatory authorities.

Identifying and Assessing the Risks of Material Misstatement

2.57 As noted in paragraphs .26–27 of AU-C section 315, to provide a basis for designing and performing further audit procedures, the auditor should identify and assess the risks of material misstatement at

 a. the financial statement level, and

 b. the relevant assertion level for classes of transactions, account balances, and disclosures.

2.58 The auditor should

 a. identify risks throughout the process of obtaining an understanding of the entity and its environment, including relevant controls that relate to the risks, by considering the classes of transactions, account balances, and disclosures in the financial statements;

 b. assess the identified risks and evaluate whether they relate more pervasively to the financial statements as a whole and potentially affect many assertions;

 c. relate the identified risks to what can go wrong at the relevant assertion level, taking account of relevant controls that the auditor intends to test; and

 d. consider the likelihood of misstatement, including the possibility of multiple misstatements, and whether the potential misstatement is of a magnitude that could result in a material misstatement.

2.59 As part of the risk assessment described in paragraph 2.57, the auditor should determine whether any of the risks identified are, in the auditor's professional judgment, a significant risk. In exercising this judgment, the auditor should exclude the effects of identified controls related to the risk. In exercising professional judgment about which risks are significant risks, the auditor should consider at least

 a. whether the risk is a risk of fraud;

 b. whether the risk is related to recent significant economic, accounting, or other developments and, therefore, requires specific attention;

Audit Considerations

c. the complexity of transactions;

d. whether the risk involves significant transactions with related parties;

e. the degree of subjectivity in the measurement of financial information related to the risk, especially those measurements involving a wide range of measurement uncertainty; and

f. whether the risk involves significant transactions that are outside the normal course of business for the entity or that otherwise appear to be unusual.

2.60 As discussed in paragraph .30 of AU-C section 315, if the auditor has determined that a significant risk exists, the auditor should obtain an understanding of the entity's controls, including control activities, relevant to that risk and, based on that understanding, evaluate whether such controls have been suitably designed and implemented to mitigate such risks.

Performing Audit Procedures In Response to Assessed Risks

2.61 As stated in paragraph .03 of AU-C section 330, the objective of the auditor is to obtain sufficient appropriate audit evidence regarding the assessed risks of material misstatement through designing and implementing appropriate responses to those risks. To reduce audit risk to an acceptably low level, paragraphs .05–.06 require that the auditor (a) should determine overall responses to address the assessed risks of material misstatement at the financial statement level, and (b) should design and perform further audit procedures whose nature, timing, and extent are responsive to the assessed risks of material misstatement at the relevant assertion level. As discussed in paragraph .A4 of AU-C section 330, the auditor's assessment of the identified risks at the relevant assertion level provides a basis for considering the appropriate audit approach for designing and performing further audit procedures. The purpose is to provide a clear linkage between the nature, timing, and extent of the auditor's further audit procedures and the assessed risks. The overall responses and the nature, timing, and extent of the further audit procedures to be performed are matters for the professional judgment of the auditor and should be based on the auditor's assessment of the risks of material misstatement.

Overall Responses

2.62 The auditor's overall responses to address the assessed risks of material misstatement at the financial statement level may include emphasizing to the audit team the need to maintain professional skepticism in gathering and evaluating audit evidence, assigning more experienced staff or those with specialized skills or using specialists, providing more supervision, or incorporating additional elements of unpredictability in the selection of further audit procedures to be performed. Additionally, the auditor may make general changes to the nature, timing, or extent of further audit procedures as an overall response, for example, performing substantive procedures at period end instead of at an interim date.

> *Considerations for Audits Performed in Accordance With PCAOB Standards*
>
> PCAOB Auditing Standard No. 13 paragraph 5, includes guidance stating the auditor should design and implement overall responses

focused on the assessed risk of material misstatement, including incorporating elements of unpredictability in the selection of the audit procedures to be performed and evaluating the company's selection and application of significant accounting principles.

Paragraph 6 of Auditing Standard No. 13 states the auditor also should determine whether it is necessary to make pervasive changes to the nature, timing, or extent of audit procedures to adequately address the assess risks of material misstatement.

Paragraph 11 of Auditing Standard No. 13 states the auditor should perform substantive procedures, including tests of details, that are specifically responsive to the significant risks assessed in planning.

Further Audit Procedures

2.63 Further audit procedures provide important audit evidence to support an audit opinion. These procedures consist of tests of controls and substantive tests. The nature, timing, and extent of the further audit procedures to be performed by the auditor should be based on the auditor's assessment of risks of material misstatement at the relevant assertion level. In some cases, an auditor may determine that performing only substantive procedures is appropriate. However, the auditor often may determine that a combined audit approach using both tests of the operating effectiveness of controls and substantive procedures is an effective audit approach.

2.64 The auditor should design and perform further audit procedures whose nature, timing, and extent are based on, and are responsive to, the assessed risks of material misstatement at the relevant assertion level. As stated in paragraph .07 of AU-C section 330, in designing the further audit procedures to be performed, the auditor should

    a. consider the reasons for the assessed risk of material misstatement at the relevant assertion level for each class of transactions, account balance, and disclosure, including

        i. the likelihood of material misstatement due to the particular characteristics of the relevant class of transactions, account balance, or disclosure (the inherent risk), and

        ii. whether the risk assessment takes account of relevant controls (the control risk), thereby requiring the auditor to obtain audit evidence to determine whether the controls are operating effectively (that is, the auditor intends to rely on the operating effectiveness of controls in determining the nature, timing, and extent of substantive procedures), and

    b. obtain more persuasive audit evidence the higher the auditor's assessment of risk.

2.65 Although some risk assessment procedures that the auditor performs to evaluate the design of controls and to determine that they have been implemented may not have been specifically designed as tests of controls, they may nevertheless provide audit evidence about the operating effectiveness of the controls and, consequently, serve as tests of controls. In such circumstances, the auditor should consider whether the audit evidence provided by those audit procedures is sufficient.

Audit Considerations

2.66 The auditor's substantive procedures should include the following audit procedures related to the financial statement reporting process:

- Agreeing the financial statements, including their accompanying notes, to the underlying accounting records
- Examining material journal entries and other adjustments made during the course of preparing the financial statements

2.67 The nature and extent of the auditor's examination of journal entries and other adjustments depend on the nature and complexity of the entity's financial reporting system and the associated risks of material misstatement.

Use of Assertions in Obtaining Audit Evidence

2.68 In representing that the financial statements are fairly presented in accordance with GAAP, management implicitly or explicitly makes assertions regarding the recognition, measurement, and disclosure of information in the financial statements and related disclosures. Assertions used by the auditor fall into the following categories.

Categories of Assertions

	Description of Assertions		
	Classes of Transactions and Events During the Period	Account Balances at the End of the Period	Presentation and Disclosure
Occurrence and existence	Transactions and events that have been recorded have occurred and pertain to the entity.	Assets, liabilities, and equity interests exist.	Disclosed events and transactions have occurred.
Rights and obligations	—	The entity holds or controls the rights to assets, and liabilities are the obligations of the entity.	Disclosed events and transactions pertain to the entity.
Completeness	All transactions and events that should have been recorded have been recorded.	All assets, liabilities, and equity interests that should have been recorded have been recorded.	All disclosures that should have been included in the financial statements have been included.

(continued)

AAG-PLI 2.68

	Description of Assertions		
	Classes of Transactions and Events During the Period	Account Balances at the End of the Period	Presentation and Disclosure
Accuracy or valuation and allocation	Amounts and other data relating to recorded transactions and events have been recorded appropriately.	Assets, liabilities, and equity interests are included in the financial statements at appropriate amounts and any resulting valuation or allocation adjustments are recorded appropriately.	Financial and other information is disclosed fairly and at appropriate amounts.
Cut-off	Transactions and events have been recorded in the correct accounting period.	—	—
Classification and understandability	Transactions and events have been recorded in the proper accounts.	—	Financial information is appropriately presented and described and information in disclosures is expressed clearly.

Revision of Risk Assessment

2.69 As discussed in paragraph .32 of AU-C section 315, the auditor's assessment of the risks of material misstatement at the assertion level may change during the course of the audit as additional audit evidence is obtained. In circumstances in which the auditor obtains audit evidence from performing further audit procedures or if new information is obtained, either of which is inconsistent with the audit evidence on which the auditor originally based the assessment, the auditor should revise the assessment and modify the further planned audit procedures accordingly. The auditor should consider the guidance in paragraph .10a of AU-C section 500, *Audit Evidence* (AICPA, *Professional Standards*), regarding what modifications or additions to audit procedures are necessary when audit evidence obtained from one source that is inconsistent with that obtained from another.

Other Risk Assessment Activities and Considerations

Planning Materiality

2.70 The auditor's consideration of materiality is a matter of professional judgment and is influenced by the auditor's perception of the needs of users of financial statements. Materiality judgments are made in light of surrounding circumstances and necessarily involve both quantitative and qualitative considerations.

2.71 In accordance with paragraph .10 of AU-C section 320, when establishing the overall audit strategy, the auditor should determine materiality for the financial statements as a whole. If, in the specific circumstances of the entity, one or more particular classes of transactions, account balances, or disclosures exist for which misstatements of lesser amounts than materiality for the financial statements as a whole could reasonably be expected to influence the economic decisions of users, then, taken on the basis of the financial statements, the auditor also should determine the materiality level or levels to be applied to those particular classes of transactions, account balances, or disclosures. As discussed in paragraph .A5 of AU-C section 320, a percentage is often applied to a chosen benchmark as a starting point in determining materiality for the financial statements taken as a whole. Examples of benchmarks for property and liability insurance entities include (*a*) percentage of surplus, (*b*) percentage of revenue, (*c*) percentage of after tax income, and (*d*) percentage of total assets.

2.72 As discussed in paragraphs .12–.13 of AU-C section 320, the auditor should revise materiality for the financial statements as a whole (and, if applicable, the materiality level or levels for particular classes of transactions, account balances, or disclosures) in the event of becoming aware of information during the audit that would have caused the auditor to have determined a different amount (or amounts) initially. If the auditor concludes that a lower materiality than that initially determined for the financial statements as a whole (and, if applicable, materiality level or levels for particular classes of transactions, account balances, or disclosures) is appropriate, the auditor should determine whether it is necessary to revise performance materiality and whether the nature, timing, and extent of the further audit procedures remain appropriate. For example, if, during the audit, it appears as though actual financial results are likely to be substantially different from the anticipated period-end financial results that were used initially to determine materiality for the financial statements as a whole, the auditor may be required, in accordance with paragraph .12 of AU-C section 320, to revise materiality. The auditor should include information related to materiality as noted in paragraph .14 of AU-C section 320 in the audit documentation.

Considerations for Audits Performed in Accordance With PCAOB Standards

PCAOB Auditing Standard No. 5 paragraph 20 states that the auditor should use the same materiality considerations he or she would use in planning the audit of the company's annual financial statements in planning the audit of internal control over financial reporting.

Performance Materiality and Tolerable Misstatement

2.73 As discussed in paragraph .A14 of AU-C section 320, planning the audit solely to detect individual material misstatements overlooks the fact that the aggregate of individually immaterial misstatements may cause the financial statements to be materially misstated and leaves no margin for possible undetected misstatements. *Performance materiality* (which, as defined, is one or more amounts) is set to reduce to an appropriately low level the probability that the aggregate of uncorrected and undetected misstatements in the financial statements exceeds materiality for the financial statements as a whole.

Similarly, performance materiality relating to a materiality level determined for a particular class of transactions, account balance, or disclosure is set to reduce to an appropriately low level the probability that the aggregate of uncorrected and undetected misstatements in that particular class of transactions, account balance, or disclosure exceeds the materiality level for that particular class of transactions, account balance, or disclosure. The determination of performance materiality is not a simple mechanical calculation and involves the exercise of professional judgment. It is affected by the auditor's understanding of the entity, updated during the performance of the risk assessment procedures, and the nature and extent of misstatements identified in previous audits and, thereby, the auditor's expectations regarding misstatements in the current period.

2.74 However, the auditor should allow for the possibility that some misstatements of lesser amounts than these materiality levels could, in the aggregate, result in a material misstatement of the financial statements. To do so, the auditor should determine one or more levels of tolerable misstatement. As discussed in AU-C section 530, *Audit Sampling* (AICPA, *Professional Standards*), *tolerable misstatement* is the application of performance materiality to a particular sampling procedure. Tolerable misstatement may be the same amount or an amount smaller than performance materiality (for example, when the population from which the sample is selected is smaller than the account balance). Such levels of tolerable misstatement are normally lower than the materiality levels.

> *Considerations for Audits Performed in Accordance With PCAOB Standards*
>
> Paragraph 10 of PCAOB Auditing Standard No. 11 states that for companies with multiple locations or business units the tolerable misstatement at an individual location should be less than the materiality level for the financial statements taken as a whole.

Consideration of Fraud in a Financial Statement Audit

2.75 Risks are inherent in all audit engagements, including the possibility that fraudulent acts may cause a material misstatement of financial statements. AU-C section 240 is the primary source of authoritative guidance about an auditor's responsibilities concerning the consideration of fraud in a financial statement audit. AU-C section 240 addresses the auditor's responsibilities relating to fraud in an audit of financial statements.

> *Considerations for Audits Performed in Accordance With PCAOB Standards*
>
> Paragraph .01 of AU section 316, *Consideration of Fraud in a Financial Statement Audit* (AICPA, *PCAOB Standards and Related Rules*, Interim Standards), states that when performing an integrated audit of financial statements and internal control over financial reporting, refer to paragraphs 14–15 of PCAOB Auditing Standard No. 5 regarding fraud considerations, in addition to the fraud considerations set forth in AU section 316. In addition, PCAOB Auditing Standard No. 12 paragraphs 65–69 provide guidance for the auditor about factors relevant to identifying fraud risks; PCAOB Auditing Standard No. 13 paragraphs 12–15 discuss audit procedures to address the assessed fraud risks; and PCAOB Auditing Standard No. 14 paragraphs 9, 20–23, and 28–29 discuss evaluation

of audit results including evaluating conditions relating to the assessment of fraud risks.

2.76 As noted in paragraphs .02–.03 of AU-C section 240, misstatements in the financial statements can arise from either fraud or error. The distinguishing factor between fraud and error is whether the underlying action that results in the misstatement of the financial statements is intentional or unintentional. Although fraud is a broad legal concept, for the purposes of GAAS, the auditor is primarily concerned with fraud that causes a material misstatement in the financial statements. Two types of intentional misstatements are relevant to the auditor—misstatements resulting from fraudulent financial reporting and misstatements resulting from misappropriation of assets. Although the auditor may suspect or, in rare cases, identify the occurrence of fraud, the auditor does not make legal determinations of whether fraud has actually occurred.

Insurance Industry—Fraud Risk Factors

2.77 An auditor's interest specifically relates to fraudulent acts that may cause a material misstatement of the financial statements. Some of the following factors and conditions are present in insurance entities where specific circumstances *do not present a risk of material misstatement*. Also, specific controls may exist that mitigate the risk of material misstatement due to fraud, even though risk factors or conditions are present. When identifying risk factors and other conditions, the auditor assesses whether those risk factors and conditions, individually and in combination, present a risk of material misstatement of the financial statements. The industry-specific fraud risk factors that follow include interpretations of some of the AU-C section 240 examples of fraud risk factors tailored to the insurance industry. Each section supplements, but does not replace, the examples of fraud risk factors included in AU-C section 240.

2.78 Tables 2-1 and 2-2 are not meant to be inclusive. The order of the examples of fraud risk factors provided in tables 2-1 and 2-2 is not intended to reflect their relative importance or frequency of occurrence. Finally, some of the fraud risk factors related to misstatements arising from fraudulent financial reporting may also be present when misstatements arising from misappropriation of assets occur. For example, ineffective monitoring of management and weakness in internal control may be present when misstatements due to either fraudulent financial reporting or misappropriation of assets exist.

Table 2-1

Fraud Risk Factors—Fraudulent Financial Reporting

Incentive or pressure		
Financial stability or profitability is threatened by economic, industry, or entity operating conditions such as the following:	a. New accounting, statutory, or regulatory requirements	1. New criteria used by rating agencies to assign ratings to insurers 2. Impact of GAAP or SAP 3. Demutualization 4. Changes in risk-based capital requirements 5. Changes in consolidation criteria (for example, special purpose entities)
	b. High vulnerability to rapid changes, such as changes in technology, product obsolescence, or interest rates	1. Rapidly changing distribution network results in different sales channels without adequate controls (for example, possible use of the Internet) 2. Changes in interest rates or in the fair value of invested securities may have a significant impact on the financial results of many insurance entities
	c. Rapid growth or unusual profitability especially compared to that of other entities in the same industry	1. Unusual and considerable increases in the number of policyholders over a short period of time 2. Loss ratios significantly different from entities offering similar insurance coverage 3. Significant concentrations of policyholders in the same geographic region causing greater exposure to catastrophe 4. Unusual increases in the number of policies in mature lines of business, potentially indicating inadequate pricing to gain business from competitors
	d. Emerging trends in claims settlement and litigation	1. Identification of emerging new classes of claims 2. Plaintiffs expanded theory of liability 3. Court coverage decisions and judicial interpretations 4. Expanded liability due to changes in legislation such as with asbestos litigation reform

AAG-PLI 2.78

Fraud Risk Factors—Fraudulent Financial Reporting—continued

	e. High degree of competition or market saturation, accompanied by declining margins	1. Rapid development of new products reacting to the market environment without adequate review of long-term strategies 2. Volatility of earnings due to market environment that could cause an entity to manipulate earnings 3. Large inflow of additional capital putting pricing pressure on current insurers
	f. Volatility of earnings due to catastrophic losses could cause the entity to manipulate earnings in other areas	1. Overstatement of adjustable features on reinsurance contracts such as profit sharing or sliding scale commissions in light of increasing ceded losses
Incentive or pressure		
Excess pressure for management to meet the requirements or expectations of third parties due to the following:	a. Pressure to meet profitability or trend expectations of investment analysts	
	b. Pressure from rating agencies to maintain or improve ratings	1. Favorable trends not in line with the industry 2. Pressures exerted over internal or external valuation actuaries 3. Smoothing of earnings through changes to IBNR reserves
	c. Pressure to meet risk-based capital requirements	1. Close to triggering regulatory actions in prior periods based on declining surplus and thus affecting risk-based capital 2. Failure to achieve forecasts provided to regulators
Opportunity		
The nature of the industry or the entity's operations provides opportunities to engage in fraudulent financial reporting that can arise from the following:	a. Significant related-party transactions not in the ordinary course of business or with related entities not audited or audited by another firm	1. Unusual or complex intercompany reinsurance transactions 2. Transactions entered into with affiliates, the impact of which is to increase statutory surplus 3. Complex or inconsistent, or both, expense allocation agreements

(continued)

Fraud Risk Factors—Fraudulent Financial Reporting—continued

	b. Assets, liabilities, revenues, or expenses based on significant estimates that involve subjective judgments or uncertainties that are difficult to corroborate	1. Estimates for loss and loss adjustment expenses, reinsurance recoverables, deferred acquisitions costs, recoverability of net deferred tax assets, goodwill recoverability, fair value of investments, other than temporary impairments, litigation reserves and others based on unusually subjective judgments 2. Significant purchases and sales of securities that do not have an active market, which could indicate "parking losses" 3. Aggressive policies related to revenue recognition for administrative-service type contracts. 4. Improper classification of normal operating losses as "catastrophe-related" in financial reporting (for example, management discussion and analysis, footnote disclosure). Also, the diversion of an insurer's resources in dealing with a catastrophe could put a strain on internal controls
	c. Significant, unusual, or highly complex transactions, especially those close to period end, that pose difficult "substance over form" questions	1. High yields on investments that appear to be low risk 2. Transactions that "convert" nonadmitted assets to admitted assets 3. Numerous and complex off-balance-sheet financing transactions 4. Reinsurance transactions that embody loss assumptions which are very different from industry or historical trends in order to pass the "transfer of risk" rules 5. Transactions that "convert" realized capital gains and losses to ordinary income or vice versa 6. Significant closing journal entries for insurers that maintain their books on a statutory basis of accounting, which results in

Audit Considerations

Fraud Risk Factors—Fraudulent Financial Reporting—continued

		posting several statutory-to-GAAP adjusting entries 7. Significant or unusual amount of quarter-end or year-end manual entries posted after consolidation 8. Absence of a review process for estimates of the value of closely held securities 9. Agreements accounted for as reinsurance transactions that do not transfer risk
Opportunity		
Ineffective monitoring of management due to the following:	a. Domination of the board of directors because it is composed primarily of an entity's close business partners (for example, agents, bankers, and lawyers)	1. Resignation of independent members
Opportunity		
There is a complex organizational structure as evidenced by the following:	a. Significant transactions included in noninsurance affiliates with the sole purpose of excluding such activity from the statutory-basis financial statements filed with insurance regulators	1. Use of related party management agreements 2. Significant due to or due from between insurance entity and its affiliates
Opportunity		
Internal control components are deficient as a result of the following:	a. Information systems that cannot account for complex features of insurance policies issued (for example, policies with complex deductible features) or reinsurance policies (for example, adjustable features)	

(continued)

AAG-PLI 2.78

Fraud Risk Factors—Fraudulent Financial Reporting—continued

Attitude and rationalization		
Excessive interest by management in maintaining or increasing the entity's stock price or earnings trend or statutory capital position:	a. Risk transfer criteria for reinsurance transactions are rarely met	1. Use of contracts with structured payout patterns 2. Inclusion of loss corridors within reinsurance agreements 3. Adjustable features that could have a material effect on cash flows between the ceding and assuming entities (for example, profit sharing, sliding scale commissions, adjustable coverage)
	b. Use of discretionary reserves to manipulate earnings	1. Management records a reserve estimate different than the estimate from the loss reserve specialist without analysis to support the deviation 2. Catastrophe reserves
Attitude and rationalization		
A failure by management to display and communicate an appropriate attitude regarding internal control and the financial reporting process:	a. Lack of board or management oversight of critical processes	1. Underwriting-control risk, price risk 2. IT systems or resources to effectively administer complex insurance or reinsurance contract provisions 3. Monitoring of creditworthiness of reinsurers 4. Suspense account clearance 5. Derivative valuation (selection of models, methodologies, and assumptions) 6. Establishment of loss and loss adjustment expense reserves 7. Investment decisions 8. Understanding of critical accounting policies and significant estimates 9. Agents or third-party administrators with underwriting or claims settling authority
	b. No business risk management responsibility or function	
	c. No accounting policy responsibility or function	

AAG-PLI 2.78

Fraud Risk Factors—Fraudulent Financial Reporting—continued

	d. Management's inattention to establish independent reporting lines for key assurance functions (for example, internal audit and quality control reviews of claims and underwriting)	
	e. Lack of insurance-industry or finance experience on the audit committee	
Attitude and rationalization		
Management displaying a significant disregard for regulatory authorities:	a. Existence of a regulatory enforcement action	
	b. Prior examination findings not addressed or inadequately addressed	
	c. Mandated restatements of regulatory financial reports due to inappropriate accounting treatment	
	d. Assessment of market conduct fines	
Attitude and rationalization		
A strained relationship between management and the current or predecessor auditor, as exhibited by the following:	a. Frequent disputes with the current or predecessor auditor on accounting, auditing, or reporting matters such as the reasonableness of sensitive estimates (for example, loss and loss adjustment expense reserves,	1. Internal or external auditors not allowed to report directly to the board of directors

(continued)

Fraud Risk Factors—Fraudulent Financial Reporting—continued

	allowances for uncollectible reinsurance, and other amounts)	
	b. Issuance of reportable condition or material weakness letters	
	c. Failure of management to address reportable condition or material weakness issues on a timely basis	
Attitude and rationalization		
Nonfinancial management's excessive participation in or preoccupation with the selection of the accounting principles or the determination of significant estimates:	a. Lack of management to establish controls over accounting policy issues	

Table 2-2

Fraud Risk Factors—Misappropriation of Assets

Incentive or pressure		
Adverse relationships between the entity and employees with authority over cash and assets could motivate employees to misappropriate those assets	a. History of workforce reductions	1. For example, combining regional claims offices
	b. Dissatisfaction with compensation	1. Inequality in pay scale 2. Unachievable incentive compensation goals
Opportunity		
Certain characteristics or circumstances may increase the susceptibility of assets to misappropriation, for example, opportunities to misappropriate assets increase when there are the following factors:	a. Significant activity and balances present in suspense accounts	
	b. Large volume premium checks received by the insurance entity rather than being sent to a lock box	
	c. Premiums are not directly remitted to the insurer but are instead collected by the agent	
Opportunity		
Inadequate internal control over assets may increase the susceptibility of misappropriation of those assets. For example, misappropriation of assets may occur because of the following factors:	a. Inadequate segregation of duties or independent checks	1. Lack of review of claim adjusters on long-term claims 2. Custodial reconciliations performed by an individual who records the amount to the ledger 3. Bank reconciliations performed by individual with access to cash receipts

(continued)

AAG-PLI 2.78

Fraud Risk Factors—Misappropriation of Assets—continued

	b. Inadequate management oversight of employees responsible for assets	1. Lack of adequate monitoring of underwriting policies and procedures 2. Lack of management review or control processes over year-end or month-end transactions 3. Extensive use of managing general agents with little or no supervision by management 4. Lack of internal audit or claim quality review functions 5. Inadequate payment approval process 6. Lack of review or inadequate controls over system overrides (for example, claim payments and commissions) 7. Lack of strong custodial controls over cash and investments
	c. Large volume of duplicate claims processed	
	d. Large volume of claims paid to post office boxes	1. No controls to ensure that claim adjustment payments are made only to authorized vendors
	e. Large volume of claims paid to the same claimant	1. No monitoring or enforcement of claims settlement authorities
	f. Claims paid to employees	
Attitude and rationalization		
Failure to report all instances of fraud to the audit committee		
Attitude and rationalization		
Failure to properly staff internal audit and other (claims or underwriting) quality control functions		
Attitude and rationalization		
Poor relationships between management, employees, and agents that may appear to justify misappropriations of assets		

Fraud Risk Factors—Misappropriation of Assets—continued

Attitude and rationalization		
Disregard for internal control over misappropriation of assets by overriding existing controls or by failing to correct known internal control deficiencies		

The Importance of Exercising Professional Skepticism

2.79 Because of the characteristics of fraud, the auditor's exercise of professional skepticism is particularly important when considering the risk of material misstatement due to fraud. Professional skepticism is an attitude that includes a questioning mind and a critical assessment of audit evidence. The auditor should conduct the engagement with a mindset that recognizes the possibility that a material misstatement due to fraud could be present, regardless of any past experience with the entity and regardless of the auditor's belief about management's honesty and integrity. Furthermore, professional skepticism requires an ongoing questioning of whether the information and evidence obtained suggests that a material misstatement due to fraud has occurred. As noted in paragraphs .13–.14 of AU-C section 240, unless the auditor has reason to believe the contrary, the auditor may accept records and documents as genuine. If conditions identified during the audit cause the auditor to believe that a document may not be authentic or that terms in a document have been modified but not disclosed to the auditor, the auditor should investigate further. When responses to inquiries of management, those charged with governance, or others are inconsistent or otherwise unsatisfactory (for example, vague or implausible), the auditor should further investigate the inconsistencies or unsatisfactory responses.

Discussion Among Engagement Personnel Regarding the Risks of Material Misstatement Due to Fraud[8]

2.80 AU-C section 315 requires a discussion among the key engagement team members, including the engagement partner, and a determination by the engagement partner of which matters are to be communicated to those team members not involved in the discussion.[9] This discussion should include an exchange of ideas or brainstorming among the engagement team members about how and where the entity's financial statements might be susceptible to material misstatement due to fraud, how management could perpetrate and conceal fraudulent financial reporting, and how assets of the entity could be misappropriated. The discussion should occur setting aside beliefs that the engagement team members may have that management and those charged with governance are honest and have integrity, and should, in particular, also address

---

[8] The brainstorming session to discuss the entity's susceptibility to material misstatements due to fraud could be held concurrently with the brainstorming session required under AU-C section 315 to discuss the potential of the risks of material misstatement.

[9] See paragraph .11 of AU-C section 315.

a. known external and internal factors affecting the entity that may create an incentive or pressure for management or others to commit fraud, provide the opportunity for fraud to be perpetrated, and indicate a culture or environment that enables management or others to rationalize committing fraud;

b. the risk of management override of controls;

c. consideration of circumstances that might be indicative of earnings management or manipulation of other financial measures and the practices that might be followed by management to manage earnings or other financial measures that could lead to fraudulent financial reporting;

d. the importance of maintaining professional skepticism throughout the audit regarding the potential for material misstatement due to fraud; and

e. how the auditor might respond to the susceptibility of the entity's financial statements to material misstatement due to fraud.

2.81 Communication among the engagement team members about the risks of material misstatement due to fraud should continue throughout the audit, particularly upon discovery of new facts during the audit.

2.82 Factors that may increase the risk of material misstatement due to fraud as a result of the items described in the preceding paragraphs include, but are not limited to, the following:

a. Internal factor. A significant portion of management compensation (that is, bonuses and stock options) is contingent upon achieving aggressive targets for stock price, operating results, financial position, or cash flow. Incentives specific to the insurance industry may include

  i. pressures motivating the underwriting department to become more profitable.

  ii. the investment department's evaluation based upon investment yields.

  iii. management or reserving actuaries to be included in short-term profit-sharing plan or incentive compensation arrangements linked to net income or surplus.

b. External factor. A slow economy: because insurers have such a large number of investments, equity market declines and reduced market interest rates will significantly lower investment returns. Such conditions could result in insurers looking to new investment vehicles to secure sufficient investment margins including derivatives, real estate, mortgage loans, and joint venture arrangements. Insurers should have controls in place to ensure adequate underwriting, due diligence, and accounting controls on new investments. Pressure exists to have investment results improve overall results in periods where underwriting operation is underperforming.

c. Internal factor. Significant dependency on information systems for support in day-to-day operations, and a lack of controls regarding access to information systems. For example, a risk of loss exists from employees who have access to the claim system. They could make unauthorized changes to policyholder account balances, ceded reinsurance account balances, or third-party claim payments. They could also approve fraudulent claims payable to themselves or excess payments to others (such as auto repair centers).

 d. Internal factor. Failure by management to communicate and demonstrate an appropriate attitude regarding internal control, as well as management's ability to override internal controls in financial reporting related to

  i. numerous manual adjustments to determine amounts recorded in financial statements (that is, accrual entries booked to a cash-basis ledger or statutory-to-GAAP adjustments).

  ii. correcting entries or adjustments made by management, particularly at or near year-end.

  iii. adjusting entries made directly to the financial statements.

 Considerations for Audits Performed in Accordance With PCAOB Standards

 PCAOB Auditing Standard No. 12 paragraph 11 requires the auditor to consider factors, such as terms of management compensation arrangements, company prepared press releases, analyst reports, and transactions by significant shareholders, in performing the risk assessment.

2.83 The risk factors are further classified based on the three conditions generally present when material misstatements due to fraud occur: incentives and pressures, opportunities, and attitudes and rationalizations. Although the risk factors cover a broad range of situations, they are only examples and, accordingly, the auditor may consider additional or different risk factors.

 Considerations for Audits Performed in Accordance With PCAOB Standards

 PCAOB Auditing Standard No. 12 paragraphs 49–53 provide additional guidance related to the discussion and the matters to be emphasized to all engagement team members.

Obtaining the Information Needed to Identify the Risks of Material Misstatement Due to Fraud

2.84 AU-C section 315 addresses the auditor's responsibility to obtain an understanding of the entity and its environment, including its internal control for the purpose of assessing the risks of material misstatement. In performing that work, information may come to the auditor's attention that should be considered in identifying risks of material misstatement due to fraud. As part of this work, the auditor should perform the procedures in paragraphs .17–.24 of AU-C section 240 to obtain information for use in identifying the risks of material misstatement due to fraud, such as the following:

 a. Make inquiries of management and others within the entity to obtain their views about the risks of fraud and how they are addressed

  Considerations for Audits Performed in Accordance With PCAOB Standards

  PCAOB Auditing Standard No. 12 paragraphs 54–56 require expanded inquiry of the audit committee, management, and internal audit. These inquiries include any known tips or complaints regarding financial reporting, controls established to address fraud risks and any instances of known override of controls.

    b. Obtain an understanding of how oversight is exercised by those charged with governance; it is important that the auditor understands the respective responsibilities of those charged with governance and management to enable the auditor to obtain an understanding of the oversight exercised by the appropriate individuals

    c. Consider any unusual or unexpected relationships that have been identified in performing analytical procedures in planning the audit

    d. Consider other information that may be helpful in the identification of risks of material misstatement due to fraud

2.85 In planning the audit, the property and liability insurance auditor should also perform analytical procedures relating to revenue with the objective of identifying unusual or unexpected relationships involving revenue accounts that may indicate a material misstatement due to fraudulent financial reporting. Measurements and fluctuations indicative of potential fraudulent practice may include the following:

- Changes in loss ratios that differ from changes experienced by the industry for a given line of business
- Changes in the relationships between unearned premium reserve and earned premiums
- Changes in the relationships between deferred acquisition costs (DAC) and unearned premiums
- Changes in the relationships between agents' balances and premiums
- Significant fluctuations in the gross to net reporting in premiums and losses
- Significant fluctuations in premiums written by agents or managing general agents

Identifying Risks That May Result in a Material Misstatement Due to Fraud

2.86 In identifying risks of material misstatement due to fraud, it is helpful for the auditor to consider the information that has been gathered in accordance with the requirements established in paragraphs .25–.27 of AU-C section 240. The auditor's identification of fraud risks may be influenced by characteristics such as the size, complexity, and ownership attributes of the entity. In addition, the auditor should evaluate whether identified risks of material misstatement due to fraud can be related to specific financial statement account balances or classes of transactions and related assertions, or whether they relate more pervasively to the financial statements as a whole.

Accounts, Classes of Transactions, and Assertions

2.87 The following key estimates may involve a high degree of management judgment and subjectivity and may present risks of material misstatement due to fraud because they are susceptible to manipulation by management:

  a. Investments:

   i. Fair value for privately placed securities and derivatives and hard to value investments

   ii. Assessment of securities for impairments that are other than temporary and recognition of related impairment losses

   iii. Yields assumed on mortgage-backed and asset-backed securities

  b. DAC:

   i. Deferral of acquisition costs and whether there is consistent application of accounting guidance and allocation techniques across lines of business annually

   ii. Data utilized to develop the DAC deferral

   iii. Recoverability of DAC

   iv. Determination of substantial change for internal replacements in accordance with Financial Accounting Standards Board (FASB) *Accounting Standards Codification* (ASC) 944-30[10]

  c. Reinsurance:

   i. Evaluation of risk transfer

   ii. Accrual of adjustable features on reinsurance contracts

   iii. Reinsurance transactions near year-end with little evidence to support agreement among the parties prior to the effective date

   iv. For assumed reinsurance, estimates due to time lags in the receipt of reports from cedants

  d. Reserves:

   i. Reasonableness of assumptions used to calculate reserves including payment patterns and development factors on both a paid and incurred basis

   ii. Manipulation of discount factors used in certain lines of business (for example, workers' compensation, group disability, and medical malpractice)

   iii. Misclassification of claim costs by line of business

   iv. Over reserving in one line of business to cover a deficiency in another line of business

---

[10] Financial Accounting Standards Board (FASB) *Accounting Standards Codification* (ASC) 944-30 provides guidance on accounting by insurance enterprises for deferred acquisition costs on internal replacements of insurance and investment contracts.

v. Accruing or releasing reserves related to prior underwriting years

vi. Reasonableness of assumptions for long-tailed exposures, such as asbestos and environmental

vii. Assumptions used in calculating reinsurance recoveries on unpaid losses and determining the effects of reinsurance on the net reserves

viii. Changes in assumptions used to calculate reserves and premium deficiencies by line of business

ix. Consistency of methodologies utilized by management from period to period

e. Other:

i. Goodwill and intangibles impairment:

(1) Reasonableness of assumptions used in evaluating potential impairment of goodwill and intangibles

ii. Recoverability of deferred tax assets

iii. Evaluation of uncertain tax positions

iv. Accrual and calculation of guarantee fund assessments

v. Evaluation of pension liability

A Presumption That Improper Revenue Recognition Is a Fraud Risk

2.88 Paragraph .A33 of AU-C section 240 states that material misstatements due to fraudulent financial reporting often result from an overstatement of revenues (for example, through premature revenue recognition or recording fictitious revenues) or an understatement of revenues (for example, through improperly shifting revenues to a later period). Therefore, the auditor should ordinarily presume that there is a risk of material misstatement due to fraud relating to revenue recognition for premiums or other insurance or investment fees.

A Consideration of the Risk of Management Override of Controls

2.89 Even if specific risks of material misstatement due to fraud are not identified by the auditor, there is a possibility that management override of controls could occur, and accordingly, the auditor should address that risk (see AU-C section 240 paragraph .08) apart from any conclusions regarding the existence of more specifically identifiable risks. Specifically, the procedures described in paragraphs .31–.33 of AU-C section 240 should be performed to further address the risk of management override of controls. These procedures include (*a*) examining journal entries and other adjustments for evidence of possible material misstatement due to fraud, (*b*) reviewing accounting estimates for biases that could result in material misstatement due to fraud, and (*c*) evaluating the business rationale for significant unusual transactions.

2.90 In conjunction with the evaluation of risk factors that could result in material misstatements due to fraud, auditors should obtain an understanding of the entity's financial reporting process and controls over journal entries and other adjustments. The auditor should obtain an understanding of the approval process for both standard and nonstandard journal entries and the types of entries that can be authorized and made by members of management. The auditor should identify and select journal entries and other adjustments for testing based on his or her understanding of the entity's controls over journal entries and other adjustments. The auditor should use professional judgment in determining the nature, timing, and extent of the testing of journal entries and other adjustments. The auditor focuses procedures on evaluating inappropriate or unauthorized entries, as well as consolidating adjustments or reclassifications in the financial statements that are not reflected in the general ledger. Inappropriate or unauthorized journal entries and adjustments often have unique identifying characteristics. Such characteristics may include entries made to unrelated, unusual, or seldom-used accounts or business segments, entries recorded at the end of the period or as postclosing entries, entries made before or during the preparation of the financial statements that do not have account numbers, and entries that contain round numbers or a consistent ending number.

Considerations for Audits Performed in Accordance With PCAOB Standards

PCAOB Auditing Standard No. 12 paragraph 67 requires the auditor to include an evaluation of how fraud could be perpetrated or concealed by presenting incomplete or inaccurate disclosures or by omitting necessary disclosures.

Assessing the Identified Risks After Taking an Evaluation of the Entity's Programs and Controls That Address the Risks Into Account

2.91 As part of the understanding of internal control sufficient to plan the audit, the auditor of a property and liability insurance entity should treat assessed risks of material misstatement due to fraud as significant risks and, accordingly, to the extent not already done so, the auditor should obtain an understanding of the entity's related controls, including control activities, relevant to such risks, including the evaluation of whether such controls have been suitably designed and implemented to mitigate such fraud risks. These programs and controls may involve

   a. specific controls designed to mitigate specific risks of fraud and may include controls to address specific assets susceptible to misappropriation. Examples of such controls include

   i. use of a lock box for the remittance of premium receipts.

   ii. management quality control review of claim payments.

   iii. established authorization and approval levels for underwriters and claim adjusters.

   b. broader programs designed to prevent, deter, and detect fraud. Examples of such controls include

   i. programs to promote a culture of honesty and ethical behavior. Management sets the tone at the top by establishing a code of conduct and promoting a strong value system.

   ii. evaluating and monitoring appropriate controls and monitoring activities. Because of the importance of information technology in supporting operations and the processing of transactions, management also needs to implement and maintain appropriate controls, whether automated or manual, over computer-generated information.

2.92 The auditor should consider whether such programs and controls mitigate the identified risks of material misstatement due to fraud or whether specific control deficiencies may exacerbate the risks. After the auditor has evaluated whether the entity's programs and controls have been suitably designed and placed in operation, the auditor should assess these risks taking that evaluation into account. This assessment should be considered when developing the auditor's response to the identified risks of material misstatement due to fraud.

Responding to the Results of the Assessment

2.93 Paragraphs .28–.33 of AU-C section 240 address an auditor's response to the results of the assessment of the risks of material misstatement due to fraud at the financial statement level and at the assertion level. The auditor's responses to address the assessed risks of material misstatement due to fraud include the following:

 a. A response that has an overall effect on how the audit is conducted—that is, a response that addresses the assessed risks of fraud at the financial statement level by involving more general considerations apart from the specific procedures otherwise planned. Such overall responses include, for example, assigning and supervising personnel consistent with the auditor's assessment of risk or incorporating an element of unpredictability in the selection of audit procedures.

 b. A response to identified risks involving the nature, timing, and extent of the auditing procedures to be performed. The property and liability insurance auditor's responses to address the assessed risks of material misstatement due to fraud at the assertion level may include changing the nature, timing, and extent of auditing procedures in the following ways:

   i. The nature of audit procedures to be performed may need to be changed to obtain audit evidence that is more reliable and relevant or to obtain additional corroborative information. This may affect both the type of audit procedures to be performed and their combination. For example:

      (1) More audit evidence may be needed from independent sources outside the entity, such as confirmations regarding reinsurance transactions or collateral account balances.

      (2) Physical observation or inspection of certain assets may become more important or the auditor may choose to use computer-assisted audit techniques to gather more evidence about data contained in significant accounts or electronic transaction files.

      (3) The auditor may design procedures to obtain additional corroborative information.

   ii. The timing of substantive procedures may need to be modified. The auditor may conclude that performing substantive testing at or near the period end better addresses an assessed risk of material misstatement due to fraud. The auditor may conclude that, given the assessed risks of intentional misstatement or manipulation, audit procedures to extend audit conclusions from an interim date to the period end would not be effective. In contrast, because an intentional misstatement—for example, a misstatement involving improper revenue recognition—may have been initiated in an interim period, the auditor may elect to apply substantive procedures to transactions occurring earlier in or throughout the reporting period. Such accounts that could be tested at year-end may include reserves and market-value testing for investments.

    iii. The extent of the procedures applied reflects the assessment of the risks of material misstatement due to fraud. For example, increasing sample sizes or performing analytical procedures at a more detailed level (that is, by product line) may be appropriate for premiums or reserves. Also, computer-assisted audit techniques may enable more extensive testing of electronic transactions and account files. Such techniques can be used to select sample transactions from key electronic files, to sort transactions with specific characteristics, or to test an entire population instead of a sample.

    iv. The auditor may wish to consider the controls in place to prevent unauthorized access and changes to policyholder information or the auditor may find it necessary to confirm certain policy information directly with the policyholder. The auditor may also consider the controls in place related to proper authorization, due diligence, and underwriting of new investments, as well as accounting controls over investment valuation.

  c. A response involving the performance of certain procedures to further address the risk of material misstatement due to fraud involving management override of controls, given the unpredictable ways in which such override could occur.

Evaluating Audit Evidence

2.94 In accordance with paragraphs .34–.37 of AU-C section 240, the auditor should evaluate, at or near the end of the audit, whether the accumulated results of auditing procedures (including analytical procedures that were performed as substantive tests or when forming an overall conclusion) affect the assessment of the risks of material misstatement due to fraud made earlier in the audit or indicate a previously unrecognized risk of material misstatement due to fraud. If not already performed when forming an overall conclusion, the analytical procedures relating to revenue, required by paragraph .22 of AU-C section 240, should be performed through the end of the reporting period.

Responding to Misstatements That May Be the Result of Fraud

2.95 As noted in paragraph .35 of AU-C section 240, when audit test results identify misstatements in the financial statements, the auditor should consider whether such misstatements may be indicative of fraud. If such an indication exists, the auditor should evaluate the implications of the misstatement with regard to other aspects of the audit, particularly the auditor's evaluation of materiality, management and employee integrity, and the reliability of management representations, recognizing that an instance of fraud is unlikely to be an isolated occurrence. If the auditor identifies a misstatement, whether material or not, and the auditor has reason to believe that it is, or may be, the result of fraud and that management (in particular, senior management) is involved, the auditor should reevaluate the assessment of the risks of material misstatement due to fraud and its resulting effect on the nature, timing, and extent of audit procedures to respond to the assessed risks. The auditor should also consider whether circumstances or conditions indicate possible collusion involving employees, management, or third parties when reconsidering the reliability of evidence previously obtained. If the auditor concludes that, or is unable to conclude whether, the financial statements are materially misstated as a result of fraud, the auditor should evaluate the implications for the audit.

2.96 As noted in paragraph .38 of AU-C section 240, if, as a result of identified fraud or suspected fraud, the auditor encounters circumstances that bring into question the auditor's ability to continue performing the audit, the auditor should

    a. determine the professional and legal responsibilities applicable in the circumstances, including whether a requirement exists for the auditor to report to the person or persons who engaged the auditor or, in some cases, to regulatory authorities;

    b. consider whether it is appropriate to withdraw from the engagement, when withdrawal is possible under applicable law or regulation; and

    c. if the auditor withdraws

        i. discuss with the appropriate level of management and those charged with governance the auditor's withdrawal from the engagement and the reasons for the withdrawal, and

        ii. determine whether a professional or legal requirement exists to report to the person or persons who engaged the auditor or, in some cases, to regulatory authorities, the auditor's withdrawal from the engagement and the reasons for the withdrawal.

Communicating About Possible Fraud to Management, Those Charged With Governance, and Others

2.97 Whenever the auditor has identified a fraud or has obtained information that indicates that a fraud may exist, that matter should be brought to the attention of an appropriate level of management. See paragraphs .39–.41 of AU section 240 for further requirements about communications with management, those charged with governance, and others. If the auditor suspects fraud involving management, the auditor should communicate these suspicions to those charged with governance and discuss the nature, timing, and extent of audit procedures necessary to complete the audit.

2.98 As stated in paragraph .42 of AU-C section 240, if the auditor has identified or suspects a fraud, the auditor should determine whether the auditor has a responsibility to report the occurrence or suspicion to a party outside the entity. Although the auditor's professional duty to maintain the confidentiality of client information may preclude such reporting, the auditor's

Documentation and Guidance

2.99 Paragraph .43 of AU-C section 240 addresses certain items and events that the auditor is required to document regarding fraud. AU-C section 580, *Written Representations* (AICPA, *Professional Standards*), addresses written representations related to fraud that the auditor should obtain from management.

Use of Information Technology

2.100 Because of large volumes of premium and claims transactions and the need to maintain accountability for individual policies, most property and liability insurance entities use IT systems to maintain statistical and accounting records. Typically, policy and agent master files are maintained on computerized systems and entities may use telecommunications, including direct access capability by agents and insureds, integrated premium and claims databases, and processing systems that lack traditional audit trails. Many entities have made significant investments in computer hardware and software and large staffs of programmers, systems analysts, and technicians to maintain day-to-day operations. Dependence on IT systems and controls may affect control risk, particularly for larger multiple-line insurance entities.

2.101 An entity's use of IT may affect any of the five components of internal control relevant to the achievement of the entity's financial reporting, operations, compliance objectives, operating units,[11] or business functions. In obtaining an understanding of internal control sufficient to assess the risk of material misstatement, the auditor considers how an entity's use of IT and manual procedures may affect controls relevant to the audit. The use of IT also affects the fundamental manner in which transactions are initiated, authorized, recorded, processed, and reported. In a manual system, an entity uses manual procedures and records in paper format. Controls in such a system are manual and should include such procedures as approvals and reviews of activities and reconciliations and follow-up of reconciling items. Alternatively, an entity may have information systems that use automated procedures to initiate, authorize, record, process, and report transactions in which case records in electronic format replace such paper documents as applications, claims payment authorizations, underwriting reviews and approvals, and related accounting records. Controls in systems that use IT consist of a combination of automated controls and manual controls. Further, manual controls may be independent of IT, may use information produced by IT, or may be limited to monitoring the effective functioning of IT and of automated controls, and to handling exceptions. When IT is used to initiate, authorize, record, process, or report transactions or other financial data for inclusion in financial statements, the systems and programs may include controls related to the corresponding assertions for material accounts or may be critical to the effective functioning of manual controls that depend on IT. An entity's mix of manual and automated controls varies with the nature and complexity of the entity's use of IT. Insurance entities have been leading users of advanced IT methods.

---

[11] When performing an audit in accordance with PCAOB standards, refer to appendix B, "Special Topics," of PCAOB Auditing Standard No. 5 for discussion of considerations when an entity has multiple locations or business units.

Consequently, the control issues involving IT have received considerable attention within the industry. The auditor should obtain an understanding of how IT affects control activities that are relevant to planning the audit. The auditor should consider whether the entity has responded adequately to the risks arising from IT by establishing effective controls, including effective general controls upon which application controls depend. Such general controls may include the following:

- Organization and operations controls:
  - IT department and user department functions should be segregated.
  - Guidelines for the general authorization of executing transactions should be provided. For example, the IT department should be prohibited from initiating or authorizing transactions.
  - Functions within the IT department should be segregated.
- Systems development and documentation controls:
  - The procedures for system design, including the acquisition of software packages, should encourage active participation by representatives of the users and, as appropriate, the accounting department and internal auditors.
  - Each system should have written specifications that are reviewed and approved by an appropriate level of management and applicable user departments.
  - System testing should be a joint effort of users and IT personnel and should include both the manual and computerized phases of the system.
  - Final approval should be obtained prior to placing a new system into operation.
  - All master file and transaction file conversion should be controlled to prevent unauthorized changes and to provide accurate and complete results.
  - After a new system has been placed in operation, all program changes should be approved before implementation to determine whether they have been authorized, tested, and documented.
  - Management should document the system and establish formal procedures to define the system at appropriate levels of detail.
- Hardware and systems software controls:
  - The control features inherent in the computer hardware, operating system, and other supporting software should be used to the maximum possible extent to provide control over operations and to detect and report hardware malfunctions.
  - Systems software should be subjected to the same control activities as those applied to installation of and changes to application programs.
- Access controls:
  - Access to program documentation should be limited to those persons who need access to perform their duties.

AAG-PLI 2.101

Audit Considerations

- Access to data files and programs should be limited to those individuals authorized to process or maintain particular systems.
- Access to computer hardware should be limited to authorized individuals.

• Data and procedural controls:

- A control function should be responsible for receiving all data to be processed, for ensuring that all data are recorded, for following up on errors detected during processing to ensure that the transactions are corrected and resubmitted by the proper party, and for verifying the proper distribution of output.
- A written manual of systems and procedures should be prepared for all computer operations and should provide for management's general or specific authorization to process transactions.
- Internal auditors or some other independent group within an organization should review and evaluate proposed systems at critical stages of development.
- On a continuing basis, internal auditors or some other independent group within an organization should review and test computer processing activities.

2.102 The sophistication of insurance IT systems is often an element of competition regarding an entity's ability to service accounts. The IT operations are characterized by one or several large installations, extensive use of telecommunications equipment, including some direct-access capability by independent agents and insureds, large premium and claims databases, some of which are integrated, and operating systems and applications that lack visible audit trails.

2.103 This guide does not address the major effects of IT on an audit. Guidance on auditing records for which IT is a significant factor is contained in the following:

a. AU-C section 315

b. AU-C section 402, *Audit Considerations Relating to an Entity Using a Service Organization* (AICPA, *Professional Standards*)[12]

c. AICPA Audit Guide *Assessing and Responding to Audit Risk in a Financial Statement Audit*

Considerations for Audits Performed in Accordance With PCAOB Standards

PCAOB Auditing Standard No. 12, *Identifying and Assessing Risks of Material Misstatement*, paragraph B4, states the auditor should obtain an understanding of specific risks to a company's internal

---

[12] The Audit Guide *Service Organizations—Applying SSAE No. 16, Reporting on Controls at a Service Organization (SOC 1)* provides guidance to practitioners engaged to examine and report on a service organization's controls over the services it provides to user entities when those controls are likely to be relevant to user entities' internal control over financial reporting. For audits performed in accordance with PCAOB Auditing Standards, the PCAOB staff has issued a series of nonauthoritative questions and answers on various topics. Questions 24–26 and 29 at www.pcaobus.org pertain to service organizations.

control over financial reporting resulting from information technology.

Going Concern Considerations

2.104 AU-C section 570, *The Auditor's Consideration of an Entity's Ability to Continue as a Going Concern* (AICPA, *Professional Standards*), addresses the auditor's responsibilities in an audit of financial statements with respect to evaluating whether there is substantial doubt about the entity's ability to continue as a going concern. The auditor can utilize the results of the RBC assessment in connection with evaluating a property and liability insurance enterprise's ability to continue as a going concern.

2.105 As required in paragraphs .08–.09 of AU-C section 570, the auditor should evaluate whether there is substantial doubt about the entity's ability to continue as a going concern for a reasonable period of time based on the results of the audit procedures performed. The auditor should consider whether the results of the procedures performed during the course of the audit identify conditions or events that, when considered in the aggregate, indicate there could be substantial doubt about the entity's ability to continue as a going concern for a reasonable period of time. The auditor should consider the need to obtain additional information about such conditions or events, as well as the appropriate audit evidence to support information that mitigates the auditor's doubt.

2.106 As noted in paragraphs .10–.11 of AU-C section 570, if, after considering the identified conditions or events in the aggregate, the auditor believes there is substantial doubt about the entity's ability to continue as a going concern for a reasonable period of time, the auditor should obtain information about management's plans that are intended to mitigate the adverse effects of such conditions or events. The auditor should

a. assess whether it is likely that the adverse effects would be mitigated by management's plans for a reasonable period of time;

b. identify those elements of management's plans that are particularly significant to overcoming the adverse effects of the conditions or events and plan and perform procedures to obtain audit evidence about them including, when applicable, the consideration of the adequacy of support regarding the ability to obtain additional financing or the planned disposal of assets; and

c. assess whether it is likely that such plans can be effectively implemented.

2.107 When prospective financial information is particularly significant to management's plans, the auditor should request management to provide that information and should consider the adequacy of support for significant assumptions underlying that information. The auditor should give particular attention to assumptions that are

- material to the prospective financial information.
- especially sensitive or susceptible to change.
- inconsistent with historical trends.

2.108 The auditor's consideration should be based on knowledge of the entity, its business, and its management and should include (*a*) reading the

Audit Considerations

prospective financial information and the underlying assumptions and (*b*) comparing prospective financial information from prior periods with actual results and comparing prospective information for the current period with results achieved to date. If the auditor becomes aware of factors, the effects of which are not reflected in such prospective financial information, the auditor should discuss those factors with management and, if necessary, request revision of the prospective financial information.

2.109 Paragraph .14 of AU-C section 570 states that the auditor should obtain written representations from management

> *a.* regarding its plans that are intended to mitigate the adverse effects of conditions or events that indicate there is substantial doubt about the entity's ability to continue as a going concern for a reasonable period of time and the likelihood that those plans can be effectively implemented, and
>
> *b.* that the financial statements disclose all of the matters of which management is aware that are relevant to the entity's ability to continue as a going concern, including principal conditions or events, and management's plans.

2.110 In accordance with paragraph .12 of AU-C section 570 when, after considering management's plans, the auditor concludes there is substantial doubt about the entity's ability to continue as a going concern for a reasonable period of time, the auditor should consider the possible effects on the financial statements and the adequacy of the related disclosure.

2.111 In accordance with paragraph .13 of AU-C section 570, when the auditor concludes, primarily because of the auditor's consideration of management's plans, that substantial doubt about the entity's ability to continue as a going concern for a reasonable period of time has been alleviated, the auditor should consider the need for, and evaluate the adequacy of, disclosure of the principal conditions or events that initially caused the auditor to believe there was substantial doubt. The auditor's consideration of disclosure should include the possible effects of such conditions or events, and any mitigating factors, including management's plans.

2.112 In accordance with paragraph .15 of AU-C section 570 if, after considering identified conditions or events and management's plans, the auditor concludes that substantial doubt about the entity's ability to continue as a going concern for a reasonable period of time remains, the auditor should include an emphasis-of-matter paragraph[13] in the auditor's report to reflect that conclusion. Readers should refer to paragraph 10.24 for an example of a modified opinion for a going concern.

Evaluating Misstatements

2.113 Based on the results of substantive procedures, the auditor may identify misstatements in accounts or notes to the financial statements. Paragraph .05 of AU-C section 450, *Evaluation of Misstatements Identified During the Audit* (AICPA, *Professional Standards*), states that the auditor should accumulate misstatements identified during the audit other than those that are

---

[13] Paragraphs .06–.07 of AU-C section 706, *Emphasis-of-Matter Paragraphs and Other-Matter Paragraphs in the Independent Auditor's Report* (AICPA, *Professional Standards*), address requirements concerning emphasis-of-matter paragraphs.

clearly trivial. As noted in paragraph .06 of AU-C section 450 the auditor should determine whether the overall audit strategy and audit plan need to be revised if

    a. the nature of identified misstatements and the circumstances of their occurrence indicate that other misstatements may exist that, when aggregated with misstatements accumulated during the audit, could be material, or

    b. the aggregate of misstatements accumulated during the audit approaches materiality determined in accordance with AU-C section 320.[14]

2.114 When evaluating misstatements, the auditor should consider management's assessment of materiality, (that is, how management has determined whether a misstatement is material or immaterial). As discussed in paragraph 2.104, the SEC has issued guidance for assessing materiality when evaluating misstatements identified within a registrant's financial statements that might also be useful for audits of nonissuers.

2.115 In accordance with paragraph .07 of AU-C section 450, the auditor should communicate on a timely basis with the appropriate level of management all misstatements accumulated during the audit. The auditor should request management to correct those misstatements.

2.116 For detailed guidance on evaluating audit findings and audit evidence, refer to AU-C sections 450 and 500, respectively.

    Considerations for Audits Performed in Accordance With PCAOB Standards

    PCAOB Auditing Standard No. 14 paragraph 16 states that when management has made corrections based on items detected by the auditor, the auditor should evaluate management's work to determine whether the corrections have been recorded properly and whether uncorrected misstatements remain.

    PCAOB Auditing Standard No. 14 paragraphs 25–26 provide guidance when management identifies additional entries that offset misstatements accumulated by the auditor and where the auditor identifies bias on judgments about amounts and disclosures within the financial statements.

    The SEC has issued guidance for assessing materiality when evaluating misstatements identified within a registrant's financial statements in Staff Accounting Bulletin (SAB) Topic 1(M), *Assessing Materiality*. The SEC staff indicated that management may utilize a rule of thumb, such as 5 percent of a line item, as a preliminary assessment of materiality of an error. The assessment of materiality requires management to view the facts in "total mix" of information. The SEC staff provided a listing of example factors that would cause a quantitatively immaterial misstatement to be considered material, including whether the misstatement arises from an item capable of precise measurement or whether it arises from an estimate, if the misstatement masks a change in earnings or other trends or hides a failure to meet earnings estimates, and if the misstatement relates to an unlawful transaction.

---

[14] See paragraph .10 of AU-C section 320, *Materiality in Planning and Performing an Audit* (AICPA, *Professional Standards*).

The SEC has also provided guidance in SAB Topic 1(N), *Considering the Effects of Prior Year Misstatements When Quantifying Misstatements in Current Year Financial Statements*, which provides interpretive guidance on how the effects of the carryover or reversal of prior year misstatements is considered in quantifying a current year misstatement. The SEC staff believes registrants should quantify the impact of correcting all misstatements, including both the carryover and reversing effects of prior year misstatements, on the current year financial statements. The staff believes that this can be accomplished by quantifying errors under both a balance sheet ("iron curtain") and an income statement ("rollover") approach, and by evaluating errors measured under each approach. The iron curtain approach quantifies the misstatement based on the effect of correcting the balance sheet at the end of the current period. The rollover approach quantifies the misstatement based on the error originating in the current year income statement and does not consider the carryover effect of prior year misstatements in the income statement.

Thus, a registrant's financial statements would require adjustment when either approach results in quantifying a material misstatement after considering all relevant quantitative and qualitative factors. For example, the SEC staff indicated that an error that may be immaterial to the income statement in a single year, but has accumulated over time to require a larger adjustment to a balance sheet asset or liability should be evaluated based on both approaches.

If in correcting an error in the current year an error is material to the current year's income statement, the prior year financial statements should be corrected even though such a revision previously was and continues to be immaterial to the prior year financial statements. Correcting prior year financial statements for immaterial errors would not require previously filed reports to be amended. Such correction may be made the next time the registrant files the prior year financial statements. However, registrants electing not to restate prior periods should follow the disclosure requirements specified in the SAB. Additional specifics on SAB No. 108 can be obtained at www.sec.gov/interps/account/sab108.pdf.

Audit Documentation

2.117 AU-C section 230, *Audit Documentation* (AICPA, *Professional Standards*), addresses the auditor's responsibility to prepare audit documentation for an audit of financial statements. Audit documentation is an essential element of audit quality. Although documentation alone does not guarantee audit quality, the process of preparing sufficient and appropriate documentation contributes to the quality of an audit.

2.118 Audit documentation is the record of audit procedures performed, relevant audit evidence obtained, and conclusions the auditor reached. Audit documentation, also known as working papers, may be recorded on paper or on electronic or other media. When transferring or copying paper documentation to another media, the auditor should apply procedures to generate a copy that is faithful in form and content to the original paper document.

2.119 Audit documentation includes, for example, audit plans, analyses, issues memorandums, summaries of significant findings or issues, letters of confirmation and representation, checklists, abstracts or copies of important documents, correspondence (including e-mail) concerning significant findings or issues, and schedules of the work the auditor performed. Abstracts or copies of the entity's records (for example, significant and specific contracts and agreements) should be included as part of the audit documentation if they are needed to enable an experienced auditor to understand the work performed and conclusions reached. The audit documentation for a specific engagement is assembled in an audit file.

2.120 As noted in paragraphs .07–.09 of AU-C section 230, the auditor should prepare audit documentation on a timely basis. The auditor should prepare audit documentation that is sufficient to enable an experienced auditor, having no previous connection with the audit, to understand

    a. the nature, timing, and extent of the audit procedures performed to comply with GAAS and applicable legal and regulatory requirements;

    b. the results of the audit procedures performed and the audit evidence obtained; and

    c. significant findings or issues arising during the audit, the conclusions reached thereon and significant professional judgments made in reaching those conclusions.

2.121 In documenting the nature, timing, and extent of audit procedures performed, the auditor should record

    a. the identifying characteristics of the specific items or matters tested;

    b. who performed the audit work and the date such work was completed; and

    c. who reviewed the audit work performed and the date and extent of such review.

2.122 For audit procedures related to the inspection of significant contracts or agreements, the auditor should include abstracts or copies of those contracts or agreements in the audit documentation. The auditor should document discussions of significant findings or issues with management, those charged with governance, and others, including the nature of the significant findings or issues discussed, and when and with whom the discussions took place. If the auditor identified information that is inconsistent with the auditor's final conclusion regarding a significant finding or issue, the auditor should document how the auditor addressed the inconsistency. The auditor should consider the guidance in paragraph .12 of AU-C section 230 regarding documentation of how the auditor addressed information that is inconsistent with the auditor's final conclusion, and in paragraph .10*a* of AU-C section 500, regarding what modifications or additions to audit procedures are necessary when audit evidence obtained from one source that is inconsistent with that obtained from another.

2.123 AU-C section 230 also addresses documentation when there is a departure from a relevant requirement, revisions to audit documentation made after the date of the auditor's report, and the assembly and retention of the final audit file. See AU-C section 230 for specific guidance.

Considerations for Audits Performed in Accordance With PCAOB Standards

PCAOB Auditing Standard No. 3, *Audit Documentation* (AICPA, *PCAOB Standards and Related Rules*, Auditing Standards), establishes the documentation requirements for audits performed in accordance with PCAOB standards.

Consideration of the Work of Internal Auditors

2.124 When evaluating the potential for the use of the work of others, the auditor needs to make a judgment about the competence and objectivity of internal audit. In audits of property and liability insurance entities, auditors may consider using the work of internal auditors in areas including, but not limited to, the following:

- Testing IT general and application controls
- Testing premiums and claims processing
- Testing the integrity of the databases underlying the loss-reserving systems
- Testing of investment activity

2.125 AU-C section 610, *The Auditor's Consideration of the Internal Audit Function in an Audit of Financial Statements* (AICPA, *Professional Standards*), addresses the auditor's responsibility when using the work of, or receiving direct assistance from, the entity's internal auditors.

Considerations for Audits Performed in Accordance With PCAOB Standards

Paragraphs 16–19 of PCAOB Auditing Standard No. 5 establish requirements and provide direction for auditors using the work of others to reduce the work that otherwise would have been performed by the auditor to test controls.

Communication of Matters Related to Internal Control

2.126 For audits conducted under GAAS, AU-C section 265, *Communicating Internal Control Related Matters Identified in an Audit* (AICPA, *Professional Standards*), addresses the auditor's responsibility to appropriately communicate to those charged with governance and management deficiencies in internal control that the auditor has identified in an audit of financial statements. AU-C section 260, *The Auditor's Communication With Those Charged With Governance* (AICPA, *Professional Standards*), establishes further requirements and provides guidance regarding the auditor's responsibility to communicate with those charged with governance certain other matters regarding the audit (see discussion in paragraphs 2.134–.138).

Identification of Deficiencies in Internal Control

2.127 As noted in paragraph .08 of AU-C section 265, the auditor should determine whether, on the basis of the audit work performed, the auditor has identified one or more deficiencies in internal control.

2.128 If the auditor has identified one or more deficiencies in internal control, the auditor should evaluate each deficiency to determine, on the basis of the audit work performed, whether, individually or in combination, they

Communication of Deficiencies in Internal Control

2.129 As required in paragraphs .11–.12 of AU-C section 265, the auditor should communicate in writing to those charged with governance on a timely basis significant deficiencies and material weaknesses identified during the audit, including those that were remediated during the audit. The auditor also should communicate to management at an appropriate level of responsibility, on a timely basis

    a. in writing, significant deficiencies and material weaknesses that the auditor has communicated or intends to communicate to those charged with governance, unless it would be inappropriate to communicate directly to management in the circumstances.

    b. in writing or orally, other deficiencies in internal control identified during the audit that have not been communicated to management by other parties and that, in the auditor's professional judgment, are of sufficient importance to merit management's attention. If other deficiencies in internal control are communicated orally, the auditor should document the communication.

2.130 The communications referred to in paragraphs .11–.12 should be made no later than 60 days following the report release date.

2.131 As noted in paragraph .14 of AU-C section 265, the auditor should include in the auditor's written communication of significant deficiencies and material weaknesses

    a. the definition of the term *material weakness* and, when relevant, the definition of the term *significant deficiency*.

    b. a description of the significant deficiencies and material weaknesses and an explanation of their potential effects.

    c. sufficient information to enable those charged with governance and management to understand the context of the communication. In particular, the auditor should include in the communication the following elements that explain that

        i. the purpose of the audit was for the auditor to express an opinion on the financial statements.

        ii. the audit included consideration of internal control over financial reporting in order to design audit procedures that are appropriate in the circumstances but not for the purpose of expressing an opinion on the effectiveness of internal control.

        iii. the auditor is not expressing an opinion on the effectiveness of internal control.

        iv. the auditor's consideration of internal control was not designed to identify all deficiencies in internal control that might be material weaknesses or significant deficiencies, and therefore,

Audit Considerations

material weaknesses or significant deficiencies may exist that were not identified.

    d. an appropriate alert in accordance with AU-C section 905, *Alert That Restricts the Use of the Auditor's Written Communication.*[15]

2.132 As discussed in paragraph .15 of AU-C section 265, when the auditor issues a written communication stating that no material weaknesses were identified during the audit, the communication should include the matters in paragraph .14*a* and .14*c–d* of AU-C section 265. As required in paragraph .16 of AU-C section 265, the auditor should not issue a written communication stating that no significant deficiencies were identified during the audit.

2.133 Under SAP, section 11, "Communication of Internal Control Related Matters Noted in an Audit," of the NAIC Model Audit Rule requires that each insurer furnish the commissioner with a written communication as to any unremediated material weaknesses in its internal control over financial reporting noted during the audit. Section 16, "Management's Report of Internal Control over Financial Reporting," of the NAIC revised Model Audit rule also requires management to prepare a report of internal controls on financial reporting if certain premium thresholds are met. See additional discussion on section 11 and section 16 of the Model Audit Rule in paragraphs 2.158–.160 and 2.163–.165.

Considerations for Audits Performed in Accordance With PCAOB Standards

AU section 325, *Communications About Control Deficiencies in an Audit of Financial Statements* (AICPA, *PCAOB Standards and Related Rules*, Interim Standards), and paragraphs 78–84 of Auditing Standard No. 5 provide guidance on identifying and reporting deficiencies that relate to an entity's internal control for audits of financial statements only and integrated audits, respectively. The auditor must communicate in writing to management and the audit committee control deficiencies that are either significant deficiencies or material weaknesses as defined in paragraphs .02–.03 of AU section 325. For integrated audits, all deficiencies in internal control with a lesser magnitude than a significant deficiency must be reported in writing to management and the audit committee notified when communication is made.

Written communications are best made prior to the issuance of the auditor's report on the financial statements for nonissuers and should be made prior to the issuance of the auditor's report for issuers. According to AU section 325 paragraph .04, the auditor's communications should distinguish clearly between those matters considered significant deficiencies and those considered material weaknesses, The audit committee or other proper equivalent level of authority is defined in AU section 325 paragraph .04 and footnote 8 in paragraph 9 of Auditing Standard No. 5. For additional information on internal control communications, see the applicable standard.

Additionally, among other matters, Section 404 of the Sarbanes-Oxley Act of 2002 requires a report on management's assessment of internal control over financial reporting of the public accounting firm to be included in an issuer's annual report. Section 989G of the

---

[15] See paragraphs .06*c*, .07, and .11 of AU-C section 905, *Alert That Restricts the Use of the Auditor's Written Communication* (AICPA, *Professional Standards*).

Dodd-Frank Act added SOX Section 404(c) to exempt from the attestation requirement smaller issuers that are neither accelerated filers nor large accelerated filers under Rule 12b-2. This report may or may not be combined with the audit opinion. Refer to paragraphs C16–C17 of appendix C, "Special Reporting Situations," of Auditing Standard No. 5, which provides direction when an auditor's report on internal control over financial reporting is included or incorporated by reference in filing under federal securities statutes.

Communication of Other Matters With Those Charged With Governance[16]

2.134 AU-C section 260 addresses the auditor's responsibility to communicate with those charged with governance in an audit of financial statements. Particular considerations apply where all of those charged with governance are involved in managing an entity.

Considerations for Audits Performed in Accordance With PCAOB Standards

Auditing Standard No. 16 (AICPA, *PCAOB Standards and Related Rules*, Auditing Standards), establishes requirements that enhance the relevance and timeliness of the communications between the auditor and the audit committee, and is intended to foster constructive dialogue between the two on significant audit and financial statement matters.

2.135 Paragraph .07 of AU-C section 260 states that the auditor should determine the appropriate person(s) within the entity's governance structure with whom to communicate. If the auditor communicates with a subgroup of those charged with governance, such as the audit committee or an individual, the auditor should determine whether the auditor also needs to communicate with the governing body.

Matters To Be Communicated

2.136 As required in paragraph .10 of AU-C section 260, the auditor should communicate with those charged with governance the auditor's responsibilities with regard to the financial statement audit, including that

    a. the auditor is responsible for forming and expressing an opinion about whether the financial statements that have been prepared by

---

[16] As discussed in paragraph 2.146, Section 14(F)(1) of the NAIC Model Audit Rule requires the auditor to communicate to the audit committee specific requirements as follows:

The Audit committee shall require the accountant that performs for an insurer any audit required by this regulation to timely report to the Audit committee in accordance with the requirements of SAS No. 61, *Communication with Audit Committees*, or its replacement, including:

    (a) All significant accounting policies and material permitted practices;

    (b) All material alternative treatments of financial information within statutory accounting principles that have been discussed with management officials of the insurer, ramifications of the use of the alternative disclosures and treatments, and the treatment preferred by the accountant; and

    (c) Other material written communications between the accountant and the management of the insurer, such as any management letter or schedule of unadjusted differences.

Audit Considerations

management, with the oversight of those charged with governance, are prepared, in all material respects, in conformity with the applicable financial reporting framework.

   b. the audit of the financial statements does not relieve management or those charged with governance of their responsibilities.

2.137 In accordance with paragraphs .12–.13 of AU-C section 260, the auditor should communicate with those charged with governance

   a. the auditor's views about qualitative aspects of the entity's significant accounting practices, including accounting policies, accounting estimates, and financial statement disclosures. When applicable, the auditor should

   i. explain to those charged with governance why the auditor considers a significant accounting practice that is acceptable under the applicable financial reporting framework not to be most appropriate to the particular circumstances of the entity, and

   ii. determine that those charged with governance are informed about the process used by management in formulating particularly sensitive accounting estimates, including fair value estimates, and about the basis for the auditor's conclusions regarding the reasonableness of those estimates.

   b. significant difficulties, if any, encountered during the audit.

   c. disagreements with management, if any.

   d. other findings or issues, if any, arising from the audit that are, in the auditor's professional judgment, significant and relevant to those charged with governance regarding their responsibility to oversee the financial reporting process.

2.138 The auditor should communicate with those charged with governance

   a. uncorrected misstatements accumulated by the auditor and the effect that they, individually or in the aggregate, may have on the opinion in the auditor's report. The auditor's communication should identify material uncorrected misstatements individually. The auditor should request that uncorrected misstatements be corrected.

   b. the effect of uncorrected misstatements related to prior periods on the relevant classes of transactions, account balances or disclosures, and the financial statements as a whole.

Communications by Successor Auditors[17]

2.139 AU-C section 510, *Opening Balances—Initial Audit Engagements, Including Reaudit Engagements* (AICPA, *Professional Standards*), and AU-C section 210 address the auditor's responsibility for communications with predecessor auditors when a change of auditors has taken place or is in process.

---

[17] Additionally, the PCAOB has issued the Staff Questions and Answers document titled *Adjustments to Prior-Period Financial Statements Audited By A Predecessor Auditor,* which is available at www.pcaobus.org.

Auditor Independence

2.140 Prohibitions and restrictions exist related to the performance of nonaudit services for audit clients, including certain actuarial services. Practitioners should be aware of and comply with these prohibitions and restrictions, including the AICPA independence rules (Interpretation No. 101-3, "Nonattest Services," of Rule 101, *Independence* [AICPA, *Professional Standards*, ET sec. 101 par. .05]), SEC independence rules, PCAOB independence rules, as well as rules passed by Government Accountability Office, state licensing boards, and others. Section 7, "Qualifications of Independent Certified Public Accountant," of the NAIC revised Model Audit Rule has been revised, for the list of nonaudit services that cannot be performed by the auditor, to generally agree with those designated by the SEC (see paragraph 2.149 for additional discussion).

Auditing Fair Value Measurements and Disclosures[18]

2.141 Fair value measurements of assets, liabilities, and components of equity may arise from both the initial recording of transactions and later changes in value. AU-C section 540, *Auditing Accounting Estimates, Including Fair Value Accounting Estimates, and Related Disclosures* (AICPA, *Professional Standards*), addresses the auditor's responsibilities relating to accounting estimates, including fair value accounting estimates and related disclosures, in an audit of financial statements. Specifically, it expands on how AU-C sections 315, 330, and other relevant AU-C sections are to be applied with regard to accounting estimates. It also includes requirements and guidance related to misstatements of individual accounting estimates and indicators of possible management bias.

2.142 Evidence obtained outside the scope of AU-C section 540 also may provide relevant information in regards to the measurement and disclosure of fair values. For example, inspection procedures to verify existence of an asset measured at fair value may provide relevant evidence about its valuation.

2.143 An auditor should be aware that simply receiving a confirmation from a third-party (including a trustee) does not in and of itself constitute adequate audit evidence with respect to the valuation assertion of interests in trusts or investments in securities. It is the responsibility of management to institute accounting and financial reporting processes for the determination of fair value measurements. In accordance with AU-C section 540, if the auditor

---

[18] FASB ASC 820, *Fair Value Measurement*, establishes a framework for measuring fair value that applies broadly to financial and nonfinancial assets and liabilities and improves the consistency, comparability, and reliability of the measurements. The fair value hierarchy gives the highest priority to quoted prices in active markets and the lowest priority to unobservable data, for example, the reporting entity's own data. Under the standard, fair value measurements would be separately disclosed by level within the fair value hierarchy. The expanded disclosures about the use of fair value to measure assets and liabilities will provide users of financial statements with better information about the extent to which fair value is used to measure recognized assets and liabilities, the inputs used to develop the measurements, and the effect of certain of the measurements on earnings (or changes in net assets) for the period.

FASB ASC 825, *Financial Instruments*, addresses the fair value option under which an entity may irrevocably elect fair value as the initial and subsequent measurement attribute for certain financial assets and financial liabilities on a contract-by-contract basis, with changes in fair value recognized in earnings as those changes occur. Insurance and reinsurance contracts that meet the definition of a financial instrument are defined within the scope of FASB ASC 825, as are insurance contracts that do not prohibit settlement of the insurer's obligation by payment to a third-party provider of goods or services rather than by payment to the insured or other claimant and certain nonfinancial assets and nonfinancial liabilities.

Audit Considerations

is unable to audit the existence or measurement of interests in investments in securities at the financial statement date, the auditor should consider whether that scope limitation requires the auditor to qualify his or her opinion or disclaim an opinion.[19]

Considerations for Auditors to Comply With the NAIC Model Audit Rule

2.144 The NAIC's Model Audit Rule requires auditors to communicate in a certain form and content with state insurance regulators. The subsequent paragraphs summarize the information in the Model Audit Rule that an auditor performing a statutory audit of an insurance entity should be aware of. Readers should refer to the full text of the Model Audit Rule for a complete understanding of the requirements for auditors and management. Further, not all states have adopted the Model Audit Rule in its entirely and could include other provisions. Auditors should be familiar with the applicable state requirements for insurance entities being audited.

Awareness

2.145 Section 6 of the Model Audit Rule requires that the insurer notify the insurance commissioner of the state of domicile of the name and address of the insurer's auditor. In connection with that notification, the insurer is required to obtain an awareness letter from its auditor stating that the auditor

   a. is aware of the provisions of the insurance code and the rules and regulations of the insurance department of the state of domicile that relate to accounting and financial matters.

   b. will issue a report on the financial statements in the terms of their conformity to the SAP prescribed or otherwise permitted by the insurance department of the state of domicile, specifying exceptions as appropriate. Readers should refer to paragraph 10.71 for an example of an "Illustration of the Accountant's Awareness Letter."

2.146 In addition, certain states require additional assertions. For most states, the awareness letter is only required to be filed once, in the first year engaged to perform the audit (within 60 days of becoming subject to the rules). For states where an annual letter is required, the filing deadline is generally December 31 of the year being audited. A few states require a letter to be filed annually. Some states have more specific requirements regarding contracts, licensure, and rules of domicile. Practitioners can check individual state regulations for the complete requirements of that state.

Change in Auditor

2.147 Section 6 of the Model Audit Rule requires that insurers notify the insurance department of the state of domicile within 5 business days of the dismissal or resignation of the auditor for the immediately preceding filed

---

[19] The AICPA Audit Guide *Special Considerations in Auditing Financial Instruments*, which is applicable to both financial assets and financial liabilities, includes the following:
- Background information about financial instruments
- Guidance about audit considerations relating to financial instruments
- Guidance on valuation—relevant information for financial instruments measured or disclosed at fair value

audited statutory financial statements. Within 10 business days of that notification, the insurer is also required to provide a separate letter stating whether there were any disagreements, subsequently resolved or not, in the 24 months preceding the event with the former auditor on any matter of accounting principles or practices, financial statement disclosure, or auditing scope or procedure and which disagreements, if not resolved to the satisfaction of the former auditor, would cause the auditor to make reference to the subject matter of the disagreement in connection with the auditor's opinion. The Model Audit Rule requires that the insurer provide the insurance department of the state of domicile a letter from the former auditor to the insurer indicating whether the auditor agrees with the statements in the insurer's letter and, if not, stating the reasons for the disagreement. The disagreements required to be reported in response to this section include both those resolved to the former accountant's satisfaction and those not resolved to the former accountant's satisfaction. Disagreements contemplated by this section are those that occur at the decision-making level; that is, between personnel of the insurer responsible for presentation of its financial statements and personnel of the accounting firm responsible for rendering its report. The insurer should also request, in writing, the former accountant to furnish a letter addressed to the insurer stating whether the accountant agrees with the statements contained in the insurer's letter and, if not, stating the reasons for which he or she does not agree; the insurer should furnish the responsive letter from the former accountant to the commissioner together with its own. Readers should refer to paragraph 10.73 for an example of an "Illustration of the Change in Auditor Letter."

Auditor's Letter of Qualifications

2.148 Section 12 of the Model Audit Rule requires the auditor to provide a letter to the insurer to be included in the annual financial report stating

    a. the auditor is independent with respect to the insurer and conforms with the standards of his or her profession as contained in the Code of Professional Conduct and pronouncements of the AICPA and the Rules of Professional Conduct of the appropriate state board of public accountancy.

    b. the background and experience in general of the individuals used for an engagement and whether each is a CPA. Nothing within this regulation shall be construed as prohibiting the auditor from utilizing such staff as he or she deems appropriate where use is consistent with the standards prescribed by GAAS.

    c. the auditor understands that the annual audited statutory financial statements and his or her opinion thereon will be filed in compliance with the requirements of the revised Model Audit Rule and that the domiciliary commissioner will be relying on the information in the monitoring and regulating of the financial position of insurers.

    d. the auditor consents to the working paper requirement contained in the revised Model Audit Rule and agrees to make the working papers and other audit documentation available for review by the domiciliary commissioner or the commissioner's designee under the auditor's control, the working papers, as defined in Section 13 of the revised Model Audit Rule.

Audit Considerations

    e. a representation that the auditor is properly licensed by an appropriate state licensing authority and is a member in good standing in the AICPA.

    f. the auditor meets the qualifications and is in compliance with the Section 7, "Qualifications of Independent Certified Public Accountant," of the Model Audit Rule.

Qualifications of the Auditor

2.149 Section 7 of the Model Audit Rule has certain requirements to which an auditor must adhere in order to be considered an independent CPA. In general, the requirements are based on the principle that the auditor cannot function in the role of management, cannot audit his or her own work, and cannot serve in an advocacy role for the insurer.

Indemnification

2.150 Section 7(A)(2) of the Model Audit Rule explains that the auditor is not considered an independent CPA by the insurance commissioner if the auditor either directly or indirectly enters into an agreement of indemnity or release from liability (collectively referred to as indemnification) with respect to the audit of the insurer. The qualified independent CPA may enter into an agreement with an insurer to have disputes relating to an audit resolved by mediation or arbitration. However, in the event of a delinquency proceeding commenced against the insurer under the applicable receivership statute, the mediation or arbitration provisions shall operate at the option of the statutory successor.

Partner Rotation

2.151 Section 7(D) of the Model Audit Rule states that the lead (or coordinating) audit partner (having primary responsibility for the audit) may not act in that capacity for more than 5 consecutive years. The person will be disqualified from acting in that or a similar capacity for the same company or its insurance subsidiaries or affiliates for a period of 5 consecutive years. An insurer may make application to the insurance commissioner for relief from the previous rotation requirement on the basis of unusual circumstances. This application should be made at least 30 days before the end of the calendar year. The insurance commissioner may consider the following factors in determining if the relief should be granted:

    a. Number of partners, expertise of the partners, or the number of insurance clients in the currently registered firm

    b. Premium volume of the insurer

    c. Number of jurisdictions in which the insurer transacts business

Prohibited Services

2.152 Section 7(G) of the Model Audit Rule lists out certain nonaudit services that if performed by the auditor contemporaneously with the audit, the commissioner will not recognize the auditor as a qualified independent CPA, nor accept an annual audited financial report. These nonaudit services are as follows:

a. Bookkeeping or other services related to the accounting records or financial statements of the insurer.

   b. Financial information systems design and implementation.

   c. Appraisal or valuation services, fairness opinions, or contribution-in-kind reports.

   d. Actuarially oriented advisory services involving the determination of amounts recorded in the financial statements. The accountant may assist an insurer in understanding the methods, assumptions, and inputs used in the determination of amounts recorded in the financial statement only if it is reasonable to conclude that the services provided will not be subject to audit procedures during an audit of the insurer's financial statements. An accountant's actuary may also issue an actuarial opinion or certification on an insurer's reserves if the following conditions have been met:

      i. Neither the accountant nor the accountant's actuary has performed any management functions or made any management decisions.

      ii. The insurer has competent personnel (or engages a third-party actuary) to estimate the reserves for which management takes responsibility.

      iii. The accountant's actuary tests the reasonableness of the reserves after the insurer's management has determined the amount of the reserves.

   e. Internal audit outsourcing services.

   f. Management functions or human resources.

   g. Broker or dealer, investment adviser, or investment banking services.

   h. Legal services or expert services unrelated to the audit.

   i. Any other services that the commissioner determines, by regulation, are impermissible.

2.153 Section 7(I) of the Model Audit Rule notes that an auditor that performs the audit may engage in other nonaudit services, including tax services that are not described in Section 7G or conflict with the principle that the auditor cannot function in the role of management, cannot audit his or her own work, and cannot serve in an advocacy role for the insurer. Any such activity must be approved in advance by the audit committee.

2.154 Readers can also refer to the *Implementation Guide for the Annual Financial Reporting Model Regulation*, located in appendix G of the NAIC *Accounting Practices and Procedure Manual*. Readers should refer to paragraph 10.85 for an example of an "Illustrative Accountant's Letter of Qualification."

Consideration of Internal Controls in a Financial Statement Audit

2.155 Section 9 of the Model Audit Rule notes that in accordance with AU section 319,[20] the auditor should obtain an understanding of internal control

---

[20] AU section 319 was superseded by AU-C section 315.

Audit Considerations

sufficient to plan the audit, and for those insurers required to file a "Management's Report of Internal Control over Financial Reporting" under Section 16 of the Model Audit Rule, consider the most recently available report in planning and performing the audit of the statutory financial statements. Section 9 of the Model Audit Rule also notes that consideration should be given to the procedures illustrated in the *Financial Condition Examiners Handbook* promulgated by the NAIC as the auditor deems necessary.

Notification of Adverse Financial Condition

2.156 Section 10 of the Model Audit Rule requires that the auditor notify the insurer's board of directors or audit committee in writing within five business days of determination of either of the following:

  a. The insurer has materially misstated its financial condition as reported to the domiciliary commissioner as of the balance-sheet date currently under audit

  b. The insurer does not meet the minimum capital and surplus requirements of the state insurance statute as of the balance-sheet date

2.157 An insurer that has received a notification of adverse financial condition is required to forward a copy of that notification within five day of its receipt to the insurance commissioner of the state of domicile and provide the auditor with evidence that the notification has been provided to the insurance commissioner. If the auditor receives no such evidence, the Model Audit Rule requires the auditor to send the notification to the insurance commissioner directly within the next five business days. (Certain states require direct notification to the insurance commissioner from the auditor as a matter of course.) Readers should refer to paragraph 10.79 for an example; "Illustration of Notification of Financial Condition Letter When the Audit Is Complete" indicates adverse financial conditions.

Report on Internal Controls

2.158 Section 11 of the Model Audit Rule requires that auditors should prepare a written communication of any unremediated material weaknesses that the insurer will furnish the domiciliary commissioner. Such communication should be prepared by the auditor and should contain a description of any unremediated material weakness (as the term *material weakness* is defined by Statement on Auditing Standards No. 60, *Communication of Internal Control Related Matters Noted in an Audit*, or its replacement[21]) as of December 31 immediately preceding (so as to coincide with the audited financial report discussed in Section 4(A) of the revised Model Audit Rule) in the insurer's internal control over financial reporting noted by the auditor during the course of the audit of the financial statements. If no unremediated material weaknesses were noted, the communication should so state. Readers should refer to paragraphs 10.82–.83 for examples of the following letters: "Material Weaknesses Defined and Identified in the Same Letter" and "Material Weaknesses Defined, But No Material Weaknesses Identified."

2.159 The insurer is also required to provide a description of remedial actions taken or proposed to correct unremediated material weaknesses if the

---

[21] SAS No. 60, *Communication of Internal Control Related Matters Noted in an Audit*, was superseded by SAS No. 122 section 265, "Communicating Internal Control Related Matters Identified in an Audit" (AICPA, *Professional Standards*, AU-C section 265).

actions are not described in the auditor's communication. The insurer is expected to maintain information about significant deficiencies communicated by the auditor. Such information should be made available to the examiner conducting a financial condition examination for review and kept in such a manner as to remain confidential.

2.160 AU-C section 265 defines a *significant deficiency* as a deficiency, or a combination of deficiencies, in internal control that is less severe than a material weakness, yet important enough to merit attention by those charged with governance. AU-C section 265 defines a *material weakness* as a deficiency, or combination of deficiencies, in internal control such that there is a reasonable possibility that a material misstatement of the entity's financial statements will not be prevented, or detected and corrected on a timely basis. For purposes other than satisfying Section 11 of the revised Model Audit Rule, the auditor also has to consider any additional reporting requirements under AU-C section 265.

Working Papers

2.161 Section 13 of the Model Audit Rule defines auditor working papers and requires that in conjunction with an examination by an insurance department examiner, photocopies of pertinent audit working papers may be made and retained by the insurance department. It also notes that such reviews by the insurance department examiners should be considered investigations and all working papers and communications obtained during the course of such investigations should be afforded the same confidentiality as other examination working papers generated by the insurance department.

Communications to Audit Committees

2.162 Section 14(F)(1) of the Model Audit Rule requires the auditor to communicate to the audit committee specific requirements:

    a. All significant accounting policies and material permitted practices

    b. All material alternative treatments of financial information within SAP that have been discussed with management officials of the insurer, ramifications of the use of the alternative disclosures and treatments, and the treatment preferred by the accountant

    c. Other material written communications between the accountant and the management of the insurer, such as any management letter or schedule of unadjusted differences

Management's Report on Internal Controls Over Financial Reporting

2.163 Section 16 of the Model Audit Rule requires every insurer that is required to file an audited financial report (that has annual direct written and assumed premiums of $500 million or more) to prepare a report of the insurer or group of insurers' internal control over financial reporting. See the *Implementation Guide for the Annual Financial Reporting Model Regulation* for additional information on effective dates for those companies moving above and below the threshold. The report should be filed with the commissioner along with the communication of internal control related matters noted in an audit described under Section 11 of the Model Audit Rule (as discussed in paragraphs

Audit Considerations

2.141–.143). As noted in Section 9 of the Model Audit Rule (as discussed in paragraph 2.139), the auditor is required to consider the most recently available report in planning and performing the audit of the statutory financial statements.

2.164 Management's report of internal control over financial reporting shall be on the internal controls as of December 31 immediately preceding. An insurer or a group of insurers that is (a) directly subject to Section 404, (b) part of a holding company system whose parent is directly subject to Section 404, (c) not directly subject to Section 404 but is a Sarbanes-Oxley Act of 2002 compliant entity, or (d) a member of a holding company system whose parent is not directly subject to Section 404 but is a Sarbanes-Oxley Act of 2002 compliant entity may file its or its parent's Section 404 report and an addendum in satisfaction of this Section 16 of the Model Audit Rule requirement. This filing and addendum is permitted provided that those internal controls of the insurer or group of insurers having a material impact on the preparation of the insurer's or group of insurers' audited statutory financial statements (those items included in Sections 5B–5G of this regulation) were included in the scope of the Section 404 report.

2.165 Management's report of internal control over financial reporting as required under Section 16 of the Model Audit Rule should include the following:

    a. A statement that management is responsible for establishing and maintaining adequate internal control over financial reporting.

    b. A statement that management has established internal control over financial reporting and an assertion, to the best of management's knowledge and belief, after diligent inquiry, whether its internal control over financial reporting is effective to provide reasonable assurance regarding the reliability of financial statements in accordance with statutory accounting principles.

    c. A statement that briefly describes the approach or processes by which management evaluated the effectiveness of its internal control over financial reporting.

    d. A statement that briefly describes the scope of work that is included and whether any internal controls were excluded.

    e. Disclosure of any unremediated material weaknesses in the internal control over financial reporting identified by management as of December 31 immediately preceding. Management is not permitted to conclude that the internal control over financial reporting is effective to provide reasonable assurance regarding the reliability of financial statements in accordance with statutory accounting principles if there is one or more unremediated material weaknesses in its internal control over financial reporting.

    f. A statement regarding the inherent limitations of internal control systems.

    g. Signatures of the chief executive officer and the chief financial officer (or equivalent position or title).

Management should document and make available upon financial condition examination the basis upon which its assertions are made. Management may base its assertions, in part, upon its review, monitoring, and testing of internal controls undertaken in the normal course of its activities.

a. Management shall have discretion as to the nature of the internal control framework used, and the nature and extent of documentation, in order to make its assertion in a cost effective manner and, as such, may include assembly of or reference to existing documentation.

b. Management's Report on Internal Control over Financial Reporting, and any documentation provided in support thereof during the course of a financial condition examination, shall be kept confidential by the state insurance department.

Auditor's Consideration of State Regulatory Examinations

2.166 The auditor should consider evaluating information contained in regulatory or examination reports, supervisory correspondence, and similar materials from applicable regulatory agencies. As noted in paragraph .12 of AU-C section 250, *Consideration of Laws and Regulations in an Audit of Financial Statements* (AICPA, *Professional Standards*), as part of obtaining an understanding of the entity and its environment, in accordance with AU-C section 315, the auditor should obtain a general understanding of the following:[22]

a. The legal and regulatory framework applicable to the entity and the industry or sector in which the entity operates

b. How the entity is complying with that framework

2.167 As noted in paragraphs .13–.14 of AU-C section 250, the auditor should obtain sufficient appropriate audit evidence regarding material amounts and disclosures in the financial statements that are determined by the provisions of those laws and regulations generally recognized to have a direct effect on their determination. The auditor should perform the following audit procedures that may identify instances of noncompliance with other laws and regulations that may have a material effect on the financial statements:

a. Inquiring of management and, when appropriate, those charged with governance about whether the entity is in compliance with such laws and regulations

b. Inspecting correspondence, if any, with the relevant licensing or regulatory authorities

2.168 Regulators are developing what they believe to be a more effective, integrated, and efficient approach to insurance regulation. The focus of their examination process is shifting to a broader and more qualitative assessment of the risks inherent in each insurer's operations and the insurer's efforts to identify and mitigate those risks.

2.169 The auditor may review reports of examinations and communications between regulators and the insurance entity and make inquiries of the regulators. The auditor may

- request that management provide access to all reports of examinations and related correspondence including correspondence relating to financial conditions.

---

[22] See paragraph .12 of AU-C section 315.

- read reports of examinations and related correspondence between regulators and the insurance enterprise during the period under audit through the date of the auditor's report.
- inquire of management and communicate with the regulators, with the prior approval of the insurance enterprise, when the regulators' examination of the enterprise is in process or a report on an examination has not been received by the insurance enterprise regarding conclusions reached during the examination.

2.170 AU-C section 705, *Modifications to the Opinion in the Independent Auditor's Report* (AICPA, *Professional Standards*), establishes requirements and guidance regarding scope limitations and auditors' reports issued in connection with audits of historical financial statements that are intended to present financial position, results of operations, and cash flows in conformity with GAAP. If management refuses to allow the auditor to communicate with the regulator or review communications with the regulator or if the regulator refuses to communicate with the auditor, then the auditor may qualify his or her opinion due to a limitation on the scope of the audit depending on the auditor's assessment of other relevant facts and circumstances.

Auditor's Consideration of Permitted Statutory Accounting Practices

2.171 Prescribed statutory accounting practices are those practices incorporated directly or by reference in state laws, regulations, and general administrative rules applicable to all insurance enterprises domiciled in a particular state. States may adopt the *NAIC Accounting Practices and Procedures Manual* in whole, or in part, as an element of prescribed statutory accounting practices in those states. If, however, the requirements of state laws, regulations, and administrative rules differ from the guidance provided in the manual or subsequent revisions, those state laws, regulations, and administrative rules will take precedence. Auditors of insurance enterprises should be aware of the provisions of the insurance code and the rules and regulations of the insurance department of the state of domicile that relate to accounting and financial matters to determine the specific prescribed statutory accounting practices applicable in each state.

2.172 Permitted statutory accounting practices include practices not prescribed by the domiciliary state, but allowed by the domiciliary state regulatory authority. An insurance enterprise may request permission from the domiciliary state regulatory authority to use a specific accounting practice in the preparation of the enterprise's statutory financial statements (*a*) if it wishes to depart from the prescribed statutory accounting practice or (*b*) if prescribed statutory accounting practices do not address the accounting for the transaction. Accordingly, permitted accounting practices differ from state to state, may differ from entity to entity within a state, and may change in the future.

2.173 Auditors should exercise professional judgment in concluding that an accounting treatment is permitted, and should consider the adequacy of disclosures in the financial statements regarding such matters. For each examination, auditors should obtain sufficient appropriate audit evidence to corroborate management's assertion that permitted statutory accounting practices that are material to an insurance enterprise's financial statements are permitted by the domiciliary state regulatory authority.

2.174 Auditors should use professional judgment to determine the type of corroboration that is necessary in the circumstances, noting audit evidence in documentary form, obtained directly by the auditor, would be more reliable than other evidence, such as a management representation.

2.175 If the auditor is unable to obtain sufficient appropriate audit evidence to corroborate management's assertion regarding a permitted statutory accounting practice that is material to the financial statements, the auditor should qualify or disclaim an opinion on the statutory financial statements in accordance with AU-C section 705 because of the limitation on the scope of the audit.

SEC Requirements for Management's Report on Internal Control Over Financial Reporting

2.176 As directed by Section 404 of the Sarbanes-Oxley Act of 2002, the SEC adopted final rules requiring entities subject to the reporting requirements of the Securities Exchange Act of 1934, other than registered investment entities, to include in their annual reports a report of management on the entity's internal control over financial reporting. Section 989(G) of the Dodd-Frank Act added Sarbanes-Oxley Section 404(c) to exempt from the attestation requirement smaller issuers that are neither accelerated filers nor large accelerated filers under Rule 12b-2. Section 404(c) essentially provides that a nonaccelerated filer will not be required to include in the annual reports it files with the SEC an attestation report from its registered public-accounting firm on internal control over financial reporting. See the SEC website at www.sec.gov/rules/final/33-8238.htm for the full text of the regulation. In its Final Rule Release No. 33-8238, *Management's Report on Internal Control Over Financial Reporting and Certification of Disclosure in Exchange Act Periodic Reports*, the SEC directs entities subject to the reporting requirements of the Securities Exchange Act of 1934, other than registered investment entities, to include in their annual reports a report of management on the entity's internal control over financial reporting. Issued for the purpose of implementing Section 404 of the Sarbanes-Oxley Act of 2002, this rule is effective August 14, 2003, and requires registrants to (*a*) take responsibility for establishing and maintaining adequate internal control structure and procedures for financial reporting and (*b*) assess their effectiveness at the end of each fiscal year. Moreover, the final rule requires an entity's annual report to include an internal control report of management that contains a statement of management's responsibility for establishing and maintaining adequate internal control over financial reporting for the entity. This requirement includes

- a statement identifying the framework used by management to evaluate the effectiveness of this internal control.
- management's assessment of the effectiveness of internal control over financial reporting as of the end of the entity's most recent fiscal year, including a statement concerning whether or not internal control over financial reporting is effective.
- disclosure of any material weaknesses in internal control over financial reporting. Management is not permitted to conclude that the entity's internal control over financial reporting is effective if there are one or more material weaknesses.

2.177 With respect to the application of this rule to quarterly reporting required under the Securities Exchange Act of 1934, management's responsibilities are less extensive than those required for annual reporting. Management must, with the participation of the principal executive and financial officers, evaluate any change in the entity's internal control over financial reporting that occurred during a fiscal quarter that has materially affected, or is reasonably likely to materially affect, the entity's internal control over financial reporting.

2.178 The SEC rules clarify that management's assessment and report is limited to internal control over financial reporting. Management does not consider other aspects of control, such as controls pertaining to operating efficiency. The SEC's definition of internal control encompasses the Committee of Sponsoring Organizations of the Treadway Commission (COSO) definition, but the SEC does not mandate that the entity use COSO as its criteria for judging effectiveness.

2.179 For quarterly reporting, the SEC rules also require management to evaluate any change in the entity's internal control that occurred during a fiscal quarter and that has materially affected, or is reasonably likely to materially affect, the entity's internal control over financial reporting. Additionally, management is required to evaluate the effectiveness of the entity's disclosure controls and procedures and issue a report concerning their effectiveness on a quarterly basis. With these rules, the SEC introduced the new term *disclosure controls and procedures*, which is different from internal controls over financial reporting and much broader.

2.180 As defined, *disclosure controls and procedures* encompass the controls over all material financial and nonfinancial information in Securities Exchange Act of 1934 reports. Information that would fall under this definition that would not be part of an entity's internal control over financial reporting might include the signing of a significant contract, changes in a strategic relationship, management compensation, or legal proceedings. See paragraphs 1.51–.56 and the preface of this guide for additional information.

Chapter 3

Premiums

Background

3.01 Insurance entities charge premiums to spread the total cost of similar risks among large groups of policyholders as well as relieve the policyholder of all or part of a risk. Such risks include (*a*) damage to, or loss of, property caused by various perils (for example, fire and theft), and (*b*) legal liability resulting from injuries to other persons or damage to their property. The premiums charged plus investment income earned on the premium received are used to cover underwriting expenses, pay the ultimate costs of claims reported on the policies, and provide a profit margin. Premiums are also used as a basis for paying certain underwriting expenses, including commissions to agents, premium taxes, and guaranty fund and other premium-based assessments (expenses are discussed in detail in chapter 8, "Insurance-Related Expenses, Taxes, and Assessments," of this guide).

3.02 The following are definitions of premiums charged for insurance policies and reinsurance agreements:

> **Direct premiums.** Premium income less return premiums arising from policies issued by the entity collecting the premiums and acting as the primary insurance carrier.
>
> **Assumed reinsurance premiums.** Premium income less return premiums arising from contracts entered into to reinsure other insurance companies that provide the related insurance or reinsurance coverage. The accounting for assumed reinsurance premiums is discussed in chapter 6, "Reinsurance," of this guide.
>
> **Ceded reinsurance premiums.** Outgoing premiums less return premiums arising from reinsurance purchased from other insurance entities. The accounting for ceded reinsurance premiums is discussed in chapter 6 of this guide.
>
> **Premium adjustments.** Additional premiums due to or from insureds or reinsurers arising from endorsements, cancellations, experience-rated features, and audits.

3.03 Premiums are generally established by one of three methods—class or manual rating, individual or judgment rating, or merit rating—which are explained as follows:

- *Class or manual rating* is used primarily to establish rates for various coverages for individuals, families, and small businesses. Based on statistical data, these large groups of similar risks can be classified by a few important and easily identifiable characteristics. These classifications result in standard rates.

- *Individual or judgment rating* is used when the rates for large or unusual risks are established almost entirely by the skill and experience of the rate maker, such as ocean marine risks.

- *Merit rating* is generally used for larger risks of commercial lines and is divided into the following three types:

AAG-PLI 3.03

— *Schedule rating* starts with an assumed standard rate, frequently the manual rate, and adjusts the standard rate according to an evaluation of greater or lesser exposure to risk. Schedule rating is often used in fire insurance or commercial properties; however, some companies use this type of rating for all lines of business.

— *Experience rating* departs from manual rates based on the insured's past experiences under the coverage. Premiums are adjusted prospectively based on average past experience. Experience rating is widely used in workers' compensation insurance, but some companies use this type of rating for commercial auto and commercial general liability to a lesser extent.

— *Retrospective experience rating* differs from experience rating in that it adjusts the premium during the period of coverage based on actual experience during that same period. Policies that are retrospectively rated often specify minimum and maximum premiums and, in effect, may leave a portion of the risk uninsured (paragraph 3.04 discusses retrospective premium adjustments).

Types of Premiums Adjustments

3.04 Adjustments to premiums written and unearned premiums can result from the following:

- *Cancellation* is a complete termination of an existing policy before expiration. Cancellations may generally be requested by the insured or occur by reason of nonpayment of premium. If, at the time of cancellation, the insured has paid more premium than has been earned through the cancellation date, the insured will typically receive a return of premium, subject to a cancellation penalty, when permitted by regulations. If the insured owes additional premium at the time of cancellation, the insurer will bill for the balance due or, if the insurer cannot collect the balance due, write off the premium receivable.

- *Endorsements* are changes in existing policies that may result in additional premiums or return premiums, such as increases or decreases in coverage limits, additions or deletions of property or risks covered, or changes in location or status of insureds.

- *Audit premiums* are premiums determined from data developed by periodic audits of insureds' records or from periodic reports submitted by insureds. An audit may result in an additional premium or a return premium. An example of a policy subject to audit premiums is a workers' compensation policy for which the premium is based on the payroll of the employer.

- *Retrospective premium adjustments* are modifications of the premiums after expiration of the policies. An adjustment is based on the experience of an individual risk during the term of the policy and is generally subject to maximum and minimum premium limits specified in the policy.

Summary of Premium Transaction Flow

3.05 The premium cycle normally includes the following functions that generate most premium-related transactions:

- Evaluating and accepting risks, including the evaluation of reinsurance needs
- Issuing policies, including coding and policy maintenance
- Billing and collecting premiums
- Paying commissions and other costs of acquiring business
- Financial and statistical reporting

3.06 Rates used by an insurance entity are based on the entity's experience by line of insurance or the industry loss experience compiled by advisory rating organizations, which are subject to supervision and regulation by state insurance departments. The principal rating organizations are the National Council on Compensation Insurance, Inc. (NCCI) for workers' compensation insurance; the Surety & Fidelity Association of America; surplus lines associations; and the Insurance Services Office for all other property and liability lines of insurance.

3.07 The states regulate insurance premium rates to ensure that premium rates shall not be inadequate, excessive, or unfairly discriminatory. In a 1944 decision, the Supreme Court held that insurance is interstate commerce and, as such, is subject to regulation by the federal government. However, in 1945, Congress passed the McCarran-Ferguson Act, which exempts the insurance business from antitrust laws. Although Congress insisted that the federal government has the right to regulate the insurance industry, it stated in the McCarran-Ferguson Act that the federal government would not regulate insurance as long as state legislation provided for the supervision of insurance companies, including rate making. All states have passed legislation requiring insurance commissioners to review, with or without prior approval, most rates charged by insurance companies. An entity must file most rates with the insurance department of each state in which it is authorized to do business. A number of states also require formal or tacit approval of rates by respective state insurance departments.

Evaluating and Accepting Risks

3.08 The evaluation and risk accepting function has three general objectives: to evaluate the acceptability of the risk, to determine the premium, and to evaluate the entity's capacity to retain the entire risk.

3.09 To initiate new business, companies may solicit consumers directly, such as with some personal lines insurance, or through a producer, such as an agent or a broker. Whether solicited directly or through a producer, sales employees and underwriters of the insurance entity must have the appropriate state licenses. If new business is sold directly to the consumer, the insurance entity typically obtains information over the phone or through the Internet and provides the applicant with a quote. If the quote is accepted, the applicant is required to send in a signed application to complete the underwriting process. If new business is submitted through an agent or a broker, the producer submits to the entity an application for a policy, often with a deposit from the customer for a portion of the estimated premium. The cash is recorded in a clearing (suspense) account and deposited, and the application is either forwarded to the

AAG-PLI 3.09

entity's underwriting department for evaluation or reviewed against fully automated underwriting criteria. If the application is sent electronically, the payment is typically sent separately to a lockbox or remittance operation. The risks of a potential new policy are evaluated in accordance with the entity's procedures; these may include a review of the exposure and potential for loss based on the application for new business. For example, applications for automobile insurance may be checked by requesting motor vehicle reports issued by a state department of motor vehicles. Applications for surety and large deductible policies may include a review of the financial stability of the insured. Applications for certain property coverages may require engineering surveys or fire hazard surveys. Often, companies will complete the underwriting process before a quote is released to the agent or broker. Companies may also perform an underwriting evaluation for certain renewals and endorsement transactions.

3.10 If the quote is accepted, insurance coverage may be "bound," pending issuance of the policy. In these cases, the agent or broker may provide the insured with a *binder*, which is a temporary contract that may be oral or written. The period covered by the binder is usually short, often limited to 30 days or less. A written binder is evidence of an understanding by both parties of what the insurance covers, the amount of insurance, the premium charged, and the entity writing the insurance. Typically, once coverage is bound, the significant insurance terms are agreed upon by both parties, with minor contract terms finalized when the policy is issued.

3.11 If the underwriter determines that the applicant falls within the entity's underwriting guidelines and is an acceptable risk, the underwriting approval is documented and the risk is coded so the entity can prepare reports concerning premiums such as the following:

  a. Premiums by state, line of business, and underwriting year, which are required to be included in the entity's annual statement or other regulatory filings

  b. Premiums written by territory and class of risk, which are required by the entity or rating bureaus to aid in ratemaking

  c. Premiums by producer, which are required to prepare agents' production reports and compute any contingent commissions due at the end of a year

3.12 If an application is denied, the deposit premium is returned to the applicant with an explanation. When the refund is sent, the suspense account is cleared. In the case in which the entity does not require a deposit premium, the agent or broker is notified of the application being denied.

3.13 Accounting entries are made for accepted applications by crediting premiums written, clearing the premium cash-suspense account for the deposits, and recording the balances due as agents' balances or premiums receivable. The combination of the rating codes entered into the policy processing system becomes the basis for the premium rates charged. Premiums are typically recorded when the policy is bound, as long as the relevant terms are agreed upon by both parties. Premiums are initially recorded as deferred revenue and then as premium earned. See the discussion on revenue recognition in paragraphs 3.30–.49.

3.14 Generally, a renewal of a policy is a new contract, but unless otherwise stated, the terms are those of the original policy. The risk insured under the original policy expires when the policy expires and each renewal must be considered as an application for a new risk. When a policy is renewed, the premium is determined in the same manner as for a new business policy.

3.15 Finally, after a risk has been accepted and the premium has been calculated, a determination must be made about whether the entire risk should be retained or all or part of it should be reinsured. If reinsurance is chosen, treaty or facultative reinsurance is purchased, or the reinsurance entity(s) on an existing agreement is notified, and the amount of ceded premium is determined and paid. In some cases, the availability of reinsurance is taken into consideration in deciding whether to write the direct business. Reinsurance is discussed in detail in chapter 6 of this guide.

3.16 Personal lines policies, applications, and endorsements may be submitted electronically (typically through the Internet or agency interface systems) or by paper. If submitted by paper, applications and endorsements are keyed into the policy processing system by customer service representatives. For commercial lines policies, an agent or a broker obtains the pertinent information from the customer and submits an application to the underwriting department for review. For personal lines policies, whether keyed into the system or interfaced electronically, information from the application or endorsement is reviewed by an underwriter or passed through automated underwriting criteria. Although some commercial lines policies may be passed through automated underwriting criteria, in most cases, applications for commercial lines policies are evaluated by an underwriter. For transactions that meet the entity's underwriting criteria, the policies are coded to the appropriate line of business. If policy transactions cannot be coded or processed automatically by the systems, they may be forwarded to a coding unit, which verifies data to the application or supplemental information received from the agent or insured. Once verified, manually coded applications and endorsements are then entered into the policy processing system. If not processed in real time, policy transactions may be batched and processed nightly. Typically, transactions entered into a policy processing system are interfaced with policy master files and statistical reporting systems at which point a policy number is assigned. This typically comprises an alphanumeric string, with the alpha prefix component of the policy identifier representing an abbreviated policy symbol designation of the type of coverage being provided. Companies should have controls to ensure that all processed transactions are balanced between the policy processing system and policy master file and statistical reporting systems. There should be controls that reconcile written premium and commissions processed in the policy processing system or policy master file to what is recorded in the billing systems. For personal lines policies, processing the information generates an insurance ID card as well as information such as terms of the policy, lines of coverage, premiums, and agent information. The policy, including any endorsements, is prepared, assigned a policy number, and sent directly to the insured or agent or broker for distribution. Underwriting files containing original documentation will be maintained at the branch or home office locations where underwriting was conducted.

Billing and Collecting Premiums

3.17 The two basic methods for billing premiums are agency billing and direct billing. Some companies use only one of these methods; others use both. Under direct billing, the entity sends bills directly to the policyholders and the policyholders remit the premiums directly to the entity. Uncollected premiums from policyholders represent premiums due to the entity that may have been directly solicited from policyholders either by an agent or the company. Customers typically have the option of remitting premiums on an installment basis. Billing may be on a monthly, quarterly, annual, or other installment schedule. If an agent solicited the business, the entity, after receiving payments from the policyholders, either sends the agent a check or otherwise credits the agent's account for his or her commission.

3.18 The following are several variations of agency billing, also called *account current*:

- *Account current item basis.* For individual policies, the agent collects the premiums directly from the insureds, subtracts his or her commissions, and remits the net premiums due the entity. If the agent cannot collect a premium during the credit period allowed by the entity, he or she may request cancellation of the policy.

- *Account current rendering basis.* The agent submits a statement of all the policies issued or due during the current month to the insurance entity and the net amount of the statement is subsequently to be paid in accordance with the agency agreement. The statement, which includes all known current activity, such as endorsements, cancellations, and audits, is compared with the entity's accounts receivable and adjusted as necessary.

- *Account current billing basis.* The entity sends the agent a statement that contains a listing of all the policies written or due minus the policies cancelled during the month. The net amount of the statement is to be paid in accordance with the agency agreements.

3.19 The credit terms to agents are usually outlined in the agency agreement. The agent's account current is usually payable within a specified period after the last day of the month of the account.

3.20 Uncollected premiums from an agent represent premiums due the entity from the agent based on his or her contract with the entity to write insurance, collect the necessary premiums, and remit the collected premiums net of commissions. For balances due from agents, companies maintain a record or register of balances due and collected by policy. This register may include information by line of business, such as current premiums, commissions, year-to-date premiums, current expired, premiums in force, and earned and unearned premiums. The entity reconciles accounts current submitted by the agent with transactions as reflected in the entity's records. An agent's aged trial balance includes information such as the current month's premiums, net premiums, prior balance, cash received, net balance, installment fees, and balance due. In addition, the agent's trial balance is reviewed to determine any uncollectible accounts.

3.21 The premium collection or remittance department is responsible for accounting for customer remittances and the agent's account current. Adequate control over these documents and the related cash must be maintained to ensure that all payments received are processed. Customers and agents may pay by check, electronic check, debit card, credit card, or wire transfer and may remit payment by Internet, phone, or mail. If customers send payment by mail, they are typically asked to send a preprinted remittance form along with the check. Many remittance processing systems can scan or read policy information from the remittance form electronically through technology such as imaging or optical character recognition. Some remittances must be keyed in manually. Customer and agent remittances should be batched, and the amount of cash deposited should be reconciled to the amount of cash applied to outstanding agents' balances and premiums receivable. Some companies may outsource these functions to a lockbox or other third-party service provider. Procedures should be in place to maintain unapplied collections in a suspense account and to clear items from the suspense account timely. Billing functions typically have customer service departments that perform a number of activities, including extending payment terms, collecting outstanding balances, and charging off uncollectible balances.

Paying Commissions and Other Costs of Acquiring Business

3.22 Agents, both independent and exclusive, and brokers are compensated for their services by commissions. Some commissions are paid on the basis of a standard percentage of premiums or an agreed upon scale known as level commissions. Commission can be paid to agents either as the insurance entity receives payments or entirely upfront when the installment down payment is received. Retroactive commissions are used in areas such as workers' compensation in which the final premium may be experience rated and the commissions would therefore require adjustment. Contingent commissions result from agreements with agents and brokers whereby the amounts of commissions are contingent on premium volume or favorable loss experience of the business placed with the entity. Establishing accounting provisions for contingent commissions is difficult because they are based on estimates of the ultimate loss experience, and in many cases, the commission period does not coincide with the entity's fiscal year. Readers should note that contingent commissions have been under regulatory scrutiny in recent years and understand what arrangements are acceptable. Insurance entities may also have other incentive compensation arrangements, such as an incentive paid to an agent's customer service representatives for each policy issued.

Financial and Statistical Reporting

3.23 Typically, companies have frontend policy processing application systems that interface with a policy master file or system. This information is automatically carried over to the general ledger and statistical reporting systems. There should be balancing controls in place to ensure that transaction counts and amounts are in agreement when one application system updates another. Proper coding of premiums is important because it affects areas such as loss reserving; future underwriting and pricing decisions; ceding to treaty reinsurance; and the accrual of premium taxes, premium-based assessments, and contingent commission arrangements.

3.24 Each state insurance department requires all insurance entities licensed to write business in that state to file an annual statement, also referred to as the convention blank, statutory blank, or simply the blank, with the state insurance commissioner for each individual insurance entity. The blank includes numerous schedules on premiums, including premiums written by the state. See paragraph 1.74 of this guide for additional discussion of the annual statement.

3.25 An entity should have appropriate controls to ensure that data file transfers from one system to another are complete and accurate, including job scheduling controls and balancing routines. An entity should also have data validation edits, required fields, and other application controls to check the completeness and accuracy of information entered by consumers or agents over the Internet or through agency interface systems. Appropriate change management controls should be in place to ensure that only authorized changes are made to key application systems.

3.26 An entity should also have controls to protect data integrity in the physical environment, including, for example, making servers accessible only to network administrators and protecting hardware and storage media from power surges. In addition to controls over physical access, there should be controls over logical access, including passwords to access networks, databases, and application systems. An entity should also maintain current authorization levels for all users, document system administration procedures, and create disaster recovery plans for occurrences such as power outages, server failure, and virus attacks. There should also be appropriate protocols over data interchange at the hardware device level and application program level. Some of these protocols for the Internet include transmission control protocol, Internet protocol, hypertext transfer protocol, and file transfer protocol. An entity should also have appropriate security over data exchanged over the Internet, including, for example, the use of data encryption and firewalls. Logical access controls should be sufficient to protect nonpublic personal information of consumers, as required under the Gramm- Leach-Bliley Act of 1999.

Involuntary Markets

3.27 As discussed in paragraph 1.08, states have established mechanisms to provide insurance to those with high risks who would otherwise be excluded from obtaining coverage. For property in high risk areas, Fair Access to Insurance Requirements (FAIR) Plans, which are federally approved and state supervised, provide insurance to owners. Companies that operate in a state are assessed for any underwriting loss experienced by the FAIR Plan in the state. Many insurers make flood insurance available to their customers through the National Flood Insurance Program (NFIP) offered by the federal government. The huge volume of claims driven by the 2005 storms, primarily Hurricane Katrina, was unprecedented and resulted in congressional action to fund NFIP payments. During 2005 and 2006, Congress passed several bills increasing the borrowing authority of the NFIP to provide funds for payment of existing claims. Some states, most notably Florida, have established catastrophe funds or state sponsored insurance companies to provide property coverage in high exposure locations where insurers are not willing to provide such coverage. In some cases, the fund or state sponsored insurance entity is authorized to assess a portion or all of the state's accumulated deficit if premiums are insufficient to cover losses and expenses. The Citizens Property Insurance Corporation in Florida is an example of this arrangement.

3.28 Similar to FAIR Plans, states also provide workers' compensation insurance through workers' compensation pools. The most significant of these workers' compensation arrangements are the NCCI pools that operate in the great majority of states that do not have their own state specific workers' compensation involuntary arrangement. Companies operating in a given state are assigned a proportionate share of the pool's results based on direct writings of the underwriting results of the pool. States also provide medical malpractice insurance through medical malpractice pools. These pools were established by law and currently exist in the majority of states. All insurers writing related liability insurance in such states are considered mandatory participants in the pools as a condition for their continuing authority to transact business in such states. States also have several methods of apportioning involuntary automobile insurance. These methods include automobile insurance plans, joint underwriting associations, and reinsurance pools or associations. However, certain states allow the insurance entity the option to not participate in the involuntary pool and to write the high risk business on their own paper, which is called a direct assignment.

3.29 Thus, involuntary mechanisms may be summarized as follows:

- Premiums assumed from an involuntary pool, such as NCCI, based on direct voluntary writings in the state.
- Premiums written directly as a "takeout" in lieu of an involuntary apportionment (that is, direct assignments).
- Assessments charged by a state that are recoupable as part of the premium or incorporated into the approved premium rate. These assessments may be based on voluntary premium writings or losses incurred in a given line(s) of business. Refer to chapter 8 of this guide for a further discussion of assessments.
- Passthrough surcharges imposed by a state or municipality. Such surcharges are usually specified as a percentage of premiums. The insurer records the collection and payments through the balance sheet only because it is functioning solely as a collections facility.

Accounting for Premiums and Acquisition Cost[1]

Premium Revenue and Premium Adjustments

Generally Accepted Accounting Principles

3.30 Under generally accepted accounting principles (GAAP), many specialized industry accounting principles for revenue recognition for property and liability insurance enterprises are specified in Financial Accounting Standards Board (FASB) *Accounting Standards Codification* (ASC) 944, *Financial Services—Insurance*. Most property and liability insurance contracts are classified as short duration contracts, and this guide generally focuses on such contracts. In

---

[1] On August 2, 2007, the Financial Accounting Standards Board (FASB) issued an invitation to comment on *An FASB Agenda Proposal: Accounting for Insurance Contracts by Insurers and Policyholders*. That invitation to comment included the discussion paper issued by the IASB *Preliminary Views on Insurance Contracts* that set forth the IASB's preliminary views on the main components of an accounting model for an issuer's rights and obligations (assets and liabilities) under an insurance contract. FASB issued the invitation to comment to gather information from its constituents to help decide whether there was a need for a comprehensive project on accounting for insurance contracts and whether FASB should undertake such a project jointly with the IASB.

In October 2008, FASB decided to join the IASB's insurance contract project.

In July 2010, the IASB issued the exposure draft *Insurance Contracts*. In developing the IASB's exposure draft, most of the discussions about the proposed insurance accounting approaches were held jointly with FASB. Although the boards reached common decisions in many areas, they reached different conclusions in others. Some FASB members prefer the IASB's proposed measurement model; however, the majority prefers an alternative model. Regardless of FASB members' individual views and uniform commitment to convergence, FASB determined that additional information was needed about whether the possible new accounting guidance would represent a sufficient improvement to generally accepted accounting principles to justify issuing new guidance. On September 17, 2010, FASB issued, for public comment, the discussion paper *Preliminary Views on Insurance Contracts*.

The boards are redeliberating significant issues based on feedback received on the IASB exposure draft and FASB discussion paper. FASB is expected to release an exposure draft, and the IASB is expected to issue a targeted revised exposure draft, during the first half of 2013. Readers should remain alert to any final pronouncements.

order for a contract to be accounted for using insurance accounting, the contract must provide for the indemnification of the insured against loss or liability, as noted in FASB ASC 720-20-25-1. GAAP accounting for insurance contracts that do not transfer insurance risk is discussed briefly in paragraph 3.64 and in more detail in chapter 6, "Reinsurance," of this guide.

3.31 As noted in FASB ASC 944-20-15-2, insurance contracts shall be classified as short- or long-duration contracts depending on whether the contracts are expected to remain in force for an extended period. As discussed in FASB ASC 944-20-15-7, the factors that shall be considered in determining whether a particular contract can be expected to remain in force for an extended period for a short-duration contract are as follows:

    a. The contract provides insurance protection for a fixed period of short duration

    b. The contract enables the insurer to cancel the contract or adjust the provisions of the contract at the end of any contract period, such as adjusting the amount of premiums charged or coverage provided

3.32 Also discussed in FASB ASC 944-10-15-10 are the factors that shall be considered in determining whether a particular contract can be expected to remain in force for an extended period for a long-duration contract. These factors are as follows:

    a. The contract generally is not subject to unilateral changes in its provisions, such as a noncancellable or guaranteed renewable contract

    b. The contract requires the performance of various functions and services, including insurance protection, for an extended period

3.33 A short duration contract is not necessarily synonymous with a term of one year or less. Examples exist of short duration contracts that extend beyond one year, such as multiyear retrospectively rated policies, residential contractors' policies, surety policies that remain in force over the term of a project, and product warranty and residual value contracts that may extend over several years.

3.34 As noted in FASB ASC 944-605-25-1, premiums from short duration contracts shall be recognized as revenue over the period of the contract in proportion to the amount of insurance protection provided. For those few types of contracts for which the period of risk differs significantly from the contract period, premiums shall be recognized as revenue over the period of risk in proportion to the amount of insurance protection provided. That generally results in premiums being recognized as revenue evenly over the contract period or period of risk, if different, except for those few cases in which the amount of insurance protection declines according to a predetermined schedule.

3.35 Under several types of contracts, the period of risk differs significantly from the contract period. An example is insurance for recreational vehicles issued for an annual period and covering claims that are incurred primarily in the summer months. Under other kinds of contracts, the amount of coverage declines over the contract period on a scheduled basis. An example is an insurance policy covering the residual value of a vehicle that is leased or financed. In those cases, the premium is recognized as revenue over the period of risk in proportion to the amount of insurance protection provided.

3.36 As discussed in FASB ASC 944-605-25-2, if premiums are subject to adjustment (for example, retrospectively rated or other experience rated insurance contracts for which the premium is determined after the period of the contract based on claim experience, or reporting form contracts for which the premium is adjusted after the period of the contract based on the value of the insured property), premium revenue shall be recognized as follows:

   a. If, as is usually the case, the ultimate premium is reasonably estimable, the estimated ultimate premium shall be recognized as revenue over the period of the contract. The estimated ultimate premium shall be revised to reflect current experience.

   b. If the ultimate premium cannot be reasonably estimated, the cost recovery method or deposit method may be used until the ultimate premium becomes reasonably estimable.

3.37 For retrospectively rated contracts, the additional premium or premium reduction determined after the period of the contract is based on current experience, as noted in paragraph 3.36*a*. Examples of variables affecting insurance premiums include the following:

- For retrospectively rated contracts, the premium is adjusted during and after the period based on the actual loss experience of the insurance contract.

- For reporting form contracts, the premium is adjusted after the period of the contract based on the value of insured property.

- For workers' compensation policies subject to audit premiums, the premium adjustment is based on a review of actual payroll during the policy period versus the estimated payroll that was used to determine the initial premiums.

3.38 As defined in the FASB ASC glossary, under the cost recovery method, premiums are recognized as revenue in amounts equal to estimated claims as insured events occur until the ultimate premium is reasonably estimable, and recognition of income is postponed until then. Also defined in the FASB ASC glossary, under the deposit method, premiums are not recognized as revenue, claims are not charged to expense until the ultimate premium is reasonably estimable, and income recognition is postponed until that time.

3.39 Readers should also be aware that a portion of the premium may be deferred because the billed premiums are for coverage to be provided by the insurance entity over the term of the policy. At the end of each reporting period, unearned premiums (premiums related to future insurance coverage to be provided during the contract term) are calculated, and the change in unearned premiums is recorded as a charge or credit to premium income. Consistent with the guidance in FASB ASC 944-605-25-1, 944-30-25-1, and 944-30-45- 1, unearned premium is recognized as revenue over the period of the contract in proportion to the amount of insurance protection provided.

3.40 GAAP does not reflect written premiums in the income statement (see paragraphs 3.41–.49 for statutory accounting), but disclosures are required, as discussed in FASB ASC 944-605-50-1(b). GAAP also does not have a similar requirement to statutory accounting to nonadmit a portion of receivables due for audit premiums, although a bad debt allowance should be provided for amounts deemed uncollectible.

Statutory Accounting Principles

3.41 Paragraph 3 of Statement on Statutory Accounting Principles (SSAP) No. 53, *Property Casualty Contracts—Premiums*, notes that, except for workers' compensation contracts, written premium is defined as the contractually determined amount charged by the reporting entity to the policyholder for the effective period of the contract based on the expectation of risk, policy benefits, and expenses associated with the coverage provided by the terms of the insurance contract.

3.42 Paragraph 4 of SSAP No. 53 also notes that

[f]or workers' compensation contracts, which have a premium that may periodically vary based upon changes in the activities of the insured, written premiums may be recorded on an installment basis to match the billing to the policyholder. Under this type of arrangement, the premium is determined and billed according to the frequency stated in the contract, and written premium is recorded on the basis of that frequency.

3.43 Written premiums do not affect the statement of income but are used as a means of tracking the amount of business written by type or location. As discussed in paragraph 3.24, the blank includes numerous schedules on premiums, including premiums written by state.

3.44 Paragraph 5 of SSAP No. 53 states

[w]ritten premiums for all other contracts shall be recorded as of the effective date of the contract. Upon recording written premium, a liability, the unearned premium reserve, shall be established to reflect the amount of premium for the portion of the insurance coverage that has not yet expired.

3.45 Paragraph 6 of SSAP No. 53 also notes that

[t]he exposure to insurance risk for most property and casualty insurance contracts does not vary significantly during the contract period. Therefore, premiums from those types of contracts shall be recognized in the statement of income, as earned premium, using either the daily pro-rata or monthly pro-rata methods as described in paragraph 7 of SSAP No. 53.

3.46 Paragraph 13 of SSAP No. 53 states that

[a]dvance premiums result when the policies have been processed, and the premiums have been paid prior to the effective date. These advance premiums are reported as a liability in the statutory financial statement and not considered income until due. Such amounts are not included in written premium or the unearned premium reserve.

3.47 As discussed in paragraphs 9–12 of SSAP No. 53

[a]djustments to the premium charged for changes in the level of exposure to insurance risk (e.g., audit premiums on workers' compensation policies) are generally determined based upon audits conducted after the policy has expired. Reporting entities shall estimate audit premium, which is generally referred to as earned but unbilled (EBUB) premium, and shall record the adjustment to premium either through written and earned premium or as only an adjustment to

earned premium. The estimate for EBUB may be determined using actuarially or statistically supported aggregate calculations using historical entity unearned premium data, or per policy calculations.

EBUB shall be adjusted upon completion of the audit, with the adjustment recognized as revenue immediately. Upon completion of an audit that results in a return of premiums to the policyholder, earned premiums shall be reduced.

[r]eporting entities shall establish all of the requisite liabilities associated with the asset such as commissions and premium taxes.

[t]en percent of the EBUB asset in excess of collateral specifically held and identifiable on a per policy basis shall be reported as a non-admitted asset. To the extent that amounts in excess of 10% are not anticipated to be collected, they shall be written off in the period the determination is made.

3.48 As noted in paragraph 5 of SSAP No. 66, *Retrospectively Rated Contracts*, initial premiums from retrospectively rated contracts shall be recognized in accordance with SSAP No. 53 or other SSAPs, depending on whether the contracts are life, property, casualty, or accident and health contracts. Also, as discussed in paragraph 8 of SSAP No. 66

[r]etrospective premium adjustments are estimated for the portion of the policy period that has expired and shall be considered an immediate adjustment to premium. Additional retrospective premiums and return retrospective premiums shall be recorded as follows:

  a. Property and Liability Reporting Entities:

   i. Accrued additional retrospective premiums shall be recorded as a receivable with a corresponding entry made to written and earned premiums or as only an adjustment to earned premiums. Premium not recorded through written premium when accrued shall be recorded through written premium when billed.

   ii. Accrued return retrospective premiums payable shall be recorded as a write-in liability with a corresponding entry made to written and earned premiums or only as an adjustment to earned premiums. Premiums not recorded through written premium when accrued shall be recorded through written premium when billed.

   iii. Ceded retrospective premium balances payable shall be recorded as liabilities, consistent with SSAP No. 62, *Property and Casualty Reinsurance*. Ceded retrospective premiums recoverable shall be recorded as an asset. Consistent with SSAP No. 64, *Offsetting and Netting of Assets and Liabilities*, ceded retrospective premium balances payable may be deducted from ceded retrospective premiums recoverable when a legal right of setoff exists.

3.49 Paragraph 9 of SSAP No. 66 fully explains how to determine the amount of accrued estimated retrospective premiums to be recorded as a nonadmitted asset. If the retrospective premium receivable is due from an insured for whom any agent's balance or uncollected premiums are classified as nonadmitted, or the amounts are not billed in accordance with policy or contract provisions, then 100 percent of the asset shall be treated as nonadmitted. Similar to EBUB, 10 percent of accrued additional retrospective premiums in excess of collateral identifiable on a per policy basis shall also be reported as a nonadmitted asset.

Premium Receivable

Generally Accepted Accounting Principles

3.50 Uncollected premiums due from an agent, net of commissions payable, are generally reflected as agents' balances or uncollected premiums. Under direct billing, the entire amount of uncollected premiums recorded within agents' balances is generally referred to as uncollected premiums. Commissions due to agents on premiums billed directly to the insured are recorded as a liability. Some insurance companies issue bill receivables, which are generally interest bearing and used as a method of financing premiums. These amounts are also included in agents' balances. Companies should consider FASB ASC 210-10. The FASB ASC glossary defines *right of setoff* and FASB ASC 210-10- 45-1 specifies what conditions must be met to have that right.

3.51 Under FASB ASC 310-10-35, *Receivables*, and FASB ASC 450, *Contingencies*, an allowance should be recorded for the amount of the receivable that is deemed uncollectible. The allowance is recorded as a contra-asset to the agents' balances and premium receivable account. The expense is generally recorded as bad debt expense in the income statement.

3.52 Under GAAP, FASB ASC 450-20-50-3 similarly notes that disclosure of the contingency shall be made when at least a reasonable possibility exists that a loss or an additional loss may have been incurred, and either of the following conditions exists:

> *a.* An accrual is not made for a loss contingency because any of the conditions in FASB ASC 450-20-25-2 are not met
>
> *b.* An exposure to loss exists in excess of the amount accrued pursuant to the provisions of FASB ASC 450-20-30-1

Statutory Accounting Principles

3.53 Paragraph 7 of SSAP No. 6, *Uncollected Premium Balances, Bills Receivable for Premiums, and Amounts Due From Agents and Brokers*, states that

> [t]he due date for all premium balances addressed by this statement is determined as follows:
>
> > *a.* Original and deposit premiums—governed by the effective date of the underlying insurance contract and not the agent/reporting entity contractual relationship;
> >
> > *b.* Endorsement premiums—governed by the effective date of the insurance policy endorsement;
> >
> > *c.* Installment premiums—governed by the contractual due date of the installment from the insured;
> >
> > *d.* Audit premiums and retrospective premiums—governed by insurance policy or insurance contract provisions. If the due

Premiums

date for receivables relating to these policies is not addressed by insurance policy provisions or insurance contract provisions, any uncollected audit premium (either accrued or billed) is nonadmitted.

3.54 Paragraph 9 of SSAP No. 6 states that

[n]onadmitted assets are determined:

    a. Uncollected Premium—To the extent that there is no related unearned premium, any uncollected premium balances which are over ninety days shall be nonadmitted. If an installment premium is over ninety days due, the amount over ninety days due plus all future installments that have been recorded on that policy shall be nonadmitted;

    b. Bills Receivable—Bills receivable shall be nonadmitted if either of the following conditions are present:

        i. If any installment is past due, the entire bills receivable balance from that policy is nonadmitted; or

        ii. If the bills receivable balance due exceeds the unearned premium on the policy for which the note was accepted, the amount in excess of the unearned premium is nonadmitted.

    c. Agents' Balances—The uncollected agent's receivable on a policy by policy basis which is over ninety days shall be nonadmitted regardless of any unearned premiums;

        i. If amounts are both payable to and receivable from an agent on the same underlying policy, and the contractual agreements between the agent and the reporting entity permit offsetting, the nonadmitted portion of amounts due from that agent shall not be greater than the net balance due, by agent;

        ii. If reconciling items between a reporting entity's account and an agent's account are over ninety days due, the amounts shall be nonadmitted.

3.55 As outlined in paragraph 10 of SSAP No. 6

[a]fter calculation of non-admitted amounts, an evaluation shall be made of the remaining admitted assets in accordance with SSAP No. 5, *Liabilities, Contingencies, and Impairments of Assets*, to determine if there is impairment. If, in accordance with SSAP No. 5, it is probable the balance is uncollectible, any uncollectible receivable shall be written off and charged to income in the period the determination is made. If it is reasonably possible a portion of the balance is uncollectible and is therefore not written off, disclosure requirements outlined in SSAP No. 5 shall be followed.

Acquisition Costs

Generally Accepted Accounting Principles

3.56 Under GAAP, FASB Accounting Standards Update (ASU) No. 2010-26, *Financial Services—Insurance (Topic 944): Accounting for Costs Associated* with *Acquiring or Renewing Insurance Contracts (a consensus of the FASB Emerging Issues Task Force)*, states that only acquisition costs that are directly related to the successful acquisition of a contract can be capitalized as deferred acquisition costs (DAC). As noted in ASU No. 2010-26, if the initial application of the amendments in ASU No. 2010-26 results in the capitalization of acquisition costs that had not been capitalized previously by an entity, the entity may elect not to capitalize those types of costs.[2] These deferred amounts are recorded as an asset on the balance sheet and amortized to income in a systematic manner based on related contract revenues. Previously, the guidance of FASB ASC 944-30 did not address successful versus unsuccessful efforts.

3.57 *Determination of deferrable costs.* The FASB ASC glossary defines acquisition costs as costs that are related directly to the successful acquisition of new or renewal insurance contracts.

3.58 As discussed in FASB ASC 944-30-25-1A, an insurance entity shall capitalize only the following as acquisition costs related directly to the successful acquisition of new or renewal insurance contracts:

    a. Incremental direct costs of contract acquisition

    b. The portion of the employee's total compensation, excluding any compensation that is capitalized as incremental direct costs of contract acquisition, and payroll related fringe benefits related directly to time spent performing any of the following acquisition activities for a contract that actually has been acquired:

        i. Underwriting

        ii. Policy issuance and processing

        iii. Medical and inspection

        iv. Sales force contract selling

    c. Other costs related directly to the insurer's acquisition activities in (b) that would not have been incurred by the insurance entity had the acquisition contract transaction(s) not occurred

    d. Advertising costs that meet the capitalization criteria in FASB ASC 340-20-25-4

3.59 *Incremental direct costs of contract acquisition.* The FASB ASC glossary defines incremental direct costs of contract acquisition as a cost to acquire an insurance contract that has both of the following characteristics:

    a. It results directly from, and is essential to, the contract transaction(s)

    b. It would not have been incurred by the insurance entity had the contract transaction(s) not occurred

3.60 FASB ASC 944-30-55-1 discusses the types of incremental direct cost of contract acquisition to be capitalized under item (a) FASB ASC 944-30-25-1A. Such costs include the following:

---

[2] A number of property and liability insurance entities have historically limited their deferral of acquisition costs to only commissions and premium-based taxes. As noted in paragraph 3.56, at the initial implementation date of FASB Accounting Standards Update No. 2010-26, *Financial Services—Insurance (Topic 944): Accounting for Costs Associated with Acquiring or Renewing Insurance Contracts (a consensus of the FASB Emerging Issues Task Force)*, an entity may elect not to capitalize costs that were not capitalized previously.

Premiums

a. An agent or a broker commission or bonus for successful contract acquisition(s)

b. Medical and inspection fees for successful contract acquisition(s)

3.61 *Total compensation, benefits, and other costs directly related to acquisition activities.* Items (b)–(c) of FASB ASC 944-30-25-1A requires that only the portion of costs related directly to time spent performing specified acquisition activities for a contract that actually has been acquired (that is, successful efforts) may be deferred.

3.62 FASB ASC 944-30-55-1C discusses that payroll related fringe benefits include any costs incurred for employees as part of the total compensation and benefits program. Examples of such benefits include all of the following:

a. Payroll taxes

b. Dental and medical insurance

c. Group life insurance

d. Retirement plans

e. 401(k) plans

f. Stock compensation plans, such as stock options and stock appreciation rights

g. Overtime meal allowances

3.63 FASB ASC 944-30-55-1G discusses that the portion of total compensation of executive employees that relates directly to the time spent approving successful contracts may be deferred as acquisition costs. For example, the amount of compensation allocable to time spent by members of a contract approval committee is a component of acquisition costs.

3.64 FASB ASC 944-30-55-1A discusses that examples of other costs related directly to the insurer's acquisition activities in item (b) of FASB ASC 944-30-25-1A that would not have been incurred by the insurance entity had the acquisition contract transaction(s) not occurred include all of the following:

a. Reimbursement of costs for air travel, hotel accommodations, automobile mileage, and similar costs incurred by personnel relating to the specified activities

b. Costs of itemized long distance telephone calls related to contract underwriting

c. Reimbursement for mileage and tolls to personnel involved in onsite reviews of individuals before the contract is executed

3.65 *Direct response advertising.* FASB ASC 340-20-25-4 notes that the costs of direct response advertising should be capitalized if both of the following conditions are met:

a. The primary purpose of the advertising is to elicit sales to customers who could be shown to have responded specifically to the advertising

b. The direct response advertising results in probable future benefits

3.66 FASB ASC 340-20-25-6 specifies that in order to conclude that advertising elicits sales to customers who could be shown to have responded specifically to the advertising, there must be a means of documenting that response, including a record that can identify the name of the customer and the advertising that elicited the direct response. Examples of such documentation include the following:

   a. Files indicating the customer names and related direct response advertisement
   b. A coded order form, coupon, or response card included with an advertisement indicating the customer name
   c. A log of customers who have made phone calls to a number appearing in an advertisement, linking those calls to the advertisement

3.67 Additional guidance for issuers to consider can be found in section 1(B), "Accounting for Advertising Costs," of the Securities and Exchange Commission's *Division of Corporation Finance: Frequently Requested Accounting and Financial Reporting Interpretations and Guidance*:

> Certain direct response advertising costs may be deferred under [FASB ASC 340-20-25]. Qualifying costs relating to a specific advertising activity must meet all of the following criteria:
>
>   (a) A direct relationship between a sale and the specific advertising activity for which cost is deferred must be demonstrated clearly. More than trivial marketing effort after customer response to the advertising and before the sale is consummated (such as customer contact with a sales person or furnishing of additional product or financing information) will disqualify the sale as being deemed a direct result of the advertising. A significant lapse of time between the advertising activity and the ultimate sale in an environment of broad general advertising may disqualify the sale as being deemed a direct result of the advertising.
>
>   (b) The advertisement's purpose must be one of eliciting a direct response in the form of a sale. For example, if the primary purpose (based on either intent or most frequent actual outcome) is identification of customers to which additional marketing efforts will be targeted, the advertising costs do not qualify.
>
>   (c) Deferrable costs do not include administrative costs, occupancy costs, or depreciation of assets other than those used directly in advertising activities. Payroll related costs that are deferrable include only that portion of employees' total compensation and payroll-related fringe benefits that can be shown to directly relate to time spent performing the qualifying activities. Costs of prizes, gifts, membership kits and similar items are not deferrable under [FASB ASC 340-20-25], but are accounted for as inventory in most circumstances.
>
>   (d) The costs must be probable of recovery from future benefits. Objective historical evidence directly relevant to the particular advertising activity is necessary to demonstrate probability of recoverability. Ancillary income from sources other than the responding customer may not be included in the calculation of future benefits for the test. Future benefits to be included in the calculation are limited to revenues derived from the customer which are the direct result of the advertising activity alone,

without significant additional marketing effort. Revenues from subsequent sales and renewals may be included only if insignificant market effort is required to obtain those revenues.

3.68 If the capitalization criteria in FASB ASC 340-20-25-4 are met, the direct response advertising costs should be included as DAC for classification, subsequent measurement, and premium deficiency test purposes in accordance with FASB ASC 944 applicable to insurance industry DAC.

3.69 As noted in FASB ASC 340-20-25-12, the cost of the direct response advertising directed to all prospective customers, not only the cost related to the portion of the potential customers that are expected to respond to the advertising, should be used to measure the amounts of such reported assets.

3.70 As noted in FASB ASC 340-20-25-8, the probable future benefits of direct response advertising activities are probable future revenues arising from that advertising in excess of future costs to be incurred in realizing those revenues. FASB ASC 340-20-25-9 discusses that demonstrating that direct response advertising will result in future benefits requires persuasive evidence that its effects will be similar to the effects of responses to past direct response advertising activities of the entity that resulted in future benefits. Such evidence should include verifiable historical patterns of results for the entity. Attributes to consider in determining whether the responses will be similar include the following:

    a. The demographics of the audience

    b. The method of advertising

    c. The product

    d. The economic conditions

3.71 *Nondeferrable expenses.* As stated in FASB ASC 944-720-25-2, an insurance entity should charge to expense as incurred any of the following costs:

    a. An acquisition related cost that cannot be capitalized in accordance with FASB ASC 944-30-25-1A (for implementation guidance, see FASB ASC 944-720-55-1)

    b. An indirect cost (for implementation guidance, see FASB ASC 944-720-55-2)

3.72 FASB ASC 944-720-55-1 includes the following examples of acquisition related costs that cannot be capitalized in accordance with FASB ASC 944-30-25-1A:

    a. Soliciting potential customers (except direct response advertising capitalized in accordance with item (d) of FASB ASC 944-30-25-1A)

    b. Market research

    c. Training

    d. Administration

    e. Unsuccessful acquisition or renewal efforts (except direct response advertising capitalized in accordance with item (d) of FASB ASC 944-30-25-1A)

    f. Product development

3.73 As discussed in FASB ASC 944-30-55-1F, employees' compensation and fringe benefits related to the activities described in paragraph 3.72, unsuccessful contract acquisition efforts, and idle time should be charged to expense as incurred.

3.74 FASB ASC 944-720-55-2 includes the following examples of indirect costs, per item (b) of FASB ASC 944-720-25-2, that should be expensed as incurred:

    a. Administrative costs

    b. Rent

    c. Depreciation

    d. Occupancy costs

    e. Equipment costs, including data processing equipment dedicated to acquiring insurance contracts

    f. Other general overhead

3.75 FASB ASC 944-30-55-1B notes that costs for software dedicated to contract acquisition are not eligible for deferral as DAC under the definition of that term. Under the definition of that term, such costs are not other costs related to those activities that would not have been incurred but for that contract. Notwithstanding that the guidance, as described in paragraph 3.74, that indicates that equipment costs are expensed as incurred, insurance entities should consider the criteria in FASB ASC 350-40 to determine if the costs qualify for capitalization as internal use software.

3.76 *Cost determination.* The identification of acquisition costs requires considerable judgment, such as how to determine successful versus unsuccessful efforts and how to determine what types of activities performed by employees are considered to be directly related to sales. The determination of the costs to be deferred can often be determined separately or via a standard costing technique or through a combination of both. FASB ASC 944-30-55-1D-1E provides additional discussion.

3.77 *Allocation of DAC.* FASB ASC 944-30-25-1B requires the following:

> To associate acquisition costs with related premium revenue, capitalized acquisition costs shall be allocated by groupings of insurance contracts consistent with the entity's manner of acquiring, servicing, and measuring the profitability of its insurance contracts.

3.78 *Determining deferrable acquisition costs.* FASB ASC 944-30-25-1A (see paragraph 3.58) discusses what types of costs an insurance entity should capitalize as acquisition costs. An insurance entity should evaluate whether employee compensation and payroll related fringe benefits are related directly to time spent performing acquisition activities for contacts that actually have been acquired. This determination may be accomplished by a two-step process:

    a. Determine the portion of the employee's time spent performing acquisition activities

    b. Determine the portion of the employee's time spent in acquisition activities directly related to contracts that have been acquired (that is, successful efforts)

3.79 Both of the following examples are meant to be illustrative and the actual determination of DAC under FASB ASC 944 should be based on the facts and circumstances of an entity's specific situation:

> Example 1: In 201X, an employee of an insurance entity whose responsibility is sales force contract selling is compensated solely on a commission basis, based on the volume of business sold directly by the employee. The employee's current year commission of $125,000 is calculated as a percentage of premiums relating to business sold directly by the employee in the current year. In this fact pattern, the $125,000 commission is an incremental direct cost of contract acquisition, and the entire $125,000 would be deferrable by the insurance entity.
>
> Example 2: In 201X, an employee of an insurance entity earned a salary and payroll related fringe benefits of $120,000 and spent approximately 80 percent of his or her time on qualifying acquisition activities, as described in paragraph 3.58. Approximately 50 percent of this time resulted in successful contract acquisitions. The amount of costs that would be deferrable as acquisition costs would be $48,000 ($120,000 × 80% qualifying acquisition activities × 50% successful efforts).

3.80 In situations when an employee is compensated by both commission and salary, judgment will be needed to determine what costs can be capitalized as acquisition costs (as discussed in paragraph 3.58), based on the facts and circumstances of each specific situation.

3.81 FASB ASC 944-605-25-14 discusses accounting for contingent commission arrangements and states that if retrospective commission or experience refund arrangements exist under experience rated insurance contracts, a separate liability shall be accrued for those amounts based on experience and the provisions of the contract. Income in any period shall not include any amounts that are expected to be paid to agents or others in the form of experience refunds or additional commissions. Contingent commission receivable or payable shall be accrued over the period in which related income is recognized.

Accounting for DAC in Connection With Modifications or Exchanges of Insurance Contracts

3.82 FASB ASC 944-30-35 and 944-30-40 provide specific guidance on accounting for DAC on internal replacements and modifications of insurance and investment contracts. The AICPA also issued a series of Technical Questions and Answers (TISs) on accounting and financial reporting issues related to FASB ASC 944-30-35 and 944-30-40 (TIS sections 6300.25–.35 [AICPA, *Technical Practice Aids*]). Readers should be aware that FASB ASC 944-30-35 and 944-30-40 apply to property and liability contracts.

Statutory Accounting Principles

3.83 Under SSAP No. 71, *Policy Acquisition Costs and Commissions*, acquisition costs are expensed as incurred (see chapter 6 of this guide for a discussion of the treatment of excess ceding commission under SSAP No. 62). Refer to SSAP No. 66 for additional statutory accounting principles (SAP) guidance on accounting for contingent commissions.

Premium Deficiencies

3.84 A premium deficiency relating to short duration insurance contracts indicates a probable loss on premiums yet to be earned. FASB ASC 944-60-25-4 states that a premium deficiency shall be recognized if the sum of expected claim costs and claim adjustment expenses, expected dividends to policyholders, unamortized acquisition costs, and maintenance costs[3] exceeds related unearned premiums.

3.85 As discussed in FASB ASC 944-60-25-3, insurance contracts shall be grouped consistently with the enterprise's manner of acquiring, servicing, and measuring the profitability of its insurance contracts to determine if a premium deficiency exists. FASB ASC 944-60-25-5 states that a premium deficiency shall first be recognized by charging unamortized acquisition costs to expense to the extent required to eliminate the deficiency. As noted in FASB ASC 944-60-25-6, if the premium deficiency is greater than unamortized acquisition costs, a liability shall be accrued for the excess deficiency.

3.86 Under SAP, SSAP No. 53 incorporates the same basic premise for determining a premium deficiency reserve but notes the following in paragraph 15:

> Commission and other acquisition costs need not be considered in the premium deficiency analysis to the extent they have previously been expensed. For purposes of determining if a premium deficiency exists, insurance contracts shall be grouped in a manner consistent with how policies are marketed, serviced and measured. A liability shall be recognized for each grouping where a premium deficiency is indicated. Deficiencies shall not be offset by anticipated profits in other policy groupings.

3.87 FASB ASC 944-60-50-1 states that an insurance entity should disclose in its financial statements whether it considers anticipated investment income in determining if a premium deficiency relating to short duration contracts exists. If an entity chooses to include anticipated investment income in the premium deficiency test, which is a policy choice, no authoritative guidance exists on how to calculate the anticipated investment income. As a result, varying industry practices exist. Over the years there has been discussion within the insurance community about whether any methods are more appropriate, but there has not been any authoritative guidance issued on this topic. There are two primary methods used in practice—the expected investment income approach, which computes anticipated investment income on the cash flows generated by current in force contracts, or the discounting approach, which discounts expected future payments for claim costs, claim adjustment expenses, and maintenance costs. Both methods incorporate the time value of money. Several variations exist within the expected investment income and discounting approaches. An entity's determination of how it performs premium deficiency testing would be a policy decision that should be applied consistently and based on individual facts and circumstances. If an entity chooses to change how it performs premium deficiency testing, it would be required to apply the guidance in FASB ASC 250, *Accounting Changes and Error Corrections*.

3.88 Under the expected investment income approach, investment income is calculated on the total funds that are available from the contract for

---

[3] Per the FASB *Accounting Standards Codification* glossary, *maintenance costs* are defined as costs associated with maintaining records relating to insurance contracts and with the processing of premium collections and commissions.

investment. Cash available for investment is determined by considering all cash flows from in force policies, including premiums, commissions, and other underwriting costs; premium taxes; claims and claim adjustment expenses; investment income; and expenses on both the unexpired and expired portions of in force policies. Under one variation of this approach, investment income is determined using cash flows associated with only the unexpired portion of the in force premium (that is, unearned premium less unamortized DAC). Generally, a premium deficiency would exist under this method if the sum of the future expected ultimate losses and expenses are greater than the unearned premium liability minus unamortized DAC plus investment income.

3.89 Several variations exist under this approach in dealing with situations in which the fund goes negative. Under one approach, negative investment income would be included in the calculation, in effect imputing borrowing costs to the entity for the net cash outflows required to pay claims. An alternative approach would record only positive investment income but would not assess negative investment income when the fund is depleted. Instead, this method implicitly assumes that funds are available from surplus to cover any shortfalls. This rationale stems from the statutory notion that invested assets are expected to be maintained to support insurance liabilities.

3.90 Under the discounting approach, a premium deficiency test considers the present value of future costs (consisting of claims, claim adjustment expenses, and maintenance expenses) expected to be incurred during the remaining portion of the contract plus unamortized acquisition costs. A premium deficiency would exist when such costs exceed the related unearned premiums. A variation of this approach would consider the present value of future costs incurred and expected to be incurred on in force policies less liabilities recorded at the measurement date (both unearned premiums and any existing claim liability) plus related unamortized acquisition costs. This latter approach gives accounting recognition to the time value of money associated with both the expired and unexpired portions of the policies. By discounting all cash outflows at the anticipated investment yield rate, the discounting approach, like one version of the expected investment income approach noted previously, implicitly assumes that funds are available from surplus to cover all claim payments.

3.91 The examples of premium deficiency calculations in paragraph 3.97 show several variations of both the expected investment income and discounting approaches that are illustrative and not meant to include current actuarial assumptions.

3.92 In the situation in which companies elect not to include the time value of money in the premium deficiency calculation, they would use the same components described in FASB ASC 944-60-25 and SSAP No. 53, using nominal values for cash flows. For liabilities discounted under current GAAP and SAP guidance, such as workers' compensation tabular reserves or structured settlements, inclusion of the time value of money would be required in the premium deficiency calculation as well. The examples in this guide assume that the entity has elected to consider anticipated investment income in its premium deficiency test.

3.93 When estimating the expected cash flow used in the premium deficiency test, although companies should consider their historical experience as an indicator of future cash flows, assumptions used in the calculated premium deficiency should be adjusted to reflect more recent or expected trends. The loss and loss expense ratio used to project anticipated losses can also be adjusted for items such as expected differences in rate adequacy and loss frequency and severity.

3.94 In addition, if current year reported loss and loss expense ratios are used to project anticipated losses, the entity should exclude from the ratios the impact of reserve development on prior accident years, as well as large or unusual current accident year events. FASB ASC 944-60-25 does not provide explicit guidance on whether to include estimates in the premium deficiency calculation for losses relating to actual events occurring subsequent to the balance sheet date. In practice, this is accounted for in multiple ways, with the common starting point being that the event is probable of occurring at the balance sheet date. One method is to include estimates for losses occurring subsequent to the balance sheet date, using all available information up through the date that the financial statements are issued. Another method is to include estimates for losses if the extent of the damage is reasonably estimable at the balance sheet date, using only information that theoretically existed at the balance sheet date. The Financial Reporting Executive Committee believes that an entity's determination of how to account for losses relating to actual events occurring subsequent to the balance sheet date within the premium deficiency calculation would be a policy decision that should be applied consistently and disclosed as follows:

> a. *Probable at the balance sheet date, using all available information up through the date that the financial statements are issued.* Estimates should be based on the entity's expectation of the future loss events that are probable at the balance sheet date, using all available information up through the date that the financial statements are issued. However, the estimates should not include losses relating to actual events occurring subsequent to the balance sheet date that were not probable at the balance sheet date. Therefore, estimates for infrequent, high severity events that are included in expected loss and loss expense ratios based on historical events and trends expected to continue should be included, but the expected cash flows should not include actual events, such as hurricanes or ice storms, that occur subsequent to the balance sheet date and that were not probable of occurring at the balance sheet date. However, in those rare circumstances when an infrequent, high severity event is probable at the balance sheet date and expected to occur in the near future, expected losses relating to that probable event should be included in the premium deficiency calculation. For example, potential losses from a hurricane sitting off the coast of Florida at period end that hits the coast and causes damage shortly thereafter in the subsequent accounting period would rarely meet the criteria of being probable. In those instances, when the hurricane did hit, expected cash flows relating to the hurricane would be included in the premium deficiency calculation, using all available information up through the date that the financial statements are issued.
>
> b. *Probable and reasonably estimable at the balance sheet date, using only information that theoretically existed at the balance sheet date.* Estimates should be based on the entity's expectation of future loss events that are probable and reasonably estimable at the balance sheet date, using only information that theoretically existed at the balance sheet date. However, the estimates should not include losses relating to actual events occurring subsequent to the balance sheet date that were not probable and reasonably estimable at the balance sheet date. Therefore, estimates for infrequent, high severity events

that are included in expected loss and loss expense ratios based on historical events and trends expected to continue should be included, but expected cash flows should not include actual events, such as hurricanes or ice storms, that occur subsequent to the balance sheet date that were not both probable of occurring and reasonably estimable at the balance sheet date. The estimate should only be based on information that theoretically existed at the balance sheet date but not thereafter. In general, it would be very rare to have a situation that would meet both criteria of being probable of occurring and being able to reasonably estimate the extent of the damage, using information that theoretically existed at the balance sheet date. For example, potential losses from a hurricane sitting off the coast of Florida at period end that hits the coast and causes damage shortly thereafter in the subsequent accounting period would very rarely meet the criteria of being both probable and reasonably estimable, using information that theoretically existed at the balance sheet date. As a result, the hurricane would not be included in a premium deficiency calculation.

3.95 In selecting the interest rate to be used under the expected investment income approach or the discount rate under the discounting approach, companies typically use a rate equal to the yield expected to be earned on total invested assets (expected portfolio rate) over the period that the claim liabilities are expected to be paid. This yield is the ratio of expected interest income; dividends; and rents, net of investment expenses, to the total invested assets. At each date that the calculation is performed, this yield would be adjusted for current market information.

3.96 Care should be taken when calculating the premium deficiency for a line of business in cases in which an estimated loss ratio is used, and the liabilities for claims and claim adjustment expenses are already recorded at a discounted amount. To avoid double counting of anticipated investment income, the projected loss ratio used in the calculation should be adjusted to exclude the effect of any discount recorded under GAAP or SAP, so that the discount rates used to calculate anticipated investment income are applied to the estimated gross unpaid loss and loss adjustment expenses.

3.97 Short duration PDR calculation examples that follow:

- No premium deficiency
  - Example 1A, "Expected Investment Income Approach Using All Cash Flows From In Force Policies"
  - Example 1B, "Expected Investment Income Approach Using Only the Unexpired Portion of the Contract"
  - Example 1C, "Discounting Approach Using Only the Unexpired Portion of the Contract"
- Expected premium deficiency
  - Example 2A, "Expected Investment Income Approach Using All Cash Flows From In Force Policies"
  - Example 2B, "Expected Investment Income Approach Using Only the Unexpired Portion of the Contract"
  - Example 2C, "Discounting Approach Using Only the Unexpired Portion of the Contract"

AAG-PLI 3.97

Background

- Computation made as of December 31, 2011. All in force contracts have a policy term of one year or less.
- Earned premium on in force contracts as of December 31, 2011, is $182,000. Unearned premiums as of December 31, 2011, are $168,000, resulting in total in force premium of $350,000.
- The block of in force contracts is expected to experience a 78 percent loss and loss expense ratio on the earned premium.
- The underwriting expenses incurred were 30.16 percent of premiums written, producing a combined ratio of 108.16 percent.
- Acquisition costs amount to 25 percent of premiums written. The difference between the incurred ratio of 30.16 percent and the deferral ratio of 25 percent is expensed currently as period costs.
- Maintenance costs are $2,919 and are paid in the same pattern as claims (for simplicity).
- The payment pattern of the anticipated claims is derived using payment data from schedule P in the statutory annual statement.
- No policyholder dividends exist on these types of policies.

Example 1A—Expected Investment Income Approach Using All Cash Flows From In Force Policies

Under the expected investment income approach, the entity projects the expected claim and claim expenses and the payment pattern of those costs. The expected claim and claim adjustment expenses typically include the recorded incurred losses related to the earned premium plus losses estimated by multiplying the expected loss and loss expense ratio by unearned premium for losses that have not been incurred.

Using the expected payment pattern and making certain assumptions concerning interest rates and the timing of premium collections, underwriting, and maintenance expense payments, the future investment income related to this block of in force premiums is computed.

Anticipated Experience on Group of In Force Policies
(Example 1A—Exhibit 1)

	Earned on Unexpired	Unearned	In Force
Premium	$182,000	$168,000	$350,000
Actual loss and loss expense ratio	78%	—	—
Expected loss and loss expense ratio	—	78%	—
	$141,960	$131,040	$273,000

Assumptions

- Analysis of individual entity experience indicates that the expected loss and loss expense ratio will be 78 percent on the in force block of business.
- The earned premium on unexpired policies was earned in 2011, and the related incurred loss and loss expense on earned premium is estimated to be $141,960.
- The unearned premium of $168,000 will be earned in 2012.
- The expected loss and loss expense on the unearned premium is $131,040.

Based on historical claim payment patterns, the entity assumes that loss and loss expenses related to both the 2011 and 2012 accident years will be paid out as follows:

Loss and Loss Expense Payments as a Percentage of Total Incurred Losses
(Example 1A—Exhibit 2)

Payment Year	Percentage of Total Incurred Paid
Calendar year of accident year	32.0
Accident year +1	28.0
Accident year +2	15.0
Accident year +3	12.0
Accident year +4	8.0
Accident year +5	5.0
	100%

These percentages are used in the exhibit 3.

Settlement Pattern of Claims Related To In Force Policies
(Example 1A—Exhibit 3)

Payment Year	Claims Related to 2011 Earned Premium		Claims Related to 2012 Earned Premium		Claims Related in Force Premium	
	%	$	%	$	%	$
2011	32.0	45,427	—	—	16.6	45,427
2012	28.0	39,749	32.0	41,933	29.9	81,682
2013	15.0	21,294	28.0	36,691	21.2	57,985
2014	12.0	17,035	15.0	19,656	13.4	36,691
2015	8.0	11,357	12.0	15,725	9.9	27,082
2016	5.0	7,098	8.0	10,483	6.5	17,581
2017	—	—	5.0	6,552	2.5	6,552
	100.0	141,960	100.0	131,040	100.0	273,000

Explanation

This exhibit shows the computation of the in force payment pattern using accident year data. When in force payment data is available, it should be used. The payment data is used in the computation of investment income in the following exhibit 4.

Computation of Anticipated Investments Income
(Example 1A—Exhibit 4)

Year	Cash Opening Balance	Premiums Received	Underwriting Costs Paid	Claims	Maintenance Costs	Cash Ending Balance Before Investment Income	Cash Average Balance	Investment Income
			30.16%		0.83%			(7.0%)
2011	$—	$350,000	$(105,581)	$(45,427)	$—	$198,992	$99,496	$6,965
2012	205,957	—	—	(81,682)	(1,046)	123,229	164,593	11,522
2013	134,751	—	—	(57,985)	(742)	76,024	105,388	7,377
2014	83,401	—	—	(36,691)	(469)	46,241	64,821	4,537
2015	50,778	—	—	(27,082)	(347)	23,349	37,064	2,594
2016	25,943	—	—	(17,581)	(228)	8,134	17,038	1,193
2017	9,327	—	—	(6,552)	(87)	2,688	6,008	421
		$350,000	$(105,581)	$(273,000)	$(2,919)			$34,609

Total expected investment income for future years (2012–17) $27,644

Assumptions for Computation of Anticipated Investment Income

- Insurance contracts are issued, premiums are collected evenly throughout the year, and underwriting costs are incurred and paid as premiums are collected.
- Claims are paid evenly throughout the year.
- Maintenance costs are 0.83 percent of premiums and paid in the same pattern as claims for years after the contract term because it is the cost to maintain the contract.
- Investment income is earned on average assets and reinvested (interest rate multiplied by the average balance).
- The historical yield is 5.5 percent; however, the expected yield, which gives consideration to the historical yield, net cash invested at new money rates, and anticipated reinvestment rates, is 7.0 percent (investment portfolio yield).
- As stated in the "Background" section of these examples, underwriting costs are 30.16 percent of written premium.

Premium Deficiency Test Using Expected Investment Income Approach as of December 31, 2011
(Example 1A—Exhibit 5) (Profitable Contracts)

Unearned premiums at December 31, 2011 (example 1A—exhibit 1)		$168,000
Less expected costs (undiscounted):		
Claims and claim adjustment expenses (example 1A—exhibit 1)	$131,040	
Maintenance costs (example 1A—exhibit 4)	2,919	
Unamortized policy acquisition costs (25% of unearned premiums)	42,000	
Subtotal		$175,959
Premium deficiency before expected investment income		(7,959)
Anticipated investment income (example 1A—exhibit 4)		27,644
Excess of income over costs		$19,685

The premium deficiency test performed using the expected investment income approach indicates an excess. Therefore, no provision for premium deficiency would be made as of December 31, 2011.

Example 1B—Expected Investment Income Approach Using Only the Unexpired Portion of the Contract

Under this variation of the expected investment income approach, investment income is determined only on the cash flows associated with the unexpired portion of the in force premium and claims related to 2012 earned premiums.

Computation of Anticipated Investments Income Using Cash Flows Associated Only With the Unexpired Portion of the In Force Premium

(Example 1B—Exhibit 1)

Year	Cash Opening Balance	Premiums Received	Underwriting Costs Paid	Claims	Maintenance Costs	Cash Ending Balance Before Investment Income	Cash Average Balance	Investment Income
			30.16%		0.83%			(7.0%)
2011	$—	$168,000	$(50,669)	$—	$—	$117,331	$58,666	$4,107
2012	121,438	—	—	(41,933)	(499)	79,006	100,222	7,016
2013	86,022	—	—	(36,691)	(354)	48,977	67,500	4,725
2014	53,702	—	—	(19,656)	(224)	33,822	43,762	3,063
2015	36,885	—	—	(15,725)	(166)	20,994	28,940	2,026
2016	23,020	—	—	(10,483)	(109)	12,428	17,724	1,241
2017	13,669	—	—	(6,552)	(42)	7,075	10,372	726
		$168,000	$(50,669)	$(131,040)	$(1,394)			$22,904

Total expected investment income for future years (2012–17) $18,797

Assumptions for Computation of Anticipated Investment Income

Assumptions are the same as used in the computation of anticipated investment income on all in force policies (example 1—exhibit 4) but based on unearned premiums and claims related to 2012 earned premiums.

Premium Deficiency Test Using Expected Investment Income Approach—Anticipated Investments Income Using Cash Flows Associated Only With the Unexpired Portion of the In Force Premium as of December 31, 2011
(Example 1B—Exhibit 2)
(Profitable Contracts)

Unearned premiums at December 31, 2011 (example 1A—exhibit 1)		$168,000
Less expected costs (undiscounted):		
Claims and claim adjustment expenses (example 1A—exhibit 1)	$131,040	
Maintenance costs (example 1B—exhibit 1)	1,394	
Unamortized policy acquisition costs (25% of unearned premiums)	42,000	
Subtotal		$174,434
Premium deficiency before expected investment income		(6,434)
Anticipated investment income (example 1B—exhibit 1)		18,797
Excess of income over costs		$12,363

The premium deficiency test performed using the expected investment income approach (anticipated investments income calculated using cash flows associated only with the unexpired portion of the in force premium) indicates an excess. Therefore, no provision for premium deficiency would be made as of December 31, 2011.

Example 1C—Discounting Approach Using Only the Unexpired Portion of the Contract

This exhibit calculates the present value as of December 31, 2011, of payments for claim costs, claim adjustment expenses, and maintenance costs related to the unearned premium.

Assumptions

- The 7 percent compound annual interest rate is the same as in example 1A—exhibit 4.
- The present value factor used is the average of the beginning of the year and end of the year factors to adjust for the payment of claims and maintenance costs evenly throughout the year.
- The expected claim costs and claim adjustment expenses are related to the 2012 earned premium from example 1A—exhibit 3.

Computation of Present Value (Discounting) of Claims and Maintenance Costs to Be Incurred
(Example 1C—Exhibit 1)

Payment Year	Claims Related to 2012 Earned Premium	Maintenance Costs	Total Claims and Maintenance Costs	Present Value Interest Factor	Present Value of Claims and Maintenance Costs
2012	$41,933	$1,046	$42,979	0.965	$41,475
2013	36,691	742	37,433	0.9018692	33,760
2014	19,656	469	20,125	0.8428684	16,963
2015	15,725	347	16,072	0.7877274	12,660
2016	10,483	228	10,711	0.7361939	7,885
2017	6,552	87	6,639	0.6880316	4,568
	$131,040	$2,919	$133,959	—	$117,311

Premium Deficiency Test Using Discounting Approach
(Example 1C—Exhibit 2)
as of December 31, 2011

Unearned premiums at December 31, 2011 (example 1A—exhibit 1)		$168,000
Less expected costs:		
Present value of claims and maintenance costs to be incurred (example 1C—exhibit 1)	$117,311	
Unamortized policy acquisition costs (25% of unearned premiums)	42,000	
Subtotal		159,311
Excess of income over costs		$8,689

AAG-PLI 3.97

The premium deficiency test performed using the discounted approach also indicates an excess with no provision for premium deficiency required as of December 31, 2011.

The expected investment income approach results in a larger sufficiency in this example because the discounting approach as shown in this example does not give credit for the investment income to be earned in the future on the portion of in force premium in excess of the amount needed to satisfy future claim payments.

The premium deficiency calculation for SAP would be the same as GAAP, except DAC would be excluded for SAP.

Premiums

Example 2A—Expected Investment Income Approach Using All Cash Flows From In Force Policies

The following is an example of a premium deficiency test using the expected investment income approach that results in a deficiency.

Assumptions

Assume all the same facts as in example 1; however,

- the loss and loss expense ratio is 88 percent instead of 78 percent assumed in the first example.
- expected investment income used in the premium deficiency calculation includes only positive investment income.

Anticipated Experience On Group of In Force Policies
(Example 2A—Exhibit 1)

	Earned on Unexpired	Unearned	In Force
Premium	$182,000	$168,000	$350,000
Actual loss and loss expense ratio	88%	—	—
Expected loss and loss expense ratio	—	88%	—
	$160,160	$147,840	$308,000

Settlement Pattern of Claims Related to In Force Policies
(Example 2A—Exhibit 2)

Payment Year	Claims Related to 2011 Earned Premium %	$	Claims Related to 2012 Earned Premium %	$	Claims Related to in Force Premium %	$
2011	32.0	51,251	—	—	16.6	51,251
2012	28.0	44,845	32.0	47,309	29.9	92,154
2013	15.0	24,024	28.0	41,395	21.2	65,419
2014	12.0	19,219	15.0	22,176	13.4	41,395
2015	8.0	12,813	12.0	17,741	9.9	30,554
2016	5.0	8,008	8.0	11,827	6.5	19,835
2017	—	—	5.0	7,392	2.5	7,392
	100.0	160,160	100.0	147,840	100.0	308,000

AAG-PLI 3.97

Computation of Expected Investment Income
(Example 2A—Exhibit 3)

Year	Cash Opening Balance	Premiums Received	Underwriting Costs Paid 30.16%	Claims	Maintenance Costs 0.83%	Cash Ending Balance Before Investment Income (1)	Cash Average Balance (1)	Investment Income (1) (7.0%)
2011	$—	$350,000	($105,560)	($51,251)	—	$193,189	$96,595	$6,762
2012	199,950	—	—	(92,154)	(1,046)	106,750	153,351	10,735
2013	117,489	—	—	(65,419)	(742)	51,327	84,406	5,908
2014	57,238	—	—	(41,395)	(469)	15,373	36,304	2,541
2015	17,916	—	—	(30,554)	(347)	(12,984)	2,465	173
2016	(12,811)	—	—	(19,835)	(228)	(32,874)	(22,843)	(1,599)
2017	(34,469)	—	—	(7,392)	(87)	(41,948)	(38,211)	(2,675)
		$350,000	($105,560)	($308,000)	($2,919)			$21,845
								$15,083

Total expected investment income for future years (2012–17)

(1) Expected investment income for future positive years only is $19,357 ($10,735 + $5,908 + $2,541 + $173).

Premium Deficiency Test Using Expected Investment Income Approach As of December 31, 2011
(Example 2A—Exhibit 4) (Unprofitable Contracts)

Unearned premiums at December 31, 2011 (example 2A—exhibit 1)		$168,000
Less expected costs (undiscounted):		
Claims and claim adjustment expenses (example 2A—exhibit 1)	$147,840	
Maintenance costs (example 2A—exhibit 3)	2,919	
Unamortized policy acquisition costs (25% of unearned premiums)	42,000	
Subtotal		192,759
Premium deficiency before expected investment income		(24,759)
Alternative 1: expected investment income, including all investment income (example 2A—exhibit 3)		15,083
Alternative 1: premium deficiency		(9,676)
Alternative 2: expected investment income, including only positive investment income (example 2A— exhibit 3)		19,357
Alternative 2: premium deficiency		($5,402)

Journal Entries

GAAP (Illustrating Alternative 1)

Debit amortization expense	$9,676
Credit DAC	$9,676

To Reduce DAC for Premium Deficiency

If the deficiency for GAAP exceeded unamortized DAC, then the entity would record the following entry for the amount that the premium deficiency exceeds DAC:

Debit provision for premium deficiency	$XXXX
Credit other liability	$XXXX

The location on the statement of income for the provision for premium deficiency would be an accounting policy decision that should be consistently applied.

SAP

In this example, no premium deficiency for SAP exists because the $42,000 of remaining unamortized acquisition costs for GAAP had already been expensed for SAP. Thus, under SAP, premium sufficiency is $32,324.

If there had been a premium deficiency for SAP, the following entry would occur to set up an aggregate write-in liability:

Debit provision for premium deficiency	$XXXX
Credit aggregate write-ins	$XXXX

Example 2B—Expected Investment Income Approach Using Investment Income That Is Determined Using Cash Flows Associated With Only the Unexpired Portion of the In Force Premium

Under this variation of the expected investment income approach, investment income is determined only on the cash flows associated with the unexpired portion of the in force premium and claims related to 2012 earned premiums, with the same changes in assumptions as example 2A.

Assume all the same facts as example 1B; however,

- the loss and loss expense ratio is 88 percent instead of 78 percent assumed in the first example.
- expected investment income used in the premium deficiency calculation includes only positive investment income.

Computation of Expected Investment Income
(Example 2B—Exhibit 1)

Year	Cash Opening Balance	Premiums Received	Underwriting Costs Paid 30.16%	Claims	Maintenance Costs 0.83%	Cash Ending Balance Before Investment Income	Cash Average Balance	Investment Income (7.0%)
2011	$—	$168,000	$(50,669)	$—	$—	$117,331	$58,666	$4,107
2012	121,438	—	—	(47,309)	(499)	73,630	95,481	6,684
2013	80,314	—	—	(41,395)	(354)	38,565	56,098	3,927
2014	42,492	—	—	(22,176)	(224)	20,092	29,328	2,053
2015	22,145	—	—	(17,741)	(166)	4,238	12,165	852
2016	5,090	—	—	(11,827)	(109)	(6,846)	17,724	(183)
2017	(7,029)	—	—	(7,392)	(42)	(14,463)	(10,655)	(746)
		$168,000	$(50,669)	$(147,840)	$(1,394)			$16,694
Total expected investment income for future years (2012–17)								$12,587

(1) Expected investment income for future positive years only is $13,516 ($6,684 + $3,927 + $2,053 + $852).

Premium Deficiency Test Using Expected Investment Income Approach as of December 31, 2011
(Example 2B—Exhibit 2) (Unprofitable Contracts)

Unearned premiums at December 31, 2011 (example 2A—exhibit 1)		$168,000
Less expected costs (undiscounted):		
Claims and claim adjustment expenses (example 2A—exhibit 1)	$147,840	
Maintenance costs (example 2B—exhibit 1)	1,394	
Unamortized policy acquisition costs (25% of unearned premiums)	42,000	
Subtotal		191,234
Premium deficiency before expected investment income		(23,234)
Alternative 1: expected investment income, including all investment income (example 2B—exhibit 1)		12,587
Alternative 1: premium deficiency		(10,647)
Alternative 2: expected investment income, including only positive investment income (example 2B— exhibit 1)		13,516
Alternative 2: premium deficiency		($9,718)

Journal Entries

GAAP (Illustrating Alternative 1)

Debit amortization expense	$10,647
Credit DAC	$10,647

To Reduce DAC for Premium Deficiency

If the deficiency for GAAP exceeded unamortized DAC, then the entity would record the following entry for the amount that the premium deficiency exceeds DAC:

Debit provision for premium deficiency	$XXXX
Credit other liability	$XXXX

The location on the statement of income for the provision for premium deficiency would be an accounting policy decision that should be consistently applied.

SAP

- In this example, no premium deficiency for SAP exists because the $42,000 of remaining unamortized acquisition costs for GAAP had already been expensed for SAP. Thus, under SAP, premium sufficiency is $31,353.

- If there had been a premium deficiency for SAP, the following entry would occur to set up an aggregate write-in liability:

Debit provision for premium deficiency $XXXX
Credit aggregate write-ins $XXXX

Example 2C—Discounting Approach Using Only the Unexpired Portion of the Contract

The following is an example of a premium deficiency test using the discounting approach that results in a deficiency.

Assume all the same facts as in example 1; however, the loss and loss expense ratio is 88 percent instead of 78 percent assumed in the first example.

Computation of Present Value (Discounting) of Claims and Maintenance Costs to Be Incurred

(Example 2C—Exhibit 1)

Payment Year	Claims Related to 2012 Unearned Premium (88%)	Maintenance Costs (0.83%)	Total Claims and Maintenance Costs	Present Value Interest Factor (7%)	Present Value of Claims and Maintenance Costs
2012	$47,309	$1,046	$48,355	0.9667	$46,745
2013	41,395	742	42,137	0.9035	38,071
2014	22,176	469	22,645	0.8444	19,121
2015	17,741	347	18,088	0.7891	14,273
2016	11,827	228	12,055	0.7375	8,891
2017	7,392	87	7,479	0.6893	5,155
	$147,840	$2,919	$150,759	—	$132,256

Premium Deficiency Test Using Discounting Approach as of December 31, 2011

(Example 2C—Exhibit 2)

Unearned premiums at December 31, 2011 (example 2A—exhibit 1)		$168,000
Less expected costs:		
Present value of claims and maintenance costs to be incurred (example 2C—exhibit 1)	$132,256	
Unamortized policy acquisition costs (25% of unearned premiums)	42,000	
Subtotal		174,256
Premium deficiency		($6,256)

Journal Entries

GAAP

Debit amortization expense	$6,256	
Credit DAC		$6,256

To Reduce DAC for Premium Deficiency

If the deficiency for GAAP exceeded unamortized DAC, then the entity would record the following entry for the amount that the premium deficiency exceeds DAC:

Debit provision for premium deficiency	$XXXX
Credit other liability	$XXXX

The location on the statement of income for the provision for premium deficiency would be an accounting policy decision that should be consistently applied.

SAP

In this example, no premium deficiency for SAP exists because the $42,000 of remaining unamortized acquisition costs for GAAP had already been expensed for SAP. Thus, under SAP, premium sufficiency is $35,744.

If there had been a premium deficiency for SAP, the following entry would occur to set up an aggregate write-in liability:

Debit provision for premium deficiency	$XXXX
Credit aggregate write-ins	$XXXX

Medicare Part D

3.98 The following paragraphs provide a high level overview of the Medicare Prescription Drug, Improvement, and Modernization Act of 2003 that established a new voluntary Medicare prescription drug program (Medicare Part D) for which benefits started January 1, 2006, for health care providers. This is applicable to property and casualty insurance entities that provide such programs. Medicare Part D products can either be offered by entities as a standalone product or included as a component of a Medicare Advantage plan. The underlying contract with the beneficiary in Medicare Part D programs generally provides health insurance (prescription drug) coverage for periods of one calendar year, with premiums adjustable annually.

3.99 After total costs paid by the enrollee, including the deductible, copays, and coinsurance under the initial coverage limit, exceed the out-of-pocket threshold, the enrollee is only responsible for a proportion (namely, the coinsurance percentage subject to a minimum copay) of any further drug costs. The regulations also permit a prescription drug plan (PDP) sponsor to offer enhanced alternative coverage in which at least one key aspect of the benefit design (deductible, cost sharing, or initial coverage limit) is richer than the standard plan. Such additional benefits are referred to as supplemental benefits in the regulations. The Centers for Medicare & Medicaid Services (CMS) will reimburse PDP sponsors for a percentage or amount of all claims above the out-of- pocket threshold. This reimbursement is known as the *reinsurance subsidy*. Further, the government provides a Low Income Cost Share (LICS) subsidy to participants that fall below a certain percentage of the poverty line. CMS will reimburse PDP sponsors for any cost sharing they pay on behalf of a Low Income Subsidy (LIS) member. To the extent that the PDP sponsor's adjusted allowable risk corridor costs vary in either direction from a target amount, risk sharing exists between the CMS and PDP sponsor. Many Medicare Part D plans have a benefit design that includes a coverage gap. When a member falls within this gap, the PDP sponsor generally provides little to no benefit. Beginning in 2011, drug manufacturers agreed to provide a discount to a member's qualifying brand drug costs for claims that are incurred while the member is within this gap. The claims are initially paid by the PDP sponsor until they are reimbursed by the manufacturer.

3.100 Medicare Part D is a complex arrangement that continues to evolve and includes the following components:

- Traditional insurance in the form of health insurance for prescription drugs
- Coinsurance, subject to a minimum copay, that represents the portion paid by the enrollee after other limits are met
- Cost sharing amounts for LIS members that are paid by the federal government
- Risk corridor payments to or from Medicare by the plan sponsor based on threshold limits
- Manufacturer discounts for claims that fall within the coverage gap
- Option for supplemental benefits related to an enhanced alternative coverage
- A late enrollment fee that is a penalty assessed to beneficiaries who enroll outside the normal enrollment windows

3.101 Those components determined to be insurance should be accounted for under FASB ASC 944, and other nonrisk premiums determined to be pass-throughs (that is, the reinsurance subsidy, the LICS subsidy, and the manufacturer discounts) that do not have any insurance risk should be accounted for as a deposit under FASB ASC 340. Two methods have been utilized in practice for accounting for the risk corridor payments:

- A retrospective refund arrangement under FASB ASC 944-605-25-14 based on the experience to date following a model based on accounting for multiple year, retrospectively rated insurance contracts under FASB ASC 944.
- A retrospective premium adjustment on a retrospectively rated contract in accordance with FASB ASC 944-605-25-2. This paragraph indicates that if the ultimate premium is reasonably estimable, the estimated ultimate premium shall be recognized as revenue over the period of the contract. Retrospective premiums should be estimated at the beginning of the plan year based upon actuarially determined models and adjustments should be made based upon revisions to those estimates in each reporting period. Retrospective premium adjustments estimated for the portion of the policy period that has expired shall be considered and immediately recorded as an adjustment to premium. FASB ASC 944-605-25- 2 also requires that if the ultimate premium cannot be reasonably estimated, the cost recovery method or deposit method may be used until the ultimate premium can be reasonably estimated.

3.102 The National Association of Insurance Commissioners Emerging Accounting Issues Working Group issued Interpretation 05-05, *Accounting for Revenues Under Medicare Part D Coverage*, to provide guidance to insurers on how to present various funds to be received under the Medicare Part D program. Interpretation 05-05 requires the application of existing SAP (SSAP No. 47, *Uninsured Plans*; No. 66; and No. 54, *Individual and Group Accident and Health Contracts*, depending upon the nature of the funds received).

Accounting for Contracts That Do Not Transfer Insurance Risk

Generally Accepted Accounting Principles

3.103 FASB ASC 340-30 provides guidance on how to account for insurance and reinsurance contracts that do not transfer insurance risk. As discussed in FASB ASC 340-30-05-2, the transfer of insurance risk requires transferring both timing risk and underwriting risk. FASB ASC 340-30 applies to all entities and all insurance and reinsurance contracts that do not transfer insurance risk, except long duration life and health insurance contracts. The method used to account for insurance and reinsurance contracts that do not transfer insurance risk is referred to as deposit accounting. FASB ASC 340-30 neither addresses when deposit accounting should be applied nor provides criteria to make that determination. This determination should be made on a case-by-case basis. FASB ASC 720-20-25-1 provides guidance on when deposit accounting should be applied to insurance and reinsurance contracts. The accounting by the insured and insurer are symmetrical, except as noted in FASB ASC 340-30-35-6 when contracts transfer only significant underwriting risk and if average rates are used as the discount rate for determining the deposit asset and liability. See further discussion of deposit accounting and risk transfer evaluation in chapter 6 of this guide.

Statutory Accounting Principles

3.104 Under SAP, guidance on accounting for contracts that do not transfer risk can be found in SSAP No. 52, *Deposit-Type Contracts*, which generally follows the same principles as GAAP. Structured settlements should be recorded consistently with the accounting provided for structured settlements in SSAP No. 65, *Property and Casualty Contracts*. Additional guidance can be found in SSAP No. 75, *Reinsurance Deposit Accounting—An Amendment to SSAP No. 62, Property and Casualty Reinsurance*. See further discussion of risk transfer evaluation and deposit accounting in chapter 6 of this guide.

Disclosure Considerations

3.105 Generally, for an operating insurance entity, premiums are significant to the entity's operations and will often result in significant balances and accounts reported in the entity's financial statements. These factors should be considered when evaluating disclosures required under FASB ASC 235-10-50-1, which requires disclosure of information about the accounting policies adopted by an entity. In addition, GAAP and SAP may specify disclosures that must be made, when relevant, related to premium, acquisition costs, and premium receivable.

Premium Revenue and Premium Adjustments

3.106 As required by FASB ASC 944-20-50-7, information should be disclosed that enables financial statement users to understand the factors affecting the present and future recognition and measurement of financial guarantee insurance contracts.

Premium Receivable

3.107 The financing and lending activities of insurance entities are included in FASB ASC 310-10-50, which sets out the following disclosure requirements, unless the trade receivables have payment terms of less than 12 months and arise from sales of insurance policies. Examples of insurance contract arrangements that may require disclosures under this guidance include insurance contracts with contract terms greater than 12 months or arrangements where premiums are withheld for a period greater than 12 months and receivables resulting from reinsurance agreements.

Entities should consider whether the following disclosures are applicable:

    a. Significant Accounting Policies as required in FASB ASC 310-10-50-2, 310-10-50-45-2, and 310-10-50-4

    b. Assets Serving as Collateral as required in FASB ASC 860-30-50-1A

    c. Nonaccrual and Past Due Financing Receivables as required in paragraphs 6, 7, and 7A of FASB ASC 310-10-50

    d. Accounting Policies for Off Balance Sheet Credit Exposures as required in FASB ASC 310-10-50-9, in addition to disclosures required by FASB ASC 450-20

    e. Foreclosed and Repossessed Assets as required in FASB ASC 310-10-50-11 and 310-10-45-3

    f. Accounting Policies for Credit Loss Related to Financing Receivables as required in FASB ASC 310-10-50-11B

    g. Impaired Loans as required in FASB ASC 310-10-5-14A

    h. Credit Quality Information as required by paragraphs 28 and 29 of FASB ASC 310-10-50

    i. Modifications as required by paragraphs 33 and 34 of FASB ASC 310-10-50

Financial Guarantee Insurance Contracts

3.108 For financial guarantee insurance contracts, FASB ASC 944-310-50-3 requires insurance entities to disclose the following for each annual and interim period:

    a. For financial guarantee insurance contracts where premiums are received as payments over the period of the contract, rather than at inception, all of the following:

        1. The premium receivable as of the date(s) of the statement of financial position and the line item in the statement of financial position where the amount is reported (if not presented separately)

        2. The unearned premium revenue as of the date(s) of the statement of financial position and the line item in the statement of financial position where the amount is reported (if not presented separately)

3. The amount of accretion on the premium receivable and the line item in the statement of income where that amount is reported (if not presented separately)

4. The weighted average risk free rate used to discount the premiums expected to be collected

5. The weighted average period of the premium receivable

b. A schedule of premiums expected to be collected related to the premium receivable detailing both of the following:

1. The four quarters of the subsequent annual period and each of the next four annual periods

2. The remaining periods aggregated in five year increments

c. A rollforward of the premium receivable for the period, including all of the following:

1. The beginning premium receivable

2. Premium payments received

3. New business written

4. Adjustments to the premium receivable, including all of the following:

    i. Adjustments for changes in the period of a financial guarantee insurance contract

    ii. An explanation of why the adjustments in item (c)(4)(i) occurred

    iii. Accretion of the premium receivable discount

    iv. Other adjustments with explanations provided

5. The ending premium receivable

Acquisition Costs

3.109 The following should be disclosed for DAC, as required by FASB ASC 944-30-50-1:

a. The nature and type of acquisition costs capitalized

b. The method of amortizing capitalized acquisition costs

c. The amount of acquisition costs amortized for the period

Contracts That Do Not Transfer Insurance Risk

3.110 Paragraphs 1–2 of FASB ASC 340-30-50 require the following disclosures:

a. Entities shall disclose a description of the contracts accounted for as deposits and the separate amounts of total deposit assets and total deposit liabilities reported in the statement of financial position

b. Insurance enterprises shall disclose the following information regarding the changes in the recorded amount of the deposit arising from an insurance or reinsurance contract that transfers only significant underwriting risk:

  i. The present values of initial expected recoveries that will be reimbursed under the insurance or reinsurance contracts that have been recorded as an adjustment to incurred losses

  ii. Any adjustments of amounts initially recognized for expected recoveries (the individual components of the adjustment [meaning, interest accrual, the present value of additional expected recoveries, and the present value of reductions in expected recoveries] should be disclosed separately)

  iii. The amortization expense attributable to the expiration of coverage provided under the contract

Auditing Premiums and Acquisition Costs

Audit Planning

3.111 In accordance with AU-C section 300, *Planning an Audit* (AICPA, *Professional Standards*), the auditor should plan the audit so that it is responsive to the assessment of the risks of material misstatement based on the auditor's understanding of the entity and its environment, including its internal control. The nature, timing, and extent of planning vary with the size and complexity of the entity and with the auditor's experience with the entity and understanding of the entity. Unless an insurance entity is a startup or in runoff, premiums will generally be significant to the financial statements and related disclosures. Refer to chapter 2, "Audit Considerations," for a detailed discussion of audit planning.

Consideration of Fraud in a Financial Statement Audit

3.112 Risks are inherent in all audit engagements, including the possibility that fraudulent acts may cause a material misstatement of financial statements. AU-C section 240, *Consideration of Fraud in a Financial Statement Audit* (AICPA, *Professional Standards*), addresses the auditor's responsibilities relating to fraud in an audit of financial statements. Because of the characteristics of fraud, the auditor's exercise of professional skepticism is important when considering the risk of material misstatement due to fraud. Readers should refer to additional discussion of AU-C section 240 in chapter 2 of this guide.

Audit Risk Factors—Premiums and DAC

3.113 As discussed in paragraph .A1 of AU-C section 320, *Materiality in Planning and Performing an Audit* (AICPA, *Professional Standards*), *audit risk* is the risk that the auditor expresses an inappropriate audit opinion when the financial statements are materially misstated. Audit risk is a function of the risks of material misstatement and detection risk. Materiality and audit risk are considered throughout the audit, in particular, when

  a. determining the nature and extent of risk assessment procedures to be performed;

b. identifying and assessing the risks of material misstatement;

   c. determining the nature, timing, and extent of further audit procedures; and

   d. evaluating the effect of uncorrected misstatements, if any, on the financial statements and in forming the opinion in the auditor's report.

3.114 Experience has demonstrated that audit risk may be greater in certain areas than in others. Significant transaction cycles of property and liability insurance entities include the premium cycle, the claims cycle, the reinsurance cycle, and the investment cycle. Risk factors specific to the premium cycle include, but are not limited to, the authorization and existence of policy or contract issuance, the completeness and accuracy of the premium earned, the existence and valuation of premium receivable, and the valuation of unearned premium, including premium deficiencies. Risk factors specific to acquisition costs include, but are not limited to, acquisition costs properly identified as costs that are related directly to the successful acquisition of new or renewal insurance contracts. These risk factors, internal control considerations, and examples of audit procedures for the insurance entity are discussed further herein.

3.115 Identification of significant accounts and disclosures by the auditor is part of the planning process. As required by AU-C section 315, *Understanding the Entity and Its Environment and Assessing the Risks of Material Misstatement* (AICPA, *Professional Standards*), to enable the auditor to understand the classes of transactions, account balances, and disclosures to be expected in the financial statements, the auditor should obtain an understanding of the relevant industry, regulatory, and other external factors, including the applicable financial reporting framework, and the nature of the entity.

3.116 Significant disclosures for the premium cycle include the accounting policy for premium recognition for the various types of insurance contracts as well as the accounting policy for contracts that are accounted for as deposits. Significant disclosures for acquisition costs include information about the nature and type of acquisition costs capitalized, the method of amortizing capitalized acquisition costs, and the amount of acquisition costs amortized for the period.

Management Estimates

3.117 When evaluating risk associated with management estimates, factors for consideration include the entity and its environment, management's historical estimation reliability, management bias, understanding of relevant controls, subjectivity in underlying assumptions, and any specific significant risks associated with estimates. AU-C section 540, *Auditing Accounting Estimates, Including Fair Value Accounting Estimates, and Related Disclosures* (AICPA, *Professional Standards*), requires that the auditor obtain an understanding of how management makes the accounting estimates and the data on which they are based. As discussed in paragraph .13 of AU-C section 540, the auditor may decide, based on the nature of the accounting estimate, to do one or more of the following:

- Develop a point estimate or range to evaluate management's point estimate

- Test the operating effectiveness of the controls over how management made the accounting estimate together with appropriate substantive procedures
- Test how management made the accounting estimate and the data on which it is based

3.118 The auditor may also decide to involve an expert. The auditor should evaluate whether the data relevant to the audit used by involved parties such as management, and, as applicable, management's internal or external specialist as well as the auditor's internal or external specialist, is sufficiently reliable, including determining whether the data is complete, accurate, and consistent. AU-C section 540 sets out guidance for the auditors when auditing estimates.

3.119 Certain premium accounts may include significant management estimates, such as the following:
- Premium adjustments (for example, on workers compensation policies), retrospectively rated premiums, or reporting form policies
- Commission adjustments (for example, profit commission or volume bonuses)
- Premium estimates on coverages for which the insurance company is contractually bound or for which coverage has been cancelled however have not yet been processed in the premium system
- Estimate of uncollectable premium receivable amounts

Risk of Material Misstatement—Inherent Risk Factors

3.120 As discussed in AU-C section 330, *Performing Audit Procedures in Response to Assessed Risks and Evaluating the Audit Evidence Obtained* (AICPA, *Professional Standards*), inherent risk is the likelihood of material misstatement due to the particular characteristics of the relevant class of transactions, account balance, or disclosure. As part of the auditor's assessment of inherent risk, the auditor may consider those factors related to premium revenue recognition, including factors relating to underwriting policies, distribution channels, management, premium billing and collection operations, and product line characteristics. Such factors might encompass the following:

a. The premium rates charged are significantly below the industry averages for similar kinds of products, or the analysis of contract pricing or profitability is inadequate.

b. Relationships of cash receipts to recorded premiums are inconsistent with the kind or volume of contracts written.

c. The insurance entity's product lines include experience rated insurance arrangements.

d. There are an increasing number of cancellations and reinstatements.

e. Changes in tax legislation affect the insurance entity's products.

f. Regulations affect the insurance entity's operations relative to its market conduct (for example, content of marketing material, licensing of sales force, and contract forms).

g. Regulation of capital capacity restricts the insurance entity's ability to write new business.

Premiums

    h. The requirements for the licensing of agents or other intermediaries are not adhered to or require changes to agent contracts.

    i. Reinsurance agreements have been revised and are becoming more complex, or reinsurance has become unavailable at the insurance entity's desired retention level or cost.

    j. New specialized products are introduced or rapid growth develops in previously limited product lines.

    k. Dependency on investment and similar contracts in which the fixed rate in the contract exceeds the rate of return on the related investments.

    l. Market trends indicate a saturated demand for the entity's product.

3.121 The auditor may also consider factors related to commissions, general expenses, and DAC, including factors relating to management, commission processing, cost allocation, and expense management. Such factors might encompass the following:

    a. Management's philosophy toward deferral and amortization of contract acquisition costs, evaluation of the kind of costs that are deferred (including product development costs), and tests for premium deficiencies are considered aggressive in comparison to the industry.

    b. Management tends to change its philosophy toward the deferral and amortization of contract acquisition costs from year to year.

    c. Commission rates are significantly above industry averages for similar products and distribution systems.

    d. The entity has changed distribution methods or compensation and incentive arrangements with agents and brokers.

    e. Requirements for licensing agents or other intermediaries are not adhered to or require changes in compensation contracts.

    f. Qualified actuaries are not used in the calculation of DAC balance, recoverability testing, or loss recognition evaluation.

Internal Control

3.122 Paragraph .04 of AU-C section 315 defines internal control as

> a process effected by those charged with governance, management, and other personnel that is designed to provide reasonable assurance about the achievement of the entity's objectives with regard to the reliability of financial reporting, effectiveness and efficiency of operations, and compliance with applicable laws and regulations. Internal control over safeguarding of assets against unauthorized acquisition, use, or disposition may include controls relating to financial reporting and operations objectives.

3.123 Internal control consists of the following five interrelated components:

    a. Control environment

    b. The entity's risk assessment process

c. The information system, including the related business processes relevant to financial reporting and communication

　　　d. Control activities relevant to the audit

　　　e. Monitoring of controls

3.124 AU-C section 315 requires the auditor to obtain an understanding of these components of the entity's internal control. Paragraphs 2.31–.41 of chapter 2 of this guide discuss in detail the components of internal control. This section will discuss certain components of a property and liability insurance entity's internal control as they relate to premiums and DAC.

Control Environment

3.125 The control environment comprises the collective effect of various factors on establishing, enhancing, or mitigating the effectiveness of specific control policies or procedures on the operations of the entity. As related to premium revenue recognition of a property and liability insurance entity, conditions that could impact the effectiveness of the control environment may include the following:

　　　a. There is a substantial increase in the volume of a particular product or a significant change in the mix of business that might adversely affect control design or operating effectiveness.

　　　b. Changes to the entity's financial or regulatory reporting requirements challenge the adequacy of the premium accounting system used by the insurance entity or third-party servicing agent and coordination with key processing systems.

　　　c. Increases in the suspense accounts or level of backlogs of premium transactions exists resulting in an excessive processing error rate.

　　　d. Whether operations are highly decentralized or have significant reliance on third parties or agents for customer correspondence, premium billing, and collection or are very centralized.

　　　e. The volume and complexity of premium transactions is increasing, raising questions about whether the staff is competent and experienced to handle it.

　　　f. New products or contracts are being written that require different revenue recognition policies or accounting procedures or that have unique processing requirements.

3.126 Such factors that relate to DAC transactions include the following:

　　　a. Whether the entity has accounting systems that provide sufficient detail to accurately identify deferrable costs and allocate costs to groups of contracts or lines of business

　　　b. Whether the entity periodically performs cost studies to validate allocation methodologies

　　　c. Whether the entity has sophisticated cost allocation systems in place to perform year-to-year comparisons of acquisition costs and other expenses by appropriate contract groupings or by line of business

　　　d. Whether there is excessive reliance on one individual for DAC calculations

Risk Assessment Process

3.127 As discussed in paragraphs .16–.18 of AU-C section 315, the auditor should obtain an understanding of whether the entity has a process for

    a. identifying business risks relevant to financial reporting objectives;

    b. estimating the significance of the risks;

    c. assessing the likelihood of their occurrence; and

    d. deciding about actions to address those risks.

3.128 The auditor should obtain an understanding of the entity's risk assessment process related to premiums and DAC and the results thereof. If the entity has not established such a process or has an ad hoc process, the auditor should discuss with management whether business risks relevant to financial reporting objectives have been identified and how they have been addressed. The auditor should evaluate whether the absence of a documented risk assessment process is appropriate in the circumstances or determine whether it represents a significant deficiency or material weakness in the entity's internal control.

Control Activities

3.129 Control activities are the policies and procedures that help ensure that management's directives are carried out and that necessary actions are taken to address risks to achieve the entity's objectives. The auditors should gain an understanding of those control activities the auditor deems necessary to assess the risks of material misstatement at the assertion level and design further audit procedures responsive to assessed risks, which may include, but are not limited to, the following:

    a. Premiums

- Principal lines of business written (property or liability, commercial or personal, and so on)
- Geographic, product, or other concentrations
- Rate-making environment and policies or practices
- Changes in product mix or emphasis
- Extent of retrospectively rated or reporting form business and the estimability and timeliness of retrospective revenue or expense determinations
- Unusual, erratic, or substantial changes in premiums in force
- Propriety of premium revenue recognition methods used
- Evidence or expectations of increased competition, market saturation, or declining demand
- Significant accounting procedures performed at other locations, such as branch offices versus the home office
- Principles and policies used by the entity in recognition of premiums
- Statistical coding and processing systems used to support underwriting functions

Property and Liability Insurance Entities

  b. Receivables

- Suspense account activity and condition (for example, large or old uncleared items or numerous outstanding debt and credit items)
- Agent statement terms and financing arrangements (for example, extended credit terms, expense supplements, loans, and profit sharing arrangements)
- Agency concentration (for example, significant volume from limited numbers of agents)
- Agency profitability (for example, derivation of substantial unprofitable business from particular agents)
- Nonadmitted asset trends (for example, sizable past due or unclear balances)
- Commission arrangements (for example, contingent commissions, or unusual commission structures that may encourage agent fraud)
- Agent binding authorities to accept underwriting risks or settle claims without prior approval
- Agent commingling of insurer or insured funds collected in a fiduciary capacity (for example, use of third-party funds for operating or personal purposes)
- Reasonableness of estimates for earned but unbilled premiums
- Adequacy of premium installment payments to provide sufficient protection in the event of policy cancellation

  c. Deferred policy acquisition costs

- Guidelines and systems are in place to identify costs directly related to the successful acquisition of new or renewal insurance contracts
- Nature of costs incurred and complexity in determining if such costs are deferrable
- Frequency and adequacy of recoverability (premium deficiency) tests, particularly regarding line of business groupings and estimated loss-ratio projections

Audit Procedures Responsive to the Assessed Risks of Material Misstatement

3.130 Risk assessment activities include determining the relevant assertions related to the significant accounts identified, determining the audit objectives, and assessing inherent risk of error of other significant risks (for example, nonroutine transactions or risk of fraud), and planning the involvement of others. As required by AU-C section 330, the auditor should design and perform further audit procedures whose nature, timing, and extent are based on, and are responsive to, the assessed risks of material misstatement at the relevant assertion level. The auditor should determine planned reliance on controls and the nature, timing, and extent of substantive testing, including whether the substantive evidence is planned from tests of details or substantive analytics.

3.131 If the auditor identifies a significant risk and is only performing substantive procedures, those procedures should include a test of details. If procedures to respond to the significant risk include both a test of controls and substantive procedures, the auditor may select substantive analytical procedures if the controls are operating effectively.

Considerations for Audits Performed in Accordance With PCAOB Standards

For audits performed in accordance with the Public Company Accounting Oversight Board's (PCAOB's) auditing standards for significant risks, paragraph 11 of Auditing Standard No. 13, *The Auditor's Responses to the Risks of Material Misstatement* (AICPA, *PCAOB Standards and Related Rules*, Auditing Standards), the auditor should perform substantive procedures, including tests of details, that are specifically responsive to the assessed risks.

Audit Consideration Chart

3.132 The auditor may consider the following specific audit objectives, examples of selected control activities, and auditing procedures in auditing account balances and classes of transactions related to premiums and acquisition costs. However, these are illustrative and auditors should develop tests that are appropriate to the risk of material misstatement in the circumstances of the engagement.

Audit Consideration Chart—Premiums and Deferred Acquisition Costs

Financial Statement Assertions	Audit Objectives	Examples of Selected Control Activities	Examples of Auditing Procedures
Existence and Authorization	• Premiums, commissions, and revenue and expense amounts recorded must relate to policies issued or in force during the period. • Issued insurance contracts are properly authorized.	• Unissued policy forms are physically controlled. • Policy applications are properly registered. • System configuration and access controls. • Documented binding or underwriting authorities are verified prior to contract issuance and processing.	• Confirmation of policy and premium • Obtain evidence about proper issuance by — checking policy file for signed application and underwriting approval. — tracing to master file data such as policy number, name, effective date, kind of policy, coverage limits, premium, payment mode, and agent. — comparing premiums to cash receipts records. • Check daily reports for underwriting approval, calculation of premiums and commissions, and proper recording of premium payments. • Reconcile premiums and commissions to agents' reports. • Trace selected premiums transactions to premium register to check that policy terms, lines of business, and

AAG-PLI 3.132

Premiums

Financial Statement Assertions	Audit Objectives	Examples of Selected Control Activities	Examples of Auditing Procedures
			• premium amounts have been properly recorded.
			• Reconcile monthly summary of premiums written direct, assumed, and ceded and related commission with general ledger.
			• Test that agents submitting applications are licensed, and inspect agency agreements.
	• Recorded deferred acquisition costs (DAC) balances related to successful efforts represent actual costs that meet the entity's criteria for deferral.	• Changes in agents' contracts and reinsurance agreements that may affect commissions are reviewed for any adjustments that may be required in deferral calculations. Any related adjustments are approved by appropriate personnel.	• Test contract master file data used to calculate DAC balances, contract type, payment mode, issue date, and current status of contract). Test that transactions are correctly recorded in the in force files.
			• Review and test time or cost studies or other analyses related to determining successful efforts.
			• Review the company's process for how commissions and bonuses are paid across various distribution channels, and what are the structures for different employees.
			• Review company's assumptions for successful efforts factor.

(continued)

AAG-PLI 3.132

Financial Statement Assertions	Audit Objectives	Examples of Selected Control Activities	Examples of Auditing Procedures
Completeness	• Premium amounts include premiums from all policies and are accurately compiled.	• Policies are recorded on a timely basis in the detail policy records, and records are reviewed for recording of all policy numbers. • Guidelines are established for coding policies, and coding is reviewed for accuracy. • Input, output, and data center controls are maintained to ensure that all changes to detail policy records are processed properly.	• Test that premiums are recorded as described previously. • Assess control over policy forms and policy issuance by — testing whether policies supplied to agents are promptly entered on policy control records. — inspecting policy numbers issued and testing procedures for investigation of missing numbers. — reconciling policy allotment register to underwriting reports of new business. — testing whether daily reports are recorded before filing.
			• Check calculation of premiums to premium rate tables.
			• Compare ratios of commissions to premiums written with ratios of prior years, and investigate significant fluctuations.
	• Agents' balances include all amounts due to or from agents as of balance sheet date.	• Amounts included in commission calculations are reconciled to premiums written.	• Test that premiums and commissions are recorded as described earlier.

AAG-PLI 3.132

Premiums 169

Financial Statement Assertions	Audit Objectives	Examples of Selected Control Activities	Examples of Auditing Procedures
Rights and Obligations	• Return premiums, policyholder dividends, and retroactive premium adjustments are properly recorded.	• Detailed agent's accounts are reconciled to the general ledger. • Policy endorsements and cancellations or other changes are approved; determinations of additional or return premiums are also reviewed. • Policyholder dividends, retrospective premiums, and experience rated premiums are reviewed and approved. • Premium adjustments are compared with policy provisions, and dividends are compared with dividend declaration for compliance.	• Trace selected commission rates to commission schedules. • Test the propriety of return premiums by inspecting evidence of cancellation on policy face and by obtaining evidence about adherence to entity policy regarding cancellation method. • Test that policyholder dividends comply with authorization, and reconcile amounts with underlying policy records. • Inspect transactions on periodic reporting policies to test whether periodic reports are received according to terms of policies, audits required by policies are performed, and premium deposits and additional or return premiums are properly calculated and recorded. • Inspect premiums recorded for retrospectively rated policies to test whether entity procedures and policy terms have been followed in determining premiums and whether claims data have

(continued)

Financial Statement Assertions	Audit Objectives	Examples of Selected Control Activities	Examples of Auditing Procedures
		• Premium and loss data underlying calculations are reconciled to the records, and calculations are reviewed and approved.	been included in the calculations.
	• Reinsured policies are properly identified, and premiums on ceded reinsurance are properly recorded and reported to assuming entities.	• Risks covered by reinsurance agreements are identified, properly designated, recorded in the premium billing and in force files, and reported to the assuming entity.	• Test whether risks in excess of retention amounts are reinsured. • Test computation of reinsurance premiums and commissions; trace to reinsurance records. • Trace information from premium records to reports sent to reinsurers. • Test the propriety of reinsurance balances payable by reference to reinsurance agreements and policy records.
Valuation or Allocation	• Premium revenues and unearned premium reserve are recorded properly.	• Premium register is balanced periodically to update premiums in force. • Premiums written are recorded in the general ledger and are reconciled periodically to premiums entered in statistical records and the premium register	• Inquire about the method for recognizing premium revenue and determining unearned premium reserves; check consistency of its application with prior years. • Inspect recording of unearned premium reserves by reconciling additions and deletions in force for selected periods back

Financial Statement Assertions	Audit Objectives	Examples of Selected Control Activities	Examples of Auditing Procedures
		• Return premiums are reviewed for reasonableness by comparison to original premiums.	to original documentation and by checking calculation of unearned premiums. • Test that the unearned premium reserves are correctly reduced for ceded insurance.
	• Uncollectible agents' balances are identified and accounted for.	• Agents' balances are periodically aged in conformity with statutory requirements. • Delinquent accounts are investigated and write-offs of bad debts and unreconciled items are approved. • Advances to agents are approved in accordance with entity procedures. • Statements of transactions and balances are periodically sent to agents.	• Compare aged trial balance of agent's balances with similar trial balances of previous periods, and investigate significant fluctuations. • Test collectability by inspecting subsequent collections or by inspecting history of receipts. • Evaluate the adequacy of the allowance for doubtful accounts, including suspense items. • Test whether agents' balances considered to be nonadmitted assets were properly excluded from the statutory statements and included in the generally accepted accounting principles (GAAP) statements only to the extent deemed collectible.

(continued)

Financial Statement Assertions	Audit Objectives	Examples of Selected Control Activities	Examples of Auditing Procedures
	• Acquisition costs are properly capitalized, amortized and are recoverable.	• Acquisition costs are capitalized in accordance with accounting policy based. • Amortization of deferred costs is compared for consistency with premium recognition.	• Inspect documentation of procedures for recording acquisition costs. • Inspect the support for DAC. • Test whether acquisition costs are properly capitalized and amortized on a consistent basis. Also test whether the balance at year-end is reasonably expected to be recovered.

Chapter 4*

The Loss Reserving and Claims Cycle

Introduction

4.01 Property and liability insurance contracts are generally agreements that provide protection against damage or loss of property caused by various perils, such as fire and theft, as well as the legal liability resulting from injuries to persons or damage to property in exchange for premiums or other considerations. The liability for unpaid losses and loss and claim adjustment expenses (herein referred to as reserves) is accrued when insured events occur based on the estimated ultimate cost of settling the claims or losses associated with those contracts. *Reserves* are management's best estimate of those amounts incurred yet unpaid. Reserve estimates should include the effects of inflation and other social and economic factors, as well as estimated recoveries from salvage and subrogation, which are deducted from the reserve estimate. A reserve for loss adjustment expenses (LAEs) expected to be incurred in the settlement of unpaid claims should be accrued when the related loss reserve is accrued. These concepts are further discussed in paragraph 4.74. Throughout this guide, the term *reserves* is used in discussions of generally accepted accounting principles (GAAP) and statutory accounting principles (SAP).

4.02 An insurance entity's claims department accepts, investigates, adjusts, and settles claims that are reported by or against policyholders. This process includes the notification of the claim, determining whether the loss is covered under an active insurance policy, gathering and investigating information about the loss, and paying or denying the claim. Insurance entities generally use claims adjusters, who may be employees of the insurance entities or agents, to investigate claims. Insurance entities may also use outside organizations to adjust claims.

Types of Businesses and Their Effect on the Estimation Process

4.03 The reporting and payment characteristics of an entity's losses will differ depending on the types of policies written. Insurance policies may be categorized in several different ways:

- By policy duration (short duration or long duration)
- By the type of coverage provided (occurrence basis or claims-made basis)
- By the kind of insurance underwritten—in this chapter, the terms *line of business* and *type of risk* are used interchangeably to mean the kind of insurance underwritten (for example, property, liability, workers' compensation, and assumed reinsurance)

---

* Refer to the preface of this guide for important information about the applicability of the professional standards to audits of issuers and nonissuers (see the definition of each in the preface). As applicable, this chapter contains dual referencing to both the AICPA's and the Public Company Accounting Oversight Board's professional standards.

Policy Duration

4.04 Insurance policies are considered to be either short duration or long duration. Policies are considered short duration when the contract provides insurance coverage for a fixed period of short duration, generally one year or less, and allows the insurer to either not renew the contract or to adjust future provisions of the contract at the end of the contract period. Certain policies are considered to be short duration policies, even though they have a duration of more than one year (for a discussion of these types of policies, see chapter 3, "Premiums," of this guide). Policies are considered long duration when the contract provides insurance coverage for an extended period and is not generally subject to unilateral changes in its provisions. Because most policies written by property and liability insurance entities are short duration policies, only short duration reserving considerations are discussed in this chapter.

Type of Coverage

4.05 Property and liability insurance policies are issued on either an occurrence basis or a claims-made basis. Occurrence basis policies provide coverage for insured events occurring during the contract period, regardless of the length of time that passes between the loss event and when the insurance entity is notified of the claim. Under occurrence basis policies, claims may be filed months or years after the policy contract has expired, making it difficult to estimate the eventual number of claims that will be reported. A pure claims-made policy typically only covers claims reported to the insurer during the contract period, regardless of when the loss event occurred. In practice, claims-made policies generally cover claims reported to either the insurer or insured during the contract period. In some cases, the claims-made policy may exclude certain claims reported to the insurer during the contract period that occurred before a stated date. Even if claims have been reported to the insurer during the contract period, it may take several months for the insurer to investigate and establish a case-basis reserve for reported claims. In addition, some claims-made claims may be reported to the insurer after the contract expires. In practice, most claims-made insurance policies contain extended reporting clauses or endorsements that provide for coverage, in specified circumstances, of claims occurring during the contract period but reported after the expiration of the policy. In many states, a claims-made insurance policy is required to (*a*) contain an extended reporting clause; (*b*) provide for the purchase, at the policyholder's option, of tail coverage (that is, coverage for events occurring during the policy term but reported after the initial policy expires); or (*c*) provide for automatic tail coverage upon the death, disability, or retirement of the insured. Thus, in practice, certain claims-made policies may resemble occurrence basis policies.

Kind of Insurance Underwritten: Line of Business or Type of Risk

4.06 The kind of insurance underwritten by property and liability insurance entities typically includes property, liability, workers' compensation, surety, and fidelity. Other examples of business written by property and liability entities include credit, accident, and health and guaranty insurance.

4.07 Lines of insurance can be further classified as primary coverage or reinsurance assumed. Primary coverage involves policies written between an insurer and a customer directly. Reinsurance coverage involves the transfer of the insurer's risk to a reinsurer (see chapter 6, "Reinsurance," of this guide).

Retrocession (sometimes also called reinsurance of reinsurance) involves the further transfer of the reinsurer's risk to a retrocessionaire (sometimes called a reinsurer).

4.08 Excess claims are those in which another insurer or the insured pays a significant portion of the claim amount (called a retention) before the insurance protection responds. Retentions can be thousands of dollars or millions of dollars, depending on the situation. Policies with a large retention or deductible that is the responsibility of the insured are referred to as high deductible policies. For these types of policies, the policyholder is typically responsible for reimbursing the insurer for claim payments made up to the deductible level. The insurance entity provides coverage for the claims over the deductible level and may service the claims, although a third-party administrator is sometimes utilized in servicing claims. These types of policies have premiums that are less than traditional coverage because the insured shares in the risk. When the insurance entity is ultimately obligated to pay all claims and recover from the insured for claims paid below the retention level, the insurance entity is subject to credit risk until the deductible is reached. However, such credit risk is typically mitigated by various forms of collateral. High deductible policies are typically sold in commercial markets (workers' compensation and health insurance) and are sold in two forms: per occurrence and aggregate coverage. On a high deductible per occurrence policy, the deductible is applied to each loss event and the insured is generally responsible for reimbursing the insurance entity for losses on each claim up to a predefined level.

4.09 Property claims generally are reported and settled quickly, often within several months. Some exceptions to this general rule may include business interruption insurance and ocean marine insurance. Property claims are usually first-party claims (that is, they are direct obligations of the insurer to pay the insured, with the claimant being the policyholder). In addition, the occurrence and extent of property losses are often relatively easy to determine because the claims relate to tangible property. However, insurance entities may set up reserves in addition to case reserves in order to reflect projected deficiencies or adverse development on existing case reserves when case reserves are not easily determinable. See the discussion on components of loss reserves in paragraph 4.33.

4.10 Liability claims are reported more slowly than property claims and settlement is often delayed, especially if litigation is involved. *Liability claims* are third-party claims in which the insurer has agreed to pay, defend, or settle claims made by third parties against the insured. A single insured event may result in several claimants. In processing a liability claim, many insurance entities keep a single file for each insured event, with separate identification of each claimant.

4.11 Workers' compensation claims are reported quickly but often take many years to settle. The amount of most claim payments is set by law and may change during the life of a claim. A claim settlement is characterized by numerous payments to the claimants or survivors for medical expenses and loss of earnings, possibly over extended periods of time.

4.12 In some instances, surety or fidelity claims may be reported and settled very slowly because the loss may be discovered months or years after it has occurred. Also, determining the extent of the loss often takes a long time. Financial guarantee insurance has become a significant insured risk to some commercial entities. Financial guarantees include the guaranteeing of interest and principal payments on corporate and municipal debt, the guaranteeing of limited partnership obligations, and a number of other products in which the insurance entity takes on an obligation to pay at some later date. The ultimate exposure to a large loss can be high with financial guarantees. Financial Accounting Standards Board (FASB) *Accounting Standards Codification* (ASC) 944, *Financial Services—Insurance*, clarifies the accounting for financial guarantee insurance contracts, including the recognition and measurement to be used to account for premium revenue and claim liabilities.

4.13 Some lines of insurance are commonly referred to as long tail lines because of the extended time required before claims are ultimately settled. Examples of long tail lines are automobile bodily injury liability, workers' compensation, professional liability, and other lines, such as products and umbrella liability coverages. Some lines are long tail because the claim may take a long time to be reported (for example, professional liability), and others may take a long time to pay out (for example, workers' compensation). It is generally more difficult to estimate loss reserves for long tail lines because of the long period of time that elapses between the occurrence of a claim and its final disposition, as well as the difficulty of estimating the ultimate settlement value of the claim.

4.14 Lines of insurance in which claims are settled relatively quickly are called short tail lines. Examples of short tail lines are automobile physical damage and property coverages.

The Transaction Cycle

4.15 Although specific procedures vary from entity to entity, a common pattern exists to the flow of transactions through the claims cycle, which consists of the following major functions: claim acceptance and processing, claim adjustment and estimation, and claim settlement. The insurance entity typically uses a computer application (herein referred to as the claim system) to store claim data, process claim information, and assist in the claim estimation process, as described subsequently. Also shown is a flowchart exhibiting a typical claims cycle transaction.

The Loss Reserving and Claims Cycle

Claim Process Flowchart

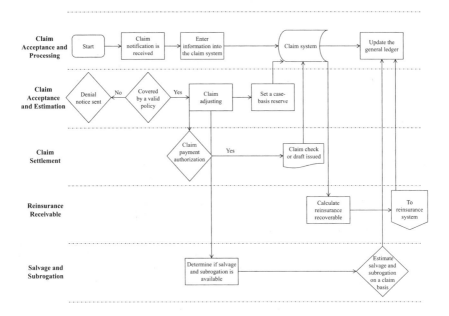

Claim Acceptance and Processing

4.16 Notice of a loss or an accident is received at the home or branch office directly from the insured or through an agent. A file number for the claim, which forms the basis for all future references, is assigned to the case, usually in numerical sequence, and a loss file and abstract are prepared. Typically, information relating to the claim is retained electronically by the insurance entity in the claim system. Policy coverage is examined to determine whether the loss is covered by an insurance policy and whether the policy was in force at the time the loss occurred. Failure to raise questions promptly may be prejudicial to an entity's rights. If it is determined that the claim is covered, the case is assigned to an adjuster. Some insurance entities establish a diary file instead of a claim file when a notice of an incident is received and when the entity is not certain that the facts require it to establish a claim file and record an estimate. For example, an insured under a liability policy may report an injury, but the injury is not expected to result in a claim.

4.17 Claim data is typically entered into the insurance entity's claim system for later use in the development of statistics used for reserve analysis. Coding of claims data is important because errors in coding data directly affect the reliability of information used to monitor historical claims experience, which may be used by the entity and auditor to evaluate the adequacy of loss reserves. Among the most important dates that might affect loss reserve developments are the accident date, policy effective date, claim report date (date reported to the entity), claim record date (date the claim is entered on the entity's claim system), claim payment date, and claim reopening date (a claim may be closed and later reopened for additional payments). Other key claim data must be properly coded, so that insurance entities can accurately meet the statutory reporting requirements of the annual statement and provide statistical information to support rate filings, including the claim state, location of risk, date of loss, and policy year.

4.18 Smaller claims or claims that are expected to be settled quickly are processed by less extensive adjudication methods. Usually, a claim file is not prepared, and a separate reserve estimate is not recorded. All statistical and accounting matters are processed on the date of payment and average reserve estimation methods are used between the report and settlement dates.

Claim Adjustment and Estimation

4.19 The process of adjusting claims involves (*a*) a field investigation; (*b*) an appraisal and a negotiation of the claim, subject to the appropriate supervision; and (*c*) approval by the entity's claims department. Through an investigation, the adjuster determines, among other things, whether the claimed loss actually occurred, his or her estimate of the amount of the loss, whether the loss may be excludable under the terms of the policy, and whether the entity has a right to recover part or all of the loss through either salvage or subrogation. *Salvage* is a contractual right of recovery that entitles the insurer to any proceeds from the disposal of damaged property for which the claim has been paid, such as the sale of a wrecked automobile to a junkyard. *Subrogation* is the legal right of the insurer to recover from a third-party who may be wholly or partly responsible for the loss paid under the terms of the policy, such as recovery from a product manufacturer for a loss resulting from the failure of a product.

4.20 Insurance entities use several different processes to adjust claims. Companies may use home or branch office adjusters, who are salaried employees of the entity, or independent adjusters, who charge fees for their investigation and adjustment services. Most insurance entities use a combination of methods to adjust claims. They may have a claim branch office established for closer supervision and better control of the cost of adjustments in territories in which they have a larger concentration of risks.

4.21 In accordance with an entity's claims settlement policy, an adjuster estimates the total expected amount that is payable on a claim as soon as it is practicable. Such an estimate may be determined by the average cost per case based on experience for the line of business or may be based on specific information on the individual case. The estimate is revised in response to changes in experience or as investigations progress and further information is received.

4.22 Insurance entities have different approaches to establishing reserves on individual claim files. For some insurance entities, the case-basis reserve represents the amount that the entity would pay as a settlement based on the facts in the file at that time. Case-basis reserves based on that approach, in the aggregate, tend to be inadequate to pay the ultimate cost of the reported claims. For other insurance entities, the claim reserve represents a worst case view of the injury and the liability or coverage issues presented by the case. Reserves based on this approach, in the aggregate, tend to exceed the ultimate cost of the reported claims.

4.23 For most insurance entities, the philosophy intended for individual claim reserving falls between the examples previously described. For purposes of establishing an appropriate financial statement reserve, the most important factors to consider are (*a*) the historical adequacy or inadequacy of total reserves, (b) the consistency in the reserving approach followed by the entity, and (c) the availability of an actuarial or a statistical analysis of reserves.

4.24 Unpredictably high jury awards; malpractice claims; bad faith claims; and the proliferation of mass tort and latent injury claims, such as those for injuries caused by pollution and asbestos, have complicated the claim estimation process. Mass tort and latent injury claims have affected insurance entities indirectly through their participation in pools and associations (for example, the significant reserves that the industry had to provide for workers' compensation injury claims). The complexity of such claims requires a higher level of claims review process. Most insurance entities now use a variety of higher level reviews, such as those by claims committees and in-house counsel, to specifically review and set loss reserves for mass tort and latent injury claims. Due to the high level of sensitivity surrounding bad faith claim cases, these claims also are often subject to a higher level of internal review.

Claim Settlement

4.25 Once all documentation, such as proof of loss, medical bills, repair bills, or invoices for fees of independent adjusters or lawyers, has been received, this information is reviewed for accuracy, consistency, and coverage under the associated policy before payment is authorized. Once all proper claim documentation is obtained and reviewed, authorization is documented within the insurance entity's claim system by the proper level of claim adjuster.

4.26 Methods of payment vary among insurance entities, generally either by check or draft. Once the claim has been approved for payment, the claim system may automatically generate the claim check or draft, or the approved documents may be electronically forwarded to the claim payment department for draft or check preparation. In many insurance entities, authority to issue drafts may be given to field offices, adjusters, and sometimes agents; in those cases, copies of the drafts and related supporting documents are forwarded to the claims department and these supporting documents are typically scanned and electronically filed in the insurance entity's claim system.

4.27 Some insurance entities record claims paid when checks or drafts are issued, and other insurance entities record claims paid when the drafts clear the bank because that is when the claimant has accepted the settlement offer and the entity's obligation for the claim is extinguished. Source records are sent to the claim system, usually in electronic control total batches, and totals of paid losses are posted to the general ledger. Changes in payment procedures or changes in the definition of payment date for coding purposes can affect loss reserve developments depending on when payments (checks or drafts) are recorded as a paid loss.

4.28 In the case of large claims, insurance entities sometimes enter into an agreement to pay the claimant in installments over an established period of time. This arrangement is referred to as a structured settlement. Often, these settlements are funded by the purchase of an annuity contract. Structured settlements funded by annuity contracts allow insurance entities to pay the present value of the ultimate claim amount immediately but, depending on who remains the primary obligor, may not allow the related reserve to be removed from the financial statements. Structured settlements are more commonly used in workers' compensation and commercial casualty lines of insurance.

Reinsurance Receivable

4.29 After the claim is entered into the claim system, the system will often automatically determine whether any right of recovery exists for that particular claim under a reinsurance agreement, based on predefined reinsurance levels coded into the claim system. When the reinsurance recovery details are not incorporated into the claim system, the determination may be performed by the claim adjuster or reinsurance department. If the entity purchases reinsurance coverage over a group of claims, any potential recovery generally has to be determined outside of the claim system, such as in the case of excess reinsurance contracts. Recoveries under quota-share reinsurance agreements are usually based on total claims figures period by period. Reinsurance arrangements on liability policies may include provisions such that if aggregate claims from a common occurrence exceed the retention, then the excess amounts are covered by the reinsurer. Recoveries under such aggregate excess reinsurance treaties are coded similarly to catastrophe claims (see chapter 6 for a further discussion about reinsurance contracts).

4.30 When it is determined that there will be a reinsurance receivable on a claim, the estimated amount receivable is usually recorded in the claim file and data processing records. Notices of losses are sent to the reinsurers in accordance with the terms of the reinsurance contracts. Although some reinsurance contracts contain provisions for immediate recovery for losses over a stated amount, recoveries are normally settled monthly or quarterly, sometimes by being deducted from the premiums due to the reinsurers.

Salvage and Subrogation

4.31 Whenever an entity incurs a claim, the possibility of salvage or subrogation may exist. As noted in FASB ASC 944-40-30-2, estimated recoveries on unsettled claims, such as salvage, subrogation, or a potential ownership interest in real estate, shall be evaluated in terms of their estimated realizable value and deducted from the liability for unpaid claims. Generally, the simplest approach to determining the anticipated receivable is to estimate loss reserves using loss data that is net of salvage and subrogation recoveries. Many of the reserving methods for losses and loss-adjustment expenses, however, can also be used to estimate salvage and subrogation recoveries.

4.32 Under SAP, as discussed in paragraph 26 of Statement of Statutory Accounting Principles (SSAP) No. 65, *Property and Casualty Contracts*, "[t]he projected losses and expenses may be reduced for expected salvage and subrogation recoveries, but may not be reduced for anticipated deductible recoveries, unless the deductibles are secured by a letter of credit (LOC) or like security." Any reduction in the liability for unpaid claims and losses for estimated anticipated recoveries on salvage and subrogation should be disclosed, as noted in paragraph 14(G) of SSAP No. 55, *Unpaid Claims, Losses, and Loss Adjustment Expenses*, and would be considered an accounting policy decision.

Components of Loss Reserves

4.33 *Loss reserves* are an insurer's estimate of its liability for the unpaid costs of insured events that have occurred. All insurance entities develop reserves for known claims on a case basis and also for the estimated cost to settle claims on insured events that occurred but were not yet reported to the insurance entity. The basic components of loss reserves or liability for unpaid claims consist of the following:

- *Case-basis reserves.* The sum of the values assigned by claims adjusters at the insurance entity to specific claims that have been reported to, and were recorded by, the insurance entity but not yet paid at the financial statement date.

- *Incurred but not reported (IBNR).* The estimated cost to settle claims arising from insured events that occurred but were not reported to the insurance entity as of the financial statement date.

    Generally, loss reserves also include a component for case development reserves that is the difference between the case-basis reserves and estimated ultimate cost of such recorded claims. This component recognizes that case-basis reserves, which are estimates based on preliminary data, will probably differ from ultimate settlement amounts. Accordingly, a summation of case-basis reserve estimates may not produce the most reasonable estimate of their ultimate cost. Depending on the insurance entity's process, this additional reserve may be specifically identified as additional case reserves or incorporated into the IBNR component. Frequently, loss reserves are reduced for salvage and subrogation, as discussed in paragraphs 4.19 and 4.31–.32.

    Some insurance entities may elect to pay claims by draft rather than by check and may not record the drafts as cash disbursed until the drafts are presented to the insurer by the bank. A liability for drafts outstanding is required only if cash disbursements and claim statistical information is not recorded concurrently, thereby creating a timing difference. Because the claim statistical information is updated to reflect the payment, no loss reserve is recorded for the claim; however, because the draft has not been presented, a draft's outstanding liability is required. In some cases, a liability for drafts outstanding is presented separately from loss reserves.

- *Reserves for LAE.* These represent expected payments for costs to be incurred in connection with the adjustment and recording of losses and commonly do not include allocated general overhead costs that will be incurred to run the business. Additional discussion on LAE can be found in paragraphs 4.54–.62.

Estimating Methods

4.34 Various analytical techniques are typically used by management or consulting actuaries in estimating and evaluating the reasonableness of loss reserves. These techniques generally consist of statistical analyses of historical information and result in estimates that may be referred to as loss reserve estimates.

4.35 Loss reserve projections are used to develop loss reserve estimates. Understanding and assessing the variability of these estimates and the reliability of historical experience as an indicator of future loss payments require a careful analysis of the historical loss data and the use of projection methods that are sensitive to the particular circumstances.

4.36 Loss reserve estimates are developed on a gross and net of reinsurance basis to enable insurance entities to report on both a GAAP (reported gross of reinsurance) and SAP (reported net of reinsurance) basis. Generally the same projection methods are used to estimate both gross and net loss reserves; gross reserve estimates are developed using data gross of reinsurance and net reserve estimates are developed using data net of reinsurance. However, some insurance entities may initially develop loss reserve estimates on a net of reinsurance basis and then gross up these estimates using more simplified assumptions in order to approximate gross reserves. In general, it is more appropriate for insurance entities to estimate gross and net reserves separately because this will enhance their ability to more effectively monitor the impact of reinsurance programs on the reserves estimates for more complex reinsurance structures.

4.37 The data used for projections is generally grouped by line of business and may be further classified by attributes such as geographic location, underwriting class, or type of coverage to improve the homogeneity of the data within each group. The data is then arranged chronologically. The following are dates that are key to classifying the chronology of the data:

- *Policy date.* The date on which the contract becomes effective (sometimes referred to as the underwriting date).
- *Accident date.* The date on which the accident (or loss) occurs.
- *Report date.* The date on which the entity first receives notice of the claim.
- *Record date.* The date on which the entity records the claim in its statistical system.
- *Closing date.* The date on which the claim is closed.

4.38 After the data has been grouped by line of business and chronology, it may then be arrayed to facilitate the analysis of the data, highlight trends, and permit ready extrapolation of the data. The following are examples of types of data that are commonly arrayed and analyzed:

- Losses paid
- Losses incurred
- Case-basis reserves
- Claim units reported
- Claim units paid
- Claim units closed
- Claim units outstanding
- Defense and cost containment (DCC) paid
- DCC outstanding
- Salvage and subrogation recovered
- Reinsurance recovered
- Reinsurance receivable
- Premiums earned
- Premiums in force
- Exposures earned
- Insured amounts
- Policy limits
- Policies in force

The Loss Reserving and Claims Cycle

4.39 The loss data may be cumulative or incremental, gross or net of reinsurance, gross or net of salvage and subrogation, or sometimes combined with DCC data. The data may be stratified by size of loss or other criteria. Because claim data and characteristics such as dates, type of loss, and claim counts significantly affect reserve estimation, controls should be established over the recording, classification, and accumulation of historical data used in the determination of loss reserves.

4.40 Loss reserve projections can be performed using a variety of mathematical approaches ranging from simple arithmetic projections using loss development factors to complex statistical models. Projection methods basically fall into three categories:

- Extrapolation of historical loss dollars
- Projection of separate frequency and severity data (the number of claims that will be paid or closed and the average costs of these claims)
- Use of expected loss ratios

4.41 Within each of these methods, a variety of techniques and loss data may be used; some methods also combine features of these basic methods. No single projection method is inherently better than any other in all circumstances.

4.42 The following is a brief summary of some commonly used projection methods:

Method	Basis
Loss extrapolation	
Paid loss	Uses only paid losses. Case-basis reserves are not considered.
Incurred loss	Uses paid losses plus case-basis reserves.
Average severities	Uses various claim count and average cost per claim data on either a paid or an incurred basis.
Loss ratio	Uses various forms of expected losses in relation to premiums earned.
Bornhuetter-Ferguson	Uses a combination of the loss ratio method and paid or incurred loss development factors to estimate reserves.

4.43 The decision to use a particular projection method and the results obtained from that method should be evaluated by considering the inherent assumptions underlying the method and the appropriateness of these assumptions to the circumstances. Stability and consistency of data are extremely important. Changes in variables, such as rates of claim payments, claims department practices, case-basis reserving adequacy, claim reporting rates, mix of business, reinsurance retention levels, and the legal environment may have a significant effect on the projection and may produce distortions or conflicting results. Reference should be made to paragraphs 4.64–.66 for a discussion of how changes in variables may affect the loss-reserving process. The results of any projection should be reviewed for reasonableness by analyzing the resultant loss ratios and losses per measure of exposure.

AAG-PLI 4.43

Illustrative Projection Data

4.44 The following tables are simple illustrations of the use of the loss extrapolation method to estimate ultimate losses, as well as the effects of considering the results of more than one projection. In these illustrations, the result of extrapolating incurred-loss data is compared with the result of extrapolating paid-loss data. These tables are presented solely for the purpose of illustrating the mathematical mechanics of the two projections. They do not illustrate the required analysis of the data and consideration of internal and external environmental variables that may affect the claim payment and loss reserving process.

4.45 Table 4-1 presents an illustration of historical incurred-loss data. It reflects, as an example, that the sum of paid losses and case-basis reserves from all claims that occurred during 20X0 at the end of 20X0 was $2,054; that sum increased to $2,717 in the next year and increased to $3,270 five years later.

Table 4-1
Case-Basis Incurred-Loss Data as of 12/31/X9

Development Period (in months)

Accident Year	12	24	36	48	60	72	84	96	108	120
20X0	$2,054	$2,717	$2,979	$3,095	$3,199	$3,348	$3,270	$3,286	$3,299	$3,301
20X1	2,213	2,980	3,269	3,461	3,551	3,592	3,631	3,643	3,651	
20X2	2,341	3,125	3,513	3,695	3,798	3,849	3,872	3,876		
20X3	2,492	3,502	3,928	4,177	4,313	4,369	4,392			
20X4	2,964	4,246	4,859	5,179	5,315	5,376				
20X5	3,394	4,929	5,605	5,957	6,131					
20X6	3,715	5,433	6,162	6,571						
20X7	4,157	5,912	6,771							
20X8	4,573	6,382								
20X9	4,785									

4.46 This incurred-loss data is first used to calculate historical period-to-period incurred-loss development factors. These factors are used to compare the amount of incurred losses at successive development stages and are illustrated in part 1 of table 4-2.

4.47 The calculation of average historical period-to-period incurred-loss development factors may be based on the use of simple averages of various period-to-period factors or more complex weighting or trending techniques. These techniques can significantly affect the reserving process and require judgment, understanding, and experience in applying. In this example, a simple average of the latest three period-to-period factors has been calculated and is presented in part 2 of table 4-2.

4.48 Once historical period-to-period incurred-loss development factors are calculated, future period-to-period incurred-loss development factors must be selected. The future period-to-period factors must reflect anticipated differences between historical and future conditions that affect loss development, such as changes in the underlying business, different inflation rates, or case-basis reserving practices. In the example, no differences are anticipated, and the average historical factors have been chosen as the selected factors, as shown in part 2 of table 4-2. The selected future period-to-period factors are then used to produce ultimate incurred development factors. The ultimate factors are presented in part 3 of table 4-2.

Table 4-2
Period-to-Period Incurred-Loss Development Factors as of 12/31/X9

Development Period (in months)

Accident Year	12–24	24–36	36–48	48–60	60–72	72–84	84–96	96–108	108–120	Est. Tail[1]
Part 1: Period-to-Period Historical Loss Development Factors										
20X0	1.323[2]	1.096	1.039	1.034	1.047	0.977	1.005	1.004	1.001	
20X1	1.347	1.097	1.059	1.026	1.012	1.011	1.003	1.002		
20X2	1.335	1.124	1.052	1.028	1.013	1.006	1.001			
20X3	1.405	1.122	1.063	1.033	1.013	1.005				
20X4	1.433	1.144	1.066	1.026	1.011					
20X5	1.452	1.137	1.063	1.029						
20X6	1.462	1.134	1.066							
20X7	1.422	1.145								
20X8	1.396									
Part 2: Period-to-Period Average Development Factors										
Simple Average of Latest Three Years										
	1.427	1.139	1.065	1.029	1.012	1.007	1.003	1.003	1.001	1.000
Selected Factors										
	1.427	1.139	1.065	1.029	1.012	1.007	1.003	1.003	1.001	1.000
Part 3: Ultimate Development Factors Selected for the Projection										
	1.828[3]	1.281	1.125	1.056	1.026	1.014	1.007	1.004	1.001	1.000

---

[1] Applies when the development period is determined to be longer than the period covered by the model (assumed to be 1.000 in this illustration).

[2] The 24-month developed losses are divided by the 12-month developed losses from table 4-1 ($2,717/$2,054 = $1.323).

[3] The product of the remaining factors (1.427 × 1.139 × 1.065 × 1.029 × 1.012 × 1.007 × 1.003 × 1.003 × 1.001 × 1.000 = 1.828) or the product of the 12–24 month selected factor multiplied by the 24–36 month ultimate factor (1.427 × 1.281 = 1.828).

4.49 The loss reserve analysis has now reached the point where an initial projection of ultimate losses, as well as an indicated provision for unreported losses for each accident year, can be made by using the historical incurred-loss data and ultimate incurred-loss development factors. This initial projection of ultimate losses is presented in table 4-3.

Table 4-3
Incurred-Loss Projection as of 12/31/X9

Accident Year	Case-Basis Incurred Loss as of 20X9[4]	Ultimate Incurred-Losses Development Factors[5]	Projected Ultimate Losses (2) x (3)	Projected Unreported Loss (4) – (2)
(1)	(2)	(3)	(4)	(5)
20X0	$3,301	1.000	$3,301	$ 0
20X1	3,651	1.001	3,655	4
20X2	3,876	1.004	3,892	16
20X3	4,392	1.007	4,423	31
20X4	5,376	1.014	5,451	75
20X5	6,131	1.026	6,290	159
20X6	6,571	1.056	6,939	368
20X7	6,771	1.125	7,617	846
20X8	6,382	1.281	8,175	1,793
20X9	4,785	1.828	8,747	3,962
Total	$51,236	—	$58,490	$7,254

4.50 Tables 4-5 and 4-6 present paid-loss data for the same entity whose incurred-loss data was presented in table 4-1. The array of paid-loss period-to-period development factors presented in table 4-5 is derived from table 4-4 using the same calculation methods used for incurred losses in table 4-2. The importance of the use of a tail factor in this calculation is apparent from the period-to-period historical loss development factors calculated in table 4-5. The tail factor represents an estimate of the development of losses beyond the period covered by the data array. In this instance, a tail factor of 1.01 was selected to project an additional 1 percent of losses to be paid from the 10th development year to ultimate. Selection of a tail factor requires careful judgment based on consideration of entity and industry experience for the line of business, actuarial studies, case-basis reserves, and any other relevant information. The initial projection of ultimate losses, using the historical paid losses and paid-loss ultimate development factors, is presented in table 4-6.

---

[4] From table 4-1.
[5] From part 3 of table 4-2.

Table 4-4
Paid-Loss Data as of 12/31/X9

Accident Year	Development Period (in months)									
	12	24	36	48	60	72	84	96	108	120
20X0	$896	$1,716	$2,291	$2,696	$3,041	$3,096	$3,185	$3,235	$3,262	$3,276
20X1	872	1,840	2,503	2,973	3,261	3,429	3,538	3,589	3,624	
20X2	968	1,975	2,683	3,185	3,494	3,670	3,763	3,819		
20X3	968	2,130	2,968	3,571	3,942	4,147	4,274			
20X4	1,201	2,580	3,673	4,421	4,860	5,114				
20X5	1,348	2,996	4,207	5,115	5,632					
20X6	1,340	3,146	4,520	5,496						
20X7	1,384	3,428	4,960							
20X8	1,568	3,696								
20X9	2,243									

Table 4-5
Period-to-Period Paid-Loss Development Factors as of 12/31/X9

Accident Year	Development Period (in months)									
	12–24	24–36	36–48	48–60	60–72	72–84	84–96	96–108	108–120	Est. Tail[6]
Part 1: Period-to-Period Historical Loss Development Factors[7]										
20X0	1.915	1.335	1.177	1.128	1.018	1.029	1.016	1.008	1.004	
20X1	2.110	1.360	1.188	1.097	1.052	1.032	1.014	1.010		
20X2	2.040	1.358	1.187	1.097	1.050	1.025	1.015			
20X3	2.200	1.393	1.203	1.104	1.052	1.031				
20X4	2.148	1.424	1.204	1.099	1.052					
20X5	2.223	1.404	1.216	1.101						
20X6	2.348	1.437	1.216							
20X7	2.477	1.447								
20X8	2.357									

(continued)

---

[6] Applies when the development period is determined to be longer than the period covered by the model (assumed to be 1.010 in this illustration).

[7] Computations are the same as those explained in table 4-2.

Accident Year	\multicolumn{9}{c}{Development Period (in months)}	Est. Tail[6]
	12–24	24–36	36–48	48–60	60–72	72–84	84–96	96–108	108–120	

Part 2: Period-to-Period Average Development Factors

Simple Average of Latest Three Years

	2.394	1.429	1.212	1.101	1.051	1.029	1.015	1.009	1.004	1.010

Selected Factors

	2.394	1.429	1.212	1.101	1.051	1.029	1.015	1.009	1.004	1.010

Part 3: Ultimate Development Factors Selected for the Projection[8]

	5.127	2.142	1.499	1.237	1.123	1.069	1.039	1.023	1.014	1.010

Table 4-6
Paid-Loss Projection as of 12/31/X9

Accident Year	Paid Losses as of 20X9	Ultimate Loss Development Factors	Projected Ultimate Losses (2) x (3)	Projected Unreported Losses[9]
(1)	(2)	(3)	(4)	(5)
20X1	$3,624	1.014	$3,675	$24
20X2	3,819	1.023	3,907	31
20X3	4,274	1.039	4,439	47
20X4	5,114	1.069	5,465	89
20X5	5,632	1.123	6,325	194
20X6	5,496	1.237	6,796	225
20X7	4,960	1.499	7,434	663
20X8	3,696	2.142	7,916	1,534
20X9	2,243	5.127	11,500	6,715
Total	$42,134	—	$60,766	$9,530

---

[8] See footnote 7.

[9] Represents the projected losses from column 4 of table 4-6 less the recorded case-basis incurred losses from column 2 of table 4-3.

4.51 Table 4-7 compares the results of extrapolating paid-loss data (table 4-6) with the results of extrapolating incurred-loss data (table 4-3). It is immediately clear that additional analysis of accident year 20X9 losses is needed, as well as possible review of the results of the two techniques for all accident periods. The difference between the results obtained from the two different projections is significant.

Table 4-7
Alternative Projections of Ultimate Losses and Unreported Losses as of 12/31/X9

Accident Year	Ultimate Losses		Unreported Losses	
	Incurred	Paid	Incurred	Paid
20X0	$3,301	$3,309	$0	$8
20X1	3,655	3,675	4	24
20X2	3,892	3,907	16	31
20X3	4,423	4,439	31	47
20X4	5,451	5,465	75	89
20X5	6,290	6,325	159	194
20X6	6,939	6,796	368	225
20X7	7,617	7,434	846	663
20X8	8,175	7,916	1,793	1,534
20X9	8,747	11,500	3,962	6,715
Total	$58,490	$60,766	$7,254	$9,530

4.52 Another projection methodology that is commonly used for more recent (that is, less mature) accident periods, such as 20X8 and 20X9, is a Bornhuetter-Ferguson approach (named for the two American actuaries who developed the methodology). Tables 4-8 and 4-9 contain examples of the Bornhuetter-Ferguson methodology using earned premiums applied for accident years 20X8 and 20X9 on an incurred-loss and a paid-loss basis, respectively. As previously indicated, the Bornhuetter-Ferguson approach uses earned premiums and is a combination of the incurred-loss or paid-loss development method and a loss ratio method. A loss ratio method assumes that loss varies directly with earned premiums; for any given accident year, a simple ultimate loss projection can be obtained by multiplying estimated ultimate earned premium by a selected ultimate loss ratio. The selected loss ratio for 20X8 and 20X9 is selected by the actuary based on expectations resulting from loss ratio trends. The Bornhuetter-Ferguson method assumes, however, that only future losses will develop based on this estimated loss ratio. For each accident year, the amount of loss yet to be developed is determined as the product of (a) the ratio of incurred loss or paid loss to ultimate loss implied by the maturity of the accident year and the incurred-loss or paid-loss development factor and (b) the ultimate loss estimate based on the loss ratio approach. Cumulative incurred loss or paid loss to date is then added to the loss-yet-to-be-developed estimate, yielding an ultimate loss estimate for each accident year.

Table 4-8
Bornhuetter-Ferguson Incurred-Loss Projection as of 12/31/X9

Accident Year (1)	Ultimate Earned Premiums (2)	Selected Loss Ratio (3)	Expected Ultimate Loss (2) × (3) (4)	Ultimate Incurred-Loss Development Factors (5)	Ratio of Incurred-Loss to Ultimate Cumulative Loss [1 / (5)] (6)	Ratio of Undeveloped Incurred Loss to Ultimate Loss [1 − (6)] (7)	Undeveloped Incurred-Loss (4) × (7) (8)	Case-Basis Incurred-Loss as of 20X9 (9)	Projected Ultimate Losses (8) + (9) (10)	Projected Unreported Losses (10) − (9) (11)
20X0	$4,126			1.000	1.000	0.000		$3,301		
20X1	4,729			1.001	0.999	0.001		3,651		
20X2	5,255			1.004	0.996	0.004		3,876		
20X3	6,043			1.007	0.993	0.007		4,392		
20X4	7,305			1.014	0.986	0.014		5,376		
20X5	8,329			1.027	0.974	0.026		6,131		
20X6	8,929			1.057	0.946	0.054		6,571		
20X7	9,632			1.126	0.888	0.112		6,771		
20X8	10,222	80.0%	$8,178	1.283	0.779	0.221	$1,804	6,382	$8,186	$1,804
20X9	11,090	80.0%	8,872	1.831	0.546	0.454	4,027	4,785	8,812	4,027
Total	$75,660							$51,236		

Table 4-9
Bornhuetter-Ferguson Paid-Loss Projections as of 12/31/X9

Accident Year	Ultimate Earned Premiums	Selected Loss Ratio	Expected Ultimate Loss (2) × (3)	Ultimate Paid-Loss Development Factors	Ratio of Cumulative Paid-Loss to Ultimate Loss [1 / (5)]	Ratio of Undeveloped Paid-Loss to Ultimate Loss [1 − (6)]	Undeveloped Paid-Loss (4) × (7)	Paid-Loss as of 20X9	Projected Ultimate Losses (8) + (9)	Case-Basis Incurred-Loss as of 20X9	Projected Unreported Losses (10) − (11)
(1)	(2)	(3)	(4)	(5)	(6)	(7)	(8)	(9)	(10)	(11)	
20X0	$4,126			1.010	0.990	0.010		$3,276		$3,301	
20X1	4,729			1.014	0.986	0.014		3,624		3,651	
20X2	5,255			1.023	0.978	0.022		3,819		3,876	
20X3	6,043			1.038	0.963	0.037		4,274		4,392	
20X4	7,305			1.068	0.936	0.064		5,114		5,376	
20X5	8,329			1.124	0.890	0.110		5,632		6,131	
20X6	8,929			1.238	0.808	0.192		5,496		6,571	
20X7	9,632			1.500	0.667	0.333		4,960		6,771	
20X8	10,222	80.0%	$8,178	2.144	0.466	0.534	$4,363	3,696	$8,059	6,382	$1,677
20X9	11,090	80.0%	8,872	5.133	0.195	0.805	7,144	2,243	9,387	4,785	4,602
Total	$75,660							$42,134		$51,236	

AAG-PLI 4.52

4.53 Table 4-10 contains a comparison of the results of all 4 actuarial techniques used in this example: incurred-loss development, paid-loss development, and the 2 Bornhuetter-Ferguson techniques based on earned premiums and incurred loss and paid loss. Based on the results of this comparison, ultimate loss amounts by accident year are selected in column 7, and indicated unreported (broad IBNR in this example) amounts and loss ratios are calculated in columns 9 and 10 based on the selected ultimate loss amounts. For accident years 20X8 and 20X9, ultimate loss amounts are selected based on the results of the Bornhuetter-Ferguson methods. A further examination of the difference in the incurred-loss and paid-loss development methods for accident year 20X9 finds that the high level of losses paid in 20X9 for accident year 20X9 relative to case-basis incurred losses for the same period causes the paid-loss development method indication to significantly exceed the incurred-loss method indication. The actuary must then examine more closely whether the high level of loss payments represents an acceleration of payment activity or an increase in the overall level of losses incurred in 20X9. The Bornhuetter-Ferguson methods are less responsive to unusual levels of incurred-loss or paid-loss activity in immature accident years, and they also avoid the distortion that could result from the application of a large development factor to a small base of incurred loss or paid loss, which may occur for long tail lines in more recent accident years. As a result, these methods are frequently used to determine loss indications for more recent accident years. This example demonstrates the benefit of using multiple actuarial methodologies in the evaluation of loss reserves because of the analysis and comparison of the ultimate loss indications from the various methodologies.

The Loss Reserving and Claims Cycle

Table 4-10
Comparison of Ultimate Loss Projections and Selected Ultimate Loss as of 12/31/X9

| Accident Year | Ultimate Earned Premiums | Ultimate Loss Projections | | | | Selected Ultimate Loss | Case-Basis Incurred-Loss as of 20X9 | Selected Unreported Loss as of 20X9 | Indicated Loss Ratio |
| | | Incurred | Paid | Bornhuetter-Ferguson Incurred | Bornhuetter-Ferguson Paid | | | | |
(1)	(2)	(3)	(4)	(5)	(6)	(7)	(8)	(7) − (8) (9)	(7) / (2) (10)
20X0	$4,126	$3,301	$3,309			$3,301	$3,301	$0	80.0%
20X1	4,729	3,655	3,675			3,665	3,651	14	77.5%
20X2	5,255	3,892	3,907			3,900	3,876	24	74.2%
20X3	6,043	4,423	4,436			4,430	4,392	38	73.3%
20X4	7,305	5,451	5,462			5,460	5,376	84	74.7%
20X5	8,329	6,297	6,330			6,310	6,131	179	75.8%
20X6	8,929	6,946	6,804			6,880	6,571	309	77.1%
20X7	9,632	7,624	7,440			7,530	6,771	759	78.2%
20X8	10,222	8,188	7,924	$8,186	$8,059	8,120	6,382	1,738	79.4%
20X9	11,090	8,761	11,513	8,812	9,387	9,100	4,785	4,315	82.1%
Total	$75,660	$58,538	$60,800	$16,997	$17,446	$58,696	$51,236	$7,460	

AAG-PLI 4.53

LAE Reserves

4.54 *LAE reserves* are the costs that will be required to settle claims that have been incurred as of the valuation date. Under GAAP, LAEs are separated as (*a*) allocated LAEs, which are expenses that are assignable or allocable to specific claims, such as fees paid to outside attorneys, experts, and investigators, and used to defend claims, and (*b*) unallocated LAEs, which are expenses that consist of all external, internal, and administrative claims-handling expenses, including determination of coverage, that are not included in allocated LAEs. For GAAP reporting purposes, total LAE expense is reported as one line or combined with incurred losses.

4.55 Under SAP, total LAE (allocated LAE plus unallocated LAE) can be classified into two broad categories: DCC and *adjusting and other* (AO). Paragraph 5 of SSAP No. 55 notes that LAE can be classified as

> Defense and Cost Containment (DCC) and Adjusting and Other (AO). DCC includes defense, litigation, and medical cost containment expenses, whether internal or external. AO are those expenses other than DCC ... and include but are not limited to the following items: (*a*) Fees and expenses of adjusters and settling agents, (*b*) LAEs for participation in voluntary and involuntary market pools if reported by calendar year, (*c*) Attorney fees incurred in the determination of coverage, including litigation between the reporting entity and the policyholder; and (*d*) Fees and salaries for appraisers, private investigators, hearing representatives, reinspectors and fraud investigators, if working in the capacity of an adjuster.

DCC Reserve Calculation Approaches

4.56 DCC is generally analyzed by line of business, utilizing methods similar to the loss methods previously described. A shift in the composition of the costs in relation to the total might affect the statistical data used in the related loss projections. This shift would need to be considered in future loss reserve projections.

4.57 Many companies calculate DCC reserves based on the relationship of DCC to losses. Underlying this approach is a basic assumption that DCC will increase or decrease in proportion to losses. The setting of reserves for DCC based on the relationship of paid DCC to paid losses is referred to as the paid-to-paid ratio approach. Separate ratios are normally developed for each accident year. Inflation in DCC is not typically evaluated separately; rather, it is estimated to occur at the same rate as the rate of inflation in the losses. The validity of this assumption can be tested by reviewing historical relationships between DCC and losses over time. The effects of a pattern of increasing or decreasing the ratio of DCC to losses should be considered in establishing DCC reserves. An understanding of the claims department's operations and philosophy over time is essential to a proper interpretation of the data.

4.58 Other approaches to DCC reserve calculation and analysis include (*a*) analyzing DCC entirely apart from the related loss costs using methods that compare the development of DCC payments at various stages and (*b*) using combined loss and DCC data in situations when it appears likely that this would produce more accurate estimates (for example, when the entity has changed its claim defense posture so that defense costs increase and loss costs decrease). In this latter approach, statistical tests and projections are based on the combined data for losses and DCC.

4.59 Some companies establish case-basis reserves for certain types of DCC or increase case-basis loss reserves by a stated percentage to provide for DCC. In either case, additional DCC reserves should be provided for the development of case-basis reserves and IBNR.

AO Reserve Calculation Approaches

4.60 AO reserves are often estimated using the calendar year paid-to-paid method rather than the accident year paid-to-paid method used for DCC reserves. Although the paid-to-paid ratios establish the relationship of the AO payments to the loss payments, the timing of the AO payments is also critical to estimation of the AO reserves. For example, some companies assume that a portion of AO costs is incurred when a claim is placed on the books and the remaining portion is incurred when the claim is settled. For reported claims, the cost of placing the claim on the books has been incurred, so it is only necessary to provide a reserve for the remaining portion at settlement. For IBNR claims, it is necessary to provide for all of the AO. Some companies perform internal studies to establish the methods and ratios to be used in their calculations. Other AO reserving methods may apply the estimated average cost per open claim to the number of open and unreported claims.

4.61 The AO reserves should provide for inflation. The assumption that AO will inflate at a rate equal to the rate at which losses inflate should be periodically reviewed. The rate should also be adjusted for expected technological or operational changes that might cause economies or inefficiencies in the claim settlement process.

4.62 If paid-to-paid AO ratios will be calculated in the aggregate for each line of business, a reasonable basis for allocating paid AO by line of business should be established.

Changes in the Environment

4.63 Loss reserve projections are used to estimate loss reporting patterns, loss payment patterns, and ultimate claim costs. An inherent assumption in such projections is that historical loss patterns can be used to predict future patterns with reasonable accuracy. Because many variables can affect past and future loss patterns, the effect of changes in such variables on the results of loss projections should be carefully considered.

4.64 Identification of changes in variables and consideration of their effect on loss reserve projections are critical steps in the loss reserving process. The evaluation of these factors requires the involvement of a loss reserve specialist as well as input from various operating departments within the entity, such as the marketing, underwriting, claims, actuarial, reinsurance, finance, and legal departments. Management's use of a specialist in determining loss reserves is discussed in paragraphs 4.69–.71.

4.65 If changes in variables have occurred, the mechanical application of loss projection methods may result in unreasonable estimates of ultimate claim costs. Changes in variables can be considered in the loss reserving process in a variety of ways, including the following:

- *Selection of the loss projection method(s).* Loss projection methods vary in their sensitivity to changes in the underlying variables and the length of the claim emergence pattern. When selecting a loss projection method, consideration should be given to how a change in the underlying data will affect that method. For example, if management has adopted a policy to defer or accelerate the settlement of claims, a paid-loss extrapolation method will probably produce unreliable results. In that case, an incurred-loss extrapolation or other methods may produce better estimates of ultimate losses.

- *Adjustment of underlying historical loss data.* In certain cases, the effect of changed variables can be isolated and appropriately reflected in the historical loss data used in the loss projection. For example, if policy limits are relatively consistent for all policies in a block of business and if these limits have recently been reduced by a constant amount, historical loss data can be adjusted to exclude amounts in excess of the revised policy limits.

- *Further segregation of historical loss data.* Certain changes in variables can be addressed by further differentiating and segregating historical loss data. For example, if an entity begins to issue claims-made policies for a line of business for which it traditionally issued occurrence basis policies, segregation of data between the two types of policies should minimize the effect of the different reporting patterns. Such segregation should produce more accurate loss reserve projections for the occurrence basis policies. However, loss development data relating to the claims-made policies will be limited in the initial years.

- *Separate calculation of the effect of variables.* The effect of certain changes in variables can be isolated and separately computed as an adjustment to the results of other loss projection methods. For example, if claim cost severity has increased (an increase in auto repair costs) or is expected to increase beyond historic trends, an additional reserve can be separately computed to reflect the effect of such actual or anticipated increases.

- *Qualitative assessments.* In many instances, the magnitude or effect of a change in a variable will be uncertain. The establishment of loss reserves in such situations requires considerable judgment and knowledge of the entity's business.

4.66 The development of pollution, asbestos, and similar mass tort claims may not follow the usual development pattern of the general liability claims with which they are usually grouped. When the activity of these claims is sufficient to distort the recorded development of the entity, the distorting activity should be isolated from the development history, so that an accurate projection of the remaining general liability claims can be made. Management's process of assessing its pollution, asbestos, and other similar exposures should include procedures to

- ensure that all data elements are recorded on each incoming claim or precautionary notice.
- assess the entity's exposure to these types of liability claims by considering such factors as the types of risks historically written, the layers of coverage provided, the policy language employed, and recent decisions rendered by courts.
- determine whether any portion of potential liability costs is probable and reasonably estimable.

Critical Accounting Policies and Estimates Disclosure

4.67 Securities and Exchange Commission (SEC) registrants should consider that the "Management's Discussion and Analysis" section of Form 10-K adequately discuss the following information:

a. The actuarial methodologies used to calculate the loss reserve projections and the differences in these methods for different lines of businesses. The discussion on the method used to develop reserve estimates might include information on the loss reserve projection methods used (for example, loss-ratio method, paid-loss development method, incurred-loss development method, and so on); the basis for selecting a certain method for different lines of business; and the reasons for any changes in the loss reserve methodology.

b. The significant assumptions, judgment, and uncertainty used in the estimation process and the potential impact of variability in this estimate to the financial statements. Uncertainties to be discussed may include any products with higher volatility or uncertainty that may affect the overall estimate (for example, asbestos reserves) and any particular assumptions that are more difficult than others to measure (for example, the length of time to reach claim settlement).

c. If available, a company should disclose the range of reasonable estimates for the loss reserves.

d. The significant changes in these assumptions during the reporting period and the effect of that change on the estimates produced. Examples of changes in assumptions that may be discussed more qualitatively include changes in the claims-handling process, policy and exposure forms, inflation, legal trends, environmental factors, mix of claimants, or timeliness of claim reporting by claimants.

e. Any development in the estimates that was identified after the fact.

4.68 In conjunction with Section 401 of the Sarbanes-Oxley Act of 2002, registrants, other than small business issuers, are required to provide an overview of certain known contractual obligations in a tabular format (referred to as a contractual obligations table). Readers should be aware that the SEC has requested that loss reserves be included as part of the contractual obligations table.

Use of Specialists by Management in Determining Loss Reserves

4.69 Management is responsible for making the accounting estimates included in the financial statements. As explained in the previous sections of this chapter, the process of estimating loss reserves is complex and involves many subjective judgments. Accordingly, the determination of loss reserves should involve an individual with a sufficient level of competence and experience in loss reserving, including knowledge about the kind(s) of insurance for which a reserve is being established and an understanding of appropriate methods available for calculating loss reserve estimates. These individuals are referred to in this chapter as *loss reserve specialists*. The specialist's level of competence and experience should be commensurate with the complexity of the entity's business, which is affected by such factors as the kind(s) of insurance underwritten and environmental and risk considerations. Criteria that may be considered in determining whether an individual qualifies as a loss reserve specialist include the aforementioned, as well as the following:

- Knowledge of various projection techniques, including their strengths and weaknesses and applicability to various lines of insurance
- Knowledge of changes in the environment in which the entity operates, including regulatory developments, social and legal trends, court decisions, and other factors described in more detail in the auditing section of this chapter, and the effect that these factors will have on the emergence and ultimate cost of these claims

4.70 The Casualty Actuarial Society offers a course of study and examinations that are designed to train individuals to be, among other things, loss reserve specialists. In addition, the American Academy of Actuaries establishes qualification standards for its members who practice in this area. Although many casualty actuaries may therefore be qualified to be loss reserve specialists, other individuals, through their experience and training, may also be qualified. Training and experience should provide individuals with knowledge about different policy forms and coverages, current developments in insurance, and environmental factors that might affect the loss reserving process. Training and experience should also provide individuals with knowledge that will enable them to apply appropriate methods of estimating loss reserves. The extent of this knowledge and ability should be commensurate with the complexity and kinds of business written.

4.71 Many insurance entities use internal loss reserve specialists who are employees or officers of the entity. In addition, many companies engage consulting casualty actuaries to either assist in the determination of the loss reserve estimate or perform a separate review of the entity's loss reserve estimate. The scope of work to be performed by the consulting actuary is a matter of judgment by entity management. Usually, the consulting actuary will issue a report summarizing the nature of the work performed and the results. Since 1990, the National Association of Insurance Commissioners *Annual Statement Instructions* has required a statement of actuarial opinion relating to loss and LAE reserves.

Guaranty Fund and Other Assessments

4.72 State guaranty funds assess entities licensed to sell insurance in the state; provide for the payment of covered claims; or meet other insurance obligations, subject to prescribed limits, of insolvent insurance enterprises. The assessments are generally based on premium volume for certain covered lines of business. Most state guaranty funds assess entities for costs related to a particular insolvency after the insolvency occurs. Many states and a number of local governmental units have established other funds supported by assessments. The most prevalent uses for such assessments are to fund operating expenses of state insurance regulatory bodies and second-injury funds. FASB ASC 405-30 provides guidance on accounting for guaranty-fund and other assessments related to insurance activities. SSAP No. 35, *Guaranty Fund and Other Assessments*, provides statutory accounting guidance on guaranty funds and other types of assessments. For further information, see chapter 8, "Insurance-Related Expenses, Taxes, and Assessments," of this guide.

The Loss Reserving and Claims Cycle 199

Accounting Principles[10]

4.73 Sources for specialized industry accounting principles for insurance enterprises include FASB ASC 944, 405-30, and 340-30.

4.74 Under GAAP, as discussed in paragraphs 1–2 of FASB ASC 944-40-25, liabilities for the cost of unpaid claims, including estimates of the cost of IBNR claims, are accrued when insured events occur. As discussed in FASB ASC 944-40-30-1, the liability for unpaid claims should be based on the estimated ultimate cost of settling the claims (that is, the total payments expected to be made) and should include the effects of inflation and other social and economic factors. Some companies select their estimate of the ultimate cost of settling claims from a selection of several different reserve methods.[11] As discussed in FASB ASC 944-40-30-2, estimated recoveries on unpaid claims, such as salvage, subrogation, or a potential ownership interest in real estate, should be evaluated in terms of their estimated realizable value and deducted from the liability for unpaid claims. As discussed in FASB ASC 944-40-25-1, a liability for those adjustment expenses expected to be incurred in the settlement of unpaid claims should be accrued when the related liability for unpaid claims is accrued. FASB ASC 944-40-35-1 notes that changes in estimates of the liabilities resulting from the continuous review process and differences between estimates and payments for claims should be recognized in income in the period in which the estimates are changed or payments are made.

Discounting Loss Reserves

4.75 The objective of discounting loss reserves is to account for the time value of money in a way that accurately reflects the anticipated future cash flows based on the characteristics of the insurance obligation. Certain liabilities for unpaid claims and claim-adjustment expenses are normally discounted (that is, the liabilities are presented at present value in the financial statements).

4.76 FASB ASC 944 provides no accounting guidance for determining if it is appropriate to discount reserves; however, it requires disclosure if reserves are discounted. In making the determination whether it is appropriate to discount liabilities for unpaid claims and claim-adjustment expenses, many insurance entities consider the following guidance to establish their policy:

- Per FASB ASC 410-30-35-12, the measurement of the liability or a component of the liability may be discounted to reflect the time value of money if the aggregate amount of the liability or component and the amount and timing of cash payments for the liability or component are fixed or reliably determinable.
- The interpretive response to question 1 in FASB ASC 944-20-S99-1 allows the following:
  — Discounting liabilities for unpaid claims and claim adjustment expenses at the same rates that it uses for reporting to state regulatory authorities with respect to the same claims liabilities

---

[10] The boards are redeliberating significant issues based on feedback received on the IASB exposure draft and FASB discussion paper. FASB is expected to release an exposure draft and the IASB is expected to issue a targeted revised exposure draft during the first half of 2013. Readers should remain alert to any final pronouncements.

[11] In practice, this amount is often referred to as management's best estimate.

AAG-PLI 4.76

Property and Liability Insurance Entities

— Discounting liabilities with respect to settled claims under the following circumstances:
- The payment pattern and ultimate cost are fixed and determinable on an individual basis claim basis
- The discount rate used is reasonable based on the facts and circumstances applicable to the registrant at the time the claims are settled

For SEC reporting, the payment pattern and ultimate costs need to be both fixed and determinable and the claim already settled versus the guidance in FASB ASC 410-30-35-12 that requires the components to be either fixed or reliably determinable and is silent with regard to whether the liability is settled.

4.77 Examples of reserves that might be discounted include workers' compensation indemnity reserves, long-term disability reserves, and short duration contract claim liabilities that meet the criteria in FASB ASC 410-30-35-12 or 944-20-S99-1, as applicable, and have payment streams that are expected to occur over a longer period of time.

4.78 Reasonable diversity exists regarding what rates should be used for discounting liabilities for unpaid claims and claim-adjustment expenses and how they are applied. If an entity decides to discount, many analogize to the following guidance in determining an appropriate discount rate:

- The interpretive response to question 1 of Topic 5(N), "Discounting by Property-Casualty Insurance Companies," of the SEC's *Codification of Staff Accounting Bulletins* notes that

    [p]ending authoritative guidance resulting from those efforts however, the staff will raise no objection if a registrant follows a policy for GAAP reporting purposes of:
    - Discounting liabilities for unpaid claims and claim adjustment expenses at the same rates that it uses for reporting to state regulatory authorities with respect to the same claims liabilities.

- Paragraph .132 of Statement of Position (SOP) 96-1, *Environmental Remediation Liabilities*, states that for entities that file with the SEC, the guidance in Staff Accounting Bulletin No. 92 with respect to the discount rate to be used—a rate that will produce an amount at which the environmental liability theoretically could be settled in an arm's-length transaction with a third-party and that should not exceed the interest rate on monetary assets that are essentially risk free and have maturities comparable to that of the environmental liability—should be followed.

- FASB ASC 340-30-35-6 concludes that for the insurer or assuming enterprise, the discount rate used to determine the deposit liability should be the current rate on a U.S. government obligation with similar cash flow characteristics.

4.79 Careful consideration of the facts and circumstances surrounding a change in the discount rate for the liabilities for unpaid claims is needed to determine the proper accounting for the change (change in accounting principle or change in accounting estimate). A change from not discounting loss reserves to discounting loss reserves would generally be a change in accounting principle.

4.80 As required by FASB ASC 944-40-50-5, the financial statements should disclose the carrying amount of liabilities for unpaid claims and claim adjustment expenses relating to short duration contracts that are presented at present value and the range of interest rates used to discount those liabilities. Insurance entities commonly disclose the effect of changes in the discount rate or unwinding of the discount rate for older accident years during the reporting period in the loss reserve roll-forward footnote because this information is beneficial to readers of financial statements.

4.81 Topic 5(W), "Contingency Disclosures Regarding Property/Casualty Insurance Reserves for Unpaid Claim Costs," of the SEC's *Codification of Staff Accounting Bulletins* provides guidance concerning those uncertainties surrounding property and casualty loss reserves that may be required to follow the guidance in FASB ASC 450, *Contingencies*. In addition, Topic 5(Y), "Accounting and Disclosures Relating to Loss Contingencies," and Topic 10(F), "Presentation of Liabilities for Environmental Costs," of the SEC's *Codification of Staff Accounting Bulletins* provide the SEC staff's interpretation of current accounting literature relating to the following:

- Recognition of liabilities for costs apportioned to other potential responsible parties
- Uncertainties in estimation of the extent of environmental or product liability
- The appropriate discount rate for environmental or product liability, if discounting is appropriate
- Accounting for exit costs
- Financial statement disclosures and disclosure of certain information outside the basic financial statements

4.82 FASB ASC 450 provides guidance for the accounting and disclosure of loss contingencies.

Structured Settlements

4.83 The treatment of structured settlements can be different between SAP and GAAP. Paragraph 18 of SSAP No. 65 states that

> [s]tatutory accounting and GAAP are consistent for the accounting of structured settlement annuities where the reporting entity is the owner and payee, and where the claimant is the owner and payee and the reporting entity has been released from its obligation. GAAP distinguishes structured settlement annuities where the owner is the claimant and a legally enforceable release from the reporting entity's liability is obtained from those where the claimant is the owner and payee but the reporting entity had not been released from its obligation. GAAP requires the deferral of any gain resulting from the purchase of a structured settlement annuity where the claimant is the owner and payee yet the reporting entity has not been released from its obligation. Statutory accounting treats these settlements as completed transactions and considers the earnings process complete, thereby allowing for immediate gain recognition.

4.84 Also see paragraph 19 of SSAP No. 65 for disclosure items for structured settlements.

4.85 As discussed in paragraph 52 of FASB Statement No. 113, *Accounting and Reporting for Reinsurance of Short-Duration and Long-Duration Contracts*, FASB concluded that unless the ceding enterprise is legally relieved of its liability to the policyholder, as described in FASB ASC 944-40-25-33, such reinsurance does not constitute a sale and immediate recognition of a gain should be precluded. The gain would therefore be deferred when the structured settlement annuity is purchased and the claimant is the owner and payee, but the reporting entity has not been released from its obligation.

Reinsurance Receivables

4.86 *Reinsurance receivables*, as discussed in paragraphs 4.29–.30, are amounts that will be recovered from reinsurers for losses and LAE accrued, including IBNR losses accrued. As stated in FASB ASC 944-310-45-5, amounts receivable from reinsurers on paid and unpaid losses shall be classified as assets.

SAP

4.87 Under SAP, as noted in paragraph 4 of SSAP No. 55

[c]laims, losses, and loss/claim adjustment expenses shall be recognized as expense when a covered or insured event occurs. ... Claim payments and related expense payments are made subsequent to the occurrence of a covered or insured event and, in order to recognize the expense of a covered or insured event that has occurred, it is necessary to establish a liability. Liabilities shall be established for any unpaid claims and unpaid losses (loss reserves), unpaid loss/claim adjustment expenses (loss/claim adjustment expense reserve) and incurred costs, with a corresponding charge to income.

4.88 Similar to GAAP, paragraph 8 of SSAP No. 55 also states that

[t]he liability for claim reserves and claim liabilities, unpaid losses and loss/claim adjustment expenses shall be based upon the estimated ultimate cost of settling claims (including the effects of inflation and other societal and economic factors), using past experience adjusted for current trends, and any other factors that would modify past experience.

4.89 As discussed in paragraph 10 of SSAP No. 55,

[b]ecause the ultimate settlement of claims (including IBNR for death claims and accident and health claims) is subject to future events, no single claim estimate can be considered accurate with certainty. Management's analysis of the reasonableness of claim or loss and loss/claim adjustment expense reserve estimates shall include an analysis of the amount of variability in the estimate. If, for a particular line of business, management develops its estimate considering a range of claim or loss and loss/claim adjustment expense reserve estimates bounded by a high and a low estimate, management's best estimate of the liability within the range shall be recorded.

4.90 Additional SAP guidance can be found in SSAP No. 62, *Property and Casualty Reinsurance*,[12] and SSAP No. 65.

4.91 As noted in paragraph 10 of SSAP No. 65, "[w]ith the exception of fixed and reasonably determinable payments such as those emanating from workers' compensation tabular indemnity reserves and long-term disability claims, property and casualty loss reserves shall not be discounted." Exhibit A of SSAP No. 65 provides guidelines for states that prescribe or permit discounting on a nontabular basis. As required under paragraphs 14–15 of SSAP No. 65, "[t]he financial statements shall disclose whether or not any of the liabilities for unpaid losses or unpaid loss adjustment expenses are discounted, including liabilities for workers' compensation."

4.92 As discussed in paragraph 26 of SSAP No. 62, "[r]einsurance recoverables on unpaid case-basis and incurred but not reported losses shall be reported as a contra-liability netted against the liability for gross losses and loss adjustment expense." Therefore, reserves in statutory financial statements for unpaid losses are presented net of reinsurance. However, under paragraph 19 of SSAP No. 62, "reinsurance recoverables on paid losses shall be reported as an asset without any available offset." For SAP and the purpose of determining the provision for reinsurance (the statutory reserve for uncollectible reinsurance), reinsurance recoverable balances are segregated between those recoverable from companies authorized by the state to transact reinsurance and those recoverable from other companies (referred to as unauthorized reinsurers). When reinsurance is placed with an unauthorized entity, the ceding entity must maintain and report a liability account(s) for reserve credits taken and the losses recoverable that have been recorded, to the extent that it has not retained funds or obtained letters of credit or other collateral.

4.93 Paragraphs 34–39 of SSAP No. 65 provide guidance on accounting for high-deductible policies. Paragraph 35 of SSAP No. 65 states that

> [t]he liability for loss reserves shall be determined in accordance with SSAP No. 5. Because the risk of loss if present from the inception date, the reporting entity shall reserve losses throughout the policy period, not over the period after the deductible has been reached. Reserves for claims arising under high deductible plans shall be established net of the deductible, however, no reserve credit shall be permitted for any claim where any amount due from the insured has been determined to be uncollectible.

Disclosures[13] of Certain Matters in the Financial Statements of Insurance Enterprises

Applicability to Statutory Financial Statements

4.94 As discussed in exhibit 1-1, "Evaluation of the Appropriateness of Informative Disclosures in Insurance Entities' Financial Statements Prepared on a Statutory Basis," in chapter 1, "Nature, Conduct, and Regulation of the Business," auditors are required to apply the same disclosure evaluation

---

[12] The Property and Casualty Reinsurance Study Group of the National Association of Insurance Commissioners Accounting Practices and Procedures Task Force is reviewing proposals to revise Statement of Statutory Accounting Principles (SSAP) No. 62, *Property and Casualty Reinsurance*.

[13] See paragraphs 1.48–.68 and the preface of this guide for additional information on rules and regulations.

criteria for statutory financial statements as they do for financial statements prepared in conformity with GAAP. Provisions of the National Association of Insurance Commissioners (NAIC) *Accounting Practices and Procedures Manual* or any other explicit rejection of a GAAP disclosure do not negate the requirements of paragraph .17 of AU-C section 800, *Special Considerations—Audits of Financial Statements Prepared in Accordance With Special Purpose Frameworks* (AICPA, *Professional Standards*). However, the manual and NAIC Emerging Accounting Issues Working Group Interpretation 04-1, *Applicability of New GAAP Disclosures Prior to NAIC Consideration*, state that GAAP pronouncements do not become part of SAP until and unless adopted by the NAIC.

Relationship to Other Pronouncements

4.95 In some circumstances, the disclosure requirements in FASB ASC 944 may be similar to, or overlap, the disclosure requirements in certain other authoritative accounting pronouncements issued by FASB, the AICPA, or the SEC. For example:

- FASB ASC 450 requires certain disclosures related to loss contingencies, including catastrophe losses of property and casualty insurance entities
- FASB ASC 275, *Risks and Uncertainties*, requires certain disclosures about reinsurance transactions
- The SEC Securities Act Guide 6, *Disclosures Concerning Unpaid Claims and Claim Adjustment Expenses of Property-Casualty Insurance Underwriters*, requires disclosures of information about liabilities for unpaid claims and claim adjustment expenses[14]

Liability for Unpaid Claims and Claim Adjustment Expenses

4.96 As discussed in FASB ASC 944-40-25-1, both of the following should be accrued when insured events occur:

    a. A liability for unpaid claims (including estimates of costs for claims relating to insured events that have occurred but have not been reported to the insurer)

    b. A liability for claim adjustment expenses; that is, a liability for all costs expected to be incurred in connection with the settlement of unpaid claims

4.97 As discussed in FASB ASC 944-40-25-2, the estimated liability includes the amount of money that will be used for future payments of (*a*) claims that have been reported to the insurer and (*b*) claims related to insured events that have occurred but that have not been reported to the insurer as of the date the liability is estimated. As discussed in FASB ASC 944-40-25-3, claim adjustment expenses include costs incurred in the claim settlement process such as legal fees; outside adjuster fees; and costs to record, process, and adjust claims.

4.98 As discussed in FASB ASC 944-40-50-3, financial statements should disclose for each fiscal year for which an income statement is presented the following information about the liability for unpaid claims and claim adjustment expenses:

---

[14] For additional information, see paragraph 1.50.

The Loss Reserving and Claims Cycle 205

    a. The balance in the liability for unpaid claims and claim adjustment expenses at the beginning and end of each fiscal year presented and the related amount of reinsurance recoverable

    b. Incurred claims and claim adjustment expenses with separate disclosure of the provision for insured events of the current fiscal year and of increases or decreases in the provision for insured events of prior fiscal years

    c. Payments of claims and claim adjustment expenses with separate disclosure of payments of claims and claim adjustment expenses attributable to insured events of the current fiscal year and to insured events of prior fiscal years

    d. The reasons for the change in incurred claims and claim adjustment expenses recognized in the income statement attributable to insured events of prior fiscal years and should indicate whether additional premiums or return premiums have been accrued as a result of the prior year effects

    4.99 In addition to the disclosures required by FASB ASC 450, paragraphs 1 and 4 of FASB ASC 944-40-50 note that insurance enterprises should disclose management's policies and methodologies for estimating the liability for unpaid claims and claim adjustment expenses for difficult-to-estimate liabilities, such as for claims for toxic waste cleanup, asbestos-related illnesses, or other environmental exposures.

Auditing Loss Reserves

Planning Considerations—Overview

    4.100 In accordance with AU-C section 300, *Planning an Audit* (AICPA, *Professional Standards*), the auditor should plan the audit so that it is responsive to the assessment of the risks of material misstatement based on the auditor's understanding of the entity and its environment, including its internal control. The nature, timing, and extent of planning vary with the size and complexity of the entity, and with the auditor's experience with the entity and understanding of the entity. Refer to chapter 2, "Audit Considerations," for a detailed discussion of audit planning.

    4.101 Given the significance loss reserves typically have on the financial statements and required disclosures of a property and liability insurance entity, and the inherent judgments necessary to estimate loss reserves, they generally give rise to significant risks that require special audit consideration in designing audit procedures to obtain sufficient appropriate audit evidence about the reasonableness of the reserve estimates. To appropriately design such procedures, the auditors should perform risk assessment procedures related to the loss reserve estimation as a part of overall engagement planning.

    4.102 The auditor's design of loss reserve auditing procedures needs to take into consideration the effects of relevant activities of the entity and changes in factors including

- changes in the entity (mergers, acquisitions, dispositions);
- underwriting and claim trends;
- the reinsurance program of the entity (including any significant transactions);

- management turnover;
- IT system changes; and
- process changes (that is, the entity's claim handling strategies).

4.103 As part of the auditor's risk assessment procedures, the auditor may consider meeting with members of an entity's management responsible for underwriting, claims, reinsurance, IT systems, internal audit, and the accounting department and actuaries (internal or external). It is helpful for the audit team members who attend these meetings to have sufficient knowledge of the entity to understand how the changes identified could impact the estimation of the loss reserves. It is recommended that the loss reserve specialist used by the auditor (including when audit firms have internal loss reserving specialists) also attend these meetings.

4.104 The auditors should identify the components of loss reserves that could be material or are of higher risk to the financial statements that have been considered in developing the overall reserve estimate. Paragraph .12 of AU-C section 300 requires that the auditor consider whether specialized skills are needed in performing the audit. Due to the varying lines of business that may be underwritten by a property and liability insurance entity, the auditor should determine that when utilizing the work of a specialist (the auditor's internal or external loss reserve specialists or management's external loss reserve specialist)[15] that specialist has the requisite experience with the lines of business underwritten by the entity in order to satisfy the requirements of AU-C section 620, *Using the Work of an Auditor's Specialist* (AICPA, *Professional Standards*), and AU-C section 500, *Audit Evidence* (AICPA, *Professional Standards*). Refer to paragraph 4.06 for a discussion on the varying types of policies and underwriting risk generally maintained by a property and liability insurance entity.

4.105 The auditor should evaluate the effects of the reporting framework of the financial statements and the associated financial statement disclosures. For example, GAAP require the gross presentation of loss reserves on the financial statements whereas SAP require reporting net of reinsurance in the financial statements supplemented by gross and ceded amounts in the disclosures. These differences may influence the nature, timing, and extent of procedures depending on local auditing requirements. Refer to appendix A, "Property and Liability Insurance Entity Specific Disclosures," for an example disclosure of permitted and prescribed accounting practices. Audits subject to Public Company Accounting Oversight Board (PCAOB) standards should integrate the requirements of the risk assessment standards during the planning phase including increased emphasis on the understanding of disclosures. Auditors should also evaluate the impacts of the requirements to audit the data within Schedule P-Part 1 of the Annual Statement under the requirements of the NAIC and in accordance with SOP 92-8, *Auditing Property/Casualty*

---

[15] AU-C section 620, *Using the Work of an Auditors' Specialist* (AICPA, *Professional Standards*), defines specialists used by management and the auditor. The guidance defines *management specialists* as "an individual or organization possessing expertise in a field other than accounting or auditing, whose work in that field is used by the entity to assist the entity in preparing the financial statements." *Auditor's specialists* are defined as
> an individual or organization possessing expertise in a field other than accounting or auditing, whose work in that field is used by the auditor to assist the auditor in obtaining sufficient appropriate audit evidence. An auditor's specialist may be either an auditor's internal specialist (who is a partner or staff, including temporary staff, of the auditor's firm or a network firm) or an auditor's external specialist.

Insurance Entities' Statutory Financial Statements—Applying Certain Requirements of the NAIC Annual Statement Instructions (AICPA, *Technical Practice Aids*, AUD sec. 14,250).

Consideration of Fraud in a Financial Statement Audit

4.106 Risks are inherent in all audit engagements, including the possibility that fraudulent acts may cause a material misstatement of financial statements. AU-C section 240, *Consideration of Fraud in a Financial Statement Audit* (AICPA, *Professional Standards*), addresses the auditor's responsibilities relating to fraud in an audit of financial statements. Because of the characteristics of fraud, the auditor's exercise of professional skepticism is important when considering the risk of material misstatement due to fraud. Readers should refer to additional discussion of AU-C section 240 in chapter 2 of this guide.

4.107 The auditor's fraud risk assessment needs to consider the potential for management to utilize the loss estimation process to intentionally misstate amounts within the financial statements. That assessment would include the auditor's understanding of the lines of business underwritten by the entity to determine which lines may be more volatile in nature and, therefore, more susceptible to misstatement via fraud.

4.108 The auditor also should evaluate the risk of management overriding controls. This process may include evaluating whether such an override might have allowed adjustments outside of the normal period-end financial reporting process to have been made to the financial statements. Such adjustments might have resulted in changes to the financial statement relationships being analyzed, causing the auditor to draw erroneous conclusions. For this reason, analytical procedures alone are not well suited to detecting fraud.

Risk of Material Misstatement—Inherent Risk Factors

4.109 As discussed in AU-C section 330, *Performing Audit Procedures in Response to Assessed Risks and Evaluating the Audit Evidence Obtained* (AICPA, *Professional Standards*), inherent risk is the likelihood of material misstatement due to the particular characteristics of the relevant class of transactions, account balance, or disclosure. Inherent risk factors relevant to the auditor's obtaining an understanding of loss reserves to assess the risks of material misstatement include factors relating to management, actuarial assumptions, product characteristics, underwriting approach, and the competitive, economic, and regulatory environment. Appendix C, "Conditions and Events That May Indicate Risks of Material Misstatement," of AU-C section 315, *Understanding the Entity and Its Environment and Assessing the Risks of Material Misstatement* (AICPA, *Professional Standards*), provides examples of conditions and events that may indicate the existence of risks of material misstatement. Such factors related to loss reserves for a property and liability insurance entity might encompass the following:

    a. Management's selection of actuarial assumptions for pricing and loss reserve calculations are unduly influenced by considerations other than realistic expectations of future performance

    b. Management's concerns with earnings and selection of its best estimate without proper support

> c. The entity has a history of entering new lines of business and actual performance is less favorable than initial projections
>
> d. Changes in regulations or application of accounting principles (SAP or GAAP) alter loss reserve requirements, assumptions, or calculation methodologies
>
> e. Changes in the entity's underwriting standards or marketing strategy result in the acceptance of higher risks or a change in business practices
>
> f. The entity's surplus position is weak in comparison to industry standards or close to minimum statutory requirements
>
> g. Unqualified specialists are involved in the calculation and review of the loss reserves

Internal Control

4.110 Paragraph .04 of AU-C section 315 defines *internal control* as

> [a] process effected by those charged with governance, management, and other personnel that is designed to provide reasonable assurance about the achievement of the entity's objectives with regard to the reliability of financial reporting, effectiveness and efficiency of operations, and compliance with applicable laws and regulations.

4.111 Internal control over safeguarding of assets against unauthorized acquisition, use, or disposition may include controls relating to financial reporting and operations objectives. Internal control consists of the following five interrelated components:

> a. Control environment
>
> b. The entity's risk assessment process
>
> c. The information system, including the related business processes relevant to financial reporting and communication
>
> d. Control activities relevant to the audit
>
> e. Monitoring of controls

4.112 AU-C section 315 requires the auditor to obtain an understanding of these components of the entity's internal control. Paragraphs 2.31–.41 of chapter 2 discuss in detail the components of internal control. This section will discuss certain components of a property and liability insurance entity's internal control as they relate to loss reserves.

Control Environment

4.113 The control environment comprises the collective effect of various factors on establishing, enhancing, or mitigating the effectiveness of specific control policies or procedures of the entity. Control environment factors related to the estimation process of loss reserves of a property and liability insurance entity may include the following:

> a. Whether operations are highly decentralized, have significant reliance on third parties to provide necessary data to calculate loss reserves, or are very centralized

b. Adequacy of existing systems to provide data for the loss reserve estimation process and adequacy of interfaces with other key processing systems

c. The extent of the use of manual processes or reliance on one individual for loss reserve calculations versus the use of systemic processes

d. The experience of the staff in relation to the complexity involved in the estimation of loss reserves

The Entity's Risk Assessment Process

4.114 As discussed in paragraphs .16–.18 of AU-C section 315, the auditor should obtain an understanding of whether the entity has a process for

a. identifying business risks relevant to financial reporting objectives;

b. estimating the significance of the risks;

c. assessing the likelihood of their occurrence; and

d. deciding about actions to address those risks.

4.115 The auditor should obtain an understanding of the entity's risk assessment process related to loss reserves and the results thereof. If the entity has not established such a process or has an ad hoc process, the auditor should discuss with management whether business risks relevant to financial reporting objectives have been identified and how they have been addressed. The auditor should evaluate whether the absence of a documented risk assessment process is appropriate in the circumstances or determine whether it represents a significant deficiency or material weakness in the entity's internal control.

Information Systems

4.116 Prior to evaluating the reasonableness of the loss reserve estimate, the auditor should obtain an understanding of the loss reserving process. This may include performing a walkthrough of the related sub-processes such as claims processing and settlement and assessing the information system. Loss reserve estimation is contingent on many other functional areas of the entity and may involve information from multiple IT systems including premiums, claim, and reinsurance.

Control Activities

4.117 *Control activities* are the policies and procedures that help ensure that management's directives are carried out and that necessary actions are taken to address risks to achieve the entity's objectives. The following are examples of typical internal control procedures and policies relating to the estimation process of loss reserves:

a. Proper authorization of transactions and activities. Written guidelines are in place that assign appropriate individuals the responsibility for initial approval and subsequent changes of actuarial assumptions and calculation methodologies.

b. Segregation of duties. Product pricing and development, loss reserve processing, premium billing and collection, key information systems functions, and general accounting activities are appropriately segregated and independent reviews of the work performed are conducted.

c. Design of adequate controls over documents and records. There are procedures to ensure that fictitious or duplicate claim records are not included in the actuarial data.

d. Independent checks on performance and proper valuation of recorded amounts. Qualified specialists are used in actuarial calculations of loss reserve amounts and policies and procedures are in place for the appropriate personnel to evaluate those calculations and the resulting liability amounts.

4.118 After identifying the relevant data related to the estimation of loss reserves as part of obtaining an understanding of the information system, the auditor should obtain an understanding of the controls related to the completeness, accuracy, and classification of that data.

> *Considerations for Audits Performed in Accordance With Public Company Accounting Oversight Board (PCAOB) Standards*
>
> Paragraph 34 of Auditing Standard No. 12, *Identifying and Assessing Risks of Material Misstatement* (AICPA, *PCAOB Standards and Related Rules*, Auditing Standards), states that a broader understanding of control activities is needed for relevant assertions for which the auditor plans to rely on controls. Also, in the audit of internal control over financial reporting, the auditor's understanding of control activities encompasses a broader range of accounts and disclosures than what is normally obtained in a financial statement audit. Also refer to paragraph 26 of Auditing Standard No. 13, *The Auditor's Responses to the Risks of Material Misstatement* (AICPA, *PCAOB Standards and Related Rules*, Auditing Standards), for a discussion on the extent of tests of controls.

Identifying and Assessing the Risks of Material Misstatement

4.119 The auditor should identify and assess the risks of material misstatement for relevant assertions about loss reserves. The auditor should use the assessment of the risks of material misstatement at the relevant assertion level as a basis to determine the nature, timing, and extent of further audit procedures.

Audit Procedures Responsive to the Assessed Risks of Material Misstatement

4.120 The auditor's assessment of risk of material misstatement include determining the relevant assertions related to the significant accounts identified, determining the audit objectives, assessing inherent risk of error of other significant risks (for example, nonroutine transactions or risk of fraud), and planning the involvement of others. As required by AU-C section 330, the auditor should design and perform further audit procedures whose nature, timing, and extent are based on, and are responsive to, the assessed risks of material misstatement at the relevant assertion level. The auditor should determine the planned reliance on controls and the nature, timing, and extent of substantive testing, including whether the substantive evidence is planned from tests of details or substantive analytics. If the auditor identifies a significant risk and is only performing substantive procedures, those procedures should include a test of details. If procedures to respond to the significant risk include both a test of controls and substantive procedures, the auditor may select substantive analytical procedures if the controls are operating effectively.

Considerations for Audits Performed in Accordance With PCAOB Standards

For audits performed in accordance with the PCAOB standards, for significant risks, paragraph 11 of Auditing Standard No. 13 (AICPA, *PCAOB Standards and Related Rules*, Auditing Standards), the auditor should perform substantive procedures, including tests of details, that are specifically responsive to the assessed risks.

4.121 A sample of other factors that the auditor may consider when determining the substantive testing approach to be utilized include the volume of transactions to be tested, reliability of data, conditions that cause variations in relationships among data, such as specific unusual transactions or events, accounting changes, business changes, or misstatements. The auditor may also consider the use of substantive analytical procedures when tests of details are performed for the same assertion.

4.122 It is the auditor's responsibility to evaluate the reasonableness of the loss reserve established by management. AU-C section 540, *Auditing Accounting Estimates, Including Fair Value Accounting Estimates, and Related Disclosures* (AICPA, *Professional Standards*), provides guidance for use by an auditor when considering the reasonableness of the loss reserve. Paragraph .08c of AU-C section 540 states that the auditor should obtain an understanding of how management developed the accounting estimates included in the financial statements and the data on which they are based. The loss reserve estimate is typically a significant estimate on the financial statements of an insurance entity. Accordingly, regardless of the approach used to audit the loss reserve estimate, the auditor should gain an understanding of how management developed the estimate.

4.123 As required by paragraph .12 of AU-C section 540, based on the assessed risks of material misstatement, the auditor should determine

 a. whether management has appropriately applied the requirements of the applicable financial reporting framework relevant to the accounting estimate; and

 b. whether the methods for making the accounting estimates are appropriate and have been applied consistently and whether changes from the prior period, if any, in accounting estimates or the method for making them are appropriate in the circumstances.

4.124 As discussed in paragraph .13 of AU-C section 540, in responding to the assessed risks of material misstatement, the auditor should undertake one or more of the following, taking into account the nature of the accounting estimate:

 a. Determine whether events occurring up to the date of the auditor's report provide audit evidence regarding the accounting estimate.

 b. Test how management made the accounting estimate and the data on which it is based. In doing so, the auditor should evaluate whether

> > i. the method of measurement used is appropriate in the circumstances;
> >
> > ii. the assumptions used by management are reasonable in light of the measurement objectives of the applicable financial reporting framework; and
> >
> > iii. the data on which the estimate is based is sufficiently reliable for the auditor's purposes.
>
> c. Test the operating effectiveness of the controls over how management made the accounting estimate together with appropriate substantive procedures.
>
> d. Develop a point estimate or range to evaluate management's point estimate. For this purpose
>
> > i. if the auditor uses assumptions or methods that differ from management's, the auditor should obtain an understanding of management's assumptions or methods sufficient to establish that the auditor's point estimate or range takes into account relevant variables and to evaluate any significant differences from management's point estimate.
> >
> > ii. if the auditor concludes that it is appropriate to use a range, the auditor should narrow the range, based on audit evidence available, until all outcomes within the range are considered reasonable.
>
> *Considerations for Audits Performed in Accordance With PCAOB Standards*
>
> When performing an integrated audit of financial statements and internal control over financial reporting, the auditor may use any of the four approaches. However, the work that the auditor performs as part of the audit of internal control over financial reporting should necessarily inform the auditor's decision about the approach he or she takes to auditing an estimate because, as part of the audit of internal control over financial reporting, the auditor would be required to obtain an understanding of the process management used to develop the estimate and to test controls over all relevant assertions related to the estimate (paragraph .10 of AU section 342, *Auditing Accounting Estimates* [AICPA, *PCAOB Standards and Related Rules*, Interim Standards]).

4.125 When auditing loss reserve estimates, usually approach (b), (c), (d), or a combination of the three is used. Normally, approach (a) alone is insufficient to provide sufficient appropriate evidence because claims are usually reported to insurance entities and settled over a period of time extending well beyond the typical auditor's report date. However, approach (a) may provide additional information concerning the reasonableness of loss reserve estimates, particularly for short tail lines of business, when used in combination with one or more of the other approaches.

4.126 When reviewing events occurring up to the date of the auditor's report for possible audit evidence regarding the estimation of loss reserves (as discussed in paragraph 4.124*a*), for statutory basis financial statements, changes in the reserve amounts as of year-end subsequent to the filing of the annual statement and prior to the issuance of audited financial statements due to the "continuous review process" should be considered a change in estimate and recorded in accordance with SSAP No. 3, *Accounting Changes and Corrections of Errors.*[16]

4.127 When planning the audit, whether the auditor chooses to use approach (b), (c), or (d), or a combination of the approaches will depend on his or her expectation of what approach will result in sufficient appropriate audit evidence in the most cost-effective manner. Each approach can be used, and, depending on client circumstances, each approach may be effective. However, when management has not used the services of a loss reserve specialist (either internal or external) in developing its loss reserve estimate, testing how management made the accounting estimate would generally not be appropriate. In this circumstance, it would be appropriate to develop a point estimate or range to evaluate management's point estimate.

4.128 The auditor should evaluate whether the data used by all involved parties (management and, as applicable, management's internal or external loss reserve specialist and the auditor's internal or external loss reserve specialist) is sufficiently reliable, including determining whether the data is complete, accurate and consistent. If the different parties will analyze the data in different groupings (that is, workers' compensation by state) the evaluation includes understanding the effect that may have on the ultimate loss reserve projections.

Use of Loss Reserve Specialists

4.129 Although AU-C section 500 does not preclude the auditor from using the work of a specialist who is employed by the insurance entity, because of the significance of loss reserves to the financial statements of insurance entities and the complexity and subjectivity involved in making loss reserve estimates, an auditor should consider using the work of either

   a. an auditor's external or internal loss reserve specialist; or

   b. management's external loss reserve specialist who is not an employee of the entity, (under the requirements of AU-C section 500 as discussed in paragraphs 4.134–.135).

Loss Reserve Specialists Engaged by the Auditor

4.130 If the auditor is developing a point estimate or range to evaluate management's point estimate, they may use loss reserve specialists within the audit firm (auditor's internal specialist) or separately engage external loss reserve specialists (auditor's external specialist). In either situation the auditor should follow all relevant requirements of AU-C section 620, including assessing the competency and objectivity of the specialist as well as the determination of the level of interaction between the parties, evaluation of the completeness and accuracy of the significant source data used, and evaluation of the relevance and reasonableness of significant assumptions in the circumstances and in relation to the auditor's other findings and conclusions.

---

[16] Paragraph 13 of SSAP No. 55, *Unpaid Claims, Losses and Loss Adjustment Expenses*, clarifies that liabilities for unpaid claims, losses, and loss adjustment expenses within the scope of SSAP No. 55 are not expected to be reestimated. Rather, additional information that is obtained after the submission of the annual statement that is not indicative of an error in the estimation process is considered part of the continuous review process and should be reflected in the statement of operations in the period the change becomes known.

4.131 If the auditor is using an internal loss reserving specialist, the working papers of the auditor's specialist form part of the audit documentation.

4.132 When using an external loss reserve specialist, the auditor should agree with the auditor's external specialist about the nature, timing and extent of communication between the auditor and the auditor's specialist, including the form of any report to be provided by the auditor's specialist, as required by AU-C section 620. Generally the working papers of the external specialist are its own and do not form part of the audit documentation. This is a factor for consideration in determining that the auditor's documentation satisfies the requirements of AU-C section 230, *Audit Documentation* (AICPA, *Professional Standards*). This may include obtaining and reviewing a copy of the auditor's external specialist's report.

> *Considerations for Audits Performed in Accordance With PCAOB Standards*
>
> The fact that generally the working papers of the external specialist are its own and do not form part of the audit documentation is a factor for consideration in determining that the auditor's documentation satisfies the requirements of Auditing Standard No. 3, *Audit Documentation* (AICPA, *PCAOB Standards and Related Rules*, Auditing Standards).

Use of Management Specialists by Auditors in Evaluating Loss Reserves

4.133 One of the procedures the auditor may consider in evaluating the reasonableness of the loss reserve is using the work of management's external specialist. AU-C section 500 provides guidance to the auditor who uses the work of management's external specialist in performing an audit of financial statements, and the relevance and reliability of the information to be used as audit evidence. The auditor is not expected to have the expertise of a person trained for or qualified to engage in the practice of another profession or occupation.

4.134 As discussed in paragraph .08 of AU-C section 500, if information to be used as audit evidence has been prepared using the work of a management's specialist, the auditor should, to the extent necessary, taking into account the significance of that specialist's work for the auditor's purposes,

    a. evaluate the competence, capabilities, and objectivity of that specialist;

    b. obtain an understanding of the work of that specialist; and

    c. evaluate the appropriateness of that specialist's work as audit evidence for the relevant assertion.

4.135 As discussed in paragraph .09 of AU-C section 500, when using information produced by the entity, the auditor should evaluate whether the information is sufficiently reliable for the auditor's purposes, including, as necessary, in the following circumstances:

    a. Obtaining audit evidence about the accuracy and completeness of the information

    b. Evaluating whether the information is sufficiently precise and detailed for the auditor's purposes

Auditor's Response to Management's Use or Non-Use of a Loss Reserve Specialist

4.136 The following are descriptions of situations involving the presence or absence of a loss reserve specialist in management's determination of loss reserves and the recommended response by the auditor in each situation.

Situation 1—The entity does not have a management loss reserve specialist involved in the determination of loss reserves.

Auditor response to situation 1—This situation may constitute a significant deficiency and possibly a material weakness in internal control. It is recommended that the auditor use an external or internal loss reserve specialist to develop a point estimate or range to evaluate management's point estimate.

Situation 2—The entity has a management internal loss reserve specialist who is involved in the determination of loss reserves and the entity does not use an outside loss reserve specialist.

Auditor response to situation 2—It is recommended that the auditor involve an auditor's external or internal loss reserve specialist to audit the reasonableness of the entity's loss reserve estimate by using an appropriate approach selected from paragraph 4.124.

Situation 3—The entity has no management internal loss reserve specialist but involves an external loss reserve specialist hired by management (that is, management's external loss reserve specialist) in the determination of loss reserves.

Auditor response to situation 3—If the auditor plans to use the work of management's external loss reserve specialist in evaluating the reasonableness of the loss reserve, the auditor should evaluate the competence, capabilities, and objectivity of a management's specialist, obtain an understanding of the work of that specialist, and evaluate the appropriateness of that specialist's work as audit evidence as required in AU-C section 500.

Situation 4—The entity involves management's internal loss reserve specialist in the determination of loss reserves and involves an external loss reserve specialist to separately review the loss reserves.

Auditor response to situation 4—In evaluating the reasonableness of the loss reserves, the auditor may wish to consider the work of management's internal and external loss reserve specialists in determining the appropriate audit approach as discussed in paragraph 4.124.

As discussed in situation 3, if the auditor plans to use the work of management's external loss reserve specialist in evaluating the reasonableness of the loss reserve, the auditor should evaluate the competence, capabilities, and objectivity of a management's specialist, obtain an understanding of the work of that specialist, and evaluate the appropriateness of that specialist's work as audit evidence as required in AU-C section 500.

Evaluating the Reasonableness of the Estimates

4.137 As required by paragraphs .18–.20 of AU-C section 540 the auditor should evaluate, based on the audit evidence, the reasonableness of the accounting estimates and disclosures related to such estimates, including the adequacy of the disclosure of estimation uncertainty for accounting estimates that give rise to significant risks, in the financial statements in the context of the applicable financial reporting framework. AU-C section 540 provides guidance that can be used by an auditor when evaluating the reasonableness of the loss reserve. This evaluation may include analytical procedures to assist the auditor in understanding changes as well as substantive procedures to obtain evidence regarding the completeness and accuracy of the amounts.

Analytical Procedures[17]

4.138 Analytical procedures are an important part of the audit process and consist of evaluations of financial information made by a study of plausible relationships among both financial and nonfinancial data. The use of analytical procedures should be considered throughout the audit cycle as a part of planning, substantive, or conclusion procedures. A basic premise underlying the application of analytical procedures is that it is reasonable to assume that plausible relationships among data exist and continue in the absence of known conditions to the contrary. Variations in these relationships may be caused by particular conditions such as unusual transactions or events, accounting changes, material business changes, random fluctuations, or misstatements.

4.139 AU-C section 520, *Analytical Procedures* (AICPA, *Professional Standards*), provides guidance on the use and documentation of analytical procedures and requires the use of analytical procedures in the overall review stage of all audits. Also, in accordance with paragraphs .05–.06 of AU-C section 315 the auditor should perform risk assessment procedures, including analytical procedures, to provide a basis for the identification and assessment of risks of material misstatement at the financial statement and relevant assertion levels.

4.140 The results of analytical procedures performed during the planning phase of the audit may affect the nature, timing, and extent of audit procedures. If there were numerous unexpected variances on a particular line of business, for example, the auditor may determine that it is more appropriate to develop a point estimate or range to evaluate management's point estimate rather than only test how management made the accounting estimate and the data on which it is based.

4.141 Various analytical procedures may be used in the evaluation of the reasonableness of loss reserve estimates, such as the analysis of

- loss and loss adjustment expense ratios.
- reserve development.
- loss frequency and severity statistics.
- claim cost by exposure units.
- average case reserves.
- claim closure rates.
- paid to incurred ratios.

4.142 Examples of sources of information for developing analytical expectations include prior period financial information, Insurance Regulatory Information System (IRIS) ratio analysis, and rating agency reports.

---

[17] The AICPA Audit Guide *Analytical Procedures* provides practical guidance to auditors on the effective use of analytical procedures. The Audit Guide includes a discussion of AU-C section 520, *Analytical Procedures* (AICPA, *Professional Standards*), concepts and definitions, a series of questions and answers, and a case study illustrating trend analysis, ratio analysis, reasonableness testing, and regression analysis.

4.143 Such analyses include comparison of significant assumptions or estimates with industry averages or other expectations. Evaluations would normally be disaggregated by line of business and accident or report year. When the auditor is able to validate the completeness and accuracy of the data used in management analytics, the auditor may elect to include these as a part of their audit evidence. It may be appropriate for the auditor to meet with management to discuss the results of analytics performed by both parties in order to understand any unexpected or unusual trends or changes.

Testing the Data, Assumptions, and Selection of the Estimate

4.144 As discussed in paragraph 4.124, an auditor may respond to the assessed risks of material misstatement for loss reserves by testing how management determined the accounting estimate and the data on which it is based. This approach may be appropriate for evaluating the reasonableness of the accounting estimates involved with loss reserves when loss reserve estimates are recommended by management's external loss reserve specialist, management has a process to evaluate the recommended reserve, and management accepts those recommendations.

4.145 An entity that uses an external loss reserve specialist to develop loss reserve recommendations may engage the external specialist to evaluate only the entity's major lines of business or only certain components of the loss reserves. In either circumstance, the auditor may determine that a different approach is needed for auditing the items not reported on by management's external loss-reserve specialist.

4.146 AU-C section 540 identifies the following as procedures the auditor may consider performing when using this approach. Some of the procedures subsequently listed apply to the process management uses to supply data to its external or internal loss reserve specialist, some apply to the process used by management's external or internal specialist to develop recommendations, some apply to the process used by management to review and evaluate those recommendations, and some apply to the process management uses to translate management's external or internal specialist's recommendations into the loss reserve estimates recorded in the financial statements:

- *Identify whether there are controls over the preparation of accounting estimates and supporting data that may be useful in the evaluation.* Controls over the preparation of accounting estimates may include
    — procedures for selecting independent external loss reserve specialists or hiring internal specialists, including procedures for determining that the specialist has the requisite competence in loss reserving, knowledge of the entity's types of business, and understanding of the different methods available for calculating loss reserve estimates.
    — procedures for reviewing and evaluating the recommendations of the external or internal loss reserve specialist.
    — procedures to ensure that the methods used to calculate the loss reserve estimate are appropriate and sufficient in the circumstances.
    — procedures to verify the clerical accuracy of the calculations in the determination of key factors, assumptions and the ultimate loss estimate, especially with regard to the use of spreadsheets,

which are susceptible to data transposition errors whether intentional or not.

Controls over the preparation of supporting data, in addition to those discussed later in this chapter, may include

— procedures for verifying that data used by the external or internal loss reserve specialist is appropriately summarized and classified from the entity's claims database.

— procedures for ensuring that data used by the external or internal loss reserve specialist is complete and accurate.

— procedures to substantiate and determine the appropriateness of industry or other external data sources used in developing assumptions (for example, data received from involuntary risk pools).

- *Identify the sources of data and factors that management used in forming the assumptions, and consider whether such data and factors are relevant, reliable, and sufficient for the purpose, based on information gathered in other audit tests.* Sources of data and factors used may include

— entity historical claims data, including changes and trends in the data.

— entity information on reinsurance levels and changes from prior years' reinsurance programs.

— data received from involuntary risk pools such as those administered by the National Council on Compensation Insurance.

— industry loss data from published sources.

— internal entity experience or information from published sources concerning recent trends in socioeconomic factors affecting claim payments, such as (*a*) general inflation rates and specific inflation rates for medical costs, wages, automobile repair costs, and the like; (*b*) judicial decisions assessing liability; (*c*) judicial decisions regarding noneconomic damages; and (*d*) changes in legislation affecting payment levels and settlement practices.

Consider whether the entity's data is sufficient to have adequate statistical credibility (for example, to allow the "law of large numbers" to work for the entity's estimates). Consider whether the types of industry data used in developing assumptions are relevant to the entity's book of business, considering policy limits, reinsurance retention, geographic and industry concentrations, and other appropriate factors.

- *Consider whether there are additional key factors or alternative assumptions about the factors.* Key factors and potential alternative assumptions that might be considered include

— changes in the entity's experience or trends in loss reporting and settlements. Increases in the speed of the settlement of claims may lead to assumptions that paid development levels will be lower in the future, or may indicate changes in the entity's procedures for processing claims that could lead to increased development in the future.

The Loss Reserving and Claims Cycle

- divergence in entity experience relative to industry experience. Such divergence might later result in entity development experience that reduces the divergence or might be indicative of a change in an entity's experience with a book of business.
- changes in an entity's practices and procedures relating to recording and settling claims.
- an entity's reinsurance programs and changes therein.
- changes in an entity's underwriting practices such as new or increased use of managing general agents.
- new or changed policy forms or coverages.
- recent catastrophic occurrences.

- *Evaluate whether the assumptions are consistent with each other, the supporting data, relevant historical data, and industry data.* In accordance with AU-C section 540, the auditor should evaluate all significant assumptions, which may include
  - paid loss projection methods, which assume that an entity's historical experience relating to the timeliness of settlement will be predictive of future results.
  - reported (incurred) loss development projection methods, which assume that an entity's experience in estimating case-basis reserves will be repeated in the future.

- *Analyze historical data used in developing the assumptions to assess whether it is comparable and consistent with data of the period under audit and consider whether the data is sufficiently reliable for the purpose.* Consider whether the entity's past methods of estimating loss reserves have resulted in appropriate estimates and whether current data (for example, current year development factors) indicate changes from prior experience. Consider the information within the loss reserve rollforward table and development commentary in the related footnotes to the financial statements. Consider how known changes in the entity's loss reporting procedures and settlement practices have been factored into the estimate. Consider how changes in reinsurance programs, in the current period and during historical periods, have been factored into management's estimates.

  The auditor should review the current year development of prior reserve estimates to assess the loss reserving process under the requirements of paragraph .09 of AU-C section 540. To understand the change in prior year reserves, the auditor should consider additional information that led to the re-estimation of prior reserve estimates.

  The evaluation should also take into account the nature of accounting estimates and whether the information obtained from the review would be relevant to identifying and assessing risks of material misstatement made in the current period. However, the review is not intended to call into question the auditor's professional judgments made in the prior periods that were based on information available at the time.

- *Consider whether changes in the business or industry may cause other factors to become significant to the assumptions.* The auditor may need the assistance of the auditor's external or internal specialist to understand the reasonableness of the drivers in the change in the

AAG-PLI 4.146

loss estimate such as unexpected claim severity, frequency, regulatory changes, or process changes. Additionally, the understanding of the factors causing development in the current period will aid in the review of the loss rollforward disclosures required under FASB ASC 944 as well as the associated discussion of the factors causing the change in the estimate disclosed as required under FASB ASC 944, FASB ASC 275, and the SEC. Examples of these disclosures are included in appendix A. Consider such changes as

— new lines of business and classes of business within lines.

— changes in reinsurance programs.

— changes in the regulatory environment such as premium rate rollbacks and regulation.

— changes in the method of establishing rates and changes in methods of underwriting business.

— changes in processing such as the timing of claim payments.

- *Review available documentation of the assumptions used in developing the accounting estimates, inquire about any other plans, goals, and objectives of the entity, and consider their relationship to the assumptions.* An entity's practices concerning settling claims, such as a practice of vigorously defending suits or of quickly settling suits, can have a significant effect on an entity's loss experience.

- *Consider using the work of a specialist regarding certain assumptions.* Using the work of a specialist is discussed in AU-C section 620.

- *Test the calculations used by management to translate the assumptions and key factors into the accounting estimate.* Consider whether all lines of business and accident years are included in the loss reserve estimate. Consider how reinsurance receivable, salvage, and subrogation have been included.

4.147 If the auditor tests how management determines the accounting estimate and the data on which it is based, and management's estimate differs significantly from the recommendations developed by management's external or internal specialists, expanded procedures should be performed by the auditor to evaluate the factors and assumptions that resulted in the differences. The auditor should consider the guidance in paragraph .12 of AU-C section 230 regarding documentation of how the auditor addressed information that is inconsistent with the auditor's final conclusion, and paragraph .10*a* of AU-C section 500, regarding what modifications or additions to audit procedures are necessary when audit evidence obtained from one source that is inconsistent with that obtained from another.

4.148 Because the process of estimating loss reserves is complex and involves many subjective judgments, the absence of involvement by a loss reserve specialist in the determination of management's estimate may constitute a significant deficiency and possibly a material weakness in the entity's internal control. AU-C section 265, *Communicating Internal Control Related Matters Identified in an Audit* (AICPA, *Professional Standards*), describes the auditor's responsibility to communicate significant deficiencies and material weaknesses to the audit committee. For an integrated audit, AU section 325, *Communications About Control Deficiencies in an Audit of Financial Statements* (AICPA, *PCAOB Standards and Related Rules*, Interim Standards), describes the auditor's responsibilities regarding communication of control deficiencies. Under SAP Section 11, "Communication of Internal Control Related Matters Noted in an Audit," of the NAIC revised Model Audit rule requires that each insurer furnish the commissioner with a written communication about any unremediated material weaknesses in its internal control over financial reporting noted during the audit.

Auditing the Underlying Data Used in the Loss Reserving Process

4.149 As subsequently noted, the *NAIC Property and Casualty Annual Statement Instructions* require the auditor to determine what historical data and methods have been used by management in developing the loss reserve estimate and whether he or she will rely on the same data or other statistical data in evaluating the reasonableness of the loss reserve estimate.

4.150 When the historical experience is the basis for significant assumptions used by management for loss reserve estimates, testing the historical data is necessary and may include

- premiums written or earned;
- losses paid or incurred;
- exposure;
- policy limits;
- claim counts; and
- third-party information.

4.151 Regardless of the audit approach selected, the auditor should perform substantive procedures for all relevant assertions related to each material class of transactions, account balance, and disclosure.[18] The auditor's substantive procedures should include agreeing on the financial statements, including their accompanying notes, to the underlying accounting records and examining material journal entries and other adjustments. Because claim data and characteristics such as dates and type of loss can significantly influence reserve estimation, the auditor should test the completeness, accuracy, and classification of the claim loss data.

> *Considerations for Audits Performed in Accordance With PCAOB Standards*
>
> For audits performed in accordance with PCAOB standards, the auditor's substantive procedures must include reconciling the financial statements with the underlying accounting records and examining material adjustments made during the course of preparing the financial statements (paragraph 41 of Auditing Standard No. 13).

4.152 The *NAIC Property and Casualty Annual Statement Instructions* require coordination among the auditor, an appointed actuary, and management and potentially require additional procedures for the auditor related to claim loss and LAE data. Section 9 of the instructions, "Scope of Examination and Report of Independent Certified Public Accountant," states

> [t]he insurer shall also require that the independent certified public accountant subject the data used by the appointed actuary to testing

---

[18] For integrated audits, the sentence reads, "Regardless of the assessed level of control risk or the assessed risk of material misstatement in connection with the audit of the financial statements, the auditor should perform substantive procedures for all relevant assertions for all significant accounts and disclosures."

procedures. The auditor is required to determine what historical data and methods have been used by management in developing the loss reserve estimate and whether he or she will rely on the same data or other statistical data in evaluating the reasonableness of the loss reserve estimate. After identifying the relevant data, the auditor should obtain an understanding of the controls related to the completeness, accuracy, and classification of loss data and perform testing as to the understanding of the controls related to the completeness, accuracy, and classification of loss data, and perform other testing as the auditor deems appropriate. Through inquiry of the appointed actuary, the auditor should obtain an understanding of the data identified by the appointed actuary as significant. It is recognized that there will be instances when data identified by the appointed actuary as significant to his or her reserve projections would not otherwise have been tested as part of the audit, and separate testing would be required. Unless otherwise agreed among the appointed actuary, management, and the auditor, the scope of the work performed by the auditor in testing the claims data in the course of the audit would be sufficient to determine whether the data tested is fairly stated in all material respects in relation to the statutory financial statements taken as a whole. The auditing procedures should be applied to the claims loss and defense and cost containment expense data used by the appointed actuary and would be applied to activity that occurred in the current calendar year (for example, tests of payments on claims paid during the current calendar year).

4.153 This does not replace the requirements to audit reconciliations of the data provided in Schedule P of the annual statement to the underlying accounting records as described in SOP 92-8. The auditor should inform management if the auditor has not planned to include in the audit all of the data identified as significant by the appointed actuary, that there may be a need for additional testing outside the scope of the statutory audit. The conclusion regarding the need for the auditor to perform additional procedures should be agreed upon by the management and the loss reserving specialist and requested of the auditor directly by management. If procedures are performed beyond those included in the statutory audit, the auditor should report on such work under the AICPA's professional standards.[19]

4.154 As previously noted, the auditor should test the information in the underwriting and claims systems as well any other information considered critical including quantitative (that is, premiums written or earned, case reserves, deductible information) and qualitative information (that is, line of business, insured location, loss accident year). If any attributes deemed critical by the appointed actuary are not tested by the auditor the auditor should document their rationale for excluding those attributes.

---

[19] The American Academy of Actuaries Committee on Property & Liability Financial Reporting published the October 2004 paper "Data Testing Requirement in 2004 P/C Annual Statement Instructions: Guidance For Actuaries Signing Statements of Actuarial Opinions on Loss and Loss Expense Reserves," which can be found on the American Academy of Actuaries website www.actuary.org.

Develop a Point Estimate or Range to Evaluate Management's Estimate

4.155 Based on his or her understanding of the facts and circumstances, the auditor may independently develop an expectation of the estimate by using other key factors or alternative assumptions about those factors. This approach is recommended whenever management has not used the services of an external or internal loss reserve specialist in developing its loss reserve estimate and may be appropriate to assist the auditor in assessing the range of reasonable possible outcomes of the entity's loss reserves and related income statement amounts, even when management does use an external or internal loss reserve specialist. The auditor frequently develops independent projections because this method may result in a more cost-effective method of obtaining sufficient appropriate audit evidence.

4.156 When this approach is used, the auditor may use either an auditor's external or internal loss reserve specialist to develop the independent expectation of the loss reserve estimate.

Loss Reserve Ranges

4.157 Estimates are based on subjective as well as objective factors and, as a result, judgment is required to estimate an amount at the date of the financial statements. Management's judgment is normally based on its knowledge and experience about past and current events and its assumptions about conditions it expects to exist and courses of action it expects to take. Accordingly, loss reserves may develop in a number of ways and a reserve for a particular line of business or accident year may prove to be redundant or deficient when analyzed in a following period. Loss reserves considered to be adequate in prior periods may need to be adjusted at a later date as a result of events outside the control of the insurance entity that create the need for a change in estimate. Such events include future court decisions and periods of inflation, in which rates may change significantly from period to period and affect the payout of claims. As a result of the circumstances described previously, the need to adjust loss reserve estimates in future periods because of future events that are not predictable at the balance sheet date should not necessarily be interpreted as evidence of an error or poor loss reserving practices in the past.

4.158 Because the ultimate settlement of claims is subject to future events, no single loss reserve estimate can be considered accurate with certainty. Auditors should refer to AU-C section 540 when considering the estimation uncertainty inherent in loss reserve estimates. The development of a single loss reserve projection, by itself, does not address estimation uncertainty (as discussed in paragraph .15 of AU-C section 540) and may not provide sufficient evidence to evaluate the reasonableness of the loss reserve provision in the financial statements. As discussed in paragraph 4.74, it is management's responsibility to record its best estimate of loss reserves in the financial statements. The auditor is responsible for evaluating the reasonableness of accounting estimates made by management in the context of the financial statements taken as a whole. As discussed in paragraph .15 of AU-C section 540, for accounting estimates that give rise to significant risks, in addition to other substantive procedures performed to meet the requirements of AU-C section 330, the auditor should evaluate the following:

a. How management has considered alternative assumptions or outcomes and why it has rejected them or how management has otherwise addressed estimation uncertainty in making the accounting estimate

b. Whether the significant assumptions used by management are reasonable

c. When relevant to the reasonableness of the significant assumptions used by management or the appropriate application of the applicable financial reporting framework, management's intent to carry out specific courses of action and its ability to do so

4.159 As discussed in paragraph .16 of AU-C section 540, if, in the auditor's professional judgment, management has not adequately addressed the effects of estimation uncertainty on the accounting estimates that give rise to significant risks, the auditor should, if considered necessary, develop a range with which to evaluate the reasonableness of the accounting estimate.

4.160 In evaluating reasonableness, the auditor should obtain an understanding of how management developed the estimate. This understanding provides the auditor with information that may be relevant to the auditor's development of an appropriate point estimate or range. As discussed in paragraph .A99 of AU-C section 540, when the auditor concludes that it is appropriate to use a range to evaluate the reasonableness of management's point estimate (the auditor's range), it is required that the range encompass all reasonable outcomes, rather than all possible outcomes. The auditor's range is useful and effective when it is sufficiently narrow to enable the auditor to conclude whether the accounting estimate is not materially misstated.

4.161 Another way to address the range of reasonable possible outcomes of the entity's loss reserves is for the auditor to develop a best estimate and to supplement it with qualitative analysis that addresses the variability of the estimate. Qualitative analysis involves consideration of the factors affecting the variability of loss reserves and integrating such factors into a determination of the range of reasonable estimates around a best estimate. Such factors, among others, include the mix of products underwritten, losses incurred by the insurance industry for similar coverages and underwriting years, and the correlation between past and current business written. Accordingly, when planning and performing procedures to evaluate accounting estimates, the auditor should consider, with an attitude of professional skepticism, both the subjective and objective factors. The audit procedures performed for this purpose will vary based on the characteristics of the business, the controls the entity uses to monitor such variability, and other audit procedures used.

4.162 The size of the loss reserve range will vary by line of business. For example, automobile physical damage claims may be estimated with greater precision than product liability claims. In extreme cases, the top-to-bottom range could extend to 50 percent and upward of the amount provided. An example of an extreme case might be a newly formed entity that writes primarily volatile types of business. The results of operations in such a situation are sensitive to future fluctuations because the loss reserve estimate is based primarily on assumptions that will undoubtedly change over time. More important, however, is the strain that any extremely adverse loss development would place on such an entity's surplus. In an opposite extreme case, the top-to-bottom range might only be 5 percent of the amount provided for an entity that only writes automobile physical damage coverages.

4.163 In evaluating whether management has identified all accounting estimates that could be material to the financial statements, the auditor considers the circumstances of the industry or industries in which the entity operates, its methods of conducting business, new accounting pronouncements, and other external factors. In other words, it is unlikely that ultimate claim settlements for each line of business will fall at the same end of the range.

Factors That Could Affect a Range of Reasonably Possible Outcomes

4.164 Because loss reserves represent both reported and unreported claims that have occurred as of the valuation date, the auditor needs to gain an understanding of the entity's exposure to risk through the business it writes as well as an understanding of environmental factors that may affect the entity's loss development at the valuation date.

4.165 The following are some factors that may affect the range of reasonable possible outcomes of the entity's loss reserves:

- *The frequency and severity of claims associated with a line of business.* Medical malpractice, directors' and officers' liability, and other lines of business that typically produce few claims with large settlement amounts tend to have a high degree of variability.
- *Policy characteristics.* Individual lines of business can be written on different policy forms. For example, loss reserving and its related variability for medical malpractice written on an occurrence basis will differ markedly when the policy is written on a claims-made basis, especially during the early years of conversion from an occurrence to a claims-made basis. Additionally lines such as workers' compensation may include varying deductible amounts and significant changes that will have an impact on variability.
- *Retention levels.* The greater an entity's retention level, the more variable the results are likely to be. This increased variability is due to the effect that one or several large losses can have on the overall book of business. For reinsurance assumed, the concepts analogous to retention levels are referred to as attachment points and limits.
- *The mix of an entity's business with respect to long tail liability lines and short tail property lines.* Typically, loss reserves on business with longer tails exhibit greater variability than on business with shorter tails because events affecting ultimate claim settlements may occur at a later date.

4.166 Some external factors that may affect the range of reasonable possible outcomes of the entity's loss reserves are

- changes in the regulatory environment.
- lack of readily available information related to catastrophes or major civil disorders.
- jury awards and social inflation arising from the legal environment in principal states in which an entity's risks are underwritten.
- the effect of inflation.
- foreign exchange fluctuations.

- tort reform and the uncertainty of the appeals process may have on certain lines of business such as medical malpractice and workers' compensation.

4.167 The auditor should obtain an understanding of both internal and external risk factors. This may be accomplished by a review of contracts, inquiries of underwriters, a review of pertinent trade publications, and any other procedures deemed necessary under the circumstances. The auditor should consider these factors in evaluating a range of reasonable possible outcomes of the entity's loss reserves. The best estimate may not necessarily be midway between in the range of reasonable possible outcomes of the entity's loss reserves, because certain factors (for example, risk retention limits and retrospectively rated contracts) may reduce the variability at one end of the range but not at the other.

4.168 The auditor needs to know about, be familiar with, and consider the workings of all significant reinsurance ceded contracts and the effect that these contracts have on best estimates and the range of reasonable possible outcomes of the entity's loss reserves. The effect of reinsurance ceded agreements on loss reserves and ceded reinsurance premiums are also important considerations.

4.169 When analyzing the range of reasonable possible outcomes of the entity's loss reserves, the auditor may wish to consider potential offsets that may serve to reduce the financial statement effects of misstatements in the recorded loss reserves. Two common examples are ceded reinsurance and retrospectively rated contracts (primary or reinsurance). It is recommended that such offsets, if material, be included in an analysis of the range of reasonable possible outcomes of the entity's loss reserves to quantify the true income statement or balance sheet effect that results from an increase or decrease in loss reserves.

4.170 A retrospectively rated feature in an insurance contract means that increases or decreases in incurred losses may be wholly or partially offset by changes to earned but unbilled premiums. As a result of such a clause, an increase in loss reserves may lead to a receivable for additional premiums, and a decrease in loss reserves may be offset by a reduction in premiums.

Evaluating the Financial Effect of a Reserve Range

4.171 To determine the amount of variability that is significant to the financial statements, an auditor may wish to consider the financial leverage of an entity. Financial leverage refers to items such as reserve-to-surplus ratios. The financial position of an entity with a 1.5-to-1 reserve-to-surplus ratio is less affected by variability in its loss reserves than is an entity operating at a 3-to-1 ratio with a similar book of business.

4.172 Additionally, an analysis comparing the difference between the net recorded loss reserves and the high and low ends of a range of reasonable outcomes with key financial statement balances, such as surplus or recorded loss reserves, might be performed. Combining financial leverage with other materiality factors pertinent to the entity (for example, loan covenant agreements) may provide insights into the amount of variability that is acceptable to the auditor. Because of the imprecise nature of estimating loss reserves, the acceptable range of loss reserve estimates will generally be higher than that of a more tangible balance such as accounts receivable or payable.

4.173 As discussed in paragraph .A122 of AU-C section 540,

> [b]ased on the audit evidence obtained, the auditor may conclude that the evidence points to an accounting estimate that differs from management's point estimate. When the audit evidence supports a point estimate, the difference between the auditor's point estimate and management's point estimate constitutes a misstatement. When the auditor has concluded that using the auditor's range provides sufficient appropriate audit evidence, a management point estimate that lies outside the auditor's range would not be supported by audit evidence. In such cases, the misstatement is no less than the difference between management's point estimate and the nearest point of the auditor's range.

4.174 As stated in paragraph .07 of AU-C section 450, *Evaluation of Misstatements Identified During the Audit* (AICPA, *Professional Standards*), the auditor should communicate on a timely basis with the appropriate level of management all misstatements accumulated during the audit, and request management to correct those misstatements.

4.175 Where the auditor has identified a judgmental misstatement involving differences in estimates, the auditor may request management to review the assumption and methods used in developing the estimate. After management has challenged the assumptions and methods used in developing an estimate for which the auditor has identified a misstatement, the auditor should reevaluate the amount of the misstatement. This includes performing additional further audit procedures, if necessary. As discussed in paragraph .09 of AU-C section 450, if management refuses to correct some or all of the misstatements communicated by the auditor, the auditor should obtain an understanding of management's reasons for not making the corrections and should take that understanding into account when evaluating whether the financial statements as a whole are free from material misstatement.

4.176 Materiality judgments involve both qualitative and quantitative considerations. As a result of the interaction of quantitative and qualitative considerations in materiality judgments, misstatements of relatively small amounts that come to the auditor's attention could have a material effect on the financial statements. Refer to paragraph .12 of AU-C section 450 for documentation requirements related to misstatements.

> *Considerations for Audits Performed in Accordance With Public Company Accounting Oversight Board (PCAOB) Standards*
>
> For audits conducted in accordance with PCAOB standards, PCAOB Auditing Standard No. 3 establishes general requirements for documentation the auditor should prepare and retain in connection with applicable engagements.

4.177 Management generally should select a single loss reserve estimate (management's best estimate)[20] that represents its judgment about the most likely circumstances and events. If management develops a reasonable range, the amount recorded could be the best estimate within that range. If the difference between the entity's recorded reserve and the farther end of the reserve range is deemed significant, the auditor may extend audit procedures to obtain additional audit evidence (such as, to understand the difference between the farther end of the range and management's estimate).

---

[20] See footnote 11.

4.178 In determining the reasonableness of loss reserves, the auditor also may consider the consistency of reserve estimates and any changes in the degree of conservatism of recorded reserves. A change in the degree of conservatism of management's estimate may be indicative of a change in management's reserve process. AU-C section 705, *Modifications to the Opinion in the Independent Auditor's Report* (AICPA, *Professional Standards*), discusses the auditor's responsibility to consider whether the financial statements include adequate disclosure of material matters in light of the circumstances and facts of which the auditor is aware.

4.179 When performing an integrated audit, additional guidance relating to audit risk and materiality can be found in Auditing Standard No. 8, *Audit Risk*, and Auditing Standard No. 11, *Consideration of Materiality in Planning and Performing an Audit* (AICPA, *PCAOB Standards and Related Rules*, Auditing Standards).

Auditor Uncertainty About the Reasonableness of Management's Estimate and Reporting Implications

4.180 Ordinarily, the auditor would look to historical data to obtain audit evidence that will provide reasonable assurance that management's estimate of loss reserves is reasonable in the circumstances. Such historical data may not currently exist for certain new entities, for entities writing significant amounts of new lines of business, or for entities with a low volume of claims. In situations where historical data is not available, the auditor should obtain other audit evidence to assist in making a determination whether management has adequately disclosed the uncertainty about management's estimate of loss reserves in the notes to the financial statements as required by FASB ASC 450 and 275.

4.181 A matter involving an uncertainty is one that is expected to be resolved at a future date at which time conclusive audit evidence concerning its outcome would be expected to become available. Conclusive audit evidence concerning the ultimate outcome of uncertainties cannot be expected to exist at the time of the audit because the outcome and related audit evidence are prospective. In these circumstances, management is responsible for estimating the effect of future events on the financial statements, or determining that a reasonable estimate cannot be made and making the required disclosures, all in accordance with GAAP, based on management's analysis of existing conditions. Absence of the existence of information related to the outcome of an uncertainty does not necessarily lead to a conclusion that the audit evidence supporting management's assertion is not sufficient. Rather, the auditor's judgment regarding the sufficiency of the audit evidence is based on the audit evidence that is available. If, after considering the existing conditions and available evidence, the auditor concludes that sufficient audit evidence supports management's assertion about the nature of a matter involving an uncertainty and its presentation or disclosure in the financial statements, an unqualified opinion ordinarily is appropriate. If the auditor is unable to obtain sufficient audit evidence to support management's assertions about the nature of a matter involving an uncertainty and its presentation or disclosure in the financial statements, the auditor should consider the need to express a modified opinion either as a qualified opinion or a disclaimer of opinion because of a scope limitation. A qualification or disclaimer of opinion because of a scope limitation is appropriate if sufficient audit evidence related to an uncertainty does or did exist but was not available to the auditor for reasons such as management's record retention policies or a restriction imposed by management.

Evaluating the Reasonableness of Loss Adjustment Expense Reserves

4.182 Evaluation of the reasonableness of LAE reserves involves many of the same skills that are needed to evaluate the reasonableness of loss reserves; therefore, such an evaluation ordinarily requires the use of an outside loss reserve specialist. Frequently, both DCC reserves and AO reserves are calculated based on formulas related to paid losses; therefore, in conjunction with the audit of LAE, the auditor should perform sufficient procedures to obtain assurance about the reliability of the paid-loss data. Although DCC and AO frequently are calculated using formulas based on paid losses, they can be calculated differently; accordingly, different procedures may be needed to evaluate those types of reserves.

4.183 The reasonableness of the AO reserve is primarily dependent on the application of sound techniques of cost accounting and expense allocation. It is recommended that the auditor review the basis of this allocation because the way that the entity allocates its expenses will have an effect on the AO reserve calculation. It is helpful for this review to focus on the allocation of costs to the loss adjustment classification as well as the allocation within that classification to the individual lines of business.

Ceded Reinsurance Recoverable and Receivable

4.184 This section discusses certain concepts and procedures that are fundamental to the auditor's evaluation of the reasonableness of the reinsurance recoverable and receivable. This section does not address the following items, which are discussed in chapter 6. Refer to chapter 6 of this guide for information about

- the purpose and nature of reinsurance.
- forms and types of reinsurance.
- accounting for reinsurance transactions.
- internal control considerations relating to ceded and assumed reinsurance and a description of audit procedures to verify the integrity of recorded transaction data pursuant to such agreements.

Understanding an Insurance Entity's Reinsurance Program

4.185 Chapter 6 of this guide recommends that the auditor obtain an understanding of an insurance entity's reinsurance program to properly perform audit procedures to verify the accuracy and completeness of recorded cessions and assess the ability of reinsurers to meet their financial obligations under such agreements. This understanding is also essential to properly evaluate the reasonableness of reinsurance recoverable balances. Because the use of historical information from reinsurance arrangements may be necessary to estimate current amounts, it is recommended that the auditor obtain an understanding of both reinsurance arrangements currently in effect and those in effect during historical periods from which loss experience will be used to project current year ultimate losses and reinsurance recoveries.

4.186 Net loss development patterns will vary from gross development to the extent that current reinsurance arrangements (coverages, levels of retention, and type and form of reinsurance) differ from arrangements in effect during the claim experience period used to project losses. Accordingly, the effect of such differences on estimates of reinsurance recoverables will need to be assessed by the auditor and the loss reserve specialist. The level of complexity involved in making this assessment is dependent on the types of reinsurance used and the amount of experience available under the program. In order to obtain audit evidence about the reasonableness of certain reinsurance accounts, the auditor may need to perform procedures to test the "gross-up" or "net-down" of balances in the financial statements and related disclosures.

4.187 Special difficulties arise in estimating reinsurance receivables on excess of loss reinsurance arrangements in which claim frequency is sporadic, retention levels have changed, or aggregate excess of loss arrangements are used. Estimates of reinsurance receivables are generally easiest for primary first dollar coverages (first dollar coverage of either property or casualty business). Additionally, relying on expected loss ratios as a guide for estimating recoveries on excess reinsurance arrangements will not be very helpful if the pricing of such arrangements has varied from year to year with little correlation to the underlying economics of these agreements. Some entities separately project reinsurance recoverable on IBNR losses by stratifying the data base by size of loss.

4.188 Several other factors that are relevant when reviewing the effects of the insurer's reinsurance program on the loss reserves include the effects of the solvency of the reinsurer as well as the effects of intercompany reinsurance agreements. Companies can effectively manage risk through their reinsurance program but they must also consider the ability of the reinsurance counterparties to settle claims. The solvency of the reinsurer is relevant to the evaluation of ceded loss reserves both paid and unpaid as the losses are ultimately the responsibility of the direct insurer and any inability to recover amounts from the reinsurers could affect the solvency, risk based capital levels and potentially the direct insurer's ability to continue as a going concern.

4.189 It is recommended that the auditor evaluate the effects of intercompany reinsurance agreements within a group of insurers to determine that they are being reported appropriately on a legal entity basis within the requirements of the reporting framework. Suggested audit procedures, include testing of the intercompany elimination entries as well as an evaluation of the intercompany agreements.

Understanding the Impacts of Foreign Exchange

4.190 Auditors of insurers with significant international operations should design procedures to determine that the entity is properly accounting for loss reserves developed in local currencies under the reporting framework (FASB ASC 830, *Foreign Currency Matters,* for GAAP financial statements and SSAP No. 23, *Foreign Exchange Transactions and Translations,* for statutory financial statements). The auditors should understand the currency in which losses may be settled as well as the currency of any potential reinsurance recoveries and evaluate the potential effects of foreign exchange fluctuations.

Audit Consideration Chart

4.191 The auditor may consider the following specific audit objectives, examples of selected control activities, and auditing procedures in auditing the claims and loss estimation processes of property and liability insurance entities. These are illustrative, however, auditors should develop tests that are appropriate to the risk of material misstatement in the circumstances of the engagement.

Claims Cycle and Estimation of Loss Reserves

Financial Statement Assertions	Audit Objectives	Examples of Selected Control Activities	Examples of Auditing Procedures
Existence or Occurrence	• Paid claims relate to transactions during the period, and unpaid claims are recorded as of the balance sheet date.	• Initial entry of claims data is appropriately controlled. • Claims are checked against daily reports for existence of coverage. • Proper documentation and proof of loss are obtained before payment. • Salvage and subrogation are noted in claims files and are followed up. • Supporting data for claims and compliance with entity policies are reviewed before approval of claim payments.	• For selected paid claims, inspect documentation of loss payments for approval and inspect canceled checks or drafts for proof of payments. • Inspect documentation of selected paid claims supporting relevant accounting and statistical data, such as amounts, incurred dates, and coding. • For selected unpaid claims (case-basis files), inspect documentation supporting relevant accounting data (such as amounts of reserves shown in the outstanding claims listing).
Completeness	• Records include all claims paid during the period and all reported claims unpaid as of the balance sheet date.	• Procedures are in effect to ensure that claims and related information are promptly reported to the claims department. • Prenumbered claim files are used or sequential claim numbers are assigned.	• Reconcile paid claims (gross and net) to the general ledger and appropriate subsidiary ledger and statistical records. • Select open claims (including reopened claims) from the files and test whether they are properly accounted for on the outstanding claims listing. • Reconcile unpaid claims (case basis, both gross and net) to the general ledger and appropriate subsidiary ledger and

AAG-PLI 4.191

The Loss Reserving and Claims Cycle

Financial Statement Assertions	Audit Objectives	Examples of Selected Control Activities	Examples of Auditing Procedures
		• Appropriate controls of input, output, and other data are maintained to ensure that all claims are processed. • Detailed control records are maintained for all reported claims.	• statistical records. Reconcile unpaid claim files to inventory. • Test whether claim processing cutoff at balance sheet date was proper and consistent with prior year. • From paid-loss transactions and the trial balance or master file of outstanding claims, test accumulation of data and balances by line of business and by accident or exposure period. • For selected claim files closed without payment, test whether they have been properly closed.
		• Statistical data are periodically reconciled to detail records. • Inventory of unpaid claims files is periodically reconciled to the master file for errors or omissions.	• Underwriting results used in actuarial analyses are agreed to accounting records.
		• Reports are generated by IT which detail any transactions not correctly interfaced between systems.	• A sample of items are selected from the report to test for proper remediation. • Record counts are reconciled between systems.

(continued)

Financial Statement Assertions	Audit Objectives	Examples of Selected Control Activities	Examples of Auditing Procedures
Rights and Obligations	• Reserves and related balances under reinsurance assumed are properly recorded.	• Current information is maintained on the status of assumed and ceded reinsurance contracts • For facultative reinsurance, reported claims are reviewed for notification of the reinsurer. • For treaty reinsurance, reinsurance recoverable estimates are recorded on a reinsurance bordereau, which is forwarded to the reinsurer in accordance with contract terms.	• Review abstracts of significant reinsurance agreements. • Trace relevant accounting data to reports provided by ceding entities. • For significant treaties or groupings of treaties, obtain or prepare a development of losses. • Evaluate whether the incurred but not reported (IBNR) reserve includes adequate provision of IBNR claims under reinsurance agreements.
	• Reinsurance recoverable on paid and unpaid losses is properly recorded.	• Reinsurance recoverable is regularly reconciled to detailed records. • Claims are reviewed for applicability of reinsurance and the reinsurers are promptly notified. • Reinsurers are promptly billed as claims are paid. • Paid claims are accumulated for recoveries under excess contracts.	• Reconcile summary of reinsurance recoverable to general ledger. • Confirm selected balances with reinsurers. • Evaluate whether loss reserves have been properly reduced for reinsurance contracts. • Trace relevant accounting data to reports provided to assuming entities. • Review Schedule F, "Assumed and Ceded Reinsurance," of the annual statement, and investigate significant or unusual items.

Financial Statement Assertions	Audit Objectives	Examples of Selected Control Activities	Examples of Auditing Procedures
			• Review the allowance for bad debt attributable to recoverable on paid and unpaid losses.
	• Liability for outstanding drafts is properly recorded.		• Obtain a list of the unpaid drafts account as of the balance sheet date and reconcile to general ledger. • On a test basis, trace draft payments subsequent to balance sheet date back to list. • Agree prepaid drafts to paid drafts on a test basis, and test unpaid claims to list. • Review supporting documents for material drafts that have been outstanding for an unreasonable length of time.
Valuation or Allocation	• Paid losses and related accounts are recorded in the proper amounts. • Estimates of loss reserves are reasonable.	• Outstanding loss reserves are balanced to monthly claims activity. • Changes in outstanding loss reserves are promptly reviewed and recorded. • For case-basis reserves, open claim files, including previous estimates of unpaid claims, are regularly reviewed and	• Test posting of losses paid, loss-adjustment expenses paid, and reinsurance recoverable for claim selected from claim register; reconcile to subsidiary registers and statistical records. • Reconcile the total amount of paid losses to cash disbursement records.

(continued)

Financial Statement Assertions	Audit Objectives	Examples of Selected Control Activities	Examples of Auditing Procedures
		analyzed for adequacy of reserves in light of current information.	• Test loss-reserve development by line of business. • Perform analytical procedures on losses incurred, losses paid, loss reserves, and loss ratios by line of business. • Review current reports of state insurance examiners and loss developments prepared for the annual statements and Schedule P, and investigate significant items.
		• Appropriate management loss reserve specialists regularly develop and analyze reserves for each line of business by accident year or by other appropriate basis. Development and analysis includes IBNR claims, claims adjustment expenses, and reserves on reinsurance assumed. • Factors and assumptions used in estimating loss reserves are documented and periodically reviewed for reasonableness.	• Obtain evidence about the entity's method of determining the reserve for IBNR losses and evaluate its reasonableness. Determine if there have been any significant changes in the entity's methods and procedures, and evaluate the effect of all current trends and conditions. • Compare current IBNR reserve against claims reported in subsequent period, and investigate significant fluctuations. • Compare entity's IBNR loss-reserve development for prior periods with actual results, and investigate causes of significant discrepancies.

AAG-PLI 4.191

The Loss Reserving and Claims Cycle

Financial Statement Assertions	Audit Objectives	Examples of Selected Control Activities	Examples of Auditing Procedures
			• Compare loss development patterns with industry results to determine reasonableness. • Determine that a qualified loss reserve specialist is involved with management's development of loss reserves.

AAG-PLI 4.191

Chapter 5
Investments and Fair Value Considerations

Introduction

Overview

5.01 A property and liability insurance entity collects funds from those who desire protection from insured loss and disburses funds to those who incur such losses. During the time between receiving premiums and the payment of losses, the entity invests the funds. These investments primarily consist of debt and equity securities. They may include mortgage loans, real estate, repurchase agreements, and derivative instruments. They may also include investments in mutual funds, hedge funds, joint ventures, and partnerships. In addition to holding long-term investments, insurance entities generally maintain short-term portfolios consisting of assets with maturities of less than one year to meet liquidity needs. Short-term investments of property and liability insurance entities typically consist of commercial paper, repurchase agreements, certificates of deposit, Treasury bills, and money market funds.

Investment Evaluation

5.02 Many insurance entities have separate investment departments responsible for managing the companies' investable funds. However, they may also use outside advisers or portfolio managers. The evaluation for purchase and subsequent purchase or sale of investments is based on the judgment of the entity's investment and finance committees. Typically, the finance committee, which usually consists of top-level management, is responsible for authorizing and monitoring all investment activity. An investment committee of the entity's investment department typically evaluates investment transactions and recommends actions to the finance committee for approval. Although some entities may not have a formal finance or investment committee, certain individuals will be responsible for carrying out similar duties of a finance or an investment committee.

5.03 The evaluation of investments includes consideration of the entity's internal investment strategies, profitability goals, current and projected cash flow needs, capital adequacy requirements, regulatory requirements, rating agency considerations, and tax implications. In addition, external factors, such as market conditions, risk and reward relationships, interest rates, and hedging opportunities, are considered.

Recordkeeping and Key Performance Indicators

5.04 The accounting department prepares investment purchase and sale transaction records as well as interest-income and dividend-income detail. This information is generally recorded on a cash basis and is reconciled periodically with cash receipts and disbursements. At the end of the period, journal entries convert the information to the accrual basis, including accruing for interest earned and dividends declared but not received and recording investment transactions with trade dates before the end of the period but not settled until after that period ends.

5.05 IT applications are not only used to record financial data relating to investments but are also used to provide investment activity, such as yield and income analyses, expected income, and market changes. This provides management with an important source of information for the evaluation of investments. Generated reports indicate whether investments owned comply with regulatory requirements. Key information includes securities by type, maturity distributions, quality ratings, issuer (for identification of concentration of credit risk), investment yields, realized and unrealized gains and losses, and nonperforming statistics.

The Transaction Cycle

5.06 The investment cycle includes all functions relating to the purchase and sale of investments. The cycle includes the recording of investment income and gains and losses, as well as the custody of investments. The functions within this cycle may be segregated into separate subcycles for each major kind of investment, such as bonds, stocks, mortgages, and real estate, because they have different activities and requirements.

5.07 Except for differences caused primarily by the regulatory environment and investment objectives, the investment transaction cycle of property and liability insurance entities is generally similar to the cycle found in other financial services industries.

Safekeeping

5.08 An entity's finance or treasury function is usually responsible for the safekeeping of securities. Generally, securities are held in the custody of banks. Coupon-bearing securities may be arranged in the vault by payment date to ensure that they are redeemed on a timely basis. A best practice would be to perform a periodic reconciliation of the entity's records to the custodian's records.

Regulation

5.09 Because insurance entities have a fiduciary responsibility to be able to meet their obligations to policyholders, state insurance statutes and regulations prescribe standards and limitations on investment holdings and activities and set requirements relating to the location and safeguarding of invested assets.

Statutory Limitations

5.10 The National Association of Insurance Commissioners (NAIC) issued two model investment laws: defined limits and defined standards. The defined limits version provides guidelines for insurers to follow and requires diversification by type of investment, issuer, and credit quality by limiting investments on both a quantitative and qualitative basis, including prohibiting certain investments. The defined standards version provides guidelines concerning investment standards by emphasizing the exercise of prudence by insurers in their investment activity and less reliance on the specific asset categories. States have the flexibility to adopt either of the NAIC's model investment laws as written or amend the guidelines for their respective state. Therefore, state insurance laws and regulations have varying investment restrictions and limitations. The regulations of the state of domicile generally have precedence.

However, several states, such as New York, have substantial compliance provisions that must also be followed by any insurance entity that writes a substantial amount of business in that state. Such requirements are considered extraterritorial because they apply to companies domiciled in another state.

5.11 Regulatory requirements and restrictions vary from state to state. However, most state statutes and regulations define the kinds of investments that insurance entities are permitted to make, limit the amount of the investments in each kind of investment and in any one issuer, and establish requirements for valuing admitted assets in the statutory financial statements.

5.12 Limitations on assets can be both quantitative and qualitative. *Quantitative limitations* are those that pertain to the total holdings of any kind of investment relative to some independent variable, such as total admitted assets or unassigned surplus. *Qualitative limitations* are those such as earnings history, minimum capital, or financial ratings that pertain to the economic condition of the investee. For example, many states limit the total amount that may be invested in noninvestment-grade securities.

5.13 Investments that do not qualify as admitted assets due to these limitations or that are not specifically authorized by state insurance laws are commonly permitted by state codes under a general basket clause or provision. Generally, the amounts of otherwise nonadmitted assets permitted by the basket provisions are limited to an amount defined as a function of admitted assets or surplus, or both.

Safeguarding of Assets

5.14 State regulations may also set requirements regarding matters such as the location and safeguarding of assets. For example, a regulatory authority may require some investments to be deposited with the state insurance department as a condition for writing business in that state. In addition, most states have laws or regulations that define permissible custodians.

Financial Accounting Standards Board *Accounting Standards Codification* 820 and 825

5.15 Financial Accounting Standards Board (FASB) *Accounting Standards Codification* (ASC) 820, *Fair Value Measurement*, defines *fair value*, establishes a framework for measuring fair value, and requires certain disclosures about fair value measurements.

Definition of *Fair Value*

5.16 FASB ASC 820-10-20-20 defines *fair value* as "the price that would be received to sell an asset or paid to transfer a liability in an orderly transaction between market participants at the measurement date." FASB ASC 820-10-05-1B states that fair value is a market-based measurement, not an entity-specific measurement. For some assets and liabilities, observable market transactions or market information might be available. For other assets and liabilities, observable market transactions and market information might not be available. However, the objective of a fair value measurement in both cases is the same—to estimate the price at which an orderly transaction to sell the asset or to transfer the liability would take place between market participants at the measurement date under current market conditions (that is, an exit price at the measurement date from the perspective of a market participant that holds the asset or owes the liability). FASB ASC 820-10-35-5 states that a fair value measurement assumes that the transaction to sell the asset or transfer the liability occurs in either the principal market for the asset or liability or, in the absence of a principal market, the most advantageous market for the asset or liability. The FASB ASC glossary defines the *principal market* as the market in which the reporting entity would sell the asset or transfer the liability with the greatest volume and level of activity for the asset or liability.

5.17 FASB ASC 820 requires that the hypothetical transaction to sell the asset or transfer the liability be considered from the perspective of a market participant that holds the asset or owes the liability. Therefore, the objective of a fair value measurement focuses on the price that would be received to sell the asset or paid to transfer the liability (an exit price), not the price that would be paid to acquire the asset or received to assume the liability (an entry price). However, FASB ASC 820-10-30-3 explains that in many cases, a transaction price will equal the fair value (for example, that might be the case when on the transaction date the transaction to buy an asset takes place in the market in which the asset would be sold). When determining whether the fair value at initial recognition equals the transaction price, a reporting entity shall take into account factors specific to the transaction and to the asset or liability, as discussed in FASB ASC 820-10-30-3A. In determining whether a transaction price represents the fair value of the asset or liability at initial recognition, the reporting entity should consider facts specific to the transaction and asset or liability.

Application to Nonfinancial Assets

5.18 FASB ASC 820-10-35-10A provides that a fair value measurement of a nonfinancial asset take into account a market participant's ability to generate economic benefits by using the asset in its highest and best use or by selling it to another market participant that would use the asset in its highest and best use.

5.19 As noted in FASB ASC 820-10-35-10B, the highest and best use of a nonfinancial asset takes into account the use that is physically possible, legally permissible, and financially feasible, as follows:

    a. A use that is physically possible takes into account the physical characteristics of the asset that market participants would take into account when pricing the asset (for example, the location or size of a property)

    b. A use that is legally permissible takes into account any legal restrictions on the use of the asset that market participants would take into account when pricing the asset (for example, the zoning regulations applicable to a property)

    c. A use that is financially feasible takes into account whether a use of the asset that is physically possible and legally permissible generates adequate income or cash flows (taking into account the costs of converting the asset to that use) to produce an investment return that market participants would require from an investment in that asset put to that use

5.20 FASB ASC 820-10-35-10C states that highest and best use is determined from the perspective of market participants, even if the reporting entity intends a different use. However, a reporting entity's current use of a nonfinancial asset is presumed to be its highest and best use unless market or other

Investments and Fair Value Considerations

factors suggest that a different use by market participants would maximize the value of the asset.

5.21 Furthermore,

FASB ASC 820-10-35-10D notes that to protect its competitive position, or for other reasons, a reporting entity may intend not to use an acquired nonfinancial asset actively or it may intend not to use the asset according to its highest and best use. For example, that might be the case for an acquired intangible asset that the reporting entity plans to use defensively by preventing others from using it. Nevertheless, the reporting entity shall measure the fair value of a nonfinancial asset assuming its highest and best use by market participants.

5.22 FASB ASC 820-10-35-10E and FASB ASC 820-10-35-11A discuss the valuation premise used to measure the fair value of the nonfinancial asset under the highest and best use. FASB ASC 820-10-55-25 illustrates the application of the highest and best use and valuation premise of concepts for nonfinancial assets.

Application to Liabilities and Instruments Classified in a Reporting Entity's Shareholders' Equity

5.23 According to FASB ASC 820-10-35-16 and FASB ASC 820-10-35-16A

[a] fair value measurement assumes that a financial or nonfinancial liability or an instrument classified in a reporting entity's shareholders' equity (for example, equity interests issued as consideration in a business combination) is transferred to a market participant at the measurement date. The transfer of a liability or an instrument classified in a reporting entity's shareholders' equity assumes the following:

   a. A liability would remain outstanding and the market participant transferee would be required to fulfill the obligation. The liability would not be settled with the counterparty or otherwise extinguished on the measurement date.

   b. An instrument classified in a reporting entity's shareholders' equity would remain outstanding and the market participant transferee would take on the rights and responsibilities associated with the instrument. The instrument would not be cancelled or otherwise extinguished on the measurement date.

Even when there is no observable market to provide pricing information about the transfer of a liability or an instrument classified in a reporting entity's shareholders' equity (for example, because contractual or other legal restrictions prevent the transfer of such items), there might be an observable market for such items if they are held by other parties as assets (for example, a corporate bond or a call option on a reporting entity's shares).

5.24 As noted in FASB ASC 820-10-35-16AA, in all cases, a reporting entity shall maximize the use of relevant observable inputs and minimize the use of unobservable inputs to meet the objective of a fair value measurement, which is to estimate the price at which an orderly transaction to transfer the liability or instrument classified in shareholders' equity would take place

AAG-PLI 5.24

between market participants at the measurement date under current market conditions.

5.25 Paragraphs 16B–16D of FASB ASC 820-10-35 discuss the guidance related to liabilities and instruments classified in a reporting entity's shareholders' equity held by other parties as assets. Paragraphs 16H–16L of FASB ASC 820-10-35 discuss the guidance related to liabilities and instruments classified in a reporting entity's shareholders'equity not held by other parties as assets.

The Fair Value Hierarchy

5.26 As explained in FASB ASC 820-10-35-37, to increase consistency and comparability in fair value measurements and related disclosures, FASB ASC 820 establishes a fair value hierarchy that categorizes the inputs to valuation techniques used to measure fair value into three broad levels. See paragraph 40–41 of FASB ASC 820-10-35, paragraphs 41B–41C of FASB ASC 820-10-35, FASB ASC 820-10-35-44, paragraphs 46–51 of FASB ASC 820-10-35, and paragraphs 52–54A of FASB ASC 820-10-35. The fair value hierarchy gives the highest priority to quoted prices (unadjusted) in active markets for identical assets or liabilities (level 1 inputs) and the lowest priority to unobservable inputs (level 3 inputs).

5.27 Paragraphs 37–54M of FASB ASC 820-10-35 establish a fair value hierarchy that distinguishes between (*a*) inputs that are developed using market data, such as publicly available information about actual events or transactions, and that reflect the assumptions that market participants would use when pricing the asset or liability (observable inputs) and (*b*) inputs for which market data are not available about the assumptions that market participants would use when pricing the asset or liability (unobservable inputs). Valuation techniques used to measure fair value should maximize the use of observable inputs and minimize the use of unobservable inputs.

5.28 The fair value hierarchy in FASB ASC 820-10-35 prioritizes the inputs to valuation techniques used to measure fair value into three broad levels. The three levels are as follows:

- Paragraphs 40–41 of FASB ASC 820-10-35 state that *level 1 inputs* are quoted prices (unadjusted) in active markets for identical assets or liabilities that the reporting entity can access at the measurement date. An *active market*, as defined by the FASB ASC glossary, is a market in which transactions for the asset or liability take place with sufficient frequency and volume to provide pricing information on an ongoing basis. A quoted price in an active market provides the most reliable evidence of fair value and should be used without adjustment to measure fair value whenever available, except as specified in paragraph 41C of FASB ASC 820-10-35. Paragraphs 47–51 of FASB ASC 820-10-35 explain that *level 2 inputs* are inputs other than quoted prices included within level 1 that are observable for the asset or liability either directly or indirectly. If the asset or liability has a specified (contractual) term, a level 2 input must be observable for substantially the full term of the asset or liability. Adjustments to level 2 inputs will vary depending on factors specific to the asset or liability. Those factors include the condition and location of the asset or liability; the extent to which the inputs relate to items that are comparable to the asset or liability, including those factors discussed in FASB ASC 820-10-35-16D; and the volume and level of activity in

Investments and Fair Value Considerations

the markets within which the inputs are observed. An adjustment that is significant to the fair value measurement in its entirety might render the measurement a level 3 measurement, depending on the level in the fair value hierarchy within which the inputs used to determine the adjustment fall. As discussed in FASB ASC 820-10-35-48, level 2 inputs include the following:

— Quoted prices for similar assets or liabilities in active markets

— Quoted prices for identical or similar assets or liabilities in markets that are not active

— Inputs other than quoted prices that are observable for the asset or liability (for example, interest rates and yield curves observable at commonly quoted intervals, implied volatilities, and credit spreads)

— Inputs that are derived principally from, or corroborated by, observable market data by correlation or other means (market-corroborated inputs)

- According to FASB ASC 820-10-35-51, an adjustment to the level 2 input that is significant to the entire measurement might result in a fair value measurement categorized within level 3 of the fair value hierarchy if the adjustment uses significant unobservable inputs.

- As discussed in paragraphs 52 of FASB ASC 820-10-35, *level 3 inputs* are unobservable inputs for the asset or liability. According to paragraphs 53–54A of FASB ASC 820-10-35

> [u]nobservable inputs shall be used to measure fair value to the extent that relevant observable inputs are not available, thereby allowing for situations in which there is little, if any, market activity for the asset or liability at the measurement date. However, the fair value measurement objective remains the same, that is, an exit price at the measurement date from the perspective of a market participant that holds the asset or owes the liability. Therefore, unobservable inputs shall reflect the assumptions that market participants would use when pricing the asset or liability, including assumptions about risk. Assumptions about risk include the risk inherent in a particular valuation technique used to measure fair value (such as a pricing model) and in the inputs to the valuation technique. A measurement that does not include an adjustment for risk would not represent a fair value measurement if market participants would include one when pricing the asset or liability. For example, it might be necessary to include a risk adjustment when there is significant measurement uncertainty (for example, when there has been a significant decrease in the volume or level of activity when compared with normal market activity for the asset or liability, or similar assets or liabilities, and the reporting entity has determined that the transaction price or quoted price does not represent fair value as described in FASB ASC 820-10-35-54C through FASB ASC 820-10-35-54J). A reporting entity should develop unobservable inputs using the best information available in the circumstances, which might include the reporting entity's own data. In developing unobservable inputs, a reporting entity may begin with its own data, but it should adjust those data if reasonably available information indicates that other market participants

AAG-PLI 5.28

would use different data or there is something particular to the reporting entity that is not available to other market participants (for example, an entity-specific synergy). A reporting entity need not undertake exhaustive efforts to obtain information about market participant assumptions. However, a reporting entity should take into account all information about market participant assumptions that is reasonably available. Unobservable inputs developed in the manner described above are considered market participant assumptions and meet the objective of a fair value measurement.

5.29 FASB ASC 820-10-55-22 provides examples of level 3 inputs for selected assets and liabilities.

5.30 As discussed in FASB ASC 820-10-35-38, the availability of relevant inputs and their relative subjectivity might affect the selection of appropriate valuation techniques. However, the fair value hierarchy prioritizes the inputs to valuation techniques, not the valuation techniques used to measure fair value. For example, a fair value measurement developed using a present value technique might be categorized within level 2 or level 3, depending on the inputs that are significant to the entire measurement and the level of the fair value hierarchy within which those inputs are categorized.

Fair Value Determination When the Volume or Level of Activity Has Significantly Decreased

5.31 FASB ASC 820-35-10-54C through FASB ASC 820-35-10-54-M clarifies the application of FASB ASC 820 in determining fair value when the volume or level of activity for the asset or liability has significantly decreased. Guidance is also included in identifying transactions that are not orderly.

5.32 As noted in FASB ASC 820-10-35-54G, when determining fair value when the volume or level of activity for the asset or liability has significantly decreased, the objective of a fair value measurement remains the same; that is, to measure fair value as the price that would be received to sell an asset or paid to transfer a liability in an orderly transaction (not a forced liquidation or distress sale) between market participants at the measurement under current market conditions. FASB ASC 820-10-35-54H further notes that estimating the price at which market participants would be willing to enter into a transaction at the measurement date under current market conditions if there has been a significant decrease in the volume or level of activity for the asset or liability depends on the facts and circumstances at the measurement date and requires judgment. A reporting entity's intention to hold the asset or to settle or otherwise fulfill the liability is not relevant when measuring fair value because fair value is a market-based measurement, not an entity-specific measurement. FASB ASC 820-10-35-54C lists a number of factors that may be evaluated to determine whether there has been a significant decrease in the volume or level of activity for an asset or liability.

5.33 This guidance does not apply to quoted prices for an identical asset or liability in an active market (level 1 inputs). For example, although the volume or level of activity for an asset or liability may significantly decrease, transactions for the asset or liability may still occur with sufficient frequency and volume to provide pricing information on an ongoing basis.

Disclosures

5.34 FASB ASC 820-10-50 discusses the disclosures required for assets and liabilities measured at fair value. FASB ASC 820-10-50-1 explains that the reporting entity should disclose information that enables users of its financial statements to assess both for (*a*) assets and liabilities measured at fair value on a recurring or nonrecurring basis in the statement of financial position after initial recognition, as well as the valuation techniques and inputs used to develop those measurements, and (*b*) recurring fair value measurements using significant unobservable inputs (level 3) and the effect of the measurements on earnings (or changes in net assets) or other comprehensive income for the period. As discussed in FASB ASC 820-10-50-1A, to meet the objectives in FASB ASC 820-10-50-1, a reporting entity should consider all of the following:

   a. The level of detail necessary to satisfy the disclosure requirements

   b. How much emphasis to place on each of the various requirements

   c. How much aggregation or disaggregation to undertake

   d. Whether users of financial statements need additional information to evaluate the quantitative information disclosed

5.35 FASC ASC 820-10-50-2 through FASB 820-10-50-10 describes the disclosures that an entity should make for each class of assets and liabilities measured at fair value.

Fair Value Option

5.36 FASB ASC 825, *Financial Instruments*, creates a fair value option under which an entity may irrevocably elect fair value as the initial and subsequent measure for many financial instruments and certain other items, with changes in fair value recognized in the statement of activities as those changes occur. FASB ASC 825-10-35-4 explains that a business entity should report unrealized gains and losses on items for which the fair value option has been elected in earnings at each subsequent reporting date. An election is made on an instrument-by-instrument basis, with certain exceptions, generally when an instrument is initially recognized in the financial statements. The fair value option need not be applied to all identical items, except as required by FASB ASC 825-10-25-7. Most financial assets and liabilities are eligible to be recognized using the fair value option, as are firm commitments for financial instruments and certain nonfinancial contracts.

5.37 As explained by FASB ASC 825-10-15-5, the following are specifically excluded from eligibility:

- An investment in a subsidiary that the entity is required to consolidate
- An interest in a variable interest entity (VIE) that the entity is required to consolidate
- An employer and a plan's obligations for pension benefits
- Other postretirement benefits, including health care and life insurance benefits
- Postemployment benefits

- Employee stock option and stock purchase plans and other forms of deferred compensation arrangements or assets representing net overfunded positions in those plans
- Financial assets and liabilities recognized under leases (this does not apply to a guarantee of a third-party lease obligation or a contingent obligation arising from a cancelled lease)
- Deposit liabilities of depository institutions
- Financial instruments that are, in whole or part, classified by the issuer as a component of shareholder's equity, including temporary equity

5.38 FASB ASC 825-10-45 and FASB ASC 825-10-50 also include presentation and disclosure requirements designed to facilitate comparisons between entities that choose different measurement attributes for similar types of assets and liabilities. The disclosure requirements are expected to provide information to enable users of its financial statements to understand management's reasons for electing or partially electing the fair value option. Paragraphs 1–2 of FASB ASC 825-10-45 state that entities should report assets and liabilities that are measured using the fair value option in a manner that separates those reported fair values from the carrying amounts of similar assets and liabilities measured using another measurement attribute. To accomplish that, an entity should either (*a*) report the aggregate of both fair value and non-fair-value items on a single line, with the fair value amount parenthetically disclosed, or (*b*) present separate lines for the fair value and nonfair-value carrying amounts. As discussed in FASB ASC 825-10-25-3, upfront costs and fees, such as debt issue costs, may not be deferred for items for which the fair value option has been elected.

Statutory Accounting

5.39 Statement of Statutory Accounting Principles (SSAP) No. 100, *Fair Value Measurements*, provides the measurement and disclosure requirements in statutory accounting for all required fair value measurements and disclosures. The statutory guidance is generally the same as the generally accepted accounting principles (GAAP) guidance, with the exception of the consideration of nonperformance risk (own credit risk) in determining the fair value measurement of liabilities.

5.40 SSAP No. 27, *Disclosure of Information About Financial Instruments with Off-Balance-Sheet Risk Financial Instruments with Concentrations of Credit Risk and Disclosure about Fair Value of Financial Instruments*, requires the same concentrations of credit risk disclosures as FASB ASC 825-10-50.

Accounting Practices[1]

5.41 As discussed in chapter 1, "Nature, Conduct, and Regulation of the Business," of this guide, insurance entities are required to file financial statements prepared in accordance with statutory accounting practices (SAP) with

---

[1] The Financial Accounting Standards Board (FASB) and the International Accounting Standards Board (IASB) have a joint project on accounting for financial instruments. The objective of this project is to significantly improve the decision usefulness of financial instrument reporting for users of financial statements. The project will replace FASB and the IASB's respective financial instruments standards with a common standard.

Investments and Fair Value Considerations

state insurance regulators. They may also prepare financial statements in accordance with GAAP. The following discussion of GAAP and statutory accounting for invested assets is not a comprehensive source of authoritative accounting literature but is intended to assist the preparers and auditors of financial statements in obtaining a general understanding of basic investment accounting practices for the most common classes of invested assets within the industry. The authoritative sources cited should be referred to in determining the appropriate accounting and reporting treatment in all cases.

Significant Differences Between GAAP and Statutory Accounting

5.42 The most significant accounting differences between GAAP and statutory accounting for investments are the valuation of debt securities; derivative accounting and reporting; other-than-temporary impairments of nonstructured debt securities and the accounting for joint ventures and partnerships; and in particular, investments in subsidiary, controlled, and affiliated (SCA) entities. These and other significant accounting differences are discussed subsequently in each investment section. In addition to accounting differences, statutory accounting requires consideration concerning whether an asset is admitted or nonadmitted for reporting purposes, which is not a GAAP concept. See paragraph 1.88 for a further discussion of nonadmitted assets. Examples of nonadmitted investments include real estate where the insurer has not obtained an appraisal in the past five years and mortgage loans that have loan-to-value ratios in excess of the maximum allowable state limit.

GAAP, Statutory, and Securities and Exchange Commission Summary Chart

Topic	GAAP	Statutory	SEC
Cash and cash equivalents	FASB ASC 210	SSAP No. 2	
	FASB ASC 230		
	FASB ASC 305		

(continued)

(footnote continued)

Effectively, the project has been split into three components: classification and measurement, impairment, and hedge accounting projects. Readers should keep track of the project on the FASB website: www.fasb.org/cs/ContentServer?c=FASBContent_C&pagename=FASB%2FFASBContent_C%2FProjectUpdatePage&cid=1175801889654.

    a. Classification and Measurement

        In May 2010, FASB issued proposed Accounting Standards Update (ASU) *Accounting for Financial Instruments and Revisions to the Accounting for Derivative Instruments and Hedging Activities—Financial Instruments (Topic 825) and Derivatives and Hedging (Topic 815).*

    b. Credit Impairment

        On January 31, 2011, FASB and the IASB proposed a common solution for impairment accounting in "Supplementary Document—Accounting for Financial Instruments and Revisions to the Accounting for Derivative Instruments and Hedging Activities—Impairment."

    c. Hedge Accounting

        On February 9, 2011, FASB issued the discussion paper "Invitation to Comment—Selected Issues About Hedge Accounting" to solicit input on the IASB's exposure draft "Hedge Accounting" in order to improve, simplify, and converge the financial reporting requirements for hedging activities.

Topic	GAAP	Statutory	SEC
Debt and equity securities	FASB ASC 220	SSAP No. 26	SAB No. 103
	FASB ASC 310	SSAP No. 30	
	FASB ASC 320	SSAP No. 32	
	FASB ASC 325	SSAP No. 43R	
	FASB ASC 940		
	FASB ASC 944		
Realized and unrealized gains and losses on debt and equity securities	FASB ASC 320	SSAP No. 30	
	FASB ASC 944	SSAP No. 32	
		SSAP No. 43R	
Mortgage loans	FASB ASC 310	SSAP No. 36	SAB No. 105
	FASB ASC 944	SSAP No. 37	
	FASB ASC 948	SSAP No. 83	
Real estate	FASB ASC 360	SSAP No. 40	
	FASB ASC 944	SSAP No. 90	
Derivatives	FASB ASC 815	SSAP No. 86	
Joint ventures and partnerships	FASB ASC 323	SSAP No. 48	
	FASB ASC 810	SSAP No. 93	
		SSAP No. 97	
Investments in subsidiary, controlled, and affiliated entities	FASB ASC 810	SSAP No. 97	SAB No. 103
Investment income due and accrued	FASB ASC 310	SSAP No. 34	
Asset transfers and extinguishments of liabilities	FASB ASC 860	SSAP No. 91R	
Repurchase agreements	FASB ASC 860	SSAP No. 91R	
Securities lending	FASB ASC 860	SSAP No. 91R	
Fair value measurements	FASB ASC 820	SSAP No. 100	
Fair value and concentrations of credit risk disclosure requirements	FASB ASC 825	SSAP No. 27	
Fair value option	FASB ASC 825	N/A	

Cash and Cash Equivalents

5.43 As defined in SSAP No. 2, *Cash, Drafts and Short-Term Investments*, *cash* constitutes a medium of exchange that a bank or other similar financial institution will accept for deposit and allow for an immediate credit to the depositor's account. Similarly, as stated in the FASB ASC glossary, cash includes not only currency on hand but demand deposits with banks or other financial institutions. Cash also includes other kinds of accounts that have the general characteristics of demand deposits in that the customer may deposit additional funds at any time and effectively withdraw funds at any time without prior notice or penalty.

5.44 No significant differences exist between GAAP and statutory accounting for cash and short-term investments.

GAAP Accounting

5.45 The FASB ASC glossary states that *cash equivalents* are short-term, highly liquid investments that are both

    a. readily convertible to known amounts of cash and

    b. so near to maturity that they present an insignificant risk of changes in value because of changes in interest rates.

Generally, only investments with original maturities of three months or less qualify under this definition.

5.46 Cash should be recognized initially at the amount received by the insurance entity or the amount received into the insurance entity's bank account. Cash equivalents should initially be recognized at cost. Treasury bills, commercial paper, and money market funds are examples of items that are commonly considered cash equivalents. However, as explained in FASB ASC 230-10-45-6, not all investments that qualify are required to be treated as cash equivalents. An entity shall establish a policy concerning which short-term, highly liquid investments satisfy the definition in FASB ASC 305-10-20 and, accordingly, are treated as cash equivalents. This policy should be disclosed, usually in the accounting policy footnote. Any change to that policy is a change in accounting principle. If a reporting entity has multiple cash accounts, any negative cash balances would need to be recorded as a liability, unless the right of offset exists under FASB ASC 210-20-45-1.

Statutory Accounting

5.47 Cash is an admitted asset to the extent that it conforms to the requirements of SSAP No. 2. For financial statement purposes, savings accounts, certificates of deposits with maturity dates within one year or less from the acquisition date, and cash equivalents are classified as cash. Paragraph 3 of SSAP No. 2, consistent with the guidance in FASB ASC 305-10-20, states that

> *cash equivalents* are short-term, highly liquid investments that are both
>
>   *a.* readily convertible to known amounts of cash and
>
>   *b.* so near their maturity that they present an insignificant risk of change in value because of changes in interest rates.

Only investments with original maturities of three months or less qualify under this definition.

5.48 *Original maturity* is defined as beginning at the time of the entity's acquisition. Footnote 1 to paragraph 3 of SSAP No. 2 provides examples that both a three-month U.S. Treasury bill and three-year Treasury note purchased three months from maturity would qualify as cash equivalents. However, a Treasury note purchased three years ago does not become a cash equivalent when its remaining maturity is three months.

5.49 If a reporting entity has multiple cash accounts, the net amount of all accounts shall be reported jointly. If, in the aggregate, the reporting entity has a net negative cash balance, it shall be reported as a negative asset, not recorded as a liability.

Debt and Equity Securities

5.50 *Debt securities* are obligations issued by business entities, governmental entities, and certain not-for-profit entities that have a fixed schedule for one or more future payments of money at specified future dates. Debt securities may include U.S. Treasury obligations and government or municipal bonds (direct obligations of any state, territory, possession, or local government unit). Some other investments that may be classified as debt securities include redeemable preferred stock; guaranteed investment contracts (GICs); and asset-backed securities, such as collateralized mortgage obligations (CMOs), mortgage participation certificates (MPCs), credit-tenant mortgages (CTMs), interest-only (IO) and principal-only (PO) certificates, and equipment trust certificates. Such investments may be public issues or private placements and are generally long-term investments. Short-term debt securities include commercial paper and negotiable certificates of deposit (CDs). Debt securities are purchased at a discount, a premium, or par value, and they generate interest income to the holder. Their sale may result in a realized gain or loss.

5.51 Equity securities represent an ownership interest in a corporation (for example, common, preferred, or other capital stock). Generally, equity securities generate cash dividends or dividends paid in the form of additional shares of stock. The sale of shares of equity securities usually results in a realized gain or loss.

5.52 The primary differences between GAAP and statutory accounting for debt and equity securities are the measurement of debt securities and the impairments of nonstructured debt securities. Investment grade bonds (NAIC rating of 1 or 2) are carried at amortized cost, and noninvestment grade bonds (NAIC rating of 3–6) are carried at the lower of amortized cost or NAIC fair value. For GAAP, bonds are classified as held to maturity, available for sale, or trading and accounted for as discussed in paragraph 5.53.

GAAP Accounting

5.53 Investments in debt securities, including redeemable preferred stocks, are classified into one of three categories at acquisition, as defined by FASB ASC 320-10-25-1. They are accounted for as follows:

> *a.* As discussed in FASB ASC 320-10-25-1, debt securities classified as held to maturity are those debt securities that the insurance entity has the positive intent and ability to hold to maturity. As noted in FASB ASC 320-10-35-1, these securities are measured at amortized

Investments and Fair Value Considerations

cost, unless there is a decline in their fair value below amortized cost that is considered other than temporary. *Amortized cost* is the original cost of the security, reduced by amortization of premiums or increased by the accretion of discounts.[2]

b. As discussed in FASB ASC 320-10-25-1, debt securities classified as trading are those acquired with the intent of being sold within hours or days. However, at acquisition, an entity is not precluded from classifying as trading a security that it plans to hold for a longer period. As discussed in FASB ASC 320-10-35-1, these securities are reported at fair value, and unrealized gains and losses are included in earnings.

c. Debt securities not classified as either trading or held to maturity shall be classified as available for sale and reported at fair value. As discussed in FASB ASC 320-10-35-1, changes in the fair value of the debt securities classified as available for sale are reported as unrealized gains or losses, net of applicable deferred income taxes, and credited or charged directly to other comprehensive income, in accordance with FASB ASC 220, *Comprehensive Income*. However, all or a portion of the unrealized holding gain and loss of an available-for-sale security that is designated as being hedged in a fair value hedge shall be recognized in earnings during the period of the hedge, pursuant to paragraphs 1–4 of FASB ASC 815-25-35.

5.54 FASB ASC 320-10-35-10 explains that the transfer of a security between categories of investments is to be accounted for at fair value and expands on how the security's unrealized gain or loss should be accounted for based on the category. Paragraphs 11–12 of FASB ASC 320-10-35 also discuss that transfers from the held-to-maturity and transfers into or from the trading category should be rare.

5.55 Amortization of premium and accretion of discount are calculated using the interest method, which results in a constant effective yield, typically using the contractual maturity date, in accordance with FASB ASC 310-20. The prepayment method, as described in FASB ASC 310-20-35-26, may also be used, particularly for high-quality asset-backed securities such as CMOs and IO and PO certificates. Amortization and accretion calculations may require the use of estimates, such as prepayment assumptions on CMOs or interest and return of investment allocations on IO and PO certificates. The current year's amortization or accretion is recorded as a charge or credit to interest income. FASB ASC 320, *Investments—Debt and Equity Securities*, provides guidance on accounting and reporting for all investments in debt securities. FASB ASC 310, *Receivables*, provides guidance on the application of the interest method and other amortization matters. Paragraphs 38–43 of FASB ASC 320-10-35 provide guidance on the accounting for certain structured notes that are in the form of debt securities. FASB ASC 310-30 should also be reviewed for guidance regarding the accrual of income.

5.56 FASB ASC 325-40 provides guidance on the recognition of interest income and impairment on retained beneficial interests in securitization transactions that are accounted for as sales under FASB ASC 860, *Transfers and*

---

[2] FASB *Accounting Standards Codification* (ASC) 320-10-25-5 states that a security may not be classified as held to maturity if that security can contractually be prepaid or otherwise settled in such a way that the holder of the security would not recover substantially all of its recorded investment. Such securities are required to be evaluated under FASB ASC 815-15 to determine if they contain an embedded derivative that should be accounted for separately.

Servicing, and purchased beneficial interests in securitized financial assets. FASB ASC 325-40-15-3 further defines *beneficial interests*.

5.57 Interest and dividend income, including the amortization of premium and the accretion of discount, are included in earnings for all three categories of investments under FASB ASC 320. Generally, interest and dividend income related to available-for-sale securities are included within net investment income on the statement of income. In practice, interest and dividend income related to trading securities have been included within net investment income or trading income on the statement of income. It is recommended that insurance entities disclose where interest and dividend components are included in the statement of income.

5.58 Equity securities that have readily determinable fair values, as defined by FASB ASC 320, are classified as either trading or available-for-sale securities and reported at fair value. Changes in the fair value of those securities are recognized as unrealized gains and losses and accounted for as described in FASB ASC 320-10-35.

5.59 Investments in equity securities that do not have readily determinable fair values (are outside the scope of FASB ASC 320) are accounted for under FASB ASC 944-325-30-1. FASB ASC 944-325-30-1 states that investments in equity securities that are not addressed by FASB ASC 320-10 or FASB ASC 958-20 because they do not have readily determinable fair values, as defined by those subtopics, shall be reported at fair value. The guidance for reporting the changes in fair value is in FASB ASC 944-325-35-1, which requires that an entity recognize changes in fair value as unrealized gains and losses, net of applicable income taxes, in other comprehensive income, except as indicated in the following sentence: All or a portion of the unrealized gain and loss of an available-for-sale security that is designated as being hedged in a fair value hedge shall be recognized in earnings during the period of the hedge, pursuant to paragraphs 1–4 of FASB ASC 815-25-35.

5.60 If an investment enables an entity (the investor) to influence the operating or financial decisions of the investee, then the entity would be required to follow the equity method under FASB ASC 323, *Investments—Equity Method and Joint Ventures*.

5.61 FASB ASC 323-10-50-2 states that the significance of an investment to the investor's financial position and results of operations should be considered in evaluating the extent of disclosures of the financial position and results of operations of an investee. If the investor has more than one investment in common stock accounted for by the equity method, disclosures wholly or partly on a combined basis may be appropriate. Disclosures that are generally applicable to the equity method of accounting for investments in common stock are discussed in FASB ASC 323-10-50-3.

5.62 Paragraphs 17–35 of FASB ASC 320-10-35 provide guidance regarding determining whether an investment is impaired and the impairment is other than temporary. The guidance requires that entities determine whether declines in the fair values of individual securities classified as either held to maturity or available for sale below their amortized cost bases are other than temporary.

5.63 As discussed in paragraphs 20–29 of FASB ASC 320-10-35, the first step in impairment testing is to determine whether an investment is impaired. Impairment is assessed at the individual investment level. An investment is considered impaired if the fair value of the investment is less than its cost. For

Investments and Fair Value Considerations

investments that are carried at cost and whose fair value is not readily determinable, but for which the investor has estimated their fair value, that fair value shall be used in determining whether the investment is impaired. For reporting periods when the fair value of a cost-method investment has not been estimated, the investor shall evaluate whether an event or change in circumstances has occurred in that period that may have a significant adverse effect on the fair value of the investment (an impairment indicator). Impairment indicators include, but are not limited to, the following:

 a. A significant deterioration in the earnings performance, credit rating, asset quality, or business prospects of the investee

 b. A significant adverse change in the regulatory, economic, or technological environment of the investee

 c. A significant adverse change in the general market condition of either the geographic area or industry in which the investee operates

 d. A bona fide offer to purchase, whether solicited or unsolicited; an offer by the investee to sell; or a completed auction process for the same or similar security for an amount less than the cost of the investment

 e. Factors that raise significant concerns about the investee's ability to continue as a going concern, such as negative cash flows from operations, working capital deficiencies, or noncompliance with statutory capital requirements or debt covenants

5.64 The second step is to evaluate whether an impairment is other than temporary. Differences exist in considering other-than-temporary impairments for equity and debt securities. However, some common factors to consider in determining whether a decline is other than temporary include (*a*) the length of time and extent to which fair value has been below cost, (*b*) the credit risk of the issuer, and (*c*) whether adverse conditions exist that are related to the issuer of the security or its industry. This is not an exhaustive list. The differences in impairment considerations between debt and equity securities are driven by the intent language in FASB ASC 320.

5.65 For equity securities, an entity must consider whether it has the intent and ability to retain the investment for a reasonable period sufficient to allow for an anticipated recovery in value. As discussed in FASB ASC 320-10-35-33, when an entity has decided to sell an impaired available-for-sale security, and the entity does not expect the fair value of the security to fully recover before the expected time of sale, the security shall be deemed other-than-temporarily impaired in the period in which the decision to sell is made, not the period in which the sale occurs. However, an entity shall recognize an impairment loss when the impairment is deemed other than temporary, even if a decision to sell has not been made. FASB ASC 320-10-35-34 notes that for equity securities, if it is determined in step 2 that the impairment is other than temporary, then an impairment loss shall be recognized in earnings equal to the entire difference between the investment's cost and its fair value at the balance sheet date of the reporting period for which the assessment is made. The measurement of the impairment shall not include partial recoveries after the balance sheet date. The fair value of the investment would then become the new amortized cost basis of the investment and shall not be adjusted for subsequent recoveries in fair value.

5.66 For debt securities, an entity is required to consider whether it intends to sell the security or whether it is more likely than not that it will be required to sell prior to an anticipated recovery of the cost basis of the security. Additionally, if the entity does not expect to recover the cost basis, then an other-than-temporary impairment shall be recognized, even if it does not intend to sell the security. As stated in FASB ASC 320-10-35-33C, in assessing whether the entire amortized cost basis of the security will be recovered, an entity shall compare the present value of cash flows expected to be collected from the security with the amortized cost basis of the security. If the present value is less than the amortized cost, then an other-than-temporary impairment (that is, a credit loss) exists. In estimating the present value of the expected cash flows to determine whether a credit loss exists, entities should consider the methodology described in FASB ASC 310-10-35 for nonstructured debt and paragraphs 4–9 of FASB ASC 325-40-35 for beneficial interests in securitized financial assets.

5.67 As discussed in FASB ASC 320-10-35-34A, the amount of an other-than-temporary impairment recognized in earnings depends on whether the entity intends to sell the security or whether it is more likely than not that it will be required to sell prior to an anticipated recovery of the cost basis.

5.68 As discussed in FASB ASC 320-10-35-34B, if the entity intends to sell the security or it is more likely than not that it will be required to sell before recovery of the amortized cost basis, an other-than-temporary impairment loss shall be recognized in earnings for the difference in the amortized cost and fair value at the balance sheet date.

5.69 As discussed in FASB ASC 320-10-35-34C, if the entity does not intend to sell the security or it is more likely than not that it will not be required to sell, the entity shall separate the other-than-temporary impairment into the amount representing the credit loss and the amount related to all other factors. FASB ASC 320-10-35-34D notes that the amount related to the credit loss is recognized in earnings, and the amount related to all other factors is recognized in other comprehensive income net of applicable taxes.

5.70 As discussed in FASB ASC 320-10-35-34E, the previous amortized cost less the other-than-temporary impairment recognized in earnings becomes the new cost basis, and it shall not be adjusted for recoveries in fair value. However, the new cost basis is adjusted for amortization and accretion, as discussed in FASB ASC 320-10-35-35.

5.71 The notes to the financial statements should include the accounting and impairment policies for debt and equity securities. FASB ASC 320-10-50 lists the extensive disclosure requirements for debt and equity securities.

Statutory Accounting

5.72 Paragraph 7 of SSAP No. 26, *Bonds, Excluding Loan-Backed and Structured Securities*, states that bonds shall be valued and reported in accordance with this statement, the *Purposes and Procedures Manual of the NAIC Securities Valuation Office* (P&P manual), and the designation assigned in *Valuations of Securities* prepared by the NAIC Securities Valuation Office (SVO). Bonds should be carried at amortized cost, except for those with an NAIC designation of 3–6, which shall be reported at the lower of amortized cost or fair value. NAIC designations of 1 and 2 are assigned to bonds that are designated highest quality and high quality, respectively. Designations 3–6 represent bonds that are designated medium quality, low quality, lowest quality, and in or near default, respectively. As with GAAP, amortization or accretion under SAP is calculated by the interest method. An acquisition or disposal of

Investments and Fair Value Considerations

a publicly traded bond shall be recorded on the trade date but shall be recorded on the funding date for private placement bonds. For bonds within the scope of SSAP No. 26, if a decline in fair value is considered other than temporary, the cost basis of the bond shall be written down to fair value, and the fair value shall become the new cost basis. As stated in paragraph 10 of SSAP No. 26, "[i]nterest income for any period consists of interest collected during the period, the change in the due and accrued interest between the beginning and end of the period as well as reductions for premium amortization and interest paid on acquisition of bonds, and the addition of discount accrual." Interest income determined to be uncollectible shall be written off through the summary of operations, and an evaluation should be made to determine nonadmitted amounts. Insurance entities are required to submit newly acquired unlisted securities not subject to the filing exemption rule to the NAIC SVO for valuation. Under the filing exemption rule, a bond is eligible for exemption if it is

   a. a U.S. government security;

   b. a CMO issued directly through any program administered by the Government National Mortgage Association (GNMA), the Federal National Mortgage Association (FNMA), the Federal Home Loan Mortgage Corporation (FHLMC), or the Federal Agricultural Mortgage Association (FAMC);

   c. a CMO whereby 100 percent of the collateral that generates principal and interest to the holders consists of mortgage pass-through securities issued or guaranteed by the GNMA, FNMA, FHLMC, or FAMC; or

   d. is rated and monitored by a nationally recognized statistical rating organization.

5.73 If the insurance entity claims that the bond is eligible, it may list the security on the statutory investment schedule as an NAIC 1 or 2, with a provisionally exempt symbol. Further information regarding the provisional exemption rule is found in the P&P manual. For loan-backed securities subject to multiple designations, the filing exemption rule is not applicable. The NAIC designation for these securities is determined by the two-step process discussed in paragraph 26 of SSAP No. 43R, *Loan-Backed and Structured Securities*.

5.74 Requirements for carrying bonds as admitted assets vary at the discretion of individual states. A bond must be classified as a nonadmitted asset if it fails a qualitative or quantitative limitation test or is otherwise unauthorized by the applicable state code.

5.75 Paragraph 9 of SSAP No. 26 discusses the impairment of bonds, excluding loan-backed and structured securities. It states that if it is determined that a decline in the fair value of a bond is other than temporary, the cost basis of the bond shall be written down to fair value as a new cost basis, and the amount of the write-down shall be accounted for as a realized loss. The new cost basis shall not be changed for subsequent recoveries in fair value; however, like GAAP, the new cost basis is adjusted for amortization and accretion. SSAP No. 26 further states that an impairment shall be considered to have occurred if it is probable that the reporting entity will be unable to collect all amounts due according to the contractual terms of a debt security in effect at the date of the acquisition. As discussed in Interpretation 06-07, *Definition of Phrase "Other Than Temporary,"* of the Emerging Accounting Issues Working Group (EAIWG), a decline in fair value that is other than temporary includes situations in which a reporting entity has made a decision to sell a security prior to its maturity at an amount below its carrying value. Additionally, if the entity does not have the intent and ability to retain the bond for a period sufficient to allow for an anticipated recovery in value, then an other-than-temporary impairment shall be recorded.

5.76 Guidance for accounting for loan-backed and structured securities, including CMOs, is provided in SSAP No. 43R,[3] the P&P manual, and the designation assigned in *Valuations of Securities* prepared by the NAIC SVO. At purchase, loan-backed and structured securities, including CMOs, are recorded at cost, including brokerage and related fees, but not at an amount in excess of fair value. Discount or premium is recorded for the difference between the purchase price and principal amount. The discount or premium is amortized using the interest method and recorded as an adjustment to investment income. The interest method results in the recognition of a constant rate of return on the investment equal to the prevailing rate at the time of purchase or at the time of subsequent adjustments of book value. Paragraph 12 of SSAP No. 43R states that prepayments are a significant variable element in the cash flow of loan-backed securities due to the way they affect the yield and determine the expected maturity against which the yield is evaluated. As noted in paragraphs 13–14 of SSAP No. 43R

> [p]repayment assumptions shall be applied consistently across portfolios to all securities backed by similar collateral (similar with respect to coupon, issuer, and age of collateral) .... Loan-backed securities shall be revalued using the currently estimated cash flows, including new prepayment assumptions, using either the prospective or retrospective adjustment methodologies, consistently applied by type of securities. However, if at anytime during the holding period, the reporting entity determines it is no longer probable that they will collect all contractual cashflows, the reporting entity shall apply the accounting requirements in paragraphs 17 through 19.

5.77 Paragraphs 26–27 of SSAP No. 43R state that

> For securities within the scope of this statement, the initial NAIC designation used to determine the carrying value method and the final NAIC designation for reporting purposes is determined using a multi-step process. The *Purposes and Procedures Manual of the NAIC Securities Valuation Office* provides detailed guidance. A general description of the processes is as follows:
>
> a. Financial Modeling: The NAIC identifies securities where financial modeling must be used to determine the NAIC designation. NAIC designation based on financial modeling incorporates the insurers' carrying value for the security. For those securities that are financially modeled, the insurer must use NAIC CUSIP specific modeled breakpoints provided by the modelers in determining initial and final designation for these identified securities. Securities where modeling results in zero expected loss in all scenarios are automatically considered to have a final NAIC designation of NAIC 1, regardless of the carrying value. The three-step process for modeled securities is as follows:

---

[3] The National Association of Insurance Commissioners (NAIC) Statutory Accounting Principles Working Group has developed appendix A, "Question and Answer Implementation Guide," of Statement of Statutory Accounting Principles (SSAP) No. 43R, *Loan-Backed and Structured Securities*, which is available on the NAIC website.

Investments and Fair Value Considerations

  i. Step 1: Determine Initial Designation – The current amortized cost (divided by remaining par amount) of a loan-backed or structured security is compared to the modeled breakpoint values assigned to the six (6) NAIC designations for each CUSIP to establish the **initial** NAIC designation.

  ii. Step 2: Determine Carrying Value Method – The carrying value method, either the amortized cost method or the lower of amortized cost or fair value method, is then determined as described in paragraph 25 based upon the **initial** NAIC designation from Step 1.

  iii. Step 3: Determine Final Designation – The final NAIC designation that shall be used for investment schedule reporting is determined by comparing the carrying value (divided by remaining par amount) of a security (based on paragraph 26a.ii.) to the NAIC CUSIP specific modeled breakpoint values assigned to the six (6) NAIC designations for each CUSIP. This final NAIC designation shall be applicable for statutory accounting and reporting purposes (including establishing the AVR charges). The final designation is not used for establishing the appropriate carrying value method in Step 2 (paragraph 26a.ii.).

b. Modified Filing Exempt Securities: The modified filing exempt method is for securities that are not subject to modeling under paragraph 26.a., and is further defined in the *Purposes and Procedures Manual of the NAIC Securities Valuation Office* and have a NAIC Acceptable Rating Organization (ARO) rating. The four-step process for these securities is similar to the three-step process described in paragraph 26.a.i. through 26a.iii.

  i. Step 1: Translate ARO Rating – Translate ARO Rating to the NAIC Designation Equivalent in accordance with the *Purposes and Procedures Manual of the NAIC Securities Valuation Office*. If the result is NAIC 1 or NAIC 6, the remaining steps do not need to be performed; use the NAIC 1 or NAIC 6 to establish the appropriate carrying value methodology per paragraph 25 and report the NAIC 1 or NAIC 6 as the Final Designation. For NAIC 2 through NAIC 5, proceed to Step 2.

  ii. Step 2: Determine Initial Designation – Use the NAIC 2 through NAIC 5 from Step 1 to identify the appropriate breakpoints from the pricing matrix (see table, "NAIC Designations Breakpoints for Loan-Backed and Structured Securities" provided in Part Three Section 3 (c) (iv) (A) of the *Purposes and Procedures Manual of the NAIC Securities Valuation Office*) and compare to the amortized cost (divided by outstanding par) to determine the **initial** NAIC designation.

  iii. Step 3: Determine Carrying Value Method – The carrying value method, either the amortized cost method or the lower of amortized cost or fair value method, is then determined as described in paragraph 25 based upon the **initial** NAIC designation determined in Step 2.

AAG-PLI 5.77

> iv. **Step 4: Determine Final Designation** – If the appropriate carrying value methodology established in Step 3 results in the security being carried at amortized cost (including securities where the carrying value method is lower of amortized cost or fair value where the amortized cost is the lower value), then the **final** NAIC designation is the same as the **initial** NAIC designation. If the appropriate carrying value methodology established in Step 3 results in the security being carried at fair value (thus the carrying value method is lower of amortized cost and fair value, and the fair value is the lower value), use the converted ARO rating NAIC designation from Step 2 to identify the appropriate breakpoints from the pricing matrix and compare to the fair value (divided by outstanding par) to determine the **final** NAIC designation. This final NAIC designation shall be applicable for statutory accounting and reporting purposes (including establishing the AVR charges). The final NAIC designation is not used for establishing the appropriate carrying value method in Step 3 (paragraph 26.b.ii.
>
> c. **All Other Loan-Backed and Structured Securities:** For loan-backed and structured securities not subject to paragraphs 26.a. (financial modeling) or 26.b. (modified filing exempt), follow the established designation procedures according to the appropriate section of the *Purposes and Procedures Manual of the NAIC Securities Valuation Office*. The NAIC designation shall be applicable for statutory accounting and reporting purposes (including determining the carrying value method and establishing the AVR charges). The carrying value method is established as described in paragraph 25. Examples of these securities include, but are not limited to, equipment trust certificates, credit tenant loans (CTL), 5*/6* securities, interest only (IO) securities, and loan-backed and structured securities with SVO assigned NAIC designations.

For reporting entities required to maintain an AVR, the accounting for unrealized gains and losses shall be in accordance with paragraph 36 of SSAP No. 43R. For reporting entities not required to maintain an AVR, unrealized gains and losses shall be recorded as a direct credit or charge to unassigned funds (surplus).

5.78 For impairments of loan-backed and structured securities, paragraphs 28–37 of SSAP No. 43R state that

> [t]he application of this reporting requirement resulting from NAIC designation (i.e., lower of cost or fair value) is not a substitute for other-than-temporary impairment recognition (paragraphs 32–36). For securities reported at fair value where an other-than-temporary impairment has been determined to have occurred, the realized loss recognized from the other-than-temporary impairment shall first be applied towards the realization of any unrealized losses previously recorded as a result of fluctuations in the security's fair value due to the reporting requirements. After the recognition of the other-than-temporary impairment, the security shall continue to report unrealized gains and losses as a result of fluctuations in fair value.

Investments and Fair Value Considerations

If the fair value of a loan-backed or structured security is less than its amortized cost basis at the balance sheet date, an entity shall assess whether the impairment is other than temporary. Amortized cost basis includes adjustments made to the cost of an investment for accretion, amortization, collection of cash, previous other-than-temporary impairments recognized as a realized loss (including any cumulative-effect adjustments recognized in accordance with paragraphs 55 through 57 of SSAP No. 43R).

If an entity intends to sell the loan-backed or structured security (that is, it has decided to sell the security), an other-than-temporary impairment shall be considered to have occurred.

If an entity does not intend to sell the loan-backed or structured security, the entity shall assess whether it has the intent and ability to retain the investment in the security for a period of time sufficient to recover the amortized cost basis. If the entity does not have the intent and ability to retain the investment for the time sufficient to recover the amortized cost basis, an other-than-temporary impairment shall be considered to have occurred.

If the entity does not expect to recover the entire amortized cost basis of the security, the entity would be unable to assert that it will recover its amortized cost basis even if it does not intend to sell the security and the entity has the intent and ability to hold. Therefore, in those situations, an other-than temporary impairment shall be considered to have occurred. In assessing whether the entire amortized cost basis of the security will be recovered, an entity shall compare the present value of cash flows expected to be collected from the security with the amortized cost basis of the security. If present value of cash flows expected to be collected is less than the amortized cost basis of the security, the entire amortized cost basis of the security will not be recovered (that is, a non-interest related decline exists), and an other-than-temporary impairment shall be considered to have occurred. A decrease in cash flows expected to be collected on a loaned-backed or structured security that results from an increase in prepayments on the underlying as-sets shall be considered in the estimate of the present value of cash flows expected to be collected.

In determining whether a non-interest related decline exists, an entity shall calculate the present value of cash flows expected to be collected based on an estimate of the expected future cash flows of the impaired loan-backed or structured security, discounted at the security's effective interest rate.

  a. For securities accounted for under paragraphs 12 through 16—the effective interest rate of the loan-backed or structured security is the rate of return implicit in the security (that is, the contractual interest rate adjusted for any net deferred fees or costs, premium, or discount existing at the origination or acquisition of the security).

  b. For securities accounted for under paragraphs 17 through 19—the effective interest rate is the rate implicit immediately prior to the recognition of the other-than-temporary impairment.

AAG-PLI 5.78

c. For securities accounted for under paragraphs 20 through 24—the reporting entity shall apply the guidance in paragraph 22.b.

When an other-than-temporary impairment has occurred because the entity intends to sell the security or has assessed that that they do not have the intent and ability to retain the investments in the security for a period of time sufficient to recover the amortized cost basis, the amount of the other-than-temporary impairment recognized in earnings as a realized loss shall equal the entire difference between the investment's amortized cost basis and its fair value at the balance sheet date. (This guidance includes loan-backed and structured securities previously held at lower of cost or market. For these securities, upon recognition of an other-than-temporary impairment, unrealized losses would be considered realized.)

When an other-than-temporary impairment has occurred because the entity does not expect to recover the entire amortized cost basis of the security even if the entity has no intent to sell and the entity has the intent and ability to hold, the amount of the other-than-temporary impairment recognized as a realized loss shall equal the difference between the investment's amortized cost basis and the present value of cash flows expected to be collected, discounted at the loan-backed or structured security's effective interest rate in accordance with paragraph 32. (This guidance includes loan-backed and structured securities previously held at lower of cost or market. For these securities, upon recognition of an other-than-temporary impairment, unrealized losses would be considered realized for the non-interest related decline. Hence, unrealized losses could continue to be reflected for these securities due to the reporting requirements.)

For situations where an other-than-temporary impairment is recognized pursuant to paragraphs 34 and 35 of this Statement, the previous amortized cost basis less the other-than-temporary impairment recognized as a realized loss shall become the new amortized cost basis of the investment. That new amortized cost basis shall not be adjusted for subsequent recoveries in fair value. Therefore, the prospective adjustment method shall be used for periods subsequent to loss recognition.

5.79 Paragraph 38 of SSAP No. 43R states that

[i]n periods subsequent to the recognition of an other than temporary impairment loss for a loan-backed or structured security, the reporting entity shall account for the other-than-temporarily impaired security as if the security had been purchased on the measurement date of the other-than-temporary impairment at an amortized cost basis equal to the previous amortized cost basis less the other-than-temporary impairment recognized as a realized loss. The difference between the new amortized cost basis and the cash flows expected to be collected shall be accreted as interest income. A reporting entity shall continue to estimate the present value of cash flows expected to be collected over the life of the loan-backed or structured security.

a. For securities accounted for under paragraphs 12 through 19, if upon subsequent evaluation, there is a significant increase in the cash flows expected to be collected or if actual cash flows are significantly greater than cash flows previously expected, such changes shall be accounted for as a prospective adjustment to

Investments and Fair Value Considerations

the accretable yield in accordance with paragraphs 17 through 19. The security shall continue to be subject to impairment analysis for each subsequent reporting period. The new amortized cost basis shall not be changed for subsequent recoveries in fair value. Future declines in fair value which are determined to be other-than-temporary shall be recorded as realized losses.

 b. For beneficial interests accounted for under paragraphs 20 through 24, a reporting entity shall apply the guidance in paragraphs 21 through 22 to account for changes in cash flows expected to be collected.

5.80 Investments in unaffiliated common stock shall be valued and reported in accordance with "Procedures for Valuing Common Stocks and Stock Warrants" of the P&P manual, in accordance with SSAP No. 30, *Investments in Common Stock (excluding investments in common stock of subsidiary, controlled, or affiliated entities).* Affiliated common stock is addressed in SSAP No. 97, *Investments in Subsidiary, Controlled, and Affiliated Entities, A Replacement of SSAP No. 88.* As discussed in paragraph 7 of SSAP No. 30, an investment in unaffiliated common stocks shall be valued at fair value. In those instances when the unit price is not available from the SVO, it is the responsibility of management to determine fair value based on analytical or pricing mechanisms.

5.81 Paragraph 15 of SSAP No. 32, *Investments in Preferred Stock (including investments in preferred stock of subsidiary, controlled, or affiliated entities)* states that redeemable preferred stock shall be classified into six quality categories (designations RP1–RP6), in accordance with the P&P manual. As noted in paragraph 16 of SSAP No. 32, preferred stock shall be valued based on (*a*) the underlying characteristics of the security; (*b*) the quality rating of the security, as defined in the P&P manual and assigned in *Valuations of Securities*; and (*c*) whether an asset valuation reserve (AVR) is maintained by the reporting entity. For reporting entities that do not maintain an AVR, redeemable preferred stocks designated highest quality and high quality (NAIC designations RP1 and RP2, respectively) shall be reported at book value; perpetual preferred stocks designated highest quality and high quality (NAIC designations P1 and P2, respectively) shall be reported at fair value; and redeemable preferred stocks and perpetual preferred stocks that are designated medium quality, low quality, and in or near default (NAIC designations RP3–RP6 and P3–P6, respectively) shall be reported at the lower of book value or fair value.

5.82 As noted in paragraph 17 of SSAP No. 32, step-up preferred stock (a security with the structure of a preferred stock, that has the cash flow characteristics of a debt instrument) is considered a security with characteristics of both debt and equity, and the accounting and valuation of such securities shall be consistent with SVO guidelines as stipulated in the P&P manual.

5.83 As noted in paragraph 18 of SSAP No. 32, for reporting entities not required to maintain an AVR, unrealized gains and losses shall be recorded as a direct credit or charge to unassigned funds (surplus). Readers should be aware that property and liability insurance entities are not required to recognize liabilities for AVR and an interest maintenance reserve (IMR), as explained in SSAP No. 7, *Asset Valuation Reserve and Interest Maintenance Reserve.*

5.84 SSAP No. 32 paragraphs 23–26 discuss accounting for other-than-temporary impairments for preferred stock:

Impairment of Redeemable Preferred Stock

An other-than-temporary impairment shall be considered to have occurred if it is probable that the reporting entity will be unable to collect all amounts due according to the contractual terms of the security in effect at the time of acquisition. A decline in fair value which is other-than-temporary includes situations where the reporting entity has made a decision to sell a security prior to its maturity at an amount below carrying value (that is, amortized cost). If it is determined that a decline in fair value of a redeemable preferred stock is other-than-temporary, an impairment loss shall be recognized as a realized loss equal to the entire difference between the redeemable preferred stock's carrying value and its fair value at the balance sheet date of the reporting period for which the assessment is made. The measurement of the impairment loss shall not include partial recoveries of fair value subsequent to the balance sheet date. For reporting entities required to maintain an AVR, realized loss shall be accounted for in accordance with SSAP No. 7, *Asset Valuation Reserve and Interest Maintenance Reserve*.

In periods subsequent to the recognition of an other-than-temporary impairment loss for a redeemable preferred stock, the reporting entity shall account for the other-than-temporary impaired security as if the security had been purchased at the measurement date of the other-than-temporary impairment, and in accordance with paragraph 19 or paragraph 21, as applicable. The fair value of the redeemable preferred stock on the measurement date shall become the new cost basis of the redeemable preferred stock and the new cost basis shall not be adjusted for subsequent recoveries in fair value. The discount or reduced premium recorded for the security, based on the new cost basis, shall be amortized over the remaining life of the security in the prospective manner based on the amount and timing of future estimated cash flows. The security shall continue to be subject to impairment analysis for each subsequent reporting period. Future declines in fair value which are determined to be other-than-temporary shall be recorded as realized losses.

Impairment of Perpetual Preferred Stock

If it is determined that a decline in the fair value of a perpetual preferred stock is other-than-temporary, an impairment loss shall be recognized as a realized loss equal to the entire difference between the perpetual preferred stock's carrying value and its fair value at the balance sheet date of the reporting period for which the assessment is made. The measurement of the impairment loss shall not include partial recoveries of fair value subsequent to the balance sheet date. For reporting entities required to maintain an AVR, realized losses shall be accounted for in accordance with SSAP No. 7, *Asset Valuation Reserve and Interest Maintenance Reserve*. A decline in fair value which is other-than-temporary includes situations where the reporting entity has made a decision to sell a security at an amount below its carrying value.

In periods subsequent to the recognition of an other-than-temporary impairment loss for a perpetual preferred stock, the reporting entity shall account for the other-than-temporary impaired security as if the security had been purchased at the measurement date of the other-than-temporary impairment, and in accordance with paragraph 20 or paragraph 22, as applicable. The fair value of the perpetual preferred stock on the measurement date shall become the new cost basis of the perpetual preferred stock and the new cost basis shall not be adjusted for subsequent recoveries in fair value. Future declines in fair value which are determined to be other-than-temporary shall be recorded as realized losses.

5.85 As noted in paragraph 5 of SSAP No. 30 and paragraph 10 of SSAP No. 32, both common and preferred stock acquisitions and dispositions shall be recorded on the trade date. Private placement stock transactions shall be recorded on the funding date.

5.86 For common stock, the basis at which the common stock is stated, a description and the amount of common stock that is restricted, and the nature of the restriction are required to be disclosed. For preferred stock, in addition to the disclosure requirements for common stock, the entity must also disclose the fair value, in accordance with SSAP No. 100, and concentrations of credit risk, in accordance of SSAP No. 27, *Disclosure of Information about Financial Instruments with Off-Balance-Sheet Risk, Financial Instruments With Concentrations of Credit Risk and Disclosures About Fair Value of Financial Instruments*. Both SSAP Nos. 30 and 32 reject the GAAP accounting guidance. Common and preferred stocks are also subject to both qualitative and quantitative limitations, as defined by the state of domicile, to qualify as admitted assets. Insurers are required to submit newly acquired unlisted securities not subject to the filing exemption rule to the NAIC SVO for valuation. Under the filing exemption rule, an insurer determines if a security is eligible for exemption based upon the nature of the rating for bonds and preferred stock and based upon market trading information for common stock.

5.87 For equity securities that are not listed in the P&P manual or are listed with no value, management must determine a fair value based on analytical or pricing mechanisms. The fair value is then substantiated by the appropriate NAIC subcommittee or regulatory agency. Property and liability insurance entities are required to submit sufficient information regarding these securities to the NAIC SVO for a determination of fair value.

5.88 Readers should look to SSAP No. 26 for the extensive disclosures required for bonds, excluding loan-backed and structured securities, and SSAP No. 43R, which requires other supplemental disclosures in addition to those required for invested assets in general.

Realized and Unrealized Gains and Losses on Debt and Equity Securities

5.89 The primary differences between GAAP and statutory accounting for realized and unrealized gains and losses on debt and equity securities are in the presentation in the financial statements. Realized gains and losses are presented on a pretax basis in the statement of earnings for GAAP and are presented net of tax for statutory accounting. Unrealized gains and losses are reported in other comprehensive income for GAAP and are included in unassigned funds (surplus) for statutory accounting. Both GAAP and statutory unrealized gains and losses are presented net of tax. Additionally, GAAP requires that other-than-temporary impairment detail be presented within the financial statements.

GAAP Accounting

5.90 FASB ASC 944-325-45-3 states that realized gains and losses on all investments, except those that are accounted for as either hedges of net investments in foreign operations or cash flow hedges, shall be reported in the statement of earnings as a component of other income and on a pretax basis. Realized gains and losses shall be presented as a separate item in the statement of earnings or disclosed in the notes to the financial statements. Realized gains and losses shall not be deferred to future periods either directly or indirectly.

5.91 FASB ASC 320-10-45-8A requires that an entity present the total other-than-temporary impairment in the statement of earnings, with an offset for the amount recognized in other comprehensive income (see an example in FASB ASC 320-10-55-21A). As discussed in FASB ASC 320-10-45-9A, the amount recognized in other comprehensive income related to securities with an other-than-temporary impairment recognized in earnings is presented separately from unrealized gains and losses for GAAP within the financial statements.

5.92 FASB ASC 320-10-35-1 states that unrealized holding gains and losses for securities categorized as trading securities are included in earnings. Unrealized gains and losses for securities categorized as available-for-sale securities, including those classified as current assets, are excluded from earnings and reported in other comprehensive income net of tax until realized. See FASB ASC 815-25-35-6 for an exception to this rule related to hedged items.

Statutory Accounting

5.93 Unrealized gains and losses on common stock and perpetual preferred stock recognized at fair value, per SSAP Nos. 30 and 32, shall be included as a direct credit or charge to unassigned funds, net of tax (surplus). Realized gains and losses are presented net of tax in the statement of operations.

Mortgage Loans

5.94 In general, mortgage loan investments represent obligations secured by first or second mortgages on industrial, commercial, residential, or farm real property and short-term construction loans. They generally provide periodic interest payments generating interest income to the holder. The principal is usually paid back on a specified schedule or specific date.

GAAP Accounting

5.95 Under GAAP, as noted in FASB ASC 944-310-35-1, mortgages purchased for investment are reported at outstanding principal, if acquired at par value, or amortized cost, if purchased at a discount or premium, with an allowance for estimated uncollectible amounts, if any. Premiums or discounts are generally amortized over the mortgage loan contract (or, in some limited cases, a shorter period based on estimated prepayment patterns; see FASB ASC 310-20-35-26) in a manner that will result in a constant effective yield. Mortgage loans held for sale are accounted for at the lower of cost or fair value less costs to sell.

5.96 Interest income and amortization amounts and other costs that are recognized as an adjustment of yield are recorded as interest income. Commitment fees should be amortized on a straight-line basis over the commitment period and recognized as service-fee income. Amounts included in income on the

Investments and Fair Value Considerations **267**

expiration of the commitment period should also be recognized as service-fee income. Note that FASB ASC 815-10-15-71 states that loan commitments relating to the origination of mortgage loans held for sale, as discussed in FASB ASC 948-310-25-3, shall be accounted for as derivative instruments by the issuer of the loan commitment. Loan origination fees should be recognized over the life of the related loan as an adjustment of yield using the interest method.

5.97 FASB ASC 310-10-35 addresses the methods for evaluating, measuring, and reporting mortgage loan impairments.

5.98 Interest income on all loans should be accrued and credited to interest income as it is earned using the interest method. FASB ASC 310-10-50-15 requires disclosure of information about the recorded investment in certain impaired loans that fall within its scope and how a creditor recognizes interest income related to those impaired loans.

5.99 FASB ASC 310 governs the accounting for loans that have evidence of credit quality deterioration and for which the purchaser does not expect to collect contractual cash flows.

5.100 FASB ASC 310 applies to certain loans acquired individually, in a portfolio, or in acquisition. This does not apply to any entity-originated loans or acquired loans without evidence of credit quality deterioration. FASB ASC 310 should be applied to loans individually to meet the scope criteria, and individual loans are not to be aggregated for determining whether they, as a group, are within the scope. Because the use of aggregation may result in different scope applicability, aggregation is only allowed for recognition, measurement, and disclosure purposes. See FASB ASC 310 for additional guidance regarding the accounting for differences between contractual cash flows and cash flows expected to be collected from an investor's initial investment in loans or debt securities acquired in a transfer if those differences are attributable, at least in part, to credit quality. FASB ASC 310 also discusses valuation allowances and new disclosure requirements.

5.101 FASB ASC 310-10-50 and 310-30-50 describe the disclosure requirements for impaired loans.

Statutory Accounting

5.102 Mortgage loans are not investment securities, but they meet the definition of *assets*, as specified in SSAP No. 4, *Assets and Nonadmitted Assets*, and are admitted assets to the extent that they conform to the requirements of SSAP No. 37, *Mortgage Loans*.

5.103 Under SAP, the amount recorded as the initial investment in a loan is the principal of the loan, net of deferred loan origination and commitment fees. If purchased, the loan is recorded at the amount paid, net of premium, or discount. Some states stipulate maximum loan values that limit the extent to which outstanding principal balances can be reported as admitted assets, and most states have restrictions that apply to the size of the individual loan in relation to the appraised value of the mortgaged property at the origination date, current valuation date, or both. In addition, many states require the mortgage to be a first mortgage only.

5.104 SSAP No. 37 provides guidance regarding amortizing premiums and discounts on mortgage loans. It also discusses when and how to impair a mortgage loan. See SSAP No. 36, *Troubled Debt Restructuring*, for the requirements regarding the accounting for troubled debt.

5.105 Interest income on mortgage loans is recorded as earned, and contingent interest may be recognized as earned or received. As noted in paragraph 14 of SSAP No. 37, if a loan in default has any investment income due and accrued that is 180 days past due and collectible, the investment income shall continue to accrue, but all interest related to the loan is to be reported as a nonadmitted asset. If accrued interest on a mortgage loan in default is not collectible, the accrued interest shall be written off immediately and no further interest accrued.

5.106 SSAP No. 83, *Mezzanine Real Estate Loans*, provides accounting and reporting guidance for mezzanine real estate loans (MRELs). Loans that meet the definition of an *MREL* are admitted assets and follow the accounting and reporting guidelines for mortgage loans contained within SSAP No. 37.

5.107 Paragraphs 20–21 of SSAP No. 37 describe the disclosure requirements regarding mortgage loans. The requirements include disclosure of fair values and concentrations of credit risk, in accordance with SSAP Nos. 27 and 100; information on interest rates on new loans; a description of the valuation basis for mortgage loans; and information on mortgages with interest 180 days past due. Paragraphs 20–21 of SSAP No. 37 also detail additional disclosures for impaired loans.

Real Estate

5.108 Real estate is classified as real estate held for investment purposes or real estate used in an entity's operations, depending on its predominant use, or real estate held for sale. Property and liability insurance entities primarily own real estate for their own use rather than as an investment, in contrast to life insurance entities that have a larger amount of real estate as investments.

5.109 For GAAP accounting, real estate encumbrances are reported as other liabilities. For statutory accounting, real estate is reported net of encumbrances, with parenthetical disclosure of the amount of the encumbrances. Real estate is depreciated over its estimated useful life. For statutory accounting, paragraph 9 of SSAP No. 40, *Real Estate Investments*, specifies that the estimated life is not to exceed 50 years.

GAAP Accounting

5.110 In accordance with paragraphs 4–6 of FASB ASC 944-360-35, real estate investments, except those held for sale, are carried at cost less accumulated depreciation. Depreciation and other related charges or credits shall be charged or credited to investment income. Reductions in the carrying amount of real estate investments resulting from the application of the "Impairment or Disposal of Long-Lived Assets" sections of FASB ASC 360-10 shall be included in realized gains and losses. FASB ASC 360-10-50-2 provides guidance regarding disclosing impairment losses.

5.111 In applying the guidance in FASB ASC 360-10-35-43, real estate held for sale shall be measured at the lower of cost or fair value less the costs to sell. Costs to sell real estate generally include legal fees, brokerage commissions, and closing costs. A long-lived asset shall not be depreciated while it is classified as held for sale. FASB ASC 360, *Property, Plant, and Equipment*, contains certain criteria that must be met in order for a long-lived asset to be sold and classified as held for sale, as well as disclosure requirements for the period during which a long-lived asset either has been sold or is classified as held for sale.

5.112 In addition to FASB ASC 360, the following is a listing of some additional FASB ASC topics and subtopics that may be useful based upon the nature of the transaction:

- FASB ASC 810-20
- FASB ASC 970, *Real Estate—General*
- FASB ASC 840, *Leases*
- FASB ASC 835-20

Statutory Accounting

5.113 Paragraph 4 of SSAP No. 40 states that real estate investments shall be reported net of encumbrances in the following balance sheet categories, with parenthetical disclosure of the amount of the related encumbrances:

a. Properties occupied by the entity

b. Properties held for the production of income

c. Properties held for sale

5.114 Per paragraph 17 of SSAP No. 90, *Accounting for the Impairment or Disposal of Real Estate Investments*, properties occupied by the entity and properties held for the production of income shall be carried at depreciated cost less encumbrances. Properties that the reporting entity has the intent to sell or is required to sell shall be classified as properties held for sale and carried at the lower of depreciated cost or fair value less encumbrances and estimated costs to sell the property.

5.115 For properties held for sale, paragraph 4 of SSAP No. 90 states that an impairment loss shall be recognized only if the carrying amount of a long-lived asset is not recoverable and exceeds the long-lived asset's fair value. The carrying amount is not recoverable if it exceeds the sum of the undiscounted cash flows expected to result from the use and eventual disposition of the asset. That assessment shall be based on the carrying amount of the asset at the date it is tested for recoverability, whether in use or under development. An impairment loss shall be measured as the amount by which the carrying amount of a long-lived asset exceeds the long-lived asset's fair value. See SSAP No. 100 for a discussion of fair value. The impairment loss shall be recorded in the summary of operations as a realized loss.

5.116 In conjunction with SSAP No. 100, paragraph 11 of SSAP No. 40 addresses the fair value of real estate by stating that the current fair value of real estate shall be determined on a property-by-property basis. If market quotes are unavailable, estimates of fair value shall be determined by an appraisal (internal or third-party) that is based upon all relevant data about the market.

5.117 For all properties held for the production of income, appraisals are required to be no more than five years old, and a current appraisal should be obtained if there has been a significant decline in fair value. If the required appraisal is not obtained, the related property shall be nonadmitted. For all properties held for sale, an appraisal shall be obtained at the time such property is classified as held for sale, and subsequently, an appraisal shall be maintained that is no more than five years old as of the reporting date. For real estate used in an entity's operations, the insurance entity is required to charge itself imputed rent. This is recorded as both investment income and an operating expense.

5.118 Readers should look to paragraphs 36–38 of SSAP No. 90 for a description of the disclosure requirements related to real estate impairments, real estate investments that either have been sold or classified as held for sale, and changes in the plans to sell an investment in real estate.

Derivatives, Including Futures, Options, and Similar Financial Instruments

5.119 Some insurance entities utilize derivative instruments as part of their overall investment management strategy. These derivative instruments include options, warrants, caps, floors, swaps, forwards, futures, and similar financial instruments.

5.120 State laws and regulations differ on the kinds of derivative transactions that an insurance entity is permitted to enter. Generally, insurance entities are permitted to utilize derivative instruments in hedging transactions, income-generation transactions, and replication (synthetic asset) transactions. However, most insurance regulators prohibit insurance entities from entering into derivative transactions for speculative purposes.

5.121 State laws and regulations also differ on the kinds of options, if any, that insurance entities are permitted to write, but some states permit insurance entities to write covered-call options, which are for securities that insurance entities own and can deliver if they are exercised by the option buyers. If an insurance entity writes a covered-call option, it transfers to the option buyer the right to benefit from appreciation of the security underlying the option above the exercise price. Insurance entities usually write covered-call options because they consider the premium received for writing the options to be either (*a*) an economic hedge against a decline in the market price of the underlying security or (*b*) an increase in yield on the underlying security.

5.122 Hedging transaction criteria may differ from state to state. At a minimum, the item to be hedged must expose the insurance entity to price, interest rate, or currency exchange risk, and the financial instrument used as a hedge must reduce the specific risk exposure.

5.123 The significant differences between GAAP and statutory accounting for derivatives are as follows:

- GAAP accounting follows a fair value measurement model, with the fair value of derivative instruments recognized in the statement of financial position; however, statutory accounting for derivative instruments applies a measurement model consistent with the qualifying hedged asset or liability (referred to as hedge accounting). Under statutory accounting, the fair value measurement is applied only when the derivative instrument is deemed an ineffective hedge or becomes an ineffective hedge (referred to as fair value accounting).
- Gains and losses on derivative instruments, such as the following:
  - Under GAAP accounting, the recognition of gains and losses on derivative instruments varies with the designation of the derivative instruments. Depending on the designation, a gain or loss may be recognized currently in earnings (no hedge designation), recognized in earnings with an offsetting gain or loss

Investments and Fair Value Considerations

on the hedged item (fair value hedge), or recognized as a component of other comprehensive income (cash flow hedge). Also, various gain or loss recognition treatments exist for foreign currency hedges.

— Under statutory accounting, the recognition of gains or losses on derivative instruments depends upon whether the derivative transaction meets the criteria for a highly effective hedge. Derivative instruments meeting the effective hedge criteria follow the valuation and recognition of gain or loss of the hedged item (hedge accounting). Derivative instruments that are deemed an ineffective hedge or become an ineffective hedge (referred to as fair value accounting) are measured at fair value, with the gain or loss recorded as unrealized investment gains or losses.

- Other GAAP and statutory derivative instrument accounting differences, such as the following:

— GAAP requires that certain financial instruments that contain an embedded derivative be bifurcated, reported separately from the host contract, and accounted for as a derivative instrument. Statutory accounting does not allow such an embedded derivative instrument to be separated from the host and accounted for separately as a derivative instrument.

— GAAP allows a portion of a derivative instrument to be designated as a hedging instrument, but under statutory accounting, the derivative instrument in its entirety is classified and accounted for as either an effective or an ineffective hedge.

GAAP Accounting

5.124 FASB ASC 815, *Derivatives and Hedging*, establishes accounting and reporting standards for derivative instruments, including certain derivative instruments embedded in other contracts (collectively referred to as derivatives), and hedging activities. It requires that an entity recognize all derivatives as either assets or liabilities in the statement of financial position and measure those derivative instruments at fair value. As noted in FASB ASC 815-10-05-4, if certain conditions are met, an insurance entity may elect to designate a derivative as follows:

a. A hedge of the exposure to changes in the fair value of a recognized asset or liability or an unrecognized firm commitment, all of which are attributable to a particular risk (referred to as a fair value hedge)

b. A hedge of the exposure to variable cash flows of a recognized asset or liability of a forecasted transaction that is attributable to a particular risk (referred to as a cash flow hedge)

c. A hedge of the foreign currency exposure of any one of the following:

 i. An unrecognized firm commitment (a foreign currency fair value hedge)

 ii. A forecasted transaction (a foreign currency fair value hedge)

 iii. A net investment in a foreign operation

5.125 The accounting for changes in the fair value of a derivative (that is, gains and losses) depends on the intended use of the derivative and the resulting designation, which is described in FASB ASC 815-10-35-2. Readers should refer to the full text of FASB ASC 815, considering accounting and reporting issues related to derivative instruments and hedging activities. The following is a list of derivative issues that are specific to property and liability insurance:

- Paragraphs 37–39 of FASB ASC 815-10-55 provide guidance for embedded derivatives in dual-trigger property and casualty insurance contracts (see chapter 6, "Reinsurance," of this guide).
- Paragraphs 32–36 of FASB ASC 815-10-55 provide guidance for embedded derivatives in dual-trigger financial guarantee contracts (see chapter 6 of this guide).
- Paragraphs 20–21 of FASB ASC 815-15-15 provide guidance for embedded derivatives in foreign currency elements of insurance contracts.
- FASB ASC 815-15-25-47, paragraphs 101–102 of FASB ASC 815-15-55, and paragraphs 107–109 of FASB ASC 815-15-55 provide guidance for embedded derivatives in modified coinsurance arrangements.
- FASB ASC 815-10-55-44 and paragraphs 135–141 of FASB ASC 815-10-55 provide guidance for scope exceptions related to physical variables.
- FASB ASC 815-20-25-16 and paragraphs 1–5 of FASB ASC 944-815-55 provide guidance for cash flow hedges: interest credited on an insurance contract liability.

5.126 Readers should review FASB ASC 815-10-50 for an extensive list of required disclosures for all derivative contracts used.

> ⓘ**Update 5-1** *Accounting and Reporting Update*: **Disclosure About Offsetting Assets and Liabilities**
>
> FASB Accounting Standards Update (ASU) No. 2011-11, *Balance Sheet (Topic 210): Disclosures about Offsetting Assets and Liabilities,* issued in December 2011, is effective for annual reporting periods beginning on or after January 1, 2013, and interim periods within those annual periods. An entity should provide the disclosures required by those amendments retrospectively for all comparative periods presented.
>
> On November 26, 2012, FASB issued proposed ASU *Balance Sheet (Topic 210): Clarifying the Scope of Disclosures about Offsetting Assets and Liabilities* to clarify the scope of ASU No. 2011-11. The proposed amendments would clarify that the scope of ASU No. 2011-11 would apply to derivatives, repurchase agreements and reverse repurchase agreements, and securities borrowing and securities lending transactions that are either offset in accordance with FASB ASC 210-20-45 or FASB ASC 815-10-45 or subject to a master netting arrangement or similar agreement.
>
> FASB Accounting Standards Board (FASB) Accounting Standards Update (ASU) No. 2013-1, *Clarifying the Scope of Disclosures about Offsetting Assets and Liabilities*, clarified that the scope of Update 2011-11 applies to derivatives accounted for in accordance with FASB ASC 815, *Derivatives and Hedging*, including bifurcated embedded derivatives, repurchase agreements and reverse repurchase agreements, and securities borrowing and securities lending transactions that are either offset in accordance with FASB ASC 210-20-45 or FASB

ASC 815-10-45 or subject to an enforceable master netting arrangement or similar agreement. An entity is required to apply the amendments for fiscal years beginning on or after January 1, 2013, and interim periods within those annual periods. An entity should provide the required disclosures retrospectively for all comparative periods presented. The effective date is the same as the effective date of FASB ASU 2011-11.

For periods after January 1, 2013, refer to section D.01 in appendix D, "Guidance Updates," which summarizes these clarifying changes that may affect an auditor's practice or methodology.

Statutory Accounting

5.127 The NAIC has incorporated certain concepts from GAAP into SSAP No. 86, *Accounting for Derivative Instruments and Hedging, Income Generation, and Replication (Synthetic Asset) Transactions*. Under SSAP No. 86, *derivatives* are defined as swaps, options, futures, caps, floors, and collars. SSAP No. 86 provides definitions for these terms.

5.128 SSAP No. 86 adopts some of the GAAP framework for fair value and cash flow hedges. It also adopts the GAAP provisions related to foreign currency hedges. It allows derivatives to be designated as hedging exposure to changes in fair value, variability in expected cash flows, or foreign currency exposures. Firm commitments and forecasted transactions are eligible for designation as hedged transactions. Forecasted transactions must meet additional specific criteria to be designated in a cash flow hedge.

5.129 To qualify for hedge accounting, a fair value, cash flow, and foreign currency hedge must, at the inception of the hedge, meet formal documentation requirements and be highly effective. *Highly effective* is specifically defined within paragraph 19(c) of SSAP No. 86 as when the change in the derivative hedging instruments is within 80 percent to 125 percent of the change in the hedged item. The concept within FASB ASC 815 of identifying and separately accounting for effective and ineffective portions of a single hedge was rejected; therefore, for statutory accounting, the ineffective portion of an effective hedge need not be separately recognized in income. An entity either has an effective hedge and follows hedge accounting or has an ineffective hedge and uses fair value accounting (recognition in unrealized gains and losses).

5.130 Under SSAP No. 86, for a gain or loss upon termination, paragraph 17 states that upon termination of a derivative that qualifies for hedge accounting, the gain or loss shall adjust the basis of the hedged item and be recognized in income in a manner that is consistent with the hedged item. Additionally, exhibit C of SSAP No. 86 provides specific hedge accounting procedures for derivatives. The redesignation of an item carried at amortized cost to another effective hedging relationship with an item carried at amortized cost shall continue to be recorded at amortized cost, with no gain or loss on the derivative recognized.

5.131 Paragraph 53 of SSAP No. 86 contains an extensive list of required disclosures for all derivative contracts used.

Joint Ventures and Partnerships

5.132 Entities may invest indirectly in real estate or other investments, such as mining or oil drilling, high-yield security partnerships, CMO partnerships, venture capital or leveraged buyout partnerships, or government-backed mortgage partnerships, through participation in joint ventures or partnerships. These investments may differ in legal form and economic substance, but the most common forms are corporate joint venture, general partnership, and limited partnership. Generally, joint venture arrangements have formal agreements that specify key terms of the arrangement for each participant, such as profit or loss allocations, cash distributions, liquidation distributions, and capital infusions.

5.133 The significant differences between GAAP and statutory accounting for joint ventures and partnerships are as follows:

- Generally, under GAAP accounting, the ownership percentage in, and degree of control over, the joint venture or partnership determines whether the investment is accounted for under the cost basis or equity method or if it is consolidated. Under statutory accounting, the equity method is applied, with differences based on whether the investee is a subsidiary or controlled or affiliated entity or whether the investor has a minor ownership interest (that is, less than 10 percent) or lacks control.

- Additionally, under GAAP accounting, a reporting entity's share of undistributed earnings and losses generally is reported in net investment income. Under statutory accounting, the insurance entity's share of undistributed earnings is recorded as unrealized investment gains and losses until a distribution is declared or received, or both. Statutory accounting defers the recognition of net investment income until a distribution is received.

GAAP Accounting

5.134 Under GAAP, the ownership percentage in, and the degree of control over, the joint venture or partnership determine whether the cost, equity, or consolidation method applies with respect to the accounting and reporting of the investment. Guidance for determining the accounting is in FASB ASC 323, *Investments—Equity Method and Joint Ventures*, and FASB ASC 810, *Consolidation*. The insurance entity should disclose any contingent obligations or commitments for additional funding or guarantees of obligations of the investee in the notes to the financial statements.

5.135 In addition, FASB ASC 810 provides the guidance for an entity to determine if it has a controlling financial interest in a VIE. FASB ASC 810 requires an entity to perform an analysis to determine whether the entity's variable interest(s) gives it a controlling financial interest in a VIE.

5.136 An entity is considered a VIE, per FASB ASC 810-10-15-14, when it has one or more of the following characteristics:

   a. The equity investment at risk is not sufficient to permit the entity to finance its activities without additional subordinated financial support provided by any parties, including the equity holders

   b. The equity investors lack one or more of the following essential characteristics of a controlling financial interest:

   i. The power, through voting or similar rights, to direct the activities of the legal entity that most significantly affect the entity's economic performance

Investments and Fair Value Considerations

ii. The obligation to absorb the expected losses of the equity

iii. The right to receive the expected residual returns of the equity

c. The voting rights of some investors are not proportional to their economic interests, and substantially all of the legal entity's activities either involve, or are conducted on behalf of, the investor that has disproportionately few voting rights

5.137 Per FASB ASC 810-10-25-38A,[4] an entity is considered to have a controlling financial interest in a VIE if it has both of the following characteristics:

a. The power to direct the activities of a VIE that most significantly affect the VIE's economic performance

b. The obligation to absorb losses of the VIE that could potentially be significant to the VIE or the right to receive benefits from the VIE that could potentially be significant to the VIE

5.138 FASB ASC 810-10-50 provides the disclosure requirements for VIEs. FASB ASC 323-10-50-3 provides the disclosure requirements for non-consolidated interests in joint ventures and partnerships.

5.139 FASB ASC 323-740 provides guidance about how an entity that invests in a qualified affordable housing project through a limited partnership should account for its investment. The guidance states that immediate recognition, at the time the investment is purchased, of the entire benefit of the tax credits to be received during the term of a limited partnership investment in a qualified affordable housing project is not appropriate (that is, affordable housing credits should not be recognized in the financial statements prior to their inclusion in the investor's tax return). The guidance also states that an entity that invests in a qualified affordable housing project through a limited partnership investment may elect to account for the investment using the effective yield method if certain conditions are met.

5.140 FASB ASC 810-20-25 and FASB ASC 810-20-55 (Emerging Issues Task Force Issue No. 04-5, *Determining Whether a General Partner, or the General Partners as a Group, Controls a Limited Partnership or Similar Entity When the Limited Partners Have Certain Rights*) provide guidance for determining whether limited partners with certain rights, that are not VIEs, should be consolidated.

Statutory Accounting

5.141 As discussed in SSAP No. 48, *Joint Ventures, Partnerships and Limited Liability Companies*, provides that joint ventures, partnerships and limited liability companies, except those with a minor ownership interest (that is, less than 10 percent), should be accounted for in accordance with the *equity method*, as defined in SSAP No. 97 paragraphs 8b(i)-8b(iv). Investments in joint ventures, partnerships, and limited liability companies for which the entity has a minor ownership interest or lacks control, as stipulated in paragraphs 9–10 of SSAP No. 48, should be recorded based on the underlying audited U.S. GAAP equity of the investee. Audited U.S. tax-basis financial statements can also be acceptable for these entities when audited GAAP financial statements of the investee are unavailable. Non-U.S. joint ventures, partnerships, and limited

---

[4] The term *entity* is used in FASB ASC 810 and may be in a different context than the rest of this document.

liability companies, for which the entity has a minor ownership interest of less than 10 percent, and where audited U.S. GAAP basis financial statements are unavailable may be recorded based on (*a*) foreign GAAP-basis financial statements with an audited footnote reconciling the investee's equity and income to GAAP or (*b*) audited International Financial Reporting Standards (IFRSs)-basis financial statements with IFRSs as adopted by the International Accounting Standards Board. The amount to be recorded shall be defined as the initial investment in an investee at cost plus subsequent capital contributions to the investee. The carrying amount of the investment shall be adjusted to recognize the reporting entity's share of the audited GAAP (or other acceptable financial statement basis) earnings or losses of the investee after the date of acquisition, adjusted for any distributions received. A reporting entity's share of adjustments, excluding changes in capital contributions to the investee, that are recorded directly to the investee's stockholder's equity shall also be recorded as adjustments to the carrying value of the investment, with an offsetting amount recorded to unrealized capital gains and losses on investments. Investments in joint ventures, partnerships, and limited liability companies should be reported in the "Other Invested Assets" section of the financial statements.

5.142 Disclosure requirements for such investments that exceed 10 percent of the total admitted assets of the reporting entity are described in paragraph 14 of SSAP No. 48. They include the name and percentage of ownership of each investment; the reporting entity's accounting policies with respect to each of these types of investments; and the difference, if any, between the amount at which the investment is carried and the amount of the underlying equity in net assets (that is, nonadmitted goodwill or other nonadmitted assets) and the accounting for the difference. In addition, for such investments for which a quoted market price is available, the aggregate value of each joint venture, partnership, or limited liability company investment based on the quoted market price and summarized information about assets, liabilities, and results of operations for these investments either individually or in groups shall be disclosed. Paragraphs 15–16 of SSAP No. 48 require that any commitments or contingent commitments to such investments be disclosed and describe the disclosure requirements regarding impairment losses.

5.143 As stated in paragraphs 12–13 of SSAP No. 48, for any decline in the fair value of an investment in joint ventures, partnerships, or limited liability companies that is determined to be other than temporary, the investment shall be written down to fair value as the new cost basis, and the amount of the write-down shall be accounted for as a realized loss.

5.144 SSAP No. 93, *Accounting for Low Income Housing Tax Credit Property Investments*, provides that investments in federal and certain state-sponsored low-income housing tax credits (LIHTC) properties having certain characteristics, as described in paragraph 1 of SSAP No. 93, shall be initially recorded at cost and carried at amortized cost, unless considered impaired, as discussed in paragraph 8(b) of SSAP No. 93. Readers should look to paragraphs 12–15 of SSAP No. 93 for discussion of the impairment of LIHTC properties and paragraphs 17–22 of SSAP No. 93 for disclosure requirements surrounding LIHTC investments.

Investments in SCA Entities

5.145 GAAP accounting requires the consolidation of subsidiaries based upon control or under the variable interest model contained in FASB ASC 810.

Statutory accounting requires that investments in subsidiary, controlled, and affiliated (SCA) entities be recorded either using a market valuation approach or one of the equity methods described in SSAP No. 97. Under SSAP No. 97, a presumption of control exists if the reporting entity and its affiliates directly or indirectly own or have the ability to control 10 percent of the voting interests of an entity. This presumption can be overcome by evaluating the facts and circumstances based on the criteria in paragraphs 10–11 of FASB ASC 323-10-15. If the presumption of control can be overcome, the insurer is required to document the disclaimer of control for review by the domiciliary commissioner.

Statutory Accounting

5.146 SSAP No. 97 requires that investments in SCA entities be recorded using either a market valuation approach or one of the equity methods described in the SSAP. Specific requirements must be met in order to use the market valuation approach, including the requirement to record the investment at a *discount to market*, as defined in paragraph 8(a) of SSAP No. 97. Under the statutory equity method, investments in U.S. insurance SCA entities shall be recorded based on the audited statutory equity of the respective entity's financial statements, adjusted for any unamortized goodwill. Paragraph 8(b)(i) of SSAP No. 97 provides additional guidance regarding the carrying value of these investments.

5.147 As explained in paragraph 9 of SSAP No. 97, investments in noninsurance SCA entities that are engaged in *specific transactions or activities*, as defined in paragraph 8(b)(ii) of SSAP No. 97, and have 20 percent or more of the SCA's revenue generated from the reporting entity and its affiliates, are valued based upon the underlying equity of the respective entity's audited GAAP financial statements adjusted to a statutory basis of accounting.

5.148 As noted in paragraph 8b(iii) of SSAP No. 97, investments in both U.S. and foreign noninsurance SCA entities that do not qualify under paragraph 8b(ii) of SSAP No. 97 should be recorded based on the audited GAAP equity of the investee. Audited foreign GAAP-basis financial statements with an audited footnote reconciling the entity's net income and equity on a foreign GAAP-basis to a U.S. GAAP basis are also acceptable.

5.149 Investments in foreign insurance SCA entities should be recorded based on the underlying audited U.S. GAAP equity of the respective entity adjusted to a statuoury basis of accounting in accordance with paragraph 9 of SSAP No. 97 and adjusted for reserves of the foreign insurance SCA with respect to business it assumes directly and indirectly from a U.S. insurer using the SAP promulgated by the NAIC in the P&P manual. The audited foreign statutory basis financial statements should include an audited footnote that reconciles net income and equity on a foreign statutory basis to a U.S. GAAP.

5.150 The admissibility of an asset may be limited when a qualified opinion is provided. Readers should look to Interpretation 03-03, *Admissibility of Investments Recorded Based on the Audited GAAP Equity of the Investee When a Qualified Opinion is Provided*, of the EAIWG for the adjustment criteria.

5.151 Per paragraph 11 of SSAP No. 97, under the equity method, the reporting entity's share of undistributed earnings and losses of an investee is included in unrealized capital gains and losses. Some other changes in the investee's surplus, such as the change in the investee's nonadmitted assets, should also be recorded as a component of unrealized capital gains and losses on investments. If the investment is recorded using the market value approach, changes in the valuation shall also be included in unrealized capital gains and losses. Dividends or distributions received should be recognized in investment income when declared, to the extent that they are not in excess of the undistributed accumulated earnings attributable to the investee. Any excess amount should reduce the carrying value of the investment. Per paragraph 12 of SSAP No. 97, for investments in entities recorded based upon the underlying audited GAAP equity of the investee, the *amount to be recorded* shall be defined as the initial investment in an investee at cost. The carrying amount of an investment shall be adjusted to recognize the reporting entity's share of the audited GAAP-basis earnings or losses of the investee after the date of acquisition, adjusted for any dividends received.

5.152 Paragraph 13 of SSAP No. 97 discusses the procedures to be followed by a reporting entity in applying the equity method of accounting to investments in SCA entities. At a minimum, these procedures should be performed on a quarterly basis.

5.153 Paragraph 14 of SSAP No. 97 states that once the reporting entity elects to use a valuation approach for a particular subsidiary, the reporting entity may not change the valuation method without approval of the domiciliary commissioner. It also describes restrictions on when changes can occur and accounting for a change.

5.154 Paragraphs 17–22 of SSAP No. 97 provide guidance on the valuation and admissibility requirements of investments in downstream holding companies.

5.155 Paragraph 28 of SSAP No. 97 states that for any decline in the fair value of an investment in an SCA that is other than temporary, the investment shall be written down to fair value because the new cost basis and the amount of the write-down shall be accounted for as a realized loss. It further states that an impairment shall be considered to have occurred if it is probable that the reporting entity will be unable to recover the carrying amount of the investment or if evidence indicates an inability of the investee to sustain earnings, which would justify the carrying amount of the investment.

5.156 Paragraphs 30–36 of SSAP No. 97 describe the disclosure requirements for these investments. It describes the disclosures that shall be made for all investments in SCA entities that exceed 10 percent of total admitted assets and those that are required for certain foreign investments. Paragraph 32 states that any commitment or contingent commitment to an SCA entity shall be disclosed (for example, guarantees or commitments to provide additional capital contributions). It also provides guidance regarding impairment loss disclosures.

Investment Income Due and Accrued

5.157 Investment income due represents certain amounts of income that are legally owed to the entity as of the financial statement date but have not yet been received. Investment income should only be accrued when it is reasonably expected to be collected. Collectability of investment income due and accrued should be reviewed following the entity's reporting cycle and in conjunction with the review of investment impairment.

5.158 Accrued investment income represents interest that is earned as of the financial statement date but not legally due to be paid until subsequent to that date. Dividends on preferred stocks and common stocks are accrued when declared.

5.159 No significant differences exist between GAAP and statutory accounting for investment income due and accrued.

Statutory Accounting

5.160 Under SAP, as described in paragraph 5 of SSAP No. 34, *Investment Income Due and Accrued*, a collectability test is used to determine whether an impairment of the investment income exists. If interest is deemed uncollectible, the amount should be written off and charged against investment income in the current period. Any remaining investment income due and accrued (that is, considered probable of collection) representing either (*a*) amounts that are over 90 days past due (generated by any invested asset, except mortgage loans in default) or (*b*) amounts designated elsewhere in the *Accounting Practices and Procedures Manual* as nonadmitted shall be considered nonadmitted assets and recognized through a direct charge to surplus in accordance with SSAP Nos. 4. These nonadmitted assets shall be subject to continuing assessments of collectability, and if determined to be uncollectible, a write-off shall be recorded in the period that such determination is made. Mortgage loan interest that is 180 days past due and deemed collectible should be considered a nonadmitted asset.

5.161 Paragraph 7 of SSAP No. 34 requires disclosure, by category, of the bases of investment income for excluding (nonadmitting) any investment income due and accrued and of the amount that is nonadmitted.

Asset Transfers and Extinguishments of Liabilities

5.162 Transfers of financial assets may include transactions in which the transferor has no continuing involvement with the transferred assets or transferee, or the transferor has continuing involvement with either the transferred assets or transferee. Examples of continuing involvement are recourse, servicing, agreements to acquire, options written or held, and pledges of collateral. Transfers of financial assets with continuing involvement may be considered sales of all or part of the assets or as secured borrowings.

5.163 An entity may settle a liability by transferring assets to the creditor or otherwise obtain an unconditional release. Alternatively, an entity may enter into other arrangements designed to set aside assets dedicated to eventually settling a liability.

5.164 Some differences exist between GAAP and statutory accounting for asset transfers and extinguishment of liabilities. The most significant differences are that the GAAP guidance no longer contains the concept of a qualifying special-purpose entity, and the requirement to achieve sale accounting is stricter than under statutory accounting. The reader should take note that the NAIC is in the process of considering the revised GAAP guidance for incorporation into statutory accounting.

GAAP Accounting

5.165 FASB ASC 860-50 and FASB ASC 405-20 provide accounting and reporting standards for transfers and servicing of financial assets and extinguishments of liabilities. Those standards are based on consistent application of a financial-components approach that focuses on control. Under that approach, after a transfer of financial assets, an entity recognizes the financial and servicing assets that it controls and the liabilities that it has incurred, derecognizes financial assets when control has been surrendered, and derecognizes liabilities when extinguished. FASB ASC 860 provides consistent standards for distinguishing transfers of financial assets that are sales from transfers that are secured borrowings. FASB ASC 860 provides guidance for assessing the isolation of transferred assets and accounting for transfers of partial interests; servicing of financial assets; securitizations; transfers of sales-type and direct-financing lease receivables; securities lending transactions; repurchase agreements, including dollar rolls, wash sales, loan syndications, and participations; risk participations in banker's acceptances; factoring arrangements; transfers of receivables with recourse; and extinguishments of liabilities.

5.166 FASB ASC 860-10-40-4 states that the objective of the guidance is to determine whether a transferor and its consolidated affiliates included in the financial statements being presented have surrendered control over transferred financial assets or third-party beneficial interests. This determination

  a. shall first consider whether the transferee would be consolidated by the transferor.

  b. shall consider the transferor's continuing involvement in the transferred financial asset.

  c. requires the use of judgment that shall consider all arrangements or agreements made contemporaneously with, or in contemplation of, the transfer, even if they were not entered into at the time of the transfer.

5.167 With respect to item (b), all continuing involvement by the transferor, its consolidated affiliates included in the financial statements being presented, or its agents shall be considered continuing involvement by the transferor. In a transfer between two subsidiaries of a common parent, the transferor subsidiary shall not consider parent involvements with the transferred financial assets in applying the following paragraph.

5.168 FASB ASC 860-10-40-5 provides the criteria to determine if a transfer is considered a sale. It states that a transfer of an entire financial asset, a group of entire financial assets, or a participating interest[5] in an entire financial asset in which the transferor surrenders control over those financial assets shall be accounted for as a sale if and only if the following conditions are met:

  a. The transferred assets have been isolated from the transferor—put presumptively beyond the reach of the transferor and its creditors, even in bankruptcy or other receivership.

  b. Each transferee (or if the transferee is an entity whose sole purpose is to engage in securitization or asset-backed financing, and that entity is constrained from pledging or exchanging the assets it receives, each third-party holder of its beneficial interests) has the right to pledge or exchange the assets (or beneficial interests) it received, and no condition both constrains the transferee (or third-party holder of its beneficial interests) from taking advantage of its right to pledge or exchange and provides more than a trivial benefit to the transferor.

---

[5] *Participating interest* as defined in FASB ASC 860-10-40-6A.

Investments and Fair Value Considerations

    c. The transferor, its consolidated affiliates included in the financial statements being presented, or its agents do not maintain effective control over the transferred financial assets or third-party beneficial interests related to those transferred assets. Examples of a transferor's effective control over the transferred financial assets include, but are not limited to, an agreement that (*a*) both entitles and obligates the transferor to repurchase or redeem them before their maturity; (*b*) provides the transferor with both the unilateral ability to cause the holder to return specific financial assets and a more-than-trivial benefit attributable to that ability, other than through a cleanup call; or (*c*) it is probable that the transferee will require the transferor to repurchase them.

5.169 If the conditions of FASB ASC 860-10-40-5 are not met, the transferor shall account for the transfer as a secured borrowing.

5.170 FASB ASC 860 requires an entity to initially measure at fair value, if practicable, a servicing asset or liability each time it undertakes an obligation to service a financial asset by entering into a servicing contract in several situations, as described in FASB ASC 860-50-25-1. FASB ASC 860-50-35-1 requires that servicing assets and liabilities be subsequently remeasured using one of the following methods:

    a. Amortization method. Amortize the servicing assets or servicing liabilities in proportion to, and over the period of, estimated net servicing income (if servicing revenues exceed servicing costs) or net servicing loss (if servicing costs exceed servicing revenues), and assess servicing assets or servicing liabilities for impairment or increased obligation based on fair value at each reporting date.

    b. Fair value measurement method. Measure servicing assets or servicing liabilities at fair value at each reporting date and report changes in fair value of servicing assets and servicing liabilities in earnings in the period in which the changes occur.

5.171 FASB ASC 860 requires that debtors reclassify financial assets pledged as collateral and report those assets in their statement of financial position separately from other assets if the secured party has the right by contract or custom to sell or repledge the collateral. Assets that have been pledged as collateral but are not required to be reclassified shall also be reported separately in the statement of financial position.

5.172 FASB ASC 405-20-40 requires that a liability be derecognized if and only if either (*a*) the debtor pays the creditor and is relieved of its obligation for the liability or (*b*) the debtor is legally released from being the primary obligor under the liability either judicially or by the creditor. A liability is not considered extinguished by an in-substance defeasance.

5.173 Readers should review FASB ASC 860-10-50 regarding the extensive disclosures requirements.

Statutory Accounting

5.174 SSAP No. 91R, *Accounting for Transfers and Servicing of Financial Assets and Extinguishments of Liabilities*, adopts portions of FASB ASC 860, with the following modifications, as noted in paragraphs 103–104 of the SSAP No. 91R:

> *a.* Servicing rights assets are to be nonadmitted.
>
> *b.* Sales treatment is not permitted for transactions when recourse provisions or removal-of-accounts provisions exist on the transferred assets; however, GAAP would permit the recognition of the transfer as a sale under some circumstances.
>
> *c.* Because statutory financial statements are prepared on a legal-entity basis, special-purpose entities should not be consolidated in a reporting entity's statutory financial statements.
>
> *d.* Leases should be accounted for in accordance with SSAP No. 22, *Leases*.
>
> *e.* Reporting entities required to maintain an IMR should account for realized and unrealized capital gains and losses in accordance with SSAP No. 7.
>
> *f.* The concepts of revolving period securitizations, banker's acceptances, and risk participation in banker's acceptances are not applicable for statutory accounting purposes.
>
> *g.* This statement does not adopt accounting for collateral, as outlined in FASB ASC 860.

This statement adopts with modification FASB ASC 860:

> *a.* This statement adopts FASB ASC 860 guidance indicating that all servicing assets and servicing liabilities should initially be measured at fair value.
>
> *b.* This statement adopts FASB ASC 860 guidance requiring the inclusion of separately recognized servicing assets and servicing liabilities in the calculation of proceeds from the sale of assets.
>
> *c.* This statement rejects the optionality provided within FASB ASC 860 for the subsequent measurement of servicing assets and servicing liabilities using either fair value or an amortization method. This statement requires application of a fair value method for subsequent measurement.
>
> *d.* This statement adopts guidance in FASB ASC 860 regarding servicing assets and servicing liabilities established from the transfer of financial assets to a qualifying special-purpose entity in a guaranteed mortgage securitization in which the transferor retains all the resulting securities.
>
> *e.* This statement adopts revisions in FASB ASC 860 replacing the term *retained interests* with *interests that continue to be held by the transferor* with amendments to the definition to exclude servicing assets and liabilities from this definition.

5.175 Paragraph 5 of SSAP No. 91R provides the criteria to account for sale accounting under statutory accounting. Paragraph 5 states that a transfer of a group of financial assets or a portion of a financial asset in which the transferor surrenders control over those financial assets shall be accounted for as a sale, to the extent that consideration other than beneficial interests in the transferred assets is received in exchange. The transferor has surrendered control over transferred assets if and only if all of the following conditions are met:

Investments and Fair Value Considerations

a. The transferred assets have been isolated from the transferor—put presumptively beyond the reach of the transferor and its creditors, even in bankruptcy or other receivership.

b. Either (i) each transferee obtains the right, free of conditions that constrain it from taking advantage of that right, to pledge or exchange the transferred assets, or (ii) the transferee is a *qualifying special-purpose entity*, as defined in paragraph 26 of SSAP No. 91R, and the holders of the beneficial interests in that entity have the right, free of conditions that constrain them from taking advantage of that right, to pledge or exchange those interests, and no condition both constrains the transferee from taking advantage of its right to pledge or exchange and provides more than a trivial benefit to the transferor.

c. The transferor does not maintain effective control over the transferred assets through (*a*) an agreement that both entitles and obligates the transferor to repurchase them before their maturity or (*b*) the ability to unilaterally cause the holder to return specific assets, other than through a cleanup call.

5.176 If the transfer does not meet the criteria to be considered a sale, the transfer is accounted for as a secured borrowing.

5.177 Paragraph 16 of SSAP No. 91R states that an exchange of debt instruments with substantially different terms is also considered a debt extinguishment and shall be accounted for in accordance with paragraph 15. A debtor's exchange of debt instruments (in a nontroubled debt situation) is accomplished with debt instruments that are substantially different if the present value of the cash flows under the terms of the new debt instrument is at least 10 percent different from the present value of the remaining cash flows under the terms of the original instrument.

5.178 Paragraph 17 of SSAP No. 91R also states that if a creditor releases a debtor from the primary obligation under the conditions that a third-party assumes the obligation and that the original debtor becomes secondarily liable, that release extinguishes the original debtor's liability. However, in those circumstances, the original debtor becomes a guarantor. As a guarantor, it shall recognize a guarantee obligation in the same manner as would a guarantor that had never been primarily liable to that creditor, with due regard for the likelihood that the third-party will carry out its obligations. The guarantee obligation shall be initially measured at fair value and that amount reduces the gain or increases the loss recognized on extinguishment.

5.179 See paragraphs 98–101 of SSAP No. 91R for the disclosure requirements for asset transfers and servicing of assets.

⟳Update 5-2 *Regulatory*: Accounting for Transfers and Servicing of Financial Assets and Extinguishments of Liabilities

NAIC SSAP No. 103, *Accounting for Transfers and Servicing of Financial Assets and Extinguishments of Liabilities*, establishes statutory accounting principles for the accounting for transfers and servicing of financial assets and extinguishments of liabilities. This statement establishes statutory accounting principles for transfers and servicing of financial assets, including asset securitizations and securitizations of policy acquisition costs, extinguishments of

(continued)

> liabilities, repurchase agreements, repurchase financing and reverse repurchase agreements, including dollar repurchase, and dollar reverse repurchase agreements.
>
> For periods after January 1, 2013, refer to section D.03 in appendix D, which summarizes these clarifying changes that may affect an auditor's practice or methodology.

Repurchase Agreements[6]

5.180 *Repurchase agreements (repos)* and *reverse repos*, which include dollar repurchase (dollar rolls) and dollar reverse repurchase agreements, are contracts to sell and repurchase or to purchase and sell back the same or similar instrument (same issuer) within a specified time. In such transactions, the underlying securities may be received by the lender or a third-party custodian or they may be designated or held by the borrower on behalf of the lender as collateral. The maturity of the agreement is fixed by the contract and based on the needs of the borrower and willingness of the lender. For example, agreements may be structured on a day-by-day basis whereby the terms are negotiated daily.

5.181 The difference between the purchase price and repurchase price (sale price) plus accrued interest on the security represents investment income or interest expense.

5.182 *Dollar rolls* are agreements to sell and repurchase similar but not identical securities (usually mortgage-backed securities [MBS], which are also referred to as pass-through certificates or mortgage-participation certificates). Dollar rolls differ from regular repurchase agreements in that the securities sold and repurchased, which are usually of the same issuer, are represented by different certificates, are collateralized by different but similar mortgage pools (for example, single-family residential mortgages), and generally have different principal amounts.

5.183 The common types of dollar rolls are fixed-coupon and yield-maintenance agreements. In a fixed-coupon agreement, the securities repurchased have the same stated interest rate as, and maturities similar to, the securities sold. They are generally priced to result in substantially the same yield. The seller-borrower retains control over the future economic benefits of the securities sold and assumes no additional market risk. In a yield-maintenance agreement, the securities repurchased may have a different stated interest rate from that of the securities sold. They are generally priced to result in different yields, as specified in the agreement. The price-spread relationship between securities with different contract interest rates does not move in tandem. The existence of yield and price disparities provides opportunities for the buyer-lender to deliver, within the terms of the agreement, certificates providing the greatest benefit to the buyer-lender. The seller-borrower surrenders control over the future economic benefits of the securities sold and assumes additional market risk. Yield-maintenance agreements may contain par cap provisions that could significantly alter the economics of the transactions. A par cap provision limits the repurchase price to a stipulated

---

[6] In March 2010, the Securities and Exchange Commission (SEC) sent an illustrative letter to certain public companies requesting information about repurchase agreements, securities lending transactions, or other transactions involving the transfer of financial assets with an obligation to repurchase the transferred assets. The letter can be found on the SEC website at www.sec.gov/divisions/corpfin/guidance/cforepurchase0310.htm.

percentage of the face amount of the certificate. Fixed-coupon agreements do not contain par cap provisions.

5.184 In a rollover and an extension, securities involved in repos are not delivered on the settlement date of the agreement, and the contract may be rolled over or extended upon mutual agreement of the buyer-lender and seller-borrower. Breakage occurs when securities repurchased under repos commonly have a principal amount that differs from the principal amount of the security originally sold under the agreement. This is particularly common to dollar rolls. The difference occurs because the principal amounts of MBS generally differ due to the monthly amortization of principal balances of mortgages collateralizing the MBS. The amount of the breakage is a factor in determining whether substantially the same security is reacquired in the repo transaction (that is, whether good delivery—one in accordance with the terms of the agreement—has been met on repurchase of the MBS). The most significant difference between GAAP and statutory accounting for repurchase agreements is the different criteria that are evaluated in order to determine if a sale has occurred.

GAAP Accounting

5.185 The accounting for repurchase and reverse repurchase agreements is in FASB ASC 860 (similar to the preceding "Asset Transfers and Extinguishments of Liabilities" section). Some dollar rolls qualify as derivatives, which should be reported at fair value under the guidance of FASB ASC 815. Other dollar rolls, that do not qualify as derivatives, are recorded as secured financing transactions.

5.186 If the criteria in FASB ASC 860-10-40-5 (discussed in paragraph 5.167) are met, FASB ASC 860-10-55-55 states that the transferor should account for the repurchase agreement as a sale of financial assets and a forward repurchase commitment, and the transferee should account for the agreement as a purchase of financial assets and a forward resale commitment. Agreements to repurchase the transferred financial assets at maturity may be accounted for as sales.

5.187 As noted in FASB ASC 860-10-55-57, wash sales shall be accounted for as sales. Unless a concurrent contract exists to repurchase or redeem the transferred financial assets from the transferee, the transferor does not maintain effective control over the transferred financial assets.

5.188 FASB ASC 860-10-55-51 states that under many agreements to repurchase the transferred financial assets before their maturity, the transferor maintains effective control over those financial assets. Repurchase agreements that do not meet all the conditions of FASB ASC 860-10-40-5 shall be accounted for as secured borrowings. Fixed-coupon and dollar-roll repurchase agreements, and other contracts under which the securities to be repurchased need not be the same as the securities sold, qualify as borrowings if the return of substantially the same securities as those concurrently transferred is assured. Therefore, those transactions shall be accounted for as secured borrowings by both parties to the transfer.

5.189 If a transferor has transferred securities to an independent third-party custodian or a transferee under conditions that preclude the transferee from selling or repledging the assets during the term of the repurchase agreement, as in most triparty repurchase agreements, the transferor has not surrendered control over those assets.

5.190 FASB ASC 210-20-05-1 states that it is a general principle of accounting that the offsetting of assets and liabilities in the balance sheet is improper except where a right of setoff exists. FASB ASC 942-210-45-3, FASB ASC 210, *Balance Sheet*, permits offsetting in the statement of financial position of only payables and receivables that represent repos and reverse repos and that meet all of the conditions specified therein and does not apply to securities borrowing or lending transactions.

5.191 See paragraphs 5.162–.173 for sources of additional guidance on the transfers and servicing of financial assets.

Statutory Accounting

5.192 The accounting guidance for statutory accounting is similar to the GAAP accounting guidance previously discussed. Under SAP, paragraph 67 of SSAP No. 91R notes that if the transferor has surrendered control over transferred assets (sales criteria, as discussed in paragraph 5 of SSAP No. 91), the transferor should account for the repurchase agreement as a sale of financial assets and forward repurchase commitment, and the transferee should account for the agreement as a purchase of financial assets and forward resale commitment. As discussed in paragraph 67 of SSAP No. 91R, repurchase agreements that do meet the sales criteria (see paragraph 5 of SSAP No. 91R) should be treated as secured borrowings. Under SAP, SSAP No. 91R adopts FASB ASC 860 for accounting for wash sales to permit sales recognition but also requires expanded disclosures (see paragraphs 99–102 of SSAP No. 91R for a listing of information to be disclosed).

Securities Lending[7]

5.193 Insurance entities occasionally loan their bonds and stocks to securities brokers or dealers for temporary purposes, usually to cover a broker's short sale or fail transactions that arise when securities are not delivered in proper form. In exchange for lending the securities, the insurance entity should receive cash collateral from the broker in an amount exceeding the market values of the securities on that day; this collateral is immediately invested for the entity's benefit. The market values of the securities on loan should be closely monitored and changes in excess of an agreed upon range cause the release of the collateral or an increase in collateral.

5.194 An insurance entity or other financial institution may advance cash, pledge other securities, or issue letters of credit as collateral for borrowed securities. If the collateral is cash, the transferor typically earns a return by investing that cash at a rate higher than the rate paid or rebated to the transferee. If the collateral is other than cash, the transferor typically receives a fee. Because of the protection of collateral (typically valued daily and adjusted frequently for changes in the market price of the securities transferred) and the short time periods of the transactions, many securities lending transactions do not pose significant credit risks for either party. However, the parties may be subject to other risks, such as interest rate and liquidity risks. The amount of cash or other collateral required might increase or decrease depending on changes in the value of the securities.

5.195 The differences between GAAP and statutory accounting for securities lending agreements relate to the recording and required amount of

---

[7] See footnote 5.

collateral. Under GAAP, collateral is not recorded as an asset unless the secured party has the ability to sell or repledge the collateral. In this case, the entity recognizes the collateral as an asset and the obligation to return the collateral. Under statutory accounting, if the collateral pledged by the transferee can be sold or pledged by custom or contract by the company or its agent, then the transferor shall record the collateral as an asset and record the obligation to return the collateral as a liability. For securities lending programs in which the collateral is not available for the general use of the entity (restricted), the collateral assets should be reflected as a one-line entry on the balance sheet (securities lending collateral), and a detailed schedule is required at each quarter- and year-end describing the collateral asset. Additionally, statutory accounting requires insurers to receive collateral at least equal to 102 percent of the fair value of their loaned securities at the transaction date and maintain a minimum of 100 percent throughout the contract term. If an insurer fails to maintain the required collateral level, the undercollateralized portion is nonadmitted. GAAP does not contain any collateral requirements.

GAAP Accounting

5.196 FASB ASC 860-10-55-48 notes that in some securities lending transactions, the criteria in FASB ASC 860-10-40-5 are met, including the effective control criterion in FASB ASC 860-10-40-5(c), and consideration other than beneficial interests in the transferred assets is received. Those transactions should be accounted for

> *a.* by the transferor as a sale of the loaned securities for proceeds consisting of the cash collateral and a forward repurchase commitment. If the collateral in a transaction that meets the criteria in FASB ASC 860-10-40-5 is a financial asset that the holder is permitted by contract or custom to sell or repledge, that financial asset is proceeds of the sale of the loaned securities.
>
> *b.* by the transferee as a purchase of the borrowed securities in exchange for the collateral and a forward resale commitment.

5.197 According to FASB ASC 860-10-55-49, during the term of that agreement, the transferor has surrendered control over the securities transferred, and the transferee has obtained control over those securities, with the ability to sell or transfer them at will. In that case, creditors of the transferor have a claim only to the collateral and the forward repurchase commitment.

5.198 However, FASB ASC 860-30-25-7 states that some securities lending transactions are accompanied by an agreement that entitles and obligates the transferor to repurchase or redeem the transferred assets before their maturity and under which the transferor maintains effective control over those assets. FASB ASC 860-10-40-24 requires that an agreement that entitles and obligates the transferor to repurchase or redeem transferred assets from the transferee maintain the transferor's effective control over those assets under FASB ASC 860-10-40-5(c)(1), and the transfer is therefore to be accounted for as a secured borrowing if, and only if, all of the conditions in FASB ASC 860-10-40-24 are met.[8] Those transactions should be accounted for as secured borrowings in which cash (or securities that the holder is permitted by contract

---

[8] FASB ASU No. 2011-03, *Transfers and Servicing (Topic 860): Reconsideration of Effective Control for Repurchase Agreements*, removes from the assessment of effective control (*a*) the criterion requiring the transferor to have the ability to repurchase or redeem the financial assets on substantially the agreed terms, even in the event of default by the transferee, and (2) the collateral maintenance implementation guidance related to that criterion.

or custom to sell or repledge) received as collateral is considered the amount borrowed, the securities loaned are considered pledged as collateral against the cash borrowed and reclassified as set forth in FASB ASC 860-30-25-5(a), and any rebate of securities paid to the transferee is interest on the cash that the transferor is considered to have borrowed.

5.199 FASB ASC 860-30-25-8 states that the transferor of securities being loaned accounts for cash received in the same way, regardless of whether the transfer is accounted for as a sale or secured borrowing. The cash received should be recognized as the transferor's asset—as should investments made with that cash, even if made by agents or in pools with other securities lenders—along with the obligation to return the cash. If securities that may be sold or repledged are received, the transferor of the securities being loaned accounts for those securities in the same way as it would account for cash received.

5.200 See paragraphs 5.162–.173 for sources of additional guidance on the transfers and servicing of financial assets.

Statutory Accounting

5.201 Under SAP, the collateral received is reflected in the appropriate investment section, and the liability is reflected on the balance sheet as a write-in line. Specific collateral requirements for securities lending and repurchase and reverse repurchase transactions are set forth in SSAP No. 91R. The collateral requirement varies based upon the type of transaction (securities lending, repurchase, reverse repurchase) or denomination of the collateral. Substantive revisions in paragraphs 13–14, 57–81, and 98–101 of SSAP No. 91R regarding securities lending transactions and repurchase agreements and additional disclosures are effective December 31, 2010, and incorporate guidance regarding the determination of whether collateral is on balance sheet or off balance sheet. Readers should familiarize themselves with the new collateral requirements in these paragraphs of SSAP No. 91R. SSAP No. 91R adopts portions of FASB ASC 860, with modifications, as noted in paragraphs 103–104 of SSAP No. 91R, as discussed in paragraph 5.173.

Other Information

5.202 The Securities and Exchange Commission (SEC) has issued Financial Reporting Release No. 36, *Management's Discussion and Analysis of Financial Condition and Results of Operations; Certain Investment Company Disclosures*. This sets forth the SEC's views concerning several disclosure matters, such as disclosures for participation in high-yield financing, highly-leveraged transactions, or noninvestment-grade loans and investments that should be considered by registrants in preparing management's discussion and analysis. Additionally, guidance for investment companies and investment contracts is provided in the Audit and Accounting Guide *Investment Companies*.

Auditing Investments

Audit Planning

5.203 In accordance with AU-C section 300, *Planning an Audit* (AICPA, *Professional Standards*), the auditor should plan the audit so that it is responsive to the assessment of the risks of material misstatement based on the

Investments and Fair Value Considerations

auditor's understanding of the entity and its environment, including its internal control. The nature, timing, and extent of planning vary with the size and complexity of the entity, and with the auditor's experience with the entity and understanding of the entity. Refer to chapter 2, "Audit Considerations," for a detailed discussion of audit planning.

Consideration of Fraud in a Financial Statement Audit

5.204 Risks are inherent in all audit engagements, including the possibility that fraudulent acts may cause a material misstatement of financial statements. AU-C section 240, *Consideration of Fraud in a Financial Statement Audit* (AICPA, *Professional Standards*), addresses the auditor's responsibilities relating to fraud in an audit of financial statements. Because of the characteristics of fraud, the auditor's exercise of professional skepticism is important when considering the risk of material misstatement due to fraud. Readers should refer to additional discussion of AU-C section 240 in chapter 2 of this guide.

Audit Risk Factors—Investments

5.205 As discussed in paragraph .A1 of AU-C section 320, *Materiality in Planning and Performing an Audit* (AICPA, *Professional Standards*), *audit risk* is the risk that the auditor expresses an inappropriate audit opinion when the financial statements are materially misstated. Audit risk is a function of the risks of material misstatement and detection risk. Materiality and audit risk are considered throughout the audit, in particular, when

   a. determining the nature and extent of risk assessment procedures to be performed;

   b. identifying and assessing the risks of material misstatement;

   c. determining the nature, timing, and extent of further audit procedures; and

   d. evaluating the effect of uncorrected misstatements, if any, on the financial statements and in forming the opinion in the auditor's report.

5.206 Experience has demonstrated that audit risk may be greater in certain areas than in others. Significant transaction cycles of property and liability insurance entities include the premium cycle, the claims cycle, the reinsurance cycle, and the investment cycle. Risk factors specific to the investment cycle include determination of the ownership and existence of investments, valuation of securities (particularly those that are not actively traded), accounting for derivative instruments, determining whether an investment is impaired and if the impairment is other than temporary, and the property and liability insurance entity's use of service organizations for investment accounting and administration. These risk factors, internal control considerations, and examples of audit procedures for the insurance entity are discussed further herein.

5.207 Identification of significant accounts and disclosures by the auditor is part of the planning process. As required by AU-C section 315, *Understanding the Entity and its Environment and Assessing the Risks of Material Misstatement* (AICPA, *Professional Standards*), to enable the auditor to understand the classes of transactions, account balances, and disclosures to be expected in the financial statements, the auditor should obtain an understanding of the relevant industry, regulatory, and other external factors, including the applicable financial reporting framework and the nature of the entity. There are various significant disclosures related to the investment cycle, such as those within FASB ASC 320-10-50, FASB ASC 820-10-50, those required by ASU No. 2011-04 that focus on level 3 investments and derivatives and under SSAP No. 100, *Fair Value Measurements*.

5.208 Property and liability insurance entities will earn investment income by investing premiums collected until any losses related to the underlying policies issued are paid, commonly referred to as "float." Companies may consider expectations of future investment income, as well as management's views on the insurance market cycle, in pricing business. These factors may result in increased underwriting losses as a consequence of a willingness to adopt a less restrictive underwriting philosophy to obtain more premium dollars to invest. This could be done as long as investment income exceeds expected underwriting losses by a sufficient margin, sometimes known as cash flow underwriting. When losses continue to increase and interest rates decline, management may revise this strategy through increasing premium rates and tightening underwriting standards.

Risk of Material Misstatement—Inherent Risk

5.209 As discussed in AU-C section 330, *Performing Audit Procedures in Response to Assessed Risks and Evaluating the Audit Evidence Obtained* (AICPA, *Professional Standards*), inherent risk is the likelihood of material misstatement due to the particular characteristics of the relevant class of transactions, account balance, or disclosure. As part of the auditor's assessment of inherent risks, the auditor may consider those factors related to investments, including factors relating to management, investment operations, and portfolio characteristics. Such factors might encompass the following:

    a. Investments in general. These include the following:

        i. The entity's general investment policy is very aggressive and encourages the use of new and innovative kinds of securities or other investment vehicles that are susceptible to investment valuation adjustments

        ii. The kinds of investments, length to maturity, rates of return, and other investment strategies are not well matched to the expected claim payment cash flows of the entity

        iii. Changing regulations, including those concerning related party transactions, current tax rules, and reporting requirements, may establish specific practices allowed in the valuation and diversification of an investment portfolio

        iv. Investments are concentrated either by certain kinds (for example, high yield securities), issues (for example, specific industry or municipal bonds), geographical areas (for example, regional concentrations of mortgage loans or real estate projects), or single issuer

        v. There is a high concentration of investments in securities subject to prepayment risk, such as CMOs, IOs, POs, and GNMA securities

Investments and Fair Value Considerations

vi. Foreign investments are threatened by actions of foreign governments (for example, foreign exchange controls or risk of government seizure of corporate assets)

vii. The amount of higher risk or unusual investment vehicles has increased (for example, private equity funds or fund of funds, joint ventures, interest rate swaps, or securities lending)

viii. The competitive environment requires the use of investment strategies that seek high rates of return

ix. Turnover in the investment portfolio, other than that caused by the maturity of securities, has increased and may affect the balance sheet classification and carrying value of certain assets

x. If the insurance company is part of a group, the cash flow expectations of the parent entity or the subsidiaries' needs for surplus are high

xi. A large percentage of compensation of investment personnel is closely linked to investment returns

xii. The entity uses subsidiaries, limited partnerships, or other legal organization forms as vehicles for higher risk investments

xiii. Management relies on a third-party pricing service for investment valuation and does not have an understanding of which securities were being valued using quoted prices from an active market, observable inputs (such as prices for similar assets), or based on a model

b. *Debt and equity securities.* These include the following:

i. The entity places substantial reliance on outside investment managers, brokers, and traders, who have significant discretionary authority over investment decisions

ii. The entity uses sophisticated cash management techniques, or cash flow projections presume utilization of float

iii. Various economic factors cause rapid fluctuations in market interest rates and securities prices

iv. There is a high concentration of investments classified as held-to-maturity under FASB ASC 320

c. *Futures, options, and other derivatives.* These include the following:

i. The entity uses sophisticated investing techniques such as hedging of interest rate and foreign currency exposure or computerized or programmed trading that may affect investment risk

ii. There is a high use of structured notes

iii. There is uncertainty regarding the financial stability of a counterparty

iv. High volatility in interest rates, currencies or other factors are affecting the value of derivatives and possibly their continued accounting for as a hedge

AAG-PLI 5.209

d. *Mortgage loans and real estate.* These include the following:

  i. Existing liens, imperfect deeds, or title positions exist that prevent the insurance entity from having clear title to real property or collateral

  ii. Adverse environmental conditions are caused by materials used in construction (for example, asbestos) or the location of the site (for example, a site located near a toxic dump or contaminated water supply)

  iii. Adequate insurance is not maintained on the property to protect the value of the collateral or real estate investment in the event of a catastrophe

  iv. There are master leases on mortgaged or owned real estate properties

  v. Government regulations are becoming more prohibitive in relation to rent controls, mandated upgrading to comply with new or existing building codes, or foreclosure ability

  vi. There is a significant decline in the market values of real properties or collateral

  vii. Significant doubt exists regarding the collection of rent (for example, tenants in bankruptcy), the ability to dispose of foreclosed property, or the ability to refinance bullet mortgage loans

  viii. Troubled mortgage loans are restructured without due consideration given to the value of the underlying collateral

  ix. Significant doubt exists regarding the financial solvency or stability of private mortgage insurers, loan servicers or title insurers utilized by the entity

  x. Loan servicers or other service organizations with inadequate internal controls to support the preparation of information used by the investor

e. *Joint ventures and other investments.* The nature of the joint venture may expose the insurance entity to large or unusual risks, such as guarantees for future contributions of capital and other contingent liabilities that may exist. The entity has a complex organizational structure with diverse, restructured, or both, investment transactions leading to potential variable interest entities.

5.210 The investment community regularly develops new kinds of securities or other investment vehicles (for example, asset backed products or other derivative products). The auditor should obtain an understanding of the kinds of investments in the entity's portfolio and the related risks in designing appropriate audit procedures and tests as deemed necessary under the circumstances. In addition, the auditor may consider using a specialist, as appropriate. Paragraph .12 of AU-C section 300 requires that the auditor consider whether specialized skills are needed in performing the audit. AU-C section 620, *Using the Work of an Auditor's Specialist* (AICPA, *Professional Standards*), provides guidance on using the work of an auditor's specialist.

5.211 In addition, the auditor may consider the following risk factors relating to the investment cycle that may affect carrying values, pricing, and other-than-temporary impairments:

- Investment concentration, by issuer, industry, geography, or other and management monitoring thereof.
- Investment liquidity, including investments with terms and maturities that extend beyond the expected timing of cash outflows for claim obligations.
- Investment valuation, such as improper or inadequate valuation methods, documentation, or impairments that are other-than-temporary, and significant amounts of investments that are not readily marketable, and downgrading of securities by rating agencies.
- Investment yield trends (that is, the indicated ability to manage the investment portfolio at maximum yields commensurate with prudent risk considerations).
- Investment policy, such as lack of documented approval of investment strategies and asset allocation targets that emphasis on speculative or high-risk investments or lack of a defined investment strategy.
- Compliance with regulatory or self-imposed investment restrictions, such as those issued by state insurance departments that restrict the types of invested assets that can be owned and related asset allocation limitations; as well as if and how derivatives may be used. Investment holdings in excess of thresholds or limitations by type may result in nonadmission of assets that exceed the thresholds. In addition, the company may require specific preapprove prior to the use of derivatives for hedging or other purposes.
- Investment repurchase agreements, such as (*a*) the risk that the seller-borrower may not be able to complete the transaction and repurchase the security—credit risk, (*b*) the risk that the collateral is not secure—particularly if it remains with the seller-borrower (guidance on such matters is provided by the AICPA's *Report of the Special Task Force on Audits of Repurchase Securities Transactions*), or (*c*) the risk that these transactions are used at period end to present an appearance of reduced leverage or increased asset quality within the portfolio.
- Significant changes in interest rates.

Internal Control

5.212 Paragraph .04 of AU-C section 315 defines internal control as

> a process effected by those charged with governance, management, and other personnel that is designed to provide reasonable assurance about the achievement of the entity's objectives with regard to the reliability of financial reporting, effectiveness and efficiency of operations, and compliance with applicable laws and regulations. Internal control over safeguarding of assets against unauthorized acquisition, use, or disposition may include controls relating to financial reporting and operations objectives.

5.213 Internal control consists of the following five interrelated components:

    a. Control environment

    b. The entity's risk assessment process

    c. The information system, including the related business processes relevant to financial reporting and communication

    d. Control activities relevant to the audit

    e. Monitoring of controls

5.214 AU-C section 315 requires the auditor to obtain an understanding of these components of the entity's internal control. Paragraphs 2.31–.41 of chapter 2 discuss the components of internal control in detail. This section will discuss certain components of a property and liability insurance entity's internal control as they relate to investments.

Control Environment

5.215 The control environment comprises the collective effect of various factors on establishing, enhancing, or mitigating the effectiveness of specific control policies or procedures on the investment operations of the entity. As related to investments of a property and liability insurance entity, conditions that could impact the effectiveness of the control environment may include the following:

    a. Investments in general. These include the following:

        i. Formal investment policies do not exist or are limited in scope.

        ii. Periodic reviews of investments for other than temporary impairments are not performed or are inadequate.

        iii. There are frequent or unusual interentity or related party transactions.

        iv. Forecasts and analysis of investment operations results are limited.

        v. When valuations are based on modeling, whether internally by management or externally by a pricing service or other third-party vendor, the details of the model and support for the assumptions used are not available.

        vi. An independent valuation specialist is not used to value certain nonmarketable or illiquid investments.

        vii. The investment information systems used by the entity or third-party managers are unsophisticated or inadequate to meet the needs of the entity's financial reporting or asset management requirements. Systems cannot cope with the diverse reporting required by regulatory agencies.

        viii. Investment department personnel are unsophisticated or given limited training in relation to the investment portfolio managed.

Investments and Fair Value Considerations

b. *Debt and equity securities.* These include the following:

   i. Holding of securities exists in-house rather than at an independent third-party custodian

   ii. The entity does not periodically assess the appropriateness of debt and equity classifications as held-to-maturity, trading, or available-for-sale

   iii. The entity does not properly monitor transfers between the debt and equity security categories

   iv. The entity does not take physical control of the underlying collateral for reverse repurchase agreements or other forms of borrowed securities

   v. Formal policies do not exist that would provide for a review of all reverse repo and dollar reverse repo contracts to determine whether they have been appropriately reported as financing or sales transactions

c. *Futures, options, and other derivatives.* These include the following:

   i. The entity depends on one individual for all organizational expertise on derivatives activities

   ii. There is inadequate information available to monitor effectively derivatives transactions, including inadequate or untimely information about derivatives values

   iii. There is significant use of derivatives without relevant expertise within the entity

   iv. There is a lack of appropriate documentation of strategies and purpose for utilization of derivatives, including compliance with New York State regulations for an approved Derivatives Use Plan

d. *Private equity, joint ventures, and other investments.* These include the following:

   i. Fund manager or joint venture management fails to provide appropriate information to the entity regarding financial transactions or valuation of the related assets in the venture

   ii. Management does not receive final net asset values on a timely basis for financial reporting purposes, resulting in a lag

   iii. Significant audit adjustments are reported by the fund or joint venture management

   iv. Subsidiary or equity investee financial statements are not available or are not reliable (for example, audited financial statements are not prepared, are prepared on a different basis of accounting, or do not have an unqualified opinion)

   v. Investment department personnel provide poor documentation for evaluation of substance over form analysis for accounting treatment of private equity or joint venture transactions

   vi. The investment department personnel do not have controls to assess the reported fair value, such as comparison of the reported net asset values to relevant benchmarks, or direct discussions with fund management to understand drivers of performance and retrospective review of reported unaudited net asset values to audited financial statements when they become available

Risk Assessment Process

5.216 As discussed in paragraphs .16–.18 of AU-C section 315, the auditor should obtain an understanding of whether the entity has a process for

    a. identifying business risks relevant to financial reporting objectives;

    b. estimating the significance of the risks;

    c. assessing the likelihood of their occurrence; and

    d. deciding about actions to address those risks.

5.217 The auditor should obtain an understanding of the entity's risk assessment process related to investments, investment income, realized gains and losses, and related account balances and the results thereof. If the entity has not established such a process or has an ad hoc process, the auditor should discuss with management whether business risks relevant to financial reporting objectives have been identified and how they have been addressed. The auditor should evaluate whether the absence of a documented risk assessment process is appropriate in the circumstances or determine whether it represents a significant deficiency or material weakness in the entity's internal control. The auditor may consider how management's risk assessment considers compliance risk from investment related regulations of state insurance departments, as well as capital allocation, asset liability matching, and other factors.

Information System

5.218 AU-C section 315 discusses that the information system relevant to financial reporting objectives, which includes the accounting system, consists of the procedures, whether automated or manual, and records established to initiate, authorize, record, process, and report an entity's transactions (as well as events and conditions) and to maintain accountability for related assets, liabilities, and equity.

5.219 The flow of accounting records for investment transactions encompasses all functions relating to the purchase and sale of investments, the recording of investment income, and realized and unrealized investment gains and losses, as well as the custody and safekeeping of invested assets. The functions within this cycle may be segregated into areas for each major investment category because of the different activities and expertise required for each.

Control Activities

5.220 Control activities are the policies and procedures that help ensure that management's directives are carried out and that necessary actions are taken to address risks in order to achieve the entity's objectives. The auditors should gain an understanding of those control activities the auditor deems necessary to assess the risks of material misstatement at the assertion level and design further audit procedures responsive to assessed risks. The following are examples of internal control procedures and policies relating to investment operations:

a. *Proper authorization of transactions and activities.* Written policy statements detailing investment guidelines, objectives, hedging techniques, asset-liability matching policies, authorization levels, and limitations are adopted and monitored by those charged with governance and designated levels of management. Potential investment transactions and investment policy changes are also reviewed and approved by those charged with governance and are recorded in the minutes. System security violations and failures are adequately monitored.

b. *Segregation of duties.* Different individuals or areas are responsible for authorizing investment transactions, recording transactions, and maintaining custody of asset records. Different individuals are responsible for authorizing mortgage loans and current valuations and appraisals of those loans.

c. *Design and use of adequate controls over documents and records.* Authorized lists of signatures, brokers, derivative counterparties, and other third parties exist, are adhered to, and are reviewed and updated on a timely basis.

d. *Adequate safeguards over access to and use of assets and accounting records.* Securities, property deeds, and other evidence of ownership are safeguarded in vaults with limited access or with third-party custodians. Documentation for evidence of ownership is made out in the name of the entity.

e. *Independent checks on performance and proper valuation of recorded amounts.* Accounting entries and supporting documentation for investment transactions are periodically reviewed by supervisory personnel to ensure accurate classification and proper recording. Recorded amounts of investments are periodically compared and reconciled to custodial ledgers and third-party custodial confirmations; differences are investigated and resolved on a timely basis; appropriate personnel review and approve reconciliations. Adjustments to investment accounts are reviewed and approved by authorized personnel.

f. *Appropriate controls to understand valuation methods classifications for fair value hierarchy disclosures.* When management utilizes a third-party pricing service, personnel with the appropriate level of knowledge and experience actively work with the vendor to determine which securities were being valued using quoted prices from an active market, observable inputs (such as prices for similar assets), or fair value measurements based on a model. In instances where modeling was used, management maintains documentation of their understanding of the model and the evaluation whether the assumptions were reasonable. Such documentation may include retrospective reviews of changes in valuations from prior periods for securities subsequently sold or sensitivities documenting how changes to the assumptions would affect the fair value conclusion.

Considerations for Audits Performed in Accordance With Public Company Accounting Oversight Board (PCAOB) Standards

Paragraph 34 of Auditing Standard No. 12, *Identifying and Assessing Risks of Material Misstatement* (AICPA, *PCAOB Standards and*

Related Rules, Auditing Standards), states that a broader understanding of control activities is needed for relevant assertions for which the auditor plans to rely on controls. In addition, in the audit of internal control over financial reporting, the auditor's understanding of control activities encompasses a broader range of accounts and disclosures than what is normally obtained in a financial statement audit. Also refer to paragraph 26 of Auditing Standard No. 13, *The Auditor's Responses to the Risks of Material Misstatement* (AICPA, *PCAOB Standards and Related Rules*, Auditing Standards), for a discussion on the extent of tests of controls.

Service Organizations

5.221 Property and liabilities entities often utilize service organizations for the investment accounting and administration. When auditing controls within the investments transaction cycle, the auditor may wish to consider the controls that are executed within the service organization and the information prepared by the service organization in both the evaluation of the design of internal control, as well as tests of operating effectiveness.

5.222 Service organizations may have an auditor test controls that the service organization has in place to support the accurate reporting of information to its clients. The service auditors will often have service organization controls (SOC) reports (SSAE No. 16, *Reporting on Controls at a Service Organization* [AICPA, *Professional Standards*, AT sec. 801]) available. In an SSAE No. 16 engagement to issue a type 2 report, the objectives of the service auditor are to (*a*) obtain reasonable assurance about whether management's description of controls of the service organization's systems presents the system designed and implemented, (*b*) confirm the controls related to the control objectives are suitably designed throughout the period, and (*c*) confirm the controls operated effectively to provide reasonable assurance that the stated objectives were achieved throughout the service period.

5.223 If an auditor plans to use a type 2 SSAE No. 16 report as audit evidence that controls at the service organization are operating effectively, the auditor needs to evaluate the audit evidence provided by the report. The auditor may consider the following factors in concluding if the service auditors report is appropriate in the circumstance:

- Evaluating whether the description, design, and operating effectiveness of controls at the service organization is for a period that is appropriate for the auditor's purposes and consistent with the user entity's intended use, considering the consistency of the period of the report with the period under audit.

- Evaluating the service auditor's report (opinion) by assessing the objectivity and competence of the service auditor.

- Evaluating if the controls tested are relevant financial statement assertions that are being considered and assessing any qualifications in the service auditor report or testing exceptions identified in the detailed results of the controls testing that are relevant to the user entity's controls. The service auditor may not have included controls related to the valuation assertion within the testing procedures performed and covered within the opinion provided.

5.224 In addition, the auditor should review the complementary user entity controls identified by the service auditor. The auditor should consider the

Investments and Fair Value Considerations

design and implementation of those complementary user entity controls. If the auditor is performing an integrated audit or relying on controls to reduce the level of substantive testing, operating effectiveness of those controls also needs to be tested.

Audit Procedures Responsive to the Assessed Risks of Material Misstatement

5.225 During planning, the auditor determines the relevant assertions related to the significant accounts identified, determines the audit objectives, assesses inherent risk of error of other significant risks (that is, nonroutine transactions or risk of fraud), and plans the involvement of others. As required by AU-C section 330, the auditor should design and perform further audit procedures whose nature, timing, and extent are based on, and are responsive to, the assessed risks of material misstatement at the relevant assertion level. The auditor determines planned reliance on controls and the nature, timing, and extent of substantive testing, including whether the substantive evidence is planned from tests of details or substantive analytics.

5.226 If the auditor identifies a significant risk and is only performing substantive procedures, those procedures should include a test of details. If procedures to respond to the significant risk include both a test of controls and substantive procedures, the auditor may select substantive analytical procedures if the controls are operating effectively.

> *Considerations for Audits Performed in Accordance With PCAOB Standards*
>
> For audits performed in accordance with the PCAOB auditing standards, for significant risks, paragraph 11 of Auditing Standard No. 13 states the auditor should perform substantive procedures, including tests of details, that are specifically responsive to the assessed risks.

Audit Consideration Chart and Procedures

5.227 The auditor may consider the following specific audit objectives, examples of selected control activities, and auditing procedures in auditing the investment cycle of property and liability insurance entities. These are illustrative; however, auditors should develop tests that are appropriate to the risk of material misstatement in the circumstances of the engagement.

5.228 Additionally AU-C section 501, *Audit Evidence—Specific Considerations for Selected Items* (AICPA, *Professional Standards*), provides guidance to auditors in planning and performing auditing procedures for assertions about derivative instruments, hedging activities, investments in debt and equity securities as defined in FASB ASC 320, and investments accounted for under FASB ASC 323. Practitioners applying AU-C section 501 may refer to the guidance in the Audit Guide *Special Considerations in Auditing Financial Instruments* for information about planning and performing audit procedures related to investments. Additionally AU-C section 540, *Auditing Accounting Estimates, Including Fair Value Accounting Estimates, and Related Disclosures* (AICPA, *Professional Standards*), establishes standards and provides guidance on auditing fair value measurements and disclosures contained in financial statements.

Audit Consideration Chart—Investments

Financial Statement Assertions	Audit Objectives	Examples of Selected Control Activities	Examples of Auditing Procedures
Existence	• Securities and investment assets included in the balance sheet physically exist.	• Transactions settled after year-end are reviewed for recording in the proper period (as of the trade date). • Custodial function is independent of investment and accounting functions and provides security commensurate with the risks involved. • Securities and evidence of ownership held by the entity are kept in vault with access limited to authorized personnel. • Management reviews and approves the journal entries and supporting documentation for investment transactions.	• Inspect and count the securities held on the client's premises as of the date that the securities amounts are reconciled to the general ledger control accounts. • Obtain confirmations from the custodians of securities held for the client. Compare the confirmed lists with the trial balance and investigate discrepancies. • Obtain confirmations that securities purchased under repurchase agreements but not delivered are being held by the sellers or the sellers' custodian on the entity's behalf. • Confirm with brokers the status of securities in transit. • Compare the face amounts or number of shares and the cost of investments recorded in the investment ledger with forms and documents created at the time of purchase. Examine forms and documents for proper completion and authorization.

Investments and Fair Value Considerations

Financial Statement Assertions	Audit Objectives	Examples of Selected Control Activities	Examples of Auditing Procedures
		• Reports and confirmations of securities held by outside custodians are reconciled to entity records. • Financial responsibility and capability of outside custodians are periodically reviewed.	• Obtain and read custodial agreements and available reports regarding the adequacy of the custodians' internal controls and financial stability.
Completeness	• Investment assets include all investments of the entity.		• Inspect and count securities held by the client. Obtain confirmation from custodian of securities held for the account of the client.
	• Investment amounts include all transactions during the period.	• Buy and sell orders to brokers are compared to brokers' advices. • Authorized lists of signatures, brokers, and so forth are maintained.	• Read finance committee minutes and test whether investment transactions have been properly authorized. • Determine that only securities dealers approved by the finance committee are used.
		• Written policy statements detailing investment guidelines and limitations are prepared by designated levels of management. • Potential investment transactions are reviewed by an investment advisory committee and approved by a finance committee.	• Compare investment yields during the period with expected yields based on previous results and current market trends; investigate significant discrepancies. • Test transactions settled after the end of the period for recording in the proper period (as of the trade date).

(continued)

Financial Statement Assertions	Audit Objectives	Examples of Selected Control Activities	Examples of Auditing Procedures
			• Review mortgages, real estate, leases, and other loans and investments for significant controlling interests.
	• Investment records are properly compiled, and totals are properly included in the investment accounts.	• Questions concerning compliance with regulatory restrictions are referred to the legal department before transactions are executed. • New, current, and restructured transactions are reviewed for completeness. • Recorded amounts of investments are periodically compared to safekeeping ledgers or custody statements and to current market values.	• Examine input and output data and balances in individual investment accounts to test whether transactions are properly recorded. • Compare investment totals to the client's reconciliation of the investment ledger to the general ledger control accounts. Investigate significant discrepancies and any large or unusual reconciling items.
		• Batch balancing, logging, and cash totals are used to provide assurance that all purchases and sales have been properly posted to master files.	
Rights and Obligations	• The entity has legal title or similar rights of ownership.	• Securities and other evidence of ownership are in the entity's name.	• Review legal department compliance records concerning statutory requirements and limitations. • Examine securities to determine whether they are

AAG-PLI 5.228

Investments and Fair Value Considerations

Financial Statement Assertions	Audit Objectives	Examples of Selected Control Activities	Examples of Auditing Procedures
			• registered or payable to the entity, an authorized nominee, or the bearer.
			• Examine bonds to determine whether interest coupons due after the count date are attached.
Valuation or Allocation	• Investments in marketable securities are recorded at their proper amounts.	• When preparing GAAP financial statements, finance personnel maintain appropriate documentation for classification of investments as trading, available-for-sale or held-to-maturity with documentation to support the classification.	• Compare recorded costs of investments to published market quotations at trade date. Consider reasonableness of commission rates, taxes, and so on.
		• Interim securities valuations are obtained from outside brokers.	• Compare recorded market values of investments to published market quotations at the end of the period and obtain other evidence, such as evidence of sufficient volume of trades or a detailed understanding of how quotes were prepared to support management's valuation.
		• Valuations for statutory reporting purposes are reviewed for conformity with National Association of Insurance Commissioners published values.	
		• Market prices for purchases and sales are compared with independent sources.	• Examine summaries of interest, dividend, and principal payments for indication of security value impairment.

(continued)

AAG-PLI 5.228

Financial Statement Assertions	Audit Objectives	Examples of Selected Control Activities	Examples of Auditing Procedures
			• Examine past-due bonds and notes for endorsements or evidence of reductions in principal through receipt of partial payments.
	• Investments that do not have a readily determinable fair value are recorded at their proper amounts.	• The valuation model, including significant assumptions and underlying data are reviewed and approved by management with appropriate knowledge. • If there are sales or dispositions, management performs a retrospective analysis to compare proceeds received to balances reported in the most recent financial statements.	• Evaluate the valuation methodology used by management to conclude the method is appropriate in the circumstances. • Evaluate the assumptions used by management by agreeing them to supporting documentation or other external sources obtained directly by the auditor.
	• Investments valued using a practical expedient qualify as per the requirements within FASB ASC 820-10 income and losses are recorded in the proper amounts.	• Personnel with requisite experience and knowledge of the framework prepare documentation to support the valuation methodology used.	• Evaluate the appropriateness of management's analysis based on the criteria within the accounting guidance.
	• Investment income and losses are recorded in the proper amounts.	• Unrealized gains and losses are substantiated by reconciliation with prior values. • Adjustments of investment accounts are reviewed and approved by an authorized official.	• Test determination of interest earned, accrued interest receivable, and amortization of discount or premium. • Test dividend income by reference to published dividend records.

Investments and Fair Value Considerations

Financial Statement Assertions	Audit Objectives	Examples of Selected Control Activities	Examples of Auditing Procedures
			• Test computations of realized gains and losses by appropriate cost method. • Obtain financial reports of joint ventures or managed real estate and compare reported amounts of dividends, net rentals, and so on, to the records.
		• Interest and dividends are reviewed for accuracy by reference to reliable sources. • Income amounts are compared to cash receipts records and are reconciled to the bond and stock master listings. • Interest and dividends due but not received are reconciled to estimated and paid income lists.	• Review purchases and sales for indications of possible wash sales.
	• Securities with market value below amortized cost may have indicators of other-than-temporary impairment indicators.	• Management reviews analysis prepared related to the investee, including the duration and size of the impairment, operational results of the issuer, external data, and confirmation of management's intentions to hold to recovery.	• Evaluate the expertise of management performing and reviewing the analysis. • Consider the results of analyses performed in prior periods, as applicable, and any recovery in value of those securities to provide a basis for relying on current year information.

(continued)

AAG-PLI 5.228

306 Property and Liability Insurance Entities

Financial Statement Assertions	Audit Objectives	Examples of Selected Control Activities	Examples of Auditing Procedures
			• Perform independent procedures to search for analyst reports or other information to support management's analysis. • Evaluate management's cash flow needs and ability to hold the investment to recovery and obtain management representations.
Presentation and Disclosure	• Investments are properly classified, described, and disclosed.	• Realized capital gains and losses are properly recorded and classified. They are then submitted on a timely basis to the tax department. • Management monitors any accounting standards for any additional disclosure requirements in the current period.	• Test whether disclosures comply with GAAP. • Inquire about pledging, assignment, or other restrictions. • Read finance committee minutes. • Examine loan agreements. • Perform procedures to understand the entities use of investments and derivatives to determine what disclosures would be required to comply with GAAP or SAP and evaluate the completeness of management's proposed disclosures.

AAG-PLI 5.228

Investments and Fair Value Considerations

Financial Statement Assertions	Audit Objectives	Examples of Selected Control Activities	Examples of Auditing Procedures
		• Management reviews footnote disclosures for completeness and accuracy, including agreement of amounts back to the basic financial statements and appropriate source documentation used in financial reporting.	• Inquire as to management's process for preparing the footnote disclosures and the sources of information contained therein. • Agree information in reports used by management to information subject to substantive testing. • Perform procedures to test the accuracy of items, such as the aging of investments in an unrealized loss position.
		• Management with appropriate knowledge and experience review analyses prepared by the Company to support the classification of investments carried at fair value in accordance with FASB ASC 820-10-35 and SSAP No. 100 within the footnote disclosures.	• Review asset classifications for appropriateness. • Reconcile information in reports used by management to information subject to substantive testing. • Obtain independent information about trade volume or availability of price quotations from multiple sources to support management's classification. • Compare changes in each category of the investment portfolio between periods.

(continued)

AAG-PLI 5.228

Financial Statement Assertions	Audit Objectives	Examples of Selected Control Activities	Examples of Auditing Procedures
		• Management with appropriate knowledge and experience review analyses prepared by the company to support the classification of investments carried at fair value in accordance with FASB ASC 815 within the footnote disclosures.	• Determine whether appropriate disclosures are made for derivative instruments. • Reconcile information in reports used by management to information subject to substantive testing.

Chapter 6[*]

Reinsurance

6.01 Insurance entities bring together people and entities subject to insurable hazards and collect from them premium amounts expected in the aggregate to be sufficient to pay all losses sustained by the insureds during the policy periods, in addition to acquisition, settlement, and administrative costs and a return on the capital employed. From the insurer's perspective, the number of insureds must be large enough and diverse enough for the statistical properties of the law of large numbers to operate effectively. However, frequently an insurance entity may be offered or may accept, for business reasons, insurance of a class or amount that does not permit the law of large numbers to operate or that could result in claims that the insurer does not have the financial capacity to absorb. Such risks are spread (or ceded) among other insurance entities through *reinsurance*, which is the indemnification (or assumption) by one insurer of all or part of a risk originally undertaken by another insurer.

6.02 In addition to using reinsurance to spread the risk of its insurance contracts, an insurer may use reinsurance contracts to finance the growth of its business. In this regard, an insurance entity's capacity (ability to write business) is limited by law or regulation based on the amount of its statutory surplus. The greater the ratio of net premiums written or liabilities to such surplus, the less likely it is that the surplus will be sufficient to withstand adverse claim experience. Through reinsurance contracts, an insurer can increase its underwriting capacity to grow its direct written premium without increasing its net written premium, effectively using reinsurance to facilitate the growth of its business.

6.03 Basically, the following four kinds of private reinsurance entities exist in the United States:

    a. Professional reinsurers that engage almost exclusively in reinsurance, although they are usually permitted by their charters and licenses to operate as primary insurance companies.

    b. Reinsurance departments of primary insurance companies that function as units of primary insurers and engage in reinsurance.

    c. Groups or syndicates of insurers, referred to as reinsurance pools or associations, that may be organized to provide their members with reinsurance protection and management for certain specialized, high risk coverage or with general access to the reinsurance market for traditional lines of business. In addition, reinsurance intermediaries, including brokers, agents, managing general agents, and similar entities, facilitate reinsurance by bringing together ceding companies and reinsurers. Reinsurance intermediaries may underwrite, design, and negotiate the terms of reinsurance. They usually place reinsurance, accumulate and report transactions, distribute premiums, and collect and settle claims.

---

[*] Refer to the preface of this guide for important information about the applicability of the professional standards to audits of *issuers* and *nonissuers* (see the definitions for each in the preface). As applicable, this chapter contains dual referencing to both the AICPA and the Public Company Accounting Oversight Board's (PCAOB's) professional standards.

d. Groups or syndicates of professional investors, such as sidecars, cat bonds, or transformers, that are designed to allow their investors to assume the risk and earn a profit on a group of insurance policies ceded by a specific insurer or retroceded by a specific reinsurer.

6.04 In addition to private reinsurance entities, reinsurance coverage can also be obtained from certain governmental entities. Examples of such governmental entities are the Florida Hurricane Catastrophe Fund and the Terrorism Risk Insurance Program of the Department of the Treasury.

6.05 The following are major reasons insurance companies enter into reinsurance contracts:

- To help balance their risks and capital
- To reduce their exposure to particular risks or classes of risks
- To protect against accumulations of losses arising out of catastrophes
- To reduce total liabilities to a level appropriate to their statutory capital
- To provide financial capacity to accept risks and policies involving amounts larger than could otherwise be accepted
- To help stabilize operating results
- To obtain assistance with new products and lines of insurance
- To limit liabilities of captive insurance companies, as discussed in chapter 9, "Captive Insurance Entities," of this guide, created for the purpose of supplying insurance to noninsurance companies

6.06 For similar reasons, reinsurers may transfer a portion of their assumed risks to other insurance and reinsurance companies, which is a practice known as retrocession.

Types of Reinsurance

6.07 *Indemnity reinsurance* agreements are transactions by which the ceding entity remains primarily liable to the policyholder. In addition, the ceding entity bears the risks that the reinsurer may be unable to meet its obligations for the risks assumed under the reinsurance agreement. The policyholder is generally not aware of any indemnity reinsurance transactions that may occur and continues to hold the original contract.

6.08 Assumption reinsurance agreements are often used to legally replace one insurer with another (through a novation) and thereby extinguish the ceding company's liability to the policyholder. Under a novation, the policyholder must consent to releasing the ceding company from risk.

Reinsurance Contracts

6.09 Flexibility is one of the characteristics of the reinsurance business. Reinsurance contracts are usually negotiated individually and can reflect a variety of terms in custom-tailored agreements. Contracts are occasionally encountered that cannot be readily classified. However, the principal kinds of reinsurance are pro rata reinsurance and excess reinsurance. These contracts may either be prospective or retroactive. Prospective reinsurance requires the reinsurer to reimburse the ceding company for losses incurred resulting from future insurable events, but retroactive reinsurance requires the reinsurer to reimburse the ceding company for liabilities incurred as a result of past insurable events. A reinsurance contract may include both prospective and retroactive provisions.

6.10 *Pro rata reinsurance* is a sharing, on a predetermined basis, by the insurer and reinsurer of premiums and losses on a risk, class of risks, or particular portion of the insurer's business. For a predetermined portion of the insurer's premium(s), the reinsurer agrees to pay a similar portion of claims and claim-adjustment expenses incurred on the business reinsured. The reinsurer's participation in the claims is set without regard to the actual frequency and severity of claims. Pro rata reinsurance can be affected by means of quota share or surplus share reinsurance, which are described as follows:

   a. *Quota share reinsurance* is a kind of pro rata reinsurance in which the ceding company cedes a proportional part (a percentage) of risks to the reinsurer and, in turn, will recover from the reinsurer the same percentage of all losses on those risks. For example, under a 50 percent quota share treaty, the reinsurer receives 50 percent of the insurer's premiums, less ceding commissions, and is obligated to pay 50 percent of each claim and claim-adjustment expense incurred by the insurer. Such reinsurance is frequently used for new lines or by new companies (for example, a company just entering the casualty field may arrange for quota share reinsurance only for its casualty business).

   b. *Surplus share reinsurance* is insurance that reinsures on a pro rata basis only those risks for which the coverage exceeds a stated amount. For example, under a surplus treaty, an insurer might reinsure what it considers to be surplus exposure under each large dwelling policy that it writes. The insurer might reinsure the amount of each dwelling policy above $25,000; the insurer would reinsure $15,000 on a dwelling policy for $40,000. Premiums and losses are shared by the reinsurer and insurer on a pro rata basis in proportion to the amount of risk insured or reinsured by each. The reinsurer would not participate at all in any losses incurred on policies with limits of $25,000 or less.

6.11 Under excess reinsurance, the insurer limits its liability in excess of a predetermined deductible or retention. Above the retention level, the reinsurer assumes all or a portion of the liability up to a stated amount (that is, the limit). The relationship between the premium and claims of the insurer and reinsurer is not proportional. Excess reinsurance takes three basic forms, which are described as follows:

   a. *Excess of loss per risk reinsurance.* Excess of loss per risk reinsurance requires the insurer to retain all claims up to a stated amount or retention on each risk covered under the reinsurance, such as all fire policies written. The reinsurer reimburses the insurer for the portion of any claim in excess of the insurer's retention, subject to the limit stated in the reinsurance agreement.

   b. *Excess of loss per occurrence reinsurance.* Excess of loss per occurrence reinsurance requires the insurer to retain all claims up to a stated amount or retention on all losses arising from a single occurrence. The reinsurer pays claims in excess of the insurer's retention, subject to the limit stated in the reinsurance agreement. One purpose of obtaining per occurrence excess reinsurance is to protect a company from the accumulation of losses arising from earthquakes, hurricanes, tornadoes, or similar occurrences. Such reinsurance is also referred to as catastrophe reinsurance.

c. *Aggregate excess of loss reinsurance.* Aggregate excess of loss reinsurance requires the insurer to retain all claims during a specified period up to a predetermined limit for the period on all its business or any definable portion of the business. The limit is sometimes expressed as a loss ratio. The reinsurer reimburses the insurer for losses above the specified loss ratio. Such reinsurance is also referred to as stop loss reinsurance.

6.12 *Fronting* is a form of an indemnity reinsurance agreement between two or more insurers whereby the fronting entity will issue contracts and then cede all or substantially all of the risk through a reinsurance agreement to the other insurer(s) for a ceding commission. Such arrangements must comply with any regulatory requirements applicable to fronting to ensure avoidance of any illegal acts. AU-C section 250, *Consideration of Laws and Regulations in an Audit of Financial Statements* (AICPA, *Professional Standards*), addresses the auditor's responsibility to consider laws and regulations in an audit of financial statements. As with other indemnity reinsurance agreements, the fronting entity remains primarily liable to the policyholder.

6.13 A *special-purpose vehicle*, generally referred to as a sidecar, is a professional reinsurer that is designed to allow its investors to assume the risk and earn the profit on a group of insurance policies (a book of business) ceded by a specific insurer or retroceded by a specific reinsurer (the ceding company). The ceding entity will usually only cede the premiums associated with a book of business to such an entity if the investors place sufficient funds in the vehicle to ensure that the sidecar can meet claims, should they arise. Typically, the investors' exposure to loss is limited to the funds invested. The sidecar is usually formed as a separate entity that provides additional capacity to the ceding company to write property catastrophe business or other short-tail lines. The risk is transferred from the ceding company to the sidecar generally through a quota share or similar type of arrangement. The ceding entity normally charges a fee (ceding commission) for originating and managing the sidecar business and may sometimes also receive a profit commission if the book of business is profitable. Because the investors' capital is usually intended to be invested in this vehicle for a short term, the sidecar has a limited existence, often for only one year, after which investors may withdraw their investment. These structures have become quite prominent in the aftermath of Hurricane Katrina as a vehicle for insurers and reinsurers to add risk-bearing capacity and for investors to participate in the potential profits resulting from sharp price increases in insurance and reinsurance. Ceding entities should evaluate whether the sidecar is a variable interest entity (VIE) and, if so, whether the ceding company is the primary beneficiary of the variable interest in the sidecar and should consolidate the sidecar under Financial Accounting Standards Board (FASB) *Accounting Standards Codification* (ASC) 810, *Consolidation.*

6.14 Recently, noninsurance entities have begun to provide products to insurers that are similar to reinsurance. Typically, the insurer and noninsurance entity use an intervening special-purpose vehicle (transformer insurance entity), so that the ceding company can apply reinsurance accounting to the transaction. The transformer insurance entity is usually associated with the noninsurance entity. Recoverables under these arrangements are typically

Reinsurance

collateralized to assure collectability. For example, transformers can be used to issue catastrophe bonds to investors, with the proceeds supporting the reinsurance of an insurance entity's catastrophe risk. Ceding entities should evaluate whether the transformer insurance company is a VIE and, if so, whether the ceding entity is the primary beneficiary of the variable interest in the transformer insurance entity and should consolidate the transformer insurance entity under FASB ASC 810.

Bases of Reinsurance Transactions

6.15 Reinsurance is transacted either on a facultative or treaty basis. Under facultative reinsurance, each risk or portion of a risk is reinsured individually, and the reinsurer has the option to accept or reject each risk. Risks are separately underwritten by the reinsurer in much the same manner as if a direct policy were being issued. The reinsurer therefore has all the policy information necessary to maintain all the accounting records, including gross premiums and reinsurance premiums, term of the policy, reinsurance commissions, and individual claims data. Because the reinsurer must specifically obligate itself before assuming the risk, the company is aware of all the risks assumed at any point. The reinsurer maintains complete records about all facultative business assumed and, therefore, has the information needed to account for premiums written and receivable, commissions incurred and payable, and losses and expenses incurred and payable.

6.16 Under treaty-basis reinsurance, any agreed portion of business written is automatically reinsured, thereby eliminating the need for the reinsurer to accept or reject each risk. Because of the time lag in reporting by the ceding entity, the reinsurer is likely to be unaware of some of the risks it has assumed at any particular point in time. The bordereaux (reports) received by the reinsurer from the ceding entity may either contain detailed information on each underlying policy or risk reinsured, such as individual policy effective dates and premiums, or only summarized reinsurance treaty-level information, such as total written premiums ceded to the reinsurance treaty for the quarter. The ceding entity will generally provide the reinsurer with information regarding ceded premiums, ceded unearned premiums, and ceded losses and loss adjustment expenses (paid, case, and incurred but not reported [IBNR]).

6.17 When the ceding entity reports only summarized information, the reinsurer reviews the information and incorporates the ceding entity's estimates of reserves for unearned premiums, losses, and loss adjustment expenses into its estimation process for those reserves to the appropriate extent. Although the reinsurer may receive untimely or incomplete information, or both, from the ceding entity, the reinsurer's financial statements must still reflect its best estimates of the business it assumes.

6.18 Reinsurance may be transacted and serviced directly between the ceding entity and reinsurer or through reinsurance intermediaries, brokers, agents, or managing general agents. Reporting of information to the reinsurer is negotiated as part of a reinsurance transaction.

Frequently Used Terms in Reinsurance Contracts

6.19 Commonly used terms in reinsurance contracts may include the following:

> **Caps.** Caps are used to limit the reinsurer's aggregate exposure by imposing a dollar limit or a limit expressed as a percentage of premiums

on the amount of claims to be paid by the reinsurer. For example, the reinsurer will not be responsible for losses in excess of 150 percent of the premium paid.

Dual triggers. A coverage feature that requires the occurrence of both an insurable event and changes in a separate preidentified variable to trigger payment of a claim. For example, a policy entered into by a trucking entity that insures costs associated with rerouting trucks over a certain time period if snowfall exceeds a specified level during that time period. For the reinsurer to reimburse the ceding entity, not only does snowfall have to exceed the specified level, but the ceding entity has to have incurred losses due to the rerouting of trucks. FASB ASC 815-10-55 prescribes the accounting treatment for property and casualty contracts for which payments are based upon the occurrence of two events.

Loss corridor. A mechanism that requires the ceding insurer to be responsible for a certain amount of the ultimate net loss above the ceding entity's designated retention, and below the designated limit, that would otherwise be reimbursed under the reinsurance agreement. A loss corridor is usually expressed as a loss ratio percentage of the reinsurer's earned premium or a combined ratio if the reinsurance agreement provides for a ceding commission to the ceding entity. For example, under a quota share agreement, the reinsurer will be responsible for losses up to 80 percent of premiums, will not be responsible for losses in excess of 80 percent of premiums up to 95 percent of premiums, and will then be responsible for losses in excess of 95 percent of premiums.

Payment schedules. Features that are designed to delay the timing of reimbursement of losses so that investment income mitigates exposure to insurance risk. Payment schedules prevent the reinsurer's payments to the ceding entity from depending on, and directly varying with, the amount and timing of claims settled under the reinsured contracts. For example, a payment schedule may provide that no losses will be payable under the reinsurance contract by the reinsurer prior to year 8, regardless of when the insured incurs or pays a loss, at which time the reinsurer will pay losses ceded up to 25 percent of the contract limit each year until the experience is complete, or the contract limit has been reached.

Experience account. An arrangement whereby the ceding entity shares in the favorable experience of the contract by reference to an experience account that typically tracks ceded premiums, less fees, less ceded losses incurred, plus interest. Experience provisions can also require the ceding entity to share in unfavorable experience by requiring additional payments to the reinsurer in the event that the experience account becomes negative.

Profit commission. A commission feature whereby the ceding entity is provided a commission based on the reinsurer's profitability under the reinsurance contract. One form of a profit commission is a no-claims bonus whereby the ceding entity receives a stated percentage of the premium ceded in the event no claims are ceded to the reinsurer.

Retrospectively rated premiums. Premiums are determined after the inception of the agreement based on the loss experience under the agreement.

Sliding scale commission. A commission adjustment on earned premiums whereby the actual ceding commission varies inversely with the loss ratio (for example, increasing payments back to the ceding entity as losses decrease and decreasing payments back to the ceding entity as losses increase), subject to a maximum and minimum.

Contingent commissions. A provision in a reinsurance agreement that provides a commission to an insurer contingent upon a specified event happening. It is intended to allow the ceding insurer to share in the profits or losses realized by the reinsurer on the business subject to the contract.

Reinstatement clause. To the extent coverage provided by the contract is absorbed by losses incurred, the contract provides for the ceding entity to reinstate coverage for the balance of the contract period for a stated additional premium. Reinsurance contracts may provide for an unlimited or a specific number of reinstatements and can either be obligatory or nonmandatory. Mandatory reinstatement premiums may require the ceding entity to pay additional amounts if a certain level of losses is incurred.

Funds withheld. A provision under which the premium due to the reinsurer is withheld and not paid by the ceding entity.

Commutation clause. A clause in a reinsurance agreement that provides for the valuation, payment, and complete discharge of some or all obligations between the ceding entity and reinsurer, including current and future obligations for reinsurance losses incurred.

Unauthorized reinsurer and nonadmitted reinsurer. A reinsurer not authorized or licensed to do business in the state in which the ceding entity is domiciled. Licensed companies can write direct business in the state; if licensed, an entity is also authorized to assume reinsurance in that state. A nonlicensed entity can assume reinsurance if the state authorizes it to do so, and it is then considered to be an authorized reinsurer.

Accounting Practices[1]

Generally Accepted Accounting Principles Accounting Practices

6.20 FASB ASC 944, *Financial Services—Insurance*, specifies the accounting by insurance enterprises for the reinsurance (ceding) of insurance contracts, and FASB ASC 340-30 provides guidance for accounting for reinsurance contracts that do not transfer insurance risk. FASB ASC 944-20-55 includes implementation questions and answers related to accounting for reinsurance.

6.21 In general, FASB ASC 944 requires a determination of whether a reinsurance agreement, despite its form, qualifies for reinsurance accounting.

---

[1] The boards are redeliberating significant issues based on feedback received on the IASB exposure draft and FASB discussion paper. FASB is expected to release an exposure draft, and the IASB is expected to issue a targeted revised exposure draft, during the first half of 2013. Readers should remain alert to any final pronouncements.

To qualify, a reinsurance contract must indemnify the ceding entity from loss or liability relating to insurance risk. As discussed in FASB ASC 944-20-15-43, the risk transfer assessment is made at contract inception based on facts and circumstances known at that time. Also, as noted in FASB ASC 944-20-15-64, when contractual terms are amended, risk transfer should be reassessed. For example, a contract that, upon inception, met the conditions for reinsurance accounting could later be amended, so that it no longer meets those conditions. The contract should be reclassified and accounted for as a deposit in accordance with FASB ASC 340-30.

Indemnification and Defining the Contract

6.22 As discussed in FASB ASC 944-20-15-40, a complete understanding of the contracts and other contracts or agreements between the ceding entity and reinsurer is needed to determine if a contract provides indemnification against loss or liability relating to insurance risk. Specifically, FASB ASC 944-20-15-40 states that a complete understanding includes an evaluation of all contractual features that (*a*) limit the amount of insurance risk to which the reinsurer is subject, such as through experience refunds, cancellation provisions, adjustable features, or additions of profitable lines of business to the reinsurance contract, or (*b*) delay the timely reimbursement of claims by the reinsurer, such as through payment schedules or accumulating retentions from multiple years.

6.23 The accounting guidance stresses substance over form in defining the contract that is subject to risk transfer analysis and accounting. All contracts, including contracts that may not be structured or described as reinsurance, must be assessed for potential reinsurance accounting. Although the legal form and substance of a reinsurance contract will generally be the same, and thus, the risks reinsured under a single legal document would constitute a single contract for accounting purposes, this may not always be the case. Careful analysis and judgment is required to determine the boundaries of a contract for accounting purposes. In some instances, features of other related contracts may need to be considered part of the subject contract. It is therefore important to determine whether the ceding entity and reinsurer have made any other legally binding agreements, whether oral or written, in conjunction with the reinsurance contract being assessed. If so, careful consideration should be given about whether these agreements are part of the subject contract. Such agreements may be referred to as side agreements. In some instances, the side agreements have served to negate some or all of the risk transfer existing in the reinsurance contract.

6.24 As discussed in FASB ASC 944-20-55-32, different kinds of exposures combined in a program of reinsurance shall not be evaluated for risk transfer and accounted for together because that may allow contracts that do not meet the conditions for reinsurance accounting to be accounted for as reinsurance by being designated as part of a reinsurance program. For example, for a multicoverage program combining several distinct lines of business, consideration should be given about whether each line should be evaluated separately or on a combined basis as part of the risk transfer test.

Risk Transfer Criteria

6.25 As discussed in FASB ASC 944-20-15-41, for property and casualty insurance risks, two criteria must be met in order for a reinsurance contract to

Reinsurance

be considered to indemnify the ceding entity against loss or liability. These two criteria, which are often referred to as the risk transfer criteria, are as follows:

    a. The reinsurer assumes significant insurance risk under the reinsured portions of the underlying contracts (both in amount and timing)

    b. It is reasonably possible that the reinsurer may realize a significant loss from the transaction

6.26 Also, as discussed in FASB ASC 944-20-15-46, a reinsurer shall not be considered to have assumed significant insurance risk under the reinsured contracts if the probability of a significant variation in either the amount or timing of payments by the reinsurer is remote. Contractual provisions that delay timely reimbursement to the ceding entity would prevent this condition from being met.

6.27 Neither generally accepted accounting principles (GAAP) nor statutory accounting principles (SAP) define *reasonably possible* or *significant loss* for purposes of the risk transfer criteria. Some insight can be found in FASB ASC 944-20-15-44. The assessment in FASB ASC 944-20-15-41, as discussed in paragraph 6.25, is applied to a particular scenario, not the individual assumptions used in the scenario. Therefore, a scenario is not reasonably possible unless the likelihood of the entire set of assumptions used in the scenario occurring together is reasonably possible.

6.28 FASB ASC 944-20-15-49 states that the ceding entity's evaluation of whether it is reasonably possible for a reinsurer to realize a significant loss from the transaction shall be based on the present value of all cash flows between the ceding and assuming entities under reasonably possible outcomes, without regard to how the individual cash flows are characterized. The same interest rate shall be used to compute the present value of cash flows for each reasonably possible outcome tested. To be reasonable and appropriate, that rate shall reflect both of the following:

    a. The expected timing of payments to the reinsurer

    b. The duration over which those cash flows are expected to be invested by the reinsurer.

FASB ASC 944-20-15-51 requires a quantitative test to be performed, calculated by dividing the present value of all cash flows between the ceding and assuming companies by the present value of amounts to be paid to the reinsurer before commissions. However, no bright-line quantitative threshold exists in either GAAP or SAP.

6.29 Determining the amount of risk transfer in a contract is a matter of judgment after evaluating all the facts, both qualitative and quantitative. Qualitative factors to consider include the following:

- The relationship between the possibility of loss and the potential magnitude of the loss (the lower the possibility of loss, the higher the magnitude of possible loss to meet risk transfer)
- The maximum possible loss
- The discount rate used to discount the cash flows in the risk transfer quantitative assessment
- The range of assumptions used

- The possibilities that the assumptions could all be realized at the same time

- Other indirect factors, such as the impact of the agreement on the entity's risk-based capital (RBC) and other key ratios (for example, premiums or surplus ratio and debt covenants)

6.30 Each contract needs to be analyzed based on the facts and circumstances of each transaction, the operating environment, and the contract's potential impact on the entity's financial reporting. Accordingly, the determination of risk transfer is not solely a quantitative exercise and judgment but, rather, a combination of understanding the contract and specifics involved. It is generally viewed as the following three-step process:

   a. Determine the business purpose of the contract

   b. Evaluate the cash flows and associated probabilities and outcomes

   c. Assess the qualitative and quantitative features together

6.31 A joint effort by actuaries and accountants is helpful to determine whether the contract transfers significant insurance risk.

6.32 A contract that has a relatively low probability of a relatively low loss may not qualify for risk transfer. Also, using an informal general probability of loss criterion can be problematic for certain types of reinsurance, such as catastrophe covers and other covers with an extremely low frequency of occurrence but potentially very high severity of loss. Accounting practice has evolved such that ordinary catastrophe covers have been deemed by most practitioners to be reinsurance, regardless of the probability of loss, if the potential magnitude of the loss in comparison with the premium paid is great and no material loss limiting factors exist, such as retrospective rating features.

The Paragraph 11 Exception

6.33 FASB ASC 944-20-15-51 states that significance of loss shall be evaluated by comparing the present value of all cash flows, determined, as described in FASB ASC 944-20-15-49, with the present value of the amounts paid or deemed to have been paid to the reinsurer. FASB ASC 944-20-15-53 notes that if based on this comparison the reinsurer is not exposed to the reasonable possibility of significant loss, the ceding entity shall be considered indemnified against loss or liability relating to insurance risk only if substantially all the insurance risk relating to the reinsured portions of the underlying insurance contracts has been assumed by the reinsurer. That condition is met only if insignificant insurance risk is retained by the ceding entity on the reinsured portions of the underlying insurance contracts. The assessment of that condition shall be made by comparing both of the following:

   a. The net cash flows of the reinsurer under the reinsurance contract

   b. The net cash flows of the ceding entity on the reinsured portions of the underlying insurance contracts

If the economic position of the reinsurer relative to the insurer cannot be determined, the contract shall not qualify under the exception in this paragraph.

6.34 Also, as discussed in FASB ASC 944-20-15-54, the extremely narrow and limited exemption in the preceding paragraph is for contracts that reinsure either an individual risk or underlying book of business that is inherently profitable. To qualify under that exception, no more than trivial insurance risk on the reinsured portions of the underlying insurance contracts may be retained by the ceding entity. The reinsurer's economic position shall be virtually equivalent to having written the relevant portions of the reinsured contracts directly.

6.35 There has been much discussion in the industry regarding which types of reinsurance treaties qualify for the exception discussed in paragraph 6.33, and there continues to be a divergence of views.

Risk-Limiting Features

6.36 *Risk-limiting features* are reinsurance contract provisions that limit the amount of insurance risk to which the reinsurer is subject or delay the timely reimbursement of claims by the reinsurer. To determine if a reinsurance contract indemnifies a ceding entity against loss or liability, a complete understanding of the reinsurance contract's provisions, including any risk-limiting features, is required. Many of the features used in reinsurance contracts (described in paragraph 6.19) have the effect of limiting the risk being transferred in the reinsurance treaty.

6.37 As the structures of risk-limiting reinsurance transactions become more complex, and their terms become more indefinite, the economics become increasingly difficult to quantify. Terms that make it difficult or impossible to evaluate the economics of a transaction suggest that reinsurance accounting may not be appropriate.

6.38 Accounting for reinstatement premiums requires a thorough understanding of the particular reinstatement premium terms (for example, whether they are obligatory or voluntary) to determine the period in which these additional amounts should be recognized. FASB ASC 944-605 guidance on premium recognition for retrospectively rated reinsurance contracts may be helpful in this analysis.

Reporting Assets and Liabilities

6.39 As discussed in FASB ASC 944-20-40-4, reinsurance contracts for which the ceding entity is not relieved of the legal liability to its policyholder do not result in the removal of the related assets and liabilities from the ceding entity's financial statements.

6.40 For those agreements, the ceding entity should report as assets estimated reinsurance receivables and any prepaid reinsurance premiums arising from those agreements.

6.41 As noted FASB ASC 944-20-25-4, the ceding enterprise should recognize an asset, and the assuming enterprise should recognize a liability to the extent that any cash or other consideration would be payable from the assuming enterprise to the ceding enterprise based on experience to date under the contract. This results in the requirement that certain contract provisions (for example, sliding scale commissions, profit sharing, and so on) may result in asset or liability recognition based on management's best estimate of the contract experience to date, which should be consistent with the estimates used to calculate loss and LAE reserves for the contract.

6.42 As noted in FASB ASC 944-310-45-7, amounts receivable and payable between the ceding entity and an individual reinsurer shall be offset only if a legal right of setoff exists, as defined in FASB ASC 210-20, even if the ceding entity and reinsurer are affiliated entities. However, if the ceding entity and reinsurer are affiliated entities, the amounts shall be eliminated in consolidation when the affiliated entities are included in consolidated financial statements.

6.43 As discussed in FASB ASC 210-10-45-1, a right of setoff exists when all of the following conditions are met:

   a. Each of two parties owes the other determinable amounts

   b. The reporting party has the right to set off the amount owed with the amount owed by the other party

   c. The reporting party intends to set off

   d. The right of setoff is enforceable at law

6.44 As noted in FASB ASC 210-10-45-2, a debtor having a valid right of setoff may offset the related asset and liability and report the net amount. As discussed in FASB ASC 210-10-45-8, state laws about the right of setoff may provide results different from those normally provided by contract or as a matter of common law. Similarly, the U.S. Bankruptcy Code imposes restrictions on, or prohibitions against, the right of setoff in bankruptcy under certain circumstances. Legal constraints should be considered to determine whether the right of setoff is enforceable.

6.45 As noted in FASB ASC 944-40-25-34, reinsurance receivables shall be recognized in a manner consistent with the related liabilities (estimates for IBNR claims and future policy benefits) relating to the underlying insurance contracts. Assumptions used in estimating reinsurance receivables should be consistent with those assumptions used in estimating the related liabilities.

6.46 The ceding entity should evaluate the financial soundness of the reinsurer and the collectability of reinsurance receivables, including consideration of collateral, to make a determination that the reinsurer has the ability to honor its commitment under the contract. The assessment of whether an allowance for uncollectible amounts is required is generally made on a reinsurer-by-reinsurer basis, considering the underlying individual contracts. In addition, the ceding entity should evaluate whether any portion of the ceded unpaid losses may be uncollectible due to disputes on coverage.

6.47 As discussed in FASB ASC 944-605-45-1, the amounts of earned premiums ceded and recoveries recognized under reinsurance contracts shall either be (*a*) reported in the statement of earnings as separate line items or parenthetically or (*b*) disclosed in the footnotes to financial statements under FASB ASC 944-605-50-1.

Reporting Revenues and Costs

6.48 FASB ASC 944-605 provides guidance on the recognition of revenues and costs for reinsurance of short duration contracts:

- *FASB ASC 944-605-25-20*. Amounts paid for prospective reinsurance that meets the conditions for reinsurance accounting shall be reported as prepaid reinsurance premiums.

- *FASB ASC 944-605-35-8*. Prepaid reinsurance premiums shall be amortized over the remaining contract period in proportion to the amount of insurance protection provided. If the amounts paid are

Reinsurance

subject to adjustment and can be reasonably estimated, the basis for amortization shall be the estimated ultimate amount to be paid.

- *FASB ASC 944-605-25-22*. Amounts paid for retroactive reinsurance that meets the conditions for reinsurance accounting shall be reported as reinsurance receivables to the extent those amounts do not exceed the recorded liabilities relating to the underlying reinsured contracts. If the recorded liabilities exceed the amounts paid, reinsurance receivables shall be increased to reflect the difference and the resulting gain deferred.

- *FASB ASC 944-605-35-9*. The deferred gain recognized under FASB ASC 944-605-25-22 shall be amortized over the estimated remaining settlement period. If the amounts and timing of the reinsurance recoveries can be reasonably estimated, the deferred gain shall be amortized using the effective interest rate inherent in the amount paid to the reinsurer and the estimated timing and amounts of recoveries from the reinsurer (the interest method). Otherwise, the proportion of actual recoveries to total estimated recoveries (the recovery method) shall determine the amount of amortization.

- *FASB ASC 944-605-25-23*. If the amounts paid for retroactive reinsurance exceed the recorded liabilities relating to the underlying reinsured contracts, the ceding enterprise shall increase the related liabilities or reduce the reinsurance receivable, or both, at the time the reinsurance contract is entered into, so that the excess is charged to earnings.

- *FASB ASC 944-605-35-11*. Changes in the estimated amount of the liabilities relating to the underlying reinsured contracts shall be recognized in earnings in the period of the change.

- *FASB ASC 944-605-35-12*. Reinsurance receivables shall reflect the related change in the amount recoverable from the reinsurer, and a gain to be deferred and amortized shall be adjusted or established as a result. When changes in the estimated amount recoverable from the reinsurer or in the timing of receipts related to that amount occur, a cumulative amortization adjustment shall be recognized in earnings in the period of the change so that the deferred gain reflects the balance that would have existed had the revised estimate been available at the inception of the reinsurance transaction.

- *FASB ASC 944-605-25-21*. When practicable, prospective and retroactive provisions included within a single contract shall be accounted for separately. The "Reinsurance Contracts" sections of this subtopic do not require any specific method for allocating reinsurance premiums to the prospective and retroactive portions of a contract. However, separate accounting for the prospective and retroactive portions of a contract may take place only when an allocation is practicable. Practicability requires a reasonable basis for allocating the reinsurance premiums to the risks covered by the prospective and retroactive portions of the contract, considering all amounts paid or deemed to have been paid, regardless of the timing of payment. If separate accounting for prospective and retroactive provisions included within a single contract is impracticable, the contract shall be accounted for as a retroactive contract, provided that the conditions for reinsurance accounting are met.

AAG-PLI 6.48

6.49 If the reinsurer cannot reasonably estimate the premium assumed under a reinsurance contract, FASB ASC 944-605-25-2 requires the use of either the cost recovery method or the deposit method to record premiums and losses until the premium becomes reasonably estimable.

Assumption Reinsurance

6.50 *Assumption reinsurance agreements* are legal replacements of one insurer by another by a novation and thereby extinguish the ceding entity's liability to the policyholder and should be accounted for by removing the related assets and liabilities from the financial statements of the ceding entity. Assumption and novation transactions may result in an immediate recognition of a gain or loss because they are a legal replacement of one insurer by another, as discussed in FASB ASC 944-40-25-33, and satisfy the requirements for extinguishment of a liability.

Commutation

6.51 A *commutation agreement* is a settlement agreement between a ceding insurer and reinsurer that provides for valuation, payment, and complete discharge of some or all of the obligations between the parties under a particular reinsurance contract. The full commutation of a reinsurance contract results in the discharge of any reinsurance recoverable and should be accounted for as a settlement of the loss recoverable asset, with a gain or loss recognized immediately depending on whether the consideration received is more or less than the loss recoverable asset.

Structured Settlements

6.52 When annuities are purchased to fund periodic fixed payments, and the insurance entity is the payee, no decrease in the liability to the policyholder is recorded under either GAAP or SAP. When the claimant is the payee and the insurer is legally released of its claim obligation under both GAAP and SAP, loss reserves are reduced to the extent that the annuity provides funding for future payments. When the claimant is the payee and the insurer is not released of its obligation, loss reserves are reduced under SAP but not under GAAP. For SAP purposes, structured settlements are considered completed transactions when the claimant is the payee, regardless of whether the insurer is legally released from its obligation, and any gain is recognized immediately. Paragraphs 17–20 of Statement of Statutory Accounting Practices (SSAP) No. 65, *Property and Casualty Contracts*, discuss accounting for structured settlements.

6.53 If the structured settlement legally replaces one insurer for another and thereby extinguishes the primary insurer's liability to the policyholder, FASB ASC 944 requires that an immediate gain or loss be recognized under GAAP. GAAP requires gain deferral in instances when the insurance entity purchases a structured settlement annuity for the claimant, but the insurer has not been legally released from its obligation. As discussed in FASB ASC 944-20-55-57, a structured settlement transaction that does not legally replace one insurer by another and thereby extinguishes the primary insurer's liability to the policyholder is accounted for as reinsurance if the annuity funding the settlement meets the conditions for reinsurance accounting. Otherwise, the transaction is accounted for as a deposit, in accordance with FASB ASC 340-30-05-1.

Interest Credits on Funds Withheld

6.54 Reinsurance contracts may include a clause that allows the ceding entity to keep the premium called for under the reinsurance contract while reporting it as ceded to the reinsurer—a practice known as funds withheld. This practice was developed to minimize cash transferred between the ceding entity and reinsurer when the ceding entity expected to pay the subject losses quickly. This practice is sometimes used to provide the ceding entity with collateral for reinsurance recoverables, particularly in cases when the reinsurer is an unauthorized reinsurer because unsecured reinsurance recoverables from such reinsurers are nonadmitted under SAP.

6.55 Some contracts require the ceding entity to credit the funds withheld account with interest at an above market rate. In effect, the ceding entity pays the reinsurer an extra amount but spreads the recognition of that extra amount over many years. A variation of this approach involves deferred ceding commissions that allow the reinsurer to defer payment of the ceding commission and thus earn extra investment income on that amount while the payment is deferred. These types of arrangements should be carefully reviewed to determine the accounting impact of the nonmarket term. All cash flows, including the extra cost resulting from the nonmarket terms, should be included in the risk transfer analysis.

6.56 Experience account arrangements contractually allow the ceding company to share in the favorable experience of the underlying contracts by reference to an experience account that notionally tracks premiums paid to the reinsurer by the ceding company, less commissions, less losses ceded, plus interest. Experience refund provisions can also require the ceding company to share in unfavorable experience by requiring additional payments to the reinsurer in the event that the notional experience account is negative. Experience refunds are also sometimes called profit commissions. Experience refunds mitigate the reinsurer's risk by providing it an adequate premium but allowing the ceding entity to get back some of its premium if losses are not as high.

6.57 A funds-withheld arrangement causes the reinsurer to recognize a receivable from the ceding insurer, as well as a liability representing reserves for the insurance coverage assumed under the funds-withheld arrangement. The terms of the reinsurer's receivable provide for the future payment of principal plus a rate of return that is generally based on a specified proportion of the ceding entity's return on either its general account assets or a specified block of those assets, such as a specific portfolio of the ceding entity's investment securities. That portfolio typically comprises fixed-rate debt securities.

6.58 FASB ASC 815-15-55 requires an entity to bifurcate a debt instrument into a debt host and an embedded derivative when the debt incorporates both interest rate risk and credit-risk exposures that are unrelated or only partially related to the creditworthiness of the instrument's issuer. Funds-withheld arrangements are one of the examples cited in FASB ASC. Other examples of contracts that may also have embedded derivatives are as follows:

- Funds-withheld reinsurance or deposit contracts that have an interest crediting based on the total return bond index or other pool of investments versus fixed interest rates or benchmark interest rate indexes (for example, London Interbank Offered Rate plus 2 percent) that are not total return indexes and, thus, typically do not contain embedded derivatives

- Experience accounts or refund accounts with interest crediting other than a fixed or variable interest rate
- Any trust account arrangements in reinsurance agreements that are not just collateral

6.59 FASB ASC 815-15-55, as discussed in paragraph 6.58, does not specify the precise nature of the derivative in the funds-withheld arrangement, but states that the nature of the embedded derivative should be determined based on the facts and circumstances of the individual contract. Therefore, each embedded derivative will vary based on specific facts and circumstances, although they are likely to be either total return swaps or credit default swaps.

Intercompany Pooling Arrangements

6.60 Intercompany pooling arrangements generally involve establishment of a conventional quota share reinsurance agreement under which all of the pooled business is ceded to the lead entity and then retroceded back to the pool participants in accordance with their stipulated shares. In these arrangements, only the policy issuing entity has direct liability to its policyholders or claimants; other pool participants are liable as reinsurers for their share of the issuing entity's obligations.

6.61 SAP specifically discusses the accounting for intercompany pooling arrangements in SSAP No. 63, *Underwriting Pools and Associations Including Intercompany Pools*. Paragraph 8 of SSAP No. 63 states

> [u]nderwriting results shall be accounted for on a gross basis whereby the participant's portion of premiums, losses, expenses, and other operations of the pools are recorded separately in the financial statements rather than netted against each other. Premiums and losses shall be recorded as direct, assumed, and/or ceded as applicable. If the reporting entity is a direct writer of the business, premiums shall be recorded as directly written and accounted for in the same manner as other business which is directly written by the entity. To the extent that premium is ceded to a pool, premiums and losses shall be recorded in the same manner as any other reinsurance arrangement. A reporting entity who is a member of a pool shall record its participation in the pool as assumed business as in any other reinsurance arrangement.

6.62 Also as discussed in paragraph 9 of SSAP No. 63, although it is acceptable that intercompany pooling transactions be settled through intercompany arrangements and accounts, intercompany pooling transactions shall be reported on a gross basis in the appropriate reinsurance accounts consistent with other direct, assumed and ceded business.

6.63 Under GAAP, the offsetting requirements of FASB ASC 210-10-45-1 (as discussed in paragraph 6.43) have not been met between the intercompany pool participants and the lead entity. Also as noted in FASB ASC 944-20-40-4, as long as the ceding entity is not relieved of the legal liability to its policyholder, the related assets and liabilities should not be removed from the ceding entity's financial statements. Therefore, the Financial Reporting Executive Committee believes that intercompany pooling transactions should be reported under GAAP in a similar manner to SAP.

Accounting for Foreign Property and Liability Reinsurance

6.64 In the past, there was diversity in insurance accounting and reporting practices of foreign insurance companies that led to questions of how U.S. insurance companies should account for property and liability reinsurance assumed from foreign companies (foreign reinsurance). Reinsurers assuming business from domestic companies have historically had sufficient information to monitor and account for contract results. In contrast, some reinsurers assuming business from foreign companies did not receive such information because in some foreign jurisdictions, insurance companies' accounting and reporting practices concerning periodic recognition of revenue and incurred claims were substantially different from U.S. practices. Therefore, reinsurers assuming business from foreign ceding companies could not always obtain sufficient information to periodically estimate earned premiums for the business assumed from the foreign ceding companies.

6.65 FASB ASC 944-605 provides information about accounting for foreign property and liability reinsurance. Although such issues are much less prevalent today, FASB ASC 944-605 provides guidance on using the periodic, zero balance, and open year methods if practitioners face such challenges.

Reinsurance Agreements Not Qualifying for Reinsurance Accounting Under FASB ASC 944

6.66 FASB ASC 944 does not specifically address accounting for reinsurance agreements that do not meet the conditions for reinsurance accounting, other than as follows:

- *FASB ASC 720-20-25-1.* To the extent that a reinsurance contract does not, despite its form, provide for indemnification of the ceding enterprise by the reinsurer against loss or liability, the premium paid less the premium to be retained by the reinsurer shall be accounted for as a deposit by the ceding enterprise. A net credit resulting from the contract shall be reported as a liability by the ceding enterprise. A net charge resulting from the contract shall be reported as an asset by the reinsurer.

- *FASB ASC 944-30-35-64.* Proceeds from reinsurance transactions that represent recovery of acquisition costs shall reduce applicable unamortized acquisition costs in such a manner that net acquisition costs are capitalized and charged to expense in proportion to net revenue recognized.[2]

- *FASB ASC 944-405-25-1.* If the ceding enterprise has agreed to service all the related insurance contracts without reasonable compensation, a liability shall be accrued for estimated excess future servicing costs under the reinsurance contract.

- *FASB ASC 944-30-25-13.* The net cost to the assuming enterprise shall be accounted for as an acquisition cost.

6.67 FASB ASC 340-30 provides guidance on how to account for insurance and reinsurance contracts that do not transfer insurance risk, except for long duration life and health insurance contracts. The method used to account for insurance and reinsurance contracts that do not transfer insurance risk is referred to as *deposit accounting*. FASB ASC 340-30 neither addresses when

---

[2] FASB ASC 944-30-25 and 944-30-30 address recognition and initial measurement of acquisition costs.

deposit accounting should be applied nor provides criteria to make that determination but, rather, provides guidance on how to apply the deposit method of accounting when it is determined that the insurance and reinsurance contracts do not transfer insurance risk.

6.68 FASB ASC 340-30-30-1 requires that, at inception, a deposit asset or liability be recognized for insurance or reinsurance contracts accounted for under deposit accounting and be measured based on the consideration paid or received less any explicitly identified premiums or fees to be retained by the insurer or reinsurer, regardless of the experience of the contract. Accounting for such fees should be based on the terms of the contract. FASB ASC 340-30-45-1 notes that deposit assets and liabilities should be reported on a gross basis, unless the *right of setoff* exists, as defined in FASB ASC 210-20.

6.69 Paragraphs 3–6 of FASB ASC 340-30-25, paragraphs 1–7 of FASB ASC 340-30-30, and paragraphs 2–5 of FASB ASC 340-30-45 provide guidance about the measurement of the deposit asset or liability at subsequent reporting dates. The subsequent measurement of the deposits is based upon whether the insurance and reinsurance contract (*a*) transfers only significant timing risk, (*b*) transfers only significant underwriting risk, (*c*) transfers neither significant timing nor underwriting risk, or (*d*) has indeterminate risk.

6.70 Consideration should be given about how cash flows should be classified for reinsurance contracts that do not contain adequate risk transfer. Factors to be considered for classification include, among other things, the outcomes of the four measurement criteria discussed in paragraph 6.69.

Disclosure Requirements Contained in GAAP Literature

6.71 FASB ASC 944-605-50 requires that all insurance entities shall disclose all of the following in their financial statements:

    a. For all reinsurance contracts, both of the following:

        i. Methods used for income recognition on reinsurance contracts

        ii. Under FASB ASC 944-605-45-1, if not reported in the statement of earnings as separate line items or parenthetically, the amounts of earned premiums ceded and recoveries recognized under reinsurance contracts

    b. For short duration contracts, all of the following on both a written basis and an earned basis:

        i. Premiums from direct business

        ii. Reinsurance assumed

        iii. Reinsurance ceded

    c. For foreign reinsurance accounted for by the open year method, all of the following shall be disclosed for each period for which an income statement is presented:

        i. The amounts of premiums, claims, and expenses recognized as income on closing underwriting balances

        ii. The additions to underwriting balances for the year for reported premiums, claims, and expenses

d. The amounts of premiums, claims, and expenses in the underwriting account for each balance sheet presented

6.72 FASB ASC 944-605-50-2 notes that appropriate disclosure of both of the following items is encouraged:

a. The extent to which reinsurance contracts indemnify the ceding entity against loss or liability relating to insurance risk

b. Indemnification policies as part of the required disclosure in the preceding paragraph about the nature and effect of reinsurance transactions

6.73 FASB ASC 944-605-50-3 also notes that disclosure in the financial statements of an insurance entity's accounting policies under FASB ASC 250, *Accounting Changes and Error Corrections*, shall include a description of the methods used to account for foreign reinsurance.

6.74 FASB ASC 944-825-55-1 requires disclosure of concentrations of credit risk associated with reinsurance receivables and prepaid reinsurance premiums.

6.75 Paragraphs 1–2 of FASB ASC 340-30-50 require the following disclosures:

a. Entities should disclose a description of the contracts accounted for as deposits and the separate amounts of total deposit assets and total deposit liabilities reported in the statement of financial position

b. Insurance enterprises should disclose the following information regarding the changes in the recorded amount of the deposit arising from an insurance or a reinsurance contract that transfers only significant underwriting risk:

   i. The present values of initial expected recoveries that will be reimbursed under the insurance or reinsurance contracts that have been recorded as an adjustment to incurred losses.

   ii. Any adjustments of amounts initially recognized for expected recoveries. The individual components of the adjustment (interest accrual, the present value of additional expected recoveries, and the present value of reductions in expected recoveries) should be disclosed separately.

   iii. The amortization expense attributable to the expiration of coverage provided under the contract.

Statutory Accounting Principles

6.76 Statutory accounting for reinsurance is discussed in SSAP No. 62R, *Property and Casualty Reinsurance*. SSAP No. 62R was adopted in December 2009 to allow prospective reinsurance accounting for the transfer of property and casualty runoff transactions when specific criteria are in place, including approval by the domiciliary regulators of the transferring entity and assuming entity.

6.77 Under SAP, as under GAAP, the essential ingredient of a reinsurance contract is the indemnification of risk. A number of states regulate reinsurance arrangements by disallowing the recognition of increased surplus resulting from non-risk-shifting arrangements. In general, the accounting treatment by ceding companies for reinsurance transactions is opposite from that of transactions that arise from writing direct business, and the amounts of the reinsurance transactions are netted against the direct amounts for financial statement presentation (for example, the premium accounts are netted against the direct amounts for premiums related to insurance ceded). The reinsurer's accounting for reinsurance normally parallels the original accounting for direct business.

6.78 Risk transfer provisions are generally similar under GAAP and SAP for property and casualty reinsurance contracts. The following are some differences that exist between GAAP and SAP for reinsurance accounting:

- The practice of reporting assets and liabilities relating to reinsured contracts net of the effects of reinsurance is applied for SAP but prohibited under FASB ASC 944. SAP requires that amounts paid for prospective reinsurance that meet the conditions for reinsurance accounting should be reported as a reduction of unearned premiums.
- GAAP and SAP guidance differs on the accounting for retroactive reinsurance and FASB ASC 944 precludes immediate gain recognition, unless the ceding entity's liability to its policyholders is extinguished.
- Reinsurance in business combinations may be treated differently. SAP requires a liability to be recorded for net reinsurance balances due from unauthorized reinsurers that exceed collateral held. In statutory financial statements, the ceding entity cannot obtain surplus credit for unearned premiums ceded to, and losses recoverable from, an unauthorized reinsurer, unless collateralized by assets held, a letter of credit, or other forms of qualifying collateral. A ceding entity must establish a liability for unauthorized reinsurance in an amount equal to the excess of the reserve credits taken over the funds held or letter of credit for the business ceded.
- SAP requires property and casualty insurers to establish a special formula-based liability for overdue reinsurance balances due from authorized reinsurers. Such liabilities are not required for GAAP; however, insurers assess collectability of reinsurance recoverables and may record an allowance.
- SAP requires that if the ceding commission paid under a reinsurance agreement exceeds the anticipated acquisition cost of the business ceded, the ceding entity shall establish a liability, equal to the difference between the anticipated acquisition cost and reinsurance commissions received, to be amortized pro rata over the effective period of the reinsurance agreement in proportion to the amount of coverage provided under the reinsurance contract.
- SAP recognizes that it is not uncommon for a reinsurance arrangement to be initiated before the beginning of a policy period but not finalized until after the policy period begins. Whether there was agreement in principle at the beginning of the policy period, and therefore, the agreement is substantively prospective, shall be determined based on the facts and circumstances. In addition, SAP requires that unless a reinsurance contract is finalized, reduced to a written form, and signed by the parties within nine months after the commencement of the policy period covered by the reinsurance arrangement, then the arrangement is presumed to be retroactive and shall be accounted for as a retroactive reinsurance agreement.

Disclosure Requirements Contained in the Statutory Literature

6.79 SSAP No. 62R includes the following disclosure requirements:

a. Unsecured reinsurance recoverables, as follows:

i. If the entity has, with any individual authorized or unauthorized reinsurers, an unsecured aggregate recoverable for paid and unpaid losses, including IBNR, loss adjustment expenses, and unearned premium, that exceeds 3 percent of the entity's policyholder surplus, list each individual reinsurer and the unsecured aggregate recoverable pertaining to that reinsurer

ii. If the individual reinsurer is part of a group, list the individual reinsurers, each of its related group members having reinsurance with the reporting entity, and the total unsecured aggregate recoverables for the entire group

b. *Reinsurance recoverables in dispute.* Reinsurance recoverables on paid and unpaid losses, including IBNR, in dispute by reason of notification, arbitration, or litigation shall be identified if the amounts in dispute from any entity or affiliate, or both, exceed 5 percent of the ceding entity's policyholder's surplus or if the aggregate of all disputed items exceeds 10 percent of the ceding entity's policyholder's surplus. *Notification* means a formal written communication from a reinsurer denying the validity of coverage.

c. *Uncollectible reinsurance.* Describe uncollectible reinsurance written off during the year reported in the following annual statement classifications, including the name(s) of the reinsurer(s):

i. Losses incurred

ii. Loss adjustment expenses incurred

iii. Premiums earned

iv. Other

d. *Commutation of ceded reinsurance.* Describe commutation of ceded reinsurance during the year and reported in the following annual statement classifications, including the name(s) of the reinsurer(s):

i. Losses incurred

ii. Loss adjustment expenses incurred

iii. Premiums earned

iv. Other

e. *Retroactive reinsurance.* The table illustrated in the NAIC *Annual Statement Instructions for Property and Casualty Companies* under the "Retroactive Reinsurance in the Notes to Financial Statements" section shall be completed for all retroactive reinsurance agreements that transfer liabilities for losses that have already occurred and that will generate special surplus transactions. The assuming or ceding insurer shall assign a unique number to each retroactive reinsurance agreement.

Property and Liability Insurance Entities

f. *Reinsurance assumed and ceded.* The tables illustrated in the NAIC *Annual Statement Instructions for Property and Casualty Companies* under the "Reinsurance Assumed and Ceded in the Notes to Financial Statements" section shall be completed as follows:

  i. The financial statements shall disclose the maximum amount of return commission that would have been due reinsurers if all reinsurance were cancelled with the return of the unearned premium reserve

  ii. The financial statements shall disclose the accrual of additional or return commission, predicated on loss experience or any other form of profit sharing arrangements as a result of existing contractual arrangements

g. A specific interrogatory requires information on reinsurance of risk accompanied by an agreement to release the reinsurer from liability, in whole or in part, from any loss that may occur on the risk or portion thereof.

h. Any risks that are reinsured under a quota share reinsurance contract with any other entity that includes a provision that would limit the reinsurer's losses below the stated quota share percentage (for example, a deductible, a loss ratio corridor, a loss cap, an aggregate limit, or any similar provisions). If so, indicate the number of reinsurance contracts containing such provisions and if the amount of reinsurance credit taken reflects the reduction in quota share coverage caused by any applicable limiting provision(s).

i. If the reporting entity ceded any risk under any reinsurance contract or multiple contracts with the same reinsurer or its affiliates for which during the period covered by the statement

  i. it recorded a positive or negative underwriting result greater than 3 percent of prior year-end surplus in regard to policyholders, or it reported calendar year written premium ceded or year-end loss and loss expense reserves ceded greater than 3 percent of prior year-end surplus in regard to policyholders;

  ii. it accounted for that contract as reinsurance, not a deposit; and

  iii. the contract(s) contain one or more of the following features that would have similar results:

   (1) A contract term longer than two years, and the contract is noncancellable by the reporting entity during the contract term

   (2) A limited or conditional cancellation provision under which cancellation triggers an obligation by the reporting entity or an affiliate of the reporting entity to enter into a new reinsurance contract with the reinsurer or an affiliate of the reinsurer

   (3) Aggregate stop loss reinsurance coverage

   (4) An unconditional or unilateral right by either party to commute the reinsurance contract, except for such provisions that are only triggered by a decline in the credit status of the other party

Reinsurance 331

- (5) A provision permitting reporting of losses or payment of losses less frequently than on a quarterly basis, unless no activity occurs during the period
- (6) Payment schedule, accumulating retentions from multiple years, or any features inherently designed to delay the timing of the reimbursement to the ceding entity

j. If the reporting entity, during the period covered by the statement, ceded any risk under any reinsurance contract or multiple contracts with the same reinsurer or its affiliates, excluding cessions to approved pooling arrangements or captive insurance companies that are directly or indirectly controlling, controlled by, or under common control with

  i. one or more unaffiliated policyholders of the reporting entity or

  ii. an association of which one or more unaffiliated policyholders of the reporting entity is a member, when

    (1) the written premium ceded to the reinsurer by the reporting entity or its affiliates represents 50 percent or more of the entire direct and assumed premium written by the reinsurer based on its most recently available financial statement.

    (2) 25 percent or more of the written premium ceded to the reinsurer has been retroceded back to the reporting entity or its affiliates

k. If affirmative disclosure is required for paragraph 6.79*i–j*, provide the following information:

  i. A summary of the reinsurance contract terms, and indicate whether it applies to the contracts meeting paragraph 6.79*i–j*

  ii. A brief discussion of management's principal objectives in entering into the reinsurance contract, including the economic purposes to be achieved

  iii. The aggregate financial statement impact, gross of all such ceded reinsurance contracts on the balance sheet and statement of income

l. Except for transactions meeting the requirements of paragraph 30 of SSAP No. 62R, disclose if the reporting entity ceded any risk under any reinsurance contract or multiple contracts with the same reinsurer or its affiliates during the period covered by the financial statement and either

  i. accounted for that contract as prospective or retroactive reinsurance under SAP and as a deposit under GAAP or

  ii. accounted for that contract as reinsurance under GAAP and as a deposit under SAP.

m. If affirmative disclosure is required for paragraph 6.79*l*, explain in a supplemental filing why the contract(s) is treated differently for GAAP and SAP.

AAG-PLI 6.79

Property and Liability Insurance Entities

    n. The financial statements shall disclose the following with respect to reinsurance agreements that have been accounted for as deposits:

        i. A description of the reinsurance agreements.

        ii. Any adjustment of the amounts initially recognized for expected recoveries. The individual components of the adjustment (for example, interest accrual, change due to a change in estimated or actual cash flow, and so on) shall be disclosed separately.

6.80 SSAP No. 63 includes the following disclosure requirements:

that if a reporting entity is part of a group of affiliated entities which utilizes a pooling arrangement under which the pool participants cede substantially all of their direct and assumed business to the pool, the financial statements shall include the following:

    a. A description of the basic terms of the arrangement and the related accounting

    b. Identification of the lead entity and of all affiliated entities participating in the intercompany pool (include NAIC Company Codes) and indication of their respective percentage shares of the pooled business

    c. Description of the lines and types of business subject to the pooling agreement

    d. Description of cessions to nonaffiliated reinsurers of business subject to the pooling agreement, and indication of whether such cessions were prior to or subsequent to the cession of pooled business from the affiliated pool members to the lead entity

    e. Identification of all pool members that are parties to reinsurance agreements with nonaffiliated reinsurers covering business subject to the pooling agreement and which have a contractual right of direct recovery from the nonaffiliated reinsurer per the terms of such reinsurance agreements

    f. Explanation of any discrepancies between entries regarding pooled business on the assumed and ceded reinsurance schedules of the lead entity and corresponding entries on the assumed and ceded reinsurance schedules of other pool participants

    g. Description of intercompany sharing, if other than in accordance with the pool participation percentage, of the Provision for Overdue Reinsurance (Schedule F Part 7) and the write off of uncollectible reinsurance

    h. Amounts due to/from the lead entity and all affiliated entities participating in the intercompany pool as of the balance sheet date

6.81 Refer to the preamble of the NAIC *Accounting Practices and Procedures Manual* for further discussion regarding disclosure requirements. The NAIC has adopted a supplemental filing requiring the CEO and CFO to separately attest to the appropriateness of the accounting procedures applied to the entity's ceded reinsurance arrangements.

Special Risk Considerations

6.82 As noted in paragraphs 6.25–.33, the consideration about whether a reinsurance contract contains sufficient transfer of insurance risk is a complex matter that determines which among the potentially very different accounting models should be used to account for a given treaty. As such, it is important for financial statement preparers to develop and document a risk transfer analysis for reinsurance treaties when the significance of risk transfer is not otherwise apparent.

6.83 As mentioned in paragraphs 6.13 and 6.19, the reinsurance market continues to evolve, with structures such as sidecars, transformers, and other special purpose vehicles being introduced to the marketplace. It is important for financial statement preparers to thoroughly understand both the legal form and substance of these structures and to read the related contracts to ensure that the accounting treatment and related disclosures are appropriate. In addition to the reinsurance accounting considerations previously discussed in this chapter (for example, risk transfer), financial statement preparers and auditors should be mindful of additional considerations, including, but not limited to, the potential for consolidation or equity method accounting under FASB ASC 810, the existence of any embedded derivatives, and the possibility of the existence of related party transactions. Entities should generally be considered the primary beneficiary of the sidecar, if the sidecar is determined to be a VIE, and to have a controlling financial interest if the entity has both the power to direct the activities that most significantly affect the entity's economic performance and the obligation to absorb losses of the entity that could potentially be significant to the VIE or the right to receive benefits from the entity that could potentially be significant to the VIE.

6.84 Reinsurance contracts can be complex documents. In an indemnity reinsurance contract, a ceding entity does not discharge its obligations to the insureds through reinsurance but only obtains the right to reimbursement from the reinsurer. Therefore, the ceding entity faces the risk that the reinsurer may not have the financial capacity or stability to meet its obligations when they are due. An absence of an adequate reinsurance program may expose an insurance entity (the ceding entity) to substantial risks in relation to the entity's financial position, particularly if the entity's risks are concentrated geographically or by type of risk. Also, a lack of sufficient experience to manage and underwrite assumed reinsurance may expose the reinsurer to substantial risks in relation to the entity's financial position.

6.85 When a reinsurer assumes reinsurance, special consideration should be given to the accuracy and reliability of the data received from the ceding entity either directly or through a reinsurance intermediary. The extent of the detail in the information provided to the reinsurer by the ceding entity or reinsurance intermediary can vary significantly in

- the timeliness of the information submitted.
- the detail of information relating to policies, claims, unearned premiums, and loss reserves.
- the annual statement line-of-business classification.
- foreign currency translation information on business assumed from companies domiciled in foreign countries (alien companies).

6.86 Information on IBNR claims and bulk reserves may also be reported by ceding companies under pro rata reinsurance arrangements. Generally, no

IBNR is reported on nonproportional (that is, excess reinsurance) arrangements. Based on the quality and comprehensiveness of the information received from the ceding entity, the information provided may need to be supplemented by the reinsurer.

Auditing Reinsurance

Audit Planning

6.87 In accordance with AU-C section 300, *Planning an Audit* (AICPA, *Professional Standards*), the auditor should plan the audit so that it is responsive to the assessment of the risks of material misstatement based on the auditor's understanding of the entity and its environment, including its internal control. The nature, timing, and extent of planning vary with the size and complexity of the entity, and with the auditor's experience with the entity and understanding of the entity. Refer to chapter 2, "Audit Considerations," for a detailed discussion of audit planning.

Consideration of Fraud in a Financial Statement Audit

6.88 Risks are inherent in all audit engagements, including the possibility that fraudulent acts may cause a material misstatement of financial statements. AU-C section 240, *Consideration of Fraud in a Financial Statement Audit* (AICPA, *Professional Standards*), addresses the auditor's responsibilities relating to fraud in an audit of financial statements. Because of the characteristics of fraud, the auditor's exercise of professional skepticism is important when considering the risk of material misstatement due to fraud. Readers should refer to additional discussion of AU-C section 240 in chapter 2 of this guide.

Audit Risk Factors—Reinsurance

6.89 As discussed in paragraph .A1 of AU-C section 320, *Materiality in Planning and Performing an Audit* (AICPA, Professional Standards), *audit risk* is the risk that the auditor expresses an inappropriate audit opinion when the financial statements are materially misstated. Audit risk is a function of the risks of material misstatement and detection risk. Materiality and audit risk are considered throughout the audit, in particular, when

    a. determining the nature and extent of risk assessment procedures to be performed;

    b. identifying and assessing the risks of material misstatement;

    c. determining the nature, timing, and extent of further audit procedures; and

    d. evaluating the effect of uncorrected misstatements, if any, on the financial statements and in forming the opinion in the auditor's report.

6.90 Experience has demonstrated that audit risk may be greater in certain areas than in others. Significant transaction cycles of property and liability insurance entities include the premium cycle, the claims cycle, the reinsurance cycle, and the investment cycle. Risk factors specific to the reinsurance cycle include the appropriateness of the determination of risk transfer, the completeness and accuracy of the computation of reinsurance recoverables, and the valuation of reinsurance recoverables. These risk factors, internal control considerations, and examples of audit procedures for the insurance entity are discussed further herein.

6.91 Identification of significant accounts and disclosures by the auditor is part of the planning process. As required by AU-C section 315, *Understanding the Entity and Its Environment and Assessing the Risks of Material Misstatement* (AICPA, *Professional Standards*), to enable the auditor to understand the classes of transactions, account balances, and disclosures to be expected in the financial statements, the auditor should obtain an understanding of the relevant industry, regulatory, and other external factors, including the applicable financial reporting framework, and the nature of the entity. Significant disclosures for the reinsurance cycle for GAAP and SAP include details, methodologies, and amounts of reinsurance assumed and ceded, as well as amounts accounted for as deposits (as described in paragraphs 6.71–.75 and 6.79–.81).

Risk of Material Misstatement—Inherent Risk

6.92 As discussed in AU-C section 330, *Performing Audit Procedures in Response to Assessed Risks and Evaluating the Audit Evidence Obtained* (AICPA, *Professional Standards*), inherent risk is the likelihood of material misstatement due to the particular characteristics of the relevant class of transactions, account balance, or disclosure. As part of the auditor's assessment of inherent risks, the auditor may consider those factors related to reinsurance, including factors relating to management, product characteristics, underwriting approach, marketing strategies, financial objectives, and the economic and regulatory environment. Such factors might encompass the following:

    a. The property and liability insurance entity is involved in a significant amount of international reinsurance, or reinsurers are in jurisdictions with foreign exchange controls

    b. The ceding entity's reinsurers are in financial difficulty

    c. Reinsurance has become unavailable at the property and liability insurance entity's desired retention levels and costs

    d. There are significant or unexpected changes in the entity's reinsurance programs

    e. Risk assumed under treaty arrangements is excessive

    f. Financial information is inadequate or is not received on a timely basis

    g. Regulations may not permit the treatment of certain reinsurance agreements as reinsurance

    h. Significant reinsurance agreements involve wholly owned subsidiaries or other related parties

Internal Control

6.93 Paragraph .04 of AU-C section 315 defines internal control as

> a process effected by those charged with governance, management, and other personnel that is designed to provide reasonable assurance about the achievement of the entity's objectives with regard to the

reliability of financial reporting, effectiveness and efficiency of operations, and compliance with applicable laws and regulations. Internal control over safeguarding of assets against unauthorized acquisition, use, or disposition may include controls relating to financial reporting and operations objectives.

Internal control consists of the following five interrelated components:

a. Control environment

b. The entity's risk assessment process

c. The information system, including the related business processes relevant to financial reporting and communication

d. Control activities relevant to the audit

e. Monitoring of controls

6.94 AU-C section 315 requires the auditor to obtain an understanding of these components of the entity's internal control. Paragraphs 2.31–.41 of chapter 2 of this guide discuss in detail the components of internal control. This section will discuss certain components of a property and liability insurance entity's internal control as they relate to reinsurance.

Control Environment

6.95 The control environment comprises the collective effect of various factors on establishing, enhancing, or mitigating the effectiveness of specific control policies or procedures on the operations of the entity. As related to the reinsurance transactions of a property and liability insurance entity, potential deficiencies in the control environment may include the following:

- The entity uses complex reinsurance transactions at or near the end of the period to achieve financial performance goals or improve its surplus position
- Significant reinsurance agreements involve wholly owned subsidiaries or other related parties
- The entity is involved in a significant amount of international reinsurance or reinsurers are in jurisdictions with foreign exchange controls
- Reinsurance arrangements are overly and unnecessarily complex
- Reinsurance coverage is inadequate (it does not meet the business need or reflect management's intended reinsurance program)
- Reinsurance has become unavailable at the ceding entity's desired retention levels and costs
- Significant or unexpected changes exist in the entity's reinsurance programs
- Risk assumed under treaty arrangements is excessive

Risk Assessment Process

6.96 As discussed in paragraphs .16–.18 of AU-C section 315, the auditor should obtain an understanding of whether the entity has a process for

a. identifying business risks relevant to financial reporting objectives;

b. estimating the significance of the risks;

Reinsurance

c. assessing the likelihood of their occurrence; and

d. deciding about actions to address those risks.

6.97 The auditor should obtain an understanding of the entity's risk assessment process related to reinsurance and the results thereof. If the entity has not established such a process or has an ad hoc process, the auditor should discuss with management whether business risks relevant to financial reporting objectives have been identified and how they have been addressed. The auditor should evaluate whether the absence of a documented risk assessment process is appropriate in the circumstances or determine whether it represents a significant deficiency or material weakness in the entity's internal control.

Information and Communication

6.98 As required by paragraph .19 of AU-C section 315, the auditor should obtain an understanding of the information system, including the related business processes relevant to financial reporting. This would include obtaining an understanding of the reinsurance process and assessing the information system. Reinsurance arrangements are contingent on many other functional areas of the entity and may involve information from multiple IT systems including premiums and claims.

6.99 Pertinent financial information must be identified, captured, and communicated in a form and time frame that enables people to carry out their responsibilities. The information system relevant to financial reporting objectives, which includes the accounting system, consists of the procedures and records established to initiate, authorize, record, process, and report entity transactions and to maintain accountability for the related assets, liabilities, and equity. The transaction flow of accounting records for reinsurance transactions usually encompasses all functions relating to underwriting, premium collection, commission processing, and claims payments. In addition, the accounting records should reflect the following:

- Evaluation and documentation of risk transfer that support the accounting treatment selected
- Evaluation of contractual features with accounting implications
- Timely and accurate accounting for adjustable features
- Appropriate methodology for the projection of reinsurance receivables
- Evaluation of collectability of reinsurance balances
- Adequate and timely valuation of collateral
- Appropriate review and consideration of disclosure requirements

Control Activities

6.100 Control activities are the policies and procedures that help ensure that management's directives are carried out and that necessary actions are taken to address risks to achieve the entity's objectives. The auditors should gain an understanding of those control activities the auditor deems necessary to assess the risks of material misstatement at the assertion level and design further audit procedures responsive to assessed risks. The following are examples of typical control activities relating to reinsurance transactions:

- *Proper authorization of transactions and activities.* Written guidelines for reinsurance transactions are in place, assigning appropriate responsibility for approval.
- *Segregation of duties.* Reinsurance transactions, claims processing, premium collection, key information systems functions, and general accounting activities should be appropriately segregated, and independent reviews should be conducted of the work performed.
- *Design of adequate control over documents and records.* Procedures ensure that fictitious or duplicate reinsurance transactions are not included in the records and prevent or detect the omission of valid transactions.
- *Adequate safeguards of access to, and use of, assets and accounting records.* Data files and production programs have adequate safeguards against unauthorized access, and adequate safeguards exist over access to any collateral from the reinsurer that may be held by the ceding entity.
- *Independent checks on performance.* Recorded insurance transactions are subject to independent testing or other quality control checks. Reinsurance ceded transactions are periodically confirmed directly with the reinsurer. Reviews are performed to determine that reinsurance transactions are valid and supported by appropriate documentation, as required by the reinsurance agreement.

Audit Procedures Responsive to the Assessed Risks of Material Misstatement

6.101 Planning activities include determining the relevant assertions related to the significant accounts identified, determining the audit objectives, assessing inherent risk of error of other significant risks (for example, nonroutine transactions or risk of fraud), and planning the involvement of others. As required by AU-C section 330, the auditor should design and perform further audit procedures whose nature, timing, and extent are based on, and are responsive to, the assessed risks of material misstatement at the relevant assertion level. The auditor should determine planned reliance on controls and the nature, timing, and extent of substantive testing, including whether the substantive evidence is planned from tests of details or substantive analytics.

6.102 If the auditor identifies a significant risk and is only performing substantive procedures, those procedures should include a test of details. If procedures to respond to the significant risk include both a test of controls and substantive procedures and substantive procedures, the auditor may select substantive analytical procedures if the controls are operating effectively.

Considerations for Audits Performed in Accordance With PCAOB Standards

For audits performed in accordance with the PCAOB auditing standards, for significant risks, paragraph 11 of Auditing Standard No. 13, *The Auditor's Responses to the Risks of Material Misstatement* (AICPA, *PCAOB Standards and Related Rules*, Auditing Standards), states the auditor should perform substantive procedures, including tests of details, that are specifically responsive to the assessed risks.

Internal Control of the Ceding Entity

6.103 A ceding entity should have controls or control procedures in place for (*a*) evaluating the financial responsibility and stability of the reinsurer and (*b*) providing accurate and timely information to the reinsurer. The ceding entity's control activities to evaluate the financial responsibility and stability of the reinsurer may include the following:

- Obtaining and analyzing recent financial information of the reinsurer, such as the following:
    — Financial statements and, if audited, the independent auditor's report
    — Financial reports filed with the Securities and Exchange Commission (SEC) (United States), Financial Services Authority (United Kingdom), or similar authorities in other countries
    — Financial statements filed with insurance regulatory authorities, with particular consideration of capital adequacy, quality, and liquidity of the entity's invested assets and loss reserve development
- Obtaining and reviewing available sources of information relating to the reinsurer, such as the following:
    — Insurance industry reporting and rating services, such as A.M. Best Company, Moody's, or Standard & Poor's
    — Insurance department examination reports
    — Loss reserve certifications filed with regulatory authorities
    — Letters relating to the design and operation of controls filed with regulatory authorities, such as the following:
        - Insurance Regulatory Information System and RBC results filed with regulatory authorities
        - All other publicly available documentation
- Inquiring about the reinsurer's retrocessional practices and experience
- Inquiring about the general business reputation of the reinsurer and background of its owners and management
- Ascertaining whether the reinsurer is authorized to transact reinsurance within the ceding entity's state of domicile or, if not, whether letters of credit or other means of security are provided
- Considering the need for, and evaluating the adequacy of, collateral from the reinsurer on collateralized reinsurance contracts

6.104 The ceding entity's control activities relating to the accuracy and timeliness of information reported to the assuming entity are generally similar in nature to other control activities for the recording of direct insurance transactions.

Internal Control of the Reinsurer

6.105 A significant component of a reinsurer's internal control that is related to reinsurance is the assessment of the accuracy and reliability of data received from the ceding companies. Principal control activities of the reinsurer may include the following:

- Maintaining underwriting files with information relating to the business reasons for entering into the reinsurance contracts and anticipated results of the contracts. The underwriting files may include the following:
  — Historical loss ratios and combined ratios of the ceding companies
  — Anticipated loss ratios under the contracts
  — Indications of the frequency and content of reports for the ceding companies
  — Prior business experience with the ceding companies
  — The assuming entity's experience on similar risks
  — Information regarding pricing and ceding commissions
- Monitoring the actual results reported by the ceding companies and investigating the reasons for, and effects of, significant deviations from anticipated results
- Visiting the ceding companies to review and evaluate their underwriting, claims processing, loss reserving, and loss reserve development-monitoring procedures
- Evaluating the experience and knowledge of the ceding companies' underwriting and claim staff
- Performing audits of claims at the ceding company and reviewing internal controls over the adjudication and processing of claims at the ceding company, including a review of any "SAS No. 70" reports (which was superseded by SSAE No. 16, *Reporting on Controls at a Service Organization* [AICPA, *Professional Standards*, AT sec. 801]) or similar reports on internal controls over the adjudication, and processing of claims at the ceding company

6.106 Additional control activities of the reinsurer may include the following:
- Obtaining and analyzing recent financial information of the ceding companies, such as the following:
  — Financial statements and, if audited, the independent auditor's report
  — Financial reports filed with the SEC (United States), Financial Services Authority (United Kingdom), or similar authorities in other countries
  — Financial statements filed with insurance regulatory authorities, with particular attention to loss reserve development
- Obtaining and reviewing available sources of information on the ceding companies, such as the following:
  — Insurance industry reporting and rating services, such as A.M. Best Company, Moody's, and Standard & Poor's
  — Insurance department examination reports
  — Loss reserve certifications filed with regulatory authorities
  — Letters relating to the design and operation of controls filed with regulatory authorities

- Inquiries about the general business reputation of the ceding companies and background of their owners and management

Auditing Procedures for the Ceding Entity

6.107 The ceding entity's independent auditor would generally evaluate the reinsurer's ability to honor its commitments under the reinsurance contract. Chapter 2 and chapter 4, "The Loss Reserving and Claims Cycle," of this guide discuss how the auditor assesses control risk.

6.108 The absence of adequate procedures by the ceding entity to determine the assuming entity's ability to honor its contractual commitments, or the failure to apply adequately designed procedures as planned, may constitute a significant deficiency or material weakness in the ceding entity's internal control. AU-C section 265, *Communicating Internal Control Related Matters Identified in an Audit* (AICPA, *Professional Standards*), discusses the auditor's responsibility for communication of a significant deficiency or material weakness in internal control to those charged with governance. Based on his or her assessment of the risks of material misstatement, the auditor may consider performing substantive procedures sufficient to evaluate the collectability of amounts reported in the financial statements as recoverable from the assuming entity. Regardless of the assessed risks of material misstatement, the auditor should design and perform substantive procedures for all relevant assertions related to each material class of transactions, account balance, and disclosure.[3]

> *Considerations for Audits Performed in Accordance With PCAOB Standards*
>
> For an audit of financial statements only, conducted in accordance with PCAOB standards, refer to AU section 325, *Communications About Control Deficiencies in an Audit of Financial Statements* (AICPA, *PCAOB Standards and Related Rules*, Interim Standards). For an integrated audit, refer to paragraphs 78–84 of PCAOB Auditing Standard No. 5, *An Audit of Internal Control Over Financial Reporting That Is Integrated with An Audit of Financial Statements* (AICPA, *PCAOB Standards and Related Rules*, Auditing Standards).

6.109 To obtain reasonable assurance about whether reinsurance contracts are appropriately accounted for, the independent auditor of the ceding entity might consider performing procedures for selected contracts, selected transactions, and related balances, including

- reading the reinsurance contract and related correspondence to
  - obtain an understanding of the business objective of the reinsurance contract.
  - determine whether the contract indemnifies the ceding entity against loss or liability and meets the conditions for reinsurance accounting, or whether it should be accounted for under deposit accounting, as defined in FASB ASC 340-30.
- reviewing other contracts and transactions with the reinsurer that may limit risk transfer.

---

[3] For audits performed in accordance with PCAOB standards, the sentence reads, "Regardless of the assessed level of control risk *or the assessed risk of material misstatement in connection with the audit of the financial statements*, the auditor should perform substantive procedures for all relevant assertions for all significant accounts and disclosures."

- reviewing ceded losses to determine whether losses are being properly ceded in accordance with the terms of the reinsurance contract.
- reviewing entries arising from selected reinsurance contracts to determine whether the appropriate accounting treatment has been properly applied.
- tracing selected transactions to supporting documents and testing the related receivables and payables.
- obtaining written confirmation of selected balances. In certain circumstances, confirmation of contract terms may be appropriate.

Auditing Procedures for the Assuming Entity

6.110 An assuming entity's independent auditor may obtain an understanding of the assuming entity's procedures for assessing the accuracy and reliability of data received from the ceding entities.

Considerations for Audits Performed in Accordance With PCAOB Standards

When performing an audit in accordance with PCAOB standards, paragraphs 32–34 of Auditing Standard No. 13 provide guidance on assessing control risk.

6.111 The absence of adequate procedures by the assuming entity to provide assurance regarding the accuracy and reliability of data received from the ceding entity, or not applying adequately designed procedures that are in use and operating as prescribed, may constitute a significant deficiency or material weakness in the assuming entity's internal control. Based on his or her assessment of the risks of material misstatement, the auditor should perform substantive procedures sufficient to obtain assurance regarding the accuracy and reliability of the data received from the ceding entities. The auditor's substantive procedures may include, but would not necessarily be limited to, one or more of the following:

- Reviewing the work of the ceding entities' independent auditors (see AU-C section 600, *Special Considerations—Audits of Group Financial Statements (Including the Work of Component Auditors)* [AICPA, *Professional Standards*]). Additionally for integrated audits, refer to paragraphs C8–C11 of appendix C, "Special Reporting Situations," of PCAOB Auditing Standard No. 5, which provides direction with respect to opinions based, in part, on the report of another auditor.
- Performing auditing procedures at the ceding entities or requesting their independent auditors to perform agreed upon procedures.
- Obtaining reports from the ceding entities' independent auditors on the ceding entities' internal control relating to ceded reinsurance (see AU-C section 402, *Audit Considerations Relating to an Entity Using a Service Organization* [AICPA, *Professional Standards*]). Additionally, when performing an integrated audit of financial statements and internal control over financial reporting, refer to paragraphs B10–B16 of appendix B, "Special Topics," in PCAOB Auditing Standard No. 5 regarding the use of service organizations.

6.112 The auditor's inability to perform the procedures considered necessary, whether as a result of restrictions imposed by the client or by circumstances such as the timing of the work, the inability to obtain sufficient appropriate audit evidence, or an inadequacy in the accounting records, constitutes a scope limitation that may require the auditor to qualify the opinion or disclaim an opinion (see AU-C section 705, *Modifications to the Opinion in the Independent Auditor's Report* [AICPA, *Professional Standards*]). In such circumstances, the reasons for the auditor's qualification of opinion or disclaimer of opinion should be described in the audit report.

6.113 To determine whether reinsurance contracts are appropriately accounted for, the independent auditor of the assuming entity might perform procedures for selected contracts, selected transactions, and related balances, including

- reading the reinsurance contract and related correspondence to
    - obtain an understanding of the business objective of the reinsurance contract.
    - determine whether the contract meets the conditions for reinsurance accounting, or whether it should be accounted for under deposit accounting, as defined in FASB ASC 340-30.
- reviewing other contracts and transactions with the ceding entity which may limit risk transfer.
- reviewing entries arising from selected reinsurance contracts to determine whether the appropriate accounting treatment has been properly applied.
- tracing selected transactions to supporting documents and testing the related receivables and payables.
- obtaining written confirmation of selected balances. In certain circumstances, confirmation of contract terms may be appropriate.

Pools, Associations, and Syndicates

6.114 Participation in reinsurance pools, associations, and syndicates is in some respects similar to reinsurance, and the guidance in paragraphs 6.107–.109 generally applies to audits of participating entities. Pools, associations, and syndicates often issue audited financial statements to participating entities, and auditors of participating entities may use the report of the independent auditor of the pool, association, or syndicate in their audits.

Reinsurance Intermediaries

6.115 Reinsurance intermediaries' involvement may include evaluation, underwriting, negotiations, and fund transfers. The assuming and ceding entities normally coordinate their control activities with those of the intermediaries.

6.116 An entity may delegate to a reinsurance intermediary the performance of the procedures described in the sections "Internal Control of the Ceding Entity," paragraphs 6.105–.106, and "Internal Control of the Reinsurer," paragraphs 6.103–.104. Normally an entity has procedures to satisfy itself that the reinsurance intermediary is adequately performing those procedures. The guidance provided to the independent auditor in those sections may be applied.

6.117 In addition to the functions discussed in the previous paragraphs, a reinsurance intermediary may be authorized to collect, hold, disburse, or remit funds on behalf of an insurance entity. The insurance entity controls normally provide reasonable assurance that the reinsurance intermediary is adequately performing those functions; safeguarding the funds and, if required, appropriately segregating them; and settling accounts on a timely basis. The insurance entity may accomplish this by obtaining a report from the independent auditor of the reinsurance intermediary or by visiting the reinsurance intermediary and reviewing its controls that relate to those functions. The auditor of the insurance entity should assess control risk in this area as described in chapter 4 of this guide.

6.118 The auditor may read the intermediary clauses in an assuming entity's reinsurance contracts.[4] Such clauses, which identify the specific intermediaries or brokers involved in negotiating the contracts, communicating information, and transmitting funds, typically state whether payment to the intermediaries constitutes payment to the other parties to the reinsurance contracts. An example of such a clause, under which the reinsurer assumes the credit risks in the transmission of reinsurance funds, follows:

> _____ is hereby recognized as the intermediary negotiating this contract. All communications (including but not limited to, notices, statements, premiums, return premiums, commissions, taxes, losses, loss adjustment expenses, salvages, and loss settlements) relating thereto shall be transmitted to the ceding company or the reinsurers through _____. Payments by the ceding company to the intermediary shall be deemed to constitute payment to the reinsurers. Payments by the reinsurers to the intermediary shall be deemed to constitute payment to the ceding company only to the extent that such payments are actually received by the ceding company.

Audit Consideration Chart

6.119 The auditor may consider the following specific audit objectives, examples of selected control activities, and auditing procedures in auditing the reinsurance processes of property and liability insurance entities. These are illustrative, however, auditors should develop tests that are appropriate to the risk of material misstatement in the circumstances of the engagement.

---

[4] Refer to "Auditing Procedures for the Ceding Entity" in paragraphs 6.107–.109.

Audit Consideration Chart—Reinsurance Cycle

Financial Statement Assertions	Audit Objectives	Examples of Selected Control Activities	Examples of Auditing Procedures
Existence	• Determine whether reinsurance recoverables are recorded for valid reinsurance contracts. • Determine whether reinsurance contracts are appropriately accounted for.	• Management documents process for determining appropriate accounting for reinsurance contracts. • Segregation of duties and independent review.	• Read reinsurance contracts and determine if the contract meets the requirements for reinsurance accounting or if it should be accounted for under deposit accounting. • Review entries arising from selected reinsurance contracts to determine whether the appropriate accounting treatment has been properly applied. Trace selected transactions to supporting documents. • Obtain written confirmation of selected balances.
Completeness	• Determine whether adjustable features have been properly accounted for.	• Management documents the company's process for periodic review and calculation of adjustable features.	• Review reinsurance contracts for the existence of adjustable features. • Review and test the company's calculation of adjustable features.
Rights and Obligations	• Reinsured policies are properly identified, and premiums on ceded reinsurance are	• Risks covered by reinsurance agreements are identified, properly designated, recorded	• Test whether risks in excess of retention amounts are reinsured.

(*continued*)

Financial Statement Assertions	Audit Objectives	Examples of Selected Control Activities	Examples of Auditing Procedures
	properly recorded and reported to assuming entities.	in the premium billing and in force files, and reported to the assuming entity.	• Test computation of reinsurance premiums and commissions; trace to reinsurance records. • Trace information from premium records to reports sent to reinsurers. • Test the propriety of reinsurance balances payable by reference to reinsurance agreements and policy records.
Valuation or Allocation	• Determine whether reinsurance recoverables are properly valued.	• Monitor the financial stability of reinsurers. • Perform adequate and timely valuation of collateral.	• Test calculation of reinsurance receivables for select reinsurance contracts • Evaluate collectability of reinsurance balances.

Chapter 7
Income Taxes

Introduction

7.01 In general, a property and liability insurance entity is subject to the same federal income tax laws that apply to other commercial enterprises. However, additional sections of the Internal Revenue Code (IRC) and related Treasury regulations apply specifically to property and liability insurers. IRC Sections 831–832 apply to all property and liability insurance entities.

7.02 This chapter is intended to familiarize the reader with significant and unique features of property and liability insurance taxation, including the provisions of the Tax Reform Act of 1986, the Omnibus Budget Reconciliation Act of 1990, and the Pension Funding Equity Act of 2004, as well as generally accepted accounting principles (GAAP) and statutory accounting requirements for federal and state income taxation. This chapter also highlights significant tax differences for financial guarantee or title insurance entities. Premium taxes and assessments are addressed in chapter 8, "Insurance-Related Expenses, Taxes, and Assessments," of this guide.

Federal Income Taxation

7.03 IRC Section 816(a)(2) defines an *insurance company* as any company for which "more than half of the business ... during the taxable year is the issuing of insurance or annuity contracts or the reinsuring of risks underwritten by insurance companies." The definition is based on the company's primary and predominant business activity (that is, other pursuits, such as investment activities, cannot outweigh insurance activities). Prior to the provisions of the Pension Funding Equity Act of 2004, this definition specifically applied to life insurance entities. The provisions of the Pension Funding Equity Act of 2004 created a uniform definition of an insurance company by amending IRC Section 831 to include the definition stated in IRC Section 816(a)(2). This specified definition of a property casualty insurance company may affect property casualty insurance entities that have substantial amounts of investment income relative to their insurance income.

7.04 Insurance entities that have less than $600,000 of gross receipts, of which more than 50 percent are premiums, may elect to be treated as tax exempt entities. The entity is required to convert to a taxable status once it exceeds $600,000 in gross receipts or if less than $600,000 in gross receipts with less than 50 percent of such gross receipts consists of premium.

Statutory Accounting Practices and Taxable Income

7.05 A property and liability insurance entity's taxable income is largely based on its statutory financial statements. The underwriting and investment exhibit of the annual statement approved by the National Association of Insurance Commissioners is accepted by the IRS as the net income of the entity, and insofar as it is not inconsistent with the provisions of the IRC, the exhibit is recognized and used as a basis for determining the gross amount earned from investment and underwriting income for tax purposes.

AAG-PLI 7.05

7.06 Several other similarities and differences exist between statutory and taxable income. First, commissions, premium taxes, and other costs of acquiring new business are fully deductible for tax purposes in the year that they are incurred. However, for example, using 80 percent of the unearned premium reserves to determine earned premiums for tax purposes (see paragraph 7.13) provides an offset. Second, incurred losses reported within the statutory financial statement are reduced by the use of discounted loss reserves for tax (see paragraphs 7.08–.12). Third, direct charges or credits to statutory surplus are generally not included in determining taxable income. They include premiums past due from agents, unless they are bona fide bad debts currently chargeable to statutory expense, and the provision for unauthorized reinsurance.

7.07 Although most of the accounting practices for determining taxable income, as prescribed by the IRC, follow statutory accounting practices (SAP), some items are always excluded from, or deductible in, computing taxable income, such as tax exempt interest received on certain bonds and the dividends received deduction (DRD). The IRC and regulations of the IRS also differ from statutory practices in certain respects for policyholder dividends and deposit premiums.

Special Income Tax Provisions

7.08 Unpaid losses, including loss adjustment expenses, of a property and liability insurance entity are subject to discounting for tax purposes, as referenced in IRC Sections 832(b)(5) and 846. As a result, the deduction for unpaid losses is limited to the increase in the amount of discounted unpaid losses. The amount of discounted unpaid losses is computed annually with respect to unpaid losses in each line of business (as contained in Schedule P of the annual statement) for each accident year. The discount periods are generally 3 years for property lines and 10 years for liability lines of business.

7.09 Discounting methodology is specified in the IRC. The amount of the discounted unpaid losses is the present value of such losses determined by using (*a*) the undiscounted loss reserves; (*b*) an applicable rate of interest; and (*c*) the pattern of the payment of claims, as referenced in IRC Section 846(a)(2).

7.10 Generally, the amount of the undiscounted unpaid losses subject to discounting is that shown in the annual statement. However, in some cases, reserves, such as workers' compensation, are already discounted for annual statement purposes. The Tax Reform Act of 1986 requires that these reserves be grossed up, as referenced in IRC Section 846(a)(3), and that an undiscounted loss reserve be calculated. The undiscounted amount of the loss reserve is used as the amount of unpaid losses to which the discounting rules are applied. Insurance entities are permitted to gross up these discounted loss reserves for tax purposes only if the discounting for annual statement purposes can be determined based on information disclosed in or with the annual statement. In addition, tax reserves cannot exceed annual statement reserves due to differing discount rates.

7.11 The interest rate to use in calculating the discounted reserve is an annual rate determined by the Secretary of the Treasury, as referenced in IRC Sections 846(a)(4)(A) and 1274(d). The annual rate for any calendar year is a rate equal to 100 percent of the average of the applicable federal midterm rates effective at the beginning of each of the calendar months in the test period. The *test period* is the most recent five year period ending before the beginning of the year for which the determination is made. Once an interest rate assumption is established for unpaid losses in a particular accident year, it continues to be used without change as claims for the accident year are paid.

7.12 The applicable loss-payment pattern is determined by the secretary of the Treasury for each line of business by reference to the historical loss-payment pattern, as referenced in IRC Section 846(a)(4)(B). Generally, the payment patterns are determined every five years based on published historical aggregate loss-payment data or, at the entity's election, each year based on the entity's own historical loss-payment experience. Once a payment pattern has been applied to a particular accident year, it cannot be redetermined to adjust for more recent information. All losses are considered as being paid in the middle of the year. In place of the loss-payment-pattern provisions previously described, an insurance entity can make an irrevocable election to utilize its own historical loss-payment pattern (for example, the most recent experience as reported in its annual statement) in applying the general loss discounting rules for a taxable year. The election is made for all lines of business for any determination year and applies for that determination year and the four succeeding calendar years. The *determination year* is defined as being calendar year 1987 and each 5th succeeding calendar year thereafter (1987, 1992, 1997, and so on). No election is permitted for any international or reinsurance line of business.

7.13 Historically, the unearned premium reserve, as defined in IRC Section 816(b), was not adjusted for purposes of income tax, but the Tax Reform Act of 1986 changed that because it was believed that allowing both a deferral of unearned premiums and a current deduction of the corresponding policy acquisition costs resulted in a significant mismatching of income and expenses. The Tax Reform Act of 1986 permits only 80 percent of the annual change in the unearned premium reserve to be used in determining taxable income for most lines of business, as referenced in IRC Section 832(b)(4)(B). For certain financial guarantee businesses, the limitation is 90 percent of the annual change in the unearned premium reserve is to be used in determining taxable income, as required by IRC Section 832(b)(7)(B). Congress deemed that the 20 percent not taken into account approximates policy acquisition costs. For example, in 1987, if an insurance entity's unearned premium reserve increased from $50,000 to $60,000, the net deduction for unearned premiums would be $8,000 ($60,000 less $50,000 multiplied by 80 percent). Similarly, if the unearned premium reserve decreased in 1988 from $60,000 to $40,000, the insurance entity would be required to include $16,000 (rather than $20,000, as under prior law) in determining taxable income.

7.14 For title insurance entities, no unearned premium reserve adjustment exists, but a portion of written premiums is deferred into a statutory premium reserve, similar to an incurred but not reported reserve. For tax purposes, the statutory premium reserve is combined with another reserve, the known loss reserve, and they are treated as loss reserves, as discussed starting in paragraph 7.08, and discounted to determine the deduction for unpaid losses. The amount of written premium deferred depends on the state of domicile and is based on the amount of coverage provided, not the amount of premium written; the amount is generally 4 percent to 5 percent of written premiums. The amounts deferred into the statutory premium reserve are then amortized into earned premiums over 20 years on an accelerated basis.

7.15 The Tax Reform Act of 1986 requires a property and liability insurance entity to prorate a specified portion of its investment income by reducing the deduction for losses incurred by 15 percent of its tax exempt interest income and the deductible portion of dividends received. Dividends received from affiliates that are eligible for the 100 percent DRD are also subject to proration if such dividends are funded by tax exempt interest income or dividends not eligible for the 100 percent DRD.

7.16 Among other matters, the Pension Funding Equity Act of 2004 changed certain provisions of the tax code defining tax exempt status. For entities other than mutual property and casualty entities, annual gross receipts, determined on a controlled group basis, must not exceed $600,000, and premiums received must be greater than 50 percent of gross receipts. This premium requirement determines that nonpremium (for example, investment) income must be $300,000 or less. For a mutual property and casualty entity, annual gross receipts must not exceed $150,000, and annual premiums must be greater than 35 percent of gross receipts, provided that certain requirements are met.[1]

7.17 The Tax Reform Act of 1986 enacted a provision that allows both mutual and stock property and liability entities to elect to be taxed only on investment income under certain conditions. The Pension Funding Equity Act of 2004 eliminated a $350,000 floor such that the election is available if net written premiums do not exceed $1.2 million. Additionally, the Pension Funding Equity Act of 2004 changed the definition of a control group by adding the requirement to include the receipts of foreign and tax exempt corporations in the control group.

7.18 IRC Section 832(c)(5) treats the deductions for capital losses of property and liability insurers differently from those of other corporate taxpayers in certain unusual circumstances. Property and liability insurers may claim ordinary deductions for capital losses, although this would be a very unique event, resulting from the sale or exchange of capital assets in order to obtain funds to meet abnormal insurance losses and provide for the payment of dividends and similar distributions to policyholders. Insurance entities use a prescribed calculation to determine whether securities were sold to meet abnormal losses. Capital losses are ordinary deductions to the extent that gross receipts from assets sold do not exceed the excess of cash-basis income over cash-basis expense.

7.19 Policyholder dividends may be deducted on the date declared; the date payable; or the date paid, as long as the chosen method is consistently followed.

7.20 The Tax Reform Act of 1986 repealed the corporate add on minimum tax and replaced it with an alternative minimum tax (AMT). As of 1990, adjusted current earnings (ACE) are used for calculating the AMT. ACE is equal to taxable income plus a number of adjustments and preferences. The most significant for property and casualty entities will be the inclusion of the untaxed portion of tax exempt interest and the DRD applicable to portfolio stocks (70 percent of DRD).

State Taxation

7.21 Some states tax income in addition to, or in place of, premium tax of property and liability insurance entities. The computation of state taxable

---

[1] The requirements are that no employee of the company or member of the employee's family is an employee of any other company that is exempt from tax under Internal Revenue Code Section 501(C)(15). The receipt and employee limitation for mutual entities is intended to address the inappropriate use of tax exempt insurance entities sheltering investment income.

income is generally based on federal taxable income, with certain modifications. Many states apply different tax rates to different lines of insurance and differentiate between domestic insurers and foreign insurers, and taxation methods and tax rates can vary widely among states. The GAAP accounting guidance in Financial Accounting Standards Board (FASB) *Accounting Standards Codification* (ASC) 740, *Income Taxes*, applies to state taxes based on income, as well as federal income taxes.

7.22 Apportionment and allocation of income by multistate entities are important considerations when accruing for such taxes. The prior year apportionment percentage may be indicative of the current year for computing the accrual. Significant changes in the places in which the entity does business, however, can affect apportionment. See the discussion on premium and state taxes in chapter 8 of this guide.

GAAP Accounting for Income Taxes

7.23 The primary literature for GAAP accounting for income taxes is FASB ASC 740. This section discusses some of the significant accounting found in FASB ASC 740, but readers should refer to FASB ASC 740 for complete guidance.

7.24 FASB ASC 740 prescribes an asset and a liability method of accounting for income taxes. Under the asset and liability method, the emphasis in accounting for income taxes is on the balance sheet rather than the income statement. The asset and liability method accounts for deferred income taxes by applying enacted statutory tax rates in effect at the balance sheet date to the temporary differences between the recorded financial statement balances and the related tax bases of assets and liabilities under GAAP, computed pursuant to FASB ASC 740. The resulting deferred tax liabilities and assets are adjusted to reflect changes in tax laws and rates in the period of enactment.

Basic Principles of GAAP Accounting for Income Taxes

7.25 Under GAAP, FASB ASC 740-10-25-2 states that a tax liability or asset is recognized based on the provisions of FASB ASC 740 for the estimated taxes payable or refundable on tax returns for the current year and prior years, and a deferred tax liability or asset should be recognized for the estimated future tax effects attributable to temporary differences and carryforwards.

7.26 As discussed in FASB ASC 740-10-25-17, a tax position recognized in the financial statements may also affect the tax bases of assets or liabilities and thereby change or create temporary differences. A *taxable and deductible temporary difference* is a difference between the reported amount of an item in the financial statements and the tax basis of an item as determined by applying the recognition threshold and measurement provisions for tax positions in FASB ASC 740-25.

7.27 Temporary differences that will result in taxable amounts in future years when the related asset or liability is recovered or settled are often referred to as taxable temporary differences. Likewise, temporary differences that will result in deductible amounts in future years are often referred to as deductible temporary differences.

7.28 As noted in FASB ASC 740-10-25-24, some temporary differences are deferred taxable income or tax deductions and have balances only on the income tax balance sheet and therefore cannot be identified with a particular asset or liability for financial reporting. As explained in FASB ASC 740-10-25-26, those temporary differences result from events that (*a*) have been recognized in the financial statements and (*b*) will result in taxable or deductible amounts in future years based on provisions of the tax law.

7.29 Unrealized gains and losses, to the extent that they are related to available-for-sale securities, are considered temporary differences for which deferred taxes computed under FASB ASC 740's intraperiod tax allocation provisions are measured and recorded through a direct charge or credit to other comprehensive income. The period in which net gains and losses on investment securities are realized is dependent upon management's future investment decisions.

7.30 As discussed in FASB ASC 740-10-30-8, the total deferred tax assets and liabilities are then measured using the enacted tax rate expected to apply to taxable income in the periods in which the deferred tax liability or asset is expected to be settled or realized. Deferred tax assets are measured for each type of temporary difference and carryforward.

7.31 Additionally, under GAAP, it is necessary to determine if a deferred income tax asset (DTA) valuation allowance is needed. DTAs are reduced by a valuation allowance if, based on all available evidence (both positive and negative), it is more likely than not (a likelihood of more than 50 percent) that some portion or all of the tax benefit will not be realized. The weight given to the potential effect of negative and positive evidence should be commensurate with the extent to which it can be objectively verified. The valuation allowance should be sufficient to reduce the DTA to the amount that is more likely than not to be realized.[2]

7.32 As discussed in FASB ASC 740-10-30-18,

> future realization of an existing deductible temporary difference or carryforward ultimately depends on the existence of sufficient future taxable income of the appropriate character (for example, ordinary income or capital gain) within the carryback or carryforward period available under the tax law. The following four possible sources of taxable income may be available under the tax law to realize a tax benefit for deductible temporary differences and carryforwards:
>
> *a.* Future reversals of existing taxable temporary differences
>
> *b.* Future taxable income, exclusive of reversing temporary differences and carryforwards
>
> *c.* Taxable income in prior carryback years if carryback is permitted under the tax law
>
> *d.* Tax planning strategies (see FASB ASC 740-10-30-19) that would, if necessary, be implemented to, for example
>
> > i. accelerate taxable amounts to utilize expiring carryforwards

---

[2] On May 26, 2010, the Financial Accounting Standards Board issued the proposed Accounting Standards Update (ASU) *Accounting for Financial Instruments and Revisions to the Accounting for Derivative Instruments and Hedging Activities—Financial Instruments (Topic 825) and Derivative and Hedging Instruments (Topic 815)*. Readers should be aware that this proposed ASU includes proposed guidance for the evaluation of a valuation allowance on a deferred tax asset related to investments in debt instruments.

Income Taxes

ii. change the character of taxable or deductible amounts from ordinary income or loss to capital gain or loss.

iii. switch from tax exempt to taxable investments

7.33 Evidence available about each of those possible sources of taxable income will vary for different tax jurisdictions and, possibly, from year to year. If evidence about one or more sources of taxable income is sufficient to support a conclusion that a valuation allowance is not necessary, other sources need not be considered. Consideration of each source is required, however, to determine the amount of the valuation allowance that is recognized for deferred tax assets.

7.34 As discussed in FASB ASC 740-10-30-19, in some circumstances, there are actions (including elections for tax purposes) that

a. are prudent and feasible.

b. an entity ordinarily might not take, but would take to prevent an operating loss or tax credit carryforward from expiring unused.

c. would result in realization of deferred tax assets.

7.35 FASB ASC 740 refers to those actions as tax planning strategies. An entity shall consider tax planning strategies in determining the amount of valuation allowance required. Significant expenses to implement a tax planning strategy, or any significant losses that would be recognized if that strategy were implemented (net of any recognizable tax benefits associated with those expenses or losses), shall be included in the valuation allowance.

7.36 FASB ASC 740 generally requires that the tax benefit of a loss carryforward be reported as a reduction of income tax expense.

7.37 Organizations adopt many tax positions relative to tax laws, including those adopted in determining whether tax is due, whether a refund is owed, or if a tax return needs to be filed. An entity's tax positions can change over time from a myriad of variables (for example, IRS developments, developments involving state taxing authorities, tax court cases, and so on). When a position is taken in a tax return that reduces the amount of income taxes paid to a taxing authority, the entity realizes an immediate economic benefit. However, considerable time can elapse before the acceptability of that tax position is determined. The guidance in FASB ASC 740 on uncertain tax positions clarifies the accounting for uncertainty in income taxes and requires the affirmative evaluation that it is more likely than not based on the technical merits of a tax position and that an enterprise is entitled to economic benefits resulting from positions taken in income tax returns. If a tax position does not meet the more likely than not recognition threshold, the benefit of that position is not recognized in the financial statements.

7.38 As noted in the FASB ASC glossary, a *tax position* is a position in a previously filed tax return or a position expected to be taken in a future tax return that is reflected in measuring current or deferred income tax assets and liabilities for interim or annual periods. A tax position can result in a permanent reduction of income taxes payable, a deferral of income taxes otherwise currently payable to future years, or a change in the expected realizability of DTAs.

7.39 A tax position could result in or affect the measurement of a current DTA or deferred income tax liability (DTL) in the statement of financial position.

7.40 As discussed in FASB ASC 740-10-55-3, the evaluation of a tax position in accordance with FASB ASC 740 is a two-step process that separates recognition from measurement. The first step is determining whether a tax position has met the recognition threshold; the second step is measuring a tax position that meets the recognition threshold.

7.41 As discussed in paragraphs 6–9 of FASB ASC 740-10-25, the enterprise determines whether it is more likely than not that a tax position will be sustained upon examination, including resolution of any related appeals or litigation processes, based on the technical merits of the position. As described in paragraph 6 of FASB ASC 740-10-25, the term *more likely than not* means a likelihood of more than 50 percent; the terms examined and upon examination also include resolution of the related appeals or litigation processes, if any. In evaluating whether a tax position has met the more likely than not recognition threshold, the enterprise should presume that the position will be examined by the appropriate taxing authority that has full knowledge of all relevant information.

7.42 FASB ASC 740-10-30-7 notes that a tax position that meets the more likely than not recognition threshold shall initially and subsequently be measured as the largest amount of tax benefit that is greater than 50 percent likely of being realized upon settlement with a taxing authority that has full knowledge of all relevant information. Measurement of a tax position that meets the more likely than not recognition threshold shall consider the amounts and probabilities of the outcomes that could be realized upon settlement using the facts, circumstances, and information available at the reporting date.

7.43 Differences between tax positions taken in a tax return and amounts recognized in the financial statements will generally result in one of the following:

    a. An increase in a liability for income taxes payable or a reduction of an income tax refund receivable

    b. A reduction in a DTA or an increase in a DTL

    c. Both *a* and *b*

7.44 As discussed in FASB ASC 740-10-25-8, tax positions that previously failed to meet the more likely than not recognition threshold should be recognized in the first subsequent financial reporting period in which that threshold is met. As discussed in FASB ASC 740-10-40-2, previously recognized tax positions that no longer meet the more likely than not recognition threshold should be derecognized in the first subsequent financial reporting period in which that threshold is no longer met. Use of a valuation allowance, as described under FASB ASC 740, is not an appropriate substitute for the derecognition of a tax position when the more likely than not recognition threshold is no longer met.

7.45 FASB ASC 740-10-25-9 notes that a tax position could be effectively settled upon examination by a taxing authority. Assessing whether a tax position is effectively settled is a matter of judgment because examinations occur in a variety of ways. In determining whether a tax position is effectively settled, an entity should make the assessment on a position-by-position basis, but an entity could conclude that all positions in a particular tax year are effectively settled.

Disclosure Requirements Contained in GAAP Literature

7.46 As discussed in FASB ASC 740-10-50-2, the components of the net DTL or DTA recognized in an entity's statement of financial position shall be disclosed as follows:

a. The total of all DTLs measured in FASB ASC 740-10-30-5(b)

b. The total of all DTAs measured in FASB ASC 740-10-30-5(c)–(d)

c. The total valuation allowance recognized for DTAs determined in FASB ASC 740-10-30-5(e)

7.47 The net change during the year in the total valuation allowance shall also be disclosed.

7.48 As discussed in FASB ASC 740-10-50-3, an entity shall disclose both of the following:

a. The amounts and expiration dates of operating loss and tax credit carryforwards for tax purposes

b. Any portion of the valuation allowance for DTAs for which subsequently recognized tax benefits will be credited directly to contributed capital (see FASB ASC 740-20-45-11)

7.49 As discussed in FASB ASC 740-10-50-4, in the event that a change in an entity's tax status becomes effective after year end in year 2, but before the financial statements for year 1 are issued or available to be issued, as discussed in FASB ASC 855-10-25, the entity's financial statements for year 1 shall disclose the change in the entity's tax status for year 2 and the effects of that change, if material.

7.50 As discussed in FASB ASC 740-10-50-5, the disclosures of temporary differences and carryforward information differ for public and nonpublic entities. As discussed in FASB ASC 740-10-50-6, a public entity shall disclose the approximate tax effect of each type of temporary difference and carryforward that gives rise to a significant portion of DTLs and DTAs (before allocation of valuation allowances). FASB ASC 740-10-50-8 requires a nonpublic entity to disclose the types of significant temporary differences and carryforwards, but it may omit disclosure of the tax effects of each type.

7.51 As discussed in FASB ASC 740-10-50-9, the significant components of income tax expense attributable to continuing operations for each year presented shall be disclosed in the financial statements or notes thereto. Those components would include, for example, the following:

a. Current tax expense or benefit

b. Deferred tax expense or benefit, exclusive of the effects of other components listed subsequently

c. Investment tax credits

d. Government grants to the extent recognized as a reduction of income tax expense

e. The benefits of operating loss carryforwards

f. Tax expense that results from allocating certain tax benefits directly to contributed capital or to reduce goodwill or other noncurrent intangible assets of an acquired entity

g. Adjustments of a DTL or DTA for enacted changes in tax laws or rates or a change in the tax status of the entity

h. Adjustments of the beginning of the year balance of a valuation allowance because of a change in circumstances that causes a change in judgment about the realizability of the related DTA in future years

7.52 FASB ASC 740-10-50-10 requires that the amount of income tax expense or benefit allocated to continuing operations and the amounts separately allocated to other items, in accordance with the intraperiod tax allocation provisions of paragraphs 2–14 of FASB ASC 740-20-45 and FASB ASC 852-740-45-3, be disclosed for each year for which those items are presented.

7.53 The disclosures of income tax expense compared to statutory expectations' information differ for public and nonpublic entities. FASB ASC 740-10-50-12 requires that a public entity disclose a reconciliation using percentages or dollar amounts of the reported amount of income tax expense attributable to continuing operations for the year to the amount of income tax expense that would result from applying domestic federal statutory tax rates to pretax income from continuing operations. The statutory tax rates shall be the regular tax rates if alternative tax systems exist. The estimated amount and the nature of each significant reconciling item shall be disclosed. FASB ASC 740-10-50-13 requires a nonpublic entity to disclose the nature of significant reconciling items, but it may omit a numerical reconciliation.

7.54 FASB ASC 740-10-50-15 requires that all entities disclose all of the following at the end of each annual reporting period presented:

a. The total amounts of interest and penalties recognized in the statement of operations and statement of financial position

b. For positions for which it is reasonably possible that the total amounts of unrecognized tax benefits will significantly increase or decrease within 12 months of the reporting date

   i. the nature of the uncertainty;

   ii. the nature of the event that could occur in the next 12 months that would cause the change; and

   iii. an estimate of the range of the reasonably possible change or a statement that an estimate of the range cannot be made.

c. A description of tax years that remain subject to examination by major tax jurisdictions

7.55 FASB ASC 740-10-50-15A requires public entities to disclose both of the following at the end of each annual reporting period presented:

a. A tabular reconciliation of the total amounts of unrecognized tax benefits at the beginning and end of the period, which shall include, at a minimum, the following:

   i. The gross amounts of the increases and decreases in unrecognized tax benefits as a result of tax positions taken during a prior period

ii. The gross amounts of increases and decreases in unrecognized tax benefits as a result of tax positions taken during the current period

iii. The amounts of decreases in the unrecognized tax benefits relating to settlements with taxing authorities

iv. Reductions to unrecognized tax benefits as a result of a lapse of the applicable statute of limitations

b. The total amount of unrecognized tax benefits that, if recognized, would affect the effective tax rate

Statutory Accounting for Income Taxes

7.56 Statement of Statutory Accounting Principles (SSAP) No. 101, *Income Taxes—A Replacement of SSAP No. 10R and No. 10*, provides statutory accounting principles for current and deferred federal income taxes and current state income taxes and became effective for years beginning January 1, 2012. SSAP No. 101 exhibit A, "Implementation Questions and Answers," provides additional clarification and significant implementation guidance including the primary differences between SAP and GAAP accounting for income taxes. The replaced SSAP No. 10R, *Income Taxes—Revised, a Temporary Replacement of SSAP No. 10*, was effective for year end 2009 statutory filings through year end 2011 statutory filings. One of the key provisions in SSAP No. 10R was an optional election to admit a higher deferred tax asset for qualifying companies.

7.57 For statutory reporting purposes, a current tax liability or asset is recognized for the estimated taxes payable or refundable on tax returns for the current year in accordance with paragraph 3 of SSAP No. 101. Paragraph 3 of SSAP No. 101, defines *current income taxes* as current year estimates of federal and foreign income taxes payable or refundable based on tax returns for the current and prior years and tax loss contingencies (including related interest and penalties) for current and all prior years, computed in accordance with SSAP No. 5R, *Liabilities, Contingencies and Impairments of Assets*, modified to (a) replace the term *probable* with *more likely than not*,' (b) presume that the entity will be examined by a taxing authority having full knowledge of the information, and (c) recognize the loss contingency at 100 percent of the original tax benefit if it is more likely than not.

7.58 Paragraphs 6 and 8 of SSAP No. 101 note that under SAP

[a] reporting entity's balance sheet should include deferred income tax assets (DTAs) and liabilities (DTLs), the expected future tax consequences of temporary differences generated by statutory accounting, as defined in paragraph 20 of FASB ASC 740-10-25.

Changes in DTAs and DTLs, including changes attributable to changes in tax rates and changes in tax status, if any, shall be recognized as a separate component of gains and losses in unassigned funds (surplus). Admitted adjusted gross DTAs and DTLs shall be offset and presented as a single amount on the statement of financial position.

7.59 Under paragraph 7 of SSAP No. 101, a reporting entity's deferred tax assets and liabilities are computed as follows:

　　a. Temporary differences are identified and measured using a balance sheet approach, whereby statutory and tax basis balance sheets are compared.

　　b. Temporary differences include unrealized gains and losses and non-admitted assets, but do not include asset valuation reserve (AVR), interest maintenance reserve (IMR), Schedule F penalties, and, in the case of a mortgage guaranty insurer, amounts attributable to its statutory contingency reserve to the extent that tax and loss bonds have been purchased.

　　c. Total DTAs and DTLs are computed using enacted tax rates.

　　d. A DTL is not recognized for amounts described in paragraph 3 of FASB ASC 740-10-25 (which discusses specific situations where temporary differences should not be recognized).

　　e. Gross DTAs are reduced by a statutory valuation allowance adjustment if, based on the weight of available evidence, it is more likely than not (a likelihood of more than 50 percent) that some portion or all of the gross DTAs will not be realized. The statutory valuation allowance adjustment 1, determined in a manner consistent with FASB ASC 740-10-30, shall reduce the gross DTAs to the amount that is more likely than not to be realized (the adjusted gross deferred tax assets).

7.60 SAP reporting requires an admissibility test, in addition to the statutory valuation allowance, to determine how much of the gross DTAs should be admitted. Paragraph 11 of SSAP No. 101 states that

　　adjusted gross DTA shall be admitted based upon the three component admission calculation at an amount equal to the sum of paragraphs 11.a., 11.b., and 11.c.:

　　　　a. Federal income taxes paid in prior years that can be recovered through loss carrybacks for existing temporary differences that reverse during a timeframe corresponding with IRS tax loss carryback provisions, not to exceed three years including any amounts established in accordance with the provision of SSAP No. 5R as described in paragraph 3.a. of this statement related to those periods.

　　　　b. If the reporting entity is subject to risk-based capital requirements or is required to file a Risk-Based Capital Report with the domiciliary state, the reporting entity shall use the *Realization Threshold Limitation Table—RBC Reporting Entities* (RBC Reporting Entity Table) in this component of the admission calculation. The RBC Reporting Entity Table's threshold limitations are contingent upon the ExDTA RBC ACL Ratio.

　　　　If the reporting entity is either a mortgage guaranty insurer or financial guaranty insurer that is not subject to risk-based capital requirements or is not required to file a Risk-Based Capital Report with the domiciliary state and the reporting entity meets the minimum capital and reserve requirements for the state of domicile, then the reporting entity shall use the *Realization Threshold Limitation Table—Financial Guaranty* or *Mortgage Guaranty Non-RBC Reporting Entities* (Financial Guaranty or Mortgage Guaranty Non-RBC Reporting Entity Table) in this component of the admission calculation. The Financial Guaranty or Mortgage Guaranty Non-RBC Reporting Entity Table's threshold limitations are contingent upon the ratio of surplus without admitted DTA (ExDTA Surplus) to policyholders and contingency reserves.

If the reporting entity is (1) is not subject to risk-based capital requirements, (2) is not required to file a Risk-Based Capital Report with the domiciliary state, (3) is not a mortgage guaranty or financial guaranty insurer, and (4) meets the minimum capital and reserve requirements, then the reporting entity shall use the *Realization Threshold Limitation Table—Other Non-RBC Reporting Entities* (Other Non-RBC Reporting Entity Table). The Other Non-RBC Reporting Entity Table's is threshold limitations are contingent upon the ratio of adjusted gross DTA5 (Adjusted gross DTA less the amount of DTA admitted in paragraph 11.a.) to adjusted capital and surplus.

(Refer to SSAP No. 101 for realization threshold limitation tables.)

The reporting entity shall admit

    i. the amount of adjusted gross DTAs, after the application of paragraph 11.a., expected to be realized within the applicable period (refer to the 11.b.i. column of the applicable Realization Threshold Limitation Table above; the RBC Reporting Entity Table, the Financial Guaranty or Mortgage Guaranty Non-RBC Reporting Entity Table, or the Other Non-RBC Reporting Entity Table) following the balance sheet date limited to the amount determined in paragraph 11.b.ii.

    ii. An amount that is no greater than the applicable percentage (refer to the 11.b.ii. column of the applicable Realization Threshold Limitation Table above: the RBC Reporting Entity Table, the Financial Guaranty or Mortgage Guaranty Non-RBC Reporting Entity Table, or the Other Non-RBC Reporting Entity Table) of statutory capital and surplus as required to be shown on the statutory balance sheet of the reporting entity for the current reporting period's statement filed with the domiciliary state commissioner adjusted to exclude any net DTAs, EDP equipment and operating system software and any net positive goodwill.

  c. The amount of adjusted gross DTAs, after application of paragraphs 11.a. and 11.b., that can be offset against existing gross DTLs. The reporting entity shall consider the character (i.e., ordinary versus capital) of the DTAs and DTLs such that offsetting would be permitted in the tax return under existing enacted federal income tax laws and regulations. Additionally, for purposes of this component, the reporting entity shall consider the reversal patterns of temporary differences; however, this consideration does not require scheduling beyond that required in paragraph 7.e.

Disclosure Requirements Contained in Statutory Literature

7.61 Under SAP, as discussed in paragraph 21 of SSAP No. 101, disclosures shall be made in a manner consistent with the provisions of paragraphs 2–3, 6, 8–9, and 16 of FASB ASC 740-10-50 and FASB ASC 740-30-50-2. However, required disclosures with regard to a reporting entity's GAAP valuation allowance shall be replaced with disclosures relating to the statutory valuation allowance adjustment and the nonadmittance of some portion or all of a reporting entity's DTAs. The financial statements shall include the disclosures required by paragraph 12–14 of FASB ASC 740-10-50 for nonpublic companies. SSAP No. 101 requires additional disclosures of the gross and adjusted gross DTA. Refer to paragraphs 22–28 of SSAP No. 101 for a complete listing of statutory disclosure requirements.

Changes in Tax Law

7.62 Under the GAAP asset and liability method, deferred taxes represent liabilities to be paid or assets to be received in the future. Accordingly, DTAs and DTLs are adjusted to reflect a change in tax law or rates. The effect of the change is recognized as a component of income tax expense in the period the tax law change is enacted. Under SAP, as noted in SSAP No. 10R, changes in DTAs and DTLs attributable to changes in tax rates and tax status should be recognized as a separate component of gains and losses in surplus.

Auditing Income Taxes

Audit Planning

7.63 In accordance with AU-C section 300, *Planning an Audit* (AICPA, *Professional Standards*), the auditor should plan the audit so that it is responsive to the assessment of the risks of material misstatement based on the auditor's understanding of the entity and its environment, including its internal control. The nature, timing, and extent of planning vary with the size and complexity of the entity, along with the auditor's experience with the entity and understanding of the entity. Refer to chapter 2, "Audit Considerations," for a detailed discussion of audit planning.

Consideration of Fraud in a Financial Statement Audit

7.64 Risks are inherent in all audit engagements, including the possibility that fraudulent acts may cause a material misstatement of financial statements. AU-C section 240, *Consideration of Fraud in a Financial Statement Audit* (AICPA, *Professional Standards*), addresses the auditor's responsibilities relating to fraud in an audit of financial statements. Because of the characteristics of fraud, the auditor's exercise of professional skepticism is important when considering the risk of material misstatement due to fraud. Readers should refer to additional discussion of AU-C section 240 in chapter 2 of this guide.

Audit Risk Factors—Income Taxes

7.65 As discussed in paragraph .A1 of AU-C section 320, *Materiality in Planning and Performing an Audit* (AICPA, *Professional Standards*), audit risk is the risk that the auditor expresses an inappropriate audit opinion when the

Income Taxes

financial statements are materially misstated. Audit risk is a function of the risks of material misstatement and detection risk. Materiality and audit risk are considered throughout the audit, in particular, when

 a. determining the nature and extent of risk assessment procedures to be performed;

 b. identifying and assessing the risks of material misstatement;

 c. determining the nature, timing, and extent of further audit procedures; and

 d. evaluating the effect of uncorrected misstatements, if any, on the financial statements and in forming the opinion in the auditor's report.

7.66 Experience has demonstrated that audit risk may be greater in certain areas than in others. Significant transaction cycles of property and liability insurance entities include the premium cycle, the claims cycle, the reinsurance cycle, and the investment cycle. There are also significant risk factors associated with determining the provision for income taxes. These factors include, but are not limited to, the measurement, valuation, and classification of income tax liabilities or receivables; and the assurance that deferred tax liabilities and assets accurately reflect the future tax consequences of events that have been recognized, including a valuation allowance when necessary. The auditor should also understand material transactions or agreements used in executing a tax strategy. These risk factors, internal control considerations, and examples of audit procedures for the insurance entity are discussed further herein.

7.67 Identification of significant accounts and disclosures by the auditor is part of the planning process. As required by AU-C section 315, *Understanding the Entity and Its Environment and Assessing the Risks of Material Misstatement* (AICPA, *Professional Standards*), to enable the auditor to understand the classes of transactions, account balances, and disclosures to be expected in the financial statements, the auditor should obtain an understanding of the relevant industry, regulatory, and other external factors, including the applicable financial reporting framework and the nature of the entity. Significant disclosures for federal income taxes include a tabular reconciliation of the total amounts of unrecognized tax benefits, deferred tax assets and liabilities, statutory valuation allowance adjustment, and the nonadmittance of some portion or all of a reporting entity's DTAs.

Risk of Material Misstatement—Inherent Risk

7.68 As discussed in AU-C section 330, *Performing Audit Procedures in Response to Assessed Risks and Evaluating the Audit Evidence Obtained* (AICPA, *Professional Standards*), inherent risk is the likelihood of material misstatement due to the particular characteristics of the relevant class of transactions, account balance, or disclosure. As part of the auditor's assessment of inherent risks, the auditor may consider those factors related to federal income taxes, including factors relating to management, income tax operations, and tax planning strategies. Such factors might encompass the following:

 a. Management places undue emphasis on meeting projected tax liabilities on earnings projections

 b. Significant changes in regulation or taxation have occurred

c. The entity is a member of a tax consolidated group and its tax provisions are dependent on amounts from affiliates

　　　d. The entity has a three year cumulative loss or significant other negative evidence on the realizability of DTAs

Internal Control

7.69 Paragraph .04 of AU-C section 315 defines *internal control* as

> a process effected by those charged with governance, management, and other personnel that is designed to provide reasonable assurance about the achievement of the entity's objectives with regard to the reliability of financial reporting, effectiveness and efficiency of operations, and compliance with applicable laws and regulations. Internal control over safeguarding of assets against unauthorized acquisition, use, or disposition may include controls relating to financial reporting and operations objectives.

Internal control consists of the following five interrelated components:

　　　a. Control environment

　　　b. The entity's risk assessment process

　　　c. The information system, including the related business processes relevant to financial reporting and communication

　　　d. Control activities relevant to the audit

　　　e. Monitoring of controls

7.70 AU-C section 315 requires the auditor to obtain an understanding of these components of the entity's internal control. Paragraphs 2.31–.41 of chapter 2 of this guide discuss in detail the components of internal control. This section will discuss certain components of a property and liability insurance entity's internal control as they relate to income taxes.

Control Environment

7.71 The control environment comprises the collective effect of various factors on establishing, enhancing, or mitigating the effectiveness of specific control policies or procedures on the operations of the entity. As related to federal income taxes of a property and liability insurance entity, potential deficiencies in the control environment may include the following:

　　　a. Whether a single person or qualified group dominates the decision making process with regard to tax issues and tax planning strategies

　　　b. Whether the entity uses an insurance tax specialist in determining its federal income tax provision

　　　c. Whether the entity has qualified tax professionals review the tax consequences of complex business transactions before they are finalized

Risk Assessment Process

7.72 As discussed in paragraphs .16–.18 of AU-C section 315, the auditor should obtain an understanding of whether the entity has a process for *a.* identifying business risks relevant to financial reporting objectives;

b. estimating the significance of the risks;

c. assessing the likelihood of their occurrence; and

d. deciding about actions to address those risks.

7.73 The auditor should obtain an understanding of the entity's risk assessment process related to federal income taxes and the results thereof. If the entity has not established such a process, or has an ad hoc process, the auditor should discuss with management whether business risks relevant to financial reporting objectives have been identified and how they have been addressed. The auditor should evaluate whether the absence of a documented risk assessment process is appropriate in the circumstances or determine whether it represents a significant deficiency or material weakness in the entity's internal control.

Control Activities

7.74 Control activities are the policies and procedures that help ensure that management's directives are carried out and that necessary actions are taken to address risks to achieve the entity's objectives. The auditors should gain an understanding of those control activities the auditor deems necessary to assess the risks of material misstatement at the assertion level and design further audit procedures responsive to assessed risks. When developing the understanding of internal controls over income taxes, the auditor should consider what could go wrong in the process that would lead to a risk of material misstatement in federal income taxes payable, deferred tax assets and liabilities including the valuation allowance, the income tax provision, and liabilities relating to uncertain tax positions. The following are examples of control activities that might be considered:

a. The related controls for determining the entity's income tax filing requirements

b. The process and related controls for approval of tax elections

c. The process and related controls for calculating income taxes payable

d. The process and related controls for calculating deferred taxes, including the amount of any valuation allowances for deferred taxes

e. The process for identifying and evaluating uncertain tax positions

f. The process and related controls to initiate, process, and record income tax expense and related payments

g. The process and related controls for reconciling and recording adjustments to the general ledger accounts related to income taxes

Audit Procedures Responsive to the Assessed Risks of Material Misstatement

7.75 Planning activities include determining the relevant assertions related to the significant accounts identified, determining the audit objectives, assessing inherent risk of error of other significant risks (that is, nonroutine transactions or risk of fraud), and planning the involvement of others. As required by AU-C section 330, the auditor should design and perform further audit procedures whose nature, timing, and extent are based on, and are responsive to, the assessed risks of material misstatement at the relevant assertion level. The auditor should determine planned reliance on controls and nature, timing, and extent of substantive testing, including whether the substantive evidence is planned from tests of details or substantive analytics.

7.76 If the auditor identifies a significant risk and is only performing substantive procedures, those procedures should include a test of details. If procedures to respond to the significant risk include both a test of controls and substantive procedures, the auditor may select substantive analytical procedures if the controls are operating effectively.

> *Considerations for Audits Performed in Accordance With PCAOB Standards*
>
> For audits performed in accordance with the PCAOB auditing standards, for significant risks, paragraph 11 of Auditing Standard No. 13, *The Auditor's Responses to the Risks of Material Misstatement* (AICPA, *PCAOB Standards and Related Rules*, Auditing Standards), the auditor should perform substantive procedures, including tests of details, that are specifically responsive to the assessed risks.

Audit Consideration Chart

7.77 The auditor may consider the following specific audit objectives, examples of selected control activities, and auditing procedures in auditing the federal income tax processes of property and liability insurance entities. These are illustrative, however, and auditors should develop tests that are appropriate to the risk of material misstatement in the circumstances of the engagement.

Income Taxes

Audit Consideration Chart—Federal Income Taxes

Financial Statement Assertions	Audit Objectives	Examples of Selected Control Activities	Examples of Auditing Procedures
Existence	Confirm that appropriate income tax returns have been filed on a timely basis.	Procedures for timely filing of income tax returns or extensions are documented and filing is reviewed.	Examine prior year income tax returns and ascertain the latest year for which returns have been filed.
Completeness	Confirm that all tax reporting differences have been identified.		Review classification and description of accounts to identify possible tax reporting differences, such as loss reserves, unearned premiums, capital losses, or expenses.
Rights and Obligations	Confirm that tax balance sheet accounts are accurate.		Test the roll-forward of tax balance sheet accounts. Consider vouching significant tax payments and credits.
	Confirm that taxable income used in tax calculations is accurate.		Obtain a schedule reconciling net income per books with taxable income for federal, state, and foreign income taxes. Agree entries to general ledger and supporting documents as appropriate. Consider the reasonableness of the current tax account balances.
	Review the tax status and consolidated return requirements of subsidiaries.		
Valuation or Allocation	Under GAAP and SAP, determine that deferred and current income taxes have been correctly calculated.	An insurance tax specialist is utilized.	Review tax planning strategies and assumptions utilized in the calculation of deferred income taxes under FASB ASC 740 and SSAP No. 101.
Presentation and Disclosure	Determine that tax calculations are based on current tax laws and rates.	Tax uncertainties are reviewed and approved.	For both GAAP and SAP, review and determine the need for and appropriateness of any valuation allowance
		Changes in tax laws and rates are monitored and documented.	

(continued)

AAG-PLI 7.77

Financial Statement Assertions	Audit Objectives	Examples of Selected Control Activities	Examples of Auditing Procedures
	Under SAP determine that admitted gross DTAs have been correctly calculated.	Calculations for admitted gross DTAa are reviewed and approved.	for deferred tax assets based upon available evidence.
	Determine that tax impacts of acquired entities are correctly included.	Entity monitors and documents preacquisition tax liabilities and exposures of acquired entities.	Evaluate tax contingencies and consider the appropriate accounting treatment for these items under FASB ASC 740 and SSAP No. 101.
	Determine that tax sharing agreements between affiliated entities are appropriately recorded.	Management documents current GAAP and SAP disclosure requirements.	Review schedule of net operating loss and other tax credit carryforwards.
	Determine that disclosures fulfill the requirements under GAAP and SAP.		Consider the deductibility of transactions such as profit-sharing, bonus, contributions, or stock option transactions.
			Review calculations to verify that changes in income tax laws and rates are properly reflected.
			Review calculation of admitted gross DTA and confirm that SSAP No. 101 is being properly applied (including admissibility test and valuation allowance).
			Review reconciliation of prior year tax accrual to the actual filed tax return.
			Determine the propriety of adjustments made in this regard and consider the impact on current year's tax accrual.
			Review the status of current year acquisitions of other entities and their preacquisition tax liabilities and exposures.

Financial Statement Assertions	Audit Objectives	Examples of Selected Control Activities	Examples of Auditing Procedures
			For separate financial statements of affiliates, review terms of all tax sharing agreements between affiliated entities to determine accounting treatment.
			Determine whether the institution is in compliance with the regulatory accounting rules for intercompany tax allocation and settlement.
			Review disclosures and compare with requirements under FASB ASC 740 and SSAP No. 101 for consolidated and separate financial statements of affiliates.

Chapter 8
Insurance-Related Expenses, Taxes, and Assessments

Introduction

8.01 Similar to most other organizations, compensation expense, such as salaries; payroll taxes; employee relations; and welfare, accounts for a significant proportion of expenses other than losses and loss adjustment expenses (LAEs). Other major categories of nonindustry specific expenses include rent and rent items, travel, depreciation, equipment, legal and audit, and supplies. Some expenses are also insurance specific, the most significant of which are taxes, licenses, and fees. The largest component of such expenses is premium taxes charged by states. The caption taxes, licenses, and fees also include the following:

> *a.* Guaranty association assessments that cover state obligations to noncommercial policyholders of bankrupt and liquidated companies, such as obligations to individuals under workers' compensation policies
>
> *b.* Other assessments, typically related to workers' compensation, imposed by many states as a percentage of an insurer's writings in the state or sometimes as a percentage of an insurer's loss payments for a given line of business
>
> *c.* Insurance department licenses and fees

8.02 Other insurance specific expenses include the costs of boards and bureaus, surveys, and underwriting reports. These latter categories are not significant. In addition, commissions are generally a significant expense for most insurance enterprises. See chapter 3, "Premiums," of this guide for a discussion of commissions and deferred acquisition costs (DAC).

8.03 In many cases, insurance entities are a part of a holding company system. The holding company, or an affiliated entity in the holding company group, may be responsible for the management of some or all of the operational aspects of the insurance entity's operations. In these situations, personnel are often employees of the holding company. The latter charges a management fee to the insurance entity for services provided. In the annual statement, management fee charges are required to be displayed by their underlying components, such as salaries and other expenses.

8.04 In the statutory property and casualty annual statement, the expenses described in paragraphs 8.01–.03 are shown on a page titled, "Underwriting and Investment Exhibit, Part 3—Expenses." For statutory reporting, the classification and grouping of expenses is determined by the National Association of Insurance Commissioners (NAIC) and is contained in an appendix to the *Annual Statement Instructions*. These classifications and definitions were codified by the NAIC and evolved originally from individual state regulations, such as New York's Regulation 30. The "Underwriting and Investment Exhibit" expense page also analyzes expenses by three functions: LAEs, other underwriting expenses, and investment expenses. A related exhibit, "Insurance

Expense Exhibit," filed with states April 1 annually, allocates expenses not just to function but also to line of business. These analyses allow insurers to understand profitability by line of business and allow insurance departments and rating agencies to similarly evaluate and set premium rates for coverages.

8.05 The allocation of expenses to lines of business is an important aspect of measuring profitability. The statutory property and casualty annual statement contains more than 30 predefined lines designed to capture all lines used by insurers conducting business in the United States. Some of the more common lines where the premium writings are concentrated include homeowners multiple peril, private passenger, auto physical damage, auto liability, other liability occurrence, and workers' compensation. Other major lines include fire and allied lines, commercial multiple peril, products liability, and commercial auto liability. In addition, many insurance companies choose to operate using internal divisions that specialize in one or more groups of commonly underwritten insurance policies. For example, a commercial lines insurer may have a property division, professional liability division, commercial lines division, and specialty division that provide directors and officers insurance. In many cases, an insurer will find it necessary to allocate its expenses for external reporting to predetermined statutory lines of business and internally to its management reporting lines. Also, in certain cases, a number of individual companies within an insurance company group may share expenses. In such situations, allocations are made to individual companies commonly based on variables such as gross premiums written; the number of employees; and, when warranted, time studies and management's assessments of time and resources devoted to individual companies.

Premium and State Taxes

8.06 Insurance entities are subject to premium taxes in almost all states in lieu of state income tax. In a few jurisdictions, such as Florida and Illinois, insurance entities are also subject to state income taxes (see the discussion in paragraphs 8.10–.11). These taxes usually apply to both the entities that are domiciled in the state, called domestic insurers, and the entities that conduct business in the state but are domiciled elsewhere, called foreign insurers. Some states, however, partially or totally exempt domestic insurers from premium taxes, and others allow domestic insurers special credits against premium taxes if they invest specified amounts of assets in domestic corporations. Statement of Statutory Accounting Principles (SSAP) No. 94, *Accounting for Transferable State Tax Credits*, provides guidance for credits that are consistent with the statutory accounting principles (SAP) statement of concepts. Excluded from its scope are certified capital gains companies and investments in low income housing, per SSAP No. 93, *Accounting for Low Income Housing Tax Credit Property Investments*.

8.07 Premium taxes are generally charged as a percentage of direct written premiums in a given state. The rates vary by state and often by line of business. For example, workers' compensation premiums are sometimes exempted from tax in certain states, but in other states, they may have a higher rate. Premium taxes usually range from 1 percent to 3 percent of direct premiums written. States with low premium tax rates often impose retaliatory taxes on writings in the state by entities domiciled in states that impose higher tax rates. Retaliatory taxes, as the term implies, involve a state with a lower premium tax rate charging insurers domiciled in a different state the other state's higher tax rate on those insurers' writings in the state. Insurers also pay municipal premium taxes in a few states, most notably Florida, Alabama,

Louisiana, Georgia, Kentucky, and South Carolina. In the case of Kentucky, such municipal taxes are recoupable from the insureds.

8.08 Some states require quarterly premium tax payments; however, most states require premium tax payments in February of the year following the year that the premiums were written. Thus, insurers generally have substantial premium tax liabilities as of December 31 of each year. Rather than computing the liability on a state-by-state basis, most entities estimate their total premium tax payable using their historical ratio of total premium tax expense to total premiums written. This ratio is applied to current premiums written to compute the current premium taxes for the fiscal year. The total liability is then adjusted for prepaid premium taxes to arrive at the accrued premium tax liability. The entity should evaluate the ratio annually because shifts in the concentration of the company's business from state to state and changes in state tax laws can significantly affect an insurer's premium tax liability.

8.09 Under generally accepted accounting principles (GAAP), costs that vary with, and are primarily related to, the acquisition of new and renewal insurance contracts, as discussed in Financial Accounting Standards Board (FASB) *Accounting Standards Codification* (ASC) 944-30-55-1, are generally deferred and amortized. Premium taxes generally meet the criteria for DAC. Refer to chapter 3 of this guide for additional discussion of DAC.

8.10 In addition to premium taxes of insurance entities, a few states tax the net taxable income (as defined by the respective state) of domestic insurers in one way or another. Some also tax the net taxable income of foreign insurers. Generally, however, various methods are used to avoid double taxation. The methods include (*a*) allowing the insurer to elect to be taxed on either premiums or net taxable income, (*b*) allowing a credit on one of the tax returns for taxes paid on the other, and (*c*) exempting domestic insurers from the premium tax.

8.11 States that tax the income in addition to, or in place of, the premium tax of property and liability insurance entities generally base the computation of taxable income on federal taxable income, with certain modifications. Apportionment and allocation of income by multistate entities are important considerations when accruing for such taxes. Refer to chapter 7, "Income Taxes," of this guide for additional discussion of federal income taxes.

8.12 The prior year apportionment percentage may be indicative of the current year for computing the accrual. However, significant changes in the places in which the entity does business can affect apportionment.

Guaranty Fund and Other Assessments

8.13 Guaranty fund assessments represent a funding mechanism employed by states to provide funds to cover policyholder obligations of insolvent insurance companies. Most states have enacted legislation establishing guaranty funds to provide for covered claims or meet other insurance obligations of insolvent insurers in the state.

8.14 FASB ASC 405-30 provides GAAP accounting and overall information on insurance-related assessments. As noted in FASB ASC 405-30-05-3, state guaranty funds use different methods for assessing entities. The three primary methods used to assess guaranty funds assessments for property and liability insurance entities are as follows:

> a. *Prospective premium based assessments.* Guaranty funds covering claims of insolvent property and casualty insurance enterprises typically assess entities based on premiums written in one or more years after the insolvency. Assessments in any year are generally limited to an established percentage of an entity's premiums written or received for the year preceding the assessment. Assessments for a given insolvency may be made over several years.
>
> b. *Prefunded premium based assessments.* This kind of assessment is intended to prefund the costs of future insolvencies. Assessments are imposed prior to any particular insolvency and are based on the current level of written premiums. Rates to be applied to future premiums are adjusted as necessary.
>
> c. *Administrative type assessments.* These assessments are typically a flat (annual) amount per insurer to fund operations of the guaranty association, regardless of the existence of an insolvency.

8.15 FASB ASC 405-30-05-3 also discusses the retrospective premium based assessment method that is typically used for guaranty funds covering benefit payments of insolvent life, annuity, and health insurance entities.

8.16 FASB ASC 405-30-05-4 notes that state laws often allow for recoveries of guaranty fund assessments by entities subject to assessments through such mechanisms as premium tax offsets, policy surcharges, and future premium rate increases. Policy surcharges are intended to provide an opportunity for assessed entities to recover some or all of the amounts assessed over a period of time.

8.17 In some instances, there may be policy surcharges that are required as a pass-through to the state or other regulatory bodies. Some structures require the insurer to collect policyholder surcharges from insureds for state and other structure assessments for future premiums and to remit the surcharges to the state or other regulatory body on behalf of the policyholder. A form of assessment that predominates in Florida and certain other coastal states is known as a catastrophe fund. Under this mechanism, the state either directly or, through a specially organized entity (for example, Citizens Property Insurance Corporation of Florida), imposes a surcharge on insurers based on insurer's writings in one or more lines within the state. In turn, assessable insurers may seek recoupment from their policyholders by way of a premium surcharge.

8.18 As noted in FASB ASC 405-30-5-5, insurance entities are subject to a variety of other insurance-related assessments. Many states and a number of local governmental units have established other funds supported by assessments. The most prevalent uses for such assessments are to fund (*a*) operating expenses of state insurance regulatory bodies (for example, the state insurance department or workers' compensation board) and (*b*) second injury funds that provide reimbursement to insurance carriers or employers for workers' compensation claims when the cost of a second injury combined with a prior accident or disability is greater than what the second accident alone would have produced. The employer of an injured or handicapped worker is responsible only for the workers' compensation benefit for the most recent injury; the second injury fund would cover the cost of any additional benefits for aggravation of a prior condition or injury. The intent of the fund is to help ensure that

Insurance-Related Expenses, Taxes, and Assessments

employers are not made to suffer a greater monetary loss or increased insurance costs because of hiring previously injured or handicapped employees. FASB ASC 405-30-05-6 discusses the primary methods used to assess these assessments:

> *a. Premium based.* The assessing organization imposes the assessment based on the insurer's written premiums. The base year of premiums is generally either the current year or the year preceding the assessment.
>
> *b. Loss based.* The assessing organization imposes the assessment based on the insurer's incurred losses or paid losses in relation to that amount for all entities subject to that assessment in the particular jurisdiction.

Generally Accepted Accounting Principles

8.19 FASB ASC 405-30-25-1 states that entities subject to assessments shall recognize liabilities for insurance-related assessments when all of the following conditions are met:

> *a. Probability of assessment.* An assessment that has been imposed or information available before the financial statements are issued or available to be issued, as discussed in FASB ASC 855-10-25, indicates it is probable that an assessment will be imposed.
>
> *b. Obligating event.* The event obligating an entity to pay (underlying cause of) an imposed or probable assessment has occurred on or before the date of the financial statements.
>
> *c. Ability to reasonably estimate.* The amount of the assessment can be reasonably estimated.

8.20 FASB ASC 405-30-25-6 summarizes the conclusions reached on the methods used to address guaranty fund assessments and other insurance-related assessments as follows:

> *a. Prospective premium based guaranty fund assessments.* The event that obligates the entity for the assessment liability generally is the writing of, or becoming obligated to write or renew, the premiums on which the expected future assessments are to be based (for example, multiple year contracts under which an insurance entity has no discretion to avoid writing future premiums). Therefore, the event that obligates the entity generally will not have occurred at the time of the insolvency. Law or regulatory practice affects the event that obligates the entity in either of the following ways:
>
>> i. In states that through law or regulatory practice provide that an entity cannot avoid paying a particular assessment in the future (even if the entity reduces premium writings in the future), the event that obligates the entity is a formal determination of insolvency or a similar event. An entity that has the ability to reasonably estimate the amount of the assessment shall recognize a liability for the entire amount of future assessments that cannot be avoided related to a particular insolvency when a formal determination of insolvency occurs.
>>
>> ii. In states without such a law or regulatory practice, the event that obligates the entity is the writing of, or becoming obligated

to write, the premiums on which the expected future assessments are to be based. An entity that has the ability to reasonably estimate the amount of the assessments shall recognize a liability when the related premiums are written or when the entity becomes obligated to write the premiums.

b. *Prefunded premium based guaranty fund assessments.* A liability for an assessment arises when premiums are written. Accordingly, an entity that has the ability to reasonably estimate the amount of the assessment shall recognize a liability as the related premiums are written.

c. *Other premium based assessments.* Other premium based assessments, as described in FASB ASC 405-30-05-5, would be accounted for in the same manner as prefunded premium based guaranty fund assessments.

d. *Loss based assessments.* An assessment is probable of being asserted when the loss occurs. The obligating event of the assessment also has occurred when the loss occurs. Accordingly, an entity that has the ability to reasonably estimate the amount of the assessment shall recognize a liability as the related loss is incurred.

8.21 As stated in FASB ASC 405-30-25-8, when it is probable that a paid or accrued assessment will result in an amount that is recoverable from premium tax offsets or policy surcharges, an asset shall be recognized for that recovery. FASB ASC 405-30-30-11 states that the asset recognized in the preceding sentence shall be measured based on current laws and projections of future premium collections or policy surcharges from in-force policies. In determining the asset to be recorded, in force policies do not include expected renewals of short-duration contracts but do include assumptions about persistency rates for long-duration contracts.

8.22 FASB ASC 405-30-25-11 clarifies that policy surcharges that are required as a pass-through to the state or other regulatory bodies shall be accounted for in a manner such that amounts collected or receivable are not recorded as revenues, and amounts due or paid are not expensed (meaning, similar to accounting for sales tax).

Statutory Accounting Principles

8.23 Statutory guidance on insurance-related assessments is provided in SSAP No. 35R, *Guaranty Fund and Other Assessments.* As noted in paragraph 4 of SSAP No. 35R

> [t]his statement adopts with modification guidance from Accounting Standard Codification 405-30, *Insurance-Related Assessments* (ASC 405-30), as reflected within this SSAP. Consistent with ASC 405-30-25-1, entities subject to assessments shall recognize liabilities for insurance-related assessments when all of the following conditions are met (paragraph 13 of SSAP No. 35R provides guidance on applying the recognition criteria):
>
> > a. An assessment has been imposed or information available prior to issuance of the statutory financial statements indicates that it is probable that an assessment will be imposed.

Insurance-Related Expenses, Taxes, and Assessments

  b. The event obligating an entity to pay an imposed or probable assessment has occurred on or before the date of the financial statements.

  c. The amount of the assessment can be reasonably estimated.

Guaranty fund and other assessments shall be charged to expense (Taxes, Licenses and Fees) and a liability shall be accrued when the above criteria are met except for certain health related assessments which shall be reported as a part of claims. Health related assessments that are reported as a part of claims instead of taxes, licenses and fees are those assessments that are designed for the purpose of spreading the risk of severe claims or adverse enrollment selection among all participating entities, and where the funds collected via the assessment are re-distributed back to the participating entities based upon the cost of specific claims, enrollment demographics, or other criteria affecting health care expenses. This standard does not permit liabilities for guaranty funds or other assessments to be discounted.

8.24 Paragraph 5 of SSAP No. 35R notes that for refunded guaranty or other fund assessments and assessments used to fund state operating expenses, reporting entities shall credit the refund or charge the assessment to expense when notification of the refund or assessment is made.

8.25 Paragraph 6 of SSAP No. 35R explains

[f]or premium-based guaranty fund assessments, except those that are prefunded, subparagraph 4a. is met when the insolvency has occurred. For purposes of applying the guidance, the insolvency shall be considered to have occurred when a reporting entity meets a state's (ordinarily the state of domicile of the insolvent reporting entity) statutory definition of an insolvent reporting entity. In most states, the reporting entity must be declared to be financially insolvent by a court of competent jurisdiction. In some states, there must also be a final order of liquidation. Prefunded guaranty-fund assessments and premium-based administrative type assessment are presumed probable when the premiums on which the assessments are expected to be based are written. Loss-based administrative-type and second injury fund assessments are presumed probable when the losses on which the assessments are expected to be based are incurred.

8.26 Paragraph 7 of SSAP No. 35R discusses that due to the differences in how assessment mechanisms operate, the event that makes an assessment probable may not be the event that obligates the entity. The following defines the event that obligates an entity to pay an assessment:

  a. For premium based assessments, the event that obligates the entity is generally writing the premiums or becoming obligated to write or renew (such as multiple-year, noncancelable policies) the premiums on which the assessments are expected to be based. Some states, through law or regulatory practice, provide that an insurance entity cannot avoid paying a particular assessment even if that insurance entity reduces its premium writing in the future. In such circumstances, the event that obligates the entity is a formal determination of insolvency or similar triggering event. For example, in certain states, an insurance entity may remain liable for assessments even though the insurance entity discontinues the writing of premiums. In this circumstance, the underlying cause of the liability is not the writing of the premium, but the insolvency. Regulatory practice would be determined based on the stated intentions or prior history of the insurance regulators.

 b. For loss based assessments, the event that obligates an entity is an entity's incurring the losses on which the assessments are expected to be based.

8.27 Paragraph 8 of SSAP No. 35R also explains that an entity's estimate of a liability for guaranty fund assessments shall reflect its share of the ultimate loss expected from the insolvency. The reporting entity shall also estimate any applicable premium tax credits and policy surcharges.

8.28 Paragraph 10 of SSAP No. 35R also provides guidance allowing insurers to record an asset for premium tax credits to be realized and policy surcharges to be collected:

> [t]he liability for accrued assessments shall be established gross of any probable and estimable recoveries from premium tax credits and premium surcharges. When it is probable that a paid or accrued assessment will result in an amount that is recoverable from premium tax offsets or policy surcharges, an asset shall be recognized for that recovery in an amount that is determined based on current laws, projections of future premium collections or policy surcharges from in-force policies, and as permitted in accordance with subparagraphs 10a, 10b, and 10c. Any recognized asset from premium tax credits or policy surcharges shall be re-evaluated regularly to ensure recoverability. Upon expiration, tax credits no longer meet the definition of an asset and shall be written off:
>
> *a.* For assessments paid before premium tax credits are realized or policy surcharges are collected, an asset results, which represents a receivable for premium tax credits that will be taken and policy surcharges which will be collected in the future. These receivables, to the extent it is probable they will be realized, meet the definition of assets, as specified in SSAP No. 4—*Assets and Nonadmitted Assets* and are admitted assets to the extent they conform to the requirements of this statement. The asset shall be established and reported independent from the liability (not reported net).
>
> *b.* Assets recognized from accrued liability assessments shall be determined in accordance with the type of guaranty fund assessment as detailed in the following subparagraphs. Assets recognized from accrued liability assessments meet the definition of an asset under SSAP No. 4, and are admitted assets to the extent they conform to the requirements of this statement:
>
>   i. For retrospective-premium-based and loss-based assessments, to the extent that it is probable that accrued liability assessments will result in a recoverable amount in a future period from business currently in-force considering appropriate persistency rates for long-duration contracts, an asset shall be recognized at the time the liability is recorded. (In-force policies do not include expected renewals of short-term contracts.

ii. For prospective-premium-based assessments, the recognition of assets from accrued liability assessments is limited to the amount of premium an entity has written or is obligated to write and to the amounts recoverable over the life of the in-force policies. This SSAP requires reporting entities to recognize prospective-based-premium assessments as the premium is written or obligated to be written by the reporting entity. Accordingly, the expected premium tax offset or policy surcharge asset related to the accrual of prospective-premium-based assessments shall be based on and limited to the amount recoverable as a result of premiums the insurer has written or is obligated to write.

c. An asset shall not be established for paid or accrued assessments that are recoverable through future premium rate structures.

8.29 Paragraph 11 of SSAP No. 35R notes that an evaluation of the assets recognized under paragraph 10 of SSAP No. 35R shall be made in accordance with SSAP No. 5R, *Liabilities, Contingencies and Impairments of Assets*, to determine if there is any impairment.

8.30 Paragraph 12 of SSAP No. 35R provides guidance in situations in which the insurer acts as an agent for certain state or federal agencies in the collection and remittance of fees or assessments. In these circumstances, the liability for the fees and assessments rests with the policyholder rather than the reporting entity. The reporting entity's obligation is to collect and subsequently remit the fee or assessment. When both the following conditions are met, an assessment shall not be reported in the statement of operations of a reporting entity:

a. The assessment is reflected as a separately identifiable item on the billing to the policyholder

b. Remittance of the assessment by the reporting entity to the state or federal agency is contingent upon collection from the insured

Capitalized Costs and Certain Nonadmitted Assets

8.31 Under GAAP, costs that will provide future benefits are capitalized and amortized to expense over the estimated period of use. Statutory accounting also recognizes the concept of capitalized costs but, in some cases, superimposes a nonadmissibility criterion, as outlined in SSAP No. 4, *Assets and Nonadmitted Assets*.

8.32 The primary reason for the difference in reporting methods is that SAP and GAAP reporting models have different principal objectives. The SAP model's principal objectives emphasize the measurement of the ability to pay claims in the future; the income statement effect is a secondary concern. SAP attempts to determine, at the financial statement date, an insurer's ability to satisfy its obligations to its policyholders and creditors. The primary focus of GAAP financial reporting is information about earnings and its components. GAAP is designed to meet the varying needs of different users of financial statements, but SAP is primarily focused on the needs of the regulators, who are the main users of the statutory financial statements.

8.33 Under SAP, nonadmitted assets are not recognized on the balance sheet; they are charged against surplus. Although not recognized on the balance sheet, the asset is depreciated or amortized against net income as the estimated economic benefit expires. Nonadmitted assets either hold economic value, which does not fulfill a responsibility to policyholders, or are unavailable due to hindrances or the interests of third parties. Assets may be considered nonadmitted if they are specifically labeled nonadmitted or are not specifically labeled as admitted in the *Accounting Practices and Procedures Manual*.

8.34 Some notable capitalized costs nonadmitted under SAP include the following:

a. Furniture and equipment

b. Prepaid expenses

8.35 Other than the inadmissibility of certain assets, the accounting treatment of most expenses is similar for GAAP and SAP. The main difference in accounting relates to commissions and other acquisition costs. Under SAP, these costs are expensed as incurred, and under GAAP, the costs are deferred and amortized in accordance with the provisions of FASB ASC 944-30-55-1. See the discussion of acquisition costs in chapter 3 of this guide.

Pensions

8.36 GAAP accounting for pensions, as outlined in FASB ASC 715, *Compensation—Retirement Benefits*, is incorporated into SSAP No. 89, *Accounting for Pensions, A Replacement of SSAP No. 8*, with a modification. See paragraph 16 of SSAP No. 89 for a full listing of modifications and additional information required. The following is a list of some significant items to consider:

- For defined benefit plans, the following:
  - The calculation of the pension obligation for SAP shall exclude nonvested employees. Partially vested employees are included only to the extent of their vested amounts.
  - The excess of plan assets over obligations should be treated as a nonadmitted asset for SAP.
  - Net plan obligations must be accrued, regardless of funding.
- For defined contribution plans, the following:
  - The reporting entity should expense contributions required by the plan over the period in which the employee vests in those contributions.
  - Contributions to plan participants' accounts made prior to vesting should be treated as a prepaid asset that is nonadmitted.
  - Contributions required after participants terminate or retire should be accrued, and an expense should be recorded over the working lives of the participants.

8.37 See FASB ASC 715 and SSAP No. 89 for required disclosures.

> **⊙Update 8-1 *Regulatory*: Pensions**
>
> NAIC SSAP No. 102, *Accounting for Pensions*, issued in March 2012, is effective for quarterly and annual reporting periods beginning on or after January 1, 2013 with early adoption permitted and the ability to elect a ten year phase-in period. SSAP No. 102 establishes statutory accounting principles and related reporting for employers' pension obligations. Readers are encouraged to consult the full text of the SSAP at www.naic.org. For periods after January 1, 2013, refer to section D.02 in appendix D, "Guidance Updates," which summarizes these clarifying changes that may affect an auditor's practice or methodology.

Audit Considerations

Audit Planning

8.38 In accordance with AU-C section 300, *Planning an Audit* (AICPA, *Professional Standards*), the auditor should plan the audit so that it is responsive to the assessment of the risks of material misstatement based on the auditor's understanding of the entity and its environment, including its internal control. The nature, timing, and extent of planning vary with the size and complexity of the entity, and with the auditor's experience with the entity and understanding of the entity. Refer to chapter 2, "Audit Considerations," of this guide for a detailed discussion of audit planning.

Consideration of Fraud in a Financial Statement Audit

8.39 Risks are inherent in all audit engagements, including the possibility that fraudulent acts may cause a material misstatement of financial statements. AU-C section 240, *Consideration of Fraud in a Financial Statement Audit* (AICPA, *Professional Standards*), addresses the auditor's responsibilities relating to fraud in an audit of financial statements. Because of the characteristics of fraud, the auditor's exercise of professional skepticism is important when considering the risk of material misstatement due to fraud. Readers should refer to additional discussion of AU-C section 240 in chapter 2 of this guide.

Audit Risk Factors

8.40 As discussed in paragraph .A1 of AU-C section 320, *Materiality in Planning and Performing an Audit* (AICPA, *Professional Standards*), audit risk is the risk that the auditor expresses an inappropriate audit opinion when the financial statements are materially misstated. Audit risk is a function of the risks of material misstatement and detection risk. Materiality and audit risk are considered throughout the audit, in particular, when

   a. determining the nature and extent of risk assessment procedures to be performed;

   b. identifying and assessing the risks of material misstatement;

   c. determining the nature, timing, and extent of further audit procedures; and *d.* evaluating the effect of uncorrected misstatements, if any, on the financial statements and in forming the opinion in the auditor's report.

8.41 Experience has demonstrated that audit risk may be greater in certain areas than in others. Significant transaction cycles of property and liability insurance entities include the premium cycle, the claims cycle, the reinsurance cycle, and the investment cycle. The areas discussed in this chapter may not contain significant risks of material misstatement.

8.42 Identification of significant accounts and disclosures by the auditor is part of the planning process. As required by AU-C section 315, *Understanding the Entity and Its Environment and Assessing the Risks of Material Misstatement* (AICPA, *Professional Standards*), to enable the auditor to understand the classes of transactions, account balances, and disclosures to be expected in the financial statements, the auditor should obtain an understanding of the relevant industry, regulatory, and other external factors, including the applicable financial reporting framework, and the nature of the entity.

Internal Control

8.43 Paragraph .04 of AU-C section 315 defines *internal control* as

> a process effected by those charged with governance, management, and other personnel that is designed to provide reasonable assurance about the achievement of the entity's objectives with regard to the reliability of financial reporting, effectiveness and efficiency of operations, and compliance with applicable laws and regulations. Internal control over safeguarding of assets against unauthorized acquisition, use, or disposition may include controls relating to financial reporting and operations objectives.

Internal control consists of the following five interrelated components:

   a. Control environment

   b. The entity's risk assessment process

   c. The information system, including the related business processes relevant to financial reporting and communication

   d. Control activities relevant to the audit

   e. Monitoring of controls

8.44 AU-C section 315 requires the auditor to obtain an understanding of these components of the entity's internal control. Paragraphs 2.31–.41 of chapter 2 of this guide discuss in detail the components of internal control.

8.45 Paragraph .13 of AU-C section 315 requires that the auditor should obtain an understanding of internal control relevant to the audit, and what is relevant to the audit is a matter of the auditor's professional judgment. Paragraph .A62 of AU-C section 315 identifies factors relevant to the auditor's professional judgment about whether a control, individually or in combination with others, is relevant to the audit.

Audit Procedures Responsive to the Assessed Risks of Material Misstatement

8.46 As required by AU-C section 330, *Performing Audit Procedures in Response to Assessed Risks and Evaluating the Audit Evidence Obtained* (AICPA, *Professional Standards*), the auditor should design and perform further audit procedures whose nature, timing, and extent are based on, and are responsive to, the assessed risks of material misstatement at the relevant assertion level. The audit approach described in this chapter with respect to insurance-related expenses, taxes, and assessments consists of substantive procedures. The auditor is required by paragraph .18 of AU-C section 330 to design and perform substantive procedures for all relevant assertions related to each material class of transactions, account balance, and disclosure, regardless of the assessed risks of material misstatement. The following sections include examples of typical substantive audit procedures applicable to these accounts.

Premium and State Taxes

8.47 Substantive audit procedures may include the following:

- Obtain an understanding of the premium and state taxes applicable for the insurer and the method for calculating the taxes and frequency of payment.
- Obtain a schedule reconciling net income per books with taxable income for state income taxes. Agree entries to general ledger and supporting documents as appropriate. Consider the reasonableness of the current tax account balances.
- Review the allocation, apportionment, and sourcing of income and expense applicable to state tax jurisdictions with significant income taxes.
- Compare the premium and state taxes recorded liability with prior year and investigate unexpected changes.
- Perform a predictive recalculation of the recorded premium and state taxes and compare to amounts recorded. Obtain explanation of any unusual or unexpected variations.
- Obtain the historical effective tax rates for the immediately preceding three years and compare to the current year effective rate.
- Confirm that any changes in concentration of business by state have been incorporated in the historical effective rates.
- Ascertain whether changes in income tax laws and rates have been properly reflected in the tax calculations and account balances.
- Obtain explanation of unusual fluctuations, if any.

Guaranty Fund and Other Assessments

8.48 Substantive audit procedures may include the following:

- Compare the liability for guaranty fund and other insurance-related assessments with those of prior years and investigate unexpected changes

- Determine that the liability for guaranty fund and other insurance-related assessments meets the conditions for accrual under both GAAP and statutory accounting guidance
- Confirm that liabilities are accrued for any new guaranty funds or insurance-related assessments by examining the new assessment notification
- Recalculate the liability for a sample of guaranty fund and other insurance-related assessments based on premium written for the specified line of business
- Compare the liability for guaranty fund and other insurance-related assessments with the total amount remitted to the corresponding guaranty fund subsequent to year end

Capitalized Costs and Certain Nonadmitted Assets

Generally Accepted Accounting Principles

8.49 The auditing procedures for miscellaneous assets will be dependent on the nature of the assets. They will be similar to those utilized in the performance of an audit of any other kind of business, including confirmation, calculation, examination, and any other procedure that may be applied to satisfy the auditor.

8.50 Certain GAAP receivables that are nonadmitted for statutory annual statement purposes may be subjected to the usual auditing procedures necessary to determine their existence and collectability. Furniture and fixtures may be subjected to the usual auditing procedures for additions and disposals and depreciation thereon, similar to those uses in any other kind of business entity.

Statutory Accounting Principles

8.51 When auditing assets and receivables classified as nonadmitted for SAP, the auditor should refer to the guidance on assets and nonadmitted assets under SSAP No. 4 (see discussion of nonadmittted assets in paragraphs 8.33–.35). Substantive audit procedures may include the following:

- Review the listing of nonadmitted assets and determine that they are in accordance with the guidance in SSAP No. 4
- Identify asset classes that would generally be considered nonadmitted and confirm that none are accounted for as admitted assets
- Review the listing assets that are accounted for as admitted assets and determine that they are properly classified

Other Underwriting Expenses

8.52 Based on overall materiality and results of fluctuation analysis, the auditor may deem it necessary to perform certain substantive procedures including recalculations or examining sufficient underlying documentation of selected other accounts. Consideration should be given to significant or sensitive accounts such as salaries and employee benefits, legal fees, professional contractual services regulatory fees, and other.

Chapter 9
Captive Insurance Entities

Introduction

9.01 This chapter provides an overview and background on captive insurance entities and specific areas of interest. When applicable, captives are subject to the insurance accounting literature throughout this guide.

9.02 The use of captive insurance entities as an alternative means of providing property and casualty insurance coverage continues to grow in popularity. The term *captive* is broadly used to describe a form of alternative risk transfer, and several types of captives are identified and described further in this chapter. Captive refers to the fact that the captive insurance entity is owned and controlled by some of the entities or individuals that it insures. Captives may also insure third-party risks. Although there may be many benefits of insuring risks through a captive insurer, some of the more cited include the following:

 a. The reduction or stabilization of insurance costs over time

 b. Additional control over underwriting and claims management

 c. Financial benefit for more favorable claims experience

 d. Coverage that might otherwise be unavailable or unaffordable

 e. Direct access to the reinsurance market

 f. Possible income tax benefits over traditional self-insurance

 g. Possible coverage for risks that were previously not insured for or uninsurable, such as cyber-risks, construction defects, and certain environmental risks

9.03 Captives can only offer commercial insurance. The types of risks that have recently shown growth in the use of captives include general and professional liability, commercial property, workers' compensation, auto liability, and health care.

9.04 Captive insurance entities are controlled by their owners and, in many cases, do not have employees to perform the necessary functions required to manage the operations of a captive. Most domestic captive domiciles require that the captive engage a captive manager who is experienced in operating insurance companies and who is knowledgeable of the domiciliary state's captive regulations. Typically, functions such as underwriting, billing and collecting premiums, investing and managing assets, investigating and settling claims under policies, accounting, and regulatory reporting are all outsourced to the captive manager or other third-party services providers.

9.05 Captive domiciles in the United States continue to expand as states pass legislation to facilitate the formation of domestic captives. The growth in the capital that captives control is also on the rise. The domiciles in the United States that contain the largest number of captives are Vermont, South Carolina, Hawaii, Arizona, the District of Columbia, and Nevada.

9.06 The primary offshore captive domiciles include Bermuda, Cayman Islands, British Virgin Islands, Guernsey, and Barbados. This chapter addresses offshore captives only to the extent that they are preparing financial statements in accordance with generally accepted accounting principles (GAAP).

Types of Captive Organizations

9.07 A pure captive insurance entity is the most common form of a captive that insures the risks of its parent and affiliated companies. They are also referred to as single parent captives. Typically, policies written by a pure captive insure high deductibles under original policies issued by rated insurers or through a fronting arrangement.

9.08 *Fronting* is a term that describes a specialized form of reinsurance that is frequently utilized in the captive insurance marketplace. In its most common form, a commercial insurance entity (fronting entity), licensed in the state where the insured risk is located, issues its policy to the insured. That risk is then fully or partially transferred from the fronting entity to a captive insurance entity through a reinsurance agreement known as a fronting agreement. Thus, the insured obtains a policy issued on the paper of the commercial insurance entity. However, economically, the risk of that coverage resides with the captive insurance entity. Several business reasons exist for this type of fronting arrangement:

> *a.* The need for a commercial carrier to issue the insurance policy for a particular risk
>
> *b.* To gain access to insure risks in multiple states without the burden of duplicative licensing and regulatory oversight requirements
>
> *c.* The need for a carrier with a minimum AM Best rating or the ability to meet other financial strength measures, or both, to issue the insurance policy for a particular risk

9.09 An additional use of fronting exists in which the captive, usually a single parent captive, serves as the fronting entity and issues a policy directly to the insured parent entity. That risk is then fully or partially reinsured to one or more domestic or foreign reinsurers. Consequently, the fronting captive would not retain all of the risks, and the parent entity has gained access to the reinsurance market. The risk could not be transferred to the reinsurer without the use of the single parent captive and fronting arrangement.

9.10 When the captive assumes coverage from the fronting entity, the fronting entity will generally require collateral to secure the captive's obligations to the fronting company under the fronting agreement. Collateral normally takes one of three forms:

> *a.* A captive's funds withheld by the fronting entity
>
> *b.* A trust agreement funded by investment securities of the captive
>
> *c.* A letter of credit issued on behalf of the captive by a bank, usually secured by investment securities of the captive

9.11 Group or association captive insurance entities insure the risks of similar organizations or the membership of an association. An association captive insurance entity may not insure any risks other than those of the member organizations of its association and their affiliated entities.

9.12 There are various benefits to an association and its membership in forming a captive insurance entity. Those benefits include the following:

    a. Meeting member needs for affordable insurance coverage or availability of coverages not otherwise provided by the commercial insurance market

    b. Source of revenue for the association

    c. Opportunity to increase association membership

9.13 In most states, association captive insurance companies are also allowed to take the form of a reciprocal. A *reciprocal insurance entity* is an unincorporated association formed under a state's insurance code in which participants exchange contracts of insurance in order to pool their risks. Because reciprocals are unincorporated, an attorney-in-fact, which acts as an agent or a manager, is used to enter into a contract on behalf of the reciprocal. In a reciprocal, profits (including investment income) and losses may be allocated back to each subscriber's savings account. Due to the fact that all pretax statutory income can be allocated to the subscribers, the reciprocal structure may provide an income tax advantage to groups whose members are nonprofit entities.

9.14 An attractive feature of reciprocals is that new policyholders can join in a way that is fair to both new and long standing policyholders because of the way profits and surplus contributions are accounted for. Each reciprocal is different based on the subscriber's agreement and governance rules.

9.15 Sponsored captive insurance entities insure the risks of separate, unrelated participants through participation agreements using, what are commonly known as, segregated cells. Essentially, participants "rent" a piece of the sponsored captive and may, in turn, operate as if they incorporated their own captive insurance entity.

9.16 Sponsored captive insurance entities consist of a general account that manages the general operations of the captive in exchange for a management fee charged to each segregated cell. The general account typically pays for all professional fees and general and administration fees, including, but not limited to, actuarial and accounting fees, captive management fees, premium taxes, licensing fees, and so on.

9.17 Typically, state laws provide that the assets and liabilities of each segregated cell must be kept segregated and separately identifiable from the assets and liabilities of the general account of the sponsored captive insurance entity, as well as from any other segregated cell.

9.18 Although it could vary by jurisdiction and change with case law, the liabilities of each segregated cell cannot be passed on to other segregated cells within the captive, as defined in the subscriber agreement.

9.19 Under the participation agreement, each segregated cell participant is required to make a contribution, as required by the domiciliary insurance department, in order to begin issuing policies. In addition, the participation agreement defines who holds the rights and obligations to the assets, liabilities, and activities of the segregated cell. The holder of these rights and obligations should be familiar with the guidance in Financial Accounting Standards Board (FASB) *Accounting Standards Codification* (ASC) 810, *Consolidation*, to determine if the segregated cells should be consolidated.

9.20 *Risk retention groups* (RRGs) are corporations or other limited liability associations organized under the Federal Liability Risk Retention Act (FLRRA) of 1986. Congress enacted this legislation to facilitate group insurance programs and increase the availability of liability insurance coverage that had become either unaffordable or unavailable due to a liability insurance crisis at that time. RRGs can be formed under either the traditional or captive insurance statutes.

9.21 Under the FLRRA, RRGs, once licensed by a domiciliary state, are permitted to insure risks in all states, with limited statutory oversight by the other state insurance departments. The RRG must first register with a state before writing policies but is not required to obtain a formal license to write business in that state.

9.22 Under the FLRRA, an RRG is permitted to write any form of commercial liability coverage, such as general liability, errors and omissions, directors and officers, medical malpractice, professional liability, and product liability. The FLRRA does not extend to workers' compensation, property insurance, or personal lines insurance, such as homeowners and personal auto insurance coverage.

9.23 The FLRRA requires that each policyholder of an RRG must be an owner of the RRG and each owner must also be a policyholder. Generally, policyholders are required to purchase one or more shares of the RRG's common stock, and the stock may be restricted.

9.24 RRGs are required to submit quarterly and annual statements using the National Association of Insurance Commissioners (NAIC) blank (that is, the yellow book). Even though the RRGs prepare the yellow book, most states require that the captive complete the blank using GAAP, not statutory accounting principles (SAP) prescribed or permitted by the RRG's state of domicile.

9.25 *Agency captive insurance entities* are captives owned by an insurance agency. The agency uses the captive to accept underwriting risk on some or all of the business placed by the agency. The majority of the risks insured consist of third-party risks. The agency captive operates similar to that of the traditional insurance entity in that it markets to unrelated third parties on a day to day basis.

9.26 Special purpose captives generally involve any captives that do not fit into a preceding description. Many states have written these into their captive laws to allow for new formations not previously considered, subject to approval by the state's commissioner or director of insurance.

Captive Operations

9.27 The first step to creating a captive is to determine the feasibility or cost effectiveness of the captive. The feasibility study aids in making the final determination of the projected cost effectiveness or viability of a captive. The feasibility study is generally prepared by a consulting actuary in conjunction with management and the captive manager. The study documents how the captive program will operate and projects the financial position of the captive for usually the first five years. The feasibility study is one of the most important documents of a captive in the early years of formation.

9.28 For the majority of captives, the day to day operations are generally handled by third-party service providers. The captive manager is the most significant third-party service provider outsourced by a captive insurance entity. The captive manager maintains the books and records of the captive insurer's business, transactions, and affairs at a location in the state of domicile. The captive manager prepares the necessary state required annual and quarterly statements and handles most of the correspondence with the state insurance departments.

9.29 Other third-party service providers used include auditors, actuaries, insurance brokers, reinsurance intermediaries, investment managers, attorneys, and claims adjusters.

Specific Transaction Considerations and Accounting Principles[1]

9.30 Many state's captive insurance regulators in the United States usually require captive insurance entities to maintain their accounting records using GAAP. However, some captive regulators will also permit the use of SAP prescribed and permitted in the captive's state of domicile. State insurance laws require captives to file annual financial reports, which may be in a prescribed format substantially different from the NAIC's annual statement and may also subject the captive to annual independent financial audits and periodic financial or market conduct examinations, or both, by the department of insurance.

9.31 Captive insurance entities generally follow the same GAAP reporting standards applicable to traditional insurance carriers and, consistent with other insurance entities, they must assess whether insurance and reinsurance contracts transfer insurance risk. One significant exception exists that many captive regulators permit: to allow captives to be capitalized with an irrevocable

---

[1] The International Accounting Standards Board (IASB) and its predecessor organization have been working for several years to develop guidance on accounting for insurance contracts. The project was split into two phases. Phase I addressed the application of existing International Financial Reporting Standards to entities that issue insurance contracts. Phase II, initiated in September 2004, is a comprehensive project on accounting for insurance contracts.

On August 2, 2007, the Financial Accounting Standards Board (FASB) issued the invitation to comment *An FASB Agenda Proposal: Accounting for Insurance Contracts by Insurers and Policyholders*. That invitation to comment included the discussion paper issued by the IASB Preliminary Views on Insurance Contracts that set forth the IASB's preliminary views on the main components of an accounting model for an issuer's rights and obligations (assets and liabilities) under an insurance contract. FASB issued the invitation to comment to gather information from its constituents to help decide whether there was a need for a comprehensive project on accounting for insurance contracts and whether FASB should undertake such a project jointly with the IASB.

In October 2008, FASB decided to join the IASB's insurance contract project.

In July 2010, the IASB issued the exposure draft Insurance Contracts. In developing the IASB's exposure draft, most of the discussions about the proposed insurance accounting approaches were held jointly with FASB. Although the boards reached common decisions in many areas, they reached different conclusions in others. Some FASB members prefer the IASB's proposed measurement model; however, the majority prefers an alternative model. Regardless of FASB members' individual views and uniform commitment to convergence, FASB determined that additional information was needed about whether the possible new accounting guidance would represent a sufficient improvement to generally accepted accounting principles to justify issuing new guidance. On September 17, 2010, FASB issued, for public comment, the discussion paper *Preliminary Views on Insurance Contracts*.

The boards are redeliberating significant issues based on feedback received on the IASB exposure draft and FASB discussion paper. FASB is expected to release an exposure draft and the IASB is expected to issue a targeted revised exposure draft during the first half of 2013. Readers should remain alert to any final pronouncements.

letter of credit secured by the assets of an entity or individual other than the captive. In this case, the captive may report the letter of credit as both an asset and equity; however, this accounting represents a departure from GAAP, and the auditor would have to consider this departure when reporting on the financial statements. Other departures from GAAP, although not as common, may exist and should be considered.

9.32 The following are areas of specific interest that may require accounting consideration:

   a. *Specific state captive regulatory and reporting requirements.*

   b. *Risk transfer.* Risk transfer analysis requires consideration of all related contracts in determining whether risk transfer occurs. The nature of captives often results in captive structures, guarantees, and other arrangements that may need to be considered in the analysis.

   c. *Surplus note.* Permitting the captive to treat a surplus note as a component of shareholders' equity, not a liability.

   d. *Investments.* Captive insurance entities are required to submit a board-approved investment policy or the captive's business plan to their regulators. Upon acceptance of the plan, captives may invest in any investments within the scope of that policy. One common exception is for captives operating as RRGs, which may be subject to the same investment restrictions applicable to traditional insurance companies.

   e. *Related party transactions.* Because of the close nature of the shareholders, often, several related party transactions exist involving investments in commonly owned subsidiaries, a note receivable from the parent entity, a letter of credit in which the assets of the parent entity are used as collateral, and so on.

   f. *Loans to the parent.* Pure captives are sometimes permitted to loan their capital back to the parent entity in the form of a loan-back. A *loan-back* is a promissory note from the parent to the captive, generally payable on demand, that will return any unnecessary funds to the parent or owner upon approval of the insurance commissioner. This approval is generally based on the parent or owner's ability to repay the loan-back on demand. This is often done to obtain higher investment rates of return through greater buying power of the parent or to improve the cash flows from the parent entity's standpoint.

   g. *Consolidation under FASB ASC 810.* A captive may qualify as a variable interest entity and be consolidated into the financial statements of the entity to which it provides benefits.

Taxes

9.33 Captive insurance entities fall under the same federal income tax law as commercial insurance entities. The same federal income tax provisions exist for loss reserve discounting, unearned premium reserves, dividends and tax exempt interest, small property and liability insurance entity provisions, and adjusted current earnings.

9.34 Some captives make the election to be taxed as a small insurance entity under Internal Revenue Code (IRC) Section 831(b). This election simplifies the calculation of taxable income and is only available for insurance companies that receive gross annual premium of $1.2 million or less. Under IRC Section 831(b), insurance entities are taxed on net investment income only.

9.35 One of the issues facing certain captive insurance entities is the ability to qualify as an insurance entity under the IRC. To qualify as an insurance entity, the captive insurance entity would need to have adequate risk shifting and distributions. Preparers and auditors should familiarize themselves with rulings issued by the IRS, such as Revenue Ruling 2001-31, Revenue Procedure 2002-75, Revenue Rulings 2002-89 through 2002-91, Notice 2003-34, Revenue Ruling 2005-40, and Notice 2005-49.

Audit Considerations

Audit Planning

9.36 In accordance with AU-C section 300, *Planning an Audit* (AICPA, *Professional Standards*), the auditor should plan the audit so that it is responsive to the assessment of the risks of material misstatement based on the auditor's understanding of the entity and its environment, including its internal control. The nature, timing, and extent of planning vary with the size and complexity of the entity, and with the auditor's experience with the entity and understanding of the entity. Refer to chapter 2, "Audit Considerations," of this guide for a detailed discussion of audit planning.

Consideration of Fraud in a Financial Statement Audit

9.37 Risks are inherent in all audit engagements, including the possibility that fraudulent acts may cause a material misstatement of financial statements. AU-C section 240, *Consideration of Fraud in a Financial Statement Audit* (AICPA, *Professional Standards*), addresses the auditor's responsibilities relating to fraud in an audit of financial statements. Because of the characteristics of fraud, the auditor's exercise of professional skepticism is important when considering the risk of material misstatement due to fraud. Readers should refer to additional discussion of AU-C section 240 in chapter 2 of this guide.

Audit Risk Factors

9.38 As discussed in paragraph .A1 of AU-C section 320, *Materiality in Planning and Performing an Audit* (AICPA, *Professional Standards*), *audit risk* is the risk that the auditor expresses an inappropriate audit opinion when the financial statements are materially misstated. Audit risk is a function of the risks of material misstatement and detection risk. Materiality and audit risk are considered throughout the audit, in particular, when

    a. determining the nature and extent of risk assessment procedures to be performed;

    b. identifying and assessing the risks of material misstatement;

    c. determining the nature, timing, and extent of further audit procedures; and *d.* evaluating the effect of uncorrected misstatements, if any, on the financial statements and in forming the opinion in the auditor's report.

9.39 Experience has demonstrated that audit risk may be greater in certain areas than in others. Generally, captive insurance entities pose similar specific audit risks as discussed throughout the other chapters of this guide. However, captive insurance entities by their nature, structure, or unique regulatory requirements may pose some unique audit risks. These risk factors, internal control considerations, and audit responses are discussed further herein.

9.40 Identification of significant accounts and disclosures by the auditor is part of the planning process. As required by AU-C section 315, *Understanding the Entity and Its Environment and Assessing the Risks of Material Misstatement* (AICPA, *Professional Standards*), to enable the auditor to understand the classes of transactions, account balances, and disclosures to be expected in the financial statements, the auditor should obtain an understanding of the relevant industry, regulatory, and other external factors, including the applicable financial reporting framework, and the nature of the entity.

Internal Control

9.41 Paragraph .04 of AU-C section 315 defines *internal control* as

> a process effected by those charged with governance, management, and other personnel that is designed to provide reasonable assurance about the achievement of the entity's objectives with regard to the reliability of financial reporting, effectiveness and efficiency of operations, and compliance with applicable laws and regulations. Internal control over safeguarding of assets against unauthorized acquisition, use, or disposition may include controls relating to financial reporting and operations objectives.

Internal control consists of the following five interrelated components:

    a. Control environment

    b. The entity's risk assessment process

    c. The information system, including the related business processes relevant to financial reporting and communication

    d. Control activities relevant to the audit

    e. Monitoring of controls

AU-C section 315 requires the auditor to obtain an understanding of these components of the entity's internal control. Paragraphs 2.31–.41 of chapter 2 of this guide discuss in detail the components of internal control.

9.42 Paragraph .13 of AU-C section 315 requires that the auditor should obtain an understanding of internal control relevant to the audit, and what is relevant to the audit is a matter of the auditor's professional judgment. Paragraph .A62 of AU-C section 315 identifies factors relevant to the auditor's professional judgment about whether a control, individually or in combination with others is relevant to the audit.

Audit Procedures Responsive to the Assessed Risks of Material Misstatement

9.43 Generally, the audit procedures for captive insurance entities are consistent with those procedures discussed throughout the other chapters of this guide. However, captive insurance entities, by their nature or structure, do pose some unique audit risks such as the following:

   a. *Segregation of duties.* Captives are typically small when compared to that of a traditional insurance entity and, as such, the volume of transactions in a captive insurance entity is generally low. Internal controls over the segregation of duties may often be limited given the small size of the accounting department. This risk may often be mitigated by board oversight. The captive's board of directors is typically comprised of representatives from the parent entity, shareholders, or both, and will often include a senior person from the captive management entity or their state of domicile legal counsel. Depending on the size of the captive, the board of directors may have separate underwriting, claims, investment and audit or finance committees that provide oversight of the various functions within the captive. The auditor may understand and plan the audit procedures in response to a lack of segregation of duties while considering the effectiveness of entity level compensating controls.

   b. *Completeness of the accounting records.* Generally, the captive manager is the main point of contact for the auditor in planning and executing the audit. Due to the varying structures of captive insurance entities and their use of third-party service providers and related parties, the captive manager is usually responsible for coordinating the flow of information necessary for the captive insurance entity's complete and accurate financial reporting. The auditor should consider the risks posed by the captive insurance entity's structure and develop the audit testing plans in response to these risks, which may require specific cutoff testing, subsequent event procedures, or confirmations with third parties.

   c. *Use of service providers.* Many captive insurance entities outsource key business processing functions to third-party service providers. The auditor should consider the design of the third-party service providers' internal controls and the impact on the captive insurance entity's internal controls over financial reporting. The auditor may decide to directly test the third-party service providers' internal controls. Alternatively, many service providers will have service organization controls (SOC) reports (SSAE 16 reports) available. The auditor may be able to rely on the design and effectiveness of the internal controls by obtaining a SOC 1 type 2 report and testing any related user controls at the captive insurance entity.

   d. *Communication with other auditors.* The captive insurance entity's activities may be consolidated by a parent or related party that is audited by other auditors. Depending on the materiality of the captive to the consolidating entity, the parent's auditors may plan to rely on the work of the captive insurance entity's auditor that may require additional coordination and communication between the respective auditors in accordance with generally accepted auditing standards.

e. *Communication with regulators.* The auditor should be aware of captive insurance laws and regulations that exist in the state in which the captive is domiciled. Generally, the captive insurance regulators are a separate department within the state insurance department and may promulgate rules and regulations under a separate set of state insurance laws and regulations. Many captive regulators require the auditor (in some cases the lead audit partner) to submit an application to be recognized by the regulator as an approved auditor for captive insurance entities. Certain captive insurance domiciles require specific communications from the auditor at the conclusion of the audit. The auditor should be aware of the domiciliary regulator's captive insurance laws and regulations.

f. *Departures from GAAP.* Generally, captive insurance laws require captive insurance entities to file their regulatory financial reports using GAAP. As discussed in paragraph 9.31, the regulators may permit captive insurance entities to depart from GAAP. Although these departures may be permitted by the regulators, the auditor should consider the impact to the auditor's report and the need to issue a modified opinion.

g. *Risk retention groups.* The auditor should be familiar with the constraints around the insurance that can be written by an RRG and that it is compliant with the laws of the state they are domiciled in.

Chapter 10
Reports on Audited Financial Statements

Reports on Financial Statements

10.01 AU-C section 700, *Forming an Opinion and Reporting on Financial Statements* (AICPA, *Professional Standards*), addresses the auditor's responsibilities to form an opinion on the financial statements and the form and content of the auditor's report as a result of an audit of financial statements. When, in forming an opinion in accordance with AU-C section 700, the auditor concludes that a modification to the auditor's opinion on the financial statements is necessary, AU-C section 705, *Modifications to the Opinion in the Independent Auditor's Report* (AICPA, *Professional Standards*), applies. AU-C section 706, *Emphasis-of-Matter Paragraphs and Other-Matter Paragraphs in the Independent Auditor's Report* (AICPA, *Professional Standards*), addresses additional communications in the auditor's report. This chapter provides an overview of the requirements of AU-C section Nos. 700, 705, and 706, including reporting on special purpose financial statements that, together with the auditor's report, are intended for general use or limited use. It is recommended that auditors be familiar with the overall objectives and application materials included in the AU-C sections. Such reports may contain an unmodified opinion, an unmodified opinion with additional communication, a qualified opinion, a disclaimer of opinion, or an adverse opinion. This chapter contains a brief discussion of each of these opinions for insurance entities, with an emphasis on illustrating issues that an auditor may encounter in auditing and reporting on the financial statements of insurance entities.

> *Considerations for Audits Performed in Accordance With Public Company Accounting Oversight Board (PCAOB) Standards*
>
> PCAOB Auditing Standard No. 1, *References in Auditors' Reports to the Standards of the Public Company Accounting Oversight Board* (AICPA, *PCAOB Standards and Related Rules*, Auditing Standards), provides illustrative reports for audits of financial statements under PCAOB auditing standards.
>
> PCAOB Auditing Standard No. 5, *An Audit of Internal Control Over Financial Reporting That Is Integrated With an Audit of Financial Statements* (AICPA, *PCAOB Standards and Related Rules*, Auditing Standards), establishes requirements and provides guidance for auditors engaged to audit both a company's financial statements and its internal control over financial reporting.

10.02 The illustrative auditors' reports in this chapter are presented to assist auditors in drafting their reports on insurance entities under various circumstances. Each illustration intentionally describes the same general fact situation to avoid suggesting that particular facts always lead to a particular form of opinion. The reports are illustrative; the facts and circumstances of each particular audit will govern the appropriate form of opinion.

Unmodified Opinions on GAAP Financial Statements

10.03 As stated in AU-C section 700, the objectives of the auditor are to form an opinion on the financial statements based on an evaluation of the audit evidence obtained, including evidence obtained about comparative financial statements or comparative financial information, and to express clearly that opinion on the financial statements through a written report that also describes the basis for that opinion. Paragraphs .13–.21 of AU-C section 700 contain guidance to help the auditor determine when to express an unmodified opinion. Paragraphs .22–.41 of AU-C section 700 describe the format and content of the auditor's report for audits conducted in accordance with generally accepted auditing standards (GAAS). When forming an opinion and reporting on special purpose financial statements (such as those prepared in accordance with a regulatory basis of accounting), the auditor should apply the requirements in AU-C section 700 as discussed in paragraph .14 of AU-C section 800, *Special Considerations—Audits of Financial Statements Prepared in Accordance With Special Purpose Frameworks* (AICPA, *Professional Standards*). Opinions on regulatory basis financial statements intended for general use are discussed in paragraphs 10.36–.41, and regulatory basis financial statements intended for limited use are discussed in paragraphs 10.42–.46.

10.04 The following is an illustration of an auditor's report (unmodified opinion), under GAAS, on an insurance entity's financial statements prepared in accordance with generally accepted accounting principles (GAAP):

Independent Auditor's Report[1]

[Appropriate Addressee]

Report on the Financial Statements[2]

We have audited the accompanying financial statements of ABC Property and Liability Company, which comprise the balance sheets as of December 31, 20X2 and 20X1, and the related statements of income, change in stockholders' equity, other comprehensive income, and cash flows for the years then ended, and the related notes to the financial statements.

Management's Responsibility for the Financial Statements

Management is responsible for the preparation and fair presentation of these financial statements in accordance with accounting principles generally accepted in the United States of America; this includes the design, implementation, and maintenance of internal control relevant to the preparation and fair presentation of financial statements that are free from material misstatement, whether due to fraud or error.

Auditor's Responsibility

Our responsibility is to express an opinion on these financial statements based on our audits. We conducted our audits in accordance with auditing standards generally accepted in the United States of America. Those standards require that we plan and perform the audit to obtain reasonable assurance about whether the financial statements are free from material misstatement.

An audit involves performing procedures to obtain audit evidence about the amounts and disclosures in the financial statements. The procedures selected depend on the auditor's judgment, including the assessment of the risks of material misstatement of the financial statements, whether due to fraud or error. In making those risk assessments, the auditor considers internal control

---

[1] For audits conducted in accordance with Public Company Accounting Oversight Board (PCAOB) standards, refer to PCAOB Auditing Standard No. 1, *References in Auditors' Reports to the Standards of the Public Company Accounting Oversight Board* (AICPA, *PCAOB Standards and Related Rules*, Auditing Standards).

[2] The subtitle "Report on the Financial Statements" is unnecessary in circumstances when the second subtitle "Report on Other Legal and Regulatory Requirements" is not applicable.

Reports on Audited Financial Statements

relevant to the entity's preparation and fair presentation of the financial statements in order to design audit procedures that are appropriate in the circumstances, but not for the purpose of expressing an opinion on the effectiveness of the entity's internal control.[3] Accordingly, we express no such opinion. An audit also includes evaluating the appropriateness of accounting policies used and the reasonableness of significant accounting estimates made by management, as well as evaluating the overall presentation of the financial statements.

We believe that the audit evidence we have obtained is sufficient and appropriate to provide a basis for our audit opinion.

Opinion

In our opinion, the financial statements referred to above present fairly, in all material respects, the financial position of ABC Property and Liability Company as of December 31, 20X2 and 20X1, and the results of its operations and its cash flows for the years then ended in accordance with accounting principles generally accepted in the United States of America.

Report on Other Legal and Regulatory Requirements

[*Form and content of this section of the auditor's report will vary depending on the nature of the auditor's other reporting responsibilities.*]

[*Auditor's signature*]

[*Auditor's city and state*]

[*Date of the auditor's report*]

10.05 The following is an illustration of an auditor's report, under PCAOB standards, on an insurance entity's financial statements:

Report of Independent Registered Public Accounting Firm

We have audited the accompanying balance sheets of ABC Property and Liability Company as of December 31, 20X2 and 20X1, and the related statements of income, changes in stockholders' equity, other comprehensive income, and cash flows for the years then ended. These financial statements are the responsibility of the Company's management. Our responsibility is to express an opinion on these financial statements based on our audits.

We conducted our audits in accordance with the standards of the Public Company Accounting Oversight Board (United States). Those standards require that we plan and perform the audits to obtain reasonable assurance about whether the financial statements are free of material misstatement. An audit includes examining, on a test basis, evidence supporting the amounts and disclosures in the financial statements. An audit also includes assessing the accounting principles used and significant estimates made by management, as well as evaluating the overall financial statement presentation. We believe that our audits provide a reasonable basis for our opinion.

In our opinion, the financial statements referred to above present fairly, in all material respects, the financial position of ABC Property and Liability Company as of December 31, 20X2 and 20X1, and the results of its operations and

---

[3] In circumstances when the auditor also has responsibility to express an opinion on the effectiveness of internal control in conjunction with the audit of the consolidated financial statements, this sentence would be worded as follows:

> In making those risk assessments, the auditor considers internal control relevant to the entity's preparation and fair presentation of the consolidated financial statements in order to design audit procedures that are appropriate in the circumstances.

In addition, the next sentence, "Accordingly, we express no such opinion," would not be included.

its cash flows for the years then ended, in conformity with U.S. generally accepted accounting principles.

[*Firm Signature*]

[*City, State*]

[*Date*]

Modified Opinions

10.06 As noted in paragraph .07 of AU-C section 705, the auditor should modify the opinion in the auditor's report when

> *a.* the auditor concludes that, based on the audit evidence obtained, the financial statements as a whole are materially misstated, or
>
> *b.* the auditor is unable to obtain sufficient appropriate audit evidence to conclude that the financial statements as a whole are free from material misstatement.

10.07 There are three types of modified opinions: a qualified opinion, an adverse opinion, and a disclaimer of opinion. As discussed in paragraph .02 of AU-C section 705, the decision regarding which type of modified opinion is appropriate depends upon the following:

> *a.* The nature of the matter giving rise to the modification (that is, whether the financial statements are materially misstated or, in the case of an inability to obtain sufficient appropriate audit evidence, may be materially misstated)
>
> *b.* The auditor's professional judgment about the pervasiveness of the effects or possible effects of the matter on the financial statements

10.08 Paragraphs .08–.16 of AU-C section 705 provide the requirements for determining the type of modification to the auditor's opinion.

10.09 As discussed in paragraphs .17–.23 of AU-C section 705

> [w]hen the auditor modifies the opinion on the financial statements, the auditor should, in addition to the specific elements required by AU-C section 700, include a paragraph in the auditor's report that provides a description of the matter giving rise to the modification. The auditor should place this paragraph immediately before the opinion paragraph in the auditor's report and use a heading that includes "Basis for Qualified Opinion," "Basis for Adverse Opinion," or "Basis for Disclaimer of Opinion," as appropriate. As stated in paragraph .23 of AU-C section 705, when the auditor modifies the audit opinion, the auditor should use a heading that includes "Qualified Opinion," "Adverse Opinion," or "Disclaimer of Opinion," as appropriate.
>
> If there is a material misstatement of the financial statements that relates to specific amounts in the financial statements (including quantitative disclosures), the auditor should include in the basis for modification paragraph a description and quantification of the financial effects of the misstatement, unless impracticable. If it is not practicable to quantify the financial effects, the auditor should so state in the basis for modification paragraph.

Reports on Audited Financial Statements

If there is a material misstatement of the financial statements that relates to narrative disclosures, the auditor should include in the basis for modification paragraph an explanation of how the disclosures are misstated.

If there is a material misstatement of the financial statements that relates to the omission of information required to be presented or disclosed, the auditor should

a. discuss the omission of such information with those charged with governance;

b. describe in the basis for modification paragraph the nature of the omitted information; and

c. include the omitted information, provided that it is practicable to do so and the auditor has obtained sufficient appropriate audit evidence about the omitted information.

If the modification results from an inability to obtain sufficient appropriate audit evidence, the auditor should include in the basis for modification paragraph the reasons for that inability.

Even if the auditor has expressed an adverse opinion or disclaimed an opinion on the financial statements, the auditor should

a. describe in the basis for modification paragraph any other matters of which the auditor is aware that would have required a modification to the opinion and the effects thereof, and

b. consider the need to describe in an emphasis-of-matter or other-matter paragraph(s) any other matters of which the auditor is aware that would have resulted in additional communications in the auditor's report on the financial statements that are not modifications of the auditor's opinion.

Qualified Opinion

10.10 As stated in paragraph .08 of AU-C section 705, the auditor should express a qualified opinion when

a. the auditor, having obtained sufficient appropriate audit evidence, concludes that misstatements, individually or in the aggregate, are material but not pervasive to the financial statements, or

b. the auditor is unable to obtain sufficient appropriate audit evidence on which to base the opinion, but the auditor concludes that the possible effects on the financial statements of undetected misstatements, if any, could be material but not pervasive.

10.11 As discussed in paragraph .24 of AU-C section 705, when the auditor expresses a qualified opinion due to a material misstatement in the financial statements, the auditor should state in the opinion paragraph that, in the auditor's opinion, except for the effects of the matter(s) described in the basis for qualified opinion paragraph, the financial statements are presented fairly, in all material respects, in accordance with the applicable financial reporting framework. When the modification arises from an inability to obtain sufficient appropriate audit evidence, the auditor should use the corresponding phrase, "except for the possible effects of the matter(s)..." for the modified opinion.

AAG-PLI 10.11

Disclaimer of Opinion

10.12 As stated in paragraph .10 of AU-C section 705, the auditor should disclaim an opinion when the auditor is unable to obtain sufficient appropriate audit evidence on which to base the opinion, and the auditor concludes that the possible effects on the financial statements of undetected misstatements, if any, could be both material and pervasive.

10.13 As discussed in paragraph .26 of AU-C section 705, when the auditor disclaims an opinion due to an inability to obtain sufficient appropriate audit evidence, the auditor should state in the opinion paragraph that

> a. because of the significance of the matter(s) described in the basis for disclaimer of opinion paragraph, the auditor has not been able to obtain sufficient appropriate audit evidence to provide a basis for an audit opinion, and
>
> b. accordingly, the auditor does not express an opinion on the financial statements.

10.14 Also as discussed in paragraph .28 of AU-C section 705, when the auditor disclaims an opinion due to an inability to obtain sufficient appropriate audit evidence, the auditor should amend the introductory paragraph of the auditor's report to state that the auditor was engaged to audit the financial statements. The auditor should also amend the description of the auditor's responsibility and the description of the scope of the audit to state only the following:

> Our responsibility is to express an opinion on the financial statements based on conducting the audit in accordance with auditing standards generally accepted in the United States of America. Because of the matter(s) described in the basis for disclaimer of opinion paragraph, however, we were not able to obtain sufficient appropriate audit evidence to provide a basis for an audit opinion.

Adverse Opinion

10.15 As stated in paragraph .09 of AU-C section 705, the auditor should express an adverse opinion when the auditor, having obtained sufficient appropriate audit evidence, concludes that misstatements, individually or in the aggregate, are both material and pervasive to the financial statements.

10.16 As discussed in paragraph .25 of AU-C section 705, when the auditor expresses an adverse opinion, the auditor should state in the opinion paragraph that, in the auditor's opinion, because of the significance of the matter(s) described in the basis for adverse opinion paragraph, the financial statements are not presented fairly in accordance with the applicable financial reporting framework.

10.17 As discussed in paragraph .27 of AU-C section 705, when the auditor expresses a qualified or an adverse opinion, the auditor should amend the description of the auditor's responsibility to state that the auditor believes that the audit evidence the auditor has obtained is sufficient and appropriate to provide a basis for the auditor's modified audit opinion.

Emphasis-of-Matter Paragraphs

Emphasis of a Matter

10.18 As discussed in paragraph .06 of AU-C section 706, if the auditor considers it necessary to draw users' attention to a matter appropriately presented or disclosed in the financial statements that, in the auditor's professional judgment, is of such importance that it is fundamental to users' understanding of the financial statements, the auditor should include an emphasis-of-matter paragraph in the auditor's report, provided that the auditor has obtained sufficient appropriate audit evidence that the matter is not materially misstated in the financial statements. Such a paragraph should refer only to information presented or disclosed in the financial statements.

10.19 As stated in paragraph .07 of AU-C section 706, when the auditor includes an emphasis-of-matter paragraph in the auditor's report, the auditor should

> *a.* include it immediately after the opinion paragraph in the auditor's report;
>
> *b.* use the heading "Emphasis of Matter" or other appropriate heading;
>
> *c.* include in the paragraph a clear reference to the matter being emphasized and to where relevant disclosures that fully describe the matter can be found in the financial statements; and
>
> *d.* indicate that the auditor's opinion is not modified with respect to the matter emphasized.

10.20 The following is an illustration of an unmodified opinion, under GAAS, on the financial statements of an insurance entity prepared in accordance with GAAP, and includes an emphasis-of-matter paragraph regarding the entity's adopting a new accounting standard. The circumstances described in the emphasis-of-matter paragraph of this illustrative report represent assumptions made for purposes of illustration only. A similar paragraph could be adapted for use in an opinion on statutory basis financial statements. This illustration is not intended to provide criteria or other guidelines to be used by auditors in deciding whether an emphasis-of-matter paragraph should be added to their reports.

Independent Auditor's Report[4]

[Appropriate Addressee]

Report on the Financial Statements[5]

We have audited the accompanying financial statements of ABC Property and Liability Company, which comprise the balance sheets as of December 31, 20X2 and 20X1, and the related statements of income, changes in stockholders' equity, other comprehensive income, and cash flows for the years then ended, and the related notes to the financial statements.

---

[4] See footnote 1.
[5] See footnote 2.

Management's Responsibility for the Financial Statements

Management is responsible for the preparation and fair presentation of these financial statements in accordance with accounting principles generally accepted in the United States of America; this includes the design, implementation, and maintenance of internal control relevant to the preparation and fair presentation of financial statements that are free from material misstatement, whether due to fraud or error.

Auditor's Responsibility

Our responsibility is to express an opinion on these financial statements based on our audits. We conducted our audits in accordance with auditing standards generally accepted in the United States of America. Those standards require that we plan and perform the audit to obtain reasonable assurance about whether the financial statements are free from material misstatement.

An audit involves performing procedures to obtain audit evidence about the amounts and disclosures in the financial statements. The procedures selected depend on the auditor's judgment, including the assessment of the risks of material misstatement of the financial statements, whether due to fraud or error. In making those risk assessments, the auditor considers internal control relevant to the entity's preparation and fair presentation of the financial statements in order to design audit procedures that are appropriate in the circumstances, but not for the purpose of expressing an opinion on the effectiveness of the entity's internal control.[6] Accordingly, we express no such opinion. An audit also includes evaluating the appropriateness of accounting policies used and the reasonableness of significant accounting estimates made by management, as well as evaluating the overall presentation of the financial statements.

We believe that the audit evidence we have obtained is sufficient and appropriate to provide a basis for our audit opinion.

Opinion

In our opinion, the financial statements referred to above present fairly, in all material respects, the financial position of ABC Property and Liability Company as of December 31, 20X2 and 20X1, and the results of its operations and its cash flows for the years then ended in accordance with accounting principles generally accepted in the United States of America.

Emphasis of Matter

As discussed in Note XX to the financial statements, as of 1/1/20X2 ABC Property and Liability Company adopted the accounting requirements of FASB ASU No. 2010-26, *Financial Services—Insurance (Topic 944): Accounting for Costs Associated with Acquiring or Renewing Insurance Contracts (a consensus of the FASB Emerging Issues Task Force)*, and changed its accounting for determining deferrable costs. The guidance was applied prospectively as of 1/1/20X2. Our opinion is not modified with respect to this matter.

[Auditor's signature]

[Auditor's city and state]

[Date of the auditor's report]

10.21 The following is an illustration of an unqualified opinion, under PCAOB standards, on the financial statements of an insurance entity and includes an emphasis-of-matter paragraph regarding the entity's failure to

---

[6] See footnote 3.

meet minimum risk-based capital standards. The circumstances described in the emphasis-of-matter paragraph of this illustrative report represent assumptions made for purposes of illustration only. A similar paragraph could be adapted for use in an opinion on statutory basis financial statements. This illustration is not intended to provide criteria or other guidelines to be used by auditors in deciding whether an emphasis-of-matter paragraph should be added to their reports.

Report of Independent Registered Public Accounting Firm

We have audited the accompanying balance sheets of ABC Property and Liability Company as of December 31, 20X2 and 20X1, and the related statements of income, changes in stockholders' equity, other comprehensive income, and cash flows for the years then ended. These financial statements are the responsibility of the Company's management. Our responsibility is to express an opinion on these financial statements based on our audits.

We conducted our audits in accordance with the standards of the Public Company Accounting Oversight Board (United States). Those standards require that we plan and perform the audits to obtain reasonable assurance about whether the financial statements are free of material misstatement. An audit includes examining, on a test basis, evidence supporting the amounts and disclosures in the financial statements. An audit also includes assessing the accounting principles used and significant estimates made by management, as well as evaluating the overall financial statement presentation. We believe that our audits provide a reasonable basis for our opinion.

In our opinion, the financial statements referred to above present fairly, in all material respects, the financial position of ABC Property and Liability Company as of December 31, 20X2 and 20X1, and the results of its operations and its cash flows for the years then ended, in conformity with U.S. generally accepted accounting principles.

As discussed in Note XX to the financial statements, as of 1/1/20X2 the ABC Property and Liability Company adopted the accounting requirements of FASB ASU No. 2010-26, *Financial Services—Insurance(Topic 944): Accounting for Costs Associated with Acquiring or Renewing Insurance Contracts (a consensus of the FASB Emerging Issues Task Force)*, and changed its accounting for determining deferrable costs. The guidance was applied prospectively as of 1/1/20X2.

[*Firm Signature*]

[*City, State*]

[*Date*]

Uncertainties

10.22 Conclusive audit evidence concerning the ultimate outcome of uncertainties cannot be expected to exist at the time of the audit because the outcome and related audit evidence are prospective. In these circumstances, management is responsible for estimating the effect of future events on the financial statements, or determining that a reasonable estimate cannot be made and making the required disclosures, in accordance with the applicable framework, based on management's analysis of existing conditions. An audit includes an assessment of whether the audit evidence is sufficient to support management's analysis. Absence of the existence of information related to the outcome of an uncertainty does not necessarily lead to a conclusion that the audit evidence supporting management's assertion is not sufficient. Rather, the auditor's professional judgment regarding the sufficiency of the audit evidence is based on the audit evidence that is, or should be, available. If, after considering the existing conditions and available evidence, the auditor concludes that sufficient audit evidence supports management's assertions about the nature of a matter involving an uncertainty and its presentation or disclosure in the financial statements, an unmodified opinion ordinarily is appropriate.

Going Concern

10.23 AU-C section 570, *The Auditor's Consideration of an Entity's Ability to Continue as a Going Concern* (AICPA, *Professional Standards*), establishes requirements and guidance on the auditor's responsibility in an audit of financial statements with respect to evaluating whether there is substantial doubt about the entity's ability to continue as a going concern for a reasonable period of time. Chapter 2, "Audit Considerations," describes going concern considerations as they relate to property and liability insurance entities and discusses how an insurance entity's regulatory capital position affects the auditor's assessment of whether there is substantial doubt about the insurance entity's ability to continue as a going concern. AU-C section 570 establishes requirements and guidance on going concern consideration audit documentation that is discussed in paragraphs 2.104–.112 of this guide. If the auditor concludes that there is substantial doubt about an insurance entity's ability to continue as a going concern for a reasonable period of time, the report should include an emphasis-of-matter paragraph (following the opinion paragraph) to reflect that conclusion. The auditor's conclusion about the insurance entity's ability to continue as a going concern should be expressed through the use of the phrase *substantial doubt about the insurance entity's ability to continue as a going concern*, or similar wording that includes the terms *substantial doubt* and *going concern*.

10.24 The following is an illustration of an auditor's report (unmodified opinion), under GAAS, on the financial statements of an insurance entity prepared in accordance with GAAP that includes an emphasis-of-matter paragraph because of the existence of substantial doubt about the insurance entity's ability to continue as a going concern for a reasonable period of time. The circumstances described in the emphasis-of-matter paragraph of this illustrative report represent assumptions made for purposes of illustration only. A similar paragraph could be adapted for use in an opinion on statutory basis financial statements. This illustration is not intended to provide criteria or other guidelines for the auditor to use in deciding whether an emphasis-of-matter paragraph is necessary in their reports.

Independent Auditor's Report[7]

[*Appropriate Addressee*]

Report on the Financial Statements[8]

We have audited the accompanying financial statements of ABC Property and Liability Company, which comprise the balance sheets as of December 31, 20X2 and 20X1, and the related statements of income, changes in stockholders' equity, other comprehensive income, and cash flows for the years then ended, and the related notes to the financial statements.

---

[7] See footnote 1.
[8] See footnote 2.

Management's Responsibility for the Financial Statements

Management is responsible for the preparation and fair presentation of these financial statements in accordance with accounting principles generally accepted in the United States of America; this includes the design, implementation, and maintenance of internal control relevant to the preparation and fair presentation of financial statements that are free from material misstatement, whether due to fraud or error.

Auditor's Responsibility

Our responsibility is to express an opinion on these financial statements based on our audits. We conducted our audits in accordance with auditing standards generally accepted in the United States of America. Those standards require that we plan and perform the audit to obtain reasonable assurance about whether the financial statements are free from material misstatement.

An audit involves performing procedures to obtain audit evidence about the amounts and disclosures in the financial statements. The procedures selected depend on the auditor's judgment, including the assessment of the risks of material misstatement of the financial statements, whether due to fraud or error. In making those risk assessments, the auditor considers internal control relevant to the entity's preparation and fair presentation of the financial statements in order to design audit procedures that are appropriate in the circumstances, but not for the purpose of expressing an opinion on the effectiveness of the entity's internal control.[9] Accordingly, we express no such opinion. An audit also includes evaluating the appropriateness of accounting policies used and the reasonableness of significant accounting estimates made by management, as well as evaluating the overall presentation of the consolidated financial statements.

We believe that the audit evidence we have obtained is sufficient and appropriate to provide a basis for our audit opinion.

Opinion

In our opinion, the financial statements referred to above present fairly, in all material respects, the financial position of ABC Property and Liability Company as of December 31, 20X2 and 20X1, and the results of its operations and its cash flows for the years then ended in accordance with accounting principles generally accepted in the United States of America.

Going Concern

The accompanying financial statements have been prepared assuming that ABC Property and Liability Company will continue as a going concern. As discussed in Note XX to the consolidated financial statements, [*State of domicile's insurance regulatory body*] imposes risk-based capital requirements on insurance entities, including the Company. At December 31, 20X2, the Company's total adjusted capital is at the company action level based on the risk-based capital calculation required by [*State of domicile's insurance regulatory body*]. The Company has filed a comprehensive financial plan with the commissioner outlining the Company's plans for attaining the required levels of regulatory capital by December 31, 20XX. To date, the Company has not received notification from the commissioner regarding acceptance or rejection of its comprehensive financial plan. Failure to meet the capital requirements and interim capital targets included in the Company's plan would expose the Company to regulatory sanctions that may include restrictions on operations and growth, mandatory asset dispositions, and placing the Company under

---

[9] See footnote 3.

regulatory control. These matters raise substantial doubt about the ability of ABC Property and Liability Company to continue as a going concern. The ability of the Company to continue as a going concern is dependent on many factors, one of which is regulatory action, including ultimate acceptance of the Company's comprehensive financial plan. Management's plans in regard to these matters are described in Note XX. The accompanying consolidated financial statements do not include any adjustments that might result from the outcome of this uncertainty. Our opinion is not modified with respect to this matter.

[Auditor's signature]

[Auditor's city and state]

[Date of the auditor's report]

10.25 The following is an illustration of an auditor's report (unmodified opinion), under PCAOB standards, on the financial statements of an insurance entity prepared in accordance with PCAOB standards, that includes an emphasis-of-matter paragraph because of the existence of substantial doubt about the insurance entity's ability to continue as a going concern for a reasonable period of time. The circumstances described in the emphasis-of-matter paragraph of this illustrative report represent assumptions made for purposes of illustration only. A similar paragraph could be adapted for use in an opinion on statutory basis financial statements. This illustration is not intended to provide criteria or other guidelines for the auditor to use in deciding whether an emphasis-of-matter paragraph is necessary in their reports.

Report of Independent Registered Public Accounting Firm

We have audited the accompanying balance sheets of ABC Property and Liability Company as of December 31, 20X2 and 20X1, and the related statements of income, changes in stockholders' equity, other comprehensive income, and cash flows for the years then ended. These financial statements are the responsibility of the Company's management. Our responsibility is to express an opinion on these financial statements based on our audits.

We conducted our audits in accordance with the standards of the Public Company Accounting Oversight Board (United States). Those standards require that we plan and perform the audits to obtain reasonable assurance about whether the financial statements are free of material misstatement. An audit includes examining, on a test basis, evidence supporting the amounts and disclosures in the financial statements. An audit also includes assessing the accounting principles used and significant estimates made by management, as well as evaluating the overall financial statement presentation. We believe that our audits provide a reasonable basis for our opinion.

In our opinion, the financial statements referred to above present fairly, in all material respects, the financial position of ABC Property and Liability Company as of December 31, 20X2 and 20X1, and the results of its operations and its cash flows for the years then ended, in conformity with U.S. generally accepted accounting principles.

The accompanying financial statements have been prepared assuming that ABC Property and Liability Company will continue as a going concern. As discussed in Note XX to the financial statements, [State of domicile's insurance regulatory body] imposes risk-based capital requirements on insurance entities, including the Company. At December 31, 20X2, the Company's total adjusted capital is at the company action level based on the risk-based capital calculation required by [State of domicile's insurance regulatory body]. The Company has filed a comprehensive financial plan with the commissioner outlining the

Company's plans for attaining the required levels of regulatory capital by December 31, 20XX. To date, the Company has not received notification from the commissioner regarding acceptance or rejection of its comprehensive financial plan. Failure to meet the capital requirements and interim capital targets included in the Company's plan would expose the Company to regulatory sanctions that may include restrictions on operations and growth, mandatory asset dispositions, and placing the Company under regulatory control. These matters raise substantial doubt about the ability of ABC Property and Liability Company to continue as a going concern. The ability of the Company to continue as a going concern is dependent on many factors, one of which is regulatory action, including ultimate acceptance of the Company's comprehensive financial plan. Management's plans in regard to these matters are described in Note XX. The accompanying financial statements do not include any adjustments that might result from the outcome of this uncertainty.

[Firm Signature]

[City, State]

[Date]

10.26 The inclusion of an emphasis-of-matter paragraph in the auditor's report (as described in paragraph 10.18) serves adequately to inform users of the financial statements of the auditor's substantial doubt about the entity's ability to continue as a going concern for a reasonable period of time. Nonetheless, AU-C section 570 does not preclude the auditor from declining to express an opinion in cases involving uncertainties. As discussed in paragraph .10 of AU-C section 705, the auditor should disclaim an opinion when the auditor is unable to obtain sufficient appropriate audit evidence on which to base the opinion, and the auditor concludes that the possible effects on the financial statements of undetected misstatements, if any, could be both material and pervasive. If the auditor disclaims an opinion, the uncertainties and their possible effects should be disclosed in an appropriate manner and the auditor's report should state all of the substantive reasons for the disclaimer of opinion.

10.27 The following is an illustration of an auditor's report, under GAAS, which contains a disclaimer of opinion as the result of uncertainties relating to an auditor's substantial doubt about an insurance entity's ability to continue as a going concern for a reasonable period of time.

Independent Auditor's Report[10]

[Appropriate Addressee]

Report on the Financial Statements[11]

We were engaged to audit the accompanying financial statements of ABC Property and Liability Company, which comprise the balance sheet as of December 31, 20X2, and the related statements of income, changes in stockholders' equity, other comprehensive income, and cash flows for the year then ended, and the related notes to the financial statements.

Management's Responsibility for the Financial Statements

Management is responsible for the preparation and fair presentation of these financial statements in accordance with accounting principles generally accepted in the United States of America; this includes the design, implementation, and maintenance of internal control relevant to the preparation and fair

---

[10] See footnote 1.
[11] See footnote 2.

presentation of financial statements that are free from material misstatement, whether due to fraud or error.

Auditor's Responsibility

Our responsibility is to express an opinion on these financial statements based on conducting the audit in accordance with auditing standards generally accepted in the United States of America. Because of the matter described in the Basis for Disclaimer of Opinion paragraph, however, we were not able to obtain sufficient appropriate audit evidence to provide a basis for an audit opinion.

Basis for Disclaimer of Opinion

The accompanying financial statements have been prepared assuming that ABC Property and Liability Company will continue as a going concern. As discussed in Note XX to financial statements, [*State of domicile's insurance regulatory body*] imposes risk-based capital requirements on insurance entities, including the Company. At December 31, 20X2, the Company's total adjusted capital is at the authorized control level based on the risk-based capital calculation required by [*State of domicile's insurance regulatory body*]. The Company has filed a comprehensive financial plan with the commissioner outlining its plans for attaining the required levels of regulatory capital by December 31, 20XX. To date, the Company has not received notification from the commissioner regarding acceptance or rejection of its comprehensive financial plan. Failure to meet the capital requirements and interim capital targets included in the Company's plan would expose the Company to regulatory sanctions that may include restrictions on operations and growth, mandatory asset dispositions, and placing the Company under regulatory control. These matters raise substantial doubt about the ability of ABC Property and Liability Company to continue as a going concern. The ability of the Company to continue as a going concern is dependent on many factors, one of which is regulatory action, including ultimate acceptance of the Company's comprehensive financial plan. Management's plans in regard to these matters are described in Note XX. The consolidated financial statements do not include any adjustments that might result from the outcome of this uncertainty.

Disclaimer of Opinion

Because of the significance of the matter described in the Basis for Disclaimer of Opinion paragraph, we have not been able to obtain sufficient appropriate audit evidence to provide a basis for an audit opinion. Accordingly, we do not express an opinion on these financial statements.

Report on Other Legal and Regulatory Requirements

[*Form and content of this section of the auditor's report will vary depending on the nature of the auditor's other reporting responsibilities.*]

[*Auditor's signature*]

[*Auditor's city and state*]

[*Date of the auditor's report*]

Evaluating Consistency of Financial Statements

10.28 AU-C section 708, *Consistency of Financial Statements* (AICPA, *Professional Standards*), and PCAOB Auditing Standard No. 6, *Evaluating Consistency of Financial Statements* (AICPA, *PCAOB Standards and Related Rules*, Auditing Standards), addresses the auditor's responsibilities to evaluate and report on the consistency of a company's financial statements and align the auditor's responsibilities with Financial Accounting Standards Board (FASB) *Accounting Standards Codification* (ASC) 250, *Accounting Changes and Error Corrections*. Both standards also require the auditor to recognize, in the auditor's report, an entity's correction of a material misstatement, regardless of whether it involves the application of an accounting principle. Both standards also require that the auditor's report indicate whether an adjustment to previously issued financial statements results from a change in accounting principle or the correction of a misstatement.

Additional Guidance When Performing Integrated Audits of Financial Statements and Internal Control Over Financial Reporting

10.29 Paragraph .01 of AU section 508, *Reports on Audited Financial Statements* (AICPA, *PCAOB Standards and Related Rules*, Interim Standards), states that when performing an integrated audit of financial statements and internal control over financial reporting in accordance with the standards of the PCAOB, the auditor may choose to issue a combined report or separate reports on the entity's financial statements and on internal control over financial reporting. Refer to paragraphs 85–98 and appendix C, "Special Reporting Situations," of PCAOB Auditing Standard No. 5 for direction about reporting on internal control over financial reporting. In addition, see paragraphs 86–88 of PCAOB Auditing Standard No. 5, which includes an illustrative combined audit report.

10.30 If the auditor issues separate reports on the entity's financial statements and on internal control over financial reporting, the following paragraph should be added to the auditor's report on the entity's financial statements:

> We have also audited, in accordance with the standards of the Public Company Accounting Oversight Board (United States), the effectiveness of X Company's internal control over financial reporting as of December 31, 20XX, based on [*identify control criteria*] and our report dated [*date of report, which should be the same as the date of the report on the financial statements*] expressed [*include nature of opinions*].

10.31 When performing an integrated audit of financial statements and internal control over financial reporting in accordance with the standards of the PCAOB, the auditor's report on the entity's financial statements and on internal control over financial reporting should be dated the same date. Refer to paragraph 89 of PCAOB Auditing Standard No. 5 for direction about the report date in an audit of internal control over financial reporting.

Reporting on Whether a Previously Reported Material Weakness Continues to Exist

10.32 PCAOB Auditing Standard No. 4, *Reporting on Whether a Previously Reported Material Weakness Continues to Exist* (AICPA, *PCAOB Standards and Related Rules*, Auditing Standards), establishes requirements and provides directions for auditors engaged to report on whether a previously reported material weakness in internal control over financial reporting continues to exist as of a date specified by management. The engagement described by the standard is voluntary and the standards of the PCAOB do not require an auditor to undertake an engagement to report on whether a previously reported material weakness continues to exist.

Auditors' Reports on Statutory Financial Statements of Insurance Entities

10.33 All states require domiciled insurance entities to submit to the state insurance commissioner an Annual Statement on forms developed by the National Association of Insurance Commissioners (NAIC). The states also require that audited statutory financial statements be provided as a supplement to the Annual Statements. Statutory financial statements are prepared using accounting principles and practices "prescribed or permitted by the regulatory authority of the state of domicile," referred to in this guide as Statutory Accounting Principles (SAP). As described in paragraph .07 of AU-C section 800, financial statements prepared on a statutory basis of accounting are considered special purpose financial statements (that is, financial statements prepared in accordance with a special purpose framework, in this case a regulatory basis).

NAIC—Codified Statutory Accounting

10.34 SAP applicable to U.S. insurance entities are codified in the NAIC's *Accounting Practices and Procedures Manual* (the manual). The manual is subject to an ongoing maintenance process. All states have adopted the manual as the primary basis of prescribed SAP. If, however, the requirements of state laws, regulations, and administrative rules differ from the guidance provided in the manual or subsequent revisions, those state laws, regulations, and administrative rules will take precedence.

10.35 Prescribed SAP are those practices that are incorporated directly or by reference in state laws, regulations, and general administrative rules applicable to all insurance enterprises domiciled in a particular state. States may adopt the manual in whole or in part as an element of prescribed SAP. If, however, the requirements of state laws, regulations, and administrative rules differ from the guidance provided in the manual or subsequent revisions, those state laws, regulations, and administrative rules will take precedence. Auditors of insurance enterprises should review state laws, regulations, and administrative rules to determine the specific prescribed SAP applicable in each state.

10.36 Permitted SAP includes practices not prescribed by the domiciliary state, but allowed by the domiciliary state regulatory authority. An insurance enterprise may request permission from the domiciliary state regulatory authority to use a specific accounting practice in the preparation of the enterprise's statutory financial statements (*a*) if it wishes to depart from the state prescribed SAP or (*b*) if prescribed SAP do not address the accounting for the transaction. Accordingly, permitted accounting practices differ from state to state, may differ from entity to entity within a state, and may change in the future. In instances where the domiciliary state regulator is considering approval of a request for an accounting practice that departs from the NAIC manual and state prescribed accounting practices, the domiciliary regulator must provide notice under the requirements as defined in paragraphs 55–56 of the preamble of the manual. See paragraphs 1.82–.87 of this guide for additional information.

Regulatory Basis Financial Statements Intended for General Use

10.37 As stated in paragraph .21 of AU-C section 800, if the special purpose financial statements are prepared in accordance with a regulatory basis of accounting, and the special purpose financial statements together with the auditor's report are intended for general use, the auditor should not include the emphasis-of-matter or other-matter paragraphs required by paragraphs .19–.20 of AU-C section 800. Instead, the auditor should express an opinion about whether the special purpose financial statements are presented fairly, in all material respects, in accordance with GAAP. The auditor should also, in a separate paragraph, express an opinion about whether the financial statements are prepared in accordance with the special purpose framework.

10.38 Although it may not be practicable to determine the amount of differences between GAAP and SAP, the nature of the differences is known. The differences generally exist in significant financial statement items, and are believed to be material and pervasive to most insurance entities' financial statements. Therefore, there is a rebuttable presumption that the differences between GAAP and SAP are material and pervasive. If the effects are not reasonably determinable, the report should so state and should also state that the differences are presumed to be material. Furthermore, the notes to the statutory financial statements should discuss SAP and describe how those practices differ from GAAP. As stated in paragraph .09 of AU-C section 705, the auditor should express an adverse opinion when the auditor, having obtained sufficient appropriate audit evidence, concludes that misstatements, individually or in the aggregate, are both material and pervasive to the financial statements.

10.39 Unless the insurance enterprise also has audited GAAP basis financial statements available, it is likely that the audited statutory basis financial statements will be requested by, and distributed to, third parties other than state insurance departments (for example, rating agencies, agents, brokers, bankers, policyholders, and reinsurers). When financial statements are used by these other parties, general use, rather than limited use, financial statements are appropriate.

10.40 As stated in paragraph .21 of AU-C section 800, in a separate paragraph, the auditor should express an opinion on whether the statutory financial statements are presented in conformity with SAP (express an opinion about whether the financial statements are prepared in accordance with the special purpose framework). If departures from SAP are found to exist and are considered to be material, the auditor should express a qualified or adverse opinion on the statutory financial statements in accordance with the requirements of AU-C section 705.

10.41 The following is adapted from illustration 4, "An Auditor's Report on a Complete Set of Financial Statements Prepared in Accordance With a Regulatory Basis of Accounting (the Financial Statements Together With the Auditor's Report Are Intended for General Use)," of AU-C section 800. This illustration is on the general use of financial statements of an insurance enterprise prepared in accordance with SAP, which contains an adverse opinion concerning being in accordance with GAAP and an unmodified opinion concerning being in accordance with SAP.

Independent Auditor's Report[12]

[*Appropriate Addressee*]

Report on the Financial Statements[13]

We have audited the accompanying statutory financial statements of ABC Property and Liability Company, which comprise the statutory statements of admitted assets, liabilities, and surplus of ABC Property and Liability Company as of December 31, 20X2 and 20X1, and the related statutory statements of income and changes in surplus, and cash flows for the years then ended, and the related notes to the financial statements.

Management's Responsibility for the Financial Statements

Management is responsible for the preparation and fair presentation of these financial statements in accordance with the accounting practices prescribed or permitted by the Insurance Department of the State of [*State of domicile*]. Management is also responsible for the design, implementation, and maintenance of internal control relevant to the preparation and fair presentation of financial statements that are free from material misstatement, whether due to fraud or error.

Auditor's Responsibility

Our responsibility is to express an opinion on these financial statements based on our audit. We conducted our audit in accordance with auditing standards generally accepted in the United States of America. Those standards require that we plan and perform the audit to obtain reasonable assurance about whether the financial statements are free from material misstatement.

An audit involves performing procedures to obtain audit evidence about the amounts and disclosures in the financial statements. The procedures selected depend on the auditor's judgment, including the assessment of the risks of material misstatement of the financial statements, whether due to fraud or error. In making those risk assessments, the auditor considers internal control relevant to the entity's preparation and fair presentation of the financial statements in order to design audit procedures that are appropriate in the circumstances, but not for the purpose of expressing an opinion on the effectiveness of the entity's internal control.[14] Accordingly, we express no such opinion. An audit also includes evaluating the appropriateness of accounting policies used and the reasonableness of significant accounting estimates made by management, as well as evaluating the overall presentation of the financial statements.

We believe that the audit evidence we have obtained is sufficient and appropriate to provide a basis for our audit opinions.

Basis for Adverse Opinion on U.S. Generally Accepted Accounting Principles

As described in Note X to the financial statements, the ABC Property and Liability Company prepared these financial statements using accounting practices prescribed or permitted by the Insurance Department of the State of [*State of domicile*], which is a basis of accounting other than accounting principles generally accepted in the United States of America.

The effects on the financial statements of the variances between these statutory accounting practices and accounting principles generally accepted in the United

---

[12] See footnote 1.
[13] See footnote 2.
[14] See footnote 3.

Reports on Audited Financial Statements   411

States of America, although not reasonably determinable, are presumed to be material.

Adverse Opinion on U.S. Generally Accepted Accounting Principles

In our opinion, because of the significance of the matter discussed in the "Basis for Adverse Opinion on U.S. Generally Accepted Accounting Principles" paragraph, the financial statements referred to above do not present fairly, in accordance with accounting principles generally accepted in the United States of America, the financial position of ABC Property and Liability Company as of December 31, 20X2 and 20X1, or the results of its operations or its cash flows thereof for the year then ended.

Opinion on Regulatory Basis of Accounting

In our opinion, the financial statements referred to above present fairly, in all material respects, the admitted assets, liabilities, and surplus of ABC Property and Liability Company as of December 31, 20X2 and 20X1, and the results of its operations and its cash flows for the years then ended, on the basis of accounting described in Note X.

[*Auditor's signature*]

[*Auditor's city and state*]

[*Date of the auditor's report*]

10.42 The following is an illustration of an independent auditor's report, under PCAOB standards,[15] on the general use financial statements of an insurance enterprise prepared in accordance with SAP, which contains an adverse opinion concerning being in accordance with GAAP, and an unmodified opinion concerning being in accordance with SAP:

Report of Independent Registered Public Accounting Firm

We have audited the accompanying statutory statements of admitted assets, liabilities, and surplus of ABC Property and Liability Company as of December 31, 20X2 and 20X1, and the related statutory statements of income and changes in surplus, and cash flows for the years then ended. These financial statements are the responsibility of the Company's management. Our responsibility is to express an opinion on these financial statements based on our audits.

We conducted our audits in accordance with the standards of the Public Company Accounting Oversight Board (United States). Those standards require that we plan and perform the audit to obtain reasonable assurance about whether the financial statements are free of material misstatement. An audit includes examining, on a test basis, evidence supporting the amounts and disclosures in the financial statements. An audit also includes assessing the accounting principles used and significant estimates made by management, as well as evaluating the overall financial statement presentation. We believe that our audits provide a reasonable basis for our opinion.

As described more fully in Note X to the financial statements, the Company prepared these financial statements using accounting practices prescribed or permitted by the Insurance Department of the State of [*State of domicile*], which practices differ from U.S. generally accepted accounting principles. The effects on the financial statements of the variances between these statutory accounting practices and accounting principles generally accepted in the United

---

[15] Independent auditor reports on general use financial statements of an insurance enterprise prepared in accordance with Statutory Accounting Principles (SAP) are not commonly prepared under PCAOB standards, but may be for certain situations, such as Securities and Exchange Commission filings.

States of America, although not reasonably determinable, are presumed to be material.

In our opinion, because of the effects of the matter discussed in the preceding paragraph, the financial statements referred to above do not present fairly, in conformity with U.S. generally accepted accounting principles, the financial position of ABC Property and Liability Company as of December 31, 20X2 and 20X1, or the results of its operations or its cash flows for the years then ended.

In our opinion, the financial statements referred to above present fairly, in all material respects, the admitted assets, liabilities, and surplus of ABC Property and Liability Company as of December 31, 20X2 and 20X1, and the results of its operations and its cash flows for the years then ended, on the basis of accounting described in Note X.

[*Firm Signature*]

[*City, State*]

[*Date*]

Regulatory Basis Financial Statements Intended for Limited Use

10.43 Paragraph .14 of AU-C section 800 states that when forming an opinion and reporting on special purpose financial statements, the auditor should apply the requirements in AU-C section 700. When, in forming an opinion, the auditor concludes that a modification to the auditor's opinion on the financial statements is necessary, the auditor should apply the requirements in AU-C section 705.

10.44 As discussed in paragraph .19 of AU-C section 800, except for when the financial statements and the auditor's report are intended for general use (see paragraph 10.39), the auditor's report on special purpose financial statements should include an emphasis-of-matter paragraph, under an appropriate heading, that

 a. indicates that the financial statements are prepared in accordance with the applicable special purpose framework;

 b. refers to the note to the financial statements that describes that framework; and

 c. states that the special purpose framework is a basis of accounting other than GAAP.

10.45 Also as discussed in paragraph .20 of AU-C section 800, the auditor's report should include an other-matter paragraph, under an appropriate heading, that restricts the use of the auditor's report solely to those within the entity, the parties to the contract or agreement, or the regulatory agencies to whose jurisdiction the entity is subject to when the special purpose financial statements are prepared in accordance with a regulatory basis of accounting.

10.46 Although auditing standards do not prohibit an auditor from issuing limited use and general use reports on the same statutory financial statements of an insurance enterprise, it is preferable to issue only one of those types of reports. Few, if any, insurance entities that do not prepare financial statements in conformity with GAAP will be able to fulfill all of their reporting obligations with limited use statutory financial statements. When financial statements are used by these other parties, general use rather than limited use financial statements are appropriate.

Reports on Audited Financial Statements

10.47 The following is adapted from illustration 3, "An Auditor's Report on a Complete Set of Financial Statements Prepared in Accordance With a Regulatory Basis of Accounting (the Financial Statements Together With the Auditor's Report Are Not Intended for General Use)," of AU-C section 800. This illustration contains an unmodified auditor's report, under GAAS, on limited use financial statements prepared in conformity with SAP.

Independent Auditor's Report[16]

[*Appropriate Addressee*]

Report on the Financial Statements[17]

We have audited the accompanying statutory financial statements of ABC Property and Liability Company, which comprise the statutory statements of admitted assets, liabilities, and surplus of ABC Property and Liability Company as of December 31, 20X2 and 20X1, and the related statutory statements of income and changes in surplus, and cash flows for the years then ended, and the related notes to the financial statements.

Management's Responsibility for the Financial Statements

Management is responsible for the preparation and fair presentation of these financial statements in accordance with the accounting practices prescribed or permitted by the Insurance Department of the State of [*State of domicile*]. Management is also responsible for the design, implementation, and maintenance of internal control relevant to the preparation and fair presentation of financial statements that are free from material misstatement, whether due to fraud or error.

Auditor's Responsibility

Our responsibility is to express an opinion on these financial statements based on our audit. We conducted our audit in accordance with auditing standards generally accepted in the United States of America. Those standards require that we plan and perform the audit to obtain reasonable assurance about whether the financial statements are free from material misstatement.

An audit involves performing procedures to obtain audit evidence about the amounts and disclosures in the financial statements. The procedures selected depend on the auditor's judgment, including the assessment of the risks of material misstatement of the financial statements, whether due to fraud or error. In making those risk assessments, the auditor considers internal control relevant to the entity's preparation and fair presentation of the financial statements in order to design audit procedures that are appropriate in the circumstances, but not for the purpose of expressing an opinion on the effectiveness of the entity's internal control.[18] Accordingly, we express no such opinion. An audit also includes evaluating the appropriateness of accounting policies used and the reasonableness of significant accounting estimates made by management, as well as evaluating the overall presentation of the financial statements.

We believe that the audit evidence we have obtained is sufficient and appropriate to provide a basis for our audit opinion.

Opinion

In our opinion, the financial statements referred to above present fairly, in all material respects, the admitted assets, liabilities, and surplus of ABC Property

---

[16] See footnote 1.
[17] See footnote 2.
[18] See footnote 3.

and Liability Company as of December 31, 20X2 and 20X1, and the results of its operations and its cash flows for the years then ended, on the basis of accounting described in Note X.

Basis of Accounting[19] We draw attention to Note X of the financial statements, which describes the basis of accounting. As described in Note X to the financial statements, these financial statements were prepared in conformity with accounting practices prescribed or permitted by the Insurance Department of the State of [*State of domicile*], which is a basis of accounting other than accounting principles generally accepted in the United States of America, to meet the requirements of [*State of domicile*]. Our opinion is not modified with respect to this matter.

Restriction on Use[20]

Our report is intended solely for the information and use of the board of directors and the management of ABC Property and Liability Company and state insurance departments to whose jurisdiction the Company is subject and is not intended to be and should not be used by anyone other than these specified parties.

[*Auditor's signature*]

[*Auditor's city and state*]

[*Date of the auditor's report*]

10.48 The following is an illustration of an unqualified auditor's report, under PCAOB standards,[21] on limited use financial statements prepared in conformity with SAP.

Report of Independent Registered Public Accounting Firm

We have audited the accompanying statutory statements of admitted assets, liabilities, and surplus of ABC Property and Liability Company as of December 31, 20X2 and 20X1, and the related statutory statements of income and changes in surplus, and cash flows, for the years then ended. These financial statements are the responsibility of the Company's management. Our responsibility is to express an opinion on these financial statements based on our audits. We conducted our audits in accordance with the standards of the Public Company Accounting Oversight Board (United States). Those standards require that we plan and perform the audit to obtain reasonable assurance about whether the financial statements are free of material misstatement. An audit includes examining, on a test basis, evidence supporting the amounts and disclosures in the financial statements. An audit also includes assessing the accounting principles used and significant estimates made by management, as well as evaluating the overall financial statement presentation. We believe that our audits provide a reasonable basis for our opinion.

As described more fully in Note X to the financial statements, these financial statements were prepared in conformity with accounting practices prescribed or permitted by the Insurance Department of the State of [*State of domicile*], which is a comprehensive basis of accounting other than U.S. generally accepted accounting principles.

---

[19] Another appropriate heading may be used.

[20] Another appropriate heading may be used.

[21] Independent auditor reports on limited use financial statements of an insurance enterprise prepared in accordance with SAP are not commonly prepared under PCAOB standards, but could be requested by a state insurance department.

In our opinion, the financial statements referred to above present fairly, in all material respects, the admitted assets, liabilities, and surplus of ABC Property and Liability Company as of December 31, 20X2 and 20X1, and the results of its operations and its cash flows for the years then ended, on the basis of accounting described in Note X.

This report is intended solely for the information and use of the board of directors and the management of ABC Property and Liability Company and state insurance departments to whose jurisdiction the Company is subject and is not intended to be and should not be used by anyone other than these specified parties.

[*Firm Signature*]

[*City, State*]

[*Date*]

Regulatory Basis Financial Statements—Other Issues

10.49 The notes accompanying an insurance enterprise's statutory financial statements should contain a summary of significant accounting policies that discusses SAP and describes how this basis differs from GAAP. In general use statutory financial statements, the effects of the differences should be disclosed if quantified. However, in limited use statutory financial statements, the effects of the differences need not be quantified or disclosed.

10.50 The auditor may emphasize a matter in a separate paragraph of the auditor's report. For example, in a general use report, an auditor may express an adverse opinion as to conformity with GAAP and an unmodified opinion as to conformity with the SAP, and also conclude there is a need to add an emphasis-of-matter paragraph regarding substantial doubt about the insurance entity's ability to continue as a going concern; such paragraphs should follow both opinion paragraphs. When an insurance entity prepares its financial statements using accounting practices prescribed or permitted by the regulatory authority of the state of domicile and has significant transactions that it reports using permitted accounting practices that materially affect the insurance entity's statutory capital, the auditor may include an emphasis-of-matter paragraph in the report describing the permitted practices and their effects on statutory capital.

10.51 An example of an emphasis-of-matter paragraph follows:

> As discussed in note X to the financial statements, the Company received permission from the Insurance Department of the [*state of domicile*] in 20XX to write up its home office property to appraised value; under prescribed statutory accounting practices, home office property is carried at depreciated cost. As of December 31, 20X5, that permitted accounting practice increased statutory surplus by $XX million over what it would be had the prescribed accounting practices been followed. Our opinion is not modified with respect to this matter.

10.52 As required by paragraph .07 of AU-C section 708, if there has been a change in accounting principles or in the method of their application that has a material effect on the comparability of the entity's financial statements, the auditor should evaluate the change in accounting principle to determine whether

> *a.* the newly adopted accounting principle is in accordance with the applicable financial reporting framework;

b. the method of accounting for the effect of the change is in accordance with the applicable financial reporting framework;

c. the disclosures related to the accounting change are appropriate and adequate; and

d. the entity has justified that the alternative accounting principle is preferable.

10.53 As required in paragraph .08 of AU-C section 708, if the auditor concludes that the criteria in paragraph .07 are met, and the change in accounting principle has a material effect on the financial statements, the auditor should include an emphasis-of-matter paragraph[22] in the auditor's report that describes the change in accounting principle and provides a reference to the entity's disclosure. If the criteria in paragraph .07 are not met, the auditor should evaluate whether the accounting change results in a material misstatement and whether the auditor should modify the opinion accordingly.[23] The emphasis-of-matter paragraph (following the opinion paragraph) should identify the nature of the change and refer to the note in the financial statements that discusses the change. The auditor's concurrence with a change is implicit, unless the auditor takes exception to the change in expressing the opinion as to the fair presentation of the financial statements in accordance with GAAP or the SAP.

10.54 An example of an emphasis-of-matter paragraph follows:

> As discussed in note X to the financial statements, the Company changed its method of accounting for guaranty funds and other assessments. Our opinion is not modified with respect to this matter.

Correction of Error

10.55 Under GAAP, FASB ASC 250-10-45-3 states that any error in the financial statements of a prior period discovered after the financial statements are issued or are available to be issued shall be reported as an error correction by restating the prior period financial statements.

10.56 Under SAP, paragraph 10 of SSAP No. 3, *Accounting Changes and Corrections of Errors*, states

> [c]orrections of errors in previously issued financial statements shall be reported as adjustments to unassigned funds (surplus) in the period an error is detected. If a reporting entity becomes aware of a material error in previously filed financial statement after it has been submitted to the appropriate regulatory agency, the entity shall file or be directed to file an amended financial statement if approved by its domiciliary regulator.

10.57 Despite the guidance in SSAP No. 3, with regard to the recording of a correction of an error in the current period, an auditor would not be able to reissue an unmodified opinion on prior year statutory basis financial statements if the auditor is aware that those statements contain a material error. Therefore in accordance with paragraphs .08 and .24 of AU-C section 705 (as discussed in paragraphs 10.10–.11), the auditor should express a qualified

---

[22] See paragraphs .06–.07 of AU-C section 706, *Emphasis-of-Matter Paragraphs and Other-Matter Paragraphs in the Independent Auditor's Report* (AICPA, *Professional Standards*).

[23] See AU-C section 705, *Modifications to the Opinion in the Independent Auditor's Report* (AICPA, *Professional Standards*).

opinion on the prior year statutory basis financial statements when the auditor, having obtained sufficient appropriate audit evidence, concludes that misstatements, individually or in the aggregate, are material but not pervasive to the financial statements.

10.58 If the material error is corrected in the prior year statutory basis financial statements instead of included in the current period, the auditor should apply the requirements in AU-C section 700 to form an opinion and report on the statutory basis financial statements.

Correction of an Error—Regulatory Basis Financial Statements Intended for General Use

10.59 The following is derived from illustration 1, "An Auditor's Report Containing a Qualified Opinion Due to a Material Misstatement of the Financial Statements," of AU-C section 705. This illustration is an independent auditor's report, under GAAS, on the general use financial statements of an insurance enterprise prepared in accordance with SAP, which contains an adverse opinion concerning being in accordance with GAAP, and a qualified opinion concerning the prior year statutory financial statements being in accordance with SAP. For purposes of this illustration, the error is due to a misstatement of net admitted deferred income tax assets in the prior year financial statements that was corrected as an adjustment to surplus in the current year financial statements. The misstatement is deemed to be material, but not pervasive to the financial statements.

Independent Auditor's Report

[*Appropriate Addressee*]

Report on the Financial Statements[24]

We have audited the accompanying statutory financial statements of ABC Property and Liability Company, which comprise the statutory statements of admitted assets, liabilities, and surplus of ABC Property and Liability Company as of December 31, 20X2 and 20X1, and the related statutory statements of income and changes in surplus, and cash flows for the years then ended.

Management's Responsibility for the Financial Statements

Management is responsible for the preparation and fair presentation of these financial statements in accordance with the accounting practices prescribed or permitted by the Insurance Department of the State of [*State of domicile*]. Management is also responsible for the design, implementation, and maintenance of internal control relevant to the preparation and fair presentation of financial statements that are free from material misstatement, whether due to fraud or error.

Auditor's Responsibility

Our responsibility is to express an opinion on these financial statements based on our audits. We conducted our audits in accordance with auditing standards generally accepted in the United States of America. Those standards require that we plan and perform the audit to obtain reasonable assurance about whether the financial statements are free from material misstatement.

An audit involves performing procedures to obtain audit evidence about the amounts and disclosures in the financial statements. The procedures selected depend on the auditor's judgment, including the assessment of the risks of

---

[24] See footnote 2.

material misstatement of the financial statements, whether due to fraud or error. In making those risk assessments, the auditor considers internal control relevant to the entity's preparation and fair presentation of the financial statements in order to design audit procedures that are appropriate in the circumstances, but not for the purpose of expressing an opinion on the effectiveness of the entity's internal control.[25] Accordingly, we express no such opinion. An audit also includes evaluating the appropriateness of accounting policies used and the reasonableness of significant accounting estimates made by management, as well as evaluating the overall presentation of the financial statements.

We believe that the audit evidence we have obtained is sufficient and appropriate to provide a basis for our audit opinions.

Basis for Adverse Opinion on U.S. Generally Accepted Accounting Principles

As described in Note X to the financial statements, the Company prepared these financial statements using accounting practices prescribed or permitted by the Insurance Department of the State of [*State of domicile*], which is a basis of accounting other than accounting principles generally accepted in the United States of America.

The effects on the financial statements of the variances between these statutory accounting practices and accounting principles generally accepted in the United States of America, although not reasonably determinable, are presumed to be material.

Adverse Opinion on U.S. Generally Accepted Accounting Principles

In our opinion, because of the significance of the matter discussed in the "Basis for Adverse Opinion on U.S. Generally Accepted Accounting Principles" paragraph, the financial statements referred to above do not present fairly, in accordance with accounting principles generally accepted in the United States of America, the financial position of ABC Property and Liability Company as of December 31, 20X2 and 20X1, or the results of its operations or its cash flows thereof for the years then ended.

Basis for Qualified Opinion on Regulatory Basis of Accounting

The Company's balance sheets include deferred income tax assets and liabilities related to the estimated future tax consequence of temporary differences and carryforwards, as required by statutory accounting. An error was discovered in the calculation of admitted deferred income tax assets of $XXX for the year ended December 31, 20X1. The correction of this error was recorded as an adjustment of $XXX to surplus as of January 1, 20X2, in accordance with Statement of Statutory Accounting Principles No. 3, *Accounting Changes and Corrections of Errors.*

Qualified Opinion on Regulatory Basis of Accounting

In our opinion, except for the effects on the 20X1 financial statements of the matter described in the Basis for Qualified Opinion paragraph, the financial statements referred to above present fairly, in all material respects, the admitted assets, liabilities, and surplus of ABC Property and Liability Company as of December 31, 20X2 and 20X1, and the results of its operations and its cash flows for the years then ended, on the basis of accounting described in Note X.

[*Form and content of this section of the auditor's report will vary depending on the nature of the auditor's other reporting responsibilities.*]

---

[25] See footnote 3.

[*Auditor's signature*]

[*Auditor's city and state*]

[*Date of the auditor's report*]

Correction of an Error—Regulatory Basis Financial Statements Intended for Limited Use

10.60 The following is derived from illustration 1, "An Auditor's Report Containing a Qualified Opinion Due to a Material Misstatement of the Financial Statements" of AU-C section 705. This illustration is an independent auditor's report, under GAAS, of a qualified auditor's report concerning the prior year statutory financial statements on limited use financial statements prepared in conformity with SAP. For purposes of this illustration, the error is due to a misstatement of net admitted deferred income tax assets in the prior year financial statements that was corrected as an adjustment to surplus in the current year financial statements. The misstatement is deemed to be material, but not pervasive to the financial statements.

Independent Auditor's Report

[*Appropriate Addressee*]

Report on the Financial Statements[26]

We have audited the accompanying statutory financial statements of ABC Property and Liability Company, which comprise the statutory statements of admitted assets, liabilities, and surplus of ABC Property and Liability Company as of December 31, 20X2 and 20X1, and the related statutory statements of income and changes in surplus, and cash flows for the years then ended.

Management's Responsibility for the Financial Statements

Management is responsible for the preparation and fair presentation of these financial statements in accordance with accounting practices prescribed or permitted by the Insurance Department of the State of [*State of domicile*]; this includes the design, implementation, and maintenance of internal control relevant to the preparation and fair presentation of financial statements that are free from material misstatement, whether due to fraud or error.

Auditor's Responsibility

Our responsibility is to express an opinion on these financial statements based on our audits. We conducted our audits in accordance with auditing standards generally accepted in the United States of America. Those standards require that we plan and perform the audit to obtain reasonable assurance about whether the financial statements are free from material misstatement.

An audit involves performing procedures to obtain audit evidence about the amounts and disclosures in the financial statements. The procedures selected depend on the auditor's judgment, including the assessment of the risks of material misstatement of the financial statements, whether due to fraud or error. In making those risk assessments, the auditor considers internal control relevant to the entity's preparation and fair presentation of the financial statements in order to design audit procedures that are appropriate in the circumstances, but not for the purpose of expressing an opinion on the effectiveness of the entity's internal control.[27] Accordingly, we express no such opinion. An audit also includes evaluating the appropriateness of accounting

---

[26] See footnote 2.
[27] See footnote 3.

policies used and the reasonableness of significant accounting estimates made by management, as well as evaluating the overall presentation of the financial statements.

We believe that the audit evidence we have obtained is sufficient and appropriate to provide a basis for our qualified audit opinion.

Basis for Qualified Opinion

The Company's balance sheet includes deferred income tax assets and liabilities related to the estimated future tax consequence of temporary differences and carryforwards, as required by statutory accounting. An error was discovered in the calculation of admitted deferred income tax assets of $XXX for the year ended December 31, 20X1. The correction of this error was recorded as an adjustment of $XXX to surplus as of January 1, 20X2, in accordance with Statement of Statutory Accounting Principles No. 3, *Accounting Changes and Corrections of Errors.*

Qualified Opinion

In our opinion, except for the effects on the 20X1 financial statements of the matter described in the Basis for Qualified Opinion paragraph, the financial statements referred to above present fairly, in all material respects, the admitted assets, liabilities, and surplus of ABC Property and Liability Company as of December 31, 20X2 and 20X1, and the results of its operations and its cash flows for the years then ended, on the basis of accounting described in Note X.

Basis of Accounting

We draw attention to Note X of the financial statements, which describes the basis of accounting. As described in Note X to the financial statements, these financial statements were prepared in conformity with accounting practices prescribed or permitted by the Insurance Department of the State of [*State of domicile*], which is a basis of accounting other than accounting principles generally accepted in the United States of America, to meet the requirements of [*State of domicile*]. Our opinion is not modified with respect to this matter.

Restriction on Use

Our report is intended solely for the information and use of the board of directors and the management of ABC Property and Liability Company and state insurance departments to whose jurisdiction the Company is subject and is not intended to be and should not be used by anyone other than these specified parties.

[*Form and content of this section of the auditor's report will vary depending on the nature of the auditor's other reporting responsibilities.*]

[*Auditor's signature*]

[*Auditor's city and state*]

[*Date of the auditor's report*]

Opinion on Supplemental Schedules

10.61 Some states require that certain supplemental information be included with the statutory basis financial statements and that the auditor provide an opinion on the supplemental information.

10.62 AU-C section 725, *Supplementary Information in Relation to the Financial Statements as a Whole* (AICPA, *Professional Standards*), addresses the auditor's responsibility when engaged to report on whether supplementary

Reports on Audited Financial Statements

information is fairly stated, in all material respects, in relation to the financial statements as a whole. As discussed in paragraph .09 of AU-C section 725, when the entity presents the supplementary information with the financial statements, the auditor should report on the supplementary information in either (*a*) an other matter paragraph in accordance with AU-C section 706 or (*b*) in a separate report on the supplementary information.

10.63 As discussed in paragraph 10.38, if the special purpose financial statements are prepared in accordance with a regulatory basis of accounting, and the special purpose financial statements together with the auditor's report are intended for general use, the auditor should express an opinion about whether the special purpose financial statements are presented fairly, in all material respects, in accordance with GAAP; in a separate paragraph, the auditor should also express an opinion about whether the financial statements are prepared in accordance with the special purpose framework.

10.64 As stated in paragraph .09 of AU-C section 705, the auditor should express an adverse opinion when the auditor, having obtained sufficient appropriate audit evidence, concludes that misstatements, individually or in the aggregate, are both material and pervasive to the financial statements. As discussed in paragraph 10.39, there is a rebuttable presumption that the differences between GAAP and SAP are material and pervasive.

10.65 Paragraph .11 of AU-C section 725 states

> [w]hen the auditor's report on the audited financial statements contains an adverse opinion or a disclaimer of opinion and the auditor has been engaged to report on whether supplementary information is fairly stated, in all material respects, in relation to such financial statements as a whole, the auditor is precluded from expressing an opinion on the supplementary information. When permitted by law or regulation, the auditor may withdraw from the engagement to report on the supplementary information. If the auditor does not withdraw, the auditor's report on the supplementary information should state that because of the significance of the matter disclosed in the auditor's report, it is inappropriate to, and the auditor does not, express an opinion on the supplementary information.

10.66 As the supplemental information is prepared in accordance with SAP, it is appropriate to express an opinion on the supplemental information included with general use financial statements, even though an adverse or disclaimer of opinion is included concerning being in accordance with GAAP. It would not be appropriate to express an opinion on the supplemental information if an adverse or disclaimer of opinion was expressed concerning being in accordance with SAP. Similarly, if there are other modifications to the opinion about whether the financial statements are prepared in accordance with SAP, such modifications would need to be considered in accordance with the guidance in AU-C section 725.

10.67 When reporting on the supplementary information in an other matter paragraph, the auditor should include such paragraph, with the heading "Other Matter" or other appropriate heading immediately, after the opinion paragraph and any emphasis-of-matter paragraph.

Other Reports

10.68 The following sections include some examples of letters from auditors to be provided to State Insurance Regulators in order to comply with the NAIC Model Audit Rule.

Accountant's Awareness Letter

10.69 Section 6 of the Model Audit Rule requires that the insurer notify the insurance commissioner of the state of domicile of the name and address of the insurer's independent CPA. In connection with that notification, the insurer is required to obtain an awareness letter from its auditor stating that the auditor

> a. is aware of the provisions of the insurance code and the rules and regulations of the insurance department of the state of domicile that relate to accounting and financial matters.
>
> b. will issue a report on the financial statements in the terms of their conformity to the SAP pre-scribed or otherwise permitted by the insurance department of the state of domicile, specifying exceptions as appropriate.

10.70 In addition, certain states require additional assertions. For most states, the awareness letter is only required to be filed once, in the first year engaged to perform the audit (within 60 days of becoming subject to the rules). The filing deadline for most states is December 31 of the year being audited. A few states require a letter to be filed annually. Some states have more specific requirements regarding contracts, licensure, and rules of domicile. Practitioners can check individual state regulations for the complete requirements of that state.

10.71 The following is an illustration of an "Accountant's Awareness" letter:

> To the Board of Directors of ABC Insurance Company:
>
> We were engaged by ABC Insurance Company (the Company) to perform annual audits in accordance with auditing standards generally accepted in the United States of America of the Company's statutory financial statements. In connection therewith, we acknowledge the following:
>
>> We are aware of the provisions relating to the accounting and financial reporting matters in the Insurance Code of [*name of state of domicile*] and the related rules and regulations of the Insurance Department of [*name of state of domicile*] that are applicable to audits of statutory financial statements of insurance entities. Also, after completion of our audits, we expect that we will issue our report on the statutory financial statements of ABC Insurance Company as to their conformity with accounting practices prescribed or permitted by the Insurance Department of [*name of state of domicile*].
>
> This letter is intended solely for the information and use of the Insurance Department of [*name of state of domicile*] and other state insurance departments and is not intended to be, and should not be, used for anyone other than these specified parties.
>
> [*Firm Signature*]
> Certified Public Accountants

[City, State]

[Date]

Change in Auditor Letter

10.72 Section 6 of the Model Audit Rule requires that insurers notify the insurance department of the state of domicile within 5 business days of the dismissal or resignation of the auditor for the immediately preceding filed audited statutory financial statements. Within 10 business days of that notification, the insurer is also required to provide a separate letter stating whether, in the 24 months preceding the event, there were any disagreements (subsequently resolved or not) with the former auditor on any matter of accounting principles or practices, financial statement disclosure, or auditing scope or procedure, and which disagreements (if not resolved to the satisfaction of the former auditor) would cause the auditor to make reference to the subject matter of the disagreement in connection with the auditor's opinion. The Model Audit Rule requires that the insurer provide the insurance department of the state of domicile a letter from the former auditor to the insurer indicating whether the auditor agrees with the statements in the insurer's letter and, if not, stating the reasons for the disagreement. The disagreements required to be reported in response to this section include both those resolved to the former accountant's satisfaction and those not resolved to the former accountant's satisfaction. Disagreements contemplated by this section are those that occur at the decision making level (that is, between personnel of the insurer responsible for presentation of its financial statements and personnel of the accounting firm responsible for rendering its report). The insurer should also request, in writing, the former accountant to furnish a letter addressed to the insurer stating whether the accountant agrees with the statements contained in the insurer's letter and, if not, stating the reasons for which he or she does not agree; the insurer should also furnish the responsive letter from the former accountant to the commissioner together with its own.

10.73 The following is an illustration of the "Change in Auditor" letter:

To the Board of Directors of DEF Insurance Company:

We previously were auditors for DEF Insurance Company and, under the date of [report date], we reported on the statutory financial statements of DEF Insurance Company as of and for the years ended December 31, 20X2 and 20X1. Effective [date of termination], we are no longer auditors of ABC Insurance Company. We have read DEF Insurance Company's statements in its letter dated [date of insurer's letter], which is attached hereto, and we agree with the statements therein.

[However, if the auditor is (a) not in a position to agree or disagree or (b) does not agree with the insurer's statement, the auditor's letter should state that the auditor is not in a position to agree or disagree or that the auditor does not agree with such statements and give the reasons.]

[Firm Signature]

Certified Public Accountants

[City, State]

[Date]

10.74 If the auditor had not reported on any financial statements, the first sentence should be modified as follows:

> We previously were engaged to audit the statutory financial statements of ABC Insurance Company as of and for the year ending December 31, 20X2.

10.75 The insurer's letter may contain a statement, such as the following:

> In connection with the audits of the statutory financial statements of the Company for the years ended December 31, 20X2 and 20X1, and the subsequent interim period through [*date of termination*], there were no disagreements with [*CPA Firm*] on any matter of accounting principles, statutory accounting practices (SAP) prescribed or permitted by the Insurance Department of [*name of state of domicile*], financial statement disclosure, or auditing scope or procedures, which disagreements if not resolved to their satisfaction would have caused them to make reference to the subject matter of the disagreement in their reports.

Notification of Financial Condition Letter

10.76 Section 10 of the Model Audit Rule requires that the auditor notify the insurer's board of directors or audit committee in writing within five business days of determination of one of the following:

> *a.* The insurer has materially misstated its financial condition as reported to the domiciliary commissioner as of the balance sheet date currently under audit
>
> *b.* The insurer does not meet the minimum capital and surplus requirements of the state insurance statute as of the balance sheet date

10.77 The revised Model Audit Rule also requires the insurer to provide both of the following:

> *a.* To the insurance commissioner of the state of domicile, a copy of the notification of adverse financial condition within five days of its receipt
>
> *b.* To the auditor, evidence that the notification has been provided to the insurance commissioner

10.78 If the auditor receives no such evidence, the Model Audit Rule requires the auditor to send the notification to the insurance commissioner directly within the next five business days. (Certain states require direct notification to the insurance commissioner from the auditor as a matter of course.)

10.79 The following is an illustration of a "Notification of Financial Condition When the Audit Is Complete" letter, which indicates adverse financial conditions:

> To the Board of Directors:
>
> We have audited, in accordance with auditing standards generally accepted in the United States of America, the statutory financial statements of MNO Insurance Company (the Company) as of December 31, 20X2 and 20X1, and have issued our report thereon dated [*date of report*].
>
> In connection with our audit, we determined that capital and surplus reflected in the statement of admitted assets, liabilities, and capital

Reports on Audited Financial Statements 425

and surplus of the Company as of December 31, 20X2, as reported on the 20X1 annual statement filed with the Insurance Department of [name of state] is materially misstated because [provide explanation]. Statutory capital and surplus of $___ reported on the 20X2 annual statement should be reduced by $___ as a result of the matter in the preceding sentence.

If we do not receive evidence that the Company has forwarded a copy of this letter to the insurance commissioner of [name of state] within five business days of receipt, we are required to give the insurance commissioner a copy of this letter within the next five business days.

This letter is intended solely for the information and use of the Insurance Department of [name of state of domicile] and other state insurance departments and is not intended to be, and should not be used, for anyone other than these specified parties.

[Firm Signature]

Certified Public Accountants

[City, State]

[Date]

Auditor Reports for Communicating Unremediated Material Weaknesses in Internal Control to Insurance Regulators[28]

10.80 Section 11 of the Model Audit Rule requires that insurers provide the commissioner with a written communication concerning any unremediated material weaknesses in its internal control over financial reporting noted during the audit. Such communication should be prepared by the auditor within 60 days after the filing of the annual audited financial report and should contain a description of any unremediated material weakness as of December 31 immediately preceding (so as to coincide with the audited financial report discussed in Section 4[A] of the revised Model Audit Rule) in the insurer's internal control over financial reporting noted by the auditor during the course of their audit of the financial statements. If no unremediated material weaknesses were noted, the communication should so state. The insurer is also required to provide a description of remedial actions taken or proposed to correct unremediated material weaknesses if the actions are not described in the accountant's communication. The insurer is expected to maintain information about significant deficiencies communicated by the independent CPA. Such information should be made available to the examiner conducting a financial condition examination for review and kept in such a manner as to remain confidential.

10.81 As discussed in paragraph .A33 of AU-C section 265, *Communicating Internal Control Related Matters Identified in an Audit* (AICPA, *Professional Standards*), an auditor may decide to include the following paragraph in the auditor's reports for communicating significant deficiencies and material weaknesses in internal control to insurance regulators if the auditor has reason to believe that there may be a perception by the user of the communication that he or she is associated with management's written response to the auditor

---

[28] This section provides examples of communication intended for regulators related to unremediated material weaknesses as required by Section 11 of the National Association of Insurance Commissioners Model Audit Rule. Readers should note that the auditor's obligation for communication with the audit committee related to material weaknesses and significant deficiencies is not satisfied by the communication intended for regulators.

AAG-PLI 10.81

communication regarding significant deficiencies or material weaknesses identified in the audit, or if an auditor is associated with management's written response to the auditor's communication regarding significant deficiencies or material weaknesses identified in the audit:

> ABC Company's written response to the significant deficiencies [and material weaknesses] identified in our audit has not been subjected to the auditing procedures applied in the audit of the financial statements and, accordingly, we express no opinion on it.

10.82 The following is an illustration of where the auditor has identified one or more unremediated material weaknesses.

Independent Auditor's Report

Insurance Department of the State of [*State of domicile*]

[*Name of Company*]

In planning and performing our audit of the statutory-basis financial statements of [*name of company*] as of and for the year ended [*balance sheet date*], in accordance with auditing standards generally accepted in the United States of America, we considered its internal control over financial reporting [*including, when relevant, internal control over financial reporting related to derivative instruments as defined by Statement of Statutory Accounting Principles No. 86*] as a basis for designing auditing procedures that are appropriate in the circumstances for the purpose of expressing our opinion on the statutory-basis financial statements, but not for the purpose of expressing our opinion on the effectiveness of the Company's internal control. Accordingly, we do not express an opinion on the effectiveness of the Company's internal control.

Our consideration of internal control was for the limited purpose described the preceding paragraph and was not designed to identify all deficiencies in internal control that might be material weaknesses or significant deficiencies. Therefore, unremediated material weaknesses may exist that were not identified. However, as discussed below, we identified certain deficiencies in internal control that we consider to be unremediated material weaknesses as of [*balance sheet date*].

A deficiency in internal control exists when the design or operation of a control does not allow management or employees, in the normal course of performing their assigned functions, to prevent or detect and correct misstatements on a timely basis. A material weakness is a deficiency, or a combination of deficiencies, in internal control, such that there is a reasonable possibility that a material misstatement of the entity's financial statements will not be prevented, or detected and corrected on a timely basis. We consider that the following deficiencies constitute material weaknesses as of [*balance sheet date*]:

[*Describe the material weaknesses that were identified and an explanation of their potential effects*]

This communication is intended solely for the information and use of the audit committee, [*board of directors, board of trustees, or owners in owner-managed enterprises*] management, others within the organization, and state insurance departments to whose jurisdiction the Company is subject and is not intended to be and should not be used by anyone other than these specified parties.

[ABC Company's written response to the significant deficiencies [*and material weaknesses*] identified in our audit has not been subjected to the auditing procedures applied in the audit of the financial statements and, accordingly, we express no opinion on it.]

[*Dated the same as audit report*]

10.83 The following is an illustration where the auditor has identified no unremediated material weaknesses, but when state insurance regulators require an annual report on internal control, regardless of whether or not any unremediated material weaknesses were noted during the audit. AU-C section 265 precludes auditors from issuing a communication that no significant deficiencies or material weaknesses were identified, but does not preclude an auditor from issuing a standalone "No Material Weaknesses" letter when no material weaknesses were identified.

Insurance Department of the State of [state of domicile]

[Name of Company]

In planning and performing our audit of the statutory basis financial statements of [name of company] as of and for the year ended [balance sheet date], in accordance with auditing standards generally accepted in the United States of America, we considered its internal control over financial reporting [including, when relevant, internal control over financial reporting related to derivative instruments as defined by Statement of Statutory Accounting Principles No. 86] as a basis for designing auditing procedures that are appropriate in the circumstances for the purpose of expressing our opinion on the statutory basis financial statements, but not for the purpose of expressing an opinion on the effectiveness of the Company's internal control. Accordingly, we do not express an opinion on the effectiveness of the Company's internal control.

A deficiency in internal control exists when the design or operation of a control does not allow management or employees, in the normal course of performing their assigned functions, to prevent or detect and correct misstatements on a timely basis. A material weakness is a deficiency, or a combination of deficiencies, in internal control, such that there is a reasonable possibility that a material misstatement of the entity's financial statements will not be prevented or detected and corrected on a timely basis.

Our consideration of internal control was for the limited purpose described in the first paragraph and was not designed to identify all deficiencies in internal control that might be material weaknesses or significant deficiencies. Given these limitations, during our audit we did not identify any deficiencies in internal control that we consider unremediated material weaknesses, as previously defined as of [balance sheet date]. However, unremediated material weaknesses may exist that were not identified.

This communication is intended solely for the information and use of the audit committee, [board of directors, board of trustees, or owners in owner managed enterprises] management, others within the organization, and state insurance departments to whose jurisdiction the Company is subject and is not intended to be and should not be used by anyone other than these specified parties.

[Dated the same as audit report]

Accountant's Letter of Qualifications

10.84 Section 12 of the Model Audit Rule requires the auditor to provide a letter to the insurer to be included in the annual financial report stating

Property and Liability Insurance Entities

a. the auditor is independent with respect to the insurer and conforms with the standards of his or her profession as contained in the Code of Professional Conduct and pronouncements of the AICPA and the Rules of Professional Conduct of the appropriate state board of public accountancy.

b. the background and experience in general of the individuals used for an engagement and whether each is a CPA. Nothing within this regulation shall be construed as prohibiting the auditor from utilizing such staff as he or she deems appropriate where use is consistent with the standards prescribed by generally accepted auditing standards.

c. the auditor understands that the annual audited statutory financial statements and his or her opinion thereon will be filed in compliance with the requirements of the revised Model Audit Rule and that the domiciliary commissioner will be relying on the information in the monitoring and regulating of the financial position of insurers.

d. the auditor consents to the working paper requirement contained in the revised Model Audit Rule and agrees to make the working papers and other audit documentation available for review by the domiciliary commissioner or the commissioner's designee under the auditor's control (the working papers) as defined in Section 13 of the revised Model Audit Rule.

e. a representation that the auditor is properly licensed by an appropriate state licensing authority and is a member in good standing in the AICPA.

f. the auditor meets the qualifications and is in compliance with the "Qualifications of Independent Certified Public Accountant" section of the revised Model Audit Rule. (Section 7 of the NAIC revised Model Audit Rule has been revised effective for the year 2010 statutory audits. The list of nonaudit services that cannot be performed by the auditor has been revised to generally agree with those designated by the SEC. Readers can also refer to the Implementation Guide for the Annual Financial Reporting Model Regulation, located in appendix G of the NAIC manual.)

10.85 The following is an illustration of the "Accountant's Qualifications" letter:

To the Board of Directors of GHI Insurance Company:

We have audited, in accordance with auditing standards generally accepted in the United States of America, the statutory financial statements of GHI Insurance Company (the Company) for the years ended December 31, 20X2 and 20X1 and have issued our report thereon dated [*date of report*]. In connection therewith, we advise you as follows:

a. We are independent certified public accountants with respect to the Company and conform to the standards of the accounting profession as contained in the Code of Professional Conduct and pronouncements of the American Institute of Certified Public Accountants and the Rules of Professional Conduct of the [*state*] Board of Public Accountancy.

b. The engagement partner and engagement manager, who are certified public accountants, have [*number*] years and [*number*]

Reports on Audited Financial Statements 429

years, respectively, of experience in public accounting and are experienced in auditing insurance entities. Members of the engagement team, most (some) of whom have had experience in auditing insurance entities and [*number*] percent of whom are certified public accountants, were assigned to perform tasks commensurate with their training and experience.

c. We understand that the Company intends to file its audited statutory financial statements and our report thereon with the Insurance Department of [*name of state of domicile*] and other state insurance departments in states in which the Company is licensed and that the insurance commissioners of those states will be relying on that information in monitoring and regulating the statutory financial condition of the Company.

Although we understand that an objective of issuing a report on the statutory financial statements is to satisfy regulatory requirements, our audit was not planned to satisfy all objectives or responsibilities of insurance regulators. In this context, the Company and the insurance commissioners should understand that the objective of an audit of statutory financial statements in accordance with generally accepted auditing standards is to form an opinion and issue a report on whether the statutory financial statements present fairly, in all material respects, the admitted assets, liabilities, and capital and surplus as well as the results of operations and cash flow in conformity with accounting practices prescribed or permitted by the Insurance Department of [*name of state of domicile*]. Consequently, under generally accepted auditing standards, we have the responsibility, within the inherent limitations of the auditing process, to plan and perform our audit to obtain reasonable assurance about whether the statutory financial statements are free of material misstatement, whether caused by error or fraud, and to exercise due professional care in the conduct of the audit. The concept of selective testing of the data being audited, which involves judgment both as to the number of transactions to be audited and the areas to be tested, has been generally accepted as a valid and sufficient basis for an auditor to express an opinion on financial statements. Audit procedures that are effective for detecting errors, if they exist, may be ineffective for detecting misstatement resulting from fraud. Because of the characteristics of fraud, a properly planned and performed audit may not detect a material misstatement resulting from fraud. In addition, an audit does not address the possibility that material misstatements caused by error or fraud may occur in the future. Also, our use of professional judgment and the assessment of materiality for the purpose of our audit means that matters may exist that would be assessed differently by insurance commissioners.

It is the responsibility of the management of the Company to adopt sound accounting policies, to maintain an adequate and effective system of accounts and to establish and maintain an internal control that will, among other things, provide reasonable, but not absolute, assurance that assets are safeguarded against loss from unauthorized use or disposition and that transactions are executed in accordance with management's

AAG-PLI 10.85

authorization and recorded properly to permit the preparation of financial statements in conformity with accounting practices prescribed or permitted by the Insurance Department of [*name of state of domicile*].

The insurance commissioner should exercise due diligence to obtain whatever other information may be necessary for the purpose of monitoring and regulating the statutory financial position of insurers and should not rely solely upon the independent auditor's report.

d. We will retain the working papers prepared in the conduct of our audit until the Insurance Department of [*name of state of domicile*] has filed a Report of Examination covering 20X1, but no longer than seven years. After notification to the Company, we will make the working papers available for review by the Insurance Department of [*name of state of domicile*] at the offices of the insurer, at our offices, at the insurance department, or at any other reasonable place designated by the insurance commissioner. Furthermore, in the conduct of the aforementioned periodic review by the Insurance Department of [*name of state of domicile*], photocopies of pertinent audit working papers may be made (under the control of the accountant) and such copies may be retained by the Insurance Department of [*name of state of domicile*].

e. The engagement partner has served in that capacity with respect to the Company since [*year that current term started*] is licensed by the [*state name*] Board of Public Accountancy and is a member in good standing of the American Institute of Certified Public Accountants.

f. To the best of our knowledge and belief, we are in compliance with the requirements of section 7 of the NAIC Annual Financial Reporting Model Regulation Model Rule (Regulation) Requiring Annual Audited Financial Reports regarding qualifications of independent certified public accountants.

The letter is intended solely for the information and use of the Insurance Department of [*name of state of domicile*] and other state insurance departments and is not intended to be and should not be used for anyone other than these specified parties.

[*Firm Signature*]

Certified Public Accountants

[*City, State*]

[*Date*]

Appendix A
Property and Liability Insurance Entity Specific Disclosures

The disclosures requirements listed in this appendix are specific to property and liability insurance entities for compliance with generally accepted accounting principles (GAAP). General disclosure requirements are not included in this appendix.

This appendix also includes illustrative examples of the discussed property and liability insurance entity specific disclosure requirements. The illustrative examples are included for illustration purposes only, are not intended to be comprehensive, and are not intended to establish preference among alternative principles acceptable under GAAP.

GAAP Disclosures in Financial Statements

Deferred Acquisition Costs

A.1 As discussed in Financial Accounting Standards Board (FASB) *Accounting Standards Codification* (ASC) 944-30-50-1, insurance entities should disclose all of the following in their financial statements:

    a. The nature of acquisition costs capitalized

    b. The method of amortizing capitalized acquisition costs

    c. The amount of acquisition costs amortized for the period

A.2 As noted in FASB ASC 944-30-50-4, the notes to financial statements should describe the accounting policy applied to internal replacements, including whether or not the entity has availed itself of the alternative application guidance outlined in paragraphs 44–45 of FASB ASC 944-30-35 and, if so, for which types of internal replacement transactions.

The following is an illustrative example of the deferred acquisition costs disclosures as required under FASB ASC 944-30-50-1:

> Acquisition costs directly related to the successful acquisition of new or renewal insurance contracts, primarily commissions, are deferred and amortized over the terms of the policies or reinsurance treaties to which they relate. Proceeds from reinsurance transactions that represent recovery of acquisition costs shall reduce applicable unamortized acquisition costs in such a manner that net acquisition costs are capitalized and charged to expense in proportion to net revenue recognized. Amortization in 20X2 and 20X1 was approximately $XX and $XX, respectively.

Liability for Unpaid Claims and Claim Adjustment Expenses

A.3 As discussed in FASB ASC 944-40-50-3, financial statements should disclose for each fiscal year for which an income statement is presented the following information about the liability for unpaid claims and claim adjustment expenses:

432 Property and Liability Insurance Entities

    a. The balance in the liability for unpaid claims and claim adjustment expenses at the beginning and end of each fiscal year presented, and the related amount of reinsurance recoverable

    b. Incurred claims and claim adjustment expenses with separate disclosure of the provision for insured events of the current fiscal year and of increases or decreases in the provision for insured events of prior fiscal years

    c. Payments of claims and claim adjustment expenses with separate disclosure of payments of claims and claim adjustment expenses attributable to insured events of the current fiscal year and to insured events of prior fiscal years

    d. The reasons for the change in incurred claims and claim adjustment expenses recognized in the income statement attributable to insured events of prior fiscal years and should indicate whether additional premiums or return premiums have been accrued as a result of the prior-year effects

A.4 In addition to the disclosures required by FASB ASC 450, *Contingencies*, paragraphs 1 and 4 of FASB ASC 944-40-50 note that insurance enterprises should disclose management's policies and methodologies for estimating the liability for unpaid claims and claim adjustment expenses for difficult to estimate liabilities, such as claims for toxic waste cleanup, asbestos-related illnesses, or other environmental exposures.

The following is an illustration of significant accounting policy disclosure as required under FASB ASC 250-10-50-1:

    The liability for losses and loss adjustment expenses includes an amount determined from loss reports and individual cases and an amount, based on past experience, for losses incurred but not reported. Such liabilities are necessarily based on estimates and, although management believes that the amount is adequate, the ultimate liability may be in excess of or less than the amounts provided. The methods for making such estimates and for establishing the resulting liability are continually reviewed, and any adjustments are reflected in earnings currently. The reserve for losses and loss adjustment expenses is reported net of receivables for salvage and subrogation of approximately $XX and $XX at December 31, 20X2 and 20X1, respectively.

The following is an illustration of information an insurance enterprise would disclose as required under FASB ASC 944-40-50-3. (This illustration presents amounts incurred and paid net of reinsurance. The information may also be presented before the effects of reinsurance with separate analysis of reinsurance recoveries and recoverables related to the incurred and paid amounts.)

    Activity in the liability for unpaid losses and loss adjustment expenses is summarized as follows.

Property and Liability Insurance Entity Specific Disclosures

	(Dollars in thousands)	
	20X2	20X1
Balance at January 1	$	$
Less reinsurance recoverables		
Net Balance at January 1		
Incurred related to:		
Current year		
Prior years		
Total incurred		
Paid related to:		
Current year		
Prior years		
Total paid		
Unrealized foreign exchange (gain) loss		
Effect on reserves from discounting		
Net Balance at December 31		
Plus reinsurance recoverables		
Balance at December 31	$	$

As a result of changes in estimates of insured events in prior years, the claims and claim adjustment expenses (net of reinsurance recoveries of $XX and $XX in 20X2 and 20X1, respectively) decreased by $XX million in 20X2 and increased $XX million in 20X1. The favorable development in 20X2 reflects lower than anticipated losses of $XX million on losses related Hurricane Howard offset by increased severity of claims on the workers' compensation line of business. The increased severity is the result of a newly developed medical procedure that results in higher annual costs and extended the life expectancy of the claimants. The unfavorable development in 20X1 was the result of higher than anticipated losses and related expenses for claims for asbestos related illnesses and toxic waste cleanup due to increased frequency of claims in recent accident year which resulted in an additional $XX million in reserves. Additionally during 20X1, the case *Insured vs. Company* which related to a case in the 19X9 accident year, was dismissed by the Supreme Court and the Company eliminated reserves of $XX million on its professional liability business as the result of the favorable outcome.

The following is an illustrative example of environmental and asbestos related claims disclosures as required under FASB ASC 944-40-50:

Environmental and Asbestos Related Claims

The Company continues to receive asbestos and environmental claims. Asbestos claims related primarily to bodily injury assets by people who came in contact with asbestos or products containing asbestos. Environmental claims related primarily to pollution and related cleanup services.

In establishing the liability for unpaid claims and claim adjustment expenses related to asbestos related illnesses and toxic waste cleanup, management considers facts currently known and the current state of the law and coverage litigation. Liabilities are recognized for known claims (including the cost of related litigation) when sufficient information has been developed to indicate the involvement of a specific insurance policy, and management can reasonably estimate its liability. In addition, liabilities have been established to cover additional exposures on both known and unasserted claims. Estimates of the liabilities are reviewed and updated continually. Developed case law and adequate claim history do not exist for such claims, especially because significant uncertainty exists about the outcome of coverage litigation and whether past claim experience will be representative of future claim experience.

The following is an illustrative example of the catastrophe related exposure disclosures as required under FASB ASC 450-20-50:

Catastrophe Exposure

The Company has geographic exposure to catastrophe losses, which can be caused by a variety of events, including, among others, hurricanes, tornadoes and other windstorms, earthquakes, hail, wildfires, severe winter weather, floods, and volcanic eruptions. Catastrophes can also result from a terrorist attack (including those involving nuclear, biological, chemical, or radiological events), explosions, infrastructure failures, or as a consequence of political instability. The incidence and severity of catastrophes are inherently unpredictable.

Reinsurance

A.5 As discussed in paragraphs 3–4 of FASB ASC 944-20-50, all insurance entities should disclose the nature, purpose, and effect of ceded reinsurance transactions on the insurance entity's operations. Ceding entities also should disclose the fact that the insurer is not relieved of its primary obligation to the policyholder in a reinsurance transaction.

A.6 According to FASB ASC 944-310-45-6, although amounts recoverable on unasserted claims should be reported as reinsurance receivables, separate presentation or disclosure of various types of receivables is not precluded.

A.7 As discussed in FASB ASC 944-605-50-1, all insurance entities should disclose all of the following in their financial statements:

    a. For all reinsurance contracts, both of the following:

        i. Methods used for income recognition on reinsurance contracts

        ii. If not reported under FASB ASC 944-605-45-1 in the statement of earnings, as separate line items or parenthetically, the amounts of earned premiums ceded and recoveries recognized under reinsurance contracts

    b. For short duration contracts, all of the following:

        i. Premiums from direct business

        ii. Reinsurance assumed

        iii. Reinsurance ceded on both a written and an earned basis

Property and Liability Insurance Entity Specific Disclosures 435

    c. For long duration contracts, all of the following:

        i. Premiums and amounts assessed against policyholders from direct business

        ii. Reinsurance assumed and ceded

        iii. Premiums and amounts earned

    d. For foreign reinsurance accounted for by the open year method, all of the following should be disclosed for each period for which an income statement is presented:

        i. The amounts of premiums, claims, and expenses recognized as income on closing underwriting balances

        ii. The additions to underwriting balances for the year for reported premiums, claims, and expenses

    e. The amounts of premiums, claims, and expenses in the underwriting account for each balance sheet presented

A.8 As discussed in FASB ASC 944-605-50-2, appropriate disclosure of both of the following items is encouraged:

    a. The extent to which reinsurance contracts indemnify the ceding entity against loss or liability relating to insurance risk

    b. Indemnification policies as part of the required disclosure in the preceding paragraph about the nature and effect of reinsurance transactions

A.9 FASB ASC 944-605-50-3 also notes that disclosure in the financial statements of an insurance entity's accounting policies under FASB ASC 250, *Accounting Changes and Error Corrections*, should include a description of the methods used to account for foreign reinsurance.

A.10 As noted in FASB ASC 944-825-50-1, under the provisions of FASB ASC 825-10-50, a ceding entity should disclose concentrations of credit risk associated with both of the following:

    a. Reinsurance receivables

    b. Prepaid reinsurance premiums

A.11 As discussed in paragraphs 2–3 of FASB ASC 944-825-50, even if a ceding entity does not have a significant concentration of credit risk with a single reinsurer, concentration of credit risk disclosures may be required under the provisions of FASB ASC 825-10-50. If a ceding entity is aware that reinsured risks have been retroceded to a diverse group of retrocessionaires, disclosures about concentrations of credit risk still should be made under FASB ASC 825-10-50 because the assuming entity's rights under the retrocessions generally are not available to the ceding entity to mitigate its credit risk. That is, the ceding entity's concentration of credit risk from the assuming entity is unchanged.

The following is an illustrative example of reinsurance disclosures as required under FASB ASC 944:

        The Company's consolidated financial statements reflect the effects of assumed and ceded reinsurance transactions. Assumed reinsurance refers to the acceptance of certain insurance risk that other insurance companies have underwritten. Ceded reinsurance involves transferring certain insurance risks (along with the related written and earned premiums) that the Company has underwritten to other insurance companies who agree to share these risks. Such reinsurance includes quota share, excess of loss, catastrophe, facultative, and other forms of reinsurance on essentially all property and casualty lines of insurance. Failure of reinsurers to honor their obligations could result in losses to the Company; consequently, allowances are established for amounts deemed uncollectible. The Company evaluates the financial condition of its reinsurers and monitors concentrations of credit risk arising from similar geographic regions, activities, or economic characteristics of the reinsurers to minimize its exposure to significant losses from reinsurer insolvencies. At December 31, 20X2, reinsurance receivables with a carrying value of $XX million and prepaid reinsurance premiums of $XX million were associated with a single reinsurer. The Company holds collateral under related reinsurance agreements in the form of letters of credit totaling $XX million that can be drawn on for amounts that remain unpaid for more than 120 days.

The Company limits the maximum net loss that can arise from large risks or risks in concentrated areas of exposure by reinsuring (ceding) certain levels of risks with other insurers or reinsurers, either on an automatic basis under general reinsurance contracts known as treaties or by negotiation on substantial individual risks. Ceded reinsurance is treated as the risk and liability of the assuming entities.

The Company is also required to participate in various involuntary reinsurance arrangements through assumed reinsurance. The Company provides services for several of these involuntary arrangements under which it writes such residual market business directly, then cedes 100 percent of this business to the mandatory pool.

The effect of reinsurance on premiums written and earned for 20X2 and 20X1 are as follows.

	(Dollars in thousands)			
	20X2		20X1	
	Written	Earned	Written	Earned
Direct	$	$	$	$
Assumed				
Ceded				
Net	$	$	$	$

The amounts of recoveries pertaining to reinsurance contracts that were deducted from losses incurred during 20X2 and 20X1 were approximately $XX and $XX, respectively.

Certain of the Company's reinsurance agreements include provisions, whereby the ultimate amount of premiums, reinsurance commissions, or profits shared between the Company and its reinsurers vary based on the loss experience under the agreements. The Company estimates the ultimate amounts receivable or payable under these contractual provisions consistent with the Company's current estimates for subject losses. Accordingly, these estimates are subject to the same uncertainties associated with the estimates for losses and loss adjustment expenses. The Company records the impact resulting from changes in estimated subject losses upon these reinsurance agreements in the period in which the estimates are changed.

Terrorism Risk Insurance Program

The Terrorism Risk Insurance Program (the program) is a Federal program administered by the Department of the Treasury that provides for a system of shared public and private compensation for certain insured losses resulting from acts of terrorism or war committed by or on behalf of a foreign interest. The program is authorized through 2014.

Insurance and Reinsurance Contracts That Do Not Transfer Insurance Risk

A.12 In accordance with paragraphs 1–2 of FASB ASC 340-30-50, the following should be disclosed about all insurance and reinsurance contracts that do not transfer insurance risk, except for long duration life and health insurance contracts:

    a. Entities should disclose a description of the contracts accounted for as deposits and the separate amounts of total deposit assets and total deposit liabilities reported in the statement of financial position

    b. Insurance entities should disclose the following information regarding the changes in the recorded amount of the deposit arising from an insurance or reinsurance contract that transfers only significant underwriting risk:

        i. The present values of initial expected recoveries that will be reimbursed under the insurance or reinsurance contracts that have been recorded as an adjustment to incurred losses.

        ii. Any adjustment of amounts initially recognized for expected recoveries. The individual components of the adjustment (meaning, interest accrual, the present value of additional expected recoveries, and the present value of reductions in expected recoveries) should be disclosed separately.

        iii. The amortization expense attributable to the expiration of coverage provided under the contract.

Stockholders' Equity

A.13 According to FASB ASC 944-505-50-1, insurance entities should disclose the following information in their financial statements relating to stockholders' equity, statutory capital and surplus, and the effects of SAP on the entity's ability to pay dividends to stockholders:

    a. The amount of statutory capital and surplus

    b. The amount of statutory capital and surplus necessary to satisfy regulatory requirements (based on the entity's current operations), if significant in relation to the entity's statutory capital and surplus *c.* The nature of statutory restrictions on payment of dividends and the amount of retained earnings that is not available for the payment of dividends to stockholders

A.14 As discussed in FASB ASC 944-505-50-2, the disclosure requirements beginning in the following paragraph apply to annual and complete sets of interim financial statements prepared in conformity with GAAP. The disclosures in the following paragraph should be made if both of the following conditions are met:

- *a.* The use of prescribed or permitted statutory accounting practices (individually or in the aggregate) results in reported statutory surplus or risk based capital that is significantly different from the statutory surplus or risk based capital that would have been reported had National Association of Insurance Commissioners' (NAIC's) statutory accounting practices been followed
- *b.* Either of the following conditions is met:
    - i. State prescribed statutory accounting practices differ from the NAIC's statutory accounting practices
    - ii. Permitted state statutory accounting practices differ from either state prescribed statutory accounting practices or the NAIC's statutory accounting practices

A.15 As noted in FASB ASC 944-505-50-3, if the criteria in FASB ASC 944-505-50-2 are met, insurance entities should disclose both of the following at the date each financial statement is presented:

- *a.* A description of the prescribed or permitted statutory accounting practice
- *b.* The related monetary effect on statutory surplus of using an accounting practice that differs from either state prescribed statutory accounting practices or the NAIC's statutory accounting practices

The following is an illustration of statutory net income and shareholders' equity disclosures as required under FASB ASC 944-505-50:

> The Company, which is domiciled in ABC State, prepares its statutory financial statements in accordance with accounting principles and practices prescribed or permitted by the ABC state insurance department, which [state of domicile] recognizes for determining solvency under the [state of domicile] insurance law. The commissioner of the [state of domicile] Insurance Department has the right to permit other practices that may deviate from prescribed practices. Prescribed statutory accounting practices are those practices that are incorporated directly or by reference in state laws, regulations, and general administrative rules applicable to all insurance enterprises domiciled in [state of domicile]. Permitted statutory accounting practices encompass all accounting practices that are not prescribed; such practices differ from state to state, may differ from entity to entity within a state, and may change in the future.

Note: *The following are two examples of illustrative disclosures that an insurance enterprise could make to meet the requirements of FASB ASC 944.*

Example 1:

The Company's statutory financial statements are presented on the basis of accounting practices prescribed or permitted by the [state of

Property and Liability Insurance Entity Specific Disclosures

domicile] Insurance Department. [*state of domicile*] has adopted the NAIC's *Accounting Practices and Procedures Manual* as the basis of its statutory accounting practices (NAIC statutory accounting principles [SAP]), except that it has retained the prescribed practice of writing off goodwill immediately to statutory surplus in the year of acquisition.

In addition, the commissioner of [*state of domicile*] Insurance Department has the right to permit other specific practices that may deviate from prescribed practices. The commissioner has permitted the Company to record its home office property at estimated fair value instead of at depreciated cost, as required by NAIC SAP. This accounting practice increased statutory capital and surplus by $XX million and $XX million at December 31, 20X2 and 20X1, respectively, over what it would have been had the permitted practice not been allowed. The Company's statutory capital and surplus, including the effects of the permitted practice, was $XX million and $XX million at December 31, 20X2 and 20X1, respectively.

Had the Company amortized its goodwill over ten years and recorded its home office property at depreciated cost, in accordance with NAIC SAP, the Company's capital and surplus would have been $XX million and $XX million at December 31, 20X2 and 20X1, respectively.

Example 2:

The Company's statutory financial statements are presented on the basis of accounting practices prescribed or permitted by the [*state of domicile*] Insurance Department. [*State of domicile*] has adopted the National Association of Insurance Commissioners' statutory accounting practices (NAIC SAP) as the basis of its SAP, except that it has retained the prescribed practice of writing off goodwill immediately to statutory surplus in the year of acquisition.

In addition, the commissioner of the [*state of domicile*] Insurance Department has the right to permit other specific practices that may deviate from prescribed practices. The commissioner has permitted the Company to record its home office property at estimated fair value instead of at depreciated cost, as required by NAIC SAP.

The monetary effect on statutory capital and surplus of using accounting practices prescribed or permitted by the [*state of domicile*] Insurance Department is as follows.

	December 31	
	20X2 $m	20X1 $m
Statutory capital and surplus per statutory financial statements	$XX.	$XX
Effect of permitted practice of recording home office property at estimated fair value	(X)	(X)
Effect of [*state of domicile's*] prescribed practice of immediate write-off of goodwill[1]	X	X
Statutory capital and surplus in accordance with the National Association of Insurance Commissioners statutory accounting practices[2]	$XX	XX

---

[1] This amount compared to the prior year reflects the net impact of an additional year's amortization and the fact that admitted goodwill is based on the level of statutory capital and surplus and thus can fluctuate.

[2] In the initial year of implementation of this disclosure, prior year amounts for the effect of permitted practices and prescribed practices should be disclosed.

Participating Policies

A.16 As noted in FASB ASC 944-50-50-1, insurance entities should disclose all of the following in their financial statements:

 a. The relative percentage of participating insurance

 b. The method of accounting for policyholder dividends

 c. The amount of dividends

 d. The amount of any additional income allocated to participating policyholders

The following is an illustrative example of participating contracts disclosures as required under FASB ASC 944-50-50-1:

> Participating business represents 6 percent of total premiums in force and premium income at December 31, 20X2, and 8 percent at December 31, 20X1. The majority of participating business is composed of workers' compensation policies. The amount of dividends to be paid on these policies is determined based on the terms of the individual policies.

Guaranty Fund and Other Insurance-Related Assessments

A.17 As discussed in FASB ASC 405-30-50-1, FASB ASC 275-10-50 and FASB ASC 450-20-55 address disclosures related to loss contingencies. That guidance is applicable to assessments covered by FASB ASC 405, *Liabilities*. Additionally, if amounts have been discounted, the entity should disclose in the financial statements the undiscounted amounts of the liability and any related asset for premium tax offsets or policy surcharges as well as the discount rate used. If amounts have not been discounted, the entity should disclose in the financial statements the amounts of the liability, any related asset for premium tax offsets or policy surcharges, the periods over which the assessments are

Property and Liability Insurance Entity Specific Disclosures **441**

expected to be paid, and the period over which the recorded premium tax offsets or policy surcharges are expected to be realized.

The following is an illustrative example of guaranty funds and other insurance related assessments disclosures as required under FASB ASC 405, 275 and 450:

> Included in other liabilities in the consolidated balance sheet is the Company's estimate of its liability for guaranty fund and other insurance-related assessments. The liability for expected state guaranty fund and other premium based assessments is recognized as the Company writes or becomes obligated to write or renew the premiums on which the assessments are expected to be based. The liability for loss based assessments is recognized as the related losses are incurred. At December 31, 20X2 and 20X1, the Company had a liability of $XX million and $XX million, respectively, for guaranty fund and other insurance-related assessments and related recoverables of $XX million and $XX million, respectively.

Financial Guarantee Insurance Contracts

A.18 For financial guarantee insurance contracts, FASB ASC 944-310-50-3 requires insurance entities to disclose the following for each annual and interim period:

- a. For financial guarantee insurance contracts where premiums are received as payments over the period of the contract, rather than at inception, all of the following:
    - i. The premium receivable as of the date(s) of the statement of financial position and the line item in the statement of financial position where the amount is reported (if not presented separately)
    - ii. The unearned premium revenue as of the date(s) of the statement of financial position and the line item in the statement of financial position where the amount is reported (if not presented separately)
    - iii. The amount of accretion on the premium receivable and the line item in the statement of income where that amount is reported (if not presented separately)
    - iv. The weighted average risk free rate used to discount the premiums expected to be collected
    - v. The weighted average period of the premium receivable
- b. A schedule of premiums expected to be collected related to the premium receivable detailing both of the following:
    - i. The four quarters of the subsequent annual period and each of the next four annual periods
    - ii. The remaining periods aggregated in five year increments
- c. A rollforward of the premium receivable for the period, including all of the following:
    - i. The beginning premium receivable
    - ii. Premium payments received

AAG-PLI APP A

iii. New business written

iv. Adjustments to the premium receivable, including all of the following:

(1) Adjustments for changes in the period of a financial guarantee insurance contract

(2) An explanation of why the adjustments in item (c)(iv)(1) occurred

(3) Accretion of the premium receivable discount

(4) Other adjustments with explanations provided

v. The ending premium receivable

Financing Receivables

Premium Receivable

A.19 The financing and lending activities of insurance entities are included in FASB ASC 310-10-50, which sets out the subsequent disclosure requirements, unless the trade receivables have payment terms of less than 12 months and arise from sales of insurance policies. Examples of insurance contract arrangements that may require disclosures under this guidance include insurance contracts with contract terms greater than 12 months or arrangements where premiums are withheld for a period greater than 12 months and receivables resulting from reinsurance agreements.

A.20 Entities should consider whether the following disclosures are applicable:

a. Significant Accounting Policies as required in FASB ASC 310-10-50-2, FASB ASC 310-10-50-45-2, and FASB ASC 310-10-50-4

b. Assets serving as collateral as required in FASB ASC 860-30-50-1A

c. Nonaccrual and past due financing receivables as required in paragraphs 6–7, and 7A of FASB ASC 310-10-50

d. Accounting policies for off-balance-sheet credit exposures as required in FASB ASC 310-10-50-9, in addition to disclosures required by FASB ASC 450-20

e. Foreclosed and repossessed assets as required in FASB ASC 310-10-50-11 and FASB ASC 310-10-45-3

f. Accounting policies for credit loss related to financing receivables as required in FASB ASC 310-10-50-11B

g. Impaired loans as required in FASB ASC 310-10-5-14A

h. Credit quality information as required by paragraphs 28–29 of FASB ASC 310-10-50

i. Modifications as required by paragraphs 33–34 of FASB ASC 310-10-50

SAP Disclosures in Financial Statements

A.21 Exhibit 1-1, "Evaluation of the Appropriateness of Informative Disclosures in Insurance Entities' Financial Statements Prepared on a Statutory Basis," of chapter 1 of this guide provides guidance on what kinds of informative disclosures are necessary for financial statements prepared on a statutory basis.

A.22 Refer to the NAIC *Accounting Practices and Procedures Manual* for statutory footnote disclosures that are required in audited statutory financial statements by the NAIC.

> *Note:* Public life insurance entities should refer to Regulation S-X, Article 7, *Insurance Companies*, for disclosure requirements.

Appendix B
Examples of Development Data

A common approach to estimating loss reserves for occurrence policies is to compile a history of the development of losses for each accident year, reviewing the historical patterns and projecting the ultimate expected losses using such patterns. Similarly, for claims-made policies, report year would be substituted for accident year. Two examples of this approach are included herein.

Although such developments are very useful in testing loss reserve estimates, the auditor should consider the adequacy of the entity's database and the stability of loss payment patterns. The auditor should keep in mind that there are other methods, retrospective and prospective, that may be more appropriate or that should be used in conjunction with the historical development method.

Example A

Table 1 represents a compilation of historical incurred loss development data arrayed by accident year and by development period. Development period 12, for example, displays the amount of incurred losses (paid plus outstanding) after 12 months. For 19X0, $8,123 was incurred at the end of 12 months. Likewise, the subsequent development periods display the incurred losses for a given accident year at the various points in time; for example, the developed loss for 19X2 at the end of 48 months (that is, 19X5) is $9,435 and the developed loss for 19X3 at the end of 36 months (also 19X5) is $8,208.

Table 2 provides an estimate of the incurred but not reported (IBNR) reserve by (1) computing the "period to period development factors" (section I); (2) computing the average factor for each development period (section II); (3) computing a period to ultimate factor (section III), which is the product of the successive period to period development factors; (4) estimating ultimate expected losses by multiplying the period to ultimate factor by the losses incurred to date (section IV); and estimating the IBNR reserve (section VI) as the difference between the ultimate expected losses and losses incurred to date (table 1).

This example considers only simple averages to derive the period to period factors. Actual applications of this approach also should consider weighted averages and averages of the more recent history (three or four years) in determining the appropriate period to period factors to be used. The use of various averages will aid in determining trends and minimizing the effects of random variation.

AAG-PLI APP B

Example A—Table 1 Incurred Loss Data

Development Period (Months)

Accident Year	12	24	36	48	60	72	84	96	108	120
19X0	8,123	8,593	8,896	8,919	8,929	8,932	8,933	8,933	8,933	8,933
19X1	8,345	8,459	8,621	8,894	8,992	8,890	8,885	8,886	8,886	
19X2	8,603	9,033	9,524	9,435	9,500	9,545	9,546	9,546		
19X3	8,002	8,621	8,208	8,288	8,419	8,365	8,363			
19X4	9,620	10,191	9,684	9,750	9,731	9,734				
19X5	7,443	8,448	8,870	8,975	8,988					
19X6	7,815	9,435	9,735	9,582						
19X7	11,089	12,319	12,174							
19X8	11,323	12,684								
19X9	12,533									

Example A—Table 2 Period to Period Development Factor

(Months)

	Accident Year	12–24	24–36	36–48	48–60	60–72	72–84	84–96	96–108	108–120	Estimated Tail
I.	19X0	1.058*	1.035	1.003	1.001	1.000	1.000	1.000	1.000	1.000	†
	19X1	1.014	1.019	1.032	1.011	0.989	0.999	1.000	1.000		
	19X2	1.050	1.054	0.991	1.007	1.005	1.000	1.000			
	19X3	1.077	0.952	1.010	1.016	0.994	1.000				
	19X4	1.059	0.950	1.007	0.998	1.000					
	19X5	1.135	1.050	1.012	1.001						
	19X6	1.207	1.032	0.984							
	19X7	1.111	0.988								
	19X8	1.120									
II.	Average	1.092	1.010	1.005	1.006	0.998	1.000	1.000	1.000	1.000	
III.	Ultimate	1.113‡	1.019	1.009	1.003	0.998	1.000	1.000	1.000	1.000	1.000

(continued)

Accident Year	12–24 19X9	24–36 19X8	36–48 19X7	48–60 19X6	60–72 19X5	72–84 19X4	84–96 19X3	96–108 19X2	108–120 19X1	Estimated Tail 19X0
IV. Ultimate Losses	13,949	12,923	12,279	9,613[11]	8,966	9,733	8,363	9,546	8,886	8,933
V. Last Diagonal# (paid + case outstanding)	12,533	12,684	12,174	9,582	8,988	9,734	8,363	9,546	8,886	8,933
VI. IBNR Reserve	1,416**	239	105	31	(22)	(1)	0	0	0	0

(Months)

The preceding triangle utilizes an "incurred to incurred" approach in developing an estimate for IBNR reserves.

* 24 month developed losses divided by 12 month developed loss from table 1 (8,593 ÷ 8,123 = 1.058).

† Applies only if development period is longer than the period covered by the model.

‡ The product of the remaining factors (1.092 × 1.010 × 1.005 × 1.006 × 0.988 × 1.000 = 1.113) or the product of the 12–24 average factor times the 24–36 ultimate factor (91.092 × 1.019 = 1.113).

[11] The product of the developed losses times the ultimate factor (12,533 × 1.113 = 13,949; 9,582 × 1.003 = 9,613).

\# Losses incurred to date from table 1.

** The difference between ultimate estimated losses and losses developed to date (13,949 × 12,533 = 1,416).

Example B

Example B demonstrates an approach similar to example A, except that paid loss data is used instead of incurred loss data. The computations are made in the same manner as for example A; however, the resulting estimate is an estimate of both the case and the IBNR reserves.

Example B—Table 1 Cumulative Paid Loss Data

Development Period (Months)

Accident Year	12	24	36	48	60	72	84	96	108
	($000)								
19X0	47	210	335	422	481	506	527	543	548
19X1	52	197	312	377	430	469	496	501	
19X2	52	185	273	348	407	437	479		
19X3	41	172	282	366	425	468			
19X4	41	203	319	410	479				
19X5	44	175	308	443					
19X6	44	174	282						
19X7	51	208							
19X8	68								

Example B—Table 2 Period to Period Development Factor

(Months)

Accident Year	12–24	24–36	36–48	48–60	60–72	72–84	84–96	96–108	Estimated Tail
19X0	4.468	1.595	1.260	1.140	1.052	1.042	1.030	1.009	*
19X1	3.788	1.584	1.208	1.141	1.091	1.058	1.010		
19X2	3.558	1.476	1.275	1.170	1.074	1.096			
19X3	4.195	1.640	1.298	1.161	1.101				
19X4	4.951	1.571	1.285	1.168					
19X5	3.977	1.760	1.438						
19X6	3.955	1.621							
19X7	4.078								
19X8									
19X9									
Average	4.121	1.607	1.294	1.156	1.080	1.065	1.020	1.009	
Ultimate	12.895	3.129	1.948	1.505	1.302	1.206	1.133	1.110	1.100

(continued)

Accident Year	(Months)									Estimated Tail	Total
	12-24	24-36	36-48	48-60	60-72	72-84	84-96	96-108			
	19X8	19X7	19X6	19X5	19X4	19X3	19X2	19X1		19X0	
Ultimate	877	651	549	667	624	565	543	556		515	
Last Diagonal	68	208	282	443	479	468	479	501		468	
Case + IBNR Reserve	809	443	267	224	145	97	64	55		47	2,149

The preceding triangle utilizes a paid loss approach in developing an estimate for total loss reserves. Note that both examples are prepared on an accident year basis. Models can also be prepared on a policy year basis. Computations are the same as explained in example A.

* Applies only if development period is longer than the period covered by the model.

Appendix C
List of Industry Trade and Professional Associations, Publications, and Information Resources

The following is a list of some of the industry organizations. These sources are useful to the auditor in obtaining an understanding of the insurance industry.

Trade Associations, Professional Associations, and Institutions

American Academy of Actuaries (AAA) was founded in 1965 to represent the profession by four specialty actuarial associations: The Casualty Actuarial Society, Conference of Actuaries in Public Practice, Fraternal Actuarial Association, and Society of Actuaries. It provides standards or criteria of competence as an actuary and promotes education in actuarial science, exchange of information among actuarial organizations, and maintenance of standards of conduct and competence. The Casualty Actuarial Society provides actuarial and statistical science in insurance other than life insurance. The AAA website can be accessed at www.actuary.org.

American Insurance Association (AIA) is a property casualty insurance trade organization. In 1964, the old AIA merged with the National Board of Fire Underwriters and the Association of Casualty and Surety Companies and became the present day AIA. The AIA represents its members in every state and at the federal level in legislative, regulatory, and legal forums to assure its members a role in shaping insurance public policy. The AIA website can be accessed at www.aiadc.org.

Group of North American Insurance Enterprises (GNAIE) consists of the CFOs of the leading U.S. insurance entities including life insurers, property and casualty insurers, and reinsurers. GNAIE members include entities that are the largest global providers of insurance and substantial multinational corporations. GNAIE provides commentary on international accounting standard setting and facilitates communication among insurers, FASB, and the IASB. The GNAIE website can be accessed at www.gnaie.net.

Independent Insurance Agents and Brokers of America (IIABA) promotes agent and broker education and supports legislation of interest to the public as well as the insurance industry and opposes legislation detrimental to members' interests. The IIABA website can be accessed at www.iiaba.net.

Insurance Accounting and Systems Association (IASA) provides education and training with respect to insurance accounting and systems. The IASA website can be accessed at www.iasa.org.

Insurance Information Institute (III) serves as the vehicle for a better public understanding and acceptance of the insurance business. The III website can be accessed at www.iii.org.

Insurance Regulatory Examiners Society (IRES) is an association of professional insurance regulators dedicated to consumer protection. IRES helps to promote fair, cost effective, and efficient insurance regulation by ensuring professionalism and integrity among the individuals who serve state and federal insurance regulatory bodies. Examiners come together for training and to share and exchange information on a formal and informal level. The IRES website can be accessed at www.go-ires.org.

Insurance Service Office (ISO) acts as the bureau developing rates and forms for many lines of insurance. The ISO website can be accessed at www.iso.com.

National Association of Independent Insurance Adjusters (NAIIA) is a national trade organization offering a central contract point for professionals in the business of insurance claims to network effectively by exchanging current news of the marketplace and sharing marketing contacts and methods. The NAIIA website can be accessed at www.naiia.com.

National Association of Insurance Commissioners (NAIC) is an organization of the chief insurance regulatory officials of the 50 states, the District of Columbia, and 5 U.S. territories. It provides a forum for the exchange of ideas and the formulation of uniform policy. The NAIC helps state commissioners fulfill their obligations of protecting the interests of insurance policyholders. The NAIC website can be accessed at www.naic.org.

National Association of Mutual Insurance Companies (NAMIC) comprises mutual fire and casualty insurance entities. The association gathers, compiles, and analyzes information on all matters relating to insurance and to the reduction and prevention of losses. It also conducts workshops and seminars on these matters. The NAMIC website can be accessed at www.namic.org.

National Association of Professional Insurance Agents (PIA) acts in a capacity similar to that of the Independent Insurance Agents and Brokers of America. The PIA website can be accessed at www.pianet.com.

National Council on Compensation Insurance (NCCI) develops and administers rating plans and systems for workers' compensation insurance. The NCCI website can be accessed at www.ncci.com.

Property Casualty Insurers Association of America (PCI) is a property and casualty trade association in the United States. It addresses broad questions of position on proposed legislation and regulation, establishment of good public relations, and methods of conducting the business. The PCI website can be accessed at www.pciaa.net.

Reinsurance Association of America (RAA) acts as spokesperson for reinsurance entities in regulatory matters and in promotion of the interests of the industry. The RAA website can be accessed at www.reinsurance.org.

Society of Financial Examiners (SOFE) is a professional society for examiners of insurance entities, banks, savings and loans, and credit unions where financial examiners come together for training and to share and exchange information on a formal and informal level. The SOFE website can be accessed at www.sofe.org.

Society of Insurance Financial Management (SIFM) provides a forum for discussion and dissemination of information on accounting, statistical, and management problems in the insurance industry. The SIFM website can be accessed at www.sifm.org.

Directories

Best's Insurance Reports, A.M. Best Co. Oldwick, NJ. www.ambest.com.

Best's Directory of Recommended Insurance Attorneys and Adjusters, A.M. Best Co. Oldwick, NJ. www.ambest.com.

Journals and Other

Best's Review (monthly), A.M. Best Co., Oldwick, NJ. www.ambest.com.

Best's Weekly (weekly), A.M. Best Co., Oldwick, NJ. www.ambest.com.

Business Insurance (weekly), Crain Communications, Inc., Detroit, MI. www.businessinsurance.com.

SNL Financial—News, Financial Data, and Analysis. www.snl.com.

Appendix D
Guidance Updates

> This appendix includes information on guidance issued through the "as of" date of this guide that is not yet effective but that will be effective for the next edition of this guide. References to this guidance, where applicable, are included throughout the chapters of this guide in shaded text. The references use a guidance update number that consists of the chapter number followed by the sequentially numbered guidance update number within any given chapter (for example, update 3-1 would be the first guidance update in chapter 3). The guidance in this appendix is cross referenced using the same guidance update numbers found throughout the chapters of this guide, as applicable. Readers should consider this information for the reporting period to which it applies.

Accounting and Reporting Updates

D.01 ASU No. 2011-11

Financial Accounting Standards Board (FASB) Accounting Standards Update (ASU) No. 2011-11, *Balance Sheet (Topic 210): Disclosures about Offsetting Assets and Liabilities*, issued in December 2011, is effective for annual reporting periods beginning on or after January 1, 2013, and interim periods within those annual periods. An entity should provide the disclosures required by those amendments retrospectively for all comparative periods presented.

ASU No. 2013-01, *Balance Sheet (Topic 210): Clarifying the Scope of Disclosures about Offsetting Assets and Liabilities*, clarified that the scope of ASU No. 2011-11 applies to derivatives accounted for in accordance with FASB ASC 815, *Derivatives and Hedging*, including bifurcated embedded derivatives, repurchase agreements and reverse repurchase agreements, and securities borrowing and securities lending transactions that are either offset in accordance with FASB ASC 210-20-45 or FASB ASC 815-10-45 or subject to an enforceable master netting arrangement or similar agreement. An entity is required to apply the amendments for fiscal years beginning on or after January 1, 2013, and interim periods within those annual periods. An entity should provide the required disclosures retrospectively for all comparative periods presented. The effective date is the same as the effective date of ASU No. 2011-11.

Accounting and Reporting Update: Disclosure About Offsetting Assets and Liabilities [Update 5-1]

The paragraphs that follow will be added after the existing paragraph 5.126 upon the effective date of ASU No. 2011-11.

5.127 As discussed in FASB ASC 210-20-50-2, an entity should disclose information to enable users of its financial statements to evaluate the effect or potential effect of netting arrangements on its financial position for recognized assets and liabilities within the scope of FASB ASC 210-20-50-1. This includes the effect or potential effect of *rights of setoff* associated with an entity's recognized assets and recognized liabilities that are in the scope of the preceding paragraph. To meet the objectives of FASB ASC 210-20-50-2, FASB ASC 210-20-50-3 requires that an entity should disclose at the end of the reporting period the following quantitative information separately for assets and liabilities that are within the scope of FASB ASC 210-20-50-1:

    a. The gross amounts of those recognized assets and those recognized liabilities.

    b. The amounts offset in accordance with the guidance in FASB ASC 210-20-45 and FASB ASC 815-10-45 to determine the net amounts presented in the statement of financial position.

    c. The net amounts presented in the statement of financial position.

    d. The amounts subject to an enforceable master netting arrangement or similar agreement not otherwise included in item *b:*

        i. The amounts related to recognized financial instruments and other derivative instruments that either

            (1) management makes an accounting policy election not to offset, or

            (2) do not meet some or all of the guidance in either FASB ASC 210-20-45 or FASB ASC 815-10-45.

        ii. The amounts related to financial collateral (including cash collateral).

    e. The net amount after deducting the amounts in item *d* from the amounts in item *c.*

5.128 As discussed in FASB ASC 210-20-50-4, the information discussed in paragraph 5.125 should be presented in a tabular format, separately for assets and liabilities, unless another format is more appropriate. The total amount disclosed in accordance with FASB ASC 210-20-50-3(d) for an instrument should not exceed the amount disclosed in accordance with paragraph 3(c) of FASB ASC 210-20-50 for that instrument. An entity should also provide a description of the rights of setoff associated with an entity's recognized assets and recognized liabilities subject to an enforceable master netting arrangement or similar agreement disclosed in accordance with paragraph 3(d) of FASB ASC 210-20-50, including the nature of those rights.

Regulatory Updates

D.02 Statement of Statutory Accounting Principles No. 102

Statement of Statutory Accounting Principles (SSAP) No. 102, *Accounting for Pensions, A Replacement of SSAP No. 89*, issued in March 2012, is effective January 1, 2013, with early adoption permitted.

Regulatory Update: Accounting for Pensions [Update 8-1]

The paragraphs that follow replace the existing paragraph 8.36 upon the effective date of SSAP No. 102.

    8.36 Under SAP, SSAP No. 102, *Accounting for Pensions, A Replacement of SSAP No. 89*, adopts sections of FASB ASC 715-20 and FASB

ASC 715-30 with the following modifications, according to paragraph 81 of the SSAP:

> a. All references to "other comprehensive income" or "accumulated other comprehensive income" within FASB ASC 715 have been revised to reflect unassigned funds (surplus).
>
> b. Any prepaid asset resulting from the excess of the fair value of plan assets over the projected benefit obligation shall be nonadmitted. Furthermore, any asset recognized from the cost of a participation right of an annuity contract per paragraph 49 shall also be nonadmitted.
>
> c. Provisions within FASB ASC 715 permitting a market-related value of plan assets have been eliminated with only the fair value measurement method for plan assets being retained.
>
> d. The reduced disclosure requirements for nonpublic entities described in FASB ASC 715-20-50-5 are rejected. All reporting entities shall follow the disclosure requirements included in paragraphs 1 and 5 of FASB ASC 715-20-50, 715-20-05-3, and 715-20-45-2.
>
> e. Clarification has been included within this standard to ensure both vested and nonvested employees are included within the recognition of net periodic pension cost and in the pension benefit obligation. Although this is consistent with GAAP, this is a change from previous statutory accounting. As nonvested employees were excluded from statutory accounting under SSAP No. 89, guidance has been included to indicate that the unrecognized prior service cost attributed to nonvested individuals is not required to be included in net periodic pension cost entirely in the year this standard is adopted. The unrecognized prior service cost for nonvested employees shall be amortized as a component of net periodic pension cost by assigning an equal amount to each expected future period of service before vesting occurs for nonvested employees active at the date of the amendment. Unassigned funds (surplus) is then adjusted each period as prior service cost is amortized. (Guidance is included within the transition related to the recognition of the prior service cost for nonvested employees through unassigned surplus.)
>
> f. Conclusion of *Interpretation 04-12: EITF 03-4: Determining the Classification and Benefit Attribution Method for a "Cash Balance" Pension Plan* (INT 04-12) indicating that cash balance plans are considered defined benefit plans has been incorporated within paragraph 3 of this statement.
>
> g. Conclusion of *Interpretation 99-26: Offsetting Pension Assets and Liabilities* (INT 99-26) prohibiting the offset of defined benefit liabilities of one plan with prepaid assets of another plan has been incorporated within paragraph 26 of this statement.
>
> h. Provisions within FASB ASC 715 regarding the classification of underfunded liabilities as current or noncurrent liabilities and the classification of assets from overfunded plans as noncurrent assets has been rejected as inconsistent with statutory accounting.

i. Provisions within FASB ASC 715 defining the fair value of investments have been rejected. Fair value definitions and measurement for investments shall be determined in accordance with statutory accounting guidance.

j. Provisions within FASB ASC 715 regarding the plan assets measurement date for consolidating subsidiaries or entities utilizing the equity method under APB Opinion No. 18 has been rejected. For statutory accounting, all entities shall follow the measurement date guidance within paragraph 42 of this statement.

k. Transition under FASB ASC 715 is different from this Statement. FASB ASC 715 requires entities with publicly traded equity securities to initially apply the requirement to recognize the funded status of a benefit plan; the gains/losses, prior service costs/credits and transition obligations/assets that have not yet been included in net periodic benefit cost; and the disclosure requirements as of the end of the fiscal year ending after December 15, 2006. Transition guidelines for statutory accounting are defined in paragraphs 82–90.

l. FASB ASC 715 provided two approaches for an employer to transition to a fiscal year-end measurement date. For purposes of statutory accounting, the second approach permitting reporting entities to use earlier measurements determined for year-end reporting as of the fiscal year immediately preceding the year that the measurement date provisions is rejected. For consistency purposes, all reporting entities shall follow the first approach and remeasure plan assets and benefit obligations as of the beginning of the fiscal year that the measurement date provisions are applied.

D.03 Statement of Statutory Accounting Principles No. 103

Statement of Statutory Accounting Principles (SSAP) No. 103, *Accounting for Transfers and Servicing of Financial Assets and Extinguishments of Liabilities*, issued in March 2012, is effective January 1, 2013 and should be applied prospectively. This statement must be applied as of the beginning of the reporting entity's first annual reporting period after the effective date for interim periods within that first annual reporting period and for interim and annual reporting periods thereafter. Earlier application is prohibited. This statement must be applied to transfers occurring on or after the effective date. On and after the effective date, the concept of a qualifying special purpose entity is no longer relevant for statutory accounting purposes. The disclosure provisions of this statement shall be applied to transfers that occurred both before and after the effective date of this statement.

Regulatory Update: Accounting for Transfers and Servicing of Financial Assets and Extinguishments of Liabilities [Update 5-2]

The paragraphs that follow replace the existing paragraphs in chapter 5, "Investments and Fair Value Considerations," upon the effective date of SSAP No. 103.

Asset Transfers and Extinguishments of Liabilities

5.174 *Statutory accounting practices.* Under SAP, the collateral received is reflected in the appropriate investment section and the

Guidance Updates

liability is reflected on the balance sheet as a write in line. Specific collateral requirements for securities lending, repurchase, and reverse repurchase transactions are set forth in SSAP No. 103, *Accounting for Transfers and Servicing of Financial Assets and Extinguishments of Liabilities.* As discussed in paragraph 123 of SSAP No. 103, the accounting guidance in this statement adopts, with modification FASB ASC 860, *Transfers and Servicing.* Statutory modifications from these adoptions include the following:

a. Rejects the GAAP consideration for "consolidated affiliates" because the concept of consolidation has not been adopted for statutory accounting.

b. Rejects reference to GAAP standards and GAAP methods not adopted for statutory as well as concepts that are not pertinent for insurers. For example, references to investments "held-to-maturity," "available for sale" or "trading" and reference to FASB standards are replaced with statutory terms and references to statutory standards.

c. Rejects GAAP reference and guidance regarding "Revolving-Period Securitizations" because this GAAP guidance is not applicable to statutory accounting. This concept was also deemed not applicable to statutory accounting under SSAP No. 91R.

d. Rejects GAAP guidance for "Sale-Type and Direct-Financing Lease Receivables" because leases shall be accounted for in accordance with *SSAP No. 22—Leases* (SSAP No. 22). This conclusion is consistent with SSAP No. 91R.

e. Rejects GAAP guidance for "Banker's Acceptances and Risk Participations in Them" as not applicable for statutory accounting. This GAAP guidance was also deemed not applicable to statutory accounting under SSAP No. 91R.

f. Rejects GAAP guidance for "Removal of Account Provisions" that allows recognition of sale accounting. For statutory, transfers that would empower the transferor to reclaim assets under certain conditions (considered removal of accounts provisions) are precluded from being accounted for as sales. This conclusion is consistent with SSAP No. 91R.

g. Rejects GAAP guidance for "Transfers of Receivables with Recourse" that allows transfers of receivables in their entirety with recourse to be accounted for as sales. For statutory accounting, a transfer of receivables with recourse shall be accounted for as a secured borrowing. This conclusion is consistent with SSAP No. 91R.

h. Rejects illustrations for transactions involving transfers of lease financing receivables with residual values and banker's acceptances with a risk participation as the GAAP guidance in FASB Statement No. 166, *Accounting for Transfers of Financial Assets—an amendment of FASB Statement No. 140.* related to these topics has been rejected for statutory accounting.

i. Rejects the optionality provided within FASB Statement No. 156, *Accounting for Servicing of Financial Assets—an amendment of FASB Statement No. 140,* for subsequent measurement of servicing assets and servicing liabilities using either fair value or an amortization method. This statement requires application of a fair value method for subsequent measurement.

    j. Incorporates guidance previously included in SSAP No. 91R specific to insurance entities and guidance that was adopted from GAAP guidance not revised through the issuance of FASB Statement No. 166.

5.175 Paragraph 8 of SSAP No. 103 provides the criteria to account for sale accounting under statutory accounting. Paragraph 8 states that a transfer of a group of financial assets or a portion of a financial asset in which the transferor surrenders control over those financial assets shall be accounted for as a sale, to the extent that consideration other than beneficial interests in the transferred assets is received in exchange. The transferor has surrendered control over transferred assets if and only if all of the following conditions are met:

    a. The transferred financial assets have been isolated from the transferor (put presumptively beyond the reach of the transferor and its creditors, even in bankruptcy or other receivership). Transferred financial assets are isolated in bankruptcy or other receivership only if the transferred financial assets would be beyond the reach of the powers of a bankruptcy trustee or other receiver for the transferor.

    b. Each transferee (or, if the transferee is an entity whose sole purpose is to engage in securitization or asset backed financing activities and that entity is constrained from pledging or exchanging the assets it receives, each third party holder of its *beneficial interests*) has the right to pledge or exchange the assets (or beneficial interests) it received, and no condition both constrains the transferee (or third party holder of its beneficial interests) from taking advantage of its right to pledge or exchange and provides more than a trivial benefit to the transferor (paragraphs 43–46).

    c. The transferor or its agents do not maintain effective control over the transferred financial assets or third party beneficial interests related to those transferred assets (paragraph 50). Examples of a transferor's effective control over the transferred financial assets include, but are not limited to, (i) an agreement that both entitles and obligates the transferor to repurchase or redeem them before their maturity (paragraphs 51–52), (ii) an agreement that provides the transferor with both the *unilateral ability* to cause the holder to return specific financial assets and a more than trivial benefit attributable to that ability, other than through a *cleanup call* (paragraphs 53–57), or (iii) an agreement that permits the transferee to require the transferor to repurchase the transferred financial assets at a price that is so favorable to the transferee that it is probable that the transferee will require the transferor to repurchase them (paragraph 58).

5.176 Paragraph 121 of SSAP No. 103 notes that if a creditor releases a debtor from primary obligation on the condition that a third party assumes the obligation and that the original debtor becomes secondarily liable, that release extinguishes the original debtor's liability. However, in those circumstances, whether or not explicit consideration was paid for that guarantee, the original debtor becomes a guarantor. As a guarantor, it shall recognize a guarantee obligation in the same manner as would a guarantor that had never been primarily liable to that creditor, with due regard for the likelihood that the third party will carry out its obligations. The guarantee obligation shall be initially measured at fair value, and that amount reduces the gain or increases the loss recognized on extinguishment.

Repurchase Agreements

5.192 The accounting guidance for statutory accounting is similar to the GAAP accounting guidance previously discussed. Under SAP, paragraph 88 of SSAP No. 103 notes that if the transferor has surrendered control over transferred assets (sales criteria, as discussed in paragraph 8 of SSAP No. 103), the transferor should account for the repurchase agreement as a sale of financial assets and forward repurchase commitment, and the transferee should account for the agreement as a purchase of financial assets and forward resale commitment. As discussed in paragraph 91 of SSAP No. 103, repurchase agreements that do meet the sales criteria (see paragraph 8 of SSAP No. 103) should be treated as secured borrowings.

Securities Lending

5.201 Under SAP, the collateral received is reflected in the appropriate investment section, and the liability is reflected on the balance sheet as a write in line. Specific collateral requirements for securities lending and repurchase and reverse repurchase transactions are set forth in SSAP No. 103. The collateral requirement varies based upon the type of transaction (securities lending, repurchase, reverse repurchase) or denomination of the collateral.

Appendix E
Mapping and Summarization of Changes— Clarified Auditing Standards

This appendix maps the extant[1] AU sections to the clarified AU-C sections. As a result of the Auditing Standards Board's (ASB's) Clarity Project, all extant AU sections have been modified. In some cases, individual AU sections have been revised into individual clarified standards. In addition, the ASB revised the AU section number order established by Statement on Auditing Standards No. 1, *Responsibilities and Functions of the Independent Auditor* (AICPA, *Professional Standards*, AU sec. 110), to follow the same number order used in International Standards on Auditing (ISAs) for all clarified AU sections for which there are comparable ISAs. The clarified standards are effective for audits of financial statements for periods ending on or after December 15, 2012.

Although the Clarity Project was not intended to create additional requirements, some revisions have resulted in changes that may require auditors to make adjustments in their practices. To assist auditors in the transition process, these changes have been organized into the following four types:

- Substantive changes
- Primarily clarifying changes
- Primarily formatting changes
- Standards not yet issued in the Clarity Project

This appendix identifies those AU-C sections associated with these four types of changes.

Substantive Changes

Substantive changes are considered likely to affect the firms' audit methodology and engagements because they contain *substantive* or *other changes*, defined as having one or both of the following characteristics:

- A change or changes to an audit methodology that may require effort to implement
- A number of small changes that, although not individually significant, may affect audit engagements

Primarily Clarifying Changes

Primarily clarifying changes are intended to explicitly state what may have been implicit in the extant standards, which, over time, resulted in diversity in practice.

(continued)

---

[1] The term *extant* is used throughout this appendix in reference to the standards that are superseded by the clarified standards.

Primarily Formatting Changes

Primarily formatting changes from the extant standards do not contain changes that expand the extant sections in any significant way and may not require adjustments to current practice.

Standards Not Yet Issued in the Clarity Project

Standards not yet issued in the Clarity Project contain the remaining sections that are in exposure or have not yet been reworked.

The preface of this guide and the Financial Reporting Center at www.aicpa.org/frc provide more information about the Clarity Project. You can also visit www.aicpa.org/sasclarity.

Extant AU Sections Mapped to the Clarified AU-C Sections

Extant AU Section		AU Section Superseded	New AU-C Section		Type of Change
110	Responsibilities and Functions of the Independent Auditor	All	200	Overall Objectives of the Independent Auditor and the Conduct of an Audit in Accordance With Generally Accepted Auditing Standards [1]	Primarily formatting changes
120	Defining Professional Requirements in Statements on Auditing Standards	All			
150	Generally Accepted Auditing Standards	All			
161	The Relationship of Generally Accepted Auditing Standards to Quality Control Standards	All	220	Quality Control for an Engagement Conducted in Accordance With Generally Accepted Auditing Standards	Primarily clarifying changes
201	Nature of the General Standards	All	200	Overall Objectives of the Independent Auditor and the Conduct of an Audit in Accordance With Generally Accepted Auditing Standards [1]	Primarily formatting changes
210	Training and Proficiency of the Independent Auditor	All			
220	Independence	All			
230	Due Professional Care in the Performance of Work	All			

(continued)

Extant AU Section		AU Section Superseded	New AU-C Section		Type of Change
311	Planning and Supervision	All except paragraphs .08–.10	300	Planning an Audit	Primarily formatting changes
		Paragraphs .08–.10	210	Terms of Engagement	Primarily clarifying changes
312	Audit Risk and Materiality in Conducting an Audit	All	320	Materiality in Planning and Performing an Audit	Primarily formatting changes
			450	Evaluation of Misstatements Identified During the Audit	Primarily formatting changes
314	Understanding the Entity and Its Environment and Assessing the Risks of Material Misstatement	All	315	Understanding the Entity and Its Environment and Assessing the Risks of Material Misstatement	Primarily formatting changes
315	Communications Between Predecessor and Successor Auditors	All except paragraphs .03–.10 and .14	510	Opening Balances—Initial Audit Engagements, Including Reaudit Engagements	Primarily clarifying changes
		Paragraphs .03–.10 and .14	210	Terms of Engagement	Primarily clarifying changes
316	Consideration of Fraud in a Financial Statement Audit	All	240	Consideration of Fraud in a Financial Statement Audit	Primarily formatting changes
317	Illegal Acts by Clients	All	250	Consideration of Laws and Regulations in an Audit of Financial Statements	Substantive changes

Mapping and Summarization of Changes

	Extant AU Section	AU Section Superseded	New AU-C Section		Type of Change
318	Performing Audit Procedures in Response to Assessed Risks and Evaluating the Audit Evidence Obtained	All	330	Performing Audit Procedures in Response to Assessed Risks and Evaluating the Audit Evidence Obtained	Primarily formatting changes
322	The Auditor's Consideration of the Internal Audit Function in an Audit of Financial Statements	All	Planned to be issued as AU-C section 610	The Auditor's Consideration of the Internal Audit Function in an Audit of Financial Statements	Standards not yet issued in the Clarity Project
324	Service Organizations	All	402	Audit Considerations Relating to an Entity Using a Service Organization	Primarily clarifying changes
325	Communicating Internal Control Related Matters Identified in an Audit	All	265	Communicating Internal Control Related Matters Identified in an Audit	Substantive changes
326	Audit Evidence	All	500	Audit Evidence	Primarily formatting changes
328	Auditing Fair Value Measurements and Disclosures	All	540	Auditing Accounting Estimates, Including Fair Value Accounting Estimates, and Related Disclosures [2]	Primarily formatting changes

(continued)

Extant AU Section		AU Section Superseded	New AU-C Section		Type of Change
329	Analytical Procedures	All	520	Analytical Procedures	Primarily formatting changes
330	The Confirmation Process	All	505	External Confirmations	Primarily clarifying changes
331	Inventories	All	501	Audit Evidence—Specific Considerations for Selected Items [3]	Primarily clarifying changes
332	Auditing Derivative Instruments, Hedging Activities, and Investments in Securities	All	501	Audit Evidence—Specific Considerations for Selected Items [3]	Primarily clarifying changes
333	Management Representations	All	580	Written Representations	Primarily formatting changes
334	Related Parties	All	550	Related Parties	Substantive changes
336	Using the Work of a Specialist	All	620	Using the Work of an Auditor's Specialist	Primarily Clarifying Changes
337	Inquiry of a Client's Lawyer Concerning Litigation, Claims, and Assessments	All	501	Audit Evidence—Specific Considerations for Selected Items [3]	Primarily clarifying changes
339	Audit Documentation	All	230	Audit Documentation	Primarily formatting changes

Mapping and Summarization of Changes 471

Extant AU Section		AU Section Superseded	New AU-C Section		Type of Change
341	The Auditor's Consideration of an Entity's Ability to Continue as a Going Concern	All	570	The Auditor's Consideration of an Entity's Ability to Continue as a Going Concern	Primarily formatting changes
342	Auditing Accounting Estimates	All	540	Auditing Accounting Estimates, Including Fair Value Accounting Estimates, and Related Disclosures [2]	Primarily formatting changes
350	Audit Sampling	All	530	Audit Sampling	Primarily formatting changes
380	The Auditor's Communication With Those Charged With Governance	All	260	The Auditor's Communication With Those Charged With Governance	Primarily formatting changes
390	Consideration of Omitted Procedures After the Report Date	All	585	Consideration of Omitted Procedures After the Report Release Date	Primarily formatting changes
410	Adherence to Generally Accepted Accounting Principles	All	700	Forming an Opinion and Reporting on Financial Statements [4]	Substantive changes
420	Consistency of Application of Generally Accepted Accounting Principles	All	708	Consistency of Financial Statements	Primarily clarifying changes

(continued)

AAG-PLI APP E

Extant AU Section		AU Section Superseded	New AU-C Section		Type of Change
431	Adequacy of Disclosure in Financial Statements	All	705	Modifications to the Opinion in the Independent Auditor's Report [5]	Primarily formatting changes
504	Association With Financial Statements	All	N/A	Withdrawn	
508	Reports on Audited Financial Statements	Paragraphs .01–.11, .14–.15, .19–.32, .35–.52, .58–.70, and .74–.76	700	Forming an Opinion and Reporting on Financial Statements [4]	Substantive changes
			705	Modifications to the Opinion in the Independent Auditor's Report [5]	Primarily formatting changes
			706	Emphasis-of-Matter Paragraphs and Other-Matter Paragraphs in the Independent Auditor's Report [6]	Substantive changes
		Paragraphs .12–.13	600	Special Considerations—Audits of Group Financial Statements (Including the Work of Component Auditors)	Substantive changes
		Paragraphs .16–.18 and .53–.57	708	Consistency of Financial Statements	Primarily clarifying changes

Mapping and Summarization of Changes

Extant AU Section		AU Section Superseded	New AU-C Section		Type of Change
		Paragraphs .33–.34	805	Special Considerations—Audits of Single Financial Statements and Specific Elements, Accounts, or Items of a Financial Statement	Primarily clarifying changes
		Paragraphs .71–.73	560	Subsequent Events and Subsequently Discovered Facts [7]	Primarily formatting changes
530	Dating of the Independent Auditor's Report	Paragraphs .01–.02	700	Forming an Opinion and Reporting on Financial Statements [4]	Substantive changes
		Paragraphs .03–.08	560	Subsequent Events and Subsequently Discovered Facts [7]	Primarily formatting changes
532	Restricting the Use of an Auditor's Report	All	905	Alert That Restricts the Use of the Auditor's Written Communication	Primarily clarifying changes
534	Reporting on Financial Statements Prepared for Use in Other Countries	All	910	Financial Statements Prepared in Accordance With a Financial Reporting Framework Generally Accepted in Another Country	Primarily clarifying changes

(continued)

Extant AU Section		AU Section Superseded	New AU-C Section		Type of Change
543	Part of Audit Performed by Other Independent Auditors	All	600	Special Considerations—Audits of Group Financial Statements (Including the Work of Component Auditors)	Substantive changes
544	Lack of Conformity With Generally Accepted Accounting Principles	All	800	Special Considerations—Audits of Financial Statements Prepared in Accordance With Special Purpose Frameworks [8]	Primarily clarifying changes
550	Other Information in Documents Containing Audited Financial Statements	All	720	Other Information in Documents Containing Audited Financial Statements	Primarily formatting changes
551	Supplementary Information in Relation to the Financial Statements as a Whole	All	725	Supplementary Information in Relation to the Financial Statements as a Whole	Primarily formatting changes
552	Reporting on Condensed Financial Statements and Selected Financial Data	All	810	Engagements to Report on Summary Financial Statements	Primarily clarifying changes
558	Required Supplementary Information	All	730	Required Supplementary Information	Primarily formatting changes

Mapping and Summarization of Changes

Extant AU Section		AU Section Superseded	New AU-C Section		Type of Change
560	Subsequent Events	All	560	Subsequent Events and Subsequently Discovered Facts [7]	Primarily formatting changes
561	Subsequent Discovery of Facts Existing at the Date of the Auditor's Report	All			
623	Special Reports	Paragraphs .19–.21	806	Reporting on Compliance With Aspects of Contractual Agreements or Regulatory Requirements in Connection With Audited Financial Statements	Primarily formatting changes
		Paragraphs .01–.10 and .22–.34	800	Special Considerations— Audits of Financial Statements Prepared in Accordance With Special Purpose Frameworks [8]	Primarily clarifying changes
		Paragraphs .11–.18	805	Special Considerations— Audits of Single Financial Statements and Specific Elements, Accounts, or Items of a Financial Statement	Primarily clarifying changes

(continued)

Extant AU Section		AU Section Super-seded	New AU-C Section		Type of Change
625	Reports on the Application of Accounting Principles	All	915	Reports on Application of Requirements of an Applicable Financial Reporting Framework	Primarily formatting changes
634	Letters for Underwriters and Certain Other Requesting Parties	All	920	Letters for Underwriters and Certain Other Requesting Parties	Primarily formatting changes
711	Filings Under Federal Securities Statutes	All	925	Filings With the U.S. Securities and Exchange Commission Under the Securities Act of 1933	Primarily formatting changes
722	Interim Financial Information	All	930	Interim Financial Information	Primarily formatting changes
801	Compliance Audits	All	935	Compliance Audits	Primarily formatting changes
901	Public Warehouses—Controls and Auditing Procedures for Goods Held	All	501	Audit Evidence—Specific Considerations for Selected Items [3]	Primarily clarifying changes
Legend: [n] Bracketed number indicates a clarity standard that supersedes more than one extant AU section.					

The AICPA has developed an Audit Risk Alert to assist auditors and members in practice prepare for the transition to the clarified standards. It has been organized to give you the background information on the development of the clarified standards and to identify the new requirements and changes from the extant standards. Check out the Audit Risk Alert *Understanding the Clarified Auditing Standards* (product no. ARACLA12P, ARACLA12E, and ARACLA12O), which is available in the AICPA store on www.cpa2biz.com.

Appendix F
International Financial Reporting Standards

> *Note:* The following content may include certain changes made since the original print version of the guide.

Introduction

The following information provides a brief overview of the ongoing globalization of accounting standards, International Financial Reporting Standards (IFRSs) as a body of accounting literature, the status of convergence with IFRSs in the United States, and the related issues that accounting professionals need to consider today.

Globalization of Accounting Standards

As the business world becomes more globally connected, regulators, investors, audit firms, and public and private companies of all sizes are expressing an increased interest in having common accounting standards among participants in capital markets and trading partners around the world. Proponents of convergence with, or adoption of, IFRSs for financial reporting in the United States believe that one set of financial reporting standards would improve the quality and comparability of investor information and promote fair, orderly, and efficient markets.

Many critics, however, believe that accounting principles generally accepted in the United States of America (U.S. GAAP) are the superior standards and question whether the use of IFRSs will result in more useful financial statements in the long term and whether the cost of implementing IFRSs will outweigh the benefits. Implementing IFRSs will require a staggering effort by management, auditors, and financial statement users, not to mention educators.

The increasing pressure to globalize accounting standards, both in the United States and around the world, means that now is the time to become knowledgeable about these changes. The discussion that follows explains the underpinnings of the international support for a common set of high quality global standards and many of the challenges and potential opportunities associated with such a fundamental shift in financial accounting and reporting.

The international standard setting process began several decades ago as an effort by industrialized nations to create standards that could be used by developing and smaller nations. However, as cross-border transactions and globalization increased, other nations began to take interest, and the global reach of IFRSs expanded. More than 100 nations and reporting jurisdictions permit or require IFRSs for domestic listed companies and most have fully conformed to IFRSs as promulgated by the International Accounting Standards Board (IASB) and include a statement acknowledging such conformity in audit reports. Several countries, including Argentina and Canada, adopted IFRSs on January 1, 2011, and many other countries have plans to converge (or eliminate significant differences between) their national standards and IFRSs in 2012.

For many years, the United States has been a strong leader in international efforts to develop globally accepted standards. Among other actions in support of IFRSs, the U.S. Securities and Exchange Commission (SEC) removed the requirement for foreign private issuers registered in the United States to reconcile their financial reports with U.S. GAAP if their accounts complied with IFRSs as issued by the IASB. In addition, the SEC continues to analyze and evaluate appropriate steps toward, and challenges related to, incorporating IFRSs into the U.S. financial reporting system, as subsequently described.

In addition to the support received from certain U.S. based entities, financial and economic leaders from various organizations have announced their support for global accounting standards. Most notably, in 2009, the Group of Twenty Finance Ministers and Central Bank Governors (G20), a group from 20 of the world's industrialized and developing economies (with the 20th member being the European Union, collectively), called for standard setters to redouble their efforts to complete convergence in global accounting standards.

Acceptance of a single set of high quality accounting standards may present many significant opportunities, including the improvement in financial reporting to global investors, the facilitation of cross-border investments, and the integration of capital markets. Further, U.S. entities with international operations could realize significant cost savings from the use of a single set of financial reporting standards. For example, U.S. issuers raising capital outside the United States are required to comply with the domestic reporting standards of the foreign country and U.S. GAAP. As a result, additional costs arise from the duplication and translation of financial reporting information.

Many multinational companies support the use of common accounting standards to increase comparability of financial results among reporting entities from different countries. They believe common standards will help investors better understand the entities' business activities and financial position. Large public companies with subsidiaries in multiple jurisdictions would be able to use one accounting language company-wide and present their financial statements in the same language as their competitors. In addition, some believe that in a truly global economy, financial professionals, including CPAs, will be more mobile, and companies will more easily be able to respond to the human capital needs of their subsidiaries around the world.

Although certain cost reductions are expected, the initial cost of convergence with IFRSs is expected to be one of the largest obstacles for many entities, including accounting firms and educational institutions. Substantial internal costs for U.S. corporations in the areas of employee training, IT conversions, and general ledger software have been predicted. In addition, the time and effort required from various external functions, including the education of auditors, investors, lenders, and other financial statement users, will be significant factors for consideration.

Although the likelihood of acceptance of IFRSs may lack clarity for the time being, U.S. companies should consider preparing for the costly transition to new or converged standards, which likely will include higher costs in the areas of training and software compliance.

Who is the IASB?

The IASB is the independent standard setting body of the IFRS Foundation, formerly, the International Accounting Standards Committee Foundation. As a private sector organization, the IFRS Foundation has no authority to impose funding regimes on countries. However, a levy system and national contributions through regulatory and standard-setting authorities or stock exchanges have been introduced in a number of countries to fund the organization. Although the AICPA was a founding member of the International Accounting Standards Committee, the IASB's predecessor organization, it is not affiliated with the IASB.

The IASB, founded on April 1, 2001, in London, England, is responsible for developing IFRSs and promoting the use and application of these standards. In pursuit of this objective, the IASB cooperates with national accounting standard setters to achieve convergence in accounting standards around the world.

The structure includes the following primary groups: (*a*) the IFRS Foundation, an independent organization having two main bodies: the IFRS Foundation trustees and the IASB; (*b*) the IFRS Advisory Council; and (*c*) the IFRS Interpretations Committee, formerly the International Financial Reporting Interpretations Committee (IFRIC). The trustees appoint the IASB members, exercise oversight, and raise the funds needed, but the IASB itself has responsibility for establishing IFRSs.

The IFRS Foundation is linked to a monitoring board of public authorities, including committees of the International Organization of Securities Commissions, the European Commission, and the SEC. The monitoring board's main responsibilities are to ensure that the trustees continue to discharge their duties as defined by the IFRS Foundation Constitution, as well as approving the appointment or reappointment of trustees. In addition, through the monitoring board, capital markets authorities that allow or require the use of IFRSs in their jurisdictions will be able to more effectively carry out their mandates regarding investor protection, market integrity, and capital formation.

The IASB board members are selected chiefly upon their professional competence and practical experience. The trustees are required to select members so that the IASB will comprise the best available combination of technical expertise and international business and market experience and to ensure that the IASB is not dominated by any particular geographical interest or constituency. The IASB has members from several different countries, including the United States. The members are responsible for the development and publication of IFRSs, including *International Financial Reporting Standard for Small- and Medium-sized Entities* (*IFRS for SMEs*), and for approving the interpretations of IFRSs as developed by the IFRS Interpretations Committee.

The IFRS Interpretations Committee, founded in March 2002, is the successor of the previous interpretations committee, the Standing Interpretations Committee (SIC), and is the interpretative body of the IASB. The role of the IFRS Interpretations Committee is to provide timely guidance on newly identified financial reporting issues not specifically addressed in IFRSs or issues in which interpretations are not sufficient.

IFRSs are developed through a formal system of due process and broad international consultation, similar to the development of U.S. GAAP.

Readers are encouraged to become involved in the standard-setting process by responding to open calls from the standard setting organizations.

What Are IFRSs?

The term *IFRSs* has both a narrow and broad meaning. Narrowly, IFRSs refers to the numbered series of pronouncements issued by the IASB, collectively called *standards*. More broadly, however, IFRSs refer to the entire body of authoritative IASB literature, including the following:

1. Standards, whether labeled IFRSs or International Accounting Standards (IASs)[1]

2. Interpretations, whether labeled IFRIC (the former name of the interpretive body) or SIC (the predecessor to IFRIC)[2]

The preface to the IFRS *2011 Bound Volume* states that IFRSs are designed to apply to the general purpose financial statements and other financial reporting of all profit-oriented entities, including commercial, industrial, and financial entities, regardless of legal form or organization. IFRSs are not designed to apply to not-for-profit entities or those in the public sector,[3] but these entities may find IFRSs appropriate in accounting for their activities.

The IASB's *Conceptual Framework for Financial Reporting* (conceptual framework) establishes the concepts that underlie the preparation and presentation of financial statements for external users. The IASB is guided by the conceptual framework in the development of future standards and in its review of existing standards. The conceptual framework is not an IFRS, and when there is a conflict between the conceptual framework and any IFRS, the standard will prevail. The conceptual framework is an overall statement of guidance for those interpreting financial statements, whereas IFRSs are issue and subject specific.

When an IFRS specifically applies to a transaction, other event, or condition, the accounting policy or policies applied to that item shall be determined by applying the IFRS and considering any relevant implementation guidance issued by the IASB for the IFRS.

Further, if an IFRS does not address a specific transaction, event, or condition explicitly, IAS 8, *Accounting Policies, Changes in Accounting Estimates and Errors*, states that management should use its judgment in developing and applying an accounting policy that results in information that is relevant and reliable. With respect to the reliability of financial statements, IAS 8 states that the financial statements (*a*) represent faithfully the financial position, financial performance, and cash flows of the entity; (*b*) reflect the economic substance of transactions, other events, and conditions; (*c*) are neutral; (*d*) are prudent; and (*e*) are complete in all material respects. When making this type of judgment, management should refer to, and consider the applicability of, the following in descending order:

1. The requirements and guidance in IFRSs dealing with similar and related issues

2. The definitions, recognition criteria, and measurement concepts for assets, liabilities, income, and expenses in the IASB Framework

Management may also consider the most recent pronouncements of other standard setting bodies that use a similar conceptual framework (for example, U.S. GAAP), other accounting literature, and accepted industry practices to the extent that these do not conflict with IFRSs.

IFRS for SMEs

IFRS for SMEs is a modification and simplification of full IFRSs aimed at meeting the needs of private company financial reporting users and easing the

---

[1] See www.ifrs.org for a current listing of International Financial Reporting Standards (IFRSs) and International Accounting Standards (IASs).

[2] See www.ifrs.org for a current listing of International Financial Reporting Interpretations Committee and Standing Interpretations Committee interpretations.

[3] Generally speaking, *public* means government-owned entities, and *private* means nongovernment-owned entities.

financial reporting burden on private companies through a cost-benefit approach. *IFRS for SMEs* is a self-contained, global accounting and financial reporting standard applicable to the general purpose financial statements of entities that, in many countries, are known as small- and medium-sized entities (SMEs). Full IFRSs and *IFRS for SMEs* are promulgated by the IASB.

SMEs are entities that publish general purpose financial statements for external users and do not have public accountability. An entity has public accountability under the IASB's definition if it files its financial statements with a securities commission or other regulatory organization or it holds assets in a fiduciary capacity (for example, banks, insurance companies, brokers and dealers in securities, pension funds, and mutual funds). It is not the IASB's intention to exclude entities that hold assets in a fiduciary capacity for reasons incidental to their primary business (for example, travel agents, schools, and utilities) from utilizing *IFRS for SMEs*.

The needs of users of SME financial statements often are different from the needs of users of public company financial statements and other entities that likely would use full IFRSs. Whereas full IFRSs were designed specifically to meet the needs of equity investors in the public capital markets, *IFRS for SMEs* was developed with the needs of a wide range of users in mind. Users of the financial statements of SMEs may be more focused on shorter-term cash flows, liquidity, balance sheet strength, interest coverage, and solvency issues. Full IFRSs may impose a burden on SME preparers in that full IFRSs contain topics and detailed implementation guidance that generally are not relevant to SMEs. This burden has been growing as IFRSs have become more detailed. As such, a significant need existed for an accounting and financial reporting standard for SMEs that would meet the needs of their financial statement users while balancing the costs and benefits from a preparer perspective.

Practically speaking, *IFRS for SMEs* is viewed as an accounting framework for entities that do not have the capacity or resources to use full IFRSs. In the United States, the term SME would encompass many private companies.

In May 2008, the AICPA Governing Council voted to recognize the IASB as an accounting body for purposes of establishing international financial accounting and reporting principles and amended appendix A, "Council Resolution Designating Bodies to Promulgate Technical Standards," of Rule 202, *Compliance With Standards* (AICPA, *Professional Standards*, ET sec. 202 par. .01), and Rule 203, *Accounting Principles* (AICPA, *Professional Standards*, ET sec. 203 par. .01). This amendment gives AICPA members the option to use IFRSs as an alternative to U.S. GAAP. Accordingly, IFRSs are not considered to be an other comprehensive basis of accounting. Rather, they are a source of generally accepted accounting principles.

As such, a key professional barrier to using IFRSs and, therefore, *IFRS for SMEs*, has been removed. Any remaining barriers may come in the form of unwillingness by a private company's financial statement users to accept financial statements prepared under *IFRS for SMEs* and a private company's expenditure of money, time, and effort to convert to *IFRS for SMEs*.[4]

The AICPA has developed a resource that compares *IFRS for SMEs* with corresponding requirements of U.S. GAAP. This resource is available in a Wiki format, which allows AICPA members and others to contribute to its development. To learn more about the resource, view available sections, and contribute to its content, visit the Wiki at http://wiki.ifrs.com/.

---

[4] CPAs are encouraged to consult their state boards of accountancy to determine the status of reporting on financial statements prepared in accordance with *International Financial Reporting Standard for Small- and Medium-sized Entities* within their individual state.

The Financial Accounting Standards Board and IASB Convergence Efforts[5]

To address significant differences between IFRSs and U.S. GAAP, the Financial Accounting Standards Board (FASB) and the IASB agreed to a "Memorandum of Understanding" (MoU), which was originally issued in 2006 and subsequently updated. Readers are encouraged to monitor the FASB and IASB websites for additional developments regarding the convergence efforts, such as discussion papers, exposure drafts, and requests for comments.

Comparison of U.S. GAAP and IFRSs

One of the major differences between U.S. GAAP and IFRSs lies in the conceptual approach: U.S. GAAP is based on principles, with heavy use of rules to illustrate the principles; however, IFRSs are principles based, without heavy use of rules.

In general, a principles-based set of accounting standards, such as IFRSs, is broad in scope. The standards are concise, written in plain language, and provide for limited exceptions and bright lines. Principles-based standards typically require a higher level of professional judgment, which may facilitate an enhanced focus on the economic purpose of a company's transactions and how the transactions are reflected in its financial reporting.

A noticeable result of these differences is that IFRSs provide much less overall detail. In developing an IFRS, the IASB expects preparers to rely on core principles and limited application guidance with fewer prescriptive rules. In contrast, FASB often leans more toward providing extensive prescriptive guidance and detailed rules. The guidance provided in IFRSs regarding revenue recognition, for example, is significantly less extensive than U.S. GAAP. IFRSs also contain relatively little industry-specific guidance.

An inherent issue in a principles-based system is the potential for different interpretations of similar transactions across jurisdictions and entities, which may affect the relative comparability of financial reporting.

Because of long-standing convergence projects between the IASB and FASB, the extent of the specific differences between IFRSs and U.S. GAAP is decreasing. Yet, significant differences remain, which could result in significantly different reported results, depending on a company's industry and individual facts and circumstances. For example, some differences include the following:

- IFRSs do not permit last in, first out (LIFO) inventory accounting.
- IFRSs allow for the revaluation of assets in certain circumstances.
- IFRSs use a single-step method for impairment write-downs rather than the two-step method used in U.S. GAAP, making write-downs more likely.
- IFRSs have a different probability threshold and measurement objective for contingencies.
- IFRSs generally do not allow net presentation for derivatives.

U.S. GAAP also addresses some specific transactions not currently addressed in IFRSs, such as accounting for reorganizations, including quasi reorganizations;

---

[5] Because the convergence projects discussed are active and subject to change, updates will be posted periodically to www.journalofaccountancy.com. Readers also are encouraged to monitor the progress of these projects at the respective boards' websites: www.ifrs.org and www.fasb.org.

troubled debt restructuring; spin-offs; and reverse spin-offs. In addition, U.S. GAAP is designed to apply to all nongovernmental entities, including not-for-profit entities, and includes specific guidance for not-for-profit entities, development stage entities, limited liability entities, and personal financial statements.

The difference in the amount of industry-specific guidance also illustrates the different approaches. Currently, IFRSs include only several standards (for example, IAS 41, *Agriculture*)[6] that might be regarded as primarily industry-specific guidance. However, the scope of these standards includes all entities to which the scope of IFRSs applies. In contrast, U.S. GAAP has considerable guidance for entities within specific industries. For example, on liability recognition and measurement alone, U.S. GAAP contains specific guidance for entities in the following industries, which is not found in IFRSs:

- Health care
- Contractors and construction
- Contractors and the federal government
- Entertainment, with separate guidance for casinos, films, and music
- Financial services, with separate guidance for brokers and dealers and depository and lending, insurance, and investment companies

For nonmonetary transactions, U.S. GAAP provides specific guidance for the airline, software, and entertainment industries.

SEC Work Plan

The SEC continues to affirm its support for a single set of high quality, globally accepted accounting standards; however, no decision has been made on whether or not to adopt IFRSs. In May 2011, the SEC staff produced a work plan outlining how such a possible transition might happen.

In November 2011, the SEC released a staff paper that summarizes the current status of convergence projects, which are grouped by both short term and long term, as well as by level of priority (greater priority versus lower priority). Currently, the three projects that are of greater priority are financial instruments, revenue recognition, and leases.

In July 2012, the SEC published its final staff report on the work plan, which focuses on the arguments for and against various forms of adoption of global accounting standards. When assessing the implications of incorporating IFRSs in the U.S. financial reporting system, the SEC concluded that although international standards have improved in comprehensiveness, there are still some gaps, especially in the areas of insurance, extractive industries, and rate-regulated industries. The report also states that the costs of full IFRS adoption remain to be among the most significant costs required from an accounting perspective, and that companies questioned whether the benefits would justify such a full-scale transition. Although the report does not contain information leading to any decision the SEC has made regarding in-corporation of IFRSs, the staff expects that the SEC and others in the United States will remain involved with the development and application of IFRS.

Refer to www.sec.gov for the full version of the staff paper.

---

[6] In addition to IAS 41, *Agriculture*, the other IFRSs that address issues specific to certain industries are IFRS 4, *Insurance Contracts*, and IFRS 6, *Exploration for and Evaluation of Mineral Resources*.

AICPA

In response to an SEC staff paper issued in May 2011, the AICPA issued a comment letter in August 2011, recommending that U.S. public companies be allowed the option of adopting use of IFRSs as the commission weighs a possible future framework for incorporating IFRSs into the U.S. financial reporting system. The letter states that the adoption option would be another important step towards achieving the goal of incorporating IFRSs into the U.S. financial reporting system and that the number of companies that would choose such an option would not be such that system-wide readiness would become an issue. The comment letter further states AICPA's agreement with the SEC in that FASB should continue to have an active role in the international financial reporting arena to ensure that U.S. interests are suitably addressed in the development of IFRSs. Results from an IFRS Readiness Survey conducted by the AICPA in September 2011 show that a majority of CPAs support optional adoption of IFRSs. This would allow publicly traded U.S. companies to use IFRS while the SEC decides whether to incorporate the standards into U.S. reporting requirements.

Additional Resources

Website	URL
AICPA	www.aicpa.org
AICPA International Financial Reporting Standards Resources	www.ifrs.com
International Accounting Standards Board and IFRS Foundation	www.ifrs.org
Comparison Wiki of *International Financial Reporting Standard for Small- and Medium-sized Entities* and U.S. generally accepted accounting principles	http://wiki.ifrs.com
Financial Accounting Standards Board	www.fasb.org

Glossary

The following terms can be found in Financial Accounting Standards Board (FASB) *Accounting Standards Codification* (ASC) glossary:

acquisition costs. Costs incurred in the acquisition of new and renewal insurance contracts. Acquisition costs include those costs that vary with and are primarily related to the acquisition of insurance contracts.

annuity contract. A contract in which an insurance entity unconditionally undertakes a legal obligation to provide specified pension benefits to specific individuals in return for a fixed consideration or premium. An annuity contract is irrevocable and involves the transfer of significant risk from the employer to the insurance entity. Annuity contracts are also called allocated contracts.

assuming entity. The party that receives a reinsurance premium in a reinsurance transaction. The assuming entity (or reinsurer) accepts an obligation to reimburse a ceding entity under the terms of the reinsurance contract.

captive insurer. An insurance entity that does business primarily with related entities.

ceding entity. The party that pays a reinsurance premium in a reinsurance transaction. The ceding entity receives the right to reimbursement from the assuming entity under the terms of the reinsurance contract.

claim. A demand for payment of a policy benefit because of the occurrence of an insured event.

cost recovery method. A revenue recognition method under which premiums are recognized as revenue in an amount equal to estimated claim costs as insured events occur until the ultimate premium is reasonably estimable, and recognition of income is postponed until that time.

deposit method. A revenue recognition method under which premiums are not recognized as revenue and claim costs are not charged to expense until the ultimate premium is reasonably estimable, and recognition of income is postponed until that time.

fronting arrangements. Reinsurance arrangements in which the ceding entity issues a policy and reinsures all or substantially all of the insurance risk with the assuming entity.

group insurance. Insurance protecting a group of persons, usually employees of an entity and their dependents. A single insurance contract is issued to their employer or other representative of the group. Individual certificates often are given to each insured individual or family unit. The insurance usually has an annual renewable contract period, although the insurer may guarantee premium rates for two or three years. Adjustments to premiums relating to the actual experience of the group of insured persons are common.

incremental direct costs of contract acquisition. A cost to acquire an insurance contract that has both of the following characteristics:

    a. It results directly from and is essential to the contract transaction(s).

    b. It would not have been incurred by the insurance entity had the contract transaction(s) not occurred.

incurred-but-not-reported claims. Claims relating to insured events that have occurred but have not yet been reported to the insurer or reinsurer as of the date of the financial statements.

incurred losses. Losses paid or unpaid for which the entity has become liable during a period.

liability for claim adjustment expenses. The amount needed to provide for the estimated ultimate cost required to investigate and settle losses relating to insured events that have occurred on or before a particular date (ordinarily, the balance sheet date), whether or not reported to the insurer at that date.

liability for unpaid claims. The amount needed to provide for the estimated ultimate cost of settling claims relating to insured events that have occurred on or before a particular date (ordinarily, the balance sheet date).

maintenance costs. Costs associated with maintaining records relating to insurance contracts and with the processing of premium collections and commissions.

morbidity. The relative incidence of disability because of disease or physical impairment.

mortgage guaranty insurance enterprise. An insurance enterprise that issues insurance contracts that guarantee lenders, such as savings and loan associations, against nonpayment by mortgagors.

mutual entity. An entity other than an investor-owned entity that provides dividends, lower costs, or other economic benefits directly and proportionately to its owners, members, and participants. Mutual insurance entities, credit unions, and farm and rural electric cooperatives are examples of mutual entities.

participating insurance. Insurance in which the contract holder is entitled to participate in the earnings or surplus of the insurance entity. The participation occurs through the distribution of dividends to policyholders.

property and liability insurance entity. An entity that issues insurance contracts providing protection against either of the following:

    a. Damage to, or loss of, property caused by various perils, such as fire and theft

    b. Legal liability resulting from injuries to other persons or damage to their property

Property and liability insurance entities also can issue accident and health insurance contracts. The term property and liability insurance enterprise is the current terminology used to describe a fire and casualty insurance entity. Property and liability insurance entities may be either stock or mutual entities.

reinsurance. A transaction in which a reinsurer (assuming entity), for a consideration (premium), assumes all or part of a risk undertaken originally by another insurer (ceding entity). For indemnity reinsurance, the legal rights of the insured are not affected by the reinsurance transaction and the insurance entity issuing the insurance contract remains liable to the insured for payment of policy benefits. Assumption or novation reinsurance contracts that are legal replacements of one insurer by another extinguish the ceding entity's liability to the policyholder.

reinsurance receivable. All amounts recoverable from reinsurers for paid and unpaid claims and claim settlement expenses, including estimated amounts receivable for unsettled claims, claims incurred but not reported, or policy benefits.

retroactive reinsurance. Reinsurance in which an assuming entity agrees to reimburse a ceding entity for liabilities incurred as a result of past insurable events covered under contracts subject to the reinsurance. A reinsurance contract may include both prospective and retroactive reinsurance provisions.

risk of adverse deviation. A concept used by life insurance enterprises in estimating the liability for future policy benefits relating to long-duration contracts. The risk of adverse deviation allows for possible unfavorable deviations from assumptions, such as estimates of expected investment yields, mortality, morbidity, terminations, and expenses. The concept is referred to as risk load when used by property and liability insurance entities.

subrogation. The right of an insurer to pursue any course of recovery of damages, in its name or in the name of the policyholder, against a third party who is liable for costs relating to an insured event that have been paid by the insurer.

termination. In general, the failure to renew an insurance contract. Involuntary terminations include death, expirations, and maturities of contracts. Voluntary terminations of life insurance contracts include lapses with or without cash surrender value and contract modifications that reduce paid-up whole-life benefits or term-life benefits.

The following is a list of additional terms that have been used in this guide:

abstract. A form containing basic data shown on a policy. Copies of an abstract may be used by the accounting, statistical, payroll audit, and inspection departments.

accident date. The date on which the accident (or loss) occurs.

accident year. The year in which an accident or loss occurred.

account current or agents' account. See **agency billing**.

accretion of discount on bonds. Adjustment of the purchase price of bonds purchased at less than par value to increase the value to par at maturity date. The adjustment is calculated to yield the effective rate of interest at which the purchase was made, which is called the *interest method*.

additional premium. A premium due from an insured arising from an endorsement.

adjustment bureau. An organization formed by a group of insurance entities to investigate, adjust, and negotiate claims on behalf of the entities.

advance premiums. The premiums collected in advance of the premium due dates.

agency billing. Any of various methods of premium billing and collection in which the insured is billed by the agent and the premium is collected by either the agent or the insurance entity.

agency company. An insurance entity whose business is produced through a network of agents, as distinguished from a direct writing entity whose business is produced by entity employees.

agency reinsurance. Reinsurance arranged to be assumed or ceded for an insurer by one of its agents who usually handles the details of writing the policies and collecting or paying the premiums. For example, on very large risks the agent frequently issues only one policy to the insured and then obtains reinsurance from other entities to reduce the exposure of the insurer to a desired level.

agency system. A system of producing business through a network of agents. Such agents have a contract to represent the entity and are of three classes: local, regional, and general. These classes are compensated at differing rates of commission, and general agents have much greater responsibilities and duties than local and regional agents.

agent. An independent contractor who represents one insurance entity, called an *exclusive agent*, or more than one entity, called an *independent agent*, with express authority to act for the entity or entities in dealing with insureds.

agents' balance. Premium balances, less commissions payable thereon, due from agents and brokers.

aggregate excess of loss. A stop-loss agreement designed to prevent a ceding entity's loss from exceeding a predetermined limit. For example, if under an agreement indemnifying an entity against losses

Glossary

in excess of a 70 percent loss ratio, the ceding entity's loss ratio exceeds 70 percent, then recovery will be made from the reinsurer of the amount necessary to reduce the loss ratio to 70 percent.

alien company. Insurance entity domiciled in a foreign country.

amortization of premiums on bonds. Adjustment of the purchase price of bonds purchased at more than par value to decrease the value to par at maturity. The adjustment is calculated to yield the effective rate of interest at which the purchase was made, known as the *interest method*.

annual pro rata. A basis used to calculate unearned premiums involving the assumption that the average date of issue of all policies written during the year is the middle of the year.

annual statement (convention statement or convention form). A statement furnishing information regarding the entity's condition and results at and for the year ended December 31 of each year. This annual statement must be filed on the form prescribed by the National Association of Insurance Commissioners (NAIC) with the various insurance departments by March 1 of the following year with each state in which an entity is authorized to transact business.

application. A request for insurance submitted to the insurer by or on behalf of the insured. An application usually includes sufficient information for the insurer to determine whether it wishes to accept the risk. In some lines of insurance the terms *daily* and *application* are used synonymously.

assessment enterprise. An insurance entity that sells insurance to groups with similar interests, such as church denominations or professional groups. Some assessment enterprises also sell insurance directly to the general public. If the enterprise cannot pay all claims, the members may be assessed.

asset, admitted. An asset recognized and accepted by state insurance regulatory authorities in determining the financial condition of an insurance entity.

assets, nonadmitted. Assets, or portions thereof, that are not readily convertible to cash to pay claims and, accordingly, are not permitted to be reported as admitted assets in the annual and quarterly statements filed with various insurance departments. Nonadmitted assets are either defined by the insurance laws of various states or not specifically identified as admitted assets. Major nonadmitted assets include agents' balances or uncollected premiums over three months due, certain amounts of deferred tax assets, intangible assets other than goodwill, furniture, fixtures, supplies, and equipment.

associations, pools, and syndicates. Organizations formed by several insurance entities or groups of entities as joint ventures to underwrite specialized types of insurance or to write insurance in specialized areas.

assumed reinsurance premiums. Premium income less return premiums arising from contracts entered into to reinsure other insurance companies that provide the related insurance or reinsurance coverage.

audit premiums. Earned premiums determined from data developed by periodic audits of insureds' records or from periodic reports submitted by insureds. Such audits are made and such reports are submitted either monthly, quarterly, semiannually, or annually.

automatic treaty. Reinsurance treaty, usually pro rata, under which the reinsurer is committed to accept from the ceding entity a fixed share of each risk or of specified risks. The ceding entity is obligated to cede, and the reinsurer is obligated to accept.

average reserves. A method of estimating loss liabilities by multiplying the number of outstanding claims by an average amount per claim based on past experience.

benefit. Any payment made under the terms of an insurance contract.

binder. An agreement, which may be written or oral, whereby one party agrees to insure another pending receipt of and final action on the application.

bordereau. A detailed listing of premiums or loss transactions, or both, usually prepared monthly or quarterly and given to interested parties. Frequently rendered by ceding entities to reinsurers and by large general agents to entities.

brokers. Licensed representatives who place the insurance of their clients with insurance entities. Compensation for their services consists of commissions paid to them by the insurance entities. They are not agents of the entities, and the commissions they receive are usually lower than that of agents who legally represent the entities.

bulk reinsurance. See **portfolio reinsurance**.

cancellation. Complete termination of an existing policy before expiration.

caps (reinsurance). Caps are used to limit the reinsurer's aggregate exposure by imposing a dollar limit or a limit expressed as a percentage of premiums on the amount of claims to be paid by the reinsurer. For example, the reinsurer will not be responsible for losses in excess of 150 percent of the premium paid.

captive insurance entity (defined in FASB ASC glossary, as presented in the first section of this glossary). Entity formed to insure the risks of an affiliated corporation, typically its parent. Reasons for forming a captive insurance entity include the following:

    a. Instances when insurance cannot be purchased from commercial insurance entities for business risk; in many instances, entities within an industry form a joint captive insurance entity for that reason.

    b. Premiums paid to a captive insurance entity are deductible as a business expense for tax purposes in certain circumstances. However, sums set aside in a self insurance program are not deductible as a business expense.

    c. Insurance can be obtained through the international reinsurance market at a more favorable premium with higher limits of coverage.

d. Investment returns can be obtained directly on its invested capital. However, competent personnel to manage and staff the entity could be excessively expensive and further a catastrophic occurrence or series of occurrences that could bankrupt the entity.

case reserve. A liability for loss estimated to be paid in the future on a specific claim.

case-basis reserves. The sum of the values assigned by claims adjusters at the insurance entity to specific claims that have been reported to, and were recorded by, the insurance entity but not yet paid at the financial statement date.

catastrophe. A conflagration, earthquake, windstorm, explosion, or similar event resulting in substantial losses. Catastrophe losses—the whole loss insured by an insurance entity from a single catastrophic event—are usually reinsured under excess-of-loss treaties in order to limit any one such loss to a specific dollar amount.

ceded reinsurance premiums. Outgoing premiums less return premiums arising from reinsurance purchased from other insurance entities.

cession. A unit of insurance passed on to a reinsurer by a ceding or primary entity. Under certain kinds of reinsurance treaties, many reinsurers give each transaction a number, called a *cession number*.

claim adjusting. The process of investigating, appraising, negotiating, and, sometimes, settling claims.

claim frequency. The relative incidence of claims in relation to an exposure base.

claim or loss files. All data relating to each loss or claim together in a folder or stapled together, or the like, and referred to as the *loss* or *claim file*.

claim severity. The relative magnitude of the dollar amount of claims.

class or manual rating. A method of determining premiums based on standard rates for large groups of similar risks.

closing date. The date on which the claim is closed.

combined ratios. The sum of both the loss and loss adjustment expense ratio and expense ratio used to measure underwriting performance.

commissions. Compensation paid by an insurance entity to agents or brokers for placing insurance coverage with the entity, usually determined as percentages of the premiums.

commutation agreement. A settlement agreement (a buy back) reached between a reinsured and a reinsurer by which the reinsurance obligation is terminated by an agreement by the reinsurer to pay funds at present value that are not yet due under the reinsurance agreement.

contingent commissions. A provision in an insurance or reinsurance agreement that provides a commission to an insurer or reinsurer contingent upon a specified event happening. It is intended to allow the insurer or ceding insurer to share in the profits or losses realized by the insurer or reinsurer on the business subject to the contract.

contract holder. A person who has an insurance contract in his or her possession or under his or her control. The term is frequently applied to describe the insured, regardless of the ownership of the contract.

contribution to premium in force. Net change in premiums in force for a period or net original premiums written during a period (total original premiums less original return premiums).

convention statement or convention form. See **annual statement**.

daily report or daily. A copy of a policy retained by an insurance entity or forwarded to the entity by an agent. The daily includes all special provisions and endorsements and it is one of the basic documents in an insurance office.

declaration sets. Documents generated by an insurance entity in processing policy applications and endorsements that include billing statements and insurance ID cards as well as information such as terms of the policies, lines of coverage, premiums, and agent information.

deposit premiums. Provisional premium payments by policyholders that are adjusted at the end of the policy terms based on actual coverage provided.

development (runoff) of loss reserves. Comparison of the loss reserves outstanding at a particular date with the total of the payments on such losses from the reserve date to the development date, plus the estimated losses still unpaid at the date of the development.

differences. Term applied to the differences between accounts current rendered by agents and transactions shown on the entity's records caused, for example, by the agents and the entity using different cutoff dates or by errors and omissions by the entity or the agents.

direct billing. Billing by an insurance entity directly to insureds for premiums due. On collection, the entity pays the commission to the agent.

direct writing entity. An insurance entity whose business is produced by entity employees, as distinguished from an agency entity whose business is produced by agents.

direct written premiums. The premiums on all policies an entity has issued during a period of time, as opposed to earned premiums. Excludes amounts related to both reinsurance assumed and reinsurance ceded.

discounting. Recording future claim payments and expenses at their present value.

domestic insurers. Insurance entities domiciled in a particular state.

dual triggers. A coverage feature that requires the occurrence of both an insurable event and changes in a separate preidentified variable to trigger payment of a claim.

Glossary

earned premiums. Pro rata portions of premiums applicable to the expired period of a policy.

effective date. The date when insurance coverage under a policy begins.

endorsement. Documentary evidence of a change in an existing policy that may result in a change in premium, return premium, or no premium adjustment.

excess insurance. A policy covering the insured against loss in excess of a stated amount. The underlying amount is usually insured by another policy but can be retained by the insured.

excess-of-loss treaty. A kind of reinsurance contract in which the reinsurer pays all or a specified percentage of a loss caused by a particular occurrence or event (frequently of a more or less catastrophic nature) in excess of a fixed amount and up to a stipulated limit. Most contracts do not apply to specific policies but to aggregate losses incurred under all policies subject to the particular hazards reinsured. The premium is usually a percentage of the net premiums written by the carrier for the hazards subject to such reinsurance.

expense ratio (statutory). Underwriting expenses incurred less other income divided by net written premiums.

experience account (reinsurance). An arrangement whereby the ceding entity shares in the favorable experience of the contract by reference to an experience account that typically tracks ceded premiums, less fees, less ceded losses incurred, plus interest. Experience provisions can also require the ceding entity to share in unfavorable experience by requiring additional payments to the reinsurer in the event that the experience account becomes negative.

experience rating. Prospective adjustment of premiums based on the insured's past experience under the coverage.

exposure. Measurement of the extent of a hazard assumed by the carrier. From the statistical standpoint of rate making, exposure is the product of the amount of insurance at risk and the policy period expressed in years.

face sheet. A sheet affixed to the front of a claim file containing abstracts of coverage and loss notices along with other information for later use in developing statistics for reserve analysis and product pricing.

facultative reinsurance. Arrangements under which each risk to be reinsured is offered to and accepted or rejected by the reinsurer. Such arrangements do not obligate the ceding entity to cede or the reinsurer to accept.

fair access to insurance requirements (FAIR) plan. A federally approved and state supervised program to make property insurance available in high risk areas.

fellow of the Society of Actuaries (FSA). A full member of the Society of Actuaries. The Society of Actuaries is a professional actuarial society covering North America that maintains rigorous examination requirements for admission to membership.

fidelity bond. Insurance that covers employers against dishonest acts by employees.

AAG-PLI GLO

fire and allied lines insurance. Property insurance coverage for risks such as fire, windstorm, hail, and water damage.

foreign insurers. Insurance entities domiciled outside a particular state.

funds held by a company under reinsurance treaty. An account used to record a liability from a deposit from a reinsurer or the withholding of a portion of the premiums due as a guarantee that a reinsurer will meet its loss and other obligations.

funds held by or deposited with ceding reinsurers. An asset account used by a reinsurer to record deposits made with ceding entities, pools, or associations of portions of premiums due from them to guarantee that the reinsurer will meet its loss and other obligations.

general agents. Agents assigned exclusive territories in which to produce business on behalf of an insurance entity.

general liability insurance. Liability coverage for most physical and property damages not covered by workers' compensation or automobile liability insurance.

gross in force. Aggregate premiums from all policies on direct and assumed business recorded before a specified date that have not yet expired or been cancelled.

gross net premium income. As used in reinsurance contracts, gross written premiums, less return premiums, and reinsurance premiums. This term has the same meaning as *net written premiums* or *net premiums* in the United States. In Europe, the term *net premiums* refers to gross premiums received, less return premiums, reinsurance premiums, and commissions paid on premiums.

gross written premium. Direct written premiums plus assumed reinsurance premiums.

hazard. The risk or peril or source of risk insured against. This term is frequently used interchangeably with the terms *risk* and *peril*.

high deductible policy. An insurance policy whereby the policyholder is responsible for the payment of claims under a specified deductible amount. Typically, the insurer pays all losses under the contract and seeks reimbursement from the policyholder for claims paid subject to the deductible amount.

incurred loss ratio. Ratio calculated by dividing incurred losses by earned premiums.

individual or judgment rating. A method of determining premiums for large or unusual risks based on an evaluation of the individual risk.

in-force premiums. Aggregate premiums from all policies recorded before the specified date that have not expired or been cancelled.

inland marine insurance. Insurance coverage of property capable of being transported (other than transocean).

installment premiums. Premiums payable periodically rather than in a lump sum at the inception or effective date of the policy.

insurable value. The stated value in an insurance contract. It may be the cash or market value, the declared value, or the replacement value.

Glossary

insurance expense exhibit. A supplement to the annual statement to be filed with each insurance department, usually by May 1 rather than on March 1 (the day on which the annual statement is due to be filed). This exhibit shows the net gain or loss from underwriting for each line of business written by the entity during the year reported.

Insurance Regulatory Information System (IRIS). A system of 11 tests based on studies of financially troubled entities compared to financially sound entities. Usual ranges are established under each of the tests. The system is intended to assist in identifying entities requiring close surveillance (formerly called *early warning system*).

insured. The person whose life, property, or exposure to liability is insured.

interinsurance exchange or reciprocal. An unincorporated aggregation of individuals or firms called *subscribers* who exchange insurance through an attorney-in-fact. Each subscriber is therefore both an insurer and an insured.

intermediary. A reinsurance broker who negotiates reinsurance contracts on behalf of the reinsured (ceding entity) with the reinsurer.

investment expenses. According to the uniform expense regulation, all expenses incurred wholly or partially in connection with the investing of funds and the obtaining of investment income.

judgment rating. See **individual or judgment rating**.

line. A kind of insurance. In relation to the amount an insurance entity accepts on a risk, (1) the limit an entity has fixed for itself as maximum exposure on a class of risk and (2) the actual amount the entity has in fact accepted on a single risk.

long duration contract. An insurance contract that generally is not subject to unilateral changes in its provisions, such as a noncancellable or guaranteed renewable contract, and requires the performance of various functions and services (including insurance protection) for an extended period.

loss (claim) adjustment expenses. Expenses incurred in the course of investigating and settling claims. Loss-adjustment expenses include any legal and adjusters' fees and the costs of paying claims and all related expenses.

loss corridor (reinsurance). A mechanism that requires the ceding insurer to be responsible for a certain amount of the ultimate net loss above the ceding entity's designated retention and below the designated limit and that would otherwise be reimbursed under the reinsurance agreement. A loss corridor is usually expressed as a loss ratio percentage of the reinsurer's earned premium or a combined ratio if the reinsurance agreement provides for a ceding commission to the ceding entity. For example, under a quota-share agreement, the reinsurer will be responsible for losses up to 80 percent of premiums, will not be responsible for losses in excess of 80 percent of premiums up to 95 percent of premiums, and will then be responsible for losses in excess of 95 percent of premiums.

loss ratios. Expression in terms of ratios of the relationship of losses to premiums. Two ratios in common usage are (1) paid loss ratio—paid losses divided by written premiums or earned premiums, and (2) incurred loss ratio—incurred losses divided by earned premiums.

loss reserves. A term used in statutory accounting for the liability for unpaid losses.

losses, reported. Losses resulting from accidents or occurrences that have taken place and on which the entity has received notices or reports of loss.

manual rating. See **class or manual rating**.

market conduct examination. A review of an insurance entity's sales, advertising, underwriting, risk rating, and claims practices that may affect policyholders or claimants. It may be performed by or on behalf of regulatory authorities.

merit rating. Any of various methods of determining premiums by which standard rates are adjusted for evaluation of individual risks or for the insureds' past or current experience.

monthly pro rata. A basis used for calculation of unearned premiums involving the assumption that the average date of issue of all policies written during any month is the middle of that month.

mortgage servicing agent. An agent servicing mortgage loans for the mortgagee at a prescribed rate under a contractual agreement.

National Association of Insurance Commissioners (NAIC). An association of the insurance commissioners of all 50 U.S. states, the District of Columbia, and five U.S. territories. The NAIC's purpose is to exchange ideas and information and to promote the uniformity of insurance regulation in policy, laws, and regulations where such uniformity is appropriate.

net written premiums. Direct written premiums plus assumed reinsurance premiums less ceded reinsurance premiums.

ocean marine insurance. Coverage for (1) a ship and its equipment, (2) the cargo, (3) the freight paid for use of the ship, and (4) liability to third parties for damages.

original premium. The premium for the full term of a policy. In case the policy has been changed, the original premium can be determined by multiplying the amount currently insured by the latest premium rate shown on the policy or an endorsement of the policy.

paid losses. Disbursements for losses during the period.

participating entity. An insurance entity that participates in an insurance pool, association, or syndicate.

payment schedules (reinsurance). Features that are designed to delay the timing of reimbursement of losses so that investment income mitigates exposure to insurance risk. Payment schedules prevent the reinsurer's payments to the ceding entity from depending on, and directly varying with, the amount and timing of claims settled under the reinsured contracts. For example, a payment schedule may provide that no losses will be payable under the reinsurance contract by the reinsurer prior to year 8, regardless of when the insured incurs or pays a loss, at which time the reinsurer will pay losses ceded up to 25 percent of the contract limit each year until the experience is complete or the contract limit has been reached.

peril. Classification of loss occurrences insured against, such as fire, windstorm, collision, hail, bodily injury, property damage, or loss of profits.

permitted practices. Under Statutory Accounting Practices, permitted practices include practices that are not prescribed practices, but instead specifically allowed by the domiciliary state regulatory authority. An insurance entity may request permission from the domiciliary state regulatory authority to use a specific accounting practice in the preparation of its statutory financial statements.

personal lines. Insurance policies issued to individuals.

policy date. The date on which the contract becomes effective (sometimes referred to as the underwriting date).

policy year. The year during which a policy is effective.

policyholder dividends. Payments made or credits extended to the insured by the entity, usually at the end of a policy year, which results in reducing the net insurance cost to the policyholder. Such dividends may be paid in cash to the insureds or applied by the insureds as reductions of the premiums due for the next policy year.

pooling. Practice of sharing all business of an affiliated group of insurance entities among the members of the group.

portfolio reinsurance. Reinsurance on a bulk basis. Occurs frequently at the inception or termination of a reinsurance treaty. Also used as a means by which an entity may retire from a particular agency or territory or from the insurance business entirely.

premium. The consideration paid for an insurance contract.

premium adjustments. Additional premiums due to or from insureds or reinsurers arising from endorsements, cancellations, experience rated features, and audits.

premium deficiency. For short duration contracts, the amount by which anticipated losses, loss adjustment expenses, policyholder dividends, unamortized acquisition costs, and maintenance expenses exceed unearned premiums.

premium register. Listing of policies issued, generally in policy number order. Normally computer generated.

premium taxes. Taxes levied at varying rates on insurance entities by the various states on premiums written.

prescribed practices. Under Statutory Accounting Principles, prescribed practices are incorporated directly or by reference in state laws, regulations, and general administrative rules applicable to all insurance enterprises domiciled in a particular state.

pro rata reinsurance. The reinsured and the reinsurer participate in the premiums and losses on every risk that comes within the scope of the agreement in fixed proportion.

profit commissions. The additional commissions the ceding entity is entitled to receive from the reinsurer based upon experience to date. One form of a profit commission is a no claims bonus whereby the ceding entity receives a stated percentage of the premium ceded in the event no claims are ceded to the reinsurer.

proof of loss. A sworn statement furnished by an insured to the carrier setting forth the amount of loss claimed. This form, which is usually used in the settlement of first party losses, includes the date and description of the occurrence, amount of loss claimed, interested insurers, and so on.

quota-share reinsurance. A form of pro rata reinsurance. A reinsurance of a certain percentage of all the business or certain classes of or parts of the business of the reinsured. For example, an entity may reinsure under a quota-share treaty 50 percent of all of its business or 50 percent of its automobile business.

rating bureau. An organization supervised by state regulatory authorities that assists member entities in obtaining approval for premium rates.

reciprocal or interinsurance exchanges. A group of persons, firms, or corporations (commonly referred to as subscribers) that exchange insurance contracts through an attorney-in-fact (an attorney authorized by a person to act in that person's behalf).

record date. The date on which the entity records the claim in its statistical system.

reinstatement. A restoration of a lapsed contract to an active status. All contracts contain a provision stating the conditions under which reinstatement will be allowed.

reinstatement clause. To the extent coverage provided by the contract is absorbed by losses incurred, the contract provides for the ceding entity to reinstate coverage for the balance of the contract period for a stated additional premium. Reinsurance contracts may provide for an unlimited or a specific number of reinstatements and can either be obligatory or nonmandatory. Mandatory reinstatement premiums may require the ceding entity to pay additional amounts if a certain level of losses is incurred.

reinsurance assumed premiums. All premiums (less return premiums) arising from policies issued to assume a liability, in whole or in part, of another insurance entity that is already covering the risk with a policy.

reinsurance, authorized. Reinsurance placed with entities authorized to transact business in the state of filing.

reinsurance ceded premiums. All premiums (less return premiums) arising from policies or coverage purchased from another insurance entity for the purpose of transferring a liability, in whole or in part, assumed from direct or reinsurance assumed policies.

reinsurance in force. Aggregate premiums on all reinsurance ceded business recorded before a specified date that have not yet expired or been cancelled.

Glossary

reinsurance intermediaries. Brokers, agents, managing general agents, and similar entities that bring together reinsurance purchasers and sellers.

reinsurance, unauthorized. Reinsurance placed with entities not authorized to transact business in the state of filing.

report date. The date on which the entity first receives notice of the claim.

reported claims. Claims relating to insured events that have occurred and have been reported to the insurer and reinsurer as of the date of the financial statements, as opposed to incurred-but-not-reported claims.

reporting form contract. Insurance contract for which the premium is adjusted after the contract term based on the value of the insured property.

retention. The net amount of any risk an entity does not reinsure but keeps for its own account.

retroactive commissions. Commissions paid to agents or brokers for which the final amount is determined based on the insured's loss experience.

retrocession. A reinsurance of reinsurance assumed. For example, B accepts reinsurance from A, and B in turn reinsures with C the whole or a part of the reinsurance B assumed from A. The reinsurance ceded to C by B is called a retrocession.

retrospective experience rating. A method of determining final premium in which the initial premium is adjusted during the period of coverage based on actual experience during that same period.

retrospective premium. Premium determined after expiration of the policy based on the loss experience under the policy. The initial premium charged on such policies is referred to as the *standard premium*.

return premiums. A premium refund due the insured from an endorsement or cancellation.

rider. Endorsement to an insurance contract that modifies clauses and provisions of the contract, either adding, excluding, or limiting coverage.

risk. See **hazard**.

risk based capital (RBC) requirements. Regulatory and rating agency targeted surplus based on the relationship of statutory surplus, with certain adjustments, to the sum of stated percentages of each element of a specified list of entity risk exposures. Insurers having total adjusted surplus less than that required by the RBC calculation will be subject to varying degrees of regulatory action depending on the level of capital inadequacy.

runoff data. See **development (runoff) of loss reserves**.

salvage. The amount received by an insurer from the sale of property (usually damaged) on which the insurer has paid a total claim to the insured and has obtained title to the property.

schedule rating. A method of determining the premium by which a standard rate is adjusted based on an evaluation of the relative exposure to risk.

short duration contract. A contract that provides insurance protection for a fixed period of short duration and enables the insurer to cancel the contract or to adjust the provisions of the contract at the end of any contract period, such as adjusting the amount of premiums charged or coverage provided.

sliding scale commission. A commission adjustment on earned premiums whereby the actual ceding commission varies inversely with the loss ratio (for example, increasing payments back to the ceding entity as losses decrease and decreasing payments back to the ceding entity as losses increase), subject to a maximum and minimum.

spread-loss treaty. A contract on an excess-of-loss basis designed to pay certain losses over a given or stipulated amount and to average such losses over a period of years. Five years is the usual period, with the premium adjustable within fixed minimum and maximum limits according to the entity's experience. Such a contract protects the ceding entity against shock losses and spreads those costs over the given period, subject to the maximum and minimum premium each year.

statutory accounting practices. Accounting principles required by statute, regulation, or rule, or permitted by specific approval that an insurance enterprise is required to follow in preparing its annual and quarterly statements for submission to state insurance departments.

statutory loss reserves. The amount by which reserves required by law on bodily injury and workers' compensation losses exceeds the case-basis loss and loss-expense reserves carried by an entity for such losses.

statutory surplus. Admitted assets less liabilities, determined in accordance with statutory accounting practices.

stock companies. Corporations organized for profit to offer insurance against various risks.

stop-loss reinsurance. Kind of excess reinsurance also called *excess-of-loss ratio*. Provides that the insurer will suffer the loss in its entirety until the total amount of the loss is such that the loss ratio (losses divided by premiums) exceeds an agreed loss ratio, after which the reinsurer reimburses the insurer the amount needed to bring the loss ratio down to the agreed percentage.

structured settlements. Periodic fixed payments to a claimant for a determinable period of time or for life for the settlement of a claim usually funded through the purchase of an annuity.

surety bond. Insurance coverage that provides compensation to a third party for the insured's failure to perform specified acts within a stated period.

surplus lines. Risks not fitting normal underwriting patterns, involving a degree of risk that is not commensurate with standard rates or that will not be written by standard carriers because of general market conditions. Policies are bound or accepted by carriers not licensed in the jurisdiction where the risk is located, and generally are not subject to regulations governing premium rates or policy language.

surplus share reinsurance. Reinsurance on a pro rata basis of only those risks on which coverage exceeds a stated amount.

surplus treaty reinsurance. A treaty on a pro rata basis reinsuring surplus liability on various risks. The reinsurer shares the gross lines of the ceding entity. The amount reinsured varies according to different classes of risks and the net retention that the ceding entity wishes to retain for its own account. Ceding entities frequently have several layers of surplus treaties so that they may accommodate very large risks; usually, the reinsurer's participation in any one surplus treaty is limited to a certain multiple of the ceding entity's retention. Premiums and losses are shared by the reinsurer and the ceding entity on a pro rata basis in proportion to the amount of risk insured or reinsured by each. This is one of the oldest forms of treaty reinsurance and is still in common use in fire reinsurance.

syndicates. See **associations, pools, and syndicates**.

title insurance enterprise. An enterprise that issues title insurance contracts to real estate owners, purchasers, and mortgage lenders, indemnifying them against loss or damage caused by defects in, liens on, or challenges to their titles on real estate.

treaty. A contract of reinsurance.

treaty-basis reinsurance. The automatic reinsurance of any agreed-on portion of business written as specified in the reinsurance contract.

unauthorized reinsurer and nonadmitted reinsurer. A reinsurer not authorized or licensed to do business in the state in which the ceding entity is domiciled. Licensed companies can write direct business in the state; if licensed, an entity is also authorized to assume reinsurance in that state. A nonlicensed entity can assume reinsurance if the state authorizes it to do so, and it is then considered to be an authorized reinsurer.

ultimate-developed-cost method. A method of estimating loss reserves based on a statistical average of the ultimate cost of all claims in a particular line.

underwriting. The process by which an insurance entity determines whether and for what premium it will accept an application for insurance.

unearned premiums. The pro rata portion of the premiums in force applicable to the unexpired period of the policy term.

workers' compensation insurance. Coverage that provides compensation for injuries sustained by employees in their employment.

zone examination. An examination of an insurance entity undertaken by on or behalf of regulatory authorities in a group of states.

Index of Pronouncements and Other Technical Guidance

A

Title	Paragraphs
AT Section	
101, *Attest Engagement*	2.08
AU-C Section	
200, *Overall Objectives of the Independent Auditor and the Conduct of an Audit in Accordance With Generally Accepted Auditing Standards*	2.01
210, *Terms of Engagement*	2.02, 2.139
230, *Audit Documentation*	2.117, 2.120, 2.122, 4.132, 4.147
240, *Consideration of Fraud in a Financial Statement Audit*	2.25, 2.75–.76, 2.79, 2.84, 2.88–.89, 2.93–.99, 3.112, 4.106, 5.204, 6.88, 7.64, 8.39, 9.37
250, *Consideration of Laws and Regulations in an Audit of Financial Statements*	2.166–.167, 6.12
260, *The Auditor's Communication With Those Charged With Governance*	2.126, 2.134–.137
265, *Communicating Internal Control Related Matters Identified in an Audit*	2.126–.132, 2.160, 4.148, 6.108, 10.81, 10.83
300, *Planning an Audit*	2.13–.14, 3.111, 4.100, 4.104, 5.203, 5.210, 6.87, 7.63, 8.38, 9.36
315, *Understanding the Entity and Its Environment and Assessing the Risks of Material Misstatement*	2.20–.21, 2.24–.27, 2.30, 2.32–.34, 2.60, 2.69, 2.84, 2.103, 2.141, 2.166, 3.115, 3.122, 3.124, 3.127, 4.109, 4.112, 4.114, 4.139, 5.207, 5.212, 5.214, 5.216, 5.218, 6.91, 6.94, 6.96, 6.98, 7.69–.70, 7.72, 8.42–.45, 9.40–.42
320, *Materiality in Planning and Performance of an Audit*	2.15–.16, 2.71–.72, 2.113, 3.113, 6.89, 7.65, 8.40, 9.38

AAG-PLI AU

Title	Paragraphs
330, *Performing Audit Procedures in Response to Assessed Risks and Evaluation the Audit Evidence Obtained*	2.23, 2.61, 2.64, 2.141, 3.120, 3.130, 4.109, 4.120, 4.158, 5.209, 5.225, 6.92, 6.101, 7.68, 7.75, 8.46
402, *Audit Considerations Relating to an Entity Using a Service Organization*	2.103, 6.111
450, *Evaluation of Misstatements Identified During the Audit*	2.113, 2.115–.116, 4.174–.176
500, *Audit Evidence*	2.69, 2.116, 4.104, 4.129, 4.133–.135, 4.136
501, *Audit Evidence—Specific Considerations for Selected Items*	5.228
510, *Opening Balances—Initial Audit Engagements, Including Reaudit Engagement*	2.139
520, *Analytical Procedures*	4.139
540, *Auditing Accounting Estimates, Including Fair Value Accounting Estimates, and Related Disclosures*	2.141–.143, 3.117–.118, 4.122–.124, 4.137, 4.146, 4.158–.160, 4.173, 5.228
570, *The Auditor's Consideration of an Entity's Ability to Continue as a Going Concern*	2.104–.106, 2.109–.112
580, *Written Representations*	2.99
610, *The Auditor's Consideration of the Internal Audit Function in an Audit of Financial Statements*	2.125
620, *Using The Work of an Auditor's Specialist*	4.104, 4.130, 4.132, 4.146, 5.210
700, *Forming an Opinion and Reporting on Financial Statements*	10.01, 10.03, 10.43, 10.58
705, *Modifications to the Opinion in the Independent Auditor's Report*	2.175, 4.178, 6.112, 10.01, 10.38, 10.40, 10.43, 10.57, 10.59, 10.64
706, *Emphasis-of-Matter Paragraphs and Other-Matter Paragraphs in the Independent Auditor's Report*	10.01, 10.62
708, *Consistency of Financial Statements*	10.28, 10.52–.53
725, *Supplementary Information in Relation to the Financial Statements as a Whole*	10.62, 10.65–.66
800, *Special Considerations—Audits of Financial Statements Prepared in Accordance With Special Purpose Frameworks*	1.80, 4.94, 10.03, 10.33, 10.37, 10.40–.41, 10.43–.45, 10.47

Index of Pronouncements and Other Technical Guidance

Title	Paragraphs
905, *Alert That Restricts the Use of the Auditor's Written Communication*	2.131
910, *Reporting on Financial Statements Prepared for Use in Other Countries*	2.04
AU Section	
310, *Responsibilities and Functions of the Independent Auditor*	2.03
316, *Consideration of Fraud in a Financial Statement Audit*	2.75
319, *Consideration of Internal Control in a Financial Statement Audit*	2.155
325, *Communications About Control Deficiencies in an Audit of Financial Statements*	2.133, 4.148
342, *Auditing Accounting Estimates*	4.124
508, *Reports on Audited Financial Statements*	10.29
600, *Other Types of Reports*	6.111
Audit and Accounting Guide *Investment Companies*	5.202
Audit Guide *Assessing and Responding to Audit Risk in a Financial Statement Audit*	2.103
Audit Risk Alerts	
Insurance Industry Developments	2.19
Understanding the Clarified Auditing Standards	Appendix E

C

Title	Paragraphs
Code of Professional Conduct ET Section, 101, *Independence*	2.140

F

Title	Paragraphs
FASB ASC	
210, *Balance Sheet*	5.42
210-10	3.50, 6.43–.44, 6.63
210-20	5.46, 5.190, 6.42
220, *Comprehensive Income*	5.42, 5.53

AAG-PLI FAS

Title	Paragraphs
230, *Statement of Cash Flows*	5.42
230-10	5.46
235, *Notes to Financial Statements*	
235-10	3.105
250, *Accounting Changes and Error Corrections*	6.73, 10.28
250-10	10.55
275, *Risks and Uncertainties*	4.95, 4.146, 4.180
305, *Cash and Cash Equivalents*	5.42
305-10	5.46–.47
310, *Receivables*	5.42, 5.99–.100
310-10	3.51, 3.107, 5.97–.98, 5.101
310-20	5.55, 5.95
310-30	5.55, 5.66, 5.101
320, *Investments—Debt and Equity Securities*	5.42, 5.57, 5.228
320-10	5.53–.55, 5.58–.59, 5.62–.63, 5.66–.71, 5.91–.92, 5.207
323, *Investments—Equity Method and Joint Ventures*	5.42, 5.60, 5.134, 5.228
323-10	5.61, 5.145
323-740	5.139
325, *Investments—Other*	5.42
325-40	5.56, 5.66
340, *Other Assets and Deferred Costs*	
340-20	3.65–.70
340-30	3.103, 3.110, 4.73, 4.78, 6.20–.21, 6.53, 6.75, 6.109, 6.113
350, *Intangibles—Goodwill and Other*	
350-40	3.75
360, *Property, Plant, and Equipment*	5.42, 5.112
360-10	5.110–.111
405, *Liabilities*	
405-20	5.165, 5.172
405-30	4.72–.73, 8.14–.16, 8.18–.22, 8.23

Index of Pronouncements and Other Technical Guidance

Title	Paragraphs
410, *Asset Retirement and Environmental Obligations*	
410-30	4.76–.77
450, *Contingencies*	3.51, 4.95, 4.180
450-20	3.52
715, *Compensation—Retirement Benefits*	8.36
720, *Other Expenses*	
720-20	3.30, 3.103, 6.66
740, *Income Taxes*	7.21, 7.23–.24
740-10	7.25–.26, 7.28, 7.32, 7.34–.37, 7.40–.42, 7.44–.46, 7.48–.55
740-20	7.48, 7.52
810, *Consolidation*	5.42, 5.134–.135, 5.145, 6.13–.14, 6.83, 9.19, 9.32
810-10	5.136–.137
810-20	5.112, 5.140
815, *Derivatives and Hedging*	5.42, 5.185
815-10	5.96, 5.124–.126
815-15	6.58–.59
815-25	5.53, 5.59, 5.92
820, *Fair Value Measurement*	5.15–.35, 5.42
820-10	5.16–.30, 5.32, 5.34–.35, 5.207
820-35	5.31
825, *Financial Instruments*	5.42
825-10	5.36–.38, 5.40
830, *Foreign Currency Matters*	4.190
835, *Interest*	
835-20	5.112
840, *Leases*	5.112
852, *Reorganizations*	7.52
860, *Transfers and Servicing*	5.42, 5.56, 5.171, 5.174, 5.185, 5.192, 5.201
860-10	5.165, 5.168–.169, 5.173, 5.186–.188, 5.196–.198
860-30	3.107, 5.198–.199
860-50	5.165, 5.170

AAG-PLI FAS

Title	Paragraphs
940, *Financial Services—Brokers and Dealers*	5.42
942, *Financial Services—Depository and Lending*	
942-210	5.190
944, *Financial Services—Insurance*	1.89–.95, 3.30, 3.101, 4.12, 4.73, 4.95, 4.146, 5.42, 6.66–.70
944-10	1.90, 3.32
944-20	1.89, 3.31, 3.106, 4.76–.77, 6.20–.22, 6.24–.28, 6.33–.34, 6.39, 6.41, 6.53, 6.63
944-30	1.93, 3.39, 3.56, 3.58, 3.60, 3.62–.64, 3.72–.73, 3.75, 3.77–.78, 3.82, 3.109, 6.66–.69, 8.09, 8.35
944-40	4.80, 4.85, 4.96–.99, 6.50
944-60	3.84–.85, 3.87, 3.92, 3.94
944-310	3.108, 4.86, 5.95, 6.42
944-325	5.59, 5.90
944-360	5.110
944-405	6.66
944-605	1.92, 3.34, 3.36, 3.39–.40, 3.101, 6.38, 6.47–.48, 6.65, 6.71–.73
944-720	3.71–.72, 3.74
944-825	6.74
948, *Financial Services—Mortgage Banking*	5.42
948-310	5.96
958, *Not-For-Profit Entities*	
958-20	5.59
970, *Real Estate—General*	5.112

Index of Pronouncements and Other Technical Guidance **509**

Title	Paragraphs
FASB ASU	
No. 2010-26, *Financial Services—Insurance (Topic 944): Accounting For Costs Associated With Acquiring or Renewing Insurance Contracts*	3.56
No. 2011-04, *Fair Value Measurement (Topic 820): Amendments to Achieve Common Fair Value Measurement and Disclosures Requirements in U.S. GAAP and IFRSs*	5.207
No. 2011-11, *Balance Sheet (Topic 210): Disclosures About offsetting Assets and Liabilities*	Appendix D
FASB Interpretation	
No. 03-03, *Admissibility of Investments Recorded Based on the Audited GAAP Equity of the Investee*	5.150
No. 06-07, *Definition of the Phrase "Other Than Temporary"*	5.75
FASB SFAC No. 113, *Accounting and Reporting For Reinsurance of Short-Duration and Long-Duration Contracts*	4.85
FASB Statement	
No. 95, *Statement of Cash Flows*	1.95
No. 162, *The Hierarchy of Generally Accepted Accounting Principles*	1.72
No. 168, *The Hierarchy of Generally Accepted Accounting Principles a Replacement of FASB Statement No. 162*	1.72

G

Title	Paragraphs
GASB	
Interpretation No. 3, *Financial Reporting For Reverse Repurchase Agreements*	1.95
Statement No. 9, *Reporting Cash Flows of Proprietary and Nonexpendable Trust Funds and Governmental Entities That Use Proprietary Fund Accounting*	1.95
Statement No. 10, *Accounting and Financial Reporting For Risk Financing and Related Insurance Issues*	1.95

AAG-PLI GAS

I

Title	Paragraphs
IRC Section	
816	7.03, 7.13
831	7.03, 9.34
832	7.08, 7.13, 7.18
846	7.08, 7.10, 7.11–.12
1274	7.11
IASB, IFRS	Appendix F

N

Title	Paragraphs
NAIC Guides and Publications	
Accounting Practices and Procedures Manual	1.70–.71, 1.83, 1.88, 2.154, 2.171, 4.94, 8.33, 10.34, Exhibit 1-1 at 1.96
Annual Statement Instructions	4.71, 4.105, 4.152, 6.76, 8.04
Examiners Handbook, Valuation of Securities Manual	1.73, 1.79
Financial Condition Examiners Handbook	2.155
Implementation Guide for the Annual Financial Reporting Model Regulation	2.163
"NAIC Financial Solvency Tools-Insurance Regulatory Information System (IRIS)"	2.55–.56
Purposes and Procedures Manual of the NAIC Securities Valuation Office	1.72, 5.72, 5.77
States' Prescribed Difference from NAIC Statutory Accounting Principles	1.71
Valuations of Securities	5.72, 5.76–.77
NAIC Interpretation	
No. 04-1, *Applicability of New GAAP Disclosures Prior to NAIC Consideration*	1.87, 4.94
No. 05-05, *Accounting For Revenues Under Medicare Part D Coverage*	3.102

Title	Paragraphs
NAIC Model	
NAIC Model Audit Rule	2.144–.165, 10.68–.69, 10.72, 10.76, 10.78, 10.80, 10.84
NAIC Model Audit Rule, Revised	1.76, 2.133, 2.140, 2.144–.165, 4.148, 10.84
NAIC SSAP	
No. 2, *Cash, Drafts, and Short-Term Investments*	5.42–.43, 5.47–.48
No. 3, *Accounting Changes and Corrections of Errors*	1.72, 4.126, 10.56–.57
No. 4, *Assets and Nonadmitted Assets*	1.88, 5.102, 5.160, 8.31, 8.51
No. 5R, *Liabilities, Contingencies and Impairment of Assets—Revised*	7.57
No. 6, *Uncollected Premium Balances, Bills Receivable For Premiums, and Amounts Due From Agents and Brokers*	3.53–.54
No. 7, *Asset Valuation Reserve and Interest Maintenance Reserve*	5.83–.84
No. 10R, *Income Taxes—Revised*	7.56
No. 23, *Foreign Exchange Transactions and Translations*	4.190
No. 26, *Bonds, Excluding Loan-Backed and Structured Securities*	5.42, 5.72, 5.75
No. 27, *Disclosure of Information About Financial Instruments With Off-Balance-Sheet Risk Financial Instruments With Concentrations of Credit Risk and Disclosure About Fair Value of Financial Instruments*	5.40, 5.42, 5.86
No. 30, *Investments in Common Stock*	5.42, 5.80, 5.85–.86
No. 32, *Investments in Preferred Stock*	5.42, 5.81, 5.83–.86
No. 34, *Investment Income Due and Accrued*	5.42, 5.160–.161
No. 35, *Guaranty Fund and Other Assessments*	4.72
No. 35R, *Guaranty Fund and Other Assessments*	8.23–.30
No. 36, *Troubled Debt Restructuring*	5.42, 5.104
No. 37, *Mortgage Loans*	5.42, 5.102, 5.104, 5.107

AAG-PLI NAI

Title	Paragraphs
No. 40, *Real Estate Investments*	5.42, 5.109, 5.113, 5.116
No. 43R, *Loan-Backed and Structured Settlements*	5.42, 5.73, 5.76, 5.78–.79
No. 47, *Uninsured Plans*	3.102
No. 48, *Joint Ventures, Partnerships and Limited Liability Companies*	5.42, 5.141–.143
No. 52, *Deposit-Type Contracts*	3.104
No. 53, *Property Casualty Contracts— Premiums*	3.41–.47, 3.86, 3.92
No. 54, *Individual and Group Accident and Health Contracts*	3.102
No. 55, *Unpaid Claims, Losses and Loss Adjustment Expenses*	4.32, 4.55
No. 62, *Property and Casualty Reinsurance*	4.90, 4.92
No. 62R, *Property and Casualty Reinsurance*	6.76, 6.79
No. 63, *Underwriting Pools and Associations Including Intercompany Pools*	6.61–.62
No. 65, *Property and Casualty Contracts*	3.104, 4.32, 4.83–.84, 4.90–.91, 4.93, 6.52
No. 66, *Retrospectively Rated Contracts*	3.48–.49, 3.83, 3.102
No. 71, *Policy Acquisition Costs and Commissions*	3.83
No. 75, *Reinsurance Deposit Accounting*	3.104
No. 83, *Mezzanine Real Estate Loans*	5.42, 5.106
No. 86, *Accounting For Derivative Instruments and Hedging, Income Generation and Replication*	5.42, 5.127–.131
No. 89, *Accounting For Pensions, A Replacement of SSAP No. 8*	8.36
No. 90, *Accounting For Impairment or Disposal of Real Estate Investments*	5.42, 5.114–.115, 5.118
No. 91R, *Accounting For Transfers and Servicing of Financial Assets and Extinguishments of Liabilities*	5.42, 5.174–.175, 5.177–.179, 5.192, 5.201
No. 93, *Accounting For Low Income Housing Tax Credit Property Investments*	5.42, 5.144, 6.80, 8.06
No. 94, *Accounting For Transferable State Tax Credits*	8.06
No. 97, *Investments In Subsidiary, Controlled, or Affiliated Entities: A Replacement of SSAP No. 88*	5.42, 5.80, 5.141, 5.145–.149, 5.151–.156

Index of Pronouncements and Other Technical Guidance 513

Title	Paragraphs
No. 100, *Fair Value Measurements*	5.39, 5.42, 5.86, 5.115–.116, 5.207
No. 101, *Income Taxes—A Replacement of SSAP No. 10R and No. 10*	7.56–.61
No. 102, *Accounting For Pensions, A Replacement of SSAP No. 89*	Appendix D
No. 103, *Accounting For Transfers and Servicing of Financial Assets and Extinguishments of Liabilities*	Appendix D

P

Title	Paragraphs
PCAOB Auditing Standard	
No. 1, *References in Auditor's Reports to the Standards of the PCAOB*	10.01
No. 3, *Audit Documentation*	4.132, 4.176
No. 4, *Reporting on Whether a Previously Reported Material Weakness Continues to Exist*	2.07–.08, 10.32
No. 5, *An Audit of Internal Control Over Financial Reporting That Is Integrated With an Audit of Financial Statements*	2.05–.06, 2.72, 2.75, 2.125, 2.133, 6.108, 6.111, 10.01, 10.29, 10.31
No. 6, *Evaluating Consistency of Financial Statements*	10.28
No. 8, *Audit Risk*	4.179
No. 9, *Audit Planning*	2.10, 2.14
No. 10, *Supervision of the Audit Engagement*	2.10
No. 11, *Consideration of Materiality in Planning and Performing an Audit*	2.10, 2.74, 4.179
No. 12, *Identifying and Assessing Risks of Material Misstatement*	2.10, 2.29, 2.75, 2.82–.84, 2.90, 2.103, 4.118, 5.220
No. 13, *The Auditor's Responses to the Risks of Material Misstatement*	2.10, 2.62, 2.75, 3.131, 4.118, 4.120, 4.151, 5.220, 5.226, 6.103, 6.110, 7.76
No. 14, *Evaluating Audit Results*	2.10, 2.75, 2.116
No. 15, *Audit Evidence*	2.10
No. 16, *Communications With Audit Committees*	2.11, 2.134

AAG-PLI PCA

Title	Paragraphs
PCAOB Release	
No. 2010-004, *Auditing Standards Related to the Auditor's Assessment of and Response to Risk and Related Amendments to PCAOB Standards*	2.10
No. 2011-001, *Temporary Rule For An Interim Program of Inspection Related to Audits of Brokers and Dealers*	2.09

S

Title	Paragraphs
SAS	
No. 60, *Communication of Internal Control Related Matters Noted in an Audit*	2.158
No. 70, *Service Organizations*	6.105
SEC Final Rule Release	
No. 33-8238, *Management's Report On Internal Control Over Financial Reporting and Certification of Disclosure In Exchange Act Periodic Reports*	2.176
No. 33-9142, *Internal Control Over Financial Reporting in Exchange Act Periodic Reports of Non-Accelerated Filers*	1.58
No. 34-62914, *Control Over Financial Reporting in Exchange Act Periodic Reports of Non-Accelerated Filers*	1.58
SEC Financial Reporting Release No. 36, *Management's Discussion and Analysis of Financial Condition and Results of Operations; Certain Investment Company Disclosures*	5.202
SEC Regulation G	1.52
SEC Regulation S-K	1.53
SEC Regulation S-X	1.48
SEC SAB	
No. 99, *Materiality*	2.116
No. 103, *Update of Codification of Staff Accounting Bulletins*	5.42
No. 105, *Application of Accounting Principles to Loan Commitments*	5.42

Index of Pronouncements and Other Technical Guidance

Title	Paragraphs
No. 108, *Considering the Effects of Prior Year Misstatements When Quantifying Misstatements In Current Year Financial Statements*	2.116
SEC SAB Topic	
5(N), *Discounting By Property-Casualty Insurance Companies*	4.78
5(W), *Codification of Staff Accounting Bulletins* "Contingency Disclosures Regarding Property/Casualty Insurance Reserves For Unpaid Claim Costs"	4.81
5(Y), *Codification of Staff Accounting Bulletins* "Accounting and Disclosures Relating to Loss Contingencies"	4.81
10(F), *Codification of Staff Accounting Bulletins* "Presentation of Liabilities For Environmental Costs"	4.81
SOP 92-8, *Auditing Property/Casualty Insurance Entities' Statutory Financial Statements-Applying Certain Requirements of the NAIC Annual Statement Instructions*	4.105, 4.153
SSAE No. 16, *Reporting on Controls at a Service Organization*	5.222–.223, 6.105

Subject Index

A

ACCIDENT AND HEALTH INSURANCE,
DEFINED 1.04
ACCIDENT DATE, DEFINED 4.37
ACCOUNT CURRENT (AGENCY
BILLING) 3.17–.18
ACCOUNT CURRENT BILLING BASIS ... 3.18
ACCOUNT CURRENT ITEM BASIS 3.18
ACCOUNT CURRENT RENDERING BASIS 3.18
ACCOUNT POOLS 1.09
ACCOUNTANT'S AWARENESS
LETTER 2.145–.146, 10.69–.71
ACCOUNTANT'S LETTER OF
QUALIFICATIONS 2.148–.149,
.... 2.154, 10.84
ACCOUNTING PRACTICES 1.37–.96
See also specific details within topics
· Acquisition costs 1.93–.94
· Federal regulations 1.48–.68
· GAAP See generally accepted accounting principles
· Industry associations 1.69
· Investments See investments
· Long-term contracts 1.89–.91
· Loss reserving and claims cycle See loss reserving and claims cycle
· Premiums and acquisition costs See premiums
· SAP See statutory accounting practices
· Short-duration contracts 1.89, 1.91–.92, 3.34
· State insurance regulation 1.37–.45
· Statutory accounting practices 1.82–.87
· Terrorism, federal regulations 1.64–.68
ACCOUNTS, MATERIAL MISSTATEMENT DUE
TO FRAUD 2.87
ACCRUAL OF INVESTMENT
INCOME 5.42, 5.157–.159
ACE See adjusted current earnings
ACL See authorized control level (ACL) risk-based capital
ACQUISITION COSTS 3.56–.83
· Accounting practices 1.93–.94
· Audit considerations 3.111–.132
· Deferred See deferral of acquisition costs (DAC)
· Defined 3.57, 3.59
· Disclosures .... 3.109, Appendix A
· GAAP 3.56–.81
· Risk factors 3.114
· SAP 3.83
ACTIVE MARKET, FAIR ACTIVE
HIERARCHY 5.28

ADJUDICATIONS, INSURANCE
REGULATION 1.44
ADJUSTED CURRENT EARNINGS (ACE) 7.20
ADJUSTERS, SOURCES OF 4.20
ADJUSTING AND OTHER (AO) 4.55,
.... 4.60–.62, 4.182–.183
ADJUSTMENTS, CLAIMS TRANSACTION
CYCLE 4.19–.24
ADJUSTMENTS TO PREMIUMS See premium adjustments
ADMINISTRATIVE TYPE ASSESSMENTS 8.14
ADVERSE FINANCIAL CONDITION,
NOTIFICATION OF 2.156–.157, 10.76–.79
ADVERSE OPINIONS 10.41, 10.59
ADVERTISING, DIRECT
RESPONSE 1.17, 3.65–.70
AGENCY BILLING (ACCOUNT
CURRENT) 3.17–.18
AGENCY CAPTIVE INSURANCE
ENTITIES 9.25
AGENTS
· Commissions 3.22
· Methods of producing business 1.10–.14
· Premiums due from 3.20–.21, 3.54
AGGREGATE COVERAGE POLICY 4.08
AGGREGATE EXCESS OF LOSS
REINSURANCE 6.11
ALLOCATED LOSS ADJUSTMENT
EXPENSES 4.54
ALTERNATIVE MINIMUM TAX (AMT) 7.20
ALTERNATIVE PROJECTIONS OF ULTIMATE
LOSSES AND UNREPORTED
LOSSES .... Table 4-7 at 4.52
AMERICAN ACADEMY OF ACTUARIES .. 4.70
AMERICAN INSTITUTE OF CERTIFIED PUBLIC
ACCOUNTANTS (AICPA), FINANCIAL
REPORTING EXECUTIVE
COMMITTEE 3.94, 6.62
AMORTIZATION OF ACQUIRED LOANS 5.170
AMT See alternative minimum tax
ANALYTICAL PROCEDURES, LOSS RESERVE
AUDITS 4.138–.143
ANTICIPATED INVESTMENT
INCOME 3.87, 3.92, 3.96–.97
AO See adjusting and other
APPLICATION, DENIED 3.12

AAG-PLI APP

Property and Liability Insurance Entities

ASSERTIONS
- Material misstatement due to fraud, identifying risks 2.87
- In obtaining audit evidence 2.68–.69

ASSESSMENTS
- Audit risk 2.20–.25
- Insurance-related See insurance-related expenses, taxes, and assessments
- Loss-based 3.29, 8.20
- Operating expense 8.18
- Risk See risk assessment process

ASSET AND LIABILITY METHOD, INCOME TAX ACCOUNTING **7.24**

ASSET RISK, DEFINED **2.48**

ASSET TRANSFER AND EXTINGUISHMENT OF LIABILITIES **5.42,**
.... **5.162–.180, Appendix D**

ASSET VALUATION RESERVE (AVR) **5.81, 5.83–.84**

ASSETS
- Deferred income tax See deferred income tax assets (DTAs)
- Disclosure .... Appendix D
- Misappropriation of .. 2.76, Table 2-2 at 2.78
- Nonadmitted .... 1.88, 3.49, 5.42, ... 5.72, 5.74, 8.31–.35
- Nonfinancial, fair value measurement 5.18–.22
  See also intangibles, impairment of
- Reinsurance reporting 6.39–.47
- Safeguarding 5.08, 5.14
  See also recordkeeping
- Transferred ... 5.42, 5.162–.180, Appendix D
- Transferred, isolation of 5.165, 5.168, 5.175

ASSIGNED RISK PLAN **1.08**

ASSOCIATION CAPTIVE INSURANCE ENTITY **9.11–.14**

ASSOCIATIONS, REINSURANCE **6.114**

ASSUMED REINSURANCE PREMIUMS ... **3.02**
See also premiums

ASSUMING COMPANY **1.24,**
.... **6.105–.106, 6.110–.113**
See also reinsurance

ASSUMPTION REINSURANCE **6.08, 6.50**

ASSUMPTIONS, TESTS OF **4.144–.156**
See also loss reserve ranges

ATTITUDE, AS FRAUD RISK FACTOR ...... **2.83, Table 2-1 at 2.78**

ATTORNEY-IN-FACT, INSURANCE ORGANIZATION **1.09**

AUDIT COMMITTEES, COMMUNICATION OF OTHER MATTERS WITH **2.11, 2.162**

AUDIT CONSIDERATION CHARTS
- Income taxes 7.77
- Investments 5.228
- Loss reserving and claims cycle 4.191
- Premiums and acquisition costs 3.132
- Reinsurance 6.119

AUDIT CONSIDERATIONS
- Audit evidence, assertions in obtaining 2.68–.69
- Auditor withdrawal 2.96
- Communication 2.126–.140
- Documentation .... 2.117–.125, ... 2.161, 4.131–.132
- Entity, environment, and internal control, understanding 2.26–.43
- Fair value measurements and disclosures 2.141–.143
- Fraud See fraud in a financial statement audit, consideration of
- Generally 2.01
- Going concern considerations ... 2.104–.112
- Income taxes 7.63–.77
- Information technology 2.100–.103
- Insurance entity requirements 1.45, 1.78–.79
- Insurance-related expenses, taxes, and assessments 8.38–.52
- Internal auditors, consideration of the work of 2.139
- Internal control .... 2.27–.43, ... 2.126–.133, 2.176–.180
- Investments 5.203–.228
- Loss reserving and claims 4.100–.191
- Materiality 2.70–.74
- Misstatements, evaluating 2.113–.116
- Permitted statutory accounting practices 2.171–.175
- Planning 2.12–.14, 2.85
  See also audit considerations, planning
- Premiums and acquisition costs 3.111–.132
- Previous audits 2.24
- Ratios and performance metrics ... 2.44–.56
- Reinsurance 6.87–.119
- Risk See audit risk
- Scope of the audit engagement ... 2.02–.11
- State regulatory examination 2.166–.170

AUDIT CONSIDERATIONS, CAPTIVE INSURANCE ENTITIES **9.36–.43**
- Fraud risk 9.37
- Internal control 9.41–.42
- Material misstatement risk 9.43
- Planning 9.36
- Risk factors 9.38–.40

AUDIT CONSIDERATIONS, INCOME TAXES **7.63–.77**
See also income taxes
- Audit chart 7.77
- Control activities 7.74
- Control environment 7.71
- Fraud risk 7.64
- Internal control 7.69–.70
- Material misstatement assessed risk response 7.75–.76
- Planning 7.63
- Risk assessment 7.72–.73
- Risk factors 7.65–.68

AAG-PLI ASS

Subject Index

AUDIT CONSIDERATIONS, INSURANCE-RELATED EXPENSES, TAXES, AND ASSESSMENTS **8.38–.52**
- Audit planning 8.38
- Fraud in a financial statement audit 8.39
- Internal control 8.43–.45
- Material misstatement risk 8.46–.52
- Risk factors 8.40–.42

AUDIT CONSIDERATIONS, INVESTMENTS **5.203–.228**
See also investments
- Audit chart 5.228
- Control activities 5.220
- Control environment 5.215
- Fraud risk 5.204
- Information system 5.218–.219
- Internal control 5.212–.214
- Material misstatement risk 5.209–.211
- Material misstatement risk response 5.225–.226
- Planning 5.203
- Risk assessment process 5.216–.217
- Risk factors 5.205–.208
- Service organizations 5.221–.224

AUDIT CONSIDERATIONS, LOSS RESERVING AND CLAIMS **4.100–.191**
See also loss reserving and claims cycle
- Analytical procedures 4.138–.143
- Audit chart 4.191
- Ceded reinsurance recoverable and receivable 4.184–.189
- Control activities 4.117–.118
- Control environment 4.113
- Data testing, assumptions, and estimate selection 4.144–.148
- Estimates, evaluating reasonableness of 4.137, 4.155–.156, 4.182–.183
  See also loss reserve ranges
- External risk factors 4.163
- Foreign exchange impacts 4.190
- Fraud risk 4.106–.108
- Independent expectation of estimate, developing 4.155–.156
- Information systems 4.116
- Internal control 4.110–.112
- Material misstatement risk factors 4.109, 4.119–.128
- Planning considerations 4.100–.105
- Reinsurance program, understanding 4.185–.189
- Risk assessment process 4.114–.115
- Specialists, use of .... 4.64, 4.69–.71, ... 4.104, 4.127, 4.129–.136
- Testing process 4.144–.148
- Uncertainty about management estimate 4.180–.181
- Underlying data 4.149–.154

AUDIT CONSIDERATIONS, PLANNING
- Captive insurance entities 7.63
- Generally 2.12–.14, 2.85
- Income taxes 7.63

AUDIT CONSIDERATIONS, PLANNING—continued
- Insurance-related expenses, taxes, and assessments 8.38
- Investments 5.203
- Loss reserving and claims cycle   4.100–.105
- Premiums 3.111
- Reinsurance 6.87

AUDIT CONSIDERATIONS, PREMIUMS AND ACQUISITION COSTS **3.111–.132**
See also premiums
- Acquisitions   See acquisition costs; deferral of acquisition costs (DAC)
- Audit chart 3.132
- Control activities 3.129
- Control environment 3.125–.126
- Fraud risk 3.112
- Internal control 3.122–.124
- Management estimates 3.117–.119
- Material misstatement risk 3.120–.121, 3.130–.131
- Planning 3.111
- Premiums and DAC risk factors   3.113–.116
- Risk assessment process 3.127–.128

AUDIT CONSIDERATIONS, REINSURANCE **6.87–.119**
See also reinsurance
- Assuming company 6.110–.113
- Audit chart 6.119
- Audit risk 6.89–.91
- Ceding company ... 6.103–.104, 6.107–.110
- Control activities 6.100
- Control environment 6.95
- Fraud risk 6.88
- Information and communication 6.98–.99
- Internal control 6.93–.94, 6.103–.106
- Material misstatement risk   6.92, 6.101–.102
- Planning 6.87
- Pools, associations, and syndicates .. 6.114
- Reinsurance intermediaries 6.115–.118
- Risk assessment process 6.96–.97

AUDIT ENGAGEMENT LETTER **2.02–.03**

AUDIT EVIDENCE, ASSERTIONS IN OBTAINING **2.68–.69**

AUDIT PREMIUMS, PREMIUM ADJUSTMENTS **3.04**

AUDIT RISK
See also audit considerations; risk
- Assessment procedure 2.20–.25
- Defined 3.113, 5.205, 6.89, 7.65
- Generally 2.15–.19
- Material misstatement, identifying and assessing 2.57–.60
- Performing audit procedures in response to 2.61–.67

AUDIT TEAM, DISCUSSION AMONG **2.25**

AUDITORS
- Awareness letter 2.145–.146, 10.69–.71
- Change in, notification of   2.147, 10.72–.75

AUDITORS—continued
- Communication by successor 2.139
- Indemnification of 2.150
- Independence of 2.140, 2.149
- Internal, considering work
  of 2.40, 2.124–.125
- Letters of qualification 2.148–.149,
  .... 2.154, 10.84
- Responsibility section, in auditor's reports
  See reports on audited financial statements
- Withdrawal of 2.96

AUTHORIZATION OF TRANSACTION AND ACTIVITIES ... 3.26, 4.117, 5.220, 6.100

AUTHORIZED CONTROL LEVEL (ACL) RISK-BASED CAPITAL 2.49–.50, 2.51

AUTOMOBILE INSURANCE, DEFINED ... 1.04

AUTOMOBILE INSURANCE PLAN 1.08

AVR See Asset Valuation Reserve

AWARENESS, NAIC MODEL AUDIT RULE 2.145–.146, 10.69–.71

B

BAD DEBT EXPENSE 3.51

BALANCE SHEET, OFFSETTING ASSET AND LIABILITY DISCLOSURE ..... Appendix D

BANKING POOLS 1.09

BASIS OF ACCOUNTING SECTION, IN AUDITOR'S REPORTS See reports on audited financial statements

BCFP See Bureau of Consumer Financial Protection

BENEFITS See compensation

BILLING, PREMIUM CYCLE 3.17–.21

BINDER, PROVIDING INSURED WITH ... 3.10

BLANK, FILING ANNUAL ... 1.74, 3.24, 9.24

BONDS, VALUATION AND REPORTING 5.52, 5.72–.75

BORNHUETTER-FERGUSON LOSS RESERVE PROJECTION 4.42, 4.52–.53,
.... Tables 4-8–4-10 at 4.52–.53

BROKERS
- Commissions 3.22
- Methods of producing business ... 1.10, 1.15

BUREAU OF CONSUMER FINANCIAL PROTECTION (BCFP) 1.55–.57

BUSINESS
- Acquiring ... 1.10–.17, 3.09–.16, 3.22, 7.06
  See also acquisition costs
- Lines of See lines of insurance
- Methods of producing 1.10–.15
- Nature, conduct, and regulation of
  the 1.01–.96
- Reinsurance in growth of 6.02

C

CAL See company action level (CAL) risk-based capital

CANCELLATIONS, PREMIUM ADJUSTMENTS 3.04

CAPITAL LOSSES 7.18

CAPS, IN REINSURANCE CONTRACTS .. 6.19

CAPTIVE INSURANCE ENTITIES 9.01–.43
- Audit considerations 9.36–.43
- Benefits 9.02
- Generally 1.30, 9.01–.06
- Operations 9.27–.29
- Taxes 9.33–.35
- Transaction and accounting considerations, specific 9.30–.35
- Types of 9.07–.26

CARRYFORWARDS, TAXES 7.32, 7.36, 7.50

CASE-BASIS INCURRED-LOSS DATA .... Table 4-1 at 4.46

CASE-BASIS RESERVES 4.22, 4.33, 4.59

CASE-DEVELOPMENT RESERVES ... 4.33–.34

CASH AND CASH EQUIVALENTS 5.42, 5.43–.49

CASH FLOW
- Expected, in premium deficiencies 3.93, 3.97
- Reinsurance cycle ... 6.28, 6.33, 6.55, 6.70
- Underwriting 5.208

CASUALTY ACTUARIAL SOCIETY 4.70

CAT BONDS 6.03

CATASTROPHE FUND 8.17

CEDED REINSURANCE PREMIUMS 3.02

CEDING COMMISSION 6.13

CEDING COMPANY 1.24,
.... 6.103–.104, 6.107–.109
See also reinsurance

CENTERS FOR MEDICARE & MEDICAID SERVICES (CMS) 3.99
See also Medicare Part D

CERTIFIED CAPITAL GAINS COMPANIES 8.06

CHANGE IN ACCOUNTING PRINCIPLE 4.79, 10.52–.54

CHANGE IN NET WRITINGS 1.47

CHANGE IN POLICYHOLDERS' SURPLUS 1.47

CHANGE OF AUDITOR LETTER 2.147, 10.72–.75

CITIZENS PROPERTY INSURANCE CORPORATION 3.27

CLAIM ACCEPTANCE AND PROCESSING 1.31, 4.16–.18

CLAIM ADJUSTMENT 1.31, 4.19–.24,
.... Appendix A

CLAIM SETTLEMENT, IN CLAIMS CYCLE 1.31, 4.25–.28

CLAIMS
- Acceptance and processing 4.16–.18
- Adjustment and estimation 4.19–.24
- Cycle See loss reserving and claims cycle

Subject Index

CLAIMS—continued
- Disclosure .... Appendix A
- Frequency and severity of 4.165
- Process flowchart 4.15
- Processing and payment of 1.31–.32
- Reinsurance receivable 4.29–.32
- Risk considerations 2.17
- Settlement 4.25–.28

CLAIMS-MADE POLICIES **4.05**

CLAIMS-SERVICING POOLS **1.09**

CLASS RATING, PREMIUMS **3.03**

CLASSES OF TRANSACTIONS **2.87**

CLOSING DATE, DEFINED **4.37**

CMS See Centers for Medicare & Medicaid Services

COLLATERAL 5.171, 5.180, 5.193–.201

COLLECTABILITY TEST **5.160**

COLLECTING, PREMIUM CYCLE 3.17–.21

COMBINED RATIO, DEFINED **2.45**

COMMERCIAL LINES OF INSURANCE **1.07, 3.16**

COMMISSIONS, PAYMENT OF **3.22**
See also compensation

COMMITTEE OF SPONSORING ORGANIZATIONS (COSO) **2.178**

COMMON STOCK VALUATION **5.80,**
.... **5.86, 5.88**

COMMUNICATION
- About possible fraud 2.25, 2.80–.83
- Captive entities 9.43
- With engagement team 2.25
- Internal control matters 2.126–.140
- Reinsurance cycle 6.98–.99
- Understanding entity's system of 2.37

COMMUTATION AGREEMENT **6.19,**
.... **6.51, 6.79**

COMPANY ACTION LEVEL (CAL) RISK-BASED CAPITAL **2.51**

COMPENSATION
- Business acquisition-related 3.61–.63,
.... 3.73, 3.78, 3.80–.81
- Commissions, payment of 3.22
- Executive, regulations 1.62, 3.63

CONDUCT OF THE BUSINESS See nature, conduct, and regulation of the business

CONFIDENTIALITY, LEGAL RESPONSIBILITY CONFLICT WITH **2.98**

CONSERVATISM, CHANGE IN MANAGEMENT'S DEGREE OF **4.178**

CONSISTENCY OF FINANCIAL STATEMENTS, EVALUATING **10.28**

CONSOLIDATION, CAPTIVE ENTITIES ... **9.32**

CONTINGENT COMMISSIONS 3.22, 6.19

CONTINUING OPERATIONS, TAX DISCLOSURE **7.51–.53**

CONTRACT PERIOD, DISTINGUISHING PERIOD OF RISK FROM **3.35**

CONTRACT TEMPORARY BINDER **3.10**

CONTRACTS, REINSURANCE
See also reinsurance
- Defining 6.23
- Generally 6.07–.19
- Indemnification and defining 6.22–.24
- With no transfer of insurance risk .... 3.103–.110, Appendix A
- Risk considerations 6.84
- Risk transfer 6.30–.35
- Terminology 6.19

CONTRACTUAL OBLIGATIONS, SEC **1.50**

CONTRACTUAL OBLIGATIONS TABLE ... **4.68**

CONTROL, PRESUMPTION OF **5.145**

CONTROL ACTIVITIES
See also internal control
- Income taxes 7.74
- Investments 5.220
- Loss reserving and claims 4.117–.118
- Premiums and acquisition costs 3.129
- Reinsurance 6.100

CONTROL ENVIRONMENT
See also environment, understanding
- Income taxes 7.71
- Investments 5.215
- Loss reserving and claims cycle 4.113
- Premium cycle 3.26, 3.125–.126
- Reinsurance 6.95

CONTROLS, TESTS OF See tests of controls

CONVENTION BLANK, FILING ANNUAL **1.74, 3.24, 9.24**

COSO See Committee of Sponsoring Organizations

COST RECOVERY METHOD **3.36, 3.101, 6.49**

COSTS
See also expenses
- Acquisition See acquisition costs; deferral of acquisition costs (DAC)
- Capitalized, and nonadmitted assets 8.31–.35
- Reinsurance reporting 6.48–.49

COVERAGE, TYPE OF, LOSS RESERVING AND CLAIMS CYCLE **4.05**

COVERED-CALL OPTIONS **5.121**

CREDIT RISK **2.48, 4.08**

D

DAC See deferral of acquisition costs

DATA SOURCES, LOSS RESERVE ESTIMATES **4.146, 4.166**

DATES, LOSS RESERVE ESTIMATION ... **4.36**

DCC See defense and cost containment

DEBT SECURITIES **5.42, 5.50–.93,**
.... **5.209, 5.215**

AAG-PLI DEB

DEDUCTIBLE TEMPORARY DIFFERENCES 7.26–.30

DEFENSE AND COST CONTAINMENT (DCC) 4.55–.59, 4.182

DEFERRAL OF ACQUISITION COSTS (DAC)
See also acquisition costs
- Allocation of 3.77
- Audit consideration chart 3.132
- Control activities 3.129
- Control environment 3.126
- Determining 3.78–.80
- Disclosure .... 3.109, Appendix A
- Fraud risk 2.87, 3.113–.116
- Modifications or exchanges of contracts 3.82
- Premium taxes 8.09
- Risk assessment process 3.128

DEFERRED INCOME TAX ASSETS (DTAS)
- Disclosure 7.46, 7.48, 7.50
- GAAP accounting 7.31
- Statutory accounting 7.58–.60
- Tax law change 7.62
- Tax position affecting 7.38–.39, 7.43

DEFERRED INCOME TAX LIABILITIES (DTLS)
- Disclosure 7.46, 7.50
- Statutory accounting 7.58–.60
- Tax law change 7.62
- Tax position affecting 7.39

DEFICIENCIES, INTERNAL CONTROL 2.127–.133

DEFICIENCIES, PREMIUM
See also premiums
- Anticipated investment income .... 3.87, ... 3.92, 3.96–.97
- Cash flow, expected 3.93, 3.97
- Discounting approach .... 3.87, ... 3.90–.91, 3.95, 3.97
- Examples 3.97
- Expected investment income approach 3.87, 3.88–.89, 3.91, 3.95, 3.97
- GAAP 3.84–.85, 3.87
- Interest rate and discount rate selection 3.95
- Loss accounting 3.94, 3.96–.97
- Recognizing 3.84
- Statutory accounting 3.86
- Time value of money 3.92
- Treatment of 3.85–.86

DEFINED LIMITS INVESTMENT LAWS ... 5.10

DEFINED STANDARDS INVESTMENT LAWS 5.10

DENIAL OF APPLICATION 3.12

DEPOSIT ACCOUNTING 6.67

DEPOSIT METHOD 6.49

DERIVATIVES
- Control environment 5.215
- Dollar rolls qualifying as 5.185
- Embedded 6.58–.59
- Inherent risks 5.209
- Investment in 5.42, 5.119–.131

DETERMINATION YEAR, LOSS-PAYMENT PATTERN 7.12

DEVELOPMENT DATA EXAMPLES Appendix B

DIRECT ASSIGNMENT 3.28–.29

DIRECT BILLING 3.17

DIRECT PREMIUMS 3.02
See also premiums

DIRECT RESPONSE ADVERTISING 1.17, 3.65–.70

DIRECT WRITING 1.10, 1.16

DIRECTORIES, LIST OF .... Appendix C

DISCLAIMER OF OPINION 6.112

DISCLOSURE
- Contracts that do not transfer insurance risk .... 3.105, Appendix A
- Controls and procedures, distinguishing internal control from 2.179–.180
- Debt and equity securities 5.71
- Deferral of acquisition costs (DAC) .... 3.109, Appendix A
- Deferred income tax assets (DTAs) 7.46, 7.48, 7.50
- Deferred income tax liabilities (DTLs) 7.46, 7.50
- Estimates and critical accounting policies disclosure 4.67–.68
- Fair value measurement .... 5.34–.35, ... 5.38, 5.40
See also fair value measurement
- Income tax 7.46–.55, 7.61
- Income taxes 7.46–.55, 7.61
- Investment cycle 5.207
- Joint ventures and partnerships 5.142
- Liabilities .... Appendix A, Appendix D
- Loss reserve ... 4.67–.68, 4.94–.99, 4.105
- Loss reserving and claims cycle ... 4.94–.99
- Mortgage loans 5.107
- Nonpublic entities 7.53
- Offsetting assets and liabilities ... Appendix D
- Permitted statutory accounting practices 1.83–.87
- Premium cycle 3.116
- Property and liability insurance entity specific .... Appendix A
- Public entities 7.53, 7.55
- Reinsurance 6.71–.75, 6.79–.81, 6.91
- Repurchase agreements 5.192
- Risk-based capital (RBC) 2.48
- Securities and Exchange Commission (SEC) 1.50–.53
- VIEs 5.138

DISCOUNT RATE, PREMIUM DEFICIENCY ACCOUNTING 3.95–.96

DISCOUNTING, LOSS RESERVES ... 4.75–.82

DISCOUNTING APPROACH, PREMIUM DEFICIENCIES .... 3.87, ... 3.90–.91, 3.95, 3.97

DIVIDEND RATIO, DEFINED 2.45

Subject Index

DIVIDENDS, TAX DEDUCTIONS 7.19

DIVIDENDS-RECEIVED DEDUCTION
(DRD) 7.07, 7.15, 7.20

DOCUMENTATION
See also recordkeeping
- Audit 2.117–.125, 2.161, 4.131–.132
  See also reports on audited financial statements
- Control over 4.117, 5.220
- Fraud in a financial statement audit, consideration of 2.99

DODD-FRANK ACT 1.54–.63,
.... 2.05, 2.133, 2.176

DOLLAR REPURCHASE
AGREEMENTS 5.180, 5.182–.185

DOLLAR REVERSE REPURCHASE
AGREEMENTS 5.180

DOLLAR ROLLS .. 5.180, 5.182–.185, 5.188

DOMESTIC INSURERS 8.06

DRD See dividends-received deduction

DRUG MANUFACTURER DISCOUNTS ... 3.99
See also Medicare Part D

DTAS See deferred income tax assets

DTLS See deferred income tax liabilities

DUAL TRIGGERS, REINSURANCE 6.19

DURATION OF POLICY
- Long-duration contracts 3.31–.32, 4.04
- Loss reserving and claims cycle 4.04
- Short-duration contracts 1.89, 1.91–.92,
  .... 3.31, 3.33–.34, 4.04

E

EARNED BUT UNBILLED (EBUB)
PREMIUMS 3.47

ELECTRONIC RECORDKEEPING See
information technology (IT); recordkeeping

EMBEDDED DERIVATIVES 6.58–.59

EMERGING ACCOUNTING ISSUES WORKING
GROUP 1.71–.72, 4.94

EMPHASIS-OF-MATTER
PARAGRAPH 10.50–.54

ENDORSEMENTS, PREMIUM
ADJUSTMENTS 3.04

ENGAGEMENT, SCOPE OF THE
AUDIT 2.02–.11

ENGAGEMENT TEAM, COMMUNICATION
WITH 2.25

ENTITY, UNDERSTANDING, AUDIT
CONSIDERATIONS 2.04, 2.26–.43

ENVIRONMENT, UNDERSTANDING
See also control environment
- Audit considerations 2.04, 2.26–.43
- Income taxes 7.67
- Investments 5.203
- Loss reserves 4.63–.66, 4.146, 4.166

ENVIRONMENT, UNDERSTANDING—continued
- Premiums 3.26
- Reinsurance 6.87

EQUITY METHOD, JOINT VENTURE AND
PARTNERSHIP ACCOUNTING 5.141

EQUITY SECURITIES 5.50–.93
- Accounting practices chart 5.42
- Control environment 5.215
- Gains and losses on 5.89–.93
- Inherent risk 5.209

ERRORS ON FINANCIAL STATEMENTS,
CORRECTION OF 10.55–.60

ESTIMATED CURRENT RESERVE DEFICIENCY
TO POLICYHOLDERS' SURPLUS,
NAIC 1.47

ESTIMATES
See also loss reserve ranges
- Controls over preparation of 4.146
- Loss reserving and claims cycle ... 4.03–.14,
  .... 4.19–.24, 4.67–.68
- Premium cycle 3.117–.119
- Reasonableness of 4.137

ESTIMATING METHODS, LOSS
RESERVES 4.34–.62
- Bornhuetter-Ferguson loss reserve
  projection 4.42, 4.52–.53,
  .... Tables 4-8–4-10 at 4.52–.53
- Categories 4.40–.42
- Considerations in choosing 4.43
- Controls 4.39
- Data analysis 4.38
- Generally 4.34–.35
- Gross reserve estimates 4.36
- Incurred-loss projection 4.42, 4.45–.49,
  .... 4.53, Tables 4-1–4-3 at 4.45–.49,
  .... Table 4-10 at 4.53
- Key dates 4.17, 4.37
- Net reserve estimates 4.36
- Paid-loss/incurred loss extrapolation ... 4.51,
  .... Appendix B, Table 4-7 at 4.51
- Paid-loss projection 4.42, 4.50, 4.53,
  .... Tables 4-4–4-6 at 4.50

EVALUATING CONSISTENCY OF FINANCIAL
STATEMENTS 10.28

EXCESS CLAIMS, DEFINED 4.08

EXCESS LIABILITY INSURANCE,
DEFINED 1.05

EXCESS OF LOSS PER OCCURRENCE
REINSURANCE 6.11

EXCESS OF LOSS PER RISK
REINSURANCE 6.11

EXCESS REINSURANCE 6.11

EXPECTED INVESTMENT INCOME APPROACH,
PREMIUM DEFICIENCIES 3.87–.89,
.... 3.91, 3.95, 3.97

EXPENSE RATIO, DEFINED 2.45

AAG-PLI EXP

EXPENSES
See also costs; insurance-related expenses, taxes, and assessments
- Bad debt 3.51
- LAE reserves .... 4.01, 4.33, ... 4.54–.62, 4.182–.183
- Nondeferrable expenses 3.71
- Unallocated loss adjustment expenses .. 4.54

EXPERIENCE ACCOUNT, REINSURANCE . **6.19**
EXPERIENCE RATING, PREMIUMS **3.03**
EXTINGUISHMENT OF LIABILITIES ..... **5.42,** .... **5.162–.180, Appendix D**
EXTRATERRITORIAL REQUIREMENTS, INVESTMENTS **5.10**

F

FACULTATIVE REINSURANCE **6.15**
FAIR ACCESS TO INSURANCE REQUIREMENTS (FAIR) PLANS **1.08, 3.27**
FAIR DEALING, PROMOTION OF **1.38**
FAIR VALUE, DEFINED **5.16–.17**
FAIR VALUE HIERARCHY ... **5.26–.30, 5.220**
FAIR VALUE MEASUREMENT **5.15–.40**
See also investments
- Activity level has decreased   5.28, 5.31–.33
- Asset transfers 5.170
- Audit considerations 2.141–.143
- Controls over 5.220
- Derivatives 5.123
- Disclosures 5.34–.35, 5.38, 5.40
- Fair value definition 5.16–.17
- Fair value option 5.36–.38
- Hierarchy 5.26–.30, 5.220
- Liabilities, application to 5.23–.25
- Nonfinancial assets 5.18–.22
- Objective 5.17
- Shareholders' equity, application to . 5.23–.25
- Statutory accounting 5.39–.40

FAIR VALUE OPTION **5.36–.38**
FDIC   See Federal Deposit Insurance Corporation
FEASIBILITY STUDY, CAPTIVE ENTITIES   9.27
FEDERAL DEPOSIT INSURANCE CORPORATION (FDIC) **1.55**
FEDERAL INCOME TAXATION **7.03–.20**
See also income taxes
- Special income tax provisions 7.08–.20
- Statutory accounting practices and taxable income 7.05–.07

FEDERAL LIABILITY RISK RETENTION ACT OF 1986 (FLRRA) **1.09, 9.20–.23**
FEDERAL REGULATIONS, ACCOUNTING PRACTICES **1.48–.68**
FEDERAL RESERVE, RISK REGULATION   1.55
FIDELITY BONDS, DEFINED **1.04**

FIDELITY CLAIMS **4.12**
FINANCE COMMITTEE **5.02**
See also investments
FINANCIAL CONDITION, NOTIFICATION OF ADVERSE **2.156–.157, 10.76–.79**
FINANCIAL GUARANTEE INSURANCE CONTRACTS .... **3.106, 3.108,** .... **4.12, Appendix A**
FINANCIAL MODELING, LOAN-BACKED AND STRUCTURED SECURITIES **5.77**
FINANCIAL RATIOS
- Loss reserve ranges 4.171
- Reporting regulations 1.52
- Types of 1.47

FINANCIAL REGULATION STANDARDS AND ACCREDITATION PROGRAM (NAIC) .. **1.46**
FINANCIAL REPORTING
See also financial statements
- Insurance entities 1.38, 1.74–.77
- Internal control over 10.29–.31

FINANCIAL REPORTING EXECUTIVE COMMITTEE **3.94, 6.62**
FINANCIAL STABILITY OVERSIGHT COUNCIL (FSOC) **1.55, 1.59**
FINANCIAL STATEMENTS
See also financial reporting
- Auditor's reports on   See reports on audited financial statements
- Correction of error on 10.55–.60
- Property and liability insurance entity specific .... Appendix A
- Regulatory basis financial statements for general use 10.37–.42, 10.46, 10.59
- Regulatory basis financial statements for limited use 10.43–.48, 10.60
- Regulatory basis financial statements-other issues 10.49–.54

FIRE AND ALLIED LINES OF INSURANCE **1.04**
FIXED-COUPON AGREEMENT .. **5.183, 5.188**
FLOAT **5.208**
FLORIDA HURRICANE CATASTROPHE FUND **6.04**
FLRRA   See Federal Liability Risk Retention Act of 1986
FORECLOSURE-RELATED ACTIVITIES OR EXPOSURES **1.50**
FOREIGN EXCHANGE IMPACT, LOSS RESERVING AND CLAIMS CYCLE **4.166, 4.190**
FOREIGN INSURERS **8.06**
FOREIGN INTEREST
- Joint ventures and partnerships .. 5.141–.142
- SCAs 5.149

FOREIGN REINSURANCE .... **6.64–.65,** **6.71, 6.73**
- Currency translation 6.85

Subject Index

FRAUD
- Distinguishing error from 2.76
- Risk factors 2.77–.78,
  .... Tables 2-1–2-2 at 2.78

FRAUD, MATERIAL MISSTATEMENT DUE TO
See also material misstatement risk
- Captive insurance entities 9.37
- Discussion among engagement personnel regarding risks of material misstatement due to fraud 2.80–.83
- Identifying risks that may result in a material misstatement due to fraud 2.86–.90
- Internal and external risk factors 2.82
- Loss reserving and claims cycle 4.109
- Obtaining the information needed to identify the risks of material misstatement due to fraud 2.84–.85
- Responding to the misstatements that may be the result of fraud 2.95–.96

FRAUD IN A FINANCIAL STATEMENT AUDIT, CONSIDERATION OF 2.75–.99
- Audit evidence, evaluating ... 2.91–.92, 2.94
- Communicating about possible fraud to management 2.97–.98
- Documentation and guidance 2.99
- Income taxes 7.64
- Insurance-related expenses, taxes, and assessments 8.39
- Investments 5.203
- Key estimates 2.87
- Loss reserving and claims 4.106–.108
- Management override of controls 2.89–.90, 2.93, 4.108
- Premiums and acquisition costs 3.112
- Reinsurance 6.88
- Results of assessment, responding to .. 2.93
- Risk factors 2.77–.78,
  .... Tables 2-1–2-2 at 2.78
- Skepticism, exercising 2.79–.80,
  .... 4.161, 5.204

FRONTING, REINSURANCE 1.26,
.... 6.12, 9.08–.10

FSOC See Financial Stability Oversight Council

FUNDS WITHHELD, REINSURANCE 6.19

FUTURES CONTRACTS 5.119–.131,
.... 5.209, 5.215

G

GAAP See generally accepted accounting principles

GAAS See Generally Accepted Auditing Standards

GAINS 5.42, 5.89–.93, 5.123, 5.125, 5.151

GENERALLY ACCEPTED ACCOUNTING PRINCIPLES (GAAP) 1.89–.95
See also specific details within topics
- Accounting guidance and literature 1.72
- Acquisition costs 3.56–.81
- Assertions in compliance with 2.68

GENERALLY ACCEPTED ACCOUNTING PRINCIPLES (GAAP)—continued
- Captive entities 9.43
- Contracts that do not transfer insurance risk 3.103
- Distinguishing SAP from 1.96,
  ...... Exhibit 1-1 at 1.96, Table 1-1 at 1.96
- Distinguishing SEC regulation from 5.42
- And FASB ASC 944 .... 1.89–.95
- Income taxes 7.23–.55
- Insurance-related expenses, taxes, and assessments 8.49–.50
- Investments 5.41–.201
- Loss reserving and claims cycle 4.74,
  .... 4.78, 4.83, 4.94
- Premium taxation 8.09
- Premiums 3.30–.40, 3.50–.52
- Reinsurance 6.20–.75, 6.78

GENERALLY ACCEPTED AUDITING STANDARDS (GAAS) 2.12–.13, 2.16
See also reports on audited financial statements

GOING CONCERN, AUDIT CONSIDERATIONS 2.104–.112

GOODWILL 2.87

GOVERNANCE, COMMUNICATING ABOUT POSSIBLE FRAUD TO THOSE CHARGED WITH 2.97, 2.134–.138
See also management

GOVERNMENT, REINSURANCE COVERAGE 6.04

GROSS AGENTS' BALANCES TO POLICYHOLDERS' SURPLUS 1.47

GROSS PREMIUMS WRITTEN TO POLICYHOLDERS' SURPLUS 1.47

GROSS RESERVE ESTIMATES 4.36

GUARANTY FUND
- Audit considerations 8.48
- Disclosure .... Appendix A
- Fraud risk 2.87
- GAAP accounting 4.72, 8.20
- Generally 8.13–.16
- Loss reserving and claims cycle 4.72
- Statutory accounting 4.72, 8.23,
  .... 8.25, 8.27–.28

H

HEDGING ACTIVITIES 5.122–.123, 5.129
See also derivatives

HIGH DEDUCTIBLE POLICIES, DEFINED 4.08

HOLDING COMPANIES, MANAGEMENT FEE CHARGES 8.03

I

IBNR See incurred but not reported

IMPAIRMENT OF INTANGIBLES 2.87

AAG-PLI IMP

IMPAIRMENT OF SECURITIES
- Bonds 5.75
- Debt securities 5.66
- Equity securities 5.65, 5.84, 5.88
- Indicators 5.63
- Investment income due and accrued .. 5.160
- Isolation of transferred assets 5.165, 5.168, 5.175
- Mortgage loans 5.101, 5.104
- Other than temporary 1.50, 5.62
- Real estate investments 5.115
- Testing, GAAP 5.63–.71
- Testing, statutory 5.75, 5.78–.79, 5.84

IMR See interest maintenance reserve

INCENTIVE COMPENSATION 3.22

INCENTIVES, AS FRAUD RISK FACTOR ..... 2.83, Table 2-1 at 2.78

INCOME TAXES 7.01–.77
- Alternative minimum tax 7.20
- Audit considerations 7.63–.77
- Capital losses 7.18
- Captive entities 9.33–.35
- Carryforward 7.32, 7.36, 7.50
- Continuing operations 7.51–.53
- Control activities 7.74
- Control environment 7.71
- Disclosure 7.46–.55, 7.61
- Distinguishing public from private entities 7.53, 7.55
- DTAs   See deferred income tax assets
- DTLs   See deferred income tax liabilities
- Federal 7.03–.20
- Future taxable income 7.32–.33
- GAAP accounting 7.23–.55
- Generally 7.01–.02
- Internal control 7.69–.70
- Material misstatement 2.87
- Multistate entity apportionment 7.22
- Risk-based capital 7.60
- Risk considerations 2.17
- Special provisions 7.08–.20
- State taxation 7.21–.22, 8.06, 8.11–.12, 8.47
- Status change 7.49
- Statutory accounting practices 7.05–.07, 7.56–.61
- Tax law changes 7.62
  See also Pension Funding Equity Act of 2004; Tax Reform Act of 1986
- Tax liability or asset recognition 7.25
- Tax planning strategies 7.35
- Tax positions 7.37–.45
- Temporary differences   7.26–.30, 7.32, 7.50

INCREMENTAL DIRECT COSTS OF CONTRACT ACQUISITION 3.59–.60

INCURRED BUT NOT REPORTED (IBNR) 4.33, 6.86

INCURRED LOSS DATA .... 4.46, Appendix B, Table 4-1 at 4.46

INCURRED LOSS/PAID-LOSS EXTRAPOLATION METHOD .... 4.51, Appendix B, Table 4-7 at 4.51

INCURRED-LOSS PROJECTION 4.42, 4.45–.47, 4.53, Tables 4-1 to 4-3 at 4.45–.49, Table 4-3 at 4.50, Table 4-10 at 4.53

INDEMNIFICATION, NAIC MODEL AUDIT RULE 2.150

INDEMNITY REINSURANCE 6.07, 6.12, 6.22–.24

INDEPENDENT AUDITOR'S REPORTS   See reports on audited financial statements

INDEPENDENT CHECKS ON PERFORMANCE 4.117, 5.220, 6.100

INDIRECT COSTS, ACQUISITIONS 3.74

INDIVIDUAL RATING, PREMIUMS 3.03

INDUSTRY ASSOCIATIONS ...... Appendix C

INDUSTRY ASSOCIATIONS, ACCOUNTING PRACTICES 1.69

INDUSTRY ASSOCIATIONS, NATURE, CONDUCT, AND REGULATION OF THE BUSINESS 1.69

INFLATION, LOSS RESERVE EFFECTS   4.166

INFORMATION TECHNOLOGY (IT)
- Audit considerations 2.35–.36, 2.93, 2.100–.103, 2.101
- Investment transaction cycle 5.05, 5.218–.219
- Loss reserving and claims cycle 4.17, 4.26–.27, 4.116
- Premium cycle 3.16, 3.23, 3.25–.26
- Reinsurance 6.98
- Software costs 3.75

INHERENT RISK
   See also audit risk; risk
- Audit procedures addressing 2.64
- Income taxes 7.65–.68
- Investments and fair value 5.209
- Loss reserving and claims cycle 4.109
- Premium cycle 3.120
- Reinsurance 6.92

INJURY FUND ASSESSMENTS 8.18

INLAND MARINE INSURANCE 1.04

INSTITUTIONS, LIST OF ...... Appendix C

INSURANCE, LINES OF   See lines of insurance

INSURANCE COMPANY
- Qualifying as 9.35
- Tax definition of 7.03, 9.35

INSURANCE CONTRACTS THAT DO NOT TRANSFER RISK 3.103–.104, 3.110

INSURANCE ENTITIES, STATUTORY FINANCIAL STATEMENTS OF 1.45

INSURANCE INDUSTRY, FRAUD RISK FACTORS .... 2.77–.78, Tables 2-1–2-2 at 2.78

Subject Index

INSURANCE PREMIUMS See premiums
INSURANCE-PURCHASING POOLS 1.09
INSURANCE REGULATORY INFORMATION SYSTEM (IRIS) ... 1.47, 2.54–.56, 4.142
INSURANCE-RELATED EXPENSES, TAXES, AND ASSESSMENTS 8.01–.52
- Audit considerations 8.38–.52
- Capitalized costs and certain nonadmitted assets 8.31–.35
- Expense reporting 8.01–.05
- Guaranty fund and other assessments 8.13–.30
  See also guaranty fund
- Pensions 8.31–.37
- Premium and state taxes ... 8.06–.12, 8.47
  See also income taxes

INSURANCE SERVICES OFFICE 3.06
INTANGIBLES, IMPAIRMENT OF 2.87
  See also nonfinancial assets
INTEGRATED AUDITS OF FINANCIAL STATEMENTS AND INTERNAL CONTROL OVER FINANCIAL REPORTING 10.29–.31
  See also reports on audited financial statements
INTERCOMPANY POOLING ARRANGEMENTS 6.60–.63
INTERCOMPANY REINSURANCE AGREEMENTS 4.189
INTEREST CREDITS ON FUNDS WITHHELD 6.54–.59
INTEREST MAINTENANCE RESERVE (IMR) 5.83
INTEREST RATE, PREMIUM DEFICIENCY ACCOUNTING 3.95
INTERINSURANCE OR RECIPROCAL EXCHANGES 1.09
INTERMEDIARIES, REINSURANCE 6.115–.118
INTERNAL AUDITORS, CONSIDERING WORK OF 2.40, 2.124–.125
INTERNAL CONTROL
  See also control activities; control environment; understanding the entity, its environment, and its internal control
- Audit considerations .... 2.27–.43, ... 2.126–.133, 2.176–.180
- Captive insurance entities 9.41–.42
- Communication of matters related to 2.126–.140
- Components .... 2.31, 3.123, 4.111, ... 5.213, 6.93, 7.69, 9.41
- Defined .. 2.30, 3.122, 4.110, 5.212, 6.93
- Distinguishing disclosure controls and procedures from 2.179–.180
- Income taxes 7.69–.70
- Information technology systems 2.101, 3.26
  See also information technology (IT)
- Insurance-related expenses, taxes, and assessments 8.43–.45
- Investments 5.212–.214

INTERNAL CONTROL—continued
- Loss reserve estimation .. 4.39, 4.110–.111
- Loss reserving and claims 4.110–.112
- Management override of .... 2.89–.90, ... 2.93, 4.108
- Management's report on internal control over financial reporting, SEC requirements 2.176
- Over financial reporting, audit report on 10.29–.31
- Premiums and acquisition costs 3.16, 3.122–.124
- Reinsurance 6.93–.94, 6.103–.106
- Report on, NAIC Model Rule 2.158–.160, 2.163–.165, 10.83
- SEC requirements 2.176–.180
- Testing effectiveness of 2.42–.43, 2.65

INTERNAL REVENUE CODE (IRC) 7.01
  See also income taxes
INTERNAL REVENUE SERVICE (IRS) See income taxes
INVESTMENT ADVISORS ACT OF 1940 .... 1.60–.61, 1.63
INVESTMENT COMPANY ACT OF 1940, PROSECUTION UNDER 1.61
INVESTMENT CYCLE, RISK CONSIDERATIONS 2.17
INVESTMENT INCOME
- Anticipated 3.87
- Due and accrued 5.42, 5.157–.159
- Ratio 2.45
- Tax provisions 7.15, 7.17
INVESTMENT YIELD 1.47
INVESTMENTS 5.01–.228
- Accounting practices 5.41–.202
- Asset transfer and extinguishment of liabilities 5.42, 5.162–.180
- Audit considerations 5.203–.228
- Captive insurance entities 9.32
- Cash and cash equivalents .. 5.42, 5.43–.49
- Debt and equity securities .... 5.42, ... 5.50–.93, 5.209
- Derivatives, futures, options, and similar instruments 5.42, 5.119–.131, 5.209
- Distinguishing GAAP from statutory accounting 5.41–.201
- Evaluating 5.02–.03
- Fair value considerations See fair value measurement
- Fraud risk 2.87
- Gains and losses on 5.42, 5.89–.93
- Generally 5.01
- Investment income due and accrued 5.42, 5.157–.159
- Joint ventures and partnerships 5.42, 5.132–.144
- Mortgage loans 5.42, 5.94–.107, 5.209
- Real estate 5.42, 5.108–.118, 5.209
- Recordkeeping and key performance indicators 5.04–.05
- Regulation 5.09–.14

AAG-PLI INV

528   Property and Liability Insurance Entities

INVESTMENTS—continued
- Repurchase agreements .. 5.42, 5.180–.192
- Responsibility for 5.02
- Safekeeping 5.08
- SCA entities 5.42, 5.145–.156
- Securities lending ... 1.50, 5.42, 5.193–.201
- Transaction cycle 1.33–.36, 5.06–.07

INVESTORS, REINSURANCE GROUPS ... 6.03

INVOLUNTARY MARKETS 1.08, 3.27–.29

IRIS   See Insurance Regulatory Information System

IRON CURTAIN APPROACH 2.116

IRS   See income taxes

IT   See information technology

J

JOINT VENTURES, INVESTMENT IN 5.42,
              5.132–.144, 5.209, 5.215

JOURNALS, LIST OF .... Appendix C

JUDGMENT RATING, PREMIUMS .. 1.21, 3.03

K

KEY PERFORMANCE INDICATORS, INVESTMENTS 5.04–.05

KINDS OF INSURANCE   See lines of insurance

KNOWN LOSS RESERVE 7.14

L

LAE   See loss adjustment expense (LAE) reserves

LATENT INJURY CLAIMS 4.24

LEGAL ENVIRONMENT
See also specific legislation
- Loss reserve effects 4.166
- Responsibility conflict with confidentiality 2.98
- Tax law changes 7.62

LEGAL FORMS OF INSURANCE ORGANIZATION 1.09, 2.04

LETTERS OF QUALIFICATION ... 2.148–.149,
              2.154, 10.84

LEVEL COMMISSIONS 3.22

LEVERAGE, FINANCIAL, LOSS RESERVE RANGE ANALYSIS 4.171

LIABILITIES
- Disclosure .... Appendix A, Appendix D
- Extinguishment of 5.42,
            5.162–.180, Appendix D
- Reinsurance reporting ... 6.39–.47, 6.64–.65

LIABILITIES TO LIQUID ASSETS 1.47

LIABILITY CLAIMS, DEFINED 4.09

LICS   See Low Income Cost Share (LICS) subsidy

LIHTC   See low-income housing tax credits (LIHTC) properties

LINES OF INSURANCE
- Accident and health insurance 1.04
- Allocating expenses to 8.05
- Automobile 1.04, 1.08
- Commercial lines 1.07
- Defined 1.04
- Excess liability insurance 1.05
- Fair Access to Insurance Requirements (FAIR) plans 1.08, 3.27
- Fidelity bonds 1.04
- Fire and allied lines of insurance 1.04
- Frequency and severity of claims link to 4.165
- Inland marine insurance 1.04
- Involuntary automobile insurance 1.08
- Legal forms of organization 1.09
- Loss reserving and claims cycle 4.03, 4.06–.14
- Medical malpractice pools 1.08
- Miscellaneous liability 1.04
- Multiple peril 1.04
- Ocean marine insurance 1.04
- Personal lines 1.07
- Professional liability insurance 1.04
- Surety bonds 1.04
- Surplus lines 1.05
- Workers' compensation 1.04, 1.08

LIQUIDITY RATIOS 1.47

LOAN-BACKED SECURITIES 5.76–.79

LOAN-BACKS, CAPTIVE ENTITIES 9.32

LONG-DURATION CONTRACTS 3.31–.32,
              4.04

LONG TAIL LINES 4.13, 4.165

LONG-TERM CONTRACTS 1.89–.91

LOSS ADJUSTMENT EXPENSE (LAE) RESERVES 4.01, 4.33,
              4.54–.62, 4.182–.183

LOSS-BASED ASSESSMENTS 3.29, 8.20

LOSS CONTINGENCIES, SECURITIES AND EXCHANGE COMMISSION (SEC) 1.50

LOSS CORRIDOR, REINSURANCE 6.19

LOSS-PAYMENT PATTERN 7.12

LOSS RATIO, DEFINED 2.45

LOSS RATIO PROJECTION METHOD 4.42

LOSS RESERVE
- Claims cycle   See loss reserving and claims cycle
- Components 4.33
- Defined 4.33
- Disclosure 4.67–.68, 4.94–.99, 4.105
- Discounting 4.75–.82, 7.06
- Estimating Methods 4.34–.53
- Examples of Development Data ... Appendix B

Subject Index

LOSS RESERVE—continued
- Securities and Exchange Commission .. 1.50
- Tax reporting 7.06, 7.08–.12, 7.14

LOSS RESERVE RANGES 4.157–.179
- Entity circumstances affecting 4.163
- Estimation uncertainty 4.158–.159,
  .... 4.180–.181
- Factors that could affect 4.164–.170
- Financial effect, evaluation of ... 4.171–.179
- Generally 4.157
- Point estimate development 4.124, 4.155–.156
- Reasonableness, evaluation of ... 4.160–.161
- Size of, variation in 4.162

LOSS RESERVE SPECIALISTS 4.64,
.... 4.69–.71, 4.104, 4.127, 4.129–.136

LOSS RESERVING AND CLAIMS CYCLE 4.01–.191
- Accounting principles 4.73–.93
- Alternative projections of ultimate losses and unreported losses .... Table 4-7 at 4.52
- AO reserve calculation 4.60–.62
- Audit considerations chart 4.191
  See also audit considerations, loss reserving and claims
- Case-basis incurred-loss data .... Table 4-1 at 4.46
- Claim process flowchart 4.15
- Critical accounting policies and estimates disclosure 4.67–.68
- DCC reserve calculation 4.56–.59
- Development data .... Appendix B
- Disclosures 4.94–.99
- Environment changes 4.63–.66
- Estimation process, types of business and effect on 4.03–.14
- Estimations   See estimating methods, loss reserves
- Functions in 1.31–.32
- Generally 4.01–.02
- Guaranty fund 4.72
- Incurred loss data .... Appendix B
- Incurred-loss projection .... Table 4-3 at 4.50
- LAE reserves 4.01, 4.33,
  .... 4.54–.62, 4.182–.183
- Paid-loss data .... Table 4-4 at 4.51
- Paid-loss projection .... Table 4-6 at 4.51
- Period-to-period development factor .... Appendix B
- Period-to-period incurred-loss development factors .... Table 4-2 at 4.49
- Period-to-period paid-loss development factors .... Table 4-5 at 4.51
- Policy duration 4.04

LOSSES
- DCC relationship to 4.57
- Derivatives 5.123, 5.125
- Premium deficiency accounting 3.94, 3.96–.97
- Realized and unrealized 5.42, 5.89–.93

LOSSES—continued
- SCAs 5.151
- Tax reporting ... 7.06, 7.08–.12, 7.18, 7.36

LOW INCOME COST SHARE (LICS) SUBSIDY 3.99
See also Medicare Part D

LOW INCOME HOUSING INVESTMENTS   8.06

LOW-INCOME HOUSING TAX CREDITS (LIHTC) PROPERTIES 5.144

M

MANAGEMENT
- Audit engagement terms and 2.02
- Going concern discussion 2.106–.112
- Loss reserve estimates   See loss reserve ranges
- Materiality assessment of 2.114
- Override of controls .. 2.89–.90, 2.93, 4.108
- Report on internal controls 2.163
- Responding to fraud by 2.95
- Responsibility section, in auditor's report   See reports on audited financial statements

MANAGEMENT ESTIMATES
- Loss reserving and claims cycle 4.67–.71, 4.180–.181
  See also audit considerations, loss reserving and claims
- Premiums and acquisition costs   3.117–.119
  See also audit considerations, premiums and acquisition costs

MANAGEMENT FEE CHARGES 8.03

MANDATORY CONTROL LEVEL (MCL) RISK-BASED CAPITAL 2.51

MANUAL RATING, PREMIUMS 1.21, 3.03

MASS MARKETING 1.17

MASS TORT CLAIMS 4.24, 4.66

MATERIAL MISSTATEMENT RISK
- Captive insurance entities 9.43
- Fraud   See fraud, material misstatement due to
- Income taxes 7.75–.76
- Insurance-related expenses, taxes, and assessments 8.46–.52
- Investments 5.209–.211, 5.225–.226
- Loss reserving and claims cycle 4.109, 4.119–.128
- Notification letter 10.76
- Premiums and acquisition costs 3.120–.121, 3.130–.131
- Reinsurance 6.92, 6.101–.102

MATERIAL WEAKNESSES, REPORTING .. 1.76,
... 2.131, 2.158–.160, 10.32, 10.80–.83

MATERIALITY
See also fraud, material misstatement due to; material misstatement risk
- Generally 2.15–.16
- Loss reserve estimates 4.176
- Misstatement evaluation 2.114, 2.116
- Planning 2.70–.74

AAG-PLI MAT

MCCARRAN-FERGUSON ACT OF
  1945 .... 1.39, 3.07
MCL   See mandatory control level (MCL)
  risk-based capital
MEDICAL MALPRACTICE POOLS 1.08
MEDICARE PART D 3.98–.102
MEDICARE PRESCRIPTION DRUG,
  IMPROVEMENT, AND MODERNIZATION
  ACT OF 2003 .... 3.98
MERIT RATING, PREMIUMS 1.21, 3.03
MEZZANINE REAL ESTATE LOANS
  (MREL) 5.106
MISAPPROPRIATION OF ASSETS 2.76,
  .... Table 2-2 at 2.78
MISCELLANEOUS LIABILITY 1.04
MISSTATEMENT, EVALUATING 2.12, 2.74
  See also fraud, material misstatement
  due to; material misstatement risk
MODIFIED FILING EXEMPT METHOD, LOAN-
  BACKED AND STRUCTURED
  SECURITIES 5.77
MODIFIED OPINIONS 10.06–.27
  · Adverse opinion 10.15–.17
  · Disclaimer of opinion 10.12–.14
  · Emphasis-of-matter paragraphs ... 10.18–.27
  · Generally 10.06–.10
  · Qualified opinion 10.10–.11
MORTGAGE AND FORECLOSURE-RELATED
  ACTIVITIES OR EXPOSURES 1.50
MORTGAGE LOANS   5.42, 5.94–.107, 5.209
MORTGAGE-PARTICIPATION
  CERTIFICATES 5.182
MREL   See mezzanine real estate loans
MULTIPLE PERIL, DEFINED 1.04
MUTUAL COMPANIES 1.09

N

NAIC   See National Association of Insurance
  Commissioners
NATIONAL ASSOCIATION OF INSURANCE
  COMMISSIONERS (NAIC)
  · Accounting Issues Working Group 3.102
  · Accounting Practices and Procedures Task
    Force 1.71
  · Annual report requirement 10.33
  · Codified statutory accounting 10.34–.36
  · Emerging Accounting Issues Working
    Group 1.72, 1.87, 4.94
  · Emerging Accounting Principles Working
    Group 1.71
  · Filing of audited financial report 1.75
  · Financial Regulation Standards and
    Accreditation Program 1.46
  · Insurance Regulatory Information
    System 1.47, 2.54–.56
  · Investment laws 5.10

NATIONAL ASSOCIATION OF INSURANCE
  COMMISSIONERS (NAIC)—continued
  · Nature, conduct, and regulation of the
    business 1.46–.47
  · RBC disclosure requirement 2.48
  · Securities Valuation Office 5.72
  · Statutory Accounting Principles Working
    Group 1.71
  · Statutory hierarchy 1.72
  · Tax reporting role 7.05
  · Terrorism Insurance Extension Act of
    2005 .... 1.66
  · Terrorism Insurance Implementation Working
    Group 1.68
  · Uniformity, promotion of 1.38
NATIONAL COUNCIL ON COMPENSATION
  INSURANCE, INC. (NCCI) 3.06, 3.28
NATIONAL FLOOD INSURANCE PROGRAM
  (NFIP) 3.27
NATURE, CONDUCT, AND REGULATION OF
  THE BUSINESS 1.01–.96
  · Federal regulation-Dodd-Frank Act .. 1.54–.63
    See also Dodd-Frank Act
  · Federal regulation-SEC 1.48–.53
  · Federal regulation-terrorism 1.64–.68
  · Generally 1.01–.03
  · Generally accepted accounting principles See
    U.S. GAAP
  · Industry associations 1.69
  · Kinds of insurance 1.04–.08
    See also lines of insurance
  · Legal forms of organization 1.09
  · Major transaction cycles See transaction
    cycle
  · Methods of producing business 1.10–.17
  · NAIC 1.46–.47
    See also National Association of Insurance
    Commissioners (NAIC)
  · State insurance regulations .. 1.34, 1.37–.45
  · Statutory accounting practices   See statutory
    accounting practices (SAP)
NCCI   See National Council on Compensation
  Insurance, Inc.
NET INCOME, TAX REPORTING 7.05
NET PREMIUMS WRITTEN TO
  POLICYHOLDERS' SURPLUS 1.47
NET RESERVE ESTIMATES 4.36
NFIP   See National Flood Insurance Program
NON-GAAP FINANCIAL MEASURES,
  ADDITIONAL INSURANCE INFORMATION
  FOR (SEC) 1.52
NONADMITTED ASSETS 1.88, 3.49,
  .... 5.42, 5.72, 5.74, 8.31–.35
NONADMITTED REINSURER 6.19
NONAUDIT SERVICES 2.152–.154
NONDEFERRABLE EXPENSES 3.71
NONFINANCIAL ASSETS, FAIR VALUE
  MEASUREMENT 5.18–.22
  See also intangibles, impairment of

Subject Index

NONPUBLIC ENTITIES, DISCLOSURE
 REQUIREMENTS 7.53
NOTIFICATION OF FINANCIAL
 CONDITION 2.156–.157, 10.76–.79
NOVATION TRANSACTIONS 6.08, 6.50

O

OCCURRENCE BASIS POLICIES 4.05
OCEAN MARINE INSURANCE 1.04
OFFICE OF THRIFT SUPERVISORS (OTS), RISK
 REGULATION 1.56
OFFSHORE CAPTIVE INSURANCE
 ENTITIES 9.06
OMNIBUS BUDGET RECONCILIATION ACT OF
 1990 .... 7.02
ONE-YEAR RESERVE DEVELOPMENT TO
 POLICYHOLDERS' SURPLUS 1.47
OPERATING EARNINGS, SEC 1.53
OPERATING EXPENSE ASSESSMENTS .. 8.18
OPERATING RATIO, DEFINED 2.45
OPINIONS See reports on audited financial
 statements
OPPORTUNITY, AS FRAUD RISK
 FACTOR .... 2.83, Table 2-1 at 2.78
OPTIONS, INVESTMENT
 IN 5.119–.131, 5.209, 5.215
ORGANIZATIONS, PRINCIPAL KINDS OF 1.09
ORIGINAL MATURITY 5.48
OTHER RISK, DEFINED 2.48
OTHER THAN TEMPORARY IMPAIRMENTS OF
 SECURITIES (GENERAL) 1.50
OTS See Office of Thrift Supervisors
OVERALL RATIOS 1.47
OVERALL RESPONSES 2.62
 See also risk

P

PAID-LOSS DATA .. 4.182, Table 4-4 at 4.51
PAID-LOSS/INCURRED LOSS EXTRAPOLATION
 METHOD .... 4.51, Appendix B,
 .... Table 4-7 at 4.51
PAID-LOSS PROJECTION .. 4.43, 4.50, 4.53,
 ... Table 4-6 at 4.51, Table 4-10 at 4.53,
 .... Tables 4-4–4-6 at 4.50
PAID-TO-PAID RATIO APPROACH 4.57,
 .... 4.60, 4.62
PARAGRAPH 11 EXCEPTION,
 REINSURANCE 6.33–.35
PARTNER ROTATION, NAIC MODEL AUDIT
 RULE 2.151
PARTNERSHIPS, INVESTMENT
 IN 5.42, 5.132–.144
PASS-THROUGH CERTIFICATES 5.182

PASSTHROUGH SURCHARGES 3.29
PAYMENT, METHODS OF 4.26
PAYMENT SCHEDULES, REINSURANCE 6.19
PAYROLL See compensation
PCAOB See Public Company Accounting
 Oversight Board
PDP See prescription drug plan
PENSION ACCOUNTING 8.36–.37
PENSION FUNDING EQUITY ACT OF
 2004 .... 7.02–.03, 7.16–.17
PENSION LIABILITY, FRAUD RISK 2.87
PER OCCURENCE POLICY 4.08
PERFORMANCE INDICATORS,
 INVESTMENTS 5.04–.05
PERFORMANCE MATERIALITY 2.73
PERFORMANCE METRICS, AUDIT
 CONSIDERATIONS 2.44–.56
PERIL INSURED AGAINST 1.01
 See also risk
PERIOD OF RISK, DISTINGUISHING CONTRACT
 PERIOD FROM 3.35
PERIOD-TO-PERIOD DEVELOPMENT
 FACTOR .... Appendix B
PERIOD-TO-PERIOD INCURRED-
 LOSS DEVELOPMENT
 FACTORS .... Table 4-2 at 4.49
PERIOD-TO-PERIOD INCURRED-LOSS
 PROJECTION .... 4.50, Appendix B,
 .... Tables 4-1–4-3 at 4.45–.49,
 .... Table 4-5 at 4.50
PERIOD-TO-PERIOD PAID-
 LOSS DEVELOPMENT
 FACTORS .... Table 4-5 at 4.51
PERMITTED STATUTORY ACCOUNTING
 PRACTICES 1.82–.87, 2.171–.175
PERPETUAL PREFERRED STOCK,
 IMPAIRMENT OF 5.84
PERSON OR PROPERTY PROTECTED ... 1.01
 See also risk
PERSONAL LINES OF INSURANCE 1.07, 3.16
PLANNING THE AUDIT See audit
 considerations, planning
POINT ESTIMATE, LOSS RESERVING AND
 CLAIMS CYCLE 4.124, 4.155–.156
 See also loss reserve ranges
POLICY CHARACTERISTICS, LOSS RESERVES
 EFFECTS 4.165
POLICY DATE, DEFINED 4.37
POLICY DURATION See duration of policy
POLICYHOLDER INFORMATION, AUDIT
 CONSIDERATIONS 2.93
POOLING
 · Defined 1.28
 · Reinsurance 1.08, 6.60–.63, 6.114
 · Risk-sharing 1.09, 1.77

AAG-PLI POO

PORTFOLIO REINSURANCE 1.25
PREFERRED STOCK
    VALUATION 5.81–.82, 5.84–.85, 5.88
PREFUNDED PREMIUM BASED
    ASSESSMENTS 8.14, 8.20
PREMIUM ADJUSTMENTS
  · Contracts that do not transfer insurance
    risk 3.106
  · Defined 3.02
  · GAAP 3.30–.40
  · Management estimates 3.119
  · Statutory accounting principles 3.41–.49
  · Types 3.04
PREMIUM RATE SETTING ... 1.20–.22, 1.38
PREMIUM TAXES 8.06–.12, 8.47
PREMIUMS 3.01–.132
  · Acquisition costs   See acquisition costs;
    deferral of acquisition costs (DAC)
  · Adjustment types 3.04
  · Audit considerations 3.111–.132
  · Billing and collecting 3.17–.21
  · Commissions, paying 3.22
  · Contracts that do not transfer insurance
    risk 3.103–.110
  · Control activities 3.129
  · Cost of acquiring business 3.22
  · Deficiencies   See deficiencies, premium
  · Defined 1.01, 1.20
  · Disclosures 3.116
  · Financial and statistical reporting .. 3.23–.26
  · Functions 3.05
  · Generally 3.01–.03, 3.05–.07
  · Involuntary markets 3.27–.29
  · Medicare Part D 3.98–.102
  · Receivables .... 3.50–.55, Appendix A
  · Revenue and adjustments 3.30–.49
  · Risk considerations 2.17, 3.114
  · Risk evaluation and acceptance 3.08–.16
  · Taxes on 8.06–.12, 8.47
  · Transaction cycle 3.05–.26
PRESCRIPTION DRUG PLAN (PDP) 3.99
    See also Medicare Part D
PRESSURE, AS FRAUD RISK
    FACTOR .... 2.82–.83, Table 2-1 at 2.78
PRIMARY COVERAGE, DEFINED 4.07
PRINCIPAL MARKET, INVESTMENT
    ASSETS 5.16
PRIVATE POOLS, DISTINGUISHING PUBLIC
    ENTITY POOLS FROM 1.09
PRO RATA REINSURANCE 6.10
PROFESSIONAL ASSOCIATIONS, LIST
    OF .... Appendix C
PROFESSIONAL INVESTORS, REINSURANCE
    GROUP 6.03
PROFESSIONAL LIABILITY INSURANCE,
    DEFINED 1.04
PROFESSIONAL REINSURERS 6.03
PROFESSIONAL SKEPTICISM,
    EXERCISING 2.79–.80, 4.161, 5.204
PROFIT COMMISSION, REINSURANCE .. 6.19
PROFITABILITY RATIOS 1.47
PROHIBITED SERVICES, NAIC MODEL AUDIT
    RULE 2.152–.154
PROPERTY CLAIMS 4.09
PROSPECTIVE PREMIUM BASED
    ASSESSMENTS 8.14, 8.20
PROSPECTIVE REINSURANCE 6.09
PUBLIC COMPANY ACCOUNTING OVERSIGHT
    BOARD (PCAOB)
  · Dodd-Frank Act ... 1.63, 2.05, 2.133, 2.176
  · Loss reserve disclosure 4.105
  · Sarbanes-Oxley Act 1.49, 1.51, 2.05
    See also Sarbanes-Oxley Act of 2002
PUBLIC ENTITIES, DISCLOSURE
    REQUIREMENTS 7.53, 7.55
PUBLIC ENTITY POOLS 1.09, 1.77
PURCHASING GROUPS 1.09
PURE CAPTIVE INSURANCE ENTITY 9.07
    See also captive insurance entities

Q

QUALIFICATION OF
    OPINION 6.112, 10.59.–60
    See also reports of independent
    registered public accounting firm
QUALITATIVE ANALYSIS, LOSS RESERVE
    RANGES 4.161
QUALITATIVE LIMITATIONS 5.12, 6.29
QUANTITATIVE LIMITATIONS 5.12
QUOTA SHARE REINSURANCE ... 6.10, 6.79

R

RAL   See regulatory action level (RAL) risk-
    based capital
RATE-MAKING PROCESS 1.20–.22
RATIONALIZATION, AS FRAUD RISK
    FACTOR .... 2.83, Table 2-1 at 2.78
RATIOS, FINANCIAL
  · Audit considerations 2.44–.56, 2.85
  · Insurance entities 1.47
  · IRIS 2.55
  · Premium tax estimates 8.08
RBC   See risk-based capital
REAL ESTATE 5.42, 5.108–.118, 5.209
REALIZED LOSSES ON INVESTMENTS,
    SEC 1.50
REASONABLE ASSURANCE 2.12
REASONABLY POSSIBLE LOSS 6.27–.28

Subject Index

RECEIVABLES
- Disclosure . . . . Appendix A
- Loss reserving and claims
  cycle 4.29–.32, 4.86, 4.184–.189
- Premium cycle 3.50–.55, 3.107, 3.129
- Reinsurance cycle 6.45–.46

RECIPROCAL INSURANCE ENTITY . . 9.13–.14

**RECIPROCAL OR INTERINSURANCE
EXCHANGES** 1.09

RECORD DATE, DEFINED 4.37

RECORDKEEPING
  See also documentation
- Captive entities 9.43
- Control over 4.117
- Investment cycle 5.04–.05
- Statutory accounting practices 1.70

RECOVERABLES 4.92, 4.184–.187, 6.79

RECOVERY, RIGHT OF 4.29–.30
  See also reinsurance

REGULATION
  See also specific regulatory entities
- Of the business   See nature, conduct, and regulation of the business
- Executive compensation 1.62, 3.63
- Federal, of accounting practices . . . 1.48–.68
- Investments 5.09–.14
- State insurance   See state insurance regulation

**REGULATORY ACTION LEVEL (RAL) RISK-
BASED CAPITAL** 2.51

REINSURANCE 6.01–.119
- Accounting practices 6.20–.81
- Agreements not qualifying for reinsurance accounting 6.66–.70
- Asset and liability reporting 6.39–.47
- Assuming entity 1.24
- Assumption reinsurance 6.50
- Audit considerations 6.87–.119
- Bases of reinsurance transactions . . 6.15–.18
- Business growth with 6.02
- Ceding company 1.24,
  . . . . 6.103–.104, 6.107–.109
- Commutation 6.51
- Contracts   See contracts, reinsurance
- Defined 1.24, 6.01
- Disclosures . . 6.71–.75, 6.79–.81, Appendix A
- Foreign property and liability
  insurance 6.64–.65
- Fraud risk 2.87
- Frequently used terms 6.19
- Fronting 1.26
- Generally 1.23–.27, 6.01
- Government-provided 6.04
- Interest credits on funds withheld . . 6.54–.59
- Loss reserving and claims cycle 4.29–.30,
  . . . . 4.86, 4.168–.169, 4.184–.189
- Paragraph 11 exception 6.33
- Pools 1.08, 6.60–.63
- Portfolio reinsurance 1.25

REINSURANCE—continued
- Premiums 3.02, 3.15
- Private entities 6.03
- Reasons for 6.05
- Receivables, loss reserving and claims
  cycle 4.29–.32, 4.86, 4.184–.189
- Retrocession 6.06
- Revenue and cost reporting 6.48–.49
- Risk considerations   See risk, reinsurance in managing
- Structured settlements 6.52–.53
- Types of 6.07–.08

REINSURANCE COVERAGE, DEFINED . . . 4.07

REINSURANCE DEPARTMENTS 6.03

**REINSURANCE POOLS (REINSURANCE
ASSOCIATIONS)** 6.03

REINSURANCE SUBSIDY 3.99
  See also Medicare Part D

REINSURER   See assuming company,
  reinsurance

**RELATED PARTY TRANSACTIONS, CAPTIVE
ENTITIES** 9.32

REPORT DATE, DEFINED 4.37

**REPORTING ON WHETHER A PREVIOUSLY
REPORTED MATERIAL WEAKNESS
CONTINUES TO EXIST**   10.32, 10.80–.83
  See also material weaknesses

**REPORTS, TRANSACTION
CYCLE** 3.11, 3.23–.26

**REPORTS OF INDEPENDENT REGISTERED
PUBLIC ACCOUNTING FIRM** 10.42

**REPORTS ON AUDITED FINANCIAL
STATEMENTS** 10.01–.85
- Accountant's awareness letter 10.69–.71
- Accountant's letter of
  qualifications 2.148–.149, 2.154, 10.84
- Change in auditor letter 10.72–.75
- Correction of error 10.55–.60
- Evaluating consistency 10.28
- General use reports, regulatory basis financial
  statements 10.37–.42, 10.46, 10.59
- Generally 10.01–.02
- Internal control over financial
  reporting 10.29–.31
- Limited use reports, regulatory basis financial
  statements 10.43–.48, 10.60
- Modified   See modified opinions
- NAIC-codified SAP 10.34–.36
- Notice of financial condition letter   10.76–.79
- Regulatory basis financial statement
  issues 10.49–.54
- Reporting on whether a previously reported
  material weakness continues to exist   10.32
- Special reports 1.80
- Statutory financial statements of insurance
  entities 10.33
- Supplemental schedules 10.61–.67

AAG-PLI REP

REPORTS ON AUDITED FINANCIAL STATEMENTS—continued
- Unmodified opinions on GAAP financial statements 10.03–.05
- Unremediated material weaknesses in internal control to insurance regulators .. 10.80–.83

REPURCHASE AGREEMENTS ..... 1.50, 5.42, ... 5.180–.192, 5.211, Appendix D

RESERVE RATIOS 1.47

RESERVES, DEFINED 4.01
See also loss reserve

RESTATEMENT CLAUSE, REINSURANCE   6.19

RESTRICTION ON USE SECTION, IN AUDITOR'S REPORTS See reports on audited financial statements

RETALIATORY TAXES 8.07

RETENTION LEVELS, LOSS RESERVES   4.165

RETENTIONS, DEFINED 4.08

RETROACTIVE REINSURANCE 6.09, 6.79

RETROCESSION, DEFINED 4.07, 6.06

RETROSPECTIVE EXPERIENCE RATING 3.03, 4.169–.170

RETROSPECTIVE PREMIUM ADJUSTMENTS 3.04, 3.37, 3.48

RETROSPECTIVELY RATED PREMIUMS, REINSURANCE 6.19

REVENUE FROM PREMIUMS
- Contracts that do not transfer insurance risk 3.106
- GAAP 3.30–.40
- Recognition 3.13, 3.34, 3.36, 3.38–.39
- Statutory accounting principles 3.41–.49

REVENUE RECOGNITION, AUDIT CONSIDERATIONS 2.88

REVENUES, REINSURANCE REPORTING 6.48–.49

REVERSE REPURCHASE AGREEMENTS 5.180–.192

RIGHT OF SETOFF 6.42–.44, 6.68

RISK
See also audit considerations; audit risk
- Captive insurance entities 9.37–.40
- Contracts that do not transfer 3.103–.104, 3.110
- Evaluating 1.19
- Fraud risk factors, consideration of .... 2.77–.78, Tables 2-1–2-2 at 2.78
- Insurance-related expense, tax, and assessment factors 8.40–.42
- Investment factors 5.205–.208
- Loss reserving and claims cycle 4.114–.115, 4.158
- Material misstatement due to fraud   See fraud, material misstatement due to
- Period of 3.35
- Premiums and acquisition cost audits 3.127–.128

RISK—continued
- Reinsurance   See risk, reinsurance in managing
- Significant 2.22, 2.59–.60
- Transaction cycle, evaluating and accepting risks 3.08–.16
- Types of   See lines of insurance
- Underwriting 1.18–.27

RISK, REINSURANCE
See also reinsurance
- Paragraph 11 exception 6.33–.35
- Risk-limiting features 6.36–.38
- Special considerations 6.82–.86
- Transfer criteria 6.25–.32

RISK ASSESSMENT PROCESS
- Income taxes 7.72–.73
- Investments 5.216–.217
- Loss reserving and claims cycle 4.101, 4.114–.115
- Premiums cycle 3.127–.128
- Reinsurance 6.96–.97

RISK-BASED CAPITAL (RBC) 2.47–.53
- Authorized control level 2.49–.50
- In comprehensive financial plan 2.52
- Disclosure regulations 2.48
- Generally 2.47, 2.53
- Going-concern considerations 2.104
- Income tax 7.60
- Levels and corrective actions 2.51

RISK-LIMITING FEATURES, REINSURANCE 6.36–.38

RISK RETENTION ACT   See Federal Liability Risk Retention Act of 1986 (FLRRA)

RISK RETENTION GROUPS (RRGS) 1.09, 9.20–.24, 9.43

RISK-SHARING POOLS 1.09

RISK TRANSFER CRITERIA 6.25–.35, 9.31–.32

ROLLOVER APPROACH 2.116

RRGS   See risk retention groups (RRGs)

RULINGS, INSURANCE DEPARTMENT ... 1.44

S

SAFEKEEPING OF SECURITIES .... 5.08, ... 5.14, 5.220

SALVAGE, LOSS RESERVING AND CLAIMS CYCLE 4.19, 4.31–.32

SAP   See statutory accounting practices

SARBANES-OXLEY ACT OF 2002 (SOX)
- Amendment 1.58
- Communication of internal control matters 2.133, 2.176
- Implementation 1.49, 1.51
- Internal control 2.05
- Loss reserve disclosure 4.68
- NAIC Model Rule 2.164

Subject Index

SCA See subsidiary, controlled, and affiliated (SCA) entities
SCHEDULE RATING, PREMIUMS 3.03
SCOPE OF THE AUDIT ENGAGEMENT, AUDIT CONSIDERATIONS 2.02–.11
SEC See Securities and Exchange Commission
SECURED BORROWING, DISTINGUISHING ASSET TRANSFERS FROM ...... 5.165, ... 5.169, 5.176, 5.188, 5.192
SECURITIES ACT OF 1933 ...... 1.48, 1.61
SECURITIES AND EXCHANGE COMMISSION (SEC)
- Accounting practices 1.48–.53
- Disclosure recommendations 1.50–.53
- Distinguishing GAAP and statutory regulation from 5.42
- Internal control 2.176–.180
- Loss reserve disclosure 4.67–.68
- Loss reserve discounting 4.76
- Nature, conduct, and regulation of the business 1.48–.53
- Non-GAAP financial measures, additional insurance information for 1.52
- Operating earnings 1.53

SECURITIES EXCHANGE ACT OF 1934 ..... 1.48, 1.61, 2.176–.77, 2.180
SECURITIES LENDING .... 1.50, 5.42, ... 5.193–.201, Appendix D
SEGREGATED CELLS, CAPTIVE INSURANCE ENTITIES 9.15–.19
SEGREGATION OF DUTIES .... 4.117, ... 5.220, 6.100, 9.43
SERVICE ORGANIZATIONS
- Captive insurance entities .... 9.04, ... 9.27–.29, 9.43
- Investment cycle 5.221–.224

SEVERITIES PROJECTION METHOD, AVERAGE 4.42
SHAREHOLDERS, EXECUTIVE PAY VOTE 1.62
SHAREHOLDER'S EQUITY .... Appendix A
SHORT-DURATION CONTRACTS .... 1.89, ... 1.91–.92, 3.31, 3.33–.34, 4.04
SHORT TAIL LINES 4.14, 4.165
SIDECARS 6.03, 6.13, 6.83
SIGNIFICANT DEFICIENCY, REPORTING 2.131, 2.158–.160
SIGNIFICANT LOSS 6.27
SIGNIFICANT RISK, DEFINED 2.22, 2.59–.60
See also risk
SINGLE PARENT CAPTIVES 9.07
See also captive insurance entities
SKEPTICISM, EXERCISING .... 2.79–.80, ... 4.161, 5.204

SLIDING SCALE COMMISSION, REINSURANCE 6.19
SOFTWARE COSTS 3.75
See also information technology (IT)
SOLVENCY, INSURANCE ENTITIES 1.38
SOX See Sarbanes-Oxley Act of 2002
SPECIAL PURPOSE CAPTIVES 9.26
SPECIAL-PURPOSE VEHICLES, REINSURANCE 6.13
See also sidecars
SPECIALISTS
- Investment audits 5.210
- Loss reserve .... 4.64, 4.69–.71, ... 4.127, 4.129–.136
See also loss reserving and claims cycle

SPONSORED CAPTIVE INSURANCE ENTITIES 9.15–.19
STATE INSURANCE REGULATION
See also statutory accounting practices
- Accounting practices 1.37–.45
- Audit engagement letter 2.03
- Captive entities 9.32
- Fair dealing, promotion of 1.38
- History 1.39, 3.07
- NAIC Model rule 2.166–.170
- Nature, conduct, and regulation of the business 1.06, 1.34, 1.37–.45
- Uniform financial reporting, promotion of 1.38

STATE REGULATION EXAMINATIONS, AUDITOR'S CONSIDERATION OF 2.166–.170
STATE TAXATION .... 7.21–.22, 8.06, ... 8.11–.12, 8.47
See also income taxes
STATISTICAL REPORTING, PREMIUM TRANSACTION CYCLE 3.23–.26
STATUTORY ACCOUNTING PRACTICES (SAP) 1.70–.88
See also specific topics
- Acquisition costs 3.83
- Contracts that do not transfer insurance risk 3.104
- Distinguishing GAAP from .... 1.96, ... Exhibit 1-1 at 1.96, Table 1-1 at 1.96
- Distinguishing SEC regulation from 5.42
- Distinguishing taxable income reporting from 7.05–.07, 7.56–.61
- Fair value measurement 5.39–.40
- Federal income taxation 7.05–.07
- Income taxes 7.05–.07, 7.56–.61
- Insurance-related expenses, taxes, and assessments 8.23–.30, 8.51
- Investments 5.10–.13, 5.41–.201
- Loss reserving and claims cycle ... 4.87–.93
- NAIC hierarchy 1.72
- Nonadmitted assets 1.88
- Permitted statutory accounting practices 1.82–.87, 2.171–.175
- Premium deficiencies 3.86–.97

AAG-PLI STA

STATUTORY ACCOUNTING PRACTICES (SAP)—continued
- Premiums and acquisition costs ... 3.41–.49
- Reinsurance 6.76–.81

STATUTORY ACCOUNTING PRINCIPLES
- Acquisition costs 3.83
- Premium adjustments 3.41–.49
- Premium receivables 3.53–.55
- Premium revenue 3.41–.49

STATUTORY ACCOUNTING PRINCIPLES WORKING GROUP 1.71

STATUTORY BLANK, FILING ANNUAL 1.74, 3.24, 9.24

STEP-UP PREFERRED STOCK 5.82

STOCK COMPANIES 1.09

STRUCTURED SECURITIES 5.76–.79

STRUCTURED SETTLEMENTS .... 4.28, ... 4.83–.85, 6.52–.53

SUBROGATION, LOSS RESERVING AND CLAIMS CYCLE 4.19, 4.31–.32

SUBSCRIBERS, INSURANCE ORGANIZATION 1.09

SUBSIDIARY, CONTROLLED, AND AFFILIATED (SCA) ENTITIES 5.42, 5.145–.156

SUBSTANTIVE PROCEDURES
- Distinguishing tests of controls from ... 2.42
  See also tests of controls
- Loss reserves and claims 4.120–.121, 4.151
- In response to assessed risks 2.62–.63, 2.66, 2.93
- Significant risk identification 2.23
- Timing of 2.93

SUPPLEMENTAL BENEFITS 3.99
See also Medicare Part D

SUPPLEMENTAL SCHEDULES, AUDIT OPINIONS ON 10.61–.67

SURETY BONDS, DEFINED 1.04

SURETY CLAIMS 4.12

SURETY & FIDELITY ASSOCIATION OF AMERICA 3.06

SURPLUS AID TO POLICYHOLDERS' SURPLUS 1.47

SURPLUS LINES OF INSURANCE 1.05, 3.06

SURPLUS NOTE, CAPTIVE ENTITY 9.32

SURPLUS SHARE REINSURANCE 6.10

SYNDICATES OF REINSURERS .... 1.29, ... 6.03, 6.114

T

TAC See total adjusted capital

TAX, PREMIUM AND STATE 7.21–.22, 8.06–.12, 8.47
See also income taxes

TAX-EXEMPT STATUS 7.04, 7.16

TAX LAW, CHANGES IN 7.62

TAX PLANNING STRATEGIES 7.35

TAX POSITIONS 7.37–.45

TAX REFORM ACT OF 1986 ..... 7.02, 7.10, ... 7.13, 7.15, 7.17, 7.20
See also income taxes

TAX STATUS, CHANGE IN 7.49

TAXABLE AND DEDUCTIBLE TEMPORARY DIFFERENCES 7.26–.30

TAXABLE INCOME, REPORTING 7.05

TAXES, LICENSES, AND FEES, REPORTING 8.01
See also income taxes

TEMPORARY DIFFERENCES, TAXES 7.26–.30, 7.32, 7.50

TERMINOLOGY, REINSURANCE CONTRACTS 6.19

TERRORISM, FEDERAL REGULATIONS 1.64–.68

TERRORISM INSURANCE EXTENSION ACT OF 2005 .... 1.64–.66, 1.68

TERRORISM INSURANCE IMPLEMENTATION WORKING GROUP (NAIC) 1.68

TERRORISM RISK INSURANCE ACT OF 2001 (TRIA) 1.64, 1.67–.68

TERRORISM RISK INSURANCE PROGRAM 6.04

TERRORISM RISK INSURANCE PROGRAM REAUTHORIZATION ACT OF 2007 .... 1.64, 1.67

TEST PERIOD, DISCOUNTED RESERVE INTEREST RATE 7.11

TESTS OF ASSUMPTIONS, LOSS RESERVE ESTIMATES 4.144–.156
See also loss reserve ranges

TESTS OF CONTROLS .... 2.42, 2.65, ... 4.124–.128
See also internal control; substantive procedures

TESTS OF DATA, ASSUMPTIONS, AND ESTIMATE SELECTION ...... 4.144–.148, ... 4.153–.154

TESTS OF INTERNAL AUDITOR WORK 2.124–.125

TIME VALUE OF MONEY, PREMIUM DEFICIENCIES 3.92

TITLE INSURANCE ENTITIES, TAX REGULATION 7.14

TOLERABLE MISSTATEMENT 2.74

TOTAL ADJUSTED CAPITAL (TAC) 2.50

TRADE ASSOCIATIONS, LIST OF Appendix C

TRANSACTION CYCLE 1.18–.36
- Captive insurers 1.30, 1.77
- Claims 4.15–.32
- Investments 1.33–.36, 5.06–.07

Subject Index

TRANSACTION CYCLE—continued
- Pooling 1.28
- Premiums 3.05–.26
- Syndicates 1.29
- Underwriting of risks 1.18–.27
- Underwriting pools 1.29

TRANSACTIONS, CLASSES OF, AND FRAUD 2.87

TRANSFERRED ASSETS .... 5.42, ... 5.162–.180, Appendix D

TRANSFERRED ASSETS, ISOLATION OF 5.165, 5.168, 5.175

TRANSFORMERS 6.03, 6.14

TREATY-BASIS REINSURANCE 6.16

TRIA See Terrorism Risk Insurance Act of 2001

TWO-YEAR OVERALL OPERATING RATIO 1.47

TWO-YEAR RESERVE DEVELOPMENT TO POLICYHOLDERS' SURPLUS 1.47

TYPE OF RISK See lines of insurance

U

UNALLOCATED LOSS ADJUSTMENT EXPENSES 4.54

UNAUTHORIZED REINSURER 6.19

UNCOLLECTED PREMIUMS 3.50–.52

UNDERSTANDING THE ENTITY, ITS ENVIRONMENT, AND ITS INTERNAL CONTROL 2.04, 2.26–.43
See also environment, understanding; internal control

UNDERWRITING
- Automated 3.16
- Defined 1.01
- Pools for 1.08, 1.29

UNDERWRITING RISK .. 1.18–.27, 2.48, 3.11

UNEARNED PREMIUM RESERVE 7.13

UNEARNED PREMIUMS 3.39

UNIFORM FINANCIAL REPORTING, PROMOTION OF 1.38

UNIFORMITY, PROMOTION OF 1.38

UNMODIFIED OPINIONS ON GAAP FINANCIAL STATEMENTS 10.03–.05

UNPAID CLAIMS AND CLAIM ADJUSTMENT EXPENSES
- Liability 4.96–.99

UNREALIZED GAINS AND LOSSES 1.50

UNREMEDIATED MATERIAL WEAKNESSES 10.32, 10.80–.83
See also material weaknesses

U.S. BANKRUPTCY CODE 6.44

U.S. DEPARTMENT OF TREASURY 6.04, 7.11–.12

U.S. SUPREME COURT, INSURANCE REGULATION 1.39

V

VARIABLE INTEREST ENTITY (VIE) 5.37–.38, ... 5.135–.137, 6.13–.14, 6.83
See also joint ventures

VIE See variable interest entity

W

WASH SALES 5.187, 5.192

WORKERS' COMPENSATION
- Claim settlement characteristics 4.11
- Commissions 3.22
- Experience rating 3.03
- Generally 1.04
- Rating organization 3.06
- States providing 3.28
- Statutory accounting principles 3.42

WORKERS' COMPENSATION POOLS 1.08

WORKING PAPERS (AUDIT DOCUMENTATION) ... 2.117–.125, 2.161, ... 4.131–.132

WORST CASE VIEW, LOSS RESERVES .. 4.22

Y

YIELD-MAINTENANCE AGREEMENTS .. 5.183

AAG-PLI YIE

AICPA® Online Professional Library

Powerful Online Research Tools

The AICPA Online Professional Library offers the most current access to comprehensive accounting and auditing literature, as well business and practice management information, combined with the power and speed of the Web. Through your online subscription, you'll get:

- Cross-references within and between titles — smart links give you quick access to related information and relevant materials
- First available updates — no other research tool offers access to new AICPA standards and conforming changes more quickly, guaranteeing that you are always current with all of the authoritative guidance!
- Robust search engine — helps you narrow down your research to find your results quickly
- And much more…

Choose from two comprehensive libraries or select only the titles you need!

With the *Essential A&A Research Collection*, you gain access to the following:
- AICPA Professional Standards
- AICPA Technical Practice Aids
- PCAOB Standards & Related Rules
- All current AICPA Audit and Accounting Guides
- All current Audit Risk Alerts

One-year individual online subscription
Item # ORS-XX

OR

Premium A&A Research Collection **and get everything from the *Essential A&A Research Collection* plus:**
- AICPA Audit & Accounting Manual
- All current Checklists & Illustrative Financial Statements
- eXacct: Financial Reporting Tools & Techniques
- IFRS Accounting Trends & Techniques

One-year individual online subscription
Item # WAL-BY

You can also add the FASB *Accounting Standards Codification*™ and the GASB Library to either collection.

Take advantage of a 30-day free trial!
See for yourself how these powerful online libraries can improve your productivity and simplify your accounting research.

Visit **cpa2biz.com/library** for details or to subscribe.